The Future for Philosophy

Where does philosophy, the oldest academic subject, stand at the beginning of the new millennium? This remarkable volume brings together leading figures from most major branches of the discipline to offer answers.

What remains of the 'linguistic turn' in twentieth-century philosophy? How should moral philosophy respond to and incorporate developments in empirical psychology? Where might Continental and Anglophone feminist theory profitably interact? How has our understanding of ancient philosophy been affected by the emergence of analytic philosophy? Where does the mind–body problem stand today? What role must value judgments play in science? Do Marx, Nietzsche, or Freud matter in the 21st century?

These and many other questions at the cutting edge of the discipline are addressed by distinguished philosophers from Australia, Britain, Canada, and the United States. They aim not only to stimulate philosophical debate, but to introduce those in cognate disciplines—biology, classics, economics, history, law, linguistics, literary studies, mathematics, philosophy, physics, political science, psychology, among others—to what is happening in contemporary philosophy. In a substantial introduction, the editor gives an overview of the state of philosophy today and helps orient non-philosophers.

Brian Leiter holds the Joseph D. Jamail Centennial Chair in Law and Philosophy at the University of Texas, Austin.

The Future for Philosophy

Edited by

Brian Leiter

CLARENDON PRESS · OXFORD

OXFORD
UNIVERSITY PRESS

Great Clarendon Street, Oxford OX2 6DP

Oxford University Press is a department of the University of Oxford.
It furthers the University's objective of excellence in research, scholarship,
and education by publishing worldwide in

Oxford New York

Auckland Cape Town Dar es Salaam Hong Kong Karachi
Kuala Lumpur Madrid Melbourne Mexico City Nairobi
New Delhi Shanghai Taipei Toronto

With offices in

Argentina Austria Brazil Chile Czech Republic France Greece
Guatemala Hungary Italy Japan Poland Portugal Singapore
South Korea Switzerland Thailand Turkey Ukraine Vietnam

Oxford is a registered trade mark of Oxford University Press
in the UK and in certain other countries

Published in the United States
by Oxford University Press Inc., New York

British Library Cataloguing in Publication Data
Data available

Library of Congress Cataloging in Publication Data
Data available

Typeset by Newgen Imaging Systems (P) Ltd., Chennai, India
Printed in Great Britain
on acid-free paper by
Biddles Ltd., King's Lynn, Norfolk

ISBN 0–19–924728–5   978–0–19–924728–8
ISBN 0–19–920392–X (Pbk.)   978–0–19–920392–5 (Pbk.)

1 3 5 7 9 10 8 6 4 2

For my three most treasured teachers:

Samuel James Leiter
William Elias Leiter
Celia Rose Leiter

Acknowledgements

Peter Momtchiloff at Oxford University Press conceived the idea for this project, and I am grateful to him for inviting me to execute it, and for his constructive advice and support throughout.

It has been both a pleasure and a privilege to work with the distinguished contributors to this volume: they exemplify what Nietzsche most admired in scholars, their 'reverence for every kind of mastery and competence, and [their] uncompromising opposition to everything that is semblance, half-genuine, dressed up, virtuosolike, demagogical, or histrionic in *litteris et artibus*' (*The Gay Science*, sec. 366).

The project would not have been completed without the assistance of two people: Neil Sinhababu, a doctoral student in the Department of Philosophy here, who not only provided important research assistance, but also compiled the bibliography (a wonderful resource for anyone learning about philosophy today); and my administrative assistant, Ms. Jolyn Piercy, who helped shepherd the book in to production.

The University of Texas School of Law provided, as always, exceptional material and institutional support, as well as a congenial and stimulating environment in which to pursue all manner of things philosophical.

Austin, Texas   B.L.
20 October 2003

Contents

x   Contents

Notes on Contributors

Julia Annas is Regents Professor of Philosophy at the University of Arizona, and has also taught at Oxford and Columbia Universities. She is the founder and former editor of the annual *Oxford Studies in Ancient Philosophy*. Among her many books are *An Introduction to Plato's Republic* (Oxford University Press, 1981), *The Modes of Scepticism* (Cambridge University Press, 1985) (with Jonathan Barnes), *Hellenistic Philosophy of Mind* (University of California Press, 1992), *The Morality of Happiness* (Oxford University Press, 1993), *Platonic Ethics, Old and New* (Cornell University Press, 1999), and *Ancient Philosophy: A Very Short Introduction* (Oxford University Press, 2000). She is a Fellow of the American Academy of Arts & Sciences and Past President of the Pacific Division of the American Philosophical Association.

Nancy Cartwright is Professor of Philosophy at the London School of Economics, where she is Director of the LSE Centre for Philosophy of Natural and Social Science, and is also Professor of Philosophy at the University of California, San Diego. She has also taught at Stanford and Princeton Universities, California Institute of Technology, and the Universities of California (Los Angeles), Maryland (College Park), and Pittsburgh. Her primary work is in philosophy of science, with particular interests in physics, economics, and problems about objectivity. Among her major publications are *How the Laws of Physics Lie* (Oxford University Press, 1983), *Nature's Capacities and their Measurement* (Oxford University Press, 1989), *Otto Neurath: Philosophy between Science and Politics* (Cambridge University Press, 1995) (with J. Cat, L. Fleck, and T. Uebel), and *The Dappled World: A Study of the Boundaries of Science* (Cambridge University Press, 2000). She is a Fellow of both the British Academy and the American Academy of Arts & Sciences.

David J. Chalmers is Regents Professor of Philosophy at the University of Arizona, where he is also Director of the Center for Consciousness Studies. He held appointments previously at the University of California at Santa Cruz and Washington University, St. Louis. He is best-known for *The Conscious Mind* (Oxford University Press, 1996), whose many influential ideas and arguments are discussed in a collection of 26 essays (ed. J. Shear) on *Explaining Consciousness: The Hard Problem* (MIT Press, 1997). He is also the editor of *Philosophy of Mind: Classical and Contemporary Readings* (Oxford University Press, 2002). His article 'The Extended Mind' (*Analysis*, 1998) (with A. Clark) was chosen as 'one of the ten best philosophical articles of the year' by *The Philosopher's Annual*. His many articles on topics in philosophy of mind, philosophy of language, metaphysics, and artificial intelligence have appeared in *Philosophical Review*, *Synthèse*, *Scientific American*, *Behavioral and Brain Sciences*, and elsewhere.

Don Garrett is Professor of Philosophy at New York University, and has also taught at Harvard and Johns Hopkins Universities and the Universities of North Carolina (Chapel Hill) and Utah. He is the author of *Cognition and Commitment in Hume's Philosophy* (Oxford University Press, 1997), editor of *The Cambridge Companion to Spinoza* (1996), and co-editor of *The Encyclopedia of Empiricism* (Greenwood Press, 1997). He is the North American editor of *Archiv für Geschicte der Philosophie* and former editor of *Hume Studies*. He is currently writing the volume on *Hume* in the *Routledge Philosophers* series and the volume on *Spinoza* in the Blackwell *Great Minds* series. He is also author of many articles on Hume, Spinoza, Leibniz, and other figures and topics in early modern philosophy in *Philosophical Review, Noûs, Studia Spinoza*, and elsewhere.

Alvin Goldman is Board of Governors Professor of Philosophy and Cognitive Science at Rutgers University at New Brunswick, and has also taught at Princeton and Yale Universities and the Universities of Arizona, Illinois (Chicago), Michigan (Ann Arbor), and Pittsburgh. Over the past thirty years, he has been responsible for the most sustained and influential versions of the causal theory of knowledge, epistemological externalism and reliabilism, and social epistemology. Among his major publications are *A Theory of Human Action* (Prentice-Hall, 1970), *Epistemology and Cognition* (Harvard University Press, 1986), *Liasons: Philosophy Meets the Cognitive and Social Sciences* (MIT Press, 1992), *Philosophical Applications of Cognitive Science* (Westview Press, 1993), *Knowledge in a Social World* (Oxford University Press, 1999), and *Pathways of Knowledge: Private and Public* (Oxford University Press, 2002). His work is the subject of a special, two-volume issue of the journal *Philosophical Topics* (2001). He is Past President of the Pacific Division of the American Philosophical Association and is a Fellow of the American Academy of Arts and Sciences.

Thomas Hurka is Chancellor Henry N. R. Jackman Distinguished Professor of Philosophy at the University of Toronto, and has also taught at the University of Calgary. A moral philosopher, he is known especially for his rehabilitation of perfectionism in ethics. He is the author of *Perfectionism* (Oxford University Press, 1993), *Principles: Short Essays in Ethics* (Harcourt Brace, 2nd ed., 1999), and *Virtue, Vice, and Value* (Oxford University Press, 2001), as well as many articles in *Ethics, Journal of Philosophy, Social Philosophy & Policy, Mind, Utilitas*, and elsewhere. He was also Executive Editor of the *Canadian Journal of Philosophy* and currently serves on the editorial board of *Ethics*. He is a Fellow of the Royal Society of Canada.

Jaegwon Kim is William Herbert Perry Faunce Professor of Philosophy at Brown University, and has also taught at Swarthmore College, Cornell and Johns Hopkins Universities, the City University of New York Graduate Center, and the Universities of Michigan (Ann Arbor), Notre Dame, and Pennsylvania. He is the author of many seminal papers on topics in metaphysics and philosophy of mind, which have appeared in all the leading philosophical journals in English, and some of which are collected in *Supervenience and Mind* (Cambridge University Press, 1993). He is also the author of *Philosophy of Mind* (Westview Press, 1996) and *Mind in a Physical World* (MIT Press, 1999). His work has been translated into German, Italian, Korean, and

Polish. He is Past President of the Central Division of the American Philosophical Association and is a Fellow of the American Academy of Arts & Sciences.

Philip Kitcher is Professor of Philosophy at Columbia University, and has also taught at the Universities of California (San Diego), Michigan (Ann Arbor), Minnesota (Minneapolis-St. Paul), and Vermont. The former Editor-in-Chief of the journal *Philosophy of Science*, he works in philosophy of science, philosophy of biology, epistemology, and philosophy of mathematics. Among his many publications are *Abusing Science: The Case Against Creationism* (MIT Press, 1982), *The Nature of Mathematical Knowledge* (Oxford University Press, 1983), *Vaulting Ambition: Sociobiology and the Quest for Human Nature* (MIT Press, 1985), *The Advancement of Science* (Oxford University Press, 1993), *The Lives to Come: The Genetic Revolution and Human Possibilities* (Simon & Schuster, 1996), *Truth, Science, and Democracy* (Oxford University Press, 2001), and *In Mendel's Mirror: Philosophical Reflections on Biology* (Oxford University Press, 2003). Five of his articles have been selected as among 'the ten best philosophical articles of the year' by *The Philosopher's Annual*. He has received the Lakatos Prize in philosophy of science and is a Fellow of the American Academy of Arts & Sciences.

Rae Langton is Professor of Philosophy at the Massachusetts Institute of Technology, and has also held appointments at Monash University, the Australian National University, Victoria University, Wellington in New Zealand, and the University of Edinburgh where she was the Professor of Moral Philosophy. She is the author of *Kantian Humility: Our Ignorance of Things in Themselves* (Oxford University Press, 1998) and *Sexual Solipsism* (Oxford University Press, forthcoming). Her article 'Whose Right? Ronald Dworkin, Women, and Pornographers' (*Philosophy & Public Affairs*, 1990) was selected as 'one of the ten best philosophical articles of the year' by *The Philosopher's Annual*, and has also been widely anthologized. Her articles on topics in moral philosophy, feminist philosophy, metaphysics, and the history of philosophy have also appeared in *Australasian Journal of Philosophy*, *Philosophical Topics*, *Philosophy & Phenomenological Research*, *Legal Theory*, and elsewhere.

Brian Leiter holds the Joseph D. Jamail Centennial Chair at the University of Texas at Austin, where he is also Director of the Law & Philosophy Program. He has also taught at Yale University, University College London, and the University of California, San Diego. He is co-editor of the journal *Legal Theory*, editor of the *Routledge Philosophers* book series, author of *Naturalizing Jurisprudence* (Cambridge University Press, forthcoming) and *Nietzsche on Morality* (Routledge, 2002), and co-editor of *The Oxford Handbook of Continental Philosophy* (forthcoming) and *Nietzsche* in the Oxford Readings in Philosophy series (2001). His article 'Legal Realism and Legal Positivism Reconsidered' (*Ethics*, 2001) was chosen as 'one of the ten best philosophical articles of the year' by *The Philosopher's Annual*. His other articles have appeared in *Ethics*, *Times Literary Supplement*, *European Journal of Philosophy*, *Social Philosophy & Policy*, *Journal of the History of Philosophy*, and elsewhere.

Philip Pettit is William Nelson Cromwell Professor of Politics at Princeton University, and was previously the Professor of Social & Political Theory in the

Research School of Social Sciences at the Australian National University. He has also taught at Cambridge, Columbia and Queen's (Ireland) Universities, as well as University College, Dublin and the Universities of Bradford and Cape Town. His work connects issues in moral and political theory with issues in metaphysics, philosophy of mind, and philosophy of social science. Among his many books are *The Common Mind: An Essay on Psychology, Society and Politics* (Oxford University Press, 1993; rev. ed., 1996), *Republicanism: A Theory of Freedom and Government* (Oxford: Clarendon Press, 1997), *A Theory of Freedom: From the Psychology to the Politics of Agency* (Oxford University Press, 2001), and *The Economy of Esteem* (Oxford University Press, 2004) (with G. Brennan). His article 'Free Riding and Foul Dealing' (*Journal of Philosophy*, 1986) was chosen as 'one of the ten best philosophical articles of the year' by *The Philosopher's Annual*. He is a member of the editorial boards of *Ethics, Journal of Political Philosophy*, and *European Journal of Philosophy*, and is a Fellow of the Australian Academy of Social Sciences and the Australian Academy of Humanities.

Peter Railton is John Stephenson Perrin Professor of Philosophy at the University of Michigan at Ann Arbor, and has also taught at the University of California at Berkeley and Cornell and Princeton Universities. He is also an Associate of the Centre de Recherché en Èpistmologie Appliquèe at the Ècole Polytechnique in Paris. He is the author of many seminal papers in metaethics, normative ethics, and the philosophy of science (especially on scientific explanation), three of which have been selected as among 'the ten best philosophical articles of the year' by *The Philosopher's Annual*, and many of which are reprinted in his *Facts, Values and Norms: Essays towards a Morality of Consequences* (Cambridge University Press, 2003). He is also co-editor of the widely used collection *Moral Discourse and Practice: Some Philosophical Approaches* (Oxford University Press, 1997). He sits on the editorial boards of *Ethics* and *Utilitas* and is a Fellow of the American Academy of Arts and Sciences.

Timothy Williamson is Wykeham Professor of Logic in the University of Oxford, and has also taught at Princeton University, the University of Edinburgh, Trinity College (Dublin), and the Massachussetts Institute of Technology. He works in such central philosophical areas as philosophy of language, metaphysics, epistemology, and philosophical logic. He is the author of *Identity and Discrimination* (Blackwell, 1990), *Vagueness* (Routledge, 1994), and *Knowledge and Its Limits* (Oxford University Press, 2000), as well as dozens of articles in such journals as *Mind, Philosophical Review, Journal of Philosophy, Analysis, Journal of Philosophical Logic*, and *Australasian Journal of Philosophy*. His article 'Knowing How' (*Journal of Philosophy*, 2001) (with J. Stanley) was chosen as 'one of the ten best philosophical articles of the year' by *The Philosopher's Annual*. He is a Fellow of both the British Academy and the Royal Society of Edinburgh.

Introduction
The Future for Philosophy

BRIAN LEITER

Philosophy Today

Philosophy, perhaps more than any other discipline, has been plagued by debates
about what the discipline is or ought to be. Partly, this is due to the fact that "philosophy" has a currency in everyday parlance and ordinary self-reflection that "linguistics" or "sociology" or "anthropology" do not. One doesn't need an advanced
degree to have a "philosophy of life", and this has bred an expectation, even among
those with advanced degrees, that the discipline of philosophy ought to be continuous with ordinary attempts to forge a philosophy of life.

Most of philosophy, both contemporary and—importantly—historical, does not,
alas, live up to this expectation. Earlier and contemporary philosophers worry, to be
sure, about truth, knowledge, the just society, and morally right action, as well as the
nature of science, beauty, death, law, goodness, rationality, and consciousness. From
reflections on these worries one might even extract a "philosophy of life", though it
would hardly be obvious, on an initial reading of Aristotle, Leibniz, Hume, Kant,
Hegel, or Husserl that this is what they were after.[1]

Meta-philosophical questions, i.e. questions about what philosophy is, its proper
concerns, methods, and limitations, and its rightful ambitions are inevitably on the
table in any consideration of philosophy's future. Yet "what philosophy is" is also the
implicit subtext anytime one "does philosophy". Indeed, often one of the best (and
most convincing) answers to the former question is given by the latter, by *the doing*
of philosophy. In this volume, the reader will find both approaches to philosophy's
future, essays in which some of the very best and most influential contemporary
philosophers are asking meta-philosophical questions and essays in which they are
doing philosophy of mind, language, and science, as well as ethics, epistemology,
feminist philosophy, and the history of philosophy—and in the "doing" they show
the reader what philosophy is today, and what it ought to be tomorrow.

The picture that emerges will no doubt be surprising to many readers outside philosophy. Philosophy today—especially, though not only, in the English-speaking
countries—is not a monolith, but a pluralism of methods and topics. "Analytic" philosophy, for example, the target of many polemics by those with little knowledge of
the discipline, is defunct. As Philip Kitcher has written elsewhere, there was
"a period"—roughly, the 1940s to the 1970s in the Anglophone world—when analytic

---

[1] For a compelling exploration of "philosophies of life" in post-Kantian figures (not Husserl, however), see Julian Young, *The Death of God and the Meaning of Life* (London: Routledge, 2003).

"philosophers could be confident of their professional standing, priding themselves on the presence of a method—the method of conceptual analysis—which they, and they alone, were trained to use".[2] Under the pressure of very different kinds of arguments deriving from Ludwig Wittgenstein[3] and W. V. O. Quine,[4] in particular, philosophers began to doubt that the "analysis" of "concepts" was informative or worthwhile.[5] The Wittgensteinian response to this loss of professional confidence was *quietism*. Philosophy, the quietists concluded, has no distinctive methods and philosophy can solve no problems; philosophy becomes a kind of *therapy*, dissolving philosophical problems, rather than solving them. One way it dissolves them is through the *history* of philosophy, which shows us how we came to think there were such things as *philosophical* problems and *philosophical* methods in the first place.[6]

Wittgensteinian quietism has been the minority response among English-speaking philosophers.[7] Far stronger has been the Quinean influence, manifest in the "naturalistic" revolution which has swept Anglophone philosophy over the last three decades (and which one sees reflected, in different ways, in the essays in this volume by Nancy Cartwright, David Chalmers, Alvin Goldman, Jaegwon Kim, Philip Pettit, Peter Railton, and myself).[8] The naturalists (largely) agree with the Wittgensteinians that philosophers have no *distinctive* methods that suffice for solving problems, but (unlike

---

[2] Philip Kitcher, "The Naturalists Return", *Philosophical Review* 100 (1992), 54. As Michael Rosen notes, the label "analytic" suggests "that those authors to whom the label is applied share a common commitment to a single philosophical method: analysis. But this is plainly untrue. Not only have very different ideas as to what analysis might amount to been put forward in the course of time (Bertrand Russell's conception is quite different from J. L. Austin's) but many of the most distinguished members of the analytic tradition do not seem to be practicing analysis in any very distinctive sense at all." "Continental Philosophy from Hegel", in *Philosophy 2: Further Through the Subject*, ed. A. C. Grayling (Oxford: Oxford University Press, 1998), 665.

[3] Ludwig Wittgenstein, *Philosophical Investigations*, trans. G. E. M. Anscombe (New York: Macmillan Publishing Co., 1953).

[4] See, e.g., the 1936 paper "Truth by Convention" (reprinted in Quine's *The Ways of Paradox and Other Essays* [New York: Random House, 1966]), the 1951 paper "Two Dogmas of Empiricism" (reprinted in his *From a Logical Point of View* [Cambridge, Mass.: Harvard University Press, 1953]), and the 1960 paper "Carnap and Logical Truth" (reprinted in *The Ways of Paradox*).

[5] The attitude of philosophical naturalists towards conceptual analysis is a bit more complicated, as discussed below.

[6] An influential, but little-published, Harvard philosopher, the late Burton Dreben, purportedly gave hyperbolic expression to this Wittgensteinian view in an oft-repeated line: "Philosophy is garbage. But the history of garbage is scholarship."

[7] Of the leading PhD-granting programs in the English-speaking world, there are just four where the Wittgensteinian view is strongly represented: Harvard University, the University of California at Berkeley, the University of Chicago, and the University of Pittsburgh. And even these four do not speak univocally in a Wittgensteinian vein. By contrast, the "naturalist" revolution in philosophy (discussed below in the text) enjoys a prominent place at more than a dozen of the leading graduate programs, including New York University, Rutgers University at New Brunswick, the University of Michigan at Ann Arbor, the Australian National University, and the University of California at San Diego, among others. (These programs, too, don't speak univocally.) Of course, at most programs, neither the Wittgensteinians nor the naturalists are dominant.

[8] It would be fair to say that the "naturalistic turn" has had less impact in Britain than the United States and Australasia, though there are some important philosophical naturalists based in the UK, like Simon Blackburn at Cambridge University and David Papineau at King's College, London.

the Wittgensteinians) the naturalists believe that the problems that have worried philosophers (about the nature of the mind, knowledge, action, reality, morality, and so on) are indeed real. For the naturalists, the key is for philosophers either to adopt and emulate the methods of successful sciences, or for philosophers to operate *in tandem* with the sciences, as their abstract and reflective branch. In the latter role, philosophy analyzes *only* those concepts that figure in successful empirical theories and tries to develop philosophical answers that win support from, or are entailed by, scientific evidence.[9] Neuroscientists teach us about the brain, and philosophers try to figure out how to square our best neuroscience with the ability of our minds to both *represent* what the world is like and *intend* to act upon and in it. Psychologists and biologists teach us about motivation and its sources, and philosophers try to discern how these discoveries fit with our understanding of morality and the demands it makes on us, and so on.

The Naturalistic Turn

One aspect of the naturalistic turn is well illustrated by Jaegwon Kim's contribution to this volume on the mind–body problem. Although the problem of the relationship between the mind and the body can be found in both Plato and Descartes, the contemporary problem, as Kim notes, is "shaped by physicalism ["the thesis that all things that exist in this world are bits of matter and structures aggregated out of bits of matter, all behaving in accordance with laws of physics"], a philosophical worldview that has been inspired and fostered by an appreciation of the foundational position of physics among the sciences."[10] The philosophical problem, then, is "where in the physical world our mind fits".[11] Kim defends the view, for which he is justly famous, that many aspects of mental life are reducible to physical phenomena (e.g. the neurophysiology of the brain)[12]—once we understand how reduction actually works in the sciences—but he also holds that the "qualitative characters of experience"—pains, itches, the experience of a color or of a piece of music—are not so reducible. These "subjective" aspects of our conscious experience are now *the* issue philosophers of mind must tackle, according to Kim, for an account of our subjectivity is also implicated in how we understand human agency and human freedom. "[T]he ultimate ideal of philosophy is self-understanding," notes Kim, and that means "an understanding of our nature and our place in the world", an understanding which won't be complete until philosophers have a satisfactory account of "subjectivity".[13]

[9] As Philip Pettit puts it in his contribution: "A naturalistic, more or less mechanical image of the universe is imposed on us by cumulative developments in physics, biology and neuroscience, and this challenges us to look for where in that world there can be room for phenomena that remain as vivid as ever in the manifest [ordinary, common-sense] image: consciousness, freedom, responsibility, goodness, virtue, and the like", "Existentialism, Quietism, and the Role of Philosophy", 306.

[10] "The Mind–Body Problem at Century's Turn", 129.   [11] Id.

[12] More precisely, in the essay here, he defends "conditional reductionism" (p. 138), the view that the only way that mental states like beliefs and desires can *cause* things to happen (like bodily movements), is *if* such states are reducible to physical states. For Kim's earlier, seminal discussions of reductionism and the problem of mental causation see chapters 13, 14, 16 and 17 in his *Supervenience and Mind* (Cambridge: Cambridge University Press, 1993).   [13] "The Mind–Body Problem at Century's Turn", 152.

In arguing that mental phenomena are not all physical, Kim agrees with David Chalmers,[14] whose own contribution takes up a different aspect of the philosophical problem of understanding our mental life. As Chalmers puts it: "Human beings are conscious beings: there is something it is like to be us. Human beings are intentional beings: we represent what is going on in the world."[15] As Chalmers observes, numerous historical figures, from Locke to Husserl, thought it was necessary to understand both aspects of our mental life—consciousness and intentionality—"as a single package",[16] a view that has reemerged in philosophy of mind only in the last quarter-century. On the one side, there have been those like Fred Dretske and Michael Tye who want to understand consciousness as "a certain sort of . . . intentional state"[17] (a view known as "representationalism"), while others, like Colin McGinn and John Searle, argue that the distinctive phenomenology (*experience*) of human consciousness underpins the phenomenon of intentionality.

Chalmers steers a middle course, advocating a kind of representationalist view, but one in which the the *phenomenal* character of intentionality—the fact that representing what is going on in the world is always a matter of representing things "in a certain way"[18]—is ineliminable. "[C]onsciousness and intentionality are intertwined, all the way down to the ground," argues Chalmers,[19] and "the interface between consciousness and intentionality" is the "central topic" for philosophers of mind in the new century.[20]

Nancy Cartwright's contribution on developments in philosophy of science illustrates a different way in which the sciences have impacted philosophy. For much of the twentieth century, philosophers of science sought to understand the character of "explanation" in the sciences without reference to the idea—central in actual scientific practice—of one thing "causing" another. As Cartwright notes, the great empiricist philosopher "David Hume taught that talk of causation was metaphysics and should be consigned to the flames".[21] Yet, as Cartwright shows, the attempts to account for a scientific explanation of some phenomenon purely in terms of its logical form (a genuine explanation was said to be a certain kind of deductive argument) failed.[22] *Real* sciences are interested in *causes*, and an adequate philosophical account of scientific explanation must attend to how the sciences understand *causation*. But—and this is Cartwright's central point—"there are a great variety of causal relations and a great variety of causal systems",[23] so the ambition of some

---

[14] See David J. Chalmers, *The Conscious Mind* (Oxford: Oxford University Press, 1996).

[15] "The Representational Character of Experience", 153.   [16] Id.   [17] Id. at 154.

[18] Id.   [19] Id. at 179.   [20] Id.

[21] "From Causation to Explanation and Back", 231. And for a detailed discussion, see Wesley Salmon, "Four Decades of Scientific Explanation", in P. Kitcher and W. Salmon (eds.), *Scientific Explanation* (Minneapolis: University of Minnesota Press, 1989).

[22] As Philip Kitcher notes in his contribution, the more general program of trying to "slice away statements that transcended the bounds of meaningful discourse"—i.e. "metaphysical" statements—also failed, when it turned out that "proposed criteria that eliminated metaphysics had an unfortunate tendency to stigmatize huge chunks of revered science, while those that respected scientific accomplishments tolerated the most vapid metaphysical formulae." "The Ends of the Sciences", 208.

[23] "From Causation to Explanation and Back", 243.

philosophers to produce a unitary account of "causation" must be abandoned: *real* causal relations don't work that way.

As the preceding discussion would suggest, one result of the "naturalistic turn" in philosophy is that the subject has become richly interdisciplinary. Everywhere one looks, one finds philosophers working in tandem with psychologists, computer scientists, linguists, economists, biologists, or physicists. The interdisciplinary character of the naturalistic turn is especially vivid in the essays by Peter Railton and Alvin Goldman.

Railton's essay develops one important strand of naturalism in recent moral philosophy. Railton endorses what he calls "moral compatibilism" which holds "that moral life does not require human exemption from the laws of nature—if we act rightly or wrongly, for the good or the bad, we do so *within* the natural world we inhabit as empirical beings". As a consequence, any philosophical account of "moral thought and practice must be compatible with what we know of the domain of human psychology, biology, and circumstance upon which it supervenes".[24] Analysis of concepts won't suffice for this approach to ethics. As Railton remarks:

> How could we, as philosophers, offer a "theory of rational action" or "theory of moral perception" intended to be adequate for *understanding* actual life that took no account of the best-developed empirical *explanations* of human motivation, cognition, and perception? It is all very well for a philosopher to say, with assurance, that "our concept of a free act is such-and-such"; it is quite another to say, with equal assurance, that this sort of act *actually* has a central role in human moral life. The latter claim is a claim about—among other things—*what causes what*, and concepts alone lack the authority to decide such matters. Conceptual necessity does not dictate any actual sequence of events.[25]

Railton goes on to show how several perennial topics and problems in moral philosophy—virtue ethics, responsiveness to moral reasons, and the limitations imposed by "human nature"—are recast when considered in light of what we have learned from empirical (social and cognitive) psychology over the past quarter-century.

Goldman's program for a "social epistemology", an epistemology that examines the reliability of the actual social institutions and practices by which beliefs are inculcated, also brings philosophical questions into contact with empirical ones. From "the problem of choosing among experts" (a problem for jurors, as well as patients seeking medical advice), to the problem of "trusting another *person* when I hear her make an assertion" (the "problem of testimony", that arises in trials, in choosing a school or job, indeed, any time we need to rely on others), the "social" dimension of epistemological questions—questions about what we *ought* to believe, assuming we want to believe what is *true*—is inescapable. And social epistemology, on Goldman's view, "intersects and sometimes substantially overlaps with inquiries in . . . the social studies of science, information science, legal theory, democratic theory, and organization theory".[26] If epistemology can not afford to ignore the

---

[24] Peter Railton, "Toward an Ethics that Inhabits the World", 271.   [25] Id. at 268.
[26] "The Need for Social Epistemology", 204.

social dimension of some epistemological questions, then epistemology must necessarily take the naturalistic turn and operate in tandem with other disciplines.

Language and Common Sense

It would be a mistake to conclude from the preceding that the "naturalistic turn" in recent philosophy has substituted one orthodoxy for another. "Conceptual analysis" has attracted new defenders,[27] and there has even been a wave of "old-fashioned" metaphysical theorizing about time, identity, change, and material being,[28] topics that date back in some cases to the Presocratics. As Timothy Williamson remarks, "[t]he usual stories about the history of twentieth-century philosophy fail to fit" this "revival of metaphysical theorizing, realist in spirit, often speculative, often commonsensical".[29] While "empirical knowledge constrains the attribution of essential properties"—a nod to the naturalistic turn in philosophy—it is still the case that "*a priori* arguments retain a central role" and "[t]he crucial experiments are thought experiments".[30]

Yet as Williamson goes on to observe in his essay examining whether we are really past the famous "linguistic turn" of twentieth-century philosophy, philosophers, even "in defining terms . . . must point at real specimens".[31] So even the non-naturalist philosophers are still interested in *reality*, not just *representations* (linguistic or mental) of reality. Moreover, few philosophers now subscribe to the conception of the "linguistic turn" in analytic philosophy associated with Michael Dummett's seminal work.[32] Yet—and this is Williamson's key point—none of this means that philosophers can afford to ignore language. Invoking a striking analogy, Williamson observes:

Some contemporary metaphysicians appear to believe that they can safely ignore formal semantics and the philosophy of language because their interest is in a largely extra-mental reality. They resemble an astronomer who thinks that he can safely ignore the physics of telescopes because his interest is in the extra-terrestrial universe. In delicate matters, his attitude makes him all the more likely to project features of his telescope confusedly onto the stars beyond.[33]

Language is for the philosopher what the telescope is for the astronomer: the *instrument* by which the investigator makes contact with his "real" subject-matter. But instruments, unless they are well-understood, can corrupt our understanding of

---

[27] See Frank Jackson, *From Ethics to Metaphysics: A Defence of Conceptual Analysis* (Oxford: Oxford University Press, 1998). Jackson, however, assigns conceptual analysis a quite modest role—indeed, he chastises conceptual analysis in its "immodest role", namely when "it gives intuitions . . . too big a place in determining what the world is like", id. at 43–4. Conceptual analysis, as Jackson conceives it, is hard to distinguish from banal descriptive sociology of the Gallup-poll variety—indeed, Jackson says explicitly that he advocates, when necessary, "doing serious opinion polls on people's responses to various cases". id. at 36.

[28] See, e.g., Trenton Merricks, *Objects and Persons* (Oxford: Clarendon Press, 2001); Michael Rea (ed.), *Material Constitution: A Reader* (Lanham, Md.: Rowman & Littlefield, 1997); Theodore Sider, *Four-Dimensionalism: An Ontology of Persistence and Time* (Oxford: Clarendon Press, 2001); Peter van Inwagen, *Material Beings* (Ithaca, NY: Cornell University Press, 1990).   [29] "Past the Linguistic Turn?", 111.

[30] Id.   [31] Id.   [32] Id. at 107–12.   [33] Id. at 127–8.

the "reality" to which they are our means of access. Using as his example the philosophical problem of vagueness[34]—the problem that arises when we realize that there are states of affairs (e.g. a severely receding hairline on a head not yet totally denuded of hair) to which it appears we can not decide whether certain predicates ("bald") truly apply—Williamson argues for the indispensable role of attention to language in philosophical inquiry. Indeed, Williamson goes so far as to suggest that "analytic philosophy" might be distinguished precisely by its use of "logical rigor and semantic sophistication to achieve a sharpness of philosophical vision unobtainable by other means".[35]

Plainly, Williamson has identified a distinctive feature of much contemporary philosophy called "analytic", even if other prominent figures so classified (like Thomas Nagel or Bernard Williams) seem to proceed without much attention to either formal logic or semantics. And, indeed, if one central area of philosophy, ethics, is to follow Thomas Hurka's lead in his contribution, then *formal* logic and *formal* semantics, not to mention empirical psychology (as Railton urges), will play a relatively minor role.

Indeed, Hurka sounds a distinctly anti-naturalistic note when he repudiates the relevance to ethics of the "scientizing attitude of logical positivism and successor views such as W. V. O. Quine's naturalism . . . [with its] hostility to common sense . . . [and] the everyday view of the world".[36] But it would be a mistake to assign Hurka to the Wittgensteinian camp, although he certainly thinks that ethics would do well to recapture that camp's "high regard for common sense, which it took to be the repository of . . . human learning".[37] The difficulty is that the Wittgensteinians, with their quietism, are "resolutely anti-technical and anti-theoretical",[38] "they deny that [common-sense] moral views can be systematized or captured in abstract principles", and so they conclude "that theorizing in ethics is fundamentally misguided".[39]

Hurka surely speaks for many moral philosophers in expressing skepticism about this anti-theoretical posture. He writes:

[A]n anti-theoretical position is properly open only to those who have made a serious effort to theorize a given domain and found that it cannot succeed. Anti-theorists who do not make this effort are simply being lazy, like Wittgenstein himself. His central example of a concept that cannot be given a unifying analysis was that of a game, but in one of the great underappreciated books of the 20th-century Bernard Suits [40] gives perfectly persuasive necessary and sufficient conditions for something's being a game. . . . With an exemplary lightness of touch, Suits mentions Wittgenstein only once:

'Don't say,' Wittgenstein admonishes us, ' "there must be something common or they would not be called games" —but *look and see* whether there is anything common to all.' This is unexceptionable advice. Unfortunately, Wittgenstein himself did not follow it. He looked, to be sure, but because he had decided beforehand that games are indefinable, his look was fleeting, and he saw very little.[41]

---

[34] For Williamson's own seminal contribution to the literature, see Timothy Williamson, *Vagueness* (London: Routledge, 1994).   [35] "Past the Linguistic Turn?", 128.

[36] "Normative Ethics: Back to the Future", 249.   [37] Id.   [38] Id.   [39] Id. at 25.

[40] Bernard Suits, *The Grasshopper: Games, Life and Utopia* (Toronto: University of Toronto Press, 1978).

[41] Id. at x , quoted in Hurka, "Normative Ethics", 252.

Hurka views the anti-theoretical tendency in ethics—associated with philosophers like Annette Baier, John McDowell, and Bernard Williams—as guilty of something very similar. Yet, against the naturalistic turn recommended by philosophers like Railton, Hurka sees the future of ethics in the kind of work common a century ago in philosophers like G. E. Moore, W. D. Ross, and C. D. Broad, philosophers who "described the underlying structure of common-sense judgements and in that sense unified and explained them".[42] The future of ethics, on Hurka's view, lies in taking seriously a remark of Nietzsche, who wrote in *Beyond Good and Evil* (sec. 186):

> With a stiff seriousness that inspires laughter, all our philosophers demanded something far more exalted, presumptuous, and solemn from themselves as soon as they approached the study of morality: they wanted to supply a *rational foundation* for morality—and every philosopher so far has believed that he has provided such a foundation. . . . How remote from their clumsy pride was that task which they considered insignificant and left in dust and must—the task of description—although the subtlest fingers and senses can scarcely be subtle enough for it.

The History of Philosophy

Hurka's essay suggests that moral philosophers need to look to their historical forebears—not of the ancient past, but still nearly a century ago—in order to make progress. But that proposal also raises a more general question: namely, why should philosophers study the *history* of their discipline? Wittgensteinian quietists, of course, have a clear reason to study the history of philosophy: it is the history of how we came to make the mistake of thinking philosophy had real methods or could solve real problems! But the naturalistic approach to philosophy, and its idea (shared by non-naturalists) that there are *real* philosophical problems, might seem to make puzzling the idea that the *history* of philosophy matters at all. After all, chemists don't turn to the history of chemistry to tackle today's scientific problems. Why should philosophy be any different?

There are two general kinds of answers, both represented by contributions in this volume. Both answers, implicitly, accept the view that philosophers *ought* to address philosophical problems, whether the relationship between mind and body, or the meaning of a human life. They differ on how the history of philosophy relates to that undertaking. The two answers can be summed up (perhaps a bit crudely) as the view, on the one hand, that history of philosophy is valuable because historical figures *get the right answers* to philosophical problems and, on the other hand, the view that history of philosophy is valuable because, even though historical figures are wrong (or incomplete, or misguided, and so on), *they still help us* get to the right answers to philosophical problems. I'll call the former the view that history of philosophy has "intrinsic" value, and the latter the view that history of philosophy has only "instrumental" value.

The instrumental view is, by far, the dominant view among both Anglophone and "Continental" philosophers. According to the instrumentalists, the history of

---

[42] "Normative Ethics: Back to the Future", 247.

philosophy is a *means* (an *instrument*) for problem-solving. In the strongest version, associated with Hegel, it is *indispensable*. We could not get to the point of philosophical insight into the central problems—the relationship between thought and reality, the nature of morality, the best form of government—without understanding all the philosophical views that came before. The philosophical *insight*, on the Hegelian view, arises precisely from understanding the dialectical progression through history of philosophical thinking on any question.

In a somewhat different Continental version of instrumentalism, associated with Gadamer's hermeneutics, we are always in the grip of a "tradition" whose assumptions and starting points (implicitly) shape our approach to any philosophical question. Indeed, these *enable us* to achieve philosophical understanding at all. Gadamer is answering a distinctively Kantian question, as he himself emphasizes: "How is understanding possible?"[43] Understanding is only possible by virtue of our being immersed in a tradition. It is not then that the history of philosophy has a dialectical structure whose appreciation is essential to unlocking the correct answer to philosophical problems. Rather, philosophical understanding is only possible against the background of tradition, so that only appreciation of tradition makes real philosophical insight possible. "[H]istory," says Gadamer, "does not belong to us, [rather] we belong to it."[44]

Philosophers who "belong" to history neglect history, needless to say, at their peril. As Julia Annas notes in her contribution on ancient philosophy in this volume, in reading philosophical texts we bring "our own interests . . . to the table".[45] She sees as one of the main tasks of ancient philosophy at the dawn of the twenty-first century the "complicated and difficult attempt to retain ancient texts as subjects of philosophical discussion in their own right, while keeping aware of the influence of our own philosophical concerns".[46]

There remains, however, a weaker version of instrumentalism, dominant in Anglophone philosophy, which understands history of philosophy to be *extremely helpful* for problem-solving, but nothing more. Don Garrett, in his contribution, defends this kind of instrumental answer. Following Edwin Curley,[47] for example, he notes that the history of philosophy can suggest,

> alternative answers [to philosophical questions] and the ways in which those answers can be defended; and such knowledge may be of value not only when we decide to pursue one of these alternatives ourselves, but also when we seek to establish the superiority of our own view by contrasting it with its strongest possible alternatives—for then we must explore those strongest possible alternatives, many of which are suggested by philosophy's past.[48]

Yet, as Garrett goes on to argue, there is another important *instrumental* consideration, namely, that "how [philosophical] questions are to be both understood and

---

[43] Hans-Georg Gadamer, *Truth and Method*, 2nd ed., trans. G. Barden & J. Cumming (New York: Crossroads, 1988), xviii.   [44] Id. at 245.

[45] Julia Annas, "Ancient Philosophy for the Twenty-First Century", 26.   [46] Id. at 27.

[47] Edwin M. Curley, "Dialogues with the Dead", *Synthèse* 67 (1984): 51–6.

[48] Don Garrett, "Philosophy and History in the History of Modern Philosophy", 56.

addressed often depends on the theoretical framework within which one poses and pursues them". As he explains:

A question in chemistry, such as the question of whether a particular substance (such as water or lead) changes in kind under specified circumstances, can take on an entirely different aspect depending on whether one poses it in an alchemical or a molecular theoretical framework. Similarly, a question about moral responsibility for actions can take on an entirely different aspect depending on whether one views it in a naturalistic Humean framework or a transcendental Kantian framework. But while the appropriateness of the molecular theoretical framework for understanding everyday questions in chemistry is ordinarily a given, the determination of the best theoretical framework in which to frame and pursue a philosophical question is a key and often highly controversial factor in the ultimate success or failure of philosophical problem-solving. It is precisely by offering not only relatively specific *answers* [as Curley suggests] but also by offering different yet reasonably comprehensive *frameworks* that the history of philosophy can be of aid to contemporary philosophy.[49]

For these reasons, the history of philosophy, according to Garrett, should be "a ready part of every philosopher's toolbox for formulating and approaching philosophical questions".[50] This instrumental view of the history of philosophy as a "tool" for dealing with philosophical questions may have an additional consideration in its favor, namely, that unlike chemistry (or the other natural sciences), the criteria of *success* for solutions to problems are not very clear in philosophy.[51] (That's why, after all, chemists can take as "given" the molecular framework, but moral philosophers can't just *presuppose* the correctness of Kant or Hume.) Without clear criteria of success in philosophy, it behooves us to appreciate the criteria of success other philosophers, at other times, have taken seriously. We ignore these at the risk of sinking into parochial self-congratulation for our current philosophical "insights".

Those who think history of philosophy has *intrinsic value* think, unsurprisingly, that the historical figures *in fact* have as good or better answers than contemporaries to the philosophical problems and questions that exercise us (or *ought* to exercise us) today. Julia Annas devotes most of her attention to developments in scholarship about ancient philosophy, such as the revolution wrought by "analytic" philosophers in the 1950s and 1960s in getting us to treat "works by Plato and Aristotle . . . as equal partners in philosophical debate, rather than revered authorities",[52] the increasing attention to historical context by scholars;[53] the new appreciation of philosophical

---

[49] Don Garrett, "Philosophy and History in the History of Modern Philosophy", at 56.

[50] Id. at 71.

[51] As Julia Annas points out, an historically sensitive reading of Plato throws light on, among other things, the peculiarly "modern assumption" that "a philosophical position must take the form of a theory which can in principle fall to a single counter-argument", 'Ancient Philosophy for the Twenty-First Century", 33. But this modern criterion of success is not shared by the ancients.

[52] Id. at 25. As Annas notes, by now appreciating philosophical developments after Plato and Aristotle, we can also now "see Plato and Aristotle themselves more as the ancients did: not as isolated giants, but as philosophers among others, with a broad range of philosophical interests and arguments", Id. at 34.

[53] Sometimes, as noted earlier, this is essential for appreciating our philosophical biases, but, as Annas also cautions, "added knowledge about cultural and historical background may not be helpful for a philosophical understanding of the texts. At most such background can position someone to focus on the philosophy; sometimes it can even be a distraction", Id. at 30.

developments in the ancient world after Plato and Aristotle; and the emerging *international* community of ancient philosophy scholarship that crosses Anglophone and Continental boundaries. Although Annas does not directly defend the *relevance* of studying ancient philosophers, it is clear what answer she would offer to the skeptic about "history of philosophy" (beyond her hermeneutic cautions noted earlier). She observes, for example, that "renewed [scholarly] interest in Plato's accounts of love and philosophy, and Aristotle's books on friendship . . . did a great deal to bring these themes into the mainstream of non-historical analytical philosophy itself."[54]

Similarly, "the ancient understanding of scepticism"—so different from the modern, Cartesian version that shares the same name—"has many attractions",[55] while the study of ancient ethics led to an appreciation of approaches to philosophical ethics "in which happiness and virtue are the basic concepts"[56] rather than (as in modern ethics) utility maximization or moral obligation. In short, ancient philosophers have *philosophically deep* things to say about central ethical and epistemological questions about which moderns, without the stimulus of the ancients, have been either silent or superficial.

My view of certain figures in the Continental tradition—notably, Marx, Nietzsche, and Freud—is similar. I defend the (unfashionable) view that these thinkers may be sufficiently *right* in their approach to certain problems (for example, about the nature and origin of morality) that we neglect them at the peril of being unable to make progress on the problems at all. This requires us to take seriously how these thinkers understood themselves, namely, as philosophical naturalists trying to make causal sense of phenomena that the sciences had previously ignored, but which philosophy can not afford to neglect. Accordingly, I argue against a recent tendency among Anglophone philosophers to read these figures through a moralizing lens, in which their naturalistic ambitions to *explain* are ignored or dismissed, and their possible import for traditional *justificatory* questions of moral and political philosophy is emphasized. This, I argue, both gets these thinkers wrong and makes them less interesting (and important) than they can be.

"Analytic" and "Continental" Philosophy

In light of the great variety of substantive and methodological approaches surveyed above, it is time to pronounce the "bogeyman" of analytic philosophy laid to rest: so-called "analytic" philosophers now include quietists *and* naturalists; old-fashioned metaphysical philosophers *and* twentieth-century linguistic philosophers; historians of philosophy *and* philosophers who show little interest in the history of the field. Given the methodological and substantive pluralism of Anglophone philosophy, "analytic" philosophy survives, if at all, as a certain *style* that emphasizes "logic", "rigor", and "argument"[57]—a stylistic commitment that does little to demarcate it,

---

[54] Id. at 34.   [55] Id. at 38.   [56] Id.

[57] Bernard Williams made a related point nearly two decades ago: "What distinguishes analytical philosophy from other contemporary philosophy (though not from much philosophy of other times) is a certain way of going on, which involves argument, distinctions, and, so far as it remembers to try to achieve it and succeeds, moderately plain speech. As an alternative to plain speech, it

of course, from Kant, Hegel, Descartes, or Aristotle. The oft-vaunted "clarity" of analytic philosophy—which was, indeed, a distinctive feature of many of the most gifted writers in the genre such as Bertrand Russell, H. L. A. Hart, and Carl Hempel—would, if deemed essential now to membership, place major contemporary Anglophone figures like John McDowell and Christopher Peacocke in some other, still unnamed philosophical camp.[58] Prototypical non-analytic figures, like Schopenhauer and Nietzsche, are far clearer (and more beautiful) writers than many of the dominant figures in Anglophone philosophy today.

Yet the demise of analytic philosophy has at the same time had the salutary effect of making less meaningful the divide between so-called "analytic" and "Continental" philosophy—though this is, in significant part, attributable to the fact that "Continental philosophy" has also become a meaningless category. Traditionally, "Continental philosophy" was an Anglophone term that referred to nineteenth- and twentieth-century German and French philosophy after Kant. And such a crude category could survive as long as analytic philosophy was an opposed, substantive research program and Anglophone scholarship on Continental philosophy was suitably superficial, as it largely was until the 1970s.

Now, of course, things are rather different. We now recognize that the two centuries after Kant in Germany and France actually encompass anywhere from seven to nine distinct, if occasionally, overlapping traditions:[59] German Idealism, German Materialism, Marxism, Neo-Kantianism, Phenomenology, Existentialism, Hermeneutics, Structuralism & Post-Structuralism.[60] The reaction to Hegelian Idealism that set in beginning in the 1830s[61] gave rise to Marxist and Materialist movements in nineteenth-century Germany that have no recognizable affinity with the phenomenological and hermeneutic traditions in Husserl, Heidegger, and

---

distinguishes sharply between obscurity and technicality. It always rejects the first, but the second it sometimes finds a necessity. This feature peculiarly enrages some of its enemies. Wanting philosophy to be at once profound and accessible, they resent technicality but are comforted by its obscurity", *Ethics and the Limits of Philosophy* (Cambridge, Mass.: Harvard University Press, 1985), viii. But on "plain speech" as a distinguishing stylistic feature of "analytic" philosophy, see the comments that follow in the text.

[58] See, e.g., John McDowell, *Meaning, Knowledge, and Reality* (Cambridge, Mass.: Harvard University Press, 1998); Christopher Peacocke, *Being Known* (Oxford: Clarendon Press, 1999). And contrast these writers on metaphysics and epistemology with the contributions in the same area by Jaegwon Kim and Alvin Goldman, as represented, for example, in this volume. Indeed, neither of two major historical figures in the development of twentieth-century analytic philosophy—Ludwig Wittgenstein and Michael Dummett—were paragons of lucid prose writing. Both Wittgenstein and Dummett assert a profound influence, of course, on McDowell and Peacocke (among others), yet there remain important philosophers equally influenced on philosophical matters by Wittgenstein and Dummett who remain exceptionally attractive writers (Colin McGinn is the best example).

[59] See the introduction to B. Leiter and M. Rosen (eds.), *The Oxford Handbook of Continental Philosophy* (Oxford: Oxford University Press, forthcoming).

[60] Logical Positivism—a major force in the development of analytic philosophy before its demise—was born on the European Continent, but soon migrated, literally, to the United States in the persons of Rudolf Carnap, Carl Hempel, and Hans Reichenbach, among others.

[61] See Herbert Schnädelbach, *Philosophy in Germany, 1831–1933*, trans. E Matthews (Cambridge: Cambridge University Press, 1984).

Gadamer. German Materialists like Feuerbach and Büchner have far more in common with late twentieth-century Anglophone philosophers like J. J. C. Smart and Patricia and Paul Churchland, than they do with Heidegger or Foucault. Indeed, the founders of the phenomenological tradition in "Continental" philosophy, philosophers like Franz Brentano and Edmund Husserl, share with one of the founders of the "analytic" tradition, Gottlob Frege, a *repudiation* of precisely the Materialist idea—so influential, for example, with Nietzsche and Freud, among others—that physiology and empirical psychology exhaust what there is to be said about the nature of the mind and mental life.

So, too, the hermeneutic tradition reaches back to Herder in the eighteenth century,[62] and bypasses altogether the Marxist and Materialist movements in nineteenth-century Germany. Hegelian Idealism, a dead issue in Germany by the 1850s (thanks to Schopenhauer and the German Materialists), found its primary home in Oxford and Cambridge by 1900, until Lukács re-inserted it back in to the Marxist tradition in 1923 with *History and Class Consciousness*. Yet today, the leading proponents of views that resonate with Hegel's Idealism are not German and French philosophers, but rather Anglophone figures like McDowell, the late Wilfrid Sellars, and Robert Brandom.[63] Phenomenology's conception of philosophy as a rigorous science of meaning, which arose in Brentano and Husserl as a reaction to late nineteenth-century naturalism, has since been enterred by both Continental[64] and Anglophone philosophers.[65] Such examples of discontinuities within what is often called Continental philosophy could, of course, be multiplied.

The "Continental tradition", then, is no tradition at all, but a series of partly over-lapping philosophical developments that have in common primarily that they occurred mainly in Germany and France in the nineteenth and twentieth centuries (in that sense *only* "Continental philosophy" survives as a useful label, on a par with "early modern philosophy" or "medieval philosophy").[66] Even so understood, it is hard

[62] See Michael Forster's introduction to his edition of Johann Gottfried Herder's *Philosophical Writings* (Cambridge: Cambridge University Press, 2002).

[63] See, e.g., John McDowell, *Mind and World* (Cambridge, Mass.: Harvard University Press, 1994); Wilfrid Sellars, *Empiricism and the Philosophy of Mind*, ed. R. Rorty and R. Brandom (Cambridge, Mass.: Harvard University Press, 1997); Robert B. Brandom, *Making It Explicit: Reasoning, Representing, and Discursive Commitment* (Cambridge, Mass.: Harvard University Press, 1994). For useful discussion, see Sally Sedgwick, "McDowell's Hegelianism", *European Journal of Philosophy* 5 (1997): 21–38. For pertinent criticism of this neo-Hegelian Idealism in McDowell, see Timothy Williamson's contribution to this volume, esp. 109–10. And for a lengthier, and often devastating, critique, see Crispin Wright, "Human Nature?" *European Journal of Philosophy* 4 (1996): 235–54.

[64] See Martin Heidegger, *Being and Time*, trans. J. Macquarrie and E. Robinson (New York: Harper & Row, 1962).   [65] See, e.g., David Bell, *Husserl* (London: Routledge, 1989).

[66] Some might say that "Continental" philosophers at least take Hegel seriously, in a way "analytic" philosophers don't. But it's unclear whether that is really true of, e.g., Schopenhauer (who ridicules Hegel), Nietzsche (who barely read him), or Husserl. Many Anglophone philosophers, as noted, take Hegel far more seriously and respectfully than either of these three major figures of so-called "Continental" philosophy. It is true, as Michael Rosen argues in an especially sensible discussion of this issue, that Continental philosophers are generally concerned with four questions, characterized by Rosen as follows: 1. "Is philosophy possible at all? And, if so, how—what is its method?" 2. "Is there a sharp dividing-line between [science and philosophy]?" 3. "Is the fact that philosophy is part of a process of

to say what sets it apart from "analytic" philosophy, now that the claims about stylistic distinctiveness are less tenable. Consider, for example, Timothy Williamson's observation (in his contribution) that Michael Dummett's influential understanding of "analytic" philosophy would arguably include Derrida! Dummett identifies three distinguishing features of the "linguistic turn" in "analytic" philosophy: that it is concerned with "thought"; that the account of "thought" is not to be a naturalistic (i.e. psychological) one; and that the account requires an analysis of "language".[67] Yet, as Williamson remarks, this applies to "much of what is usually called 'continental (supposedly non-analytic) philosophy.' It is not obvious that Jacques Derrida does not subscribe in his own way to Dummett's three tenets."[68] From the standpoint of demarcation, things hardly get better if we go beyond Dummett and characterize analytic philosophy as involving a "representational turn, on which the goal of philosophy is the analysis (in a generous sense) of representation", whether mental or linguistic.[69] For as Williamson observes—echoing, in effect, Chalmers—"The phenomenological tradition may constitute another form of the representational turn." Moreover, "In the hermeneutic study of interpretation and various shades of postmodernist discourse about discourse the representational turn takes a more specifically linguistic form."[70]

Similarly, as Alvin Goldman notes at the end of his essay on social epistemology, "Many scholars in the humanities assume that only 'Continental' thinkers like Foucault or [Bruno] Latour approach epistemology in a manner that interfaces with real institutional problems. But that impression need not persist if the project of social epistemology as described here is actively pursued."[71] Social epistemologists in the Goldman mode have as much reason to be interested in how society distributes "truth" as Foucauldians, even if the Goldmanesque philosophers are more

historical change itself a fact of philosophical significance?" 4. "If philosophy is something other than a form of science . . . it seems reasonable to suppose that it will affect one's attitudes and practices in a more direct way than the discovery of some new scientific fact", Rosen, "Continental Philosophy after Hegel," op. cit., 665. Question 1, however, does little to distinguish Continental philosophy from most of what usually gets called twentieth-century analytic philosophy. Question 2 typically receives an affirmative answer in many Continental figures (e.g. Hegel, Husserl, Gadamer, Habermas), but it receives such an answer from many figures in "analytic" philosophy, starting, most notably, with Frege. Moreover, it receives a negative answer from Marx (if not all his progeny), though Rosen explicitly excludes Marxism from his discussion of Continental philosophy, and arguably from Nietzsche too (though this is complicated—see my *Nietzsche on Morality* (London: Routledge, 2002), ch. 1). An affirmative answer to question 3 marks perhaps the most distinctive view held by many Continental philosophers (e.g. Hegel, Heidegger, Gadamer, Foucault), but it is surely worth noting that (a) it is not a view shared by other major Continental figures (like Schopenhauer, Nietzsche, and Husserl), and (b) it is on a continuum with views of the history of philosophy advocated by Anglophone scholars (see the discussion below in the text). The "unity of theory and practice", finally, is a striking feature of much Continental philosophy (especially Marx and the Frankfurt School), but it doesn't obviously apply to the phenomenological tradition in figures like Husserl and Merleau-Ponty, and the unity is, in any case, conceived quite differently by, e.g., the Frankfurt School.

[67] "Past the Linguistic Turn?", 107.
[68] Id. As Williamson also notes, the Dummett definition of "analytic" philosophy wouldn't apply to Bertrand Russell!   [69] Id. at 4.
[70] Id. at 108. Cf. the "third part" of Gadamer's *Truth and Method*, op. cit.
[71] "The Need for Social Epistemology", 205.

willing to ask about whether society succeeds in promoting true belief in this or that domain. But that is a dispute about the nature of "truth", not the relevance of the social dimension of knowledge, and on that issue there are reasons, as Goldman himself explains, to think French-style skepticism is hyperbolic.

Philip Kitcher's essay on "The Ends of the Sciences"—the values and goals the sciences *ought* to serve—is a particularly striking illustration of this general development. As Kitcher notes, "the general thrust of [English-speaking] philosophy of science, from 1930 to 2001, could be summed up in a simple program: Science is great, and if we can find out how it works we can improve other discussions enormously."[72] It was left to Continental theorists like Michel Foucault, Herbert Marcuse, Theodor Adorno, and Max Horkheimer to notice that the institution of natural science is "a social institution, of considerable prestige" and to ask "about the effects of this institution: are those effects always beneficial"?[73] Kitcher takes up the challenge posed by the Continental theorists, and shows how it ought to shape an agenda for philosophers of science in the twenty-first-century. On Kitcher's view, critical scrutiny of the "Science is great" mindset of twentieth-century Anglophone philosophy of science requires us to ask two primary questions:

First, are the sciences One or many? In recent years, one of the most exciting and valuable developments within philosophy of science has consisted in posing this question in a variety of ways, and writers like Nancy Cartwright, John Dupré, and Peter Galison have illuminated the diversity of the endeavors we pick out as natural sciences. Second, in what, if anything, does the greatness of the sciences consist? As several generations of post-Kuhnian historians and sociologists have made clear, the sciences profoundly affect and are affected by the societies within which scientific work is done, and it's surely appropriate to try to understand how what they contribute is (or is not) valuable. [This raises] a second Aristotelian question: what are the ends of the sciences and are our actual practices well-adapted to promoting them?[74]

This latter question particularly engages Kitcher's attention, and he argues for a distinctive answer that he has also defended elsewhere,[75] namely, "that there's no general goal of inquiry in all contexts and at all times but . . . the sciences aim to find true answers to those questions that would strike particular groups as significant if they worked out their collective will in an ideal deliberation."[76] Taking seriously a challenge first posed by Continental theorists brings questions of normative theory squarely back in to philosophy of science in a way logical positivists and other twentieth-century philosophers of science would not have anticipated.

Just as "engagement with analytical philosophy restored the study of ancient philosophy to philosophical vigour" (as Julia Annas notes),[77] the Continental traditions have similarly benefitted from attention by "analytical" or "analytically" trained philosophers since the 1970s, philosophers such as Charles Taylor,[78] G. A. Cohen,[79]

[72] "The Ends of the Sciences", 209.   [73] Id. at 208.   [74] Id. at 209–10.
[75] See Philip Kitcher, *Science, Truth, and Democracy* (New York: Oxford University Press, 2001).
[76] "The Ends of the Sciences", 228.
[77] "Ancient Philosophy for the Twenty-First Century", 41.
[78] *Hegel* (Cambridge: Cambridge University Press, 1975).
[79] *Karl Marx's Theory of History: A Defence* (Princeton: Princeton University Press, 1978).

16   Brian Leiter

Allen Wood,[80] Raymond Geuss,[81] Hubert Dreyfus,[82] Michael Forster,[83] John Richardson,[84] Maudemarie Clark,[85] Frederick Neuhouser,[86] and Michael Rosen,[87] among many others. As Julia Annas remarks, Continental scholarship on ancient texts "often treated them in broad and sweeping ways".[88] The same, alas, has been true of much Continental, especially German, scholarship on Continental figures: quotation and paraphrase, and a reverential attitude sometimes bordering on hagiography, have too often substituted for philosophical engagement with ideas and arguments. A valuable legacy of the "analytic takeover" of Continental scholarship over the past quarter-century has been precisely to restore Continental thought to "philosophical vigour". For one thing, the analytically trained philosophers typically write with greater argumentative and philosophical penetration about Continental figures than those not so trained,[89] though it seems more accurate to characterize this as the difference between better and worse philosophy, and not competing "camps". (Which "camp" of philosophy could possibly be *committed* to less careful analysis, less thorough argumentation?) For another, there is an increasing willingness to take Continental thinkers seriously as philosophers, to ask whether they are right and, if so, about what? This has been most apparent in Marx scholarship, where the development of "analytical Marxism"[90] that followed G. A. Cohen's seminal 1978 book on *Karl Marx's Theory of History* led to a wholesale reevaluation of Marx, including the discarding of many familiar Marxist theses.[91]

Rae Langton's essay in this volume illustrates another fruitful way in which "analytic" and "Continental" philosophy are merging, namely, within the burgeoning

---

[80] *Karl Marx* (London: Routledge, 1980); *Hegel's Ethical Thought* (Cambridge: Cambridge University Press, 1990).

[81] *The Idea of a Critical Theory: Habermas and the Frankfurt School* (Cambridge: Cambridge University Press, 1981).

[82] Hubert L. Dreyfus and Paul Rabinow, *Michel Foucault: Beyond Structuralism and Hermeneutics*, 2nd ed. (Chicago: University of Chicago Press, 1983); Hubert L. Dreyfus, *Being-in-the-World: A Commentary on Being and Time, Division I* (Cambridge, Mass.: MIT Press, 1990).

[83] *Hegel and Skepticism* (Cambridge, Mass.: Harvard University Press, 1989).

[84] *Existential Epistemology: A Heideggerian Critique of the Cartesian Project* (Oxford: Oxford University Press, 1986).   [85] *Nietzsche on Truth and Philosophy* (Cambridge: Cambridge University Press, 1990).

[86] *Fichte's Theory of Subjectivity* (Cambridge: Cambridge University Press, 1990); *Foundations of Hegel's Social Theory: Actualizing Freedom* (Cambridge, Mass.: Harvard University Press, 2000).

[87] *On Voluntary Servitude: False Consciousness and the Theory of Ideology* (Cambridge, Mass.: Harvard University Press, 1996).   [88] "Ancient Philosophy for the Twenty-First Century", 35.

[89] Contrast, e.g., the work on Habermas by an "analytic" philosopher like Geuss (*The Idea of a Critical Theory*, op. cit.), with work by a non-analytical philosopher like Thomas McCarthy (see, e.g., his useful, but often superficial and uncritical *The Critical Theory of Jürgen Habermas* (Cambridge, Mass.: MIT Press, 1978).

[90] See, e.g., J. Roemer (ed.), *Analytical Marxism* (Cambridge: Cambridge University Press, 1986); A. Callinicos (ed.), *Marxist Theory* (Oxford: Oxford University Press, 1989).

[91] For the extreme version—bordering on caricature—of this tendency, see Jon Elster, *Making Sense of Marx* (Cambridge: Cambridge University Press, 1985). And for some sober and warranted doubts about Elster's revisionism, see Robert Paul Wolff, "Methodological Individualism and Marx: Some Remarks on Jon Elster, Game Theory, and Other Things", *Canadian Journal of Philosophy* 20 (1990), 469–86. A more balanced assessment of Marx, one that takes appropriate account of the contribution of analytical Marxism, is Jonathan Wolff, *Why Read Marx Today?* (Oxford: Oxford University Press, 2002).

field of feminist philosophy.[92] Anglophone feminist philosophers have tended to focus on how women's oppression involves a denial of their "autonomy", while Continental theorists (especially those associated with what is often called "French feminism")[93] have focused on the "social construction" of gender, of how "women's oppression stems from the operation of large-scale pscyhological or linguistic forces, shaped by unconscious and irrational desires, or shaped by the structure of language itself, a 'language of the fathers' ".[94] As Langton notes, both concerns have a resonance in ideas that emerge from Kant's critical philosophy (a philosopher not often treated appreciatively by feminist philosophers!) but her more immediate concern is to show that the two ideas (about autonomy and the social construction of gender) may interact in important ways. As she writes:

> Feminist thinkers in one camp sometimes get impatient with feminist thinkers in the other. One side [the "Continental" side] finds the other's preoccupation with autonomy naive, a relic of oppressive, dualistic ways of thinking; finds naive her apparent focus on individual action, and local manifestation of prejudice; and finds naive her apparent neglect of the invisible forces of desire and language. The other [the "analytic" side] in turn finds naive her sister's exaggeration of the power of desire and language; finds frustrating the poetic style which seeks an alternative to the language of the fathers, an authentic woman's voice which in practice thwarts communication; and finds naive her apparent neglect of norms, whether of reason or morality, by which a case for feminism can be argued.[95]

Langton proposes to show that, in fact, the concerns of the two "camps" of feminist philosophy come together in any adequate understanding of the phenomenon of sexual objectification. For sexual objectification involves both the idea that woman's autonomy is denied *and* the idea associated with French feminism "that belief is driven by desire, and that belief shapes and constructs the world"—in other words, that a social construction of gender based on desire is then *projected* on to the world, thus obscuring the denial of autonomy.[96] "Sexual objectification", writes Langton, "emerges as the idea that certain sexual ways of treating someone may be ways of denying their autonomy, ignoring their subjective inner life, treating them as readily replaceable, treating them as the kinds of things that can be bought and sold."[97] Yet it also involves the thought—emphasized by Continental theorists—that "those who exert power over women see the world as a certain way because they '*want* to see' the world that way", that is, they *project* their desire-induced beliefs on to it.[98] By offering a careful exposition of the idea of projection, she shows how attention to philosophers like David Hume and J. L. Mackie illuminates ideas found in feminist theorists like Luce Irigaray and Catharine MacKinnon.

[92] See, e.g., Louise Antony and Charlotte Witt (eds.), *A Mind of One's Own: Feminist Essays on Reason and Objectivity* (Boulder: Westview Press, 1993); Catriona Mackenzie and Natalie Stoljar (eds.), *Relational Autonomy: Feminist Perspectives on Autonomy, Agency and the Social Self* (Oxford: Oxford University Press, 2000); Jennifer Hornsby and Miranda Fricker (eds.), *The Cambridge Companion to Feminism in Philosophy* (Cambridge: Cambridge University Press, 2000).
[93] Associated most often with the work of Julia Kristeva and Luce Irigaray.
[94] Rae Langton, "Projection and Objectification", 286.   [95] Id. at 287.   [96] Id.
[97] Id. at 288.   [98] Id. at 289.

Philosophy: Reality and Popular Myths

If *real* philosophy, then, as portrayed in the essays in this volume, is less familiar to readers and scholars outside the field, the explanation is, in part, that a handful of philosophers who have, in recent years, reached a wide audience outside the discipline have generally done a poor job representing the *actual* state of affairs. Richard Rorty is both the best-known and worst offender on this score—his depictions of philosophy are widely regarded by philosophers as shameless fabrications[99]—but even more sober-minded philosophers like the late Bernard Williams have played a role in giving non-philosophers a skewed perception of what philosophers are doing.[100] Other myths about philosophy have been put in to circulation by the media, which often take their cues about philosophy, regrettably, from non-philosophers.

The net result has been that the educated reader these days is likely to have been exposed to all the following (not even consistent!) myths about philosophy:

(1) Postmodernism—that is, far-reaching skepticism about the objectivity of morality, truth, knowledge, and science—is now triumphant in philosophy.

(2) We have reached the "end of philosophy"—the consequence of quietism—thanks to the pervasive influence of figures like Wittgenstein and Heidegger, and their contemporary interpreters like Rorty.

(3) Those remaining benighted "professors" of philosophy—the remaining few who have evaded postmodernism and Wittgenstein—are now so hopelessly

---

[99] Rorty, alas, never responds to his most serious critics, with the result that most philosophers have stopped reading him. For trenchant critical discussions, see, e.g., Jaegwon Kim, "Rorty on the Possibility of Philosophy", *Journal of Philosophy* 77 (1980), 588–97; Ernest Sosa, "Serious Philosophy and Freedom of Spirit", *Journal of Philosophy* 84 (1987), 707–27.

[100] So, e.g., in a widely noted essay on "Philosophy as a Humanistic Discipline" in *The Threepennny Review* (Spring 2001), Williams engages in a reckless polemic against what he calls the "scientism" of contemporary philosophy. He mocks, for example, the "stylistic scientism" of philosophy which embodies "the pretence, for instance, that the philosophy of mind is the more theoretical and less experimentally encumbered end of neurophysiology" (sec. 2). Yet Williams himself commends philosophers for being "better than natural science [at] . . . making sense of what we are trying to do in our intellectual activities" (sec. 3), which was exactly the point of "stylistic scientism"! He objects to the "scientistic illusion, that it is our job as rational agents to search for, or at least move as best we can towards, a system of political and ethical ideas which would be the best from an absolute point of view, a point of view that was free of contingent historical perspective" (sec. 6). But there are no philosophical naturalists who believe that; indeed, the only contemporary figures of note who believe anything close to that are the resolutely anti-naturalist, anti-scientistic American philosopher Thomas Nagel and the Continental figure Jürgen Habermas!

Even more bizarrely, Williams suggests that "the intellectual authority of science is . . . tied up with its hopes for offering an absolute conception of the world as it is independently of any local or peculiar perspective on it" (sec. 4). But the latter feature is usually attributed to science as an *explanation of its actual* source of authority: namely, that it works, whether one is American or Japanese or Iranian. In the end, it appears Williams is simply in the grips of some outdated, mid-twentieth century conception of science and scientific explanation—views usefully debunked by Nancy Cartwright and Philip Kitcher in their contributions—since he thinks "scientistic illusions" stand in the way of philosophy being "part of a wider humanistic enterprise of making sense of ourselves and of our activities" (sec. 8). But surely that is exactly the conception of philosophy recommended in the naturalistically-minded essays by Peter Railton and myself in this volume.

"technical" and "professionalized" that their work is inaccessible and irrelevant to ordinary people; they thus betray the philosophical tradition which spoke to the immediate concerns of all reflective, educated people.

These three myths, as the reader may now recognize, manage to stand reality on its head. Postmodernism is non-existent in all the leading philosophy departments throughout the English-speaking world, where it is regarded, with justice,[101] as sophomoric skeptical posturing. (It is surely a scandal that postmodernism is so often presented in the popular media as a dominant force in the academy, when it is almost completely irrelevant not only to philosophy, but also to economics, physics, classics, mathematics, cognitive psychology, most of sociology, physical anthropology, linguistics, biology, most of political science [rational choice theory, comparative politics, etc.], law, medicine—in other words, the *vast majority* of university disciplines!)[102]. The quietistic influence of Wittgenstein and Heidegger has been pervasive only among those with little knowledge of philosophy; among philosophers, as noted, quietism has been a decidedly minority posture. The non-quietistic philosophers—the naturalists and otherwise—take up *precisely* the kinds of questions that have occupied the major historical figures, in many cases back to antiquity: the objectivity of moral judgement, the nature of reality, the relationship between mind and body, the character of the just society and the good life, and so on. It is true, to be sure, that philosophy is now a "profession"—just like psychology, linguistics, sociology, physics, and mathematics—and it is also true that the discipline is often technical and unintelligible to the lay person. But only a complete ignorance of the history of philosophy could lead anyone to think that this supports a special complaint about contemporary philosophy: Leibniz, Spinoza, Kant, Hegel, and Heidegger, among many other "greats", are also technical and obscure to the lay person.[103] Yet no one, other than teenagers and anti-intellectuals, consider this an objection to their philosophy. As Timothy Williamson trenchantly puts it in his essay: "Impatience with the long haul of technical reflection is a form of shallowness, often thinly disguised by histrionic advocacy of depth. Serious philosophy is always likely to bore those with short attention-spans."[104]

Even if the myths *are* myths, this is not to say that there are not things to lament about professionalized philosophy. There is the tendency, famously remarked upon by Daniel Dennett, to invest substantial intellectual energy in irrelevant issues. In an essay widely available on the Internet,[105] Dennett points out that "you can make

---

[101] See, e.g., Alvin Goldman, *Knowledge in a Social World* (Oxford: Oxford University Press, 1999), ch. 1 "Epistemology and Postmodern Resistance", for a patient analysis and reply to representative postmodern critiques. See also the discussion in Goldman's contribution to this volume at 187–94.

[102] Apparently a disproportionate number of journalists were English or History majors, and so are convinced that "postmodernism" is a philosophical event with scope and depth. (A very different set of ideas called "postmodern" have obviously been influential in the arts and in architecture, among other fields.)

[103] No one made the point more trenchantly than Nietzsche: Kant "wrote against the scholars in favor of popular prejudice, but for scholars and not for the people", *The Gay Science*, sec. 193.

[104] "Past the Linguistic Turn?", 126–7.

[105] It is not published in a conventional journal. The essay, "Higher Order Truths about Chmess", is available, among other places, at the website www.ephilosopher.com.

philosophy out of just about anything, and this is not always a blessing". Some "philosophical projects", observes Dennett, are "like working out the truths of *chmess*", a game just like chess, "except that the king can move two squares in any direction, not one". *Chmess* involves "just as many *a priori* truths" as regular chess, and it requires some analytic penetration and clarity to identify them all. But Dennett suggests that philosophers may too often fail to heed "Hebb's dictum": "If it isn't worth doing, it isn't worth doing well." Dennett continues:

Each of us can readily think of an ongoing controversy in philosophy whose participants would be out of work if Hebb's dictum were ruthlessly applied. . . . One good test to make sure you're not exploring the higher order truths of chmess is to see if people aside from philosophers can actually play the game. Can anybody outside of academic philosophy be made to *care* whether you're right about whether Jones's counterexample works against Smith's principle? Another such test is to try to teach the stuff to uniniated undergraduates. If they don't "get it," you really should consider the hypothesis that you're following a self-supporting community of experts into an artifactual trap.

Alas, the professionalization of the discipline of philosophy has multiplied the number of "self-supporting communit[ies] of experts", which means the trap in question is often set. The contributors to this volume discuss problems that, I suspect, would easily pass Dennett's test, but that will, of course, ultimately be for future philosophers to judge.

Professional philosophy, like any hierarchical organization, also displays unpleasant bureaucratic features, such as cronyism and in-breeding.[106] Philosophers often describe their discipline as being an especially "critical" one, yet much of the time philosophers are deeply uncritical, more so than most might believe. As Hegel appreciated, most philosophers tend to capture their time in thought, that is, they end up giving expression to and trying to rationalize the most deep-seated beliefs of their culture (*vide* Hegel himself, not to mention Kant). Much philosophy takes quite seriously our ordinary "intuitions"—untutored and immediate responses to particular questions or problems—in ways that might be thought suspect.[107] Much philosophy fits the mold of a recent book by an eminent philosopher, whose publisher describes it as "reconcil[ing] our common-sense conception of ourselves as

[106] The Harvard philosopher Hilary Putnam, for example, one of the most influential figures in recent philosophy, appears to cite only to his former or current students and colleagues: one would have no idea from reading Putnam of the range of philosophers making the same or similar arguments, often more compellingly than those Putnam deems worthy of mention! (The contrast with Putnam's long-time Harvard colleague, John Rawls, is striking in this regard: Rawls was meticulous in acknowledging all influences on his work, however obscure.) One of the best-known legal philosophers, Ronald Dworkin, is often accused by specialists of misstating his opponent's views and failing to footnote the sources of criticisms to which he subsequently responds—unless the critics are from one of the annointed institutions like Oxford or Harvard.

[107] On the role of "intuition" in Rawlsian moral theory, see, e.g., R. M. Hare, *Moral Thinking* (Oxford: Clarendon Press, 1981), 11–14. And for more recent doubts about the role of intuition in epistemology, moral theory, and philosophy of mind, see Robert Cummins, "Reflection on Reflective Equilibrium", in M. DePaul and W. Ramsey (eds.), *Rethinking Intuition: The Psychology of Intuition and Its Role in Philosophical Inquiry* (Lanham: Rowman & Littlefield, 1998); Jonathan M. Weinberg, Shaun Nichols, and Stephen Stich, "Normativity and Epistemic Intuitions", *Philosophical Topics* 29 (2001), 429–60.

conscious, free, mindful, rational agents" with "a world that we believe includes brute, unconscious, mindless, meaningless, mute physical particles in fields of force". But why think such a reconciliation is in the offing? Too often, the answer is unclear in philosophy.

To be sure, there are philosophers who do not fit this mold—Hume (at least some of the time), Nietzsche, Charles Stevenson, John Mackie, Galen Strawson, among many others—and sometimes, of course, common sense gets things right, and it is useful for philosophers to work out the insights captured by common sense.

Philip Pettit, in his explicitly meta-philosophical contribution, discusses these issues directly. He notes that

We always do philosophy in dialogue with positions that already have a hold on us. Philosophy, as we might put it, is an attempt to come to terms with those opinions, endorsing them if they prove worthy of reasoned endorsement and seeking to liberate ourselves from them otherwise. It is an effort to appropriate and own the views that we take on relevant questions—to expose them to the light of reason—and not to allow them to remain with us, unseen and uninvited, in the dark of unreflective opinion.[108]

Pettit, then, situates his own view of the role of philosophy between two extremes. On the one hand, there is a kind of "quietist" view which holds that, "Philosophy has no place in practice. It is a quiet and inert presence in life, not one that radiates its influence in other spheres."[109] At the other extreme is the "existentialist" view— exemplified by Kierkegaard, but resonating in aspects of Marx, Sartre, and the Frankfurt School, among others—that philosophy "ought to change people who pursue it, shaping the way they perceive and the way they act. It ought to be capable of being lived out in practice . . . giving a new direction or quality to the experiences and the dispositions of philosophers themselves."[110] Pettit repudiates both extremes. Philosophy takes place "in a field where rival forces pull against one another . . . fidelity to the manifest [the "spontaenous, everyday"] image of how things are, on the one side; fidelity to the intellectual [scientific, rational, critical] image of how things are on the other."[111]

Pettit, as a kind of philosophical naturalist, sees "philosophy [as] continuous with the efforts of science, so far as it attempts to elaborate theory that has to be squared with scientific results".[112] But philosophy goes beyond science since it has as its task "the elaboration of a position that vindicates or can replace the views that come spontaneously to us in the ordinary course of life".[113] Pettit carefully explains how it is that our ordinary practices can commit us to philosophical presumptions and ideas before turning to the question that divides quietists from existentialists: "Is philosophical reflection impotent in relation to the practice from which it springs? Or is it a sort of reflection that can feed back in that way onto ordinary practice?"[114] Plainly, Pettit rejects the quietist answer to these questions, but why, then, does he pull back from the existentialist alternative, whether in "Continental" figures like Sartre or "analytic" figures like J. L. Mackie, or Paul Churchland?

---

[108] "Existentialism, Quietism, and the Role of Philosophy", 305.   [109] Id. at 304.   [110] Id.
[111] Id. at 306.   [112] Id.   [113] Id. at 307.   [114] Id. at 318.

The difficulty for the existential conception of philosophy is that it derives "from an inadequate understanding of the relationship between belief and practice", namely, the supposition that beliefs determine practices.[115] Yet it is crucial to Pettit's earlier account of how practice involves philosophical commitments that many beliefs are "not independent of our reasoning habits and practices"[116] and thus are not available for fundamental revision as existentialists imagine. Many of our ideas, notes Pettit, "come with the inertia of habits ingrained in us by our biology and our background" which "leave in place only restricted possibilities for revision and replacement".[117] Pettit's essay illustrates how even explicitly meta-philosophical reflections implicate basic philosophical issues about the nature of belief and reasoning.

Limitations of space have meant that many important and lively areas of philosophy and philosophical scholarship have, alas, been neglected in this volume: the new wave of "old-fashioned" metaphysics noted earlier;[118] the substantial literature in normative political philosophy that has developed in the wake of Rawls, that sometimes pursues and sometimes criticizes Rawlsian themes, but also develops libertarian, republican, and Marxian ideas, as well as branches out in to investigations of important political concepts like equality and democracy;[119] the turn to philosophy of language, metaphysics, and epistemology which has transformed philosophy of law over the last decade;[120] developments in technical philosophy of language and linguistics;[121] the explosion of specialized work in the philosophy of physics and of biology;[122] and important recent developments in scholarship on

[115] "Existentialism, Quietism, and the Role of Philosophy", at 320.   [116] Id.

[117] Id. at 321.   [118] See above, n. 28.

[119] See, e.g., Thomas Christiano, The Rule of the Many: Fundamental Issues in Democratic Theory (Boulder: Westview Press, 1996); G. A. Cohen, If You're an Egalitarian, How Come You're So Rich? (Cambridge, Mass.: Harvard University Press, 2000); David Copp, Jean Hampton, and John E. Roemer (eds.), The Idea of Democracy (Cambridge: Cambridge University Press, 1993); Samuel Freeman (ed.), The Cambridge Companion to Rawls (Cambridge: Cambridge University Press, 2003); Gerald Gaus, Justificatory Liberalism: An Essay on Epistemology and Political Theory (New York: Oxford University Press, 1996); Michael Otsuka, Libertarianism without Inequality (Oxford: Oxford University Press, 2003); Philip Pettit, Republicanism: A Theory of Freedom and Government (Oxford: Clarendon Press, 1997).

[120] See, e.g., Nicos Stavropoulos, Objectivity in Law (Oxford: Clarendon Press, 1996); Timothy A. O. Endicott, Vagueness in Law (Oxford: Clarendon Press, 2000); Brian Leiter (ed.), Objectivity in Law and Morals (Cambridge: Cambridge University Press, 2001); Michael S. Moore, Objectivity in Law and Ethics (Dartmouth: Ashgate, 2003), Brian Leiter, Naturalizing Jurisprudence (Cambridge: Cambridge University Press, forthcoming).

[121] See, e.g., James Higginbotham, Fabio Pianese, and Achille C. Varzi (eds.), Speaking of Events (New York: Oxford University Press, 2000); Hans Kamp and Uwe Reyle, From Discourse to Logic: Introduction to Modeltheoretic Semantics of Natural Language, Formal Logic and Discourse Representation Theory (Dordrecht: Kluwer Academic Publishers, 1993); Jeffrey C. King, Complex Demonstratives: A Quantificational Account (Cambridge, Mass.: MIT Press, 2001).

[122] See, e.g., David Z. Albert, Time and Chance (Cambridge, Mass.: Harvard University Press, 2000); John Earman, Bangs, Crunches, Whimpers, and Shrieks: Singularities and Acausalities in Relativistic Spacetimes (New York: Oxford University Press, 1995); Tim Maudlin, Quantum Non-Locality and Relativity: Metaphysical Intimations of Modern Physics (Oxford: Blackwell, 1994); Sahotra Sarkar, Genetics and Reductionism (Cambridge: Cambridge University Press, 1998); Sahotra Sarkar (ed.), The Philosophy and History of Molecular Biology: New Perspectives (Dordrecht: Kluwer Academic Publishers, 1996); Simon Saunders and Harvey R. Brown (eds.), The Philosophy of Vacuum (Oxford: Clarendon Press, 1991); Kenneth Schaffner, Discovery and Explanation in Biology and Medicine (Chicago: University of Chicago Press, 1993);

philosophically defunct but historically important movements like German Idealism,[123] phenomenology,[124] and logical positivism.[125]

Notwithstanding this, I am confident this volume will be instructive to both those new to philosophy and those conversant in the discipline. It gives a rich picture of philosophy's distant and recent past, and sets what will prove to be important agendas for philosophy's future.[126]

Lawrence Sklar, *Physics and Chance: Philosophical Issues in the Foundations of Statistical Mechanics* (Cambridge: Cambridge University Press, 1993); Elliott Sober, *From a Biological Point of View: Essays in Evolutionary Philosophy* (Cambridge: Cambridge University Press, 1994); Kim Sterelny, *The Evolution of Agency and Other Essays* (Cambridge: Cambridge University Press, 2001).

[123] See, e.g., Frederick C. Beiser, *German Idealism: The Struggle Against Subjectivism, 1781–1801* (Cambridge, Mass.: Harvard University Press, 2002); Frederick C. Beiser, *Hegel* (London: Routledge, forthcoming); Forster, *Hegel and the Idea of a Phenomenology of the Spirit*, op. cit.; Sebastian Gardner, *Fichte, Schelling and Early German Idealism* (London: Routledge, forthcoming); Robert Stern, *Hegel, Kant and the Structure of the Object* (London: Routledge, 1990) and *Hegel and the Phenomenology of Spirit* (London: Routledge, 2001).

[124] In addition to the books by David Bell and Hubert Dreyfus cited earlier, see also, Taylor Carman, *Merleau-Ponty* (London: Routledge, forthcoming); Pierre Keller, *Husserl, Heidegger and Human Experience* (Cambridge: Cambridge University Press, 1999); Richardson, *Existential Epistemology: A Heideggerian Critique of the Cartesian Project*, op. cit.; Barry Smith and David Woodruff Smith (eds.), *The Cambridge Companion to Husserl* (Cambridge: Cambridge University Press, 1995); David Woodruff Smith, *Husserl* (London: Routledge, forthcoming); Julian Young, *Heidegger's Philosophy of Art* (Cambridge: Cambridge University Press, 2001); Julian Young, *Heidegger's Later Philosophy* (Cambridge: Cambridge University Press, 2002).

[125] See, e.g., Nancy Cartwright, Jordi Cat, L. Fleck, and Thomas Uebel, *Otto Neurath: Philosophy Between Science and Politics* (New York: Cambridge University Press, 1996); Michael Friedman, *Reconsidering Logical Positivism* (Cambridge: Cambridge University Press, 1999); Alan W. Richardson, *Carnap's Construction of the World: The Aufbau and the Emergence of Logical Empiricism* (Cambridge: Cambridge University Press, 1998); Sahotra Sarkar (ed.), *Science and Philosophy in the Twentieth Century*, 6 vols. (New York: Garland Publishing, 1996).

[126] For comments on an earlier draft of this introduction, I am grateful to John Deigh, Thomas Hurka, Maurice Leiter, Peter Momtchiloff, and David Sosa.

I

Ancient Philosophy for the Twenty-First Century

JULIA ANNAS

It may sound peculiar to suggest that ancient philosophy can develop in a way appropriate to the twenty-first century. After all, it consists in the study of a body of texts which, apart from occasional new discoveries, remains fairly constant. Moreover, some among these texts have been studied for so long, and so intensively, that we might question whether there are any genuinely new developments to be made in their interpretation. Ancient philosophy, however, is a philosophical way of engaging with these texts; that is what distinguishes it from other ways of studying them. And philosophy develops differently at different times, so we would reasonably expect the state of ancient philosophy to reflect its engagement with philosophy.

In the twentieth century the discipline of ancient philosophy has undergone two major changes. Firstly, there was a radical shift as it joined the mainstream of analytical philosophy. Then there has been a series of developments peculiar to it, which though varied hang together and have in fact produced a more coherent situation at the beginning of the twenty-first century than has existed for some time. The future of ancient philosophy in the twenty-first century is an exciting one in large part because of its eventful history in the twentieth.

There are, of course, strands of the study of ancient philosophy which have escaped or ignored its engagement with analytical philosophy. In what follows I shall concentrate on analytical philosophy simply because it has been the main force in the field, and its effects have been felt in all areas of philosophy.

In the second half of the twentieth century ancient philosophy came to be emphatically present in philosophy departments. Before that, although philosophers taught and studied history of philosophy (with more or less enthusiasm) specialists even in Plato or Aristotle were quite likely to think of their professional home as being that of classics. (The conception of 'classics' or 'classical studies' as a subject has since become more problematic, and I shall return to this.) The scholarly skills needed to engage with ancient philosophers, even when accompanied by skills in argument, were likely to be developed in a context of historical and literary study of the ancient Graeco-Roman world.[1] Then in the late 1950s and 1960s, there was a great change. Hallowed works by Plato and Aristotle began to be treated as equal partners in philosophical debate, rather than revered authorities. A very 1960s

---

[1] So it is not surprising that in the twentieth century so many prominent figures in ancient philosophy have come from Oxford, where by historical accident philosophy was taught in a classics degree.

excitement developed as it became possible to argue on level ground with ancient thinkers, an excitement which, like much about the 1960s, can seem exaggerated in retrospect because its results have become part of our ordinary ways of thinking, but is still recalled by older scholars as the indication that something really different was happening. This excitement was increased by a surprisingly strong resentment aroused in some of the stuffier classicists by the new analytical approach to figures who *were*, for some of them, revered authorities.

For some time it has been taken for granted, in the major philosophy departments, that ancient philosophy is part of philosophy. Apart from a few eccentrics, philosophers recognize that their colleagues should include someone who teaches ancient philosophy. And those who teach ancient philosophy assume that the ancient texts are to be studied philosophically. However, the general demand that we study Plato on the parts of the soul, or Aristotle on the categories 'philosophically', raises some questions. These were not raised in the 1950s and 1960s when philosophers began reclaiming Plato and Aristotle as philosophers with arguments worth examining, rather than as historical figures important only for the influence of their conclusions. At the time, just what was most exciting was the new ability to focus on the argumentative content of an ancient text, asking directly, What exactly is the argument, and is it valid? What are the premises, and are they true?

This is unsurprising when we bear in mind that the impetus to treat Plato and Aristotle as fellow philosophers came from analytical philosophy, and is best seen simply as the application to ancient texts of the methods of analytical philosophy. Analytical philosophy, however, has as a movement been notoriously ahistorical, and on the whole hostile to the idea that the history of philosophy is relevant to it, so we might wonder how well it works to apply its methodology and techniques directly to ancient texts. Examining this issue is illuminating not just about ancient philosophy but also about the characterization of analytical philosophy itself.

Treating ancient texts philosophically can be, and in the 1950s and 1960s certainly was, regarded as methodologically quite straightforward. You read ancient texts looking for the arguments which support the philosophical positions put forward. You identify the premises and ask whether they are true; you identify the argument and find whether it is valid. If what you find fails to amount to a sound argument, you indicate which premises need to be added, or which argumentative steps need to be corrected, or both. This has appeared to many to be a neutral, transparent approach, in which every step is accountable simply to the canons of good argument. Just for this reason, it seemed for some time the only *philosophical* way to read ancient texts, the only way to treat Plato and Aristotle with respect as philosophical partners, rather than historical relics.

The excitement of discussing philosophy directly with Plato and Aristotle in this way can prevent us from being aware of just how much of our own interests we are bringing to the table, how strong our own assumptions are as to what is and what is not worth discussing. If we think that the only philosophical way to read Plato, say, is to extract an argument in the above way, and thus to get dialogue going between us as directly as possible, taking no account of any wider background presuppositions that either of us is bringing along, then we are likely to drift into thinking that these wider considerations are irrelevant, because we are simply discussing the timelessly relevant issues of philosophy. Asking why just this problem seemed to require an answer in the fourth century BC, or seems to do so at the end of the second millennium, comes to seem optional at best, or even a distraction from what is philosophically relevant.

There are dangers in an excessively ahistorical approach, dangers of which those of us working in ancient philosophy have become more aware. It is working in reaction to these dangers that has produced the best work in the field in the last half-century, and the future of ancient philosophy lies in promoting these directions. In this respect the development of ancient philosophy has been rather unlike that of non-historical analytical philosophy, which on the whole has proceeded more placidly along unquestioned lines.[2] The development of ancient philosophy, on the other hand, can best be seen as a complicated and difficult attempt to retain ancient texts as subjects of philosophical discussion in their own right, while keeping aware of the influence of our own philosophical concerns. In particular we have learned to avoid the dead-ends that have been all too thoroughly explored in excessively direct and ahistorical engagement with the ancients.

The idea that we can just ignore differences between us and Plato, and can discuss one of his arguments in a way that concedes nothing to the historical distance between us, leads to a very selective approach to the ancient tradition. In practice, only issues and problems will be discussed which contemporary philosophers can already find relevant. So it is no accident that ancient philosophy as first practiced in the philosophical mainstream centred on a handful of texts, mainly in Plato and Aristotle, in which issues were discussed that lent themselves to treatment in terms of 1950s and 1960s assumptions, in particular assumptions about language and meaning, and the centrality of these themes for the rest of philosophy. Philosophers' concern with the ancients was for some time very unbalanced, with great over-emphasis on Plato and Aristotle, and on those few of their texts which lent themselves to focus on linguistic issues.

One feature of the impetus to treat ancient philosophers as contemporary partners was, and to some extent remains, an anxiety to show that ancient authors are worth contemporary attention, rather than being archaic blunderers. This anxiety can lead to a rather odd attitude in interpretation, in which no effort is spared to show that an argument which might appear weak or fallacious really contains hidden riches which are worth our time to explore. I once heard a leading analytical interpreter of Plato defend the position that, where an argument in Plato's text emerges as feeble or lacking premises, it is the interpreter's job to supply the missing elements, bringing them in from neighbouring parts of the text or from other dialogues. At what point, he was asked, do you call a halt to this improving cooperation with the text? When I get a sound argument, he retorted without

[2] I don't mean, of course, that there have been no disputes, rather that there has been less pressure to challenge basic methodological assumptions. Non-historical analytical philosophy, however, has changed its self-conception to some extent; see below, pp. 40–1.

missing a beat. As a result of this attitude some arguments, particularly in Plato, have received from analytical philosophers more loving and respectful attention than they have from anyone since the ancient Platonist commentators. Even when the aim has been to disagree with Plato, there has been little hesitation to fortify sometimes sketchy and informal argument with modernized equipment.[3]

The irony here is just one application of a more general irony, namely that ancient philosophy got taken up into the mainstream of analytical philosophy at the latter's most ahistorical point; seldom can a tradition have been less interested in anybody's past, including its own, than at just the time that articles began to appear in analytical philosophy journals on Aristotle's principle of individuation and Plato's Third Man Argument (a notorious problem to which we will return). Only gradually, over a period of years, did it become apparent that an understanding of the structure and motivation of Plato's theory of forms, say, is unlikely to come from the format of short, snappy exchanges of journal articles arguing about the exact structure of a short piece of argument in a particular dialogue.[4]

Taking ancient philosophy up into the mainstream of analytical philosophy was a tremendous catalyst. It produced brilliant work like the articles of Gwilym Owen.[5] It made specialists in ancient philosophy realize that our training should be as rigorous as that of specialists in non-historical philosophy. And the task of explaining Plato to audiences with no background forced us to face philosophical issues in the text plainly and without compromise. It also made philosophers who had assumed that history of philosophy was just history of ideas realize that, to take one example, Aristotle's subtle and difficult account of the soul could provide real philosophical illumination in the context of modern philosophy of mind, and was worth serious, uncondescending discussion.[6]

Ancient philosophy's entry into the analytical mainstream has irreversibly altered the way ancient philosophy is studied and taught. Nonetheless, progress in ancient philosophy has taken us away from the straightforward idea that ancient texts can and should be discussed as though they were modern articles. I shall set out four

[3] It is also true, though, that the early years of analytical argument with ancient philosophers saw a lot of now fortunately forgotten journal articles in which Plato and Aristotle were dismissed in a couple of pages for having committed the 'naturalistic fallacy' or the like.

[4] From the start, there were complaints, particularly where Plato was concerned, that the analytical approach to ancient texts ignored the literary and historical context of the arguments. These complaints, however, tended to issue from sources uninterested in or contemptuous of analytical philosophy, and so it is not surprising that analytical philosophers found little in them to engage with. In recent years there has been a greater tendency (discussed below, pp. 31–2 to appreciate the significance for philosophical interpretation of literary and formal aspects of philosophical writing, Plato's in particular.

[5] Owen's work, difficult and densely argumentative, has not survived as well as has that of easier and more accessible authors. Owen always had less concern for his publications than for his practice of teaching ancient texts in a rigorously philosophical way, and he would have been happy to think of his real legacy as being his students.

[6] A good selection of articles and relevant bibliography can be found in M. C. Nussbaum and A. O. Rorty (eds.), *Essays on Aristotle's De Anima* (Oxford University Press, 1992); also useful is the section 'Psychology' by Stephen Everson in J. Barnes (ed.), *The Cambridge Companion to Aristotle* (Cambridge University Press, 1995). Substantial contributions are David Charles, *Aristotle's Philosophy of Action* (Duckworth, 1984) and Stephen Everson, *Aristotle on Perception* (Oxford University Press, 1997).

ways in which I take this to be so. Those who are suspicious of the idea of progress can make their own judgement as to whether the scene I depict is progress or regress; it is certainly different from what I just called the straightforward idea.

Ahistoricity

In recent years we have seen a rejection of the plain ahistorical approach. This of course forces us to be more specific in defining what is meant by 'ahistorical' here. There has never been a shortage of ancient historians and literary scholars chastising the study of ancient philosophers as 'ahistorical' where by this they mean that it is done without situating the works historically and culturally in a non-philosophical context. This kind of complaint refuses to take seriously the idea of studying philosophical argument in its own right, and students of ancient philosophy just have to face the fact that it is a professional hazard and will probably always be with us.

It is true that with ancient philosophers, particularly before Aristotle, we should not underestimate the possibility of important cultural factors which make the philosophical argument difficult for us to engage with. Parmenides and Empedocles, for example, write in Homeric hexameter verse, a style rather different, to put it mildly, from contemporary professional ways of writing philosophy. This introduces problems of vocabulary, style, and syntax which complicate our interpretation of the arguments, as well as issues of audience and reception. So sometimes, indeed, we do need to be reminded that there is non-philosophical background to be mastered before we can confidently proceed to discuss the philosophy. But this is not universally true; Hellenistic and later philosophy is frequently quite near in style to modern ways of producing philosophical writing. In any case, this is only one way in which study of ancient philosophy can be 'ahistorical', and surely not the most relevant one.

'[I]t is a commonplace of modern criticism that every text is to be located within a complex network of cultural practices and material.'[7] What is the relevance of this to the study of ancient philosophy? We are just not in a position, with ancient philosophers, to contextualize their work in terms of contemporary history and culture; we know too little about the background in most cases, the biographical traditions have been thoroughly contaminated by philosophical polemic and hagiography, and some authors, notably Plato, write in ways which seem designed to frustrate explanation in terms of contemporary background.[8] Moreover, many

---

[7] Kathryn A. Morgan, 'Socrates and Gorgias at Delphi and Olympia: *Phaedrus* 235d6–236b4', *Classical Quarterly* 44(ii), (1994), 375–86, 375. I am not criticizing Morgan, who does not claim to be reading the text philosophically. She points out that a reference in Plato's *Phaedrus* to the dedication of statues at Delphi probably has a historic reference to the sophist Gorgias, picturesquely underlining Plato's already evident contempt in the dialogue for famous practitioners of rhetoric. Morgan is also quite aware of the point that 'Students of the ancient world may sometimes feel at a disadvantage; we simply do not have as much information as we would like in order to contextualize thoroughly. This has been especially true in the study of the Platonic dialogues' (375).

[8] Some of Plato's dialogues have a thickly described background, and their vividness can lead us to forget that they are set at least one generation in the past. Plato further complicates things by his use of deliberate historical anachronisms.

ancient philosophers write in a way to which historical background is utterly irrelevant. The Middle Platonist Alcinous' *Handbook of Platonism*, for example, was written at some time between the first century BC and the second century AD, but nothing dates it within that period, so nothing in it can be explained by the large cultural and political changes in that period. Quite a few philosophical texts exist in this kind of multi-century limbo. But in any case added knowledge about cultural and historical background may not be helpful for a philosophical understanding of the texts. At most such background can position someone to focus on the philosophy; sometimes it can even be a distraction.

Yet the study of ancient philosophy has definitely become 'less ahistorical' in the last thirty years, so the texts are in some way being contextualized rather than being treated by contemporary philosophical analysis in a completely unmediated way. In part this naturally comes from disappointment at the results of focusing on individual arguments in isolation from their intellectual context, a disappointment which has led to the demand for more intellectual contextualization of such arguments. A case study in this kind of shift is to be found in the changing fortunes of the so-called 'Third Man' argument.

In Plato's dialogue *Parmenides* young Socrates puts forward what certainly looks like a position we find in other dialogues about what are called 'forms'. Parmenides, an older philosopher, raises against this position six objections, none of which Socrates is able to meet. The second one, a rather short passage of less than half a page, raises a problem about forms using the example of the form of *large*. Socrates' claim that there is a form of large leads, apparently, to an infinite regress. This has long been recognized as a significant argument, often referred to as the 'Third Man' argument, rather than the 'Third Large', because 'The Third Man' is Aristotle's name for an argument which looks relevantly similar to this one.

The argument itself is deceptively simple to state. When we consider a number of large things, we notice that they all share a common feature, that of being large, and we take this to be the form; the form is the one item in virtue of which all the large things are large. But then we go on to consider a second group of large things: the original large things and the form itself. And now it seems that they share a common feature, requiring a form in turn to be the one item in virtue of which they are all large. But once introduced, this line of thought leads to the conclusion that if we have even one form, we have infinitely many.

An article by Gregory Vlastos, one of the most influential figures in twentieth-century ancient philosophy, began a spurt of philosophical investigation of the argument. Vlastos suggested that the problem with the argument lies in Plato's holding a position that contains two assumptions which are not explicit in the text. The first is that the form of F is itself F. The second is that whatever is F cannot be F by virtue of itself. Suppose we say that there is a form of large but it is not itself large; or that it is large, but is large by virtue of itself; in neither case do we get the infinite regress.

Why should this particular point be crucial to Plato's interpretation, generating a flood of articles, often disagreeing very intemperately? To understand this we have to bear in mind that the background was seen as one in which Plato holds a 'Theory of Forms', that is, has a position about forms which is organized in an explanatorily ambitious way comparable to that of a modern philosophical theory. Such a theory is vulnerable to a successful counter-argument; if it depends on assumptions which, when made explicit, lead to infinite regress, then it has obviously failed as a theory. Hence the 'Third Man' was seen as the crucial counter-argument to the 'Theory of Forms'. Argument swirled for decades round the issues of whether the argument destroys the theory, or the theory withstands the argument, and of whether Plato was aware, or not, of the assumptions he was making and their implications. Vlastos held that the argument is a record of 'honest perplexity': Plato could see that there was a fundamental problem, but couldn't identify what it was. Some classicists of the old school argued that the theory withstands the argument, since the argument depends on a misconstrual of what forms are. Some argued that Plato recognized the upshot of the argument and changed his theory of forms to avoid it.

Each of these views has implications for what is often called 'the development of Plato's thought'. If the argument rests on a misunderstanding of the theory, then it gives us no reason to think that the theory ever changed. If the argument damages the theory, and Plato recognized this, then we would expect works written after the *Parmenides* to reflect this. If Plato realizes that something is wrong, but cannot identify what, we would still expect a less confident use of the 'theory of forms' than before. So a large part of the controversy involved the issue of whether Plato's thought developed in a way marked by either abandoning or modifying the 'theory of forms'. Study focused on dialogues generally considered to be later than the arguments in the *Parmenides*, but this proved inconclusive; because Plato never develops a technical terminology there can be dispute as to whether various passages do in fact constitute a reference to forms, and what appears to be the main example of a 'late' dialogue containing an account of forms vulnerable to the 'Third Man', the *Timaeus*, may well not be later than the argument.

All of this presumes that the 'theory of forms' is a defining part of Plato's thought, and that the issue of whether it can be held despite the 'Third Man' argument is one the answer to which is going to determine central issues about Plato's philosophy. This explains the ongoing activity, for over two decades, of books and articles containing ever more refined and ingenious approaches to the argument and its attendant issues, especially that of the form F being itself F (so-called 'self-predication').[9] This activity eventually died down out of exhaustion, as the relevant moves and counter-moves became clear; there was no definite winner.

Yet the 'Third Man' does not remain as a pressing unsolved problem. Rather, we can now see that a great deal of the time and fuss was off the point, and that the argument yields far better philosophical understanding if instead of plucking it out of its context and treating it as though it were straightforwardly a modern argument attacking a modern kind of theory, we try to put it into its broader philosophical context.

---

[9] A very thorough analysis, with references to the modern literature, is to be found in Gail Fine, *On Ideas* (Oxford University Press, 1993). Fine deals with Aristotle's criticisms of Plato's theory of forms, in a way sensitive to all the evidence, and to the differences in methodology between the two philosophers.

This involves, firstly, recognizing that the *Parmenides* is a dialogue, not a philosophical treatise. So much writing about the dialogue form in Plato has in the twentieth century come from literary and non-analytical sources, and it has frequently been so hostile to philosophy, that analytical philosophers have been understandably reluctant to give it a serious role. Only relatively recently has it become clear that the dialogue form has an important *epistemological* role for Plato. It distances him from what is said, even when it is said by Socrates, in a way which should inhibit the reader from simple-mindedly accepting what Socrates says as being what Plato thinks. This does not imply that Plato rejects, or is dubious about, its truth; the point is rather one about the way the reader receives it. If we accept what we find in Plato on his authority, then, even if what we have acquired is true, we have acquired it in a non-philosophical and unreflective manner. Plato presents us with arguments in a way designed to encourage us to pursue them *as arguments*. Only if we think about the conclusions, and the way they are reached, for ourselves are we making headway towards philosophical understanding. This is the most likely explanation of why we never find a 'theory of forms' laid out in the manner of a treatise; instead, we find forms in various passages and various argumentative roles which we have to pursue for ourselves. Of course, these passages are part of a larger position, but there is no writing of Plato's where the work is done for us, and all the parts of such a position are brought together for us and presented as a theory in the modern manner.

The first part of the *Parmenides*, moreover, is not just *a* dialogue, but is very like the Socratic dialogues where Socrates confronts someone who claims to be an expert, but is shown up as lacking understanding when he cannot answer Socrates' questions about the nature of his subject. In the *Parmenides* it is Socrates who is the overconfident purveyor of a position which Parmenides' questions show that he doesn't really understand. If we take this point seriously, we can appreciate that the result of Socrates' failed answers is the same as the result for others in the Socratic dialogues—*aporia*, puzzlement, the state you are in when you realize that you don't understand something that you thought you did. This is not the straightforward destruction of a theory, because failure to answer probing questions adequately doesn't prove that you are wrong. You might be right, but you still have a lot of work to do before you really understand your position. Once we take this point seriously, we can see why the result in the dialogue is not that Parmenides tells Socrates that his forms are no good, but rather that he tells him that his commitment to the idea has been premature: he must train himself further in various kinds of positive and negative abstract argument before he can claim to have understanding of it. Finally, once we take *this* point seriously we can see why the *Parmenides'* first part is followed by a long second part consisting of just this—argument for and against a number of highly abstract theses. Moreover, it is through looking carefully in the second part that philosophers have found arguments and themes that are highly illuminating about the arguments in the first part, including the 'Third Man'.[10]

[10] See M. Schofield, 'Likeness and Likenesses in the *Parmenides*', in C. Gill and M. N. McCabe (eds.), *Form and Argument in Late Plato* (Oxford University Press 1996). M. L. Gill, in her introduction to the Hackett translation of *Parmenides* by M. L. Gill and P. Ryan (1996) gives a clear account of the options, with reference to previous work.

The fate of the copious literature on the 'Third Man' gives us a cautionary tale as to what happens when an ancient text is seized upon too unreflectively and treated as though we had a confrontation of theory with counter-argument like those in analytical philosophy journals. Once the argument is taken out of its argumentative context and intellectual background, its significance becomes misunderstood and its importance overblown—and so are supposed implications about the development of Plato's thought. We gain much more understanding when our engagement with it is mediated by consideration of Plato's methodology, particularly his philosophical use of dialogue.

It is obvious, however, that our improvement in understanding both the argument and its role does not represent a falling-off from standards of analytical rigour in argument. It just makes it clear that carefulness and precision in dealing with arguments do not have to bring with them further, more locally modern assumptions, such as that a philosophical position must take the form of a theory which can in principle fall to a single counter-argument. It also shows how precision in arguing is actually increased once we bear in mind that for ancient philosophers there is nothing methodologically odd about putting forward a theory in a way which explicitly recognizes that it has problems and is not fully understood.

This kind of contextualizing obviously requires historical knowledge of, for example, much of Plato's work and not just this dialogue, as well as awareness of differences between ancient and modern methodology where theory and argument are concerned. In a perfectly good sense it is a less 'ahistorical' approach than the one visible in previous focus on the 'Third Man'. But none of this is historical in a sense opposed to philosophical rigour, implying that Plato is being treated as history of ideas. Indeed, it is only when we contextualize the argument in this kind of way that we achieve a precise philosophical understanding of it.

Broader Scope

The philosophers who made the first and strongest appeal to people wanting to treat ancient texts in an analytical way were Plato and Aristotle. This was only natural: their texts were accessible without source-criticism, they were already prominent in the teaching tradition, and various themes in them were already familiar to non-specialists. Treatment even of Plato and Aristotle, however, was at first constrained by the analytical tradition's focus on issues of meaning and language: a few of Plato's dialogues, such as the *Theaetetus* and *Sophist*, were heavily emphasized because of issues about meaning and reference that were discovered there, and interest in Aristotle focused greatly on themes of language and reality found in the *Categories* and the central books of the *Metaphysics*. Interest in philosophy of mind also led to intensive study of Aristotle's works on the 'soul'. None of these topics, it is worth mentioning, were regarded as central in ancient philosophical debate.

Once again, philosophical interest in a limited circle of topics, intensively worked on, became exhausted. From the late 1970s, however, a huge widening of concerns developed among ancient philosophers, spreading interests both within Plato and

Aristotle studies and outside it. Once again, there was no shedding of analytical exactness and rigour in argument. It was just parochial twentieth-century limitations of interest which one by one were overcome. One striking example is the renewed interest in Plato's accounts of love and philosophy, and Aristotle's books on friendship, texts which had hitherto been skirted for the most part with nervousness or embarrassment. That texts like these could be treated in philosophically rewarding ways did a great deal to bring these themes into the mainstream even of non-historical analytical philosophy itself.[11]

Another limitation that got shed fast was limitation of interest to Plato and Aristotle. Groups of ancient philosophers, both locally and internationally, focused philosophically on post-Aristotelian philosophy in particular, an area that had been thought of as the preserve of specialists: many of the major texts were available only in the original languages, and the tradition of discussion had been mainly limited to classicists. In the last two decades, however, there has been a stream of translations of later texts and philosophical debates bringing them into the mainstream of ancient philosophy teaching and research. Later ancient philosophy is now available at all teaching levels, and as a result the field has broadened in a strikingly rapid way. Stoic logic, Epicurean ethics, and Sceptical self-refutation arguments are now just as much a part of the field, as that is defined by teaching, publications, and conferences, as Plato and Aristotle. The result has been a redefining of the whole field. Not only are more ancient philosophers included, but our conception of ancient philosophy is now much less focused on large dominating figures, such as Plato and Aristotle had become, and more on continuing debates and themes. And we see Plato and Aristotle themselves more as the ancients did: not as isolated giants, but as philosophers among others, with a broad range of philosophical interests and arguments.

Unsurprisingly, the non-historical mainstream of analytical philosophy did not keep up with this expansion of historical horizons. One result of this growing divergence was the birth of a number of new philosophy periodicals devoted to ancient philosophy, and a corresponding decrease of such articles published in journals belonging to non-historical analytical philosophy. The new ancient philosophy journals, born in the late 1970s and early 1980s, are still going strong, and their content illustrates very nicely the way in which ancient philosophy has and has not moved away from analytical philosophy. In their interests the articles do not defer to the current fashions in non-analytical journals, their agenda being given by debates arising within the field. They are, however, as rigorous and exact as articles in non-historical analytical journals. Unlike pre-1950s articles on the same topics they are unlikely to contain large amounts of untranslated Greek and Latin, or to focus on philological points unless these are crucial to an argument.

---

[11] Here much is owed to the work of Martha Nussbaum on Platonic dialogues like the *Symposium* and *Phaedrus*, which had been skirted not just because of their content but because of their rich literary style, alien to contemporary analytical philosophers. Nussbaum's work on ancient moral philosophy has been of landmark importance because it benefited from consideration of the rich moral psychology involved, and this has in turn enriched her work on modern ethical and political thought.

Many of the conferences and meetings which sparked off the huge new interest in later Greek philosophy were international ones, and another result of ancient philosophy's becoming more independent of the analytical mainstream in anglophone countries was that it became more international in outlook. There was increasing cooperation with ancient philosophers working in Europe, the results of which can be seen in the increasingly internationalized ancient philosophy journals. In continental Europe, ancient philosophy has a rather different relation to analytical philosophy, which it encountered somewhat later than did the anglophones. In the European traditions, especially the French, philology had never become as atheoretical a study as it had in Britain, and it had more reserves ready for its encounter with analytical philosophy. Also, analytical philosophy was never the powerful presence in continental Europe that it was in anglophone countries, and so it was never able to impose its own sense of philosophical priorities as it first did in those countries. It is not so surprising, then, that from the first the impact of analytical ways of doing philosophy in European countries was to focus attention in a more rigorous and exact way on the ancient philosophers' arguments. This was in sharp contrast to competing philosophical ways of reading ancient texts in these countries, which often treated them in broad and sweeping ways. It fitted in well, however, with a tradition which insisted on philological erudition, and had never been interested in taking over the philosophical interests and dogmas of anglophone non-historical analytical philosophers.[12]

Methodology

As we have investigated ever more theories and arguments over the area of ancient philosophy, one thing that we have come to understand a great deal better is ancient philosophical methodology. It was philosophically exciting, in the 1960s, to replace the classicists' view of Plato as a grand sweeping synthesizer, more interested in vision than in argument, by a Plato with whom we could simply argue, laying out his arguments and debating with them. But, as the case of the 'Third Man' vividly shows, this could lead to an attitude which missed Plato's own methodology because of blindly imposing our own.

It has been a gradual process over time for philosophers to come to understand ancient philosophical arguments in terms of ancient philosophical methodology. As this has happened, it has inevitably led to increased self-awareness about our own methodology, and hence to a weakening of the ahistorical viewpoint implicit in

[12] In France, Jacques Brunschwig and André Laks should be mentioned as leading figures in this continental approach to ancient texts. See A. Laks, 'Herméneutique et argumentation' 146–54 of *Débat* 72 (1992), Gallimard. In Germany, the influence and pupils of Guenther Patzig have been notable. In a study of this scope, I cannot do more than mention a few highlights of traditions which deserve fuller investigation, but I should not pass over the vigorous Dutch contributions, particularly Jaap Mansfeld's doxographical studies at Utrecht, and the notable flourishing of ancient philosophy in Italy, particularly under the influence of the late Gabriele Giannantoni at Rome and Marcello Gigante at Naples, the latter having revitalized study of the Epicurean writings from Herculaneum. Many Italian ancient philosophers have become better-known in the anglophone world, such as Anna Maria Ioppolo and Carlo Natali.

taking ancient philosophers to be our partners in some timeless argument. Far from leading to a weakening of the philosophical impulse in discussing these texts, this has led to a deepened philosophical engagement with them, one that can have implications for modern philosophy as well as for our understanding of the ancients.

One example of this is the issue of teleology. Aristotle in particular has been the target of various criticisms to the effect that his biology depends on unacceptable 'metaphysical' ideas, such as teleology. What exactly, though, is teleology? When little attempt was made to explore Aristotle's biology, it was often assumed that teleology must imply a grossly anthropomorphic view of the natural world, in which natural things and processes were thought of as though they had desires, plans, and so on. Increased attention to the biology, and to its relations with Aristotle's epistemology of science and the rest of his science, has resulted in clarification of the whole idea of teleology. It is now clear that Aristotle's teleology is not anthropomorphic and in no way depends, as some later theories do, on the notion of divine plan in the world. It is an immanent teleology, recognizing that in the natural world there are many things and processes such that we cannot under-stand their nature until we recognize the role they play 'for the sake of some larger system'. The increase in sophistication in our understanding of teleology has had an impact on both ancient and modern studies of the topic.[13]

The really dramatic results, however, have come in the areas of epistemology and of ethics. The contrast between the way in which Plato's epistemology was regarded, for example, in the 1960s and the way it is studied now is astounding. When Plato began to be discussed in the terms of analytical philosophy, his claims about knowledge were simply interpreted in familiar terms, and the result was distinctly odd. Forms were taken to be abstract objects which we know by a pecu-liar kind of mental seeing;[14] not surprisingly, this appeared to be, as an account of knowledge, both mysterious and extravagant.

Since then, careful work has shown us that Plato's concern with knowledge is complex. In the 'Socratic' dialogues the model of knowledge is that of skill or expertise; the expert is the person who has understanding of their subject-matter, and hence, according to Plato, should be able to 'give an account' of it—that is, explain and justify what it is about the subject which they understand which grounds their successful practice of it. In the case of people who fail to meet this

[13] Understanding of Aristotle's biology has enormously increased in sophistication in the last half-century. The work of David Balme has received increased recognition; see the collection of articles in his honour edited by Allan Gotthelf, *Aristotle on Nature and Living Things* (Mathesis Publications / Bristol Classical Press, 1985). *Philosophical Issues in Aristotle's Biology*, edited by Allan Gotthelf and James Lennox, is another influential collection of pioneering articles. Also important are Pierre Pellegrin's *Aristotle's Classification of Animals*, translated by A. Preus (University of California Press, Berkeley, 1986), and *Aristotle's Philosophy of Biology*, Cambridge Studies in Philosophy and Biology (Cambridge University Press, 2001), James Lennox's collected papers.

[14] Plato was taken to 'posit . . . the existence of Ideas as real abiding entities visible to the mind, and therefore [sic] qualified to be objects of knowledge in the fullest sense' (R. M. Hare, *Plato* (Oxford University Press 1982, 37)). Hare regards this position as ridiculous, but instead of seeking a more sympathetic understanding he accuses Plato of various muddles about language and reference supposedly leading to the absurd position.

standard for understanding virtue, piety, justice, and the like we can discern what grounds Plato's requirements for knowledge of what he calls a form—the object of understanding which grounds successful practice in the ethical realm. The demand comes from the same source as the everyday demand we make on an expert to be able to articulate and communicate to us the basis of her understanding, and hence the knowledge in question, far from being a passive gaze on an abstract object, is thought of as essentially a kind of *practical* knowledge—a knowledge of how to act which is like that of the everday expert in practical matters.[15]

In dialogues like the *Republic* we can also see the influence of mathematics as a model for knowledge in general—something which in its turn has implications for the way forms are regarded. It is from the *Republic* that we get most of the imagery for knowledge of forms (particularly in the famous passage of Sun, Line and Cave). Both of these models are influential in a great deal of Plato's work, but we also find a third in the *Meno* and *Theaetetus*, one closer to modern epistemology in its focus on the individual knower's relation to a particular fact, and on the idea that knowledge might be some kind of improvement on true belief. Great progress has been made in disentangling these different strands in Plato's thinking about knowledge, and this has not just improved our interpretation of Plato, but has produced more thought about different conceptions of knowledge, and the very varied character of ancient epistemology. Especial interest has been raised by the model of practical expertise, with its implicit challenge to the twentieth-century philosophical dogma that thought about values cannot be in its nature practical.[16] And there has been much reflection on the notion of understanding, something which does not correspond readily to any modern epistemological notion, but appears in the ancient texts as a prominent and powerful idea.[17]

Work on ancient scepticism, pioneered by Myles Burnyeat and a number of other scholars,[18] has in effect rediscovered a whole ancient methodology which had

[15] The classic article showing the importance of skill or expertise for Plato's account of knowledge in the Socratic dialogues is Paul Woodruff's 'Plato's early theory of knowledge' in Stephen Everson (ed.), *Epistemology* (Cambridge University Press, 1990), ch. 4, ('Companions to Ancient Thought' 1—the volume also contains extensive relevant bibliography).

[16] My article, 'Moral Knowledge as Practical Knowledge' in Paul, Miller, and Paul (eds.), *Moral Epistemology* (Cambridge University Press, 2001), 236–56, explicitly points up the contrast between ancient and modern demands on moral epistemology.

[17] Here the work of Myles Burnyeat has been important, notably in reference to the famously difficult claims of Aristotle about *nous* (often translated 'understanding' or 'comprehension'). See Burnyeat's 'Aristotle on Understanding Knowledge', in E. Berti (ed.), *Aristotle on Science: the Posterior Analytics* (Editrice Antenore, Padua, 1981), 97–139. Christopher Taylor, in his study 'Aristotle's epistemology', in Stephen Everson (ed.), *Epistemology* (Cambridge University Press, 1990), 116–42, refers to other work on the issue by James Lesher, Aryeh Kosman, and Charles Kahn.

[18] Seminal and much discussed articles by Jonathan Barnes, Myles Burnyeat, and Michael Frede are reprinted in M. Burnyeat and M. Frede (eds.), *The Original Sceptics: A Controversy* (Hackett, 1997). Important sceptical arguments are translated and commented in *The Modes of Scepticism: Ancient Texts and Modern Interpretations*, Julia Annas and Jonathan Barnes (Cambridge University Press, 1985), and there is a recent translation of Sextus Empiricus' *Outlines of Scepticism* by Julia Annas and Jonathan Barnes in the Cambridge Texts in the History of Philosophy series (Cambridge University Press, 2000). There has been a spate of recent articles and books on many aspects of ancient scepticism, of which some of the most

remained misunderstood for some time. As developed in modern analytical philosophy, scepticism is generally understood as a claim about the possibility of knowledge, either in general or in some specific area. If this assumption is brought to the ancient texts, an obviously inadequate interpretation results. Careful study of a wide range of ancient texts has recovered a proper understanding of ancient scepticism, which is an attitude leading to the investigation of any disputable claim, and is as concerned with beliefs as with knowledge. Unlike modern scepticism, which with few exceptions assumes the viability of a philosophical position insulated from practical effect, ancient scepticism takes seriously the thought that our attitude to our beliefs will be changed if we find that they lack rational support which we previously took them to have.

In turn, as the difference between ancient and modern conceptions of scepticism became clearer, we have recovered the sense of the ancient conflict between interpretations of Plato as a sceptic and interpretations taking his work 'dogmatically', that is, as a system of doctrines. In the modern understanding of scepticism, it is bizarre to think of Plato as a sceptic; when we recover the ancient understanding of scepticism, we can see that this is a subtle and powerful interpretation, which has many attractions. This recovery of the ancient options has done a great deal to loosen the hold of contemporary preconceptions about intepreting Plato, and to lead to a more open-minded attitude as to how to read—and to teach—this most elusive of ancient philosophers.

Most dramatic, though, is the case of ethical theory. Ancient ethics has been studied throughout the twentieth century, mostly in Aristotle's version, but has generally been regarded as an object of purely historical interest. The resurgence of philosophical interest in ancient texts at first merely added to this view: various ancient arguments were convicted of 'deriving values from facts', or similar sins, and Aristotle's supposed 'function' argument was plucked out of context, given an overblown significance and mostly misunderstood. Study of ethics, however, benefited greatly from the expansion of interest into a wider range of ancient philosophy, since Aristotle's theory is only one of many ancient theories produced within the same tradition, that in which happiness and virtue are the basic concepts.

Ancient ethics begins from reflection on my life as a whole, and my attempts to live a good life, rather than one whose form is given by unreflective adherence to norms and priorities. Different ethical theories are seen as giving different answers to the question of how I can, in fact, live a good life, and ethics is thus seen as a struggle to come up with the right specification of my final end, the goal I am seeking in my life as a whole. Because this end is in ancient thought characterized as *eudaimonia* or happiness, this type of ethical theory is rightly called eudaimonist. Until the last decades, theories of this kind had been seen as being of very limited contemporary relevance, mainly because of crude and uncriticized conceptions of happiness. Aristotle's theory, for example, was frequently dismissed as egoistic, the assumption being that happiness

noteworthy are Jonathan Barnes, *The Toils of Scepticism* (Cambridge University Press, 1990), Richard Bett, *Pyrrho, His Antecedents and His Legacy* (Oxford University Press, 2000), and Charles Brittain, *Philo of Larissa: the Last of the Academic Sceptics* (Oxford University Press, 2001).

is enjoyment or some other desirable state of yourself which you are trying to bring about. Related problems of interpretation afflicted understanding of virtue in this kind of theory. It is clear just from looking at Aristotle's theory, for example, that virtue, the activity of being a certain kind of good person, is a complex and multi-faceted thing. Yet it has persistently been mistaken for a crude kind of causal build-up of tendencies to behaviour, a state somehow brought about in you.

Progress in understanding the ancient ideas better has been greatly helped by the widening of interest from Aristotle to other ancient theories. The ethical theories of Epicurus and the Stoics, for example, had traditionally been treated mostly within these theories as wholes, obscuring the point that their ethical framework is the same as Aristotle's, much though they disagree on other points. Comparative study of these and other theories enabled their common eudaimonistic framework to be seen more clearly, and in this case illumination went rather strikingly in both directions: we can now see that ancient debates about ethics to a great extent took the form of comparing and criticizing different options within a shared framework,[19] and we have a better understanding from our own side of rich and ethically promising conceptions of virtue and happiness.[20]

And so, study of virtue and happiness over a wide range of theories has had two mutually supporting results. On the one hand, we now have a far better understanding of theories like those of Epicurus and the Stoics. Epicurus had been seen simply as a hedonist, and the Stoics as implausibly high-minded about virtue. Interpreting them in a rigorously philosophical way, and seeing their theories as attempts to produce differing defensible conceptions of living a good life, has revealed these theories to be far richer and more philosophically applicable.[21] On the other hand, our improved understanding of virtue and happiness in the ancient theories has fed into the modern revival of so-called 'virtue ethics'. For some time virtue has become a prominent concept in ethical theory, but modern assumptions have limited the illumination that this can bring. Exploration of different kinds of ancient theory that base themselves on virtue and happiness has opened up the many different ways these concepts might figure in a modern ethical theory.

---

[19] Hence there has been renewed interest in Cicero's work of ethical philosophy, *De Finibus*, which takes precisely the form of debates for and against current ethical theories. There is now a new translation of it into modern English by Raphael Woolf: *Cicero On Moral Ends*, Cambridge Texts in the History of Philosophy (Cambridge University Press, 2001).

[20] My own *The Morality of Happiness* (Oxford University Press, 1993), deals with the structure of ancient eudaimonism and analyses the theories of Aristotle, Epicurus, the Stoics, and later hybrid Aristotelian/Stoic theories as options within the eudaimonistic framework. This allows the concepts of virtue and happiness in ancient ethics to emerge in some detail, in a way which minimizes the interfering factors of modern assumptions about ethical theory.

[21] As well as *The Morality of Happiness* (see last note) there has been a great deal of work on Epicurean hedonism, beginning with Phillip Mitsis, *Epicurus' Ethical Theory* (Cornell University Press, 1988) and continuing vigorously in the journals, and on Stoic ethics, beginning especially with Brad Inwood, *Ethics and Human Action in Early Stoicism* (Oxford University Press, 1985). Discussion of these theories tends to remain more at the specialist level because of the nature of our sources, but recent more widely available works are Richard Sorabji, *Emotion and Peace of Mind: from Stoic Agitation to Christian Temptation* (Oxford University Press, 2000), and Lawrence Becker, *A New Stoicism* (Princeton University Press, 1998).

Ethics always had the most to gain from a progressive detachment from the substantial priorities of analytical philosophy. Although there have been exceptions, which over the past half-century have become increasingly prominent,[22] ethical philosophy in the analytical tradition has until recently been greatly handicapped by metaphysical assumptions of an empiricist kind which, apart from their own problems, made it hard to do justice to the ancient theories, and particularly hard to get a proper understanding of the role of virtue and happiness in those theories. The recent growing prominence of 'virtue ethics' of various varieties owes much to the way ancient theories have been better understood. This is a strikingly clear example of the way ancient philosophy can feed back into the mainstream, and also of the way that analytical philosophy's own priorities and assumptions can be discarded without losing concern for clarity of argument and precision of meaning. Work on ancient ethics has become ever more 'analytical' in the sense of caring for rigour in our understanding of the ancient debates.

What Matters for Ancient Philosophy

Those of us working in ancient philosophy no longer feel called upon to show that Plato is already of interest to people uninterested in the history of philosophy (never a sensible endeavour in the first place). The project of showing that Plato is (despite appearances) interesting because he has a problem that would be solved by introducing the distinction between transparent and opaque reference, or the project of showing that Aristotle is interesting because he has some kind of functionalist theory of mind, are projects that for some time have had no future.

Ancient philosophy has increased in self-confidence and (yes) in self-esteem. We no longer defer to the interests of ahistorically minded philosophers, or take the concerns of late twentieth-century analytical philosophy to be unquestioned presuppositions of any properly philosophical enquiry. What we do do, is to apply to ancient texts the concern, associated with analytical philosophy, for precision and rigour in argument.

This result may seem meagre, and also ironic. Meagre because ancient philosophy by now shares so little of the assumptions and priorities of non-historical analytical philosophy; ironic because the influence of such an ahistorical movement seems to have produced a trend in historical philosophy whose vigour increases with its historical awareness.[23] Yet properly understood, the debt of ancient philosophy as presently practised to analytical philosophy is far from meagre. Ancient philosophy has been relocated into philosophy in a definitive way. And the irony is lessened once we reflect that the result has been to restore an interest in ancient philosophy as the practice of philosophical argument—and indeed to revive interest in periods of ancient philosophy where this took a particularly specialized and sophisticated form. And so the study of

[22] E.g. Elizabeth Anscombe, Philippa Foot, John McDowell, Bernard Williams, and Rosalind Hursthouse—philosophers whose own views are very diverse.
[23] Something similar is true, I think, of the history of early modern philosophy; but the case will have to be made independently.

ancient philosophy has ended up doing what the ancient philosophers were doing, namely argue and debate about a huge range of philosophical topics. The surprising thing now is not that we can enter into ancient philosophical debates. What is surprising is rather that in the early part of this century our tradition could have become so narrowed and so isolated from the activity of philosophers arguing in non-historical mode. Engagement with analytical philosophy restored the study of ancient philosophy to philosophical vigour. It has been so successfully invigorated that it is now clear that study of ancient philosophy, far from needing non-historical philosophy to grant it a list of interesting topics, has much to teach some strands of modern philosophy, particularly epistemology and ethics.

If philosophical study of ancient philosophers now shares few priorities and assumptions with non-historical analytical philosophy, should it be said to have parted company with it? A comparison of the latest issue of an ancient philosophy journal with one from a journal in the analytical mainstream might lead to this thought, for it is unlikely to turn up much overlap of topics or methodology. However, the very point of whether this matters raises the consideration that the self-definition of analytical philosophy has not remained static either. It is arguable that by the late twentieth century analytical philosophy has become essentially characterized as a concern for precision and rigour in argument, less tied to particular assumptions about meaning and the role of science than earlier analytical philosophers.[24] If this is taken to be the case, then ancient philosophy is still firmly in the analytical fold. Only if analytical philosophy is taken to include substantial philosophical assumptions has the study of ancient philosophy distanced itself. I take it that this is not an issue that can be easily or rapidly settled, and if the implications are understood there is no strong need to settle it.[25]

What of the relation of ancient philosophy to classics? This has been much complicated by the massive refocusing of classics as a subject. Forty years ago classics, particularly the study of the classical languages, was sufficiently entrenched in schools, in both Europe and America, that anyone going on to specialize in ancient philosophy was likely already to have a solid linguistic and cultural background. This is no longer the case; graduates wishing to specialize in ancient philosophy often learn Greek and Latin as research tools, and thus inevitably lack a wider classical background; their interest in ancient philosophy may well be unaccompanied by independent interest in ancient literature or history.[26] Further, given the pressures for publication, especially in North America, it is often difficult for aspirants to gain sufficient mastery of the material to make worthwhile contributions early enough for career advancement. As a result, classicists can find some ancient philosophers to be underequipped or insufficiently interested in textual and literary issues which can determine local points of philosophical importance.

[24] These assumptions are predominantly of an empiricist kind, and in the past some of them have led to bad misunderstandings of philosophers like Plato.

[25] I am grateful to Brian Leiter for suggestions on this issue.

[26] There has been an analogous trend with ancient history, which is now often to be found in history departments, taught by people with historians' training, rather than in classics departments.

Meanwhile, departments of classics have themselves developed in a much less specialized and philological direction, and have become more assimilated to the model of modern literary departments, with stress on gender and ethnic perspectives, and with the pedagogy influenced by currently fashionable literary theory. This has sometimes produced a distancing from, even hostility to, ancient philosophy analytically practised, since the literary theory involved is often derived from very different philosophical traditions. Also, and with a certain amount of irony, classicists are often unwilling to accept ancient philosophy on its own terms because of a theory-driven insistence on interpreting texts in terms of their non-philosophical background. One particularly strange example of this is the new *Cambridge Companion to Greek Tragedy*, which is preoccupied with the original productions of ancient dramas, and contains no discussion of Aristotle's *Poetics*, nor of any of the theoretical issues which Aristotle raises. As a result, something of a disciplinary divide has developed between ancient philosophy analytically practised, and the methodology employed by younger classicists. This is not universal (it is more pronounced in North America than in other anglophone countries) and there can be attempts to bridge the gap, successful mainly with Plato, the only philosopher with substantial appeal to both parties.[27]

Conclusion

In an interesting way, the impact of analytical philosophy on the study of ancient philosophy has been to rejuvenate it, precisely by means of the recognition that this study is not a timeless activity without substantial philosophical presuppositions. Rather, it is a study of ancient texts which brings to them the same rigour in argument and concern for well-based understanding that motivated their original authors. Like those authors, we have philosophical assumptions and methodological preferences of our own, which we do well to be aware of.

The future for ancient philosophy thus lies in carrying on what we are already doing: engaging with the ancient texts with analytical rigour, but without necessarily taking on the specific modern assumptions and concerns of non-historical analytical philosophy. How does doing this differ from doing what the ancient philosophers themselves were doing? Not much, if at all (allowing, of course, for different styles and methods). So what we should be doing is new and old at the same time. This is unsurprising if we reflect, as some in the first flush of analytical excitement forgot to do, that history of philosophy is of its nature a hybrid and impure activity. We are not doing 'pure' analytical philosophy, but we are not just doing history either. (Hence we can always expect imperceptive criticism from both sides.) We argue with the ancients, but always keeping aware of our assumptions, and of theirs. If we forget to take account of our own philosophical assumptions,

[27] Some examples of successful interdisciplinary collections on Plato are: J. C. Klagge and N. Smith (eds.), *Methods of Interpreting Plato and His Dialogues* (*Oxford Studies in Ancient Philosophy*, supplementary vol. 1992), Charles Griswold (ed.), *Platonic Readings, Platonic Writings* (Routledge, 1988), and Julia Annas and Christopher Rowe (eds.), *New Perspectives on Plato, Modern and Ancient* (Harvard University Press, 2002).

we shall get the ancients wrong. If we forget to take account of theirs, we shall also get them wrong. It is a difficult project, with, as is clear, a huge and continuing risk of getting things wrong. The future of ancient philosophy lies with a clear-headed acceptance of this and the complexity it brings. We should avoid either an attempt to retreat to a supposed purity of contextless and timeless philosophical debate, or a fallback to doing history of ideas.

I should emphasize in conclusion the already obvious point that this has not, despite its inevitably historical focus, been a survey of work done in ancient philosophy in the last decades, and makes no predictions as to which particular areas will be the winners in the research stakes. Work in ancient philosophy has never been more lively or spread over a wider area; progress and achievement lie in very diverse directions. Moreover, a survey doing justice to the wide range of excellent work done in Europe, Britain, and North America in the last decades would be a completely different kind of undertaking.[28,29,30,31]

[28] I give a survey of work in the UK, up to the 1990s, in 'Royaume-Uni: III:La philosophie antique', in *La philosophie en Europe*, sous la direction de Raymond Klibansky et David Pears (Gallimard, 1993), 398–404.

[29] The best recent introduction to ancient philosophy as a subject is *Philosophie grecque*, sous la direction de Monique Canto-Sperber, en collaboration avec Jonathan Barnes, Luc Brisson, Jacques Brunschwig et Gregory Vlastos (Presses Universitaires de France, 1997). The subject has been greatly helped by a recent increase in research tools. We have large numbers of good new translations. Translations of the Presocratics can be found both in the scholarly Cambridge presentation of Kirk, Raven, and Schofield and in more popular translations by Barnes and Waterfield. Numerous recent translations of Plato can be found in Penguin, Oxford World's Classics, and the new Hackett complete works. The older Oxford translation of the complete works of Aristotle has been revised, and numerous recent translations of individuals works are available. Post-Hellenistic philosophy is available in a number of new translations of individual authors (notably Cicero and Sextus) and in anthologies by Inwood and Gerson and Long and Sedley. Philosophical commentaries can be found in the Oxford series of Clarendon Plato, Clarendon Aristotle, and Clarendon Later Ancient Philosophy translations. Cambridge has produced useful Companions to Plato, Aristotle, Stoicism, and Early Greek Philosophy, containing topical articles and bibliography. There is a new *Encyclopaedia of Classical Philosophy* from Greenwood, a revised *Oxford Classical Dictionary*, and new histories of ancient philosophy from Blackwells, Routledge, and Harvard (taken over from Flammarion). There are recent Cambridge histories of ancient political thought and Hellenistic philosophy, as well as the Cambridge histories of texts (translated with notes) in the history of philosophy and history of political thought, and Cambridge topical Companions to Ancient Thought. Electronic resources are also expanding: the whole of Greek and Latin literature is now available on CD-ROM, the Perseus Project database is available to help learners (http:www.perseus.tufts.edu), and Project Archélogos, an argument analysis of philosophical texts, is developing on the web (http://www.archelogos.com). This list is far from exhaustive. The field has never been easier to approach or more lively and varied.

[30] Christopher Gill, 'The Impact of Greek Philosophy on Contemporary Ethical Philosophy', forthcoming in an International Plato Society volume in honour of Thomas Robinson, is a valuable survey which also provides details on prominent figures such as Terence Irwin and Nicholas White, which my narrow focus here has omitted.

[31] I would like to thank the many people with whom I have discussed these ideas, especially Brian Leiter, Christopher Rowe, Myles Burnyeat, and André Laks. Needless to say, I am solely responsible for the result, with which I do not expect everyone in the field to agree (a healthy sign, I think).

2

Philosophy and History in the History of Modern Philosophy

Don Garrett

Philosophical questions are *cognitively orienting*. That is, how one answers them—whether explicitly or implicitly—determines in fundamental ways how one thinks about a whole range of important but more specific or consequent questions. Answers to philosophical questions can provide cognitive orientation through their implications about what the answers to those more specific or consequent questions must be, through their implications about how those more specific or consequent questions should be approached, or through their implications about the significance or value of the answers to those more specific or consequent questions. Of course, it does not follow from this characterization of philosophical questions that every question is either entirely philosophical or entirely unphilosophical; nor that philosophical questions can be well addressed without knowledge of the answers to less philosophical questions; nor that there is any single method or training that is suitable for addressing all philosophical questions; nor that different cultures and eras will not find themselves confronting quite different philosophical questions or employing quite different methods.

The *history of philosophy* is the enterprise of investigating and understanding those attempts to pose and address philosophical questions that are now at a significant temporal distance—for most purposes, those that are older than half a century.[1] *Modern philosophy*, as distinguished from *ancient*, *medieval*, or *Renaissance philosophy*, is the philosophy of the period extending from the seventeenth century to the present. Modern philosophy's past—that is, modern philosophy prior to *recent* or *contemporary* philosophy—is often subdivided into *early modern philosophy* (encompassing the seventeenth century and the eighteenth century), *nineteenth-century philosophy*, and *early twentieth-century philosophy*.[2]

---

[1] The term 'history' can refer to the enterprise of investigating the past, the tangible products of such investigation, or the past so investigated. To avoid ambiguity, I will use the term 'history' only in the first sense. For the third sense, I will simply use the term 'past'—as in 'modern philosophy's past'.

[2] In some uses, 'modern philosophy' is taken to include Renaissance philosophy as well; in accordance with this use, early modern philosophy may be thought to begin as early as the late fifteenth century. If one thinks (as I do not) that philosophy has now entered a distinctively "post-modern" period, then one will hold that the period of modern philosophy extends not quite to the present.

One should perhaps add the qualification "European-influenced" to the characterization of "modern philosophy", since it is in fact almost exclusively European and European-influenced philosophy that is discussed under the heading of "modern philosophy" (and under the headings of "ancient philosophy",

The *history of modern philosophy* is of special interest to contemporary philosophers in large part because it investigates the philosophy of times and places in which, in response to new constellations of intellectual and cultural forces, many older philosophical terms, questions, methods, and answers were transformed, and many new ones arose, in such a way as to produce, collectively, a remarkable share of the most general philosophical questions, methods, and answers that still quite recognizably structure philosophy today. Because it is closer to the present, modern philosophy's past is often more readily accessible to investigation than is ancient, medieval, or Renaissance philosophy; yet the investigation remains a challenging enterprise. Some works from modern philosophy's past appear obscure, inaccessible, or alien even to most contemporary philosophers; and these appearances can make it easy to underestimate their philosophical merit. On the other hand—precisely because of their role in setting so many of the terms, questions, methods, and answers of contemporary philosophy—many of even the earliest works of the modern period feel quite familiar to contemporary philosophical readers. Yet this very familiarity can make it easy to underestimate their philosophical distance and the difficulty of determining their true meaning and significance. In what follows, my aim will be to explore and illustrate some of the opportunities and dangers facing the history of modern philosophy at the beginning of the twenty-first century and some of the ways in which philosophically-minded historians of modern philosophy can exploit those opportunities as they try to avoid the dangers.

My method of approach at the outset will be—naturally enough, given the topic—largely historical. In order to understand the prospects for the history of modern philosophy, it is important first to know something of its subject-matter—i.e. modern philosophy's past—and of the ways in which that subject-matter has already been investigated and analyzed; hence, we must briefly enter into both *the history of modern philosophy* and *the history of the history of modern philosophy*. But answers to more specific questions about the prospects for the history of modern philosophy in the twenty-first century will also necessarily depend partly on answers to some of the most fundamental cognitively orienting questions about the nature and value of the history of philosophy itself—that is, on the *philosophy of the history of philosophy*; and since many of these philosophical questions *about* the history of philosophy have themselves already been thoughtfully addressed in the past, it will also be useful to enter along the way into

---

"medieval philosophy", and "Renaissance philosophy" as well). While this restricted focus is no doubt partly due to a certain narrowness of cultural vision, it also reflects the fact that temporal divisions useful for categorizing European-influenced philosophy are naturally less appropriate for categorizing particular eras of philosophy outside that influence. By the twentieth century, philosophy (like most other human endeavors) became more globally integrated. As a result, the inclusion of the qualifier "European-influenced" in characterizing recent or contemporary modern philosophy is of less significance; most serious philosophy outside narrowly religious contexts is now "European-influenced" in at least the minimal sense that it is produced in awareness of philosophical traditions influenced by Europeans, just as most philosophy is now influenced by non-European philosophy. It is also worth noting that early modern philosophy in Europe was affected in many ways by the greater knowledge of non-European cultures that had resulted from exploration and trade. The culture of China was of particular interest to many Europeans in the early modern period.

the history of the philosophy of the history of philosophy. This three-pronged historical survey will provide a perspective from which to analyze recent and contemporary trends in the history of modern philosophy; to explore its nature and aims; and to assess its opportunities, dangers, and prospects for the future. Within the scope of the history of modern philosophy fall three-and-a-half centuries of prodigious philosophical inquiry of nearly all kinds—from ethical theory to the philosophy of mathematics, from epistemology to the philosophy of law—and it would be impossible to construct a complete research program for its future either in terms of topics or of methods. Nevertheless, I will conclude by recommending a selection of illustrative topics as particularly worth pursuing and a few strategies as particularly worth emphasizing.

I. Modern Philosophy and Its History

Philosophy and its History in the Seventeenth Century. There have been many schemes for classifying the branches of philosophy, but one of the most common in early modern philosophy recognized three main divisions: *metaphysics*, concerned with the most general and fundamental questions about whatever is real and how real beings constitute the universe; *natural philosophy*, concerned with general and fundamental questions about the operations of nature (as distinct from the human and the divine); and *moral philosophy*, concerned with general and fundamental questions about human life and thought.

Early in the seventeenth century, a series of discoveries by Galileo Galilei and Johannes Kepler provided powerful support for, and essential refinements to, the heliocentric cosmology proposed more than a half-century earlier by Nicolaus Copernicus. Accommodating the emerging cosmology required radical alterations in the broadly Aristotelian principles of natural philosophy that were then domin-ant, a process that seemed to undermine much of what had been previously accepted as knowledge. Yet the new cosmology also held out to many an exciting prospect: that *mechanics*—i.e. the science concerned with the communication of motion through contact among bodies, previously regarded as a relatively narrow field of chiefly technological value—could, if suitably corrected and expanded, provide the basis for a simplified, unified, and mathematically quantified account of all of nature, including within its scope even the heavens and living things.

These revolutionary developments within natural philosophy inevitably posed in new forms a whole range of fundamental questions that reached deeply into other areas of philosophy as well. These included questions concerning the proper metaphysics within which to place the new understanding of nature; the nature of causality; the character of sensation, thought, and knowledge; the best methods for pursuing a science of nature; the role of faith and religious authority in relation to human reason; the relations between minds and bodies; the freedom of the human will; the causes, characters, and motivational roles of the passions; and the status of both God and morality in relation to a seemingly mechanistic physical universe. Many of the leading philosophers of the seventeenth century considered their own era to constitute a kind of new beginning in knowledge—an attitude that often led, understandably enough, to the downgrading of earlier philosophies and of their study. René Descartes's negative assessment, in his *Discourse on the Method*, of his own Jesuit college education (particularly in relation to his training in philosophy) is one particularly well-known example. Early modern philosophies were nevertheless inescapably influenced by the terminology, concepts, and principles of the philosophies that preceded them—as anyone reading Descartes's subsequent accounts of the surprisingly scholastic[3] deliverances of the unaided "light of nature" has had ample occasion to observe.

Yet despite its often-revolutionary aspirations, seventeenth-century philosophy was by no means entirely anti-historical. In fact, the decline in Aristotle's reputation that began with the abandonment of his cosmology served to spark a renewed interest in other ancient authors, including atomists, Stoics, Epicureans, and skeptics. Francis Bacon—perhaps the century's most influential philosopher of scientific methodology—called for the historical collection and survey not only of observations of natural phenomena themselves but also of "the several Opinions of several Authors touching the Nature of Things" (*The Advancement of Learning* III.5)[4] as a preliminary to more rigorous modern experimental investigation. The historical part of Bacon's charge was taken up by several authors—most notably by Thomas Stanley and George Horn, each of whom published a *History of Philosophy* in 1655. These authors presented generally narrative accounts—often organized around philosophical "sects"—that aimed to present and explain the broadly philosophical views of religious figures as well as those of more systematic and argumentative writers.[5]

Near the end of the century, Pierre Bayle's *Dictionnaire Historique et Critique* (1696) offered a strikingly different and more directly argumentative approach to the history of philosophy. Encyclopedic rather than narrative in organization, it presented articles on a remarkably wide variety of thinkers, well-known and obscure, ancient, medieval, and early modern—articles that frequently served essentially as jumping-off points for discussions of whatever topics and arguments were of greatest interest to Bayle. The format allowed its author to bring the history of philosophy to bear directly on contemporary philosophical concerns, while at the same time obscuring his own intentions behind alternating professions of religious faith and demonstrations of the difficulties that reason posed for the objects of such faith. Bayle's provocative work remained much-read and deeply influential for many decades.

Philosophy and its History in the Eighteenth Century. As the popularity of the *Dictionnaire Historique et Critique* indicated, by the beginning of the eighteenth century many philosophers were already concerned not merely to reject the older

---

[3] 'Scholastic philosophy' refers to the dominant (though not the only) mode of philosophy in Europe between roughly the fifth century and the Scientific Revolution. Derived from the manner in which philosophical "dialectic" was taught in early Christian schools, it placed emphasis on reasoning and disputation concerning questions related to theology in a context of Christian revelation. Later scholastic philosophy was deeply influenced by Aristotle and by St. Thomas Aquinas's synthesis of Aristotelianism with Christianity.   [4] This passage is also cited in Armstrong (1959: 455).

[5] Stanley's included the ancient "Chaldaicks" and did not extend into the Christian era, while Horn's began with Adam and extended to the seventeenth century. Stanley's work prominently included a motto from Bacon. For more on early modern history of philosophy, see Walton (1977) and Rée (1978).

scholastic philosophy—which, indeed, had still only recently begun to lose its hold on many European universities—but also to understand and to criticize the preceding generation of more distinctively modern philosophers as well. One of the eighteenth-century's most prominent works in the history of philosophy was Johann Jakob Brucker's monumental five-volume *Critical History of Philosophy* (1744), which traced philosophy from before the Flood up to John Locke and G. W. Leibniz. Brucker treated the story of philosophy's past as essentially the story of competing schools or philosophical sects rather than of individual philosophers. In Brucker's view, the primary value of pursuing the history of philosophy lay in its contribution to *eclecticism*—that is, the selection and adoption of points and arguments from a wide variety of different sources—as a conscious philosophical method.

The seventeenth-century's promise of a simple, unified, and mathematically quantified account of nature had born impressive fruit in Isaac Newton's *Philosophiae Naturalis Principia Mathematica* (1687). Yet while Newton's achievements in natural philosophy could not ultimately be denied, they intensified as many metaphysical issues as they resolved. Newton's ontological commitment to space and time as absolute (i.e. as having reality independently of their contents and not as constituted by the relations of those contents) remained metaphysically contentious, for example, and his mathematical apparatus stimulated debate about the infinitely divisible and the infinitely small. In addition, he postulated an attractive force of gravitation that at least appeared to give rise to a non-mechanistic and hence rather mysterious action-at-a-distance, and he thereby deepened rather than resolved the metaphysical question of the nature of physical causation. Furthermore, the very successes of Newtonian natural philosophy often contributed in the eighteenth century to a sense of dissatisfaction with the relative lack of consensus in the correlative fields of metaphysics and moral philosophy. While the processes of human knowledge and cognition had been important topics of philosophical investigation at least since Plato, for many eighteenth-century philosophers these processes became the objects of increasingly systematic investigations. For David Hume and Immanuel Kant, at least, these investigations included theorizing about philosophical inquiry itself, considered as a manifestation of human cognitive processes, and were undertaken partly with the aim of clarifying the inherent resources, limitations, and potential paradoxes of metaphysical philosophy.

Philosophy and its History in the Nineteenth Century. Partly as the result of the stimulus provided by Kant's transcendental idealism (which treated space, time, and the most fundamental organizing features of reality as in some sense contributions of the mind rather than as features of things-in-themselves), the final decades of the eighteenth century and especially the early decades of the nineteenth century witnessed the remarkable philosophical and cultural phenomenon of German Idealism. Among its distinctive features was the endeavor to find rational processes imminent in the world of experience; and G. W. F. Hegel's doctrine that philosophy is a rational, dialectical process through which mind or spirit becomes increasingly self-conscious gave a striking new significance to the history of philosophy. In contrast to many previous historians of philosophy who had tended to organize philosophy's past as the repeated elaboration of a fixed set of possible doctrines on a fixed set of philosophical issues, Hegel saw the history of philosophy rather as a story of inevitable progress that matched the evident progress of natural science, a story in which partially adequate questions and answers alike were incorporated into and superceded by ever more adequate ones. In this conception, the understanding of philosophy's past and its relation to the present became an inseparable part of philosophizing itself; and whereas the leading constructive philosophers of earlier eras had largely been content to cite, assess, or argue with a limited number of important predecessors in piecemeal fashion, leaving the systematic history of philosophy to others, Hegel took the history of philosophy as a centerpiece of his philosophical project.

Later nineteenth-century philosophy—as evidenced by the works of such thinkers as Karl Marx and John Stuart Mill—was partly driven by the social, political, and moral problems posed by the Industrial Revolution. In addition, Charles Darwin's *Origin of Species* (1859) raised sharp new issues about the relation between human beings and other forms of life, about the role of purpose in the explanation of nature, about the grounding of ethics, and about the character and significance of beauty and aesthetic response—topics that had been, in very different ways, of special interest to many of the German Idealists as well. The acceptance of Darwin's theory that species resulted from biological evolution driven by natural selection was facilitated by, and contributed further support to, the increasingly explicit critiques of both scriptural Christianity and philosophical appeals to theology that had been developing from the beginning of the seventeenth century. Among those deeply concerned with the implications of Darwinism for the understanding of nature and with the critical assessment of Christian morality was Friedrich Nietzsche.

Toward the end of the nineteenth century, such philosophers as T. H. Green, J. M. E. McTaggart, and F. H. Bradley made British Idealism—inspired by German Idealism, and especially by Kant and Hegel—a dominant force in British philosophy. In keeping with their broadly Hegelian philosophy of the history of philosophy, British Idealist historians of philosophy (particularly Green) elaborated a narrative according to which early modern philosophy had consisted of two schools or movements: the "Continental Rationalism" of Descartes, Spinoza, and Leibniz; and the "British Empiricism" of Locke, Berkeley, and Hume. These movements were then synthesized, on this account, by the critical philosophy of Kant, which thereby superceded them.[6] Their broadly Hegelian conception of the significance of philosophy's modern past led not only to comprehensive narrative histories of modern philosophy but also to substantial critical commentaries on single philosophers, as well as to editions of earlier philosophical texts accompanied by substantial annotations or lengthy critical introductions.[7] For idealists of the nineteenth century, important support for one's

---

[6] For fuller accounts of this process, see Loeb (1981) and Kuklick (1984). For an account of a principled way to draw the rationalist/empiricist distinction, see Garrett (1997, ch. 1).

[7] See, e.g., Alexander Campbell Fraser's relentlessly Kantian and Hegelian annotations to his 1894 edition of Locke's *Essay Concerning Human Understanding* (which constituted the standard English edition

own philosophy—and for the philosophy of philosophy informing it—was often thought to lie in the ability of one's philosophy to give a compelling narrative explanation of the character of philosophical thinking of the past.

Philosophy and its History in the Early Twentieth Century. It is particularly ironic, then, and yet also fitting, that one of the earliest salvos from the philosophical forces that displaced British Idealism from its newly-won position of dominance in England came precisely in the form of a commentary in the history of early modern philosophy: Bertrand Russell's *A Critical Exposition of the Philosophy of Leibniz* (1900). Russell offered to make new sense of Leibniz's remarkable and comprehensive metaphysics by deriving it from the underlying premises of Leibniz's distinctive logic.[8] Moreover, Russell claimed that this derivation corresponded to the real order of Leibniz's thought, which Leibniz had supposedly obscured for the sake of popular appeal. Russell offered relatively little historical or even textual evidence for this biographical claim, apart from the coherence and power of the reconstruction of Leibniz's metaphysics that accompanied it. But just as earlier idealists had proposed to justify their philosophy in part through its capacity to explain the inadequacies of the philosophies of the past, so too Russell in effect justified his own developing methodological turn toward questions about the logical forms of propositions—a turn inspired by the tools of formal logic that had been developed by Gottlob Frege—through its ability to explain the contents, successes, and failings of the philosophies of the past.

Although Russell himself maintained a life-long interest in the history of philosophy, the turn to logical and semantic analysis that he helped to inaugurate soon led to a relative anti-historicism that often saw previous philosophy primarily as a succession of errors. The logical positivists[9]—influenced both by the desire to construct a conception of the meaning of scientific statements accommodated to Albert Einstein's theories of relativity and by Russell's project of analyzing mathematical truths so as to show them to be non-empirical truths of logic—entirely rejected traditional metaphysics. They proposed the "verifiability principle", according to which the meaning of a proposition is its method of verification, and from which it

---

for three-quarters of a century) and T. H. Green's enormous and highly critical introductions in *The Philosophical Works of David Hume*, co-edited with T. H. Grose (1874), which conclude thus:

> Our business [has been] to show that the philosophy based on the abstraction of feeling . . . was with Hume played out. . . . If this object has been in any way attained, so that the attention of Englishmen 'under five-and-twenty' may be diverted from the anachronistic systems hitherto prevalent among us to the study of Kant and Hegel, an irksome labor will not have been in vain.

[8] Particularly important in Russell's reconstruction was the logical doctrine that propositions are fundamentally of subject-predicate form—that is, that they take the form of ascribing a predicate (for example, "is tall" to a subject (for example, "John"). Propositions that do not appear to have this form—for example, those ascribing a relation among multiple subjects—must then be somehow reducible to subject-predicate form.

[9] *Logical positivism* (also called "logical empiricism") was a philosophical movement that originated in the 1920s in Austria with the "Vienna Circle", a collaborative philosophical group whose members included Moritz Schlick, Rudolf Carnap, Hans Reichenbach, Herbert Feigl, Carl Hempel, Otto Neurath, and Friedrich Waismann.

followed that whatever cannot be verified by experience is meaningless; and they took their seemingly successful use of the principle in diagnosing and explaining the meta-physical confusions of earlier philosophers to be confirmation of their own view of philosophical method. As the stock of Kant and Hegel declined under the influence of logical positivism, the stock of those early modern philosophers (such as Berkeley and Hume) who could be seen as precursors of logical positivism correspondingly rose.[10]

II. Recent and Contemporary Trends in the History of Modern Philosophy

Recent History of Modern Philosophy (1950 to 1985). The decline of logical positivism and related doctrines led, by mid-century, to a broad renewal of positive interest in the history of philosophy. Despite the popularity of "ordinary language philosophy" in some quarters and of existentialism in others, the logical positivists' program of logical and semantic analysis was not ultimately replaced by any durable philosoph-ical movement of similarly revolutionary meta-philosophical aims or corresponding anti-historical tendencies. It was replaced instead by a general conception of philo-sophy as aiming to address a wide variety of philosophical issues through careful dis-tinctions and rigorous argumentation drawing on any relevant epistemic resources. This led gradually, in turn, to history of modern philosophy that was chiefly concerned with text-based treatments of the arguments of important individual philosophers, often undertaken with the explicit aim of updating and appropriating those arguments for purposes of enriching contemporary debate. Many landmark contributions to the understanding of modern philosophy were made in this period by philosophers—such as Martial Gueroult, Michael Ayers, Edwin Curley, and Margaret Wilson—who specialized primarily in the history of modern philosophy. At the same time, a great deal of stimulating and exciting work in the history of modern philosophy was also produced by philosophers—such as J. L. Mackie, Peter Strawson, Barry Stroud, Robert Fogelin, and Jonathan Bennett—who were at least equally well known for their non-historical writings and whose views on contem-porary philosophical issues were often directly related to their historical work. Frequent dialogue among philosophers of both kinds helped to encourage the further reintegration of the history of modern philosophy into the mainstream of post-1950 philosophy. The aim of this general approach was well-captured in a series of books on individual past philosophers inaugurated in 1973 by Routledge—including contributions by Wilson (*Descartes*), Ayers (*Locke*), Stroud (*Hume*), and Fogelin (*Wittgenstein*)—under the series title "The Arguments of the Philosophers".

---

[10] Berkeley was seen (with some considerable violence to his texts) as anticipating the phenomenalist semantic analysis of statements about physical objects into statements about sensations. Hume was seen (with some considerable simplification) as offering analyses of statements about causation in terms of observable constant conjunctions of types of events. It should be emphasized that a good deal of fine work in the history of modern philosophy was done in the early twentieth century by philosophers largely uninfluenced by logical positivism: examples include Kemp Smith's important "naturalistic" inter-pretation of Hume (1905 and 1941).

Recent Philosophy of the History of Philosophy (1950 to 1985). Discussions of the practice and significance of the history of philosophy were published sporadically in academic journals through the middle decades of the twentieth century, but it was largely in the late 1970s that the philosophy of the history of philosophy again became a hotly debated topic in its own right. While it was generally agreed that historians of philosophy should strive, as at least part of their task, to reconstruct "the arguments of the philosophers", the debate that emerged concerned how best to approach that reconstruction. Bernard Williams, in the Preface to his 1978 book *Descartes: The Project of Pure Enquiry*, helped to popularize an influential distinction between the *history of ideas* and the *history of philosophy*:

> The history of ideas is history before it is philosophy, whereas the history of philosophy is the other way around. In any worthwhile work of either sort, both concerns are likely to be represented, but there is a genuine distinction. For the history of ideas, the question about a work *what does it mean?* is centrally the question *what did it mean?* . . . The history of philosophy of course has to constitute its object, the work, in genuinely historical terms, yet there is a cut-off point, where authenticity is replaced as the objective by the aim of articulating philosophical ideas. The "horizontal" search for what Descartes meant will, if it is properly done, yield an object essentially ambiguous, incomplete, imperfectly determined by the author's and his contemporaries' understanding, for that is what the work—at least if it is now of any autonomous interest at all—cannot fail to have been. The present study, while I hope that it is not unaware that it does so, prefers the direction of rational reconstruction of Descartes's thought, where the rationality of the construction is essentially and undisguisedly conceived in a contemporary style. (Williams 1978: 9–10)[11]

In an essay published in the same year and entitled "Analytic Philosophy and the History of Philosophy", Michael Ayers took "analytic philosophers" engaged in the history of early modern philosophy sharply to task.[12] Citing examples concerning Leibniz, Locke, Berkeley, and Hume, he argued that the project of translating the works of early modern philosophers into contemporary terms and then providing "rational reconstructions" of their positions and arguments—especially when carried out in explicit rejection of the strictly historical aim of determining the "original meaning" of the texts—had, in ignoring the circumstances in which their works were produced, typically yielded not philosophical riches but rather misinterpretations that trivialized and undervalued the historical texts under discussion. Reinforcing Ayers's call for greater emphasis on historical accuracy was an influential 1984 collection of essays entitled *Philosophy in History: Essays on the Historiography of Philosophy* and edited by Richard Rorty, J. B. Schneewind, and Quentin Skinner. The editors' introduction to the volume accepted a distinction between "intellectual

---

[11] In his Preface, Williams cites a discussion of the "history of ideas" in Dunn (1968). Dunn, however, had construed the history of philosophy as a branch of the history of ideas, rather than as a distinct and collateral (if still allied) enterprise. It might be remarked that, if Williams considered his own book about Descartes to be of "autonomous interest" as well (despite its containing rational reconstructions) then presumably he considered it, too, to be "ambiguous, incomplete, [and] imperfectly determined by the author's [i.e. Williams's] and his contemporaries' understanding".

[12] Among those criticized by name were Bertrand Russell, A. J. Ayer, H. H. Price, D. J. O'Connor, and Jonathan Bennett. None but Bennett was still publishing substantially in the history of philosophy in 1978.

history" (i.e. "history of ideas") and "history of philosophy", but argued for greater self-consciousness on the part of "analytic philosophers" about their own place in the ongoing process of historical philosophical conversation and about the mutual interdependence of good "intellectual history" and good "history of philosophy".[13]

In the same year in which *Philosophy in History* appeared, Jonathan Bennett set out, in his introduction to *A Study of Spinoza's 'Ethics'*, a spirited contrarian defense of intentionally limiting the degree of attention devoted to historical context:

> I want to understand the pages of the *Ethics* in a way that will let me learn philosophy from them. For that, I need to consider what Spinoza had in mind, for readings of the text which are faithful to his intentions are likely to teach me more than ones which are not—or so I believe, as I think him to be a great philosopher. And one can be helped to discover his intentions by knowing what he had been reading, whose problems he had been challenged by, and so on. But this delving into backgrounds is subject to a law of diminishing returns: while some fact about Maimonides or Averroes might provide the key to an obscure passage in Spinoza, we are more likely to get his text straight by wrestling with it directly, given just a fair grasp of his immediate background. I am sure to make mistakes because of my inattention to Spinoza's philosophical ancestry; but I will pay that price for the benefits which accrue from putting most of one's energies into philosophically interrogating Spinoza's own text. (Bennett 1984: 15–16)

The issue of the relative values of "historical reconstruction" and "rational reconstruction"—also often formulated in terms of "the history of ideas" and "the history of philosophy", or "historical accuracy" and "philosophical pay-off"—has remained an important topic of methodological discussion within the history of modern philosophy.

Contemporary History of Modern Philosophy (Since 1985). The history of modern philosophy has expanded and matured as a field in many ways in the last two decades. One obvious sign of this expansion and maturation is the proliferation of tools for scholarship. These include more complete and accurate print editions and translations of important works—with useful annotations, glossaries, notes of textual variants, and other apparatus—and also, in many cases, fully searchable electronic editions. Such developments promote—and are also promoted by—high standards of professional scholarship.[14] Just as the publication of better research tools on Leibniz (including accessible versions of many of his previously inaccessible texts) led to an explosion of good work on his philosophy earlier in the twentieth century, new editions and research tools stimulated work on many other philosophers at the end of the century. Moreover, while more accurate translations have become available for everyday use, scholars have also come increasingly to realize the value of attention to

---

[13] Rorty's own contribution famously distinguished not two but four distinct "genres": doxography (which he saw as being of little value), "rational reconstruction", "historical reconstruction", and "*Geistesgeschichte*"—with this last, somewhat Hegelian, genre operating at the level of large-scale problematics, where it sought to present narratives that would serve to situate and justify the contemporary philosopher's own approach to philosophical issues.

[14] Also worth noting is the series of *Cambridge Companions* to individual philosophers published by Cambridge University Press, each volume consisting of ten to twelve essays by specialists on central aspects of the individual's philosophy, and the *Cambridge Histories of Philosophy* series devoted to particular eras.

original languages for research purposes. In addition, historians of modern philosophy are increasingly in regular and routine contact with colleagues working in other countries and languages; and as a result, the history of modern philosophy is more international than it has ever been before.[15]

While broadening its scope linguistically and geographically, the history of modern philosophy has broadened its scope intellectually as well. As the practice of philosophy generally has become more interdisciplinary and better informed by developments in other fields, the history of modern philosophy, too, has become more informed by understanding of the broader intellectual contexts of past periods. In many cases, this broadening of scope involves topics—such as the laws of motion or techniques for moderating the passions—that were once considered central parts of natural or moral philosophy but are now regarded as falling within special sciences of more recent maturation, such as physics or psychology. Thus, for example, work by historians of philosophy knowledgeable in the history of science has allowed contemporary readers to see Descartes's epistemological project in the *Meditations*—once viewed in relative isolation by most philosophers—as intended to provide the foundations for a distinctive metaphysics designed specifically to accommodate in detail a new mechanistic and radically anti-Aristotelian physics.[16] Yet understanding the significance of that metaphysics requires not only an understanding of seventeenth-century physics but also of seventeenth-century physiology and psychology of the emotions, for one of the primary tasks of that metaphysics is to underwrite Descartes's account of the nature of the passions and his prescriptions for their control as part of a virtuous life. Indeed, it also requires an understanding of seventeenth-century theology, for Descartes's central psychophysical doctrine of "substantial union" between the human mind and the human body provides a sense in which the soul is the "form" of a human being—a claim that, in turn, can only be fully appreciated against the background of the Catholic Church's commitment to a metaphysics of form and matter and, ultimately, to its use of that metaphysics in articulating the "real presence" of Christ in the Eucharist.

In keeping with this broadening of intellectual interests, historians of modern philosophy continue to broaden the range of works to which they devote serious attention. This is true even in the case of the best-known philosophers of the past, those that have traditionally been taught as an essential part of undergraduate philosophy curricula. Thus, Berkeley's lesser-known *The Analyst* is now used to shed light on the finitist philosophy of mathematics implicated in the immaterialism of his *Principles of Human Knowledge* and *Three Dialogues*,[17] and Kant's writings about race in his anthropological works are used to question the intended application of the categorical imperative of morality in his ethical writings.[18] But the broadening of interests has also involved increasing attention to the writings of other philosophers of long-acknowledged importance but less often included at length in undergraduate

---

[15] Many of these developments are discussed in M. Wilson (1992).

[16] See especially Garber (1992). Similarly, much recent work on Leibniz focuses on the relation between his metaphysics and his dynamics.   [17] See, e.g., Jesseph (1993).

[18] See, e.g., Charles Mills (1997).

philosophy curricula, such as Francis Bacon, Nicolas Malebranche, Pierre Gassendi, Antoine Arnauld, Pierre Bayle, Joseph Butler, Thomas Reid, and John Stuart Mill.[19] In addition, it has brought to new attention many significant but somewhat lesser-known figures in metaphysics and epistemology, such as Cartesian metaphysicians Robert Desgabets, Pierre-Sylvain Régis, and Johannes Clauberg, as well as the anti-Cartesian skeptic Pierre-Daniel Huet;[20] and it has also brought new attention to such figures in ethics and political theory as Hugo Grotius, Samuel Pufendorf, Bernard Mandeville, Richard Cumberland, Frances Hutcheson, and Jeremy Bentham.[21] Moreover, there has been a groundswell of interest in early modern women philosophers such as Princess Elizabeth of Bohemia, Margaret Cavendish, Anne Conway, and Catherine Trotter Cockburn,[22] most of whom were long entirely absent from histories of modern philosophy. Especially important has been the new level of attention directed by historians of philosophy trained in the analytic tradition to the study of continental European philosophy after Kant—including Hegel, J. G. Fichte, and Friedrich Nietzsche.[23] Due partly to the internationalization of the field, this development has contributed to a reintegration of the two strands of the history of modern philosophy and to a heightened appreciation of the common interests of Anglophone and continental philosophy.

Contemporary Philosophy of the History of Philosophy (Since 1985). While discussion of the philosophy of the history of philosophy since 1985 has continued to address the relation between "rational reconstruction" and "historical reconstruction" (or "history of philosophy" and "history of ideas"), the dominant tone has been relatively conciliatory, with some (e.g. M. Wilson 1992) calling for "pluralistic tolerance" and others (e.g. Garber 1989) characterizing the two as complementary approaches rather than competing programs. Increasingly prominent, however, has been the closely related question of how, why, and to what extent studying philosophy's past can be of value to contemporary philosophy. The question is sharply posed by David Rosenthal (1989): if philosophy is a problem-solving discipline, as most contemporary philosophers believe, then why should the history of past—and presumably mostly failed—attempts to solve these problems be of serious importance to that enterprise? The history of chemistry, for example, is of relatively marginal importance to contemporary research in chemistry; why then should the history of philosophy be of any greater importance to philosophy?

Rosenthal's own answer is that charitable interpretation of the past demands that one attempt to state the content of past philosophizing in one's own terms, with the result that undertaking a charitable history of philosophy is necessarily one way—if a somewhat indirect way—of exploring contemporary philosophical problems.

---

[19] Important recent books on these figures include Gaukroger (2001) on Bacon; Nadler (1992) and Schmaltz (1996) on Malebranche; Lennon (1995) on Gassendi; Nadler (1989) on Arnauld; Lennon (1999) on Bayle; Penelhum (1985) on Butler; Lehrer (1989) and Wolterstorff (2001) on Reid; and Skorupski (1989) on Mill.   [20] See, e.g., Schmaltz (2002).

[21] See, e.g., Schneewind (1998).   [22] See, e.g., Atherton (1994) and Broad (2002).

[23] Examples include Pippin (1989) and Wood (1990) on Hegel; Zöller (1998) on Fichte; and Clark (1990), Richardson (1996), and Leiter (2002) on Nietzsche. See also Beiser (1987) and Sedgwick (2000).

Edwin Curley (1984) has argued for a more direct answer: the history of philosophy can be a kind of conversation with, or interrogation of, great and original philosophers of the past that allows us to determine how they would answer the philosophical questions that we might put to them. The result, he maintains, is that we gain valuable knowledge of alternative answers and the ways in which those answers can be defended; and such knowledge may be of value not only when we decide to pursue one of these alternatives ourselves, but also when we seek to establish the superiority of our own view by contrasting it with its strongest possible alternatives—for then we must explore those strongest possible alternatives, many of which are suggested by philosophy's past. Daniel Garber has argued (1989) that the history of philosophy is valuable to philosophy primarily for the capacity of "disinterested historical inquiry" to give philosophers an external perspective on present philosophizing, a perspective that forces them to ask themselves why they accept the suppositions and methods that they do, and which thereby aids them in formulating further and better philosophical questions.[24] Margaret Wilson (1992) has emphasized that the history of philosophy also provides a deeper understanding of the sources and meaning of current philosophical questions and of now-dominant doctrines and approaches.

Each of these claims is surely correct, and each contributes to the answer to Rosenthal's question. It may be added, however, that philosophical *problems* typically concern how to answer philosophical *questions*—and how such questions are to be both understood and addressed often depends on the theoretical framework within which one poses and pursues them, in a way that helps to explain the special relevance of the history of philosophy. A question in chemistry, such as the question of whether a particular substance (such as water or lead) changes in kind under specified circumstances, can take on an entirely different aspect depending on whether one poses it in an alchemical or a molecular theoretical framework. Similarly, a question about moral responsibility for actions can take on an entirely different aspect depending on whether one views it in a naturalistic Humean framework or a transcendental Kantian framework. But while the appropriateness of the molecular theoretical framework for understanding everyday questions in chemistry is ordinarily a given, the determination of the best theoretical framework in which to frame and pursue a philosophical question is a key and often highly controversial factor in the ultimate success or failure of philosophical problem-solving. It is precisely by offering not only relatively specific *answers* but also by offering different yet reasonably comprehensive *frameworks* that the history of philosophy can be of aid to contemporary philosophy, providing not only a valuable and disinterested *general* perspective on philosophical problem-solving activity, but a selection of promising *particular* perspectives from which to conduct it. Both the difficulties and the successes of previous detailed attempts to develop the resources of these varied frameworks and perspectives often reward philosophical investigation. Indeed, it is impossible to say in advance which aspects of these attempts—including their various concepts,

---

[24] See also Cohen (1986) for further discussion of this idea.

distinctions, examples, arguments, and criticisms of other approaches—will *not* prove to be useful to contemporary philosophy.[25]

III. The History of Philosophy and Its Aims

Four Aims in the History of Philosophy. Given that the history of philosophy is potentially of special significance to philosophy in the present, how can it best realize that potential? In order to answer this question, it is essential to distinguish four different aims that one might have in studying philosophy's past. Each aim can be pursued for its own sake, as a means to an end, or both.

The first aim is to *contextualize* philosophical works of the past. That is, one may seek to determine the various circumstances—intellectual, material, personal, social, and political—under which they were produced and which helped to determine their character. Typically, this will include acquiring personal knowledge about their authors—including facts about each author's education, reading, acquaintances, influences, conceptions of the past, vocabulary, manner of expression, interests, concerns, aims, projects, and motives for writing, as well as the ways in which these changed during the course of the author's life. Equally important, it will involve acquiring knowledge about the broader context in which the author worked—including the religious, social, and political forces at work up to that time; the content and formulation of both the shared intellectual commonplaces and the disputed intellectual issues prevalent up to that time in the widest possible range of fields, and the ways in which each of these affected or would have been likely to affect the author. Ideally, at least, it will ultimately involve integrating this knowledge in order to reconstruct a comprehensive picture of each author's world as it gave rise to the works under consideration. Thus, for example, one may seek to understand how Spinoza's program of conducting scientific scriptural hermeneutics in order to support freedom of speech and religion (as propounded in his *Theological-Political Treatise*) was influenced by his education in the Jewish community of Amsterdam, his affiliation with a close circle of non-dogmatic Christians, his reading of Hobbes, his understanding of scientific methodology, his interaction with leading figures in natural science such as Christiaan Huygens and Henry Oldenburg, and his support of the republican party in seventeenth-century Dutch politics.

---

[25] Of course, the ways just mentioned do not exhaust the ways in which the history of philosophy contributes to contemporary philosophy. Jorge Gracia (1992) has argued that dialogue and communication between Anglo-American philosophy and Continental philosophy—which were often relatively isolated and divergent from one another in the twentieth century—can best be facilitated by developing a shared understanding of their common historical antecedents. Many have remarked on the pedagogical value of the history of philosophy as well, noting that philosophy's past offers an enduring body of work particularly suitable for use in intellectual training aimed at developing the skills of philosophical interpretation, analysis, and evaluation that are required for tackling contemporary philosophical problems. Also notable is Catherine Wilson's (1998) hopeful claim that the history of philosophy provides "definitive wise answers to perennial questions" of conduct that allow philosophers to serve society more generally as "physicians of the soul". For more discussion of the distinctive relation of philosophy to its own history, see Garrett (1997, ch. 1).

The second aim is to *interpret* philosophical works of the past. That is, one may seek to understand what the author meant in them and by them. This will typically include trying to specify the meanings of various questions asked and claims made in the work; how the author intended these questions and claims to be related (for example, how an author intended some claims to be supported by other claims); what unexpressed doctrines are implicit or presupposed in the works; why the author wrote as he or she did; and what the author intended the work as a whole to convey. Thus, for example, one may seek to understand what Hume meant when he concluded in *A Treatise of Human Nature* (Hume, 2000: I.iii.6), that the inferences in which we project that unobserved cases will be like observed cases (now commonly called "inductive" inferences) are "not determin'd by reason". Does he mean that the conclusions of inductive inferences lack all epistemic merit (belief-worthiness), or merely that such inferences are not logically infallible? Or does he intend rather a claim in cognitive psychology, namely, that in every inductive inference there is a step that is itself not causally mediated by inference but rather by another causal mechanism?[26] This question is closely related to other interpretive questions concerning the meanings of the premises he gives for the claim, the uses to which he puts the claim, and his intentions with respect to the topics of reason and skepticism in the *Treatise* as a whole.

The third aim is to *evaluate* philosophical works of the past. That is, one might seek to assess the works to determine how good they are—as wholes and in their parts—in any of various respects. Typically, this will most centrally involve assessing the truth of the claims made and the strength of the arguments offered, as well as assessing the value, importance, and clarity of the questions raised, the soundness of the approaches employed, and the adequacy of the answers or solutions proposed. It may involve assessing the value and importance of philosophers' overall projects and their relative success in carrying out those projects; and it may also involve assessing the originality of philosophical works and their value as contributions to philosophy in their own period. Thus, for example, one may seek to ascertain whether any of the arguments that Descartes offers in the *Meditations* actually succeed in justifying the claim of the work's subtitle to have "demonstrated the existence of God", as well as whether Descartes's postulation of "true and immutable natures" in the course of one of those arguments is justifiable, and whether the existence of such natures can be accommodated within Descartes's own ontology of substances and modes; and one may seek to determine whether Descartes's formulations of these arguments, whether sound or not, constituted important developments in the evolution of philosophical theology.

The fourth aim is to *apply* philosophical works of the past. That is, one may seek to utilize them in the process of determining how best to answer one's own philosophical questions or solve one's own philosophical problems. In the simplest case, one may simply find oneself adopting an answer or solution proposed by a philosopher of the past. For example, many recent and contemporary philosophers

---

[26] I have argued for this third interpretation in Garrett (1997) and elsewhere.

concerned with the question, "What kind of freedom is required for moral responsibility?" have, upon consideration, largely accepted Hume's answer: it is the freedom one has whenever one's actions are responsive to and determined by one's will. But one may also apply a philosophical work of the past by borrowing, criticizing, adapting, or developing questions, problems, formulations, concepts, distinctions, vocabulary, premises, arguments, examples, methods, skills, habits of mind, insights, projects, approaches, perspectives, and frameworks. One may study philosophy's past to find inspirational or cautionary examples; to improve one's philosophical abilities or to gain a greater command of philosophical issues and their interrelations; to discover resources for defending philosophical positions or to find objections to them; to develop a sense of the importance of a philosophical question or to acquire a critical distance from it. One may seek to refine and justify one's own developing philosophy by using it to explain the successes and failures of a philosophy of the past. One need not be in complete or even substantial agreement with a philosophical text of the past in order to utilize it fruitfully. (Nor, for that matter, is agreement sufficient for fruitful application.) Thus, for example, one may disagree with many aspects of Kant's moral theory, and with the metaphysics of agency in which it is embedded, while still finding in that theory—as John Rawls did in *A Theory of Justice* (1971)—inspiration for a procedure for assessing the justness of political institutions.

These four aims—contextualization, interpretation, evaluation, and application—by no means exhaust what one might seek to do with philosophical texts of the past. For example, one might also seek to understand their reception among later philosophers or other thinkers—which is, in part, to use them to contextualize *other* writings—or to compare them with others, or to utilize them for other aesthetic, political, linguistic, or rhetorical purposes. The four aims just described, however, stand in a particularly important ordered relation to one another: success in achieving one aim makes success in achieving the next aim much more likely. Thus, the more one understands about the personal, social, and intellectual context in which a text was produced, the more likely one will be to interpret its meaning correctly. A faithful interpretation of the meaning of the questions, arguments, and claims contained in a text is, in turn, crucial to a fair and accurate evaluation of them. And although one might occasionally derive some accidental insights from a misinterpretation or misevaluation of a text, the most useful applications of a work—especially a work by a very good philosopher—are much more likely to be those that are based on an accurate understanding of its meaning and a sound evaluation of its parts.

Equally important, but perhaps less obvious, is the converse relation: success or failure in an earlier aim will often provide feedback that is crucial for assessing one's success or failure in achieving the previous aim. Thus, an inability to make any useful applications of a philosophical position, argument, or solution may cast at least some doubt on a previous favorable evaluation of it. All philosophers make mistakes, of course, and negative evaluations are often warranted; but if one is led to conclude that central arguments by a great philosopher are riddled with foolish errors of fact and outrageous fallacies of logic, that suggests the wisdom of reconsidering one's interpretation of the text in question. Difficulty in finding a coherent or convincing interpretation of a stretch of philosophical work should, in turn, call into question the adequacy of one's understanding of the context in which it was produced, indicating that further research into that context is required.

The Case of Hume's Theory of Moral Evaluation. An example may help to render these interrelations more concrete. Consider the case of Hume's theory of moral evaluation. Hume has often been read as maintaining that expressed moral evaluations are semantically equivalent to reports of the state of mind of the person making the evaluation. After all, he seems to say *exactly* that:

[W]hen you pronounce any action or character to be vicious, you mean nothing, but that from the constitution of your nature you have a feeling or sentiment of blame from the contemplation of it. (*A Treatise of Human Nature*, Hume, 2000: 3.1.1.26).

As critics have pointed out, it seems to follow straightaway that, if one person feels blame for an action while judging this feeling to result from a personal natural constitution and pronounces it *vicious* while another feels praise for it while judging this feeling to result from a personal natural constitution and pronounces the same action *virtuous*, then each may speak truly, as both should be prepared to admit. While readers have sometimes approved Hume's view so interpreted, taking it to constitute a bracing and hard-headed ethical naturalism, as a semantic doctrine its only apparent application is to serve as an object of elementary refutation—by noting that one can deny another person's moral evaluation even while accepting the corresponding claim about the other's feelings. The easy refutability of the doctrine should prompt a reconsideration of any positive assessment of Hume's position so interpreted—especially when it is noted that the doctrine does not follow from any *argument* that Hume offers. Worse, the doctrine appears flatly to contradict other passages of a few pages earlier that, taken together, seem to entail that moral evaluations are not really true or false at all:

Reason is the discovery of truth or falshood. (*A Treatise of Human Nature*, 3.1.1.9)
Morals . . . cannot be deriv'd from reason. (*A Treatise of Human Nature*, 3.1.1.6)

And yet Hume also characterizes moral distinctions as "something real, essential, and founded on nature" (*Treatise of Human Nature*, I.ii.vii.5) and as matters about which we "judge"—a term that he elsewhere limits to matters of truth and falsehood. In fact, he even offers definitions of 'virtue'—from which it is seems to follow that whatever traits satisfy the definition are *in fact* virtuous. The apparent incoherence of maintaining jointly that moral evaluations (i) merely report feelings but (ii) are neither true nor false, even while (iii) expressing judgments about something real and definable should lead one to question whether the original interpretation of Hume was accurate; and that questioning, in turn, should lead to an examination in greater depth of the context of Hume's pronouncements.

Once one does examine the context of Hume's pronouncements, one finds a number of relevant facts about his background and motivations: that he demonstrated ongoing concern with the prospects for improving the quality of moral and aesthetic judgments; that he was familiar with and strongly opposed to ethical theories (like Samuel Clarke's and William Wollaston's) according to which moral evaluation is a matter of determining, through the exercise of rational inference, the presence of "moral relations" analogous to geometrical relations; and that he was familiar with and favorably disposed toward the then-recent innovation of "moral sense" ethical theories (such as those of Shaftesbury and especially Frances Hutcheson), according to which genuine "moral distinctions" are ascertained by feeling rather than by inference. One also discovers relevant facts about his uses of terms in accordance with common eighteenth-century meanings: for example, that he uses the term 'mean' itself as a synonym for 'signify', in such a way that the phrase 'you mean nothing but' may be used to indicate what a person's *action shows* rather than what the *semantic content* of a person's utterance *is*; that by 'discovery', he means specifically a process of uncovering what is hidden, so that sensation or feeling may provide *access* to truths without "discovering" them; and that by 'reason' he means, not all ways of knowing truths or arriving at assent, but specifically the process of inference. Moreover, one finds that he treats the development of moral *predicates* from moral *feelings* as analogous to the development of color predicates from color sensations: both, he thinks, demand a kind of feeling or sensation as the original input, but both allow of "corrections" for the peculiarities of one's perspective or situation as one develops "abstract ideas" signified by the relevant terms. Furthermore, although Hume allows that science may show that a power to produce a particular kind of color sensation lies in an arrangement of parts that are not themselves colored, he does not on that account deny that things can be truly distinguished by their colors. Thus it appears that moral judgments may, for Hume, indeed be true or false, reporting what is real, and yet not be simply equivalent to statements about one's own sentiments. The result is a much more subtle and coherent Humean theory of moral judgment, and one that is supported by reasonably strong Humean arguments. Indeed, with suitable updating to reflect current psychology, it offers an important alternative approach for contemporary ethical theory. It is an alternative that supports the intuition that basic moral principles about what constitutes virtue and vice are *necessary* (i.e. true in every possible circumstance, just as identities between *redness* and particular light reflectance properties may be), while rejecting the problematic assumption that they must therefore also be a priori (i.e. knowable without epistemic reliance on experience).[27]

Historical Reconstruction and Rational Reconstruction. Some philosophers have in effect identified "history of ideas" with the *contextualization* of philosophical texts of the past and "history of philosophy" with the *application* of philosophical texts of the past to contemporary problems. But this pair of terms is ill-suited for distinguishing different pursuits or aims within the investigation of philosophy's past, whatever they may be. For *any* investigation of philosophy's past—good or bad, and

---

[27] This aspect of the application of Hume's theory was suggested by conversation with Stephen Schiffer. Further discussion of the process by which Humean moral predicates are generated may be found in Garrett (1997, ch. 9).

regardless of approach or purpose—ipso facto constitutes "history of philosophy", just as any investigation of chemistry's past, regardless of purpose, ipso facto constitutes "history of chemistry". And since philosophy consists of "ideas", in a suitably broad sense, the history of philosophy, however distinctive its nature or uses, cannot help but be one part or branch of the "history of ideas"—for the same obvious reason that such fields as the history of chemistry, the history of theology, and the history of mathematics must also be parts or branches of the history of ideas.

It does, on the other hand, make a certain amount of prima facie sense to distinguish "historical reconstruction" and "rational reconstruction" as two potentially different approaches, governed by different goals, to the study of philosophy's past: the former as the interpretation of philosophical texts on the basis of their contextualization, with the primary goal of historical accuracy; and the latter as the interpretation of philosophical texts so as to maximize their favorable evaluation, with the primary goal of useful application. Yet a historically accurate interpretation cannot be guaranteed by contextualization alone—it (and the accurate interpretation of other works constituting parts of the context) often requires the feedback of critical evaluation,[28] which, in turn, often requires the feedback provided by attempted philosophical application. By the same token, if one aims to apply a philosophical text by interpreting it as favorably as possible, it is overwhelmingly likely that the most rationally coherent and philosophically useful interpretation with which to *begin* the process of evaluation and application will also be the most historically accurate one. For the method of consciously and judiciously updating and revising a well-understood philosophical text of the past is far more likely to isolate its remediable defects without losing its original or distinctive strengths than is the method of trying to let an ill-understood text somehow suggest an important and original contribution to philosophy.[29] But finding the most historically accurate interpretation to evaluate, and apply (possibly through revision) requires, in turn, at least some knowledge of context. Thus, regardless of whether one's own interests are more historical than philosophical or vice versa, "historical reconstruction" and "rational reconstruction" must to a considerable extent go hand-in-hand. *Any* fully satisfactory reconstruction of a process that both *occurred in the past* and *involved reasoning*—such as past attempts to give a reasoned answer to a philosophical question—must be essentially both "historical" and "rational".

Division of Labor. For the history of philosophy to be fully successful, it must pursue all four aims: contextualization, interpretation, evaluation, and application. It does not follow, however, that every single project within the history of philosophy

[28] One case in point is Wolfson (1934), which provides a magnificent reconstruction of the sources that Spinoza must have read—while often giving entirely implausible interpretations of Spinoza's philosophy itself, interpretations that could have been forestalled by asking whether the doctrines attributed to Spinoza bore any rational relation to the detailed arguments that Spinoza offers.

[29] One case in point is Stove (1973), which loses nearly everything of value in Hume's treatment of induction by reconstructing it as a baldly fallacious inference in probability theory, from "inductive fallibilism" (the doctrine that the probability of a hypothesis on inductive evidence is always less than 1) to "inductive skepticism" (the doctrine that inductive evidence never increases the probability of a hypothesis). One telling sign that the text has been misunderstood is that Stove is forced to dismiss Hume's *own* detailed discussion of probability as confused and irrelevant to the argument.

must pursue all four aims equally: for example, one may aim at determining through archival research the contents of a past philosopher's library, while another aims at finding novel applications for a past philosopher's already well-understood distinction, argument, or framework. Nor does it follow that every historian of philosophy must pursue all four aims to an equal extent, even over the course of a career. Although the satisfaction of each aim is, in some measure, a means to the satisfaction of the others, each is (or can be) also an end in its own right, to be pursued even beyond the limits of its merely instrumental value for the satisfaction of the others. Furthermore, while the knowledge, talents, and skills that are most directly valuable in the pursuit of one aim may and typically do overlap with those that are most directly valuable in the pursuit of the others, they are by no means identical. Since the history of philosophy is a vast and multifaceted enterprise whose practitioners often differ in interests, knowledge, talents, and skills, a reasonable division of labor will often be in order.

The history of modern philosophy differs, however, from many other collaborative enterprises—such as an automobile assembly line—in which a division of labor is also in order. An assembly line is engineered in such a way that the whole takes shape automatically through the additive efforts of the workers, who therefore need not understand the contributions made by other workers nor the relation of those contributions to his or her own. In order for historians of philosophy to do their jobs well, in contrast, they must understand the work of others in the field who are focusing on very different tasks and aims. Accordingly, it is not enough for historians of modern philosophy simply to practice mutual "tolerance" of "multiple approaches", nor even to recognize the positive intrinsic value of each of multiple aims. Rather, to the extent possible they must seek out, master, assess, and actively incorporate into their own work the work of other historians, philosophers, and historians of philosophy whose interests, skills, and distributions of effort differ markedly from their own.

IV. Prospects for the History of Modern Philosophy

We have seen something of modern philosophy's past, the ways in which that past has been studied and understood, and the ways in which philosophers have thought about that study; and this, in turn, has helped to explain the nature, current state, and basic interrelated aims of the history of modern philosophy. What, then, are the prospects for the history of modern philosophy in the twenty-first century?

Opportunities. At least four aspects of the current state history of modern philosophy constitute special opportunities. One is its relative freedom from large-scale revolutionary ideologies of the philosophy of philosophy—such as Hegelian idealism, Marxist historical materialism, and logical positivism—that tend systematically to distort the interpretation and evaluation (whether positive or negative) of philosophical works of the past. Another is the availability of more and better research tools, which promise to enhance the understanding of well-known philosophers and encourage the exploration of those who deserve to be better known. A third is the general broadening of scope to other fields, authors, and disciplines, which offers the prospect of new works for primary investigation as well as new sources for their contextualization. The fourth is the important body of work produced in the history of modern philosophy over the past fifty years, which promises to provide both context and stimulation for future work while establishing high standards for both the quality of research and the quality of argumentation.

Dangers. The primary dangers facing the history of modern philosophy at present are dangers of fragmentation—i.e. failures of integration. If historians of modern philosophy do not appreciate the vital interrelations among the multiple aims of their endeavor, the failure to integrate their pursuit has the potential to divide historians of philosophy into two ideological camps working in substantial isolation from each another: one camp narrowly emphasizing the value of contextualization and historical exploration at the expense of philosophical application, and another camp narrowly emphasizing the value of philosophical evaluation and application at the expense of contextualization. The result would be unfortunate on both sides. Those in the latter camp would be all too easily limited to discussing anachronistic interpretations of familiar themes from a small selection of familiar canonical works, and they would soon find themselves isolated from colleagues outside of philosophy. Those in the former camp would all too easily ignore the distinction between those past philosophers whose work is of enduring philosophical significance in its own right and those past philosophers whose work is of philosophical significance primarily for the light it sheds on the work of others; and they would soon find themselves isolated from their colleagues in philosophy. Most importantly, both the contextualization and the application of modern philosophy—not to mention its interpretation and evaluation—would suffer in consequence.

In addition to avoiding the fragmentation of their aims, historians of modern philosophy must also take care to avoid the fragmentation of disciplinary expertise. The history of modern philosophy is by nature an interdisciplinary endeavor, located at the intersection of philosophy and modern history. Like many other interdisciplinary fields, it has the potential to offer distinctive insights and benefits to each of the fields it connects while drawing from both to achieve its aims; but (again like many other interdisciplinary fields) in order for it to do so, its practitioners must develop and maintain knowledge, skills, and methods relevant to each of its two related disciplines. When historians of modern philosophy fail to develop the historical knowledge, methods, and skills needed to interact fruitfully with historians, they thereby become less valuable to philosophy itself; just as when they fail to develop the philosophical knowledge, methods, and skills needed to interact with philosophers, they lose their distinctive value to the discipline of history. Similar dangers of fragmentation exist, of course, in philosophy's many other interdisciplinary endeavors, such as cognitive science, philosophy of biology, philosophy of physics, philosophy of religion, philosophy of mathematics, and philosophy of art— not to mention the history of ancient and medieval philosophy. Nevertheless, the danger is particularly acute in the history of modern philosophy, because the historian of philosophy requires at least some knowledge and training in the modern history of *many* specific fields—including, for example, cognitive psychology, biology, physics, religion, mathematics, and art.

A third danger concerns a kind of subdisciplinary fragmentation within the history of modern philosophy itself. For as the base of knowledge grows, historians of modern philosophy will quite naturally tend to specialize not only in one or another period of modern philosophy but also in the history of one or another subdiscipline of modern philosophy, such as metaphysics, epistemology, philosophy of science, logic, ethics, or political theory. Yet these subdisciplines are often quite tightly linked in the periods of modern philosophy's past, and they are tightly linked in the work of many particular philosophers of those periods, including (for example) Descartes, Spinoza, Hume, Kant, Hegel, and Mill. An understanding of Spinoza's metaphysical theory of essences, for example, is essential to understanding his theory of ethical motivation; and an understanding of Hume's conceptions of virtue and beauty illuminate his theory of causal necessity.

Directions and Strategies. Assuming that the history of modern philosophy can exploit these opportunities and avoid these dangers, what topics warrant its particular attention, and what strategies should it adopt? While the scope of the field is far too vast to permit comprehensive answers to these questions, I will offer a few suggestions, organized around the four primary aims of contextualization, interpretation, evaluation, and application.

The modern era has been marked by a series of revolutionary scientific developments, including the new cosmology of Copernicus, Galileo, and Kepler; the mathematical physics of Newton; the evolutionary biology of Darwin; and Einstein's theories of relativity. Exploring the influences of these developments on the formulation of philosophical questions and answers is a particularly rich source for the contextualization of modern philosophy, from the effect of seventeenth-century conceptions of motion on the ontology of physical properties and the metaphysics of space and time to the effect of Newtonian physics on Kant's conception of the mind's constitution of the phenomenal world, and from the effect of the theory of natural selection on the ethics of altruism and the conception of God to the effect of relativity on the logical positivists' conception of the aims and structure of science. While there has been serious attention to the influence of modern science on modern philosophy in recent years, much remains to be done—especially for periods after the seventeenth century.[30] Other particularly promising topics for investigation include the influence of Stoicism on early modern ethics; the influence of scholastic theories of sense perception on early modern epistemology; the influence of religion (including the controversial status of Jansenism and doctrines of the Eucharist) on seventeenth-century Cartesian metaphysics;[31] the influence of changing doctrines in logic on epistemology and metaphysics through the modern era; the influence of modern medical theories on modern philosophy of mind and

---

[30] Work by Michael Friedman provides a good example of valuable work on Newton's influence on Kant; see, for example, Friedman (1992). Friedman (1983) takes up the influence of relativity theory on logical positivism.   [31] See, e.g., Schmaltz (2002).

ethics;[32] and the influence of the methodology of *eclecticism* (later promoted by Brucker) on German philosophy in general and Leibniz in particular.[33]

While there are many strategies for contextualizing a philosophical text, one particularly valuable strategy is to try to determine who it is that an author is arguing *against*. This not only provides insight into an author's motivations but also often provides a key to understanding the author's argumentative strategy and technical vocabulary. Hume's previously-mentioned discussion of inductive inference, for example, has often been treated as a free-standing skeptical argument about the "rational warrant" of such inferences. More recently, some commentators have proposed that the argument is not a skeptical argument but merely a rejection of a narrow "a prioristic" or "deductivist" conception of inference identified with Descartes. In part through an investigation of early modern theories of inference, however, David Owen has shown convincingly that Hume's primary target is Locke; and that the leading issue between them is not the adequacy of "a priori" or "deductivist" theories of inference but rather the question of whether inductive inference requires a "medium". Locke (as part of his non-formalist conception of logic) sees all inference as the mediated perception of a relation of "agreement" (or "seeming agreement") between two ideas, where the perception of agreement is mediated by an intermediate idea (called a "proof") that is perceived to "agree" to each. To recognize that Hume is rejecting the application of this model to the case of inductive inference is to see Hume's argument and its terminology in an entirely new light.[34]

The interpretation of philosophical texts becomes naturally more difficult as they recede further into the past; and although the best known have had generations of careful readers and commentators in the years since their publication, many questions of interpretation remain. In some cases, these questions concern the history of an entire topic. For example, there are many interpretive issues about early modern treatments of freedom and necessity—from the meaning of Descartes's claim that assent can be free even when doubt is impossible to the reasons for Hume's concentration on establishing a "doctrine of necessity" that is compatible with causal indeterminism—that depend on the interpretation of no-longer-current distinctions among kinds of necessity and largely unfamiliar disputes about the nature of causal power. In many cases, even central aspects of the thought of very well-known philosophers still require reinterpretation, whether because of mistaken assumptions or the difficulty of the texts. For example, the assumption that Berkeley's theory of meaning should be understood as a variant of Locke's theory that the meaning of a word is typically the idea for which it stands has prevented the fundamental role of volition in his theory of meaning from being understood; while the metaphysics of Spinoza's theory of the mind's eternity has resisted many

[32] In forthcoming work, for example, Livia Guimaraes discusses the fascinating influence of medical conceptions of "melancholy" on Hume's conception of the psychology of philosophizing.
[33] See Mercer (2001). Mercer also provides a detailed refutation of Russell's thesis that Leibniz originally derived his metaphysics from his logic.
[34] See Owen (1999). See also Garrett (2000) for further discussion of how to utilize this result in the interpretation of Hume's argument.

attempts at interpretation largely through the difficulty and compression of the texts. There are a vast number of cases in which detailed interpretation is needed of the ideas of less-frequently discussed figures, from the moral epistemology of Malebranche and Clarke to the non-Cartesian skepticism of Gassendi and Bayle. Twentieth-century analytic philosophy's loss of contact with much post-Kantian continental philosophy creates a particular need for careful interpretation of the arguments and conclusions of such important and influential figures as Fichte, Hegel, Schopenhauer, Marx, Nietzsche, Edmund Husserl, and Martin Heidegger.

One useful strategy in interpretation is to pay particular attention to interpretive *puzzles*—that is, to passages or features of a text that appear to be inconsistent with other passages or features of the author's text, or radically fallacious in a way that would be surprising for the author, or otherwise seem not to make sense. If one can resolve these puzzles, one often finds a key that leads to a more satisfying interpretation of other passages and texts as well. One case in point is Mill's famous argument, in Chapter 4 of *Utilitarianism*, proceeding from the premise that "each person, so far as he believes it to be attainable, desires his own happiness", through the principle that "the sole evidence it is possible to produce that anything is desirable, is that people do actually desire it", to the conclusion that "the general happiness is a good to the aggregate of all persons". This argument has typically been interpreted as committing two gross fallacies: first, equivocating between psychological and normative senses of 'desirable' ("can be desired" vs. "is worthy of being desired—i.e. good"); and second, arguing by fallacious composition that, if each person's happiness is a good to that person, then the general happiness must be a good to the aggregate of persons. As Geoffrey Sayre-McCord (2001) has observed, however, this would be a very puzzling performance indeed on Mill's part, since he elsewhere shows himself to be sensitive to the very distinctions that this doubly fallacious version of the argument ignores. By careful attention to (i) the meaning of Mill's own claims about the level of "proof" that his argument does and does not provide, (ii) to Mill's conception of desire as constituting a (defeasible) perception of something as good (in the same way that vision provides a defeasible perception of things as colored and shaped), and (iii) to Mill's distinction between something's being good and something's being good for an individual, Sayre-McCord provides a reconstruction of the argument that is strong (albeit with debatable psychological premises) and far more plausible as an interpretation of Mill's meaning. In addition, it exhibits an unexpected parallel with the argumentative structure of Kant's argument for his formulation of the categorical imperative of morality as requiring that all rational agents treat rational nature as an end in itself.

If much remains to be interpreted in modern philosophy's past, even more remains to be evaluated or re-evaluated, either as a result of reinterpretation or as the result of new directions in contemporary philosophy. Locke's account of the ontological status of secondary qualities calls for reassessment, for example, in light of recent work in color theory and on the nature of dispositions, and his theory of the semantics of natural kind terms under conditions of compositional ignorance also deserves reassessment. Moral sense theories of moral epistemology—as found in Shaftesbury, Hutcheson, Hume, and Adam Smith—call for evaluation as alternatives to recent sophisticated expressivist and quasi-realist theories of morality. A particularly central topic for evaluation, in light of the recent concentration on practical rationality in ethics, is the merits of the competing Humean and Kantian views on the question of whether immoral action is necessarily in some way irrational. Nineteenth-century German aesthetics, marginalized in twentieth-century analytic philosophy, is another part of the history of modern philosophy potentially deserving of particular critical scrutiny. With recent developments in the philosophy of language, philosophy of logic, and epistemology (including renewed discussion of the nature and extent of a priori knowledge), the re-evaluation of Quine's thesis of the indeterminacy of translation, his treatment of the analytic/synthetic distinction, and his views about the revisability of logic—topics now newly part of modern philosophy's past—constitute other obvious examples.

One especially useful strategy for accurate evaluation is the simple one of reconstructing an author's argument formally, *in the words of the text itself*, with individual propositions as numbered steps and with relations of inferential support clearly labeled. When done well, this provides specific and accurate objects for critical assessment, since each undefended premise can be assessed for truth or falsehood, and each inference can be assessed for validity or invalidity, strength or weakness; the restriction to outlining material that is actually present in the text helps to provide an accurate version of the argument to be evaluated. A case in point is the infamous so-called "Cartesian Circle"—one of the most-discussed episodes in the history of modern philosophy. In his *Meditations on First Philosophy*, Descartes seeks to establish the proposition (sometimes dubbed "the Truth Rule") that "whatever is perceived clearly and distinctly is true". A key element in the establishment of the Truth Rule, in turn, is the proposition that "God exists and is not a deceiver". Many readers (beginning with his own contemporaries) have judged that Descartes's reasoning is *circular*, on the grounds that, although he uses the existence of a non-deceiving God to support the Truth Rule, he must also use the Truth Rule to support his acceptance of the argument that there exists a non-deceiving God. Formally outlining the argument for the Truth Rule (found in Meditation IV) indeed shows that the existence of a non-deceiving God is a crucial premise in it. However, extending that outline to encompass the full support for its premises also shows that at no point does Descartes argue (despite his opponents' claim) for the proposition that there exists a non-deceiving God on the grounds that he (Descartes) perceives God's existence and non-deception clearly and distinctly, and that whatever is perceived clearly and distinctly is true. Descartes offers two arguments for God's existence as a supremely perfect and consequently non-deceptive being in Meditation III, and another in Meditation V; but none of these arguments employs the Truth Rule as a premise, and hence there is no formal circularity. It is true, of course, that Descartes *ascribes a role* to the clarity and distinctness of the premises in his argument for God's existence and non-deception—but it is not the role of justifying their acceptance. Their acceptance is justified by the fact that they are *indubitable while Descartes is entertaining them*, in accordance with his principle that one is always entitled to accept what one cannot doubt as long as one cannot doubt it. The clarity and distinctness of Descartes's premises serve *causally* to *explain* their indubitability (in accordance with Descartes's theory of the determination of assent), not *epistemically* to justify their acceptance. To be sure, a further question remains of whether Descartes should have *stopped*, following his acceptance of each premise in his proofs for the existence of a non-deceiving God, to ask himself whether his standard grounds for doubt (such as the possibility of a powerful and malignant deceiver) could be applied to the premise immediately, rather than waiting until the *end* of the argument to raise such doubts—when, on Descartes's account, such doubts prove to be *too late* to be effective, because the doubts will then be blocked by the newly-achieved certainty of God's existence. But that is a separate question from the question of whether the argument is formally circular or not; and seeing this constitutes a real advance in assessing the strengths and weaknesses of Descartes's project.

Much of the excitement of the history of modern philosophy lies in the range of its applications to contemporary philosophical debate—which has arguably never been greater. Thus, for example, Spinoza's arguments that only virtuous action can be free and that only positive reactive attitudes such as love, praise, and approval (as opposed to negative reactive attitudes such as hatred, blame, and indignation) can be rational bear directly on contemporary debates about the "symmetry" or "asymmetry" of freedom (with respect to freedom to act rightly and wrongly) and the appropriateness of moral "reactive" attitudes.[35] Reid's attempt to ground an adequate response to skepticism in a teleological explanation of human cognitive faculties is directly relevant to both theological and evolutionary approaches to knowledge and skepticism in contemporary epistemology.[36] Kant's attempt to determine the structures necessary for data to constitute information has clear applications to contemporary cognitive science.[37] Jerry Fodor (2003) has recently credited Hume as the originator of the project of basing an empirical psychology on a theory of representation, and he has argued that many errors of twentieth-century philosophy of mind could have been avoided by more careful attention to the components and structure of Hume's theory.

The theory of mental representation is, as Fodor and many others recognize, central to contemporary philosophy of mind, philosophy of language, epistemology, and metaphysics; but the theory of mental representation was also a central topic of the entire early modern period, in part because earlier scholastic theories of perception and cognitive functioning appeared to be incompatible with the new mechanistic science of nature and so required replacement. The investigation of the full range of different early modern theories of representation—from Descartes, Arnauld, and Malebranche, through Locke, Hume, Reid, and Kant—thus has been and will continue to be among the most stimulating and fruitful pursuits in the history of early modern philosophy. Indeed, because of its underlying concern with the

---

[35] For a good discussion of the possible asymmetry of freedom, see Wolf (1990).
[36] See, e.g., Plantinga (1993).   [37] See, e.g., Kitcher (1993).

nature of abstraction and predicate-generation, early modern philosophy may even contribute to discussions of topics central to contemporary metaphysics—such as the nature of vagueness—that were not often explicitly addressed in the early modern period itself. Another striking feature of contemporary philosophy is the increasing number of contemporary philosophers who identify themselves as *naturalists*, and an especially important aspect of contemporary philosophy is its focus on exploring the philosophical adequacy of *naturalism*—roughly, the view that there are no metaphysical realms or causes distinct from ordinary nature and its causal laws—in a wide range of applications, from ethics to philosophy of mind. Thus, naturalists of the past—such as Spinoza, Hume, and Nietzsche—are likely to be particularly fertile sources of application for contemporary philosophy.[38]

As many of these cases suggest, one strategy for developing applications of the history of modern philosophy is to search for philosophical projects of the past that parallel philosophical projects of the present. An illustrative case in point is Spinoza's theory of mind. Although its expression in Spinozistic terminology and its setting in a one-substance metaphysics can make it seem alien to contemporary readers, Spinoza's aim is to explain representation and consciousness as phenomena that arise incrementally through levels of complex organization within nature—an aim very congenial to contemporary naturalists. Spinoza treats internal states of things as always representing the causes of those states (although possibly in a way that *confuses* them with other possible causes) just to the extent that the causal contribution of that cause plays a role in determining the self-preservatory activity of the thing. Because he finds some self-preservatory activity at even very rudimentary levels of organization,[39] Spinoza is able to treat representation as a phenomenon that occurs (although often, especially at lower levels of organization, in a *very* confused way) throughout nature. His identification of the degree of *consciousness* of a representation with its degree of power to determine self-preservatory activity leads to a very attractive theory of consciousness, one that avoids the difficulties of contemporary "higher-order perception" and "higher-order thought" theories and instead has important affinities with contemporary theories that treat consciousness as the recruitment of a representational state for participation in a more global state of neurological activity.[40]

Conclusion. Philosophers have approached the history of their subject in many different ways over the years—from the narrative sect-based doxology of Stanley and Horn to Bayle's highly provocative evaluations and applications of past philosophies; and from the semi-official anti-historicism of Descartes, Locke, and the logical positivists to the organic incorporation of history into philosophy by Hegel and the

---

[38] For a useful delineation of more specific naturalist doctrines found in Spinoza, Hume, and (especially) Nietzsche, see Leiter (2002, ch. 1).

[39] Indeed, self-preservatory activity is a precondition for individuation in Spinoza's metaphysics; see Garrett (2002).

[40] Robert van Gulick, for example, has recently proposed, in as-yet-unpublished work, such a "Higher Order Global State" theory of consciousness. I discuss Spinoza's theories of representation and consciousness at greater length in Garrett (2001).

British idealists. While it is difficult to share the extravagant Hegelian view that philosophy essentially *is* the study of its own history, philosophers should be prepared—as Brucker recommended over 250 years ago—to practice a thoroughgoing eclecticism, borrowing useful materials from the past wherever they find them. Historians of modern philosophy must continue to strive not only to pursue rigorous philosophical and historical training for themselves but also to integrate the philosophical study of the history of modern philosophy into the training of every philosopher, so that the intellectual resources it can provide will be a ready part of every philosopher's toolbox for formulating and approaching philosophical questions. Only in this way can the history of modern philosophy avoid the appearance of being a time-consuming detour on the road to answering philosophical questions—questions that will unfortunately already have been formulated in ignorance of their origins.

To contextualize, interpret, evaluate, and apply a very wide range of figures and topics from two and a half centuries of unprecedented philosophical activity is, of course, a daunting task, far beyond the resources of any individual. The history of modern philosophy is a truly Baconian enterprise, in the sense that it requires the coordinated efforts of many intellectual laborers, each operating in conditions of a free flow of information that make each laborer's results available to the others, and each guided by a mutual understanding of the common project. But there are today many laborers in the history of modern philosophy; and their tools, skills, and means of communication have never been better. Its scope is ever-growing, not only as more is uncovered about the past, but also as what was once philosophy of the present becomes newly past. If the enterprise is guided by good judgment and a philosophy of the history of philosophy that respects and values the reciprocal relations among its primary aims, then future historians of the history of philosophy will be able to look back on the twenty-first century as a Golden Age for the history of modern philosophy.

References

Armstrong, A. MacC. 1959. "Philosophy and its History", *Philosophy and Phenomenological Research*, 19: 447–65.

Atherton, Margaret (editor). 1994. *Women Philosophers of the Early Modern Period* (Indianapolis: Hackett Publishing Company).

Ayers, Michael. 1978. "Analytical Philosophy and the History of Philosophy", in Rée, Ayers, and Westoby 1978.

Bacon, Francis. 1605. *The Advancement of Learning* (London: Henrie Tomes).

Bayle, Pierre. 1697. *Dictionnaire Historique et Critique* (Rotterdam: Reinier Leers).

Beiser, Frederick C. 1987. *The Fate of Reason: German Philosophy from Kant to Fichte* (Cambridge, Mass.: Harvard University Press).

Bennett, Jonathan. 1984. *A Study of Spinoza's 'Ethics'* (Indianapolis: Hackett).

Broad, Jacqueline. 2002. *Women Philosophers of the Seventeenth Century* (Cambridge: Cambridge University Press).

Brucker, Jakob. 1744. *Historia Critica Philosophiæ* (Leipzig, 1744).

Clark, Maudemarie. 1990. *Nietzsche on Truth and Philosophy* (Cambridge: Cambridge University Press).

Cohen, Leslie. 1986. "Doing Philosophy is Doing its History", *Synthese* [Special issue on "The Role of History in and for Philosophy"] 67: 33–50.

Curley, Edwin. 1984. "Dialogues with the Dead", *Synthese* [Special issue on "The Role of History in and for Philosophy"] 67: 51–6.

Fodor, Jerry. 2003. *Hume Variations* (Oxford: Oxford University Press).

Friedman, Michael. 1947. *Kant and the Exact Sciences* (Cambridge, Mass.: Harvard University Press).

—— 1983. *Foundations of Space-Time Theories: Relativistic Physics and Philosophy of Science* (Princeton: Princeton University Press).

Garber, Daniel. 1992. *Descartes's Metaphysical Physics* (Chicago: University of Chicago Press).

—— 1989. "Does History Have a Future? Some Reflections on Bennett and Doing Philosophy Historically", in *Doing Philosophy Historically* (Buffalo: Pergamon Press).

Garrett, Don. 2002. "Spinoza's *Conatus* Argument", in *Spinoza: Metaphysical Themes*, edited by John I. Biro and Olli Koistinen (New York: Oxford University Press): 127–58.

—— 2001. "Spinoza's Theory of Mind and Imagination." Presented at the American Philosophical Association Eastern Division Meetings.

—— 2000. "Owen on Humean Reasoning", *Hume Studies* 26.2: 291–303.

—— 1997. *Cognition and Commitment in Hume's Philosophy* (New York: Oxford University Press).

Gaukroger, Stephen. 2001. *Francis Bacon and the Transformation of Early Modern Philosophy* (Cambridge: Cambridge University Press).

Gracia, Jorge J. E. 1992. *Philosophy and Its History: Issues in Philosophical Historiography* (Albany: State University of New York Press).

Horn, George (Georgius Hornius). 1655. *Historiae philosophicae libre VII successione sectis et vita philosophorum ab orbe condito ad nostrum aetatem agitu* (Lugdini Batavorum).

Hume, David. 2000. *A Treatise of Human Nature*, edited by David Fate Norton and Mary J. Norton (Oxford: Oxford University Press).

Jesseph, Douglas. 1993. *Berkeley's Philosophy of Mathematics* (Chicago: University of Chicago Press).

Kemp Smith, Norman. 1941. *The Philosophy of David Hume* (London: Macmillan).

—— 1905. "The Naturalism of Hume [I and II]", *Mind*, 14.

Kitcher, Patricia. 1993. *Kant's Transcendental Psychology* (New York: Oxford University Press).

Kuklick, Bruce. 1984. "Seven Thinkers and How They Grew: Descartes, Spinoza, Leibniz; Locke, Berkeley, Hume; Kant". in Rorty, Schneewind, and Skinner 1984.

Lehrer, Keith. 1989. *Thomas Reid* (London: Routledge).

Leiter, Brian. 2002. *Routledge Philosophy Guidebook to Nietzsche on Morality* (London: Routledge).

Lennon, Thomas M. 1999. *Reading Bayle* (Toronto: University of Toronto Press).

—— 1993. *The Battle of the Gods and Giants: the Legacies of Descartes and Gassendi, 1655–1715* (Princeton, New Jersey: Princeton University Press).

Loeb, Louis E. 1981. *From Descartes to Hume: Continental Metaphysics and the Development of Modern Philosophy* (Ithaca: Cornell University Press).

Mercer, Christia. 2001. *Leibniz's Metaphysics: Its Origins and Development* (Cambridge: Cambridge University Press).

Mills, Charles W. 1997. *The Racial Contract* (Ithaca, N.Y.: Cornell University Press.

Nadler, Steven M. 1992. *Malebranche and Ideas* (New York: Oxford University Press).

—— 1989. *Arnauld and the Cartesian Philosophy of Ideas* (Princeton, New Jersey Princeton University Press).

Owen, David. 1999. *Hume's Reason* (Oxford: Oxford University Press).

Penelhum, Terence. 1985. *Butler* (London: Routledge & Kegan Paul).

Pippin, Robert B. 1989. *Hegel's Idealism: the Satisfactions of Self-Consciousness* (Cambridge: Cambridge University Press).

Plantinga, Alvin. 1993. *Warrant and Proper Function* (New York: Oxford University Press).

Rawls, John. 1971. *A Theory of Justice* (Cambridge, Mass.: Harvard University Press, revised 1999).

Rée, Jonathan, Ayers, Michael, and Westoby, Adam (editors). 1978. *Philosophy and Its Past* (Hassocks, Sussex: Harvester Press).

Richardson, John. 1996. *Nietzsche's System* (New York: Oxford University Press).

Rorty, Richard, Schneewind, J. B., and Skinner, Quentin (editors). 1984. *Philosophy in History: Essays in the Historiography of Philosophy* (Cambridge: Cambridge University Press).

—— 1984. "The Historiography of Philosophy: Four Genres", in Rorty, Schneewind, and Skinner, 1984.

Rosenthal, David M. 1989. "Philosophy and its History", in *The Institution of Philosophy: A Discipline in Crisis?* edited by Avner Cohen and Marcelo Dascal (La Salle: Open Court).

Russell, Bertrand. 1900. *A Critical Exposition of the Philosophy of Leibniz* (Cambridge: Cambridge University Press).

—— 1945. *A History of Western Philosophy* (New York: Simon & Schuster).

Sayre-McCord. 2001. "Mill's Proof of the Principle of Utility: A More than Half-Hearted Defense", in *Social Philosophy & Policy* 18.2: 330–60.

Schmaltz, Tad M. 2002. *Radical Cartesianism: The French Reception of Descartes* (Cambridge: Cambridge University Press).

—— 1996. *Malebranche's Theory of the Soul: A Cartesian Interpretation* (New York: Oxford University Press).

Schneewind, Jerome B. 1998. *The Invention of Autonomy: A History of Modern Moral Philosophy* (Cambridge: Cambridge University Press).

Sedgwick, Sally. 2000. *The Reception of Kant's Critical Philosophy: Fichte, Schelling, and Hegel* (Cambridge: Cambridge University Press).

Skorupski, John. 1989. *John Stuart Mill* (London: Routledge).

Stanley, Thomas. 1655. *The History of Philosophy* (London).

Stove, D. C. 1973. *Probability and Hume's Inductive Skepticsm* (Oxford: Clarendon Press).

Walton, Craig, 1977. "Bibliography of the Historiography and Philosophy of the History of Philosophy", *International Studies in Philosophy* 5: 135–66.

Williams, Bernard. 1978. *Descartes: The Project of Pure Enquiry* (Harmondsworth: Penguin Books).

Wilson, Catherine. 1998. "The History of Modern Philosophy", in *The Future of Philosophy: Towards the Twenty-First Century* (London: Routledge).

Wilson, Margaret. 1992. "History of Philosophy Today; and the Case of the Sensible Qualities", *Philosophical Review* 101.1 (Jan.): 191–243.

Wolf, Susan. 1990. *Freedom Within Reason* (New York: Oxford University Press).

Wolfson, H. A. 1934. *The Philosophy of Spinoza: Unfolding the Latent Processes of his Reasoning* (Cambridge, Mass.: Harvard University Press).

Wolterstorff, Nicholas. 2001. *Thomas Reid and the Story of Epistemology* (Cambridge: Cambridge University Press).

Wood, Allen W. 1990. *Hegel's Ethical Thought* (Cambridge: Cambridge University Press).

Zöller, Günter. 1998. *Fichte's Transcendental Philosophy: the Original Duplicity of Intelligence and Will* (Cambridge: Cambridge University Press).

3

The Hermeneutics of Suspicion: Recovering Marx, Nietzsche, and Freud

BRIAN LEITER

Paul Ricoeur famously dubbed that great triumvirate of late nineteenth and early twentieth-century thought—Marx, Nietzsche, and Freud—"the school of suspicion",[1] by which he meant those thinkers who taught us to regard with suspicion our conscious understandings and experience,[2] whether the deliverances of ordinary psychological introspection about one's desires ("I really want to be rich!"), or the moral categories political leaders and ordinary citizens apply to themselves and the social world they inhabit ("an inheritance tax is an immoral death tax!"). "Beneath" or "behind" the surface lay causal forces that *explained* the conscious phenomena precisely because they laid bare the true *meaning* of those phenomena: I don't *really* want lots of money, I want the *love* I never got as a child; survivors have no moral claim on an inheritance, but it is in the interests of the ruling classes that we believe they do, and so on.

Recent years have been, in now familiar ways, unkind to Marx and Freud. For understandable, if philosophically frivolous, reasons the collapse of the Soviet Union has been taken—especially in the media—as signalling the defeat of Marxism *qua* philosophy.[3] Meanwhile, Freud's theory of the mind fell prey to the combined forces of the philosophical critique launched by Adolf Grünbaum[4] (especially as popularized by polemicists like Frederick Crews)[5] and market-driven models of medical care (especially in the United States), which disfavored the lengthy investment required by Freudian psychoanalysis. Only Nietzsche has remained *apparently* unscathed, his academic reputation and influence at perhaps its highest point ever.[6]

Yet instead of a frontal assault on the critiques of the explanatory programs of Marx and Freud, the defense of their legacy in the English-speaking world has

---

[1] Paul Ricoeur, *Freud and Philosophy*, trans. D. Savage (New Haven: Yale University Press, 1970), 32.

[2] "If we go back to the intention they had in common, we find in it the decision to look upon the whole of consciousness primarily as 'false' consciousness." Id. at 33.

[3] Marxism had been so long associated with the Soviet Union, that that system's collapse was taken to coincide with the collapse of its putative intellectual foundations. Of course, this association is, from a philosophical point of view, a non-sequitur. Indeed, the Soviet Union arguably collapsed for Marxian reasons: bureaucratic central planning clearly fettered the development of the forces of production, and thus was eventually supplanted by nascent market forms of production and distribution.

[4] Adolf Grünbaum, *The Foundations of Psychoanalysis: A Philosophical Critique* (Berkeley: University of California Press, 1984). [5] See below n. 85.

[6] Even analytic philosophers like Christine Korsgaard and Thomas Nagel—ones with Kantian sympathies no less!—now refer respectfully to his ideas.

gradually fallen to those I will call *moralizing* interpreters of their thought. The moralizing readers de-emphasize (or simply reject) the explanatory and causal claims in the work of Marx and Freud, and try to marry more-or-less Marxian and Freudian ideas to various themes in normative ethics and political philosophy *Explanation* of phenomena is abandoned in favor of the more traditional philosophical enterprise of *justification*, whether of the just distribution of resources or the possibility of morality's authority.

So, for example, G. A. Cohen, the most influential of English-language Marx interpreters in recent decades,[7] has declared that "Marxism has lost much or most of its [empirical] carapace, its hard shell of supposed fact"[8] and that, as a result, "Marxists . . . are increasingly impelled into normative political philosophy."[9] (Under the influence of Habermas, the Marxist tradition has taken a similar turn on the Continent.)[10] Similarly, a leading moral philosopher notes that, "Just when philosophers of science thought they had buried Freud for the last time, he has quietly reappeared in the writings of moral philosophers"[11] and goes on to claim that "Freud's theory of the superego provides a valuable psychological model for various aspects of [Kant's] Categorical Imperative."[12] On these new renderings, Marx and Freud command our attention because they are *really* just complements (or correctives) to Rawls or Korsgaard, really just normative theorists who can be made to join in a contemporary dialogue about equality and the authority of morality.[13]

Yet even Nietzsche has been transformed by moralizing interpreters, though in a somewhat different way. The crucial development here has been the retreat from the natural reading of Nietzsche as a philosopher engaged in an *attack* on morality—a reading first articulated by the Danish scholar Georg Brandes more than a century ago[14]—in favor of a reading which presents Nietzsche as fundamentally concerned with questions of truth and knowledge: the moralistic scruples of interpreters are satisfied by treating Nietzsche as concerned with *something else*, something less morally alarming than a "revaluation of values". Thus, on the European Continent, Heidegger tells us that Nietzsche is the last great metaphysician, advancing claims,

---

[7] See G. A. Cohen, *Karl Marx's Theory of History: A Defense* (Princeton: Princeton University Press, 1978).

[8] G. A. Cohen, *If You're an Egalitarian, How Come You're So Rich?* (Cambridge, Mass.: Harvard University Press, 2000), 103.   [9] Id. at 109.

[10] See, e.g., Jürgen Habermas, *Theorie des kommunikativen Handelns*, 2 vols. (Frankfurt: Suhrkamp, 1981), translated as *The Theory of Communicative Action* by Thomas McCarthy in two volumes (1984, 1987) published by Beacon Press (Boston).

[11] J. David Velleman, "A Rational Superego", *Philosophical Review* 108 (1999), 529.   [12] Id.

[13] One hopeful sign that the tide may be turning with respect to Marx is Jonathan Wolff's splendid book, *Why Read Marx Today?* (Oxford: Oxford University Press, 2002). At times, to be sure, Wolff expresses a certain uneasiness about the epistemic status of Marx's claims. "My point", he says, "is that we value the work of the greatest philosophers for their power, rigour, depth, inventiveness, insight, originality, systematic vision, and, no doubt, other virtues too. Truth, or at least the whole truth and nothing but the truth, seems way down the list . . . . There are things much more interesting than truth. Understood this way, Marx's works are as alive as anyone's." Id. at 101. Yet elsewhere—and Wolff makes the case powerfully—he notes that Marx "does say many true and inspiring things. His work is full of insight and illumination." Id. at 125.

[14] Based on lectures first given in the late 1880s, they subsequently appeared in English as *Friedrich Nietzsche*, trans. A. Chater (London: Heinemann, 1915).

like Plato, about the essence of Being,[15] while in the hands of Foucault and Derrida, Nietzsche becomes the precursor of post-modern skepticism about knowledge and determinate meaning.

In Anglophone philosophy, the development has followed a somewhat different trajectory, but arrived, nonetheless, at the same resting point. The late Walter Kaufmann, a gifted translator but unreliable scholar, saved Nietzsche from the mis-representations of the Nazis, but added his own by introducing a more straightfor-wardly moralistic interpretation: Kaufmann's Nietzsche turns out to be a congenial secular liberal, committed to self-realization.[16] Since Kaufmann, however, the prim-ary tendency among English-speaking interpreters has been, as on the Continent, to locate Nietzsche's central philosophical concerns outside of the theory of value: for example, as a certain sort of philosophical skeptic about truth, knowledge, and meaning. This approach, which dominated Nietzsche studies beginning with Arthur Danto's 1965 book *Nietzsche as Philosopher*,[17] received its most sophisticated articula-tion in Alexander Nehamas's 1985 study, *Nietzsche: Life as Literature*,[18] a book which presents a "Nietzsche" that, one suspects, Georg Brandes would not have recognized.

I shall argue that, in fact, all three of the great practitioners of the hermeneutics of suspicion have suffered at the hands of moralizing interpreters who have resisted the essentially *naturalistic* thrust of their conception of philosophical practice. The resistance, it is important to note at the beginning, has taken different forms. On Cohen's reading of Marx, for example, Marx is, indeed, a kind of naturalist, but a *failed* one: Marxists are better-served by turning to moral theory, according to Cohen, given the failure of the naturalistic project. On Nehamas's reading of Nietzsche, by contrast, the naturalism is simply ignored, in favor of a reading that makes Nietzsche morally palatable by reading him as claiming only that the best kind of life is one that displays the coherence of the ideal literary character. In the case of Freud, finally, recent interpretations have been straightforwardly moralistic: Freud is, indeed, a naturalist, on these accounts, but one whose central claims either lend support to or require supplementation by claims from—of all sources!—Kantian moral theory.

This paper argues against all three forms of moralizing readings, and in support of the claim that, as a matter of both textual exegesis and intellectual importance,

---

[15] A more compelling reading of Nietzsche along these lines than Heidegger's is presented in John Richardson, *Nietzsche's System* (Oxford: Oxford University Press, 1996). For my own doubts about this interpretation, see my review in *Mind* 107 (1998): 683–90.

[16] Although long discredited, this reading continues to resurface. For a recent example, see James Conant, "Nietzsche's Perfectionism: A Reading of *Schopenhauer as Educator*", in R. Schacht (ed.), *Nietzsche's Postmoralism* (Cambridge: Cambridge University Press, 2001). For discussion of the sloppy scholarship here, see my review in *Mind* 112 (2003): 175–8. As Thomas Hurka points out, Conant even quotes selectively from "Schopenhauer as Educator", and mistranslates a central term in order to support his (mis)reading. See Thomas Hurka, "Nietzsche: Perfectionist", in B. Leiter and N. Sinhababu (eds.), *Nietzsche and Morality* (Oxford: Oxford University Press, forthcoming).

[17] (New York: Macmillan, 1965).

[18] (Cambridge, Mass.: Harvard University Press, 1985). Nehamas does repudiate, correctly, Danto's attribution of a pragmatic theory of truth to Nietzsche. But in its overall interpretive orientation, it follows in Danto's footsteps.

Marx, Nietzsche, and Freud are best read as primarily naturalistic thinkers, that is thinkers who view philosophical inquiry as continuous with a sound empirical understanding of the natural world and the causal forces operative in it. When one understands conscious life *naturalistically*, in terms of its real causes, one contributes at the same time to a *critique* of the contents of consciousness: that, in short, is the essence of a hermeneutics of suspicion.

Now admittedly, such a rendering of the "hermeneutics of suspicion" would have seemed strange to Ricoeur, who was in the grips of a fairly crude philosophy of science. He thought the hermeneutics of suspicion stood in opposition to a "scientific" understanding of phenomena. "The statements of psychoanalysis are [not] located . . . within the causal discourse of the natural sciences," Ricoeur says, then adding that since psychoanalysis is concerned with "motives"—though not motives that "coincide with any conscious process of awareness"—"its explanations resemble causal explanations, without, however, being identically the same, for then psychoanalysis would reify all its notions and mystify interpretation itself."[19] The talk of "reification" is, shall we say, obscure. Psychoanalysis, as Freud himself understood it, offers *causal* explanations that appeal to *unconscious* motives, and while these causes are laden with meaning, they are causes nonetheless.[20] To be sure, when philosophers of science thought that *all* causal explanations had to conform to one model—usually drawn from some idealized version of physics—it seemed that a hermeneutic explanation, one that took seriously the *meaningfulness* of certain mental states *qua* causes, was necessarily not part of the causal discourse of science. But that understanding of causal explanation is now, happily, defunct,[21] replaced with a new pluralism that recognizes, as one philosopher of science puts it, that "explanatory adequacy is essentially pragmatic and field-specific".[22] Sciences may all offer consilient explanations of diverse phenomena, and generate true predictions, but beyond that, there is room for a plurality of logical forms and degrees of quantitative precision.

This last point bears emphasizing: naturalism in philosophy—certainly as it is relevant to Marx, Nietzsche, and Freud—is fundamentally a *methodological* view, which holds that philosophical inquiry should be both *modelled on* the methods of the successful sciences, and, at a minimum, *consistent with* the results of those sciences.[23] The *supernatural* finds no place in our best ontology, on this view, simply because the methods of the sciences don't require positing its existence. Because naturalism, so

---

[19] *Freud and Philosophy*, 360.

[20] As Peter Railton eloquently puts the same general point in his contribution to this volume: "How could any explanation of a human phenomenon be *causally adequate* if it failed to give us an account that accurately rendered the *lived experience* or *subjectivity* of those immersed in a practice?—such experience is surely the primary data to be accounted for. And how could an understanding of human action be *meaning adequate* if it failed to locate those ideas, images, or motives that actually played a role in bringing about the behavior and its effects?"

[21] See Nancy Cartwright's and Philip Kitcher's essays in this volume.

[22] Richard W. Miller, *Fact and Method: Explanation, Confirmation and Reality in the Natural and Social Sciences* (Princeton: Princeton University Press, 1987), 95.

[23] I have defended this view of naturalism in various places: see, e.g., my *Nietzsche on Morality* (London: Routledge, 2002), 3–6, and my "Naturalism and Naturalized Jurisprudence", in *Analyzing Law: New Essays in Legal Theory*, ed. B. Bix (Oxford: Clarendon Press, 1998), 81–4. Michael Rea, in one of the

understood, gives priority to *actual* scientific practices, it repudiates the characteristic doctrines of mid-twentieth-century scientistic philosophy, such as the idea that all genuine sciences must ultimately be reducible to physics, or the claim that all genuine explanations must have a certain logical form or at least the form of the explanations we find in physics. Physics is a successful science, but so too are evolutionary biology, cognitive psychology, and geology, despite the fact that they aren't reducible to physics, and despite the fact that they explain phenomena in ways that look unfamiliar from the austere ontological and methodological repertoire of physics.

Marx, Nietzsche, and Freud are more important, to be sure, for their methodological naturalism, brought as it is to bear on questions of great moment, than for all the details of their empirical theories. We must allow that on many particulars, these three great practitioners of the hermeneutics of suspicion are not satisfactory— indeed, *can not be* uniformly satisfactory since they sometimes contradict each other! Of course, empirical progress is the norm in all forms of inquiry that aim for a naturalistic understanding of the world. And just as evolutionary biologists find it necessary to modify parts of the explanatory framework bequeathed them by Darwin—even as they preserve the main elements of his outlook—so, too, should practitioners of the hermeneutics of suspicion expect to dispense with many of the particular theses associated with Marx, Nietzsche, and Freud, even as they retain the general explanatory framework that informs their hermeneutics of suspicion.[24] As one recent researcher, reviewing experimental evidence supporting Freud, wrote: "To reject psychodynamic thinking because Freud's instinct theory or his view of women is dated is like rejecting modern physics because Newton did not understand relativity."[25] To take Marx, Nietzsche, and Freud seriously as philosophical naturalists demands nothing less.

If we can recover the naturalistic ambitions of Marx, Nietzsche, and Freud, we will also accomplish two important meta-philosophical goals: first, it helps make philosophy "relevant"—as the critics of philosophy so often demand—and, second, it bridges the so-called analytic/Continental divide in philosophy. Philosophy becomes relevant because the world—riven as it is with hypocrisy and concealment—desperately needs a hermeneutics of suspicion to unmask it. And by taking these three seminal figures of the Continental traditions as philosophical naturalists we show their work to be continuous with the naturalistic turn that has swept Anglophone philosophy

---

most careful and systematic (albeit highly critical) considerations of philosophical naturalism, reaches a similar conclusion: see Michael C. Rea, *World Without Design: The Ontological Consequences of Naturalism* (Oxford: Clarendon Press, 2002), esp. chs. 2 and 3.

[24] Obviously, they shouldn't retain the framework if it proves empirically unsustainable. And equally obviously, this way of approaching the hermeneutics of suspicion makes it hostage to empirical fortune: but as far as I can see, that is what Marx, Nietzsche, and Freud intended, and that is what makes them genuinely interesting and significant. On recent empirical support for Nietzsche, see my essay on Nietzsche's theory of the will in *The Blackwell Companion to Nietzsche*, ed. K. Ansell-Pearson (Oxford: Blackwell, forthcoming) and the essay by Joshua Knobe and myself on the empirical foundations of Nietzsche's moral psychology in *Nietzsche and Morality*, op. cit.; on Freud, see below n. 89; on Marx, see below nn. 41–6.

[25] Drew Westen, "The Scientific Legacy of Sigmund Freud: Toward a Psychodynamically Informed Psychological Science", *Psychological Bulletin* 124 (1998), 334.

over the past several decades. Such a reconciliation of Continental and Anglophone philosophy may seem to some the *wrong* one, but it is beyond the scope of this essay to defend the importance of the *naturalistic* turn.[26] All I hope to establish here is that the antipathy to naturalism often thought to be constitutive of "the Continental tradition" is simply an artifact of cutting the joints of that tradition in certain places.[27] Much of *that* Continental tradition has earned the—sometimes justified— antipathy of Anglophone philosophers, but there is reason to hope that just as German intellectuals of the 1840s and 1850s, in the grips of the first great naturalistic turn in philosophy, gave up on Hegel as an obscurantist metaphysician,[28] that we, too, may leave behind Hegel and his progeny.

Marx: From Science of Society to Normative Theory

A quarter-century ago, G. A. Cohen's seminal work restored Marx to a central place in the Anglophone philosophy curriculum by offering a powerful and precise reconstruction of his theory of history, the centerpiece of Marx's scientific ambitions. Yet, more recently, Cohen has suggested that the real place of Marxian ideas is squarely within the familiar purview of normative moral and political theory. What happened to bring about this moralizing transformation?

Let us assume, plausibly enough, that Marxists want to bring communism into existence. Cohen's argument, then, for why Marxists should turn from Marx's naturalistic project to normative theory can be reconstructed as follows:

(1) Normative moral and political theory is *not* necessary to bring about communism if history has the teleological structure Marx says it has.

(2) History does not have the teleological structure Marx says it has.

(3) Therefore, moral and political theory is necessary to bring about communism.[29]

Cohen's arguments in support of (2) are twofold:

(2a) The imputation of teleological structure is not a scientifically sound methodological move.

(2b) The specific reasons Marx offers for thinking communism is the inevitable outcome of history are no longer sound.

---

[26] But see the introduction to this volume, and, especially, the contributions by Alvin Goldman and Peter Railton.

[27] This is not to deny that anti-naturalism is an important theme in post-Kantian philosophy on the European Continent in the nineteenth- and twentieth-centuries; it is to deny that such a theme *constitutes* an ineliminable element of Continental philosophy.

[28] No one put it better than Schopenhauer, who remarked that the emblem of a university committed to Hegel's philosophy would be "a cuttle-fish creating a cloud of obscurity around itself so that no one sees what it is, with the legend, *mea caligine tutus* [fortified by my own obscurity]". *On the Will in Nature*, trans. E. F. J. Payne (New York: Oxford University Press, 1992), 24.

[29] Thus, Cohen writes that, "Capitalism does not produce its own gravediggers. The old (partly real, partly imagined) agency of socialist transformation is gone, and there is not, and *never will be* [emphasis added], another one like it. Socialists have to settle for a less dramatic scenario, and they must engage in more moral advocacy than used to be fashionable." *If You're an Egalitarian*, 112.

I want to grant the truth of propositions (1) and (2), and simply observe that (3) does not follow: the argument is invalid.[30] From the fact that X is *not* necessary if Y is true, it doesn't follow that X is necessary just because Y is false. Something else may equally well bring about communism even if history does not have the teleological structure Marx says it has. I shall return to this point below.

This last worry is also implicated in the argument for the truth of (2). (2a) is plainly correct. In Cohen's understated formulation: the various a priori Hegelian dogmas to which Marx is often committed—about the teleological structure of history and the dialectical nature of explanation—are ideas that "few would now regard as consonant with the demands of rigorous science".[31] But this is just to say that there has been no *a posteriori* reason proferred for thinking that history will have a teleological structure (whatever the details of that structure). The truth of (2a), however, is compatible with the falsity of (2b): it could be the case, *contra* (2b), that communism is *inevitable* under the actual circumstances (or at least *very likely* given the actual historical facts), even though history doesn't have a teleological structure. Cohen's argument in support of the truth (2b) is, it turns out, problematic.

What made the nineteenth-century working class an agent of revolution—and thus made the triumph of communism inevitable (or *very* likely)—according to classical Marxism was that it possessed four features, that is, the proletariat:

1. constituted the majority of society;
2. produced the wealth of society;

---

[30] John Deigh suggests to me a different way of formulating the argument. On this reading, Cohen claims that Marxists are already committed to the value of equality, but they see no need to argue for or defend this commitment, since their theory of history guarantees its realization via the triumph of communism. Since the theory of history fails, Cohen calls on Marxists to argue for their commitment to the value of equality. On this reading, the argument is not fallacious, but it also doesn't have much force: it simply says that since *the facts* don't guarantee normative value X, you ought to give arguments for normative value X. But surely even when *the facts* guaranteed X, there was as much reason to argue for it as there is when the facts don't guarantee X—*unless* you add the supposition that giving philosophical arguments for X will help realize X. But this latter point is not argued for by Cohen, and I dispute it below. (I am also skeptical that Marxists are, in fact, committed to equality as a value. Cohen assumes it is throughout the book, without ever specifying what is meant by Marxian equality. At one point, he equates "Marxist equality" with the famous slogan "From each according to his ability, to each according to his needs". But the latter seems a slogan that contemplates vast amounts of inequality, making the exact content of the Marxist commitment to equality even more puzzling. Certainly, Marx is committed to equality in what is now the banal sense accepted by all post-Enlightenment thinkers: namely, that in moral deliberations, everyone's interests (well-being, dignity, autonomy, etc.) counts equally. I am not entitled to more or less moral consideration because I am an American, or a male, or white. At this level, however, equality as a doctrine does not do much to discriminate among possible positions. After all, Kant is an egalitarian in this sense, as is the arch-utilitarian, Bentham. As a matter of Marxology, it seems to me that, in fact, equality is not a Marxian value at all—except in the banal sense just noted—whereas well-being (human flourishing) is the central Marxian evaluative concept. Marx is a kind of utilitarian (he is surely a welfarist, but also, I would argue, a kind of maximizer) not a deontological thinker, as Cohen's employment of the equality rhetoric often suggests. Of course, Marx's view of well-being is a very particular (and Hegelian) one, and has nothing to do with desire-satisfaction, actual or idealized. But it is this implicit utilitarianism that would explain the famous slogan "From each according to his ability, to each according to his needs". Productive labor is part of the good life, according to Marx, and thus everyone is made better off by producing what they are able to produce; yet no one can flourish unless their needs are met, independent of their ability to produce.)   [31] *If You're an Egalitarian*, 64.

3. were the exploited people in society; and
4. were the needy people in society.[32]

Given propositions 1 through 4, Cohen notes, it followed that the working class "would have nothing to lose from revolution" and that therefore it "could and would transform society".[33]

A potential revolutionary agent, on this account, has to have two characteristics: it needs a source of *power* and it has to have a *reason* for acting, a reason to engage in revolutionary acts. Being *either* the majority *or* the producers of society's wealth would be a source of power; being *either* exploited *or* simply needy would provide a reason for acting, for upsetting the existing social order.

The difficulty with Cohen's argument is that he argues, plausibly, that there is no group (nor is there likely to be one) with *all four features*—there *"never will be. . . . another"* revolutionary agent like the proletariat of Classical Marxism he says—yet he fails to give us any reason for thinking that there will not be a group with both *power* and a *reason for acting*, that is, a group who satisfies just one of the two conjuncts that would suffice for each of the two features of a potential revolutionary agent.

Thus, for example, Cohen observes, correctly, that the proletariat did not become the "immense majority",[34] and that, increasingly, the immiserated of the world are not producers like the classic working class: they are just miserable.[35] Yet this could only be an argument against the likelihood of a group having both the power and the reason to bring about communism if one thinks, as Cohen does, that a group, to be an effective agent of revolution, has to have the four features that the classic nineteenth-century proletariat were supposed to have, i.e. they were the majority, they produced the wealth of society, they were exploited by the capitalist class, and they were needy. It is true, as Cohen notes, that the second and third features made the cause of the proletariat particularly appealing: they *produced* society's wealth, yet it was taken from them. But what he never explains is why it would not suffice for revolution if the majority of humanity was needy: need would be a reason for acting (they have "nothing to lose" by revolution) and being the majority would be a source of power.[36]

Sometimes, however, Cohen adds an additional condition for the "inevitable" triumph of the working class. He writes:

Two supposedly irrepressible historical trends, working together, guaranteed the future material equality. One was the rise of an organized working class, whose social emplacement,

---

[32] *If You're an Egalitarian*, at 107.   [33] Id.   [34] Id.   [35] Id. at 107–8.
[36] Would the conjunction of the two disjuncts suffice to bring about a *communist* revolution? This raises an interesting question, but it is not clear that Cohen has shown that *only* the conjunction of the *four* features of the nineteenth-century proletariat suffices for that end either. Cohen says: "when the group whose plight requires the relief supplied by socialism is conceived as having the four features [of the nineteenth-century proletariat], socialism will then present itself as a demand of democracy, justice, elementary human need, and even of the general happiness." Id. at 109. But surely if the vast majority were simply miserable, socialism would seem similarly compelling, without normative argument. (I am grateful to John Deigh for raising this issue.)

at the short end of *in*equality, directed it in favor of equality. The workers' movement would
grow in numbers and in strength, until it had the power to abolish the unequal society which
had nurtured its growth. And the other trend helping to ensure an eventual equality was the
development of the productive forces, the continual increase in the human power to transform nature for human benefit. That growth would issue in a material abundance so great
that anything anyone needed for a richly fulfilling life could be taken from the common store
at no cost to anyone.[37]

Now Cohen—who sometimes writes, I fear, as if history were over—declares that,
"History has shredded each of the predictions that I have just sketched."[38] But as we
have already argued, all Cohen has shown is that historical developments *so far* make
it rather unlikely that a social group will emerge with *all four* of the characteristics
of the nineteenth-century proletariat; he has done nothing to show that a group
capable of being a revolutionary agent in virtue of having both power and reasons for
acting isn't a likely development.

Yet in the passage just quoted, Cohen has added an additional condition for
the success of the revolutionary agent: namely, the accuracy of Marx's prediction
of productive abundance. Cohen disputes this prediction also: he says "our environment is already severely degraded" such that "if there is a way out of the crisis,
then it must include much less aggregate material consumption than what now
prevails", meaning "unwanted changes of lifestyle" for those in the affluent West.[39]
Unfortunately, these empirical propositions require support, as well as refutation of
the empirical literature that disputes them.[40] None of this is in evidence. Cohen
would, apparently, have Marxists abandon the empirical claims of the theory without any actual empirical evidence to the contrary!

But what empirical evidence, it may fairly be asked, is there *in favor* of Marx's theory? To start, of course, there is the enormous and impressive historical literature
employing a Marxian framework to make explanatory sense of historical events.[41]
Perhaps more striking is the accuracy of many of Marx's best-known *qualitative*

---

[37] *If You're an Egalitarian*, at 104.   [38] Id.   [39] Id. at 113.
[40] See, e.g., Joel A. Cohen, *How Many People Can the Earth Support?* (1995), who wryly notes that,

> The Princeton demographer Ansley J. Coale observed that, in 1890 (when the U.S. population was
> 63 million) most reasonable people would have considered it impossible for the United States to
> support 250 million people, its approximate population in 1990; how would 250 million people find
> pasture for all their horses and dispose of all their manure? Id. at 266.

See also, "Doing the Numbers", *The Nation* (14 July 1997), 7: "From the annual U.N. Human
Development Report: [D]elivering basic social services in all developing nations would cost $40 billion
a year for ten years—less than 0.2 per cent of total world income; the net worth of ten billionaires is
1.5 times the combined national income of the forty-eight poorest countries."
[41] See, e.g., Michael A. Bernstein, *The Great Depression: Delayed Recovery and Economic Change in
America, 1929–1939* (Cambridge: Cambridge University Press, 1987); Elizabeth Blackmar, *Manhattan for
Rent, 1785–1850* (Ithaca: Cornell University Press, 1989); Robert Brenner, *Merchants and Revolution:
Commercial Change, Political Conflict, and London's Overseas Traders, 1550–1653* (Princeton: Princeton
University Press, 1993); Edward G. Burrows and Mike Wallace, *Gotham: A History of New York City to 1898*
(New York: Oxford University Press, 1999); David Brion Davis, *The Problem of Slavery in the Age of
Revolution, 1770–1823* (Ithaca: Cornell University Press, 1975); Eric Foner, *Reconstruction: America's
Unfinished Revolution, 1863–1877* (New York: Harper & Row, 1988); E. J. Hobsbawm's four studies: *The Age
of Revolution, 1789–1848* (New York: New American Library, 1962), *The Age of Capital, 1848–1875*

predictions about the tendencies of capitalist development: capitalism continues to conquer the globe;[42] its effect is the gradual erasure of cultural and regional identities;[43] growing economic inequality is the norm in the advanced capitalist societies;[44] where capitalism triumphs, market norms gradually dominate all spheres of life, public and private; class position continues to be the defining determinant of political outlook;[45] the dominant class dominates the political process which, in turn, does its bidding;[46] and so on. To be sure, there are striking predictive

(London: Weidenfeld & Nicolson, 1975); *The Age of Empire, 1875–1914* (New York: Pantheon, 1987), and *The Age of Extremes: A History of the World, 1914–1991* (New York: Pantheon, 1994).

[42] See, e.g., Jeffrey D. Sachs *et al.*, "Economic Reform and the Process of Global Integration", *Brookings Papers on Economic Activity* (1995): 1–118; Lawrence H. Summers, "Reflections on Managing Global Integration", *Journal of Economic Perspectives* 13 (1999): 3–18; Linda Wong, "Privatization of Social Welfare in Post-Mao China", *Asian Survey* 34 (1994): 307–25.

[43] See, e.g., Bill Keller, "Of Famous Arches, Beeg Meks and Rubles", *New York Times* (28 January 1990), A1 (commenting on the first McDonald's to open in Moscow, " a company executive . . . summing up the company's cultural conquest" said, " 'We're going to McDonaldize them' "); Amy Wu, "For the Young, Hong Kong is the Home of Opportunity", *New York Times* (27 January 1997), C12 ("To us, as long as the paychecks go up and we are satisfied with our lives, then whatever flag we are under [British or Chinese] doesn't seem to matter"). And see more generally, Daniel Nettle and Suzanne Romaine, *Vanishing Voices—The Extinction of the World's Languages* (Oxford: Oxford University Press, 2000); George Ritzer, *The Globalization of Nothing* (New York: Sage Publications, 2004). And for scholarly case studies, see David Boyd, "The Commercialization of Ritual in the Eastern Highlands of Papua New Guinea", *Man* 20 (1985): 325–40; Michael French Smith, "Bloody Time and Bloody Scracity: Capitalism, Authority, and the Transformation of Temporal Experience in a Papua New Guinea Village", *American Ethnologist* 9 (1982): 503–18.

[44] See Frank Levy and Richard Murnane, "U.S. Earnings Levels and Earnings Inequality: A Review of Recent Trends and Proposed Explanations", *Journal of Economic Literature* 30 (1992): 1333–81, and, more generally, Edward Wolff, *Top Heavy: The Increasing Inequality of Wealth in America and What Can Be Done About It* (New York: Twentieth Century Fund, 1995). And for a more recent, popular treatment, see Paul Krugman, "For Richer: How the Permissive Capitalism of the Boom Destroyed America's Equality", *New York Times Magazine* (20 October 2002), 62 ff.

[45] See, e.g., Eric Mann, " 'Foreign Aid' for Los Angeles: Three Myths of Urban Renewal", *New York Times* (1 May 1993), A23 ("Elect a black mayor. In 1973, a multiracial movement elected Tom Bradley, a moderate who promised jobs and justice. The Bradley legacy has been a revitalized downtown business district, the transformation of the mayor's office into an adjunct to the Chamber of Commerce and the polarization of wealth and poverty. At every major juncture, the Bradley administration sided with privilege and against the poor"); Katha Pollitt, "Subject to Debate", *The Nation* (4 December 1995), 697 ("The truth is, except on a few high-profile issues—abortion rights, sexual harassment, violence against women—electoral feminism is a pretty pallid affair: a little more money for breast cancer research here, a boost for women business owners there. The main job of the women is the same as that of the men: playing toward the center, amassing campaign funds, keeping business and big donors happy, and currying favor with the leadership in hopes of receiving plums"). For one scholarly treatment, see Clem Brooks and David Brady, "Income, Economic Voting, and Long-Term Political Change in the U.S., 1952–1996", *Social Forces* 77 (1999): 1339–74.

[46] See, e.g., former Congressman Dan Hamburg's candid confession that, "The real government of our country is economic, dominated by large corporations that charter the state to do their bidding." "Inside the Money Chase", *The Nation* (5 May 1997), 25. Cf. Bob Herbert, "The Donor Class," *New York Times* (19 July 1998), 15 ("I doubt that many people are aware of just how elite and homogenous the donor class [to political campaigns] is. It's a tiny group—just one-quarter of 1 per cent of the population—and it is not representative of the nation. But its money buys plenty of access"). See, more generally, Noreena Hertz, *The Silent Takeover: Global Capitalism and the Death of Democracy* (London: Free Press, 2002); Charles Lewis, *The Buying of the President 2000* (New York: Avon, 2000).

failures in the Marxian corpus like the labor theory of value, the theory of the falling rate of profit, or his mistaken views about timing. The last failing is certainly the most notorious: for like many a giddy optimist of the nineteenth-century, Marx thought the period of limitless abundance was almost at hand, and thus the end of capitalism near. No doubt his Eurocentric focus encouraged this way of thinking, since the industrial and technological progress there was remarkable. But once we allow that the conditions Marx himself thought necessary for the demise of capitalism[47] have still not been obtained, it is far more plausible to view the broad *tendencies* of capitalist development around the world as in line with Marx's central qualitative predictions. Whether his ultimate predictions about what befalls capitalism at its productive peak are correct is still an open empirical question—though there are, ironically enough, reasons for skepticism based on what remains the most fertile part of Marx's theory: the theory of ideology.

The Marxian theory of ideology predicts that the ruling ideas in any well-functioning society will be ideas that promote the interests of the ruling class in that society, i.e. the class that is economically dominant. By the "ruling ideas" we should understand Marx to mean the central moral, political, and economic ideas that dominate discussion in the mass media and in the corridors of power in that society. The theory is not peculiar to Marx, since the "classical realists" of antiquity like the Sophists and Thucydides advanced essentially the same theory: the powerful clothe their pursuit of self-interest in the garb of morality and justice.[48] When Marx says that, "The ideas of the ruling class are in every epoch the ruling ideas" (*The German Ideology*) and that, "Law, morality, religion are to [the proletariat] so many bourgeois prejudices, behind which lurk in ambush just as many bourgeois interests" (*The Communist Manifesto*), he is simply translating into Marxian terms the Sophistic view "that the more powerful will always take advantage of the weaker, and will give the name of law and justice to whatever they lay down in their own interests."[49] (The ancients, of course, did not emphasize the close connections between political power and control over the means of production.) If the Marxist theory of ideology is correct over the long-term, then we might expect that even at its productive peak, capitalism will still sustain itself through the promulgation of an ideological framework that rationalizes the continued dominance of the capitalist class.

In one of the most important contributions to scholarship on Marxism since G. A. Cohen's seminal work, Michael Rosen has recently argued that the Marxist theory of ideology is, however, yet another failure.[50] The Marxist theory of ideology, on Rosen's (reasonable) rendering, is an answer to the question: "Why do the

---

[47] These would include the maximal development of the forces of production, the immiseration of the great mass of humanity globally, the exhaustion of potential markets for goods on a global scale, and the destruction, through market forces, of the hitherto-existing national, ethnic, and religious identities. See, e.g., *The Communist Manifesto*, 475–83, 488.

[48] See Brian Leiter, "Classical Realism", *Philosophical Issues* 11 (2001): 244–67.

[49] W. K. C. Guthrie, *The Sophists* (Cambridge: Cambridge University Press, 1971), 60.

[50] Michael Rosen, *On Voluntary Servitude: False Consciousness and the Theory of Ideology* (Cambridge, Mass.: Harvard University Press, 1996).

many accept the rule of the few, even when it seems to be plainly against their interests to do so?"[51] The Marxist answer (as Rosen puts it) is that

1. they [the few] maintain themselves in virtue of false consciousness on the part of the citizens;
2. this false consciousness occurs in response to the needs of society.[52]

Call the first "the False Consciousness Thesis", and the second, "the Society as Self-Maintaining System Thesis". Rosen complains that the Society as Self-Maintaining System Thesis "requires an ontological commitment that is not justified according to the explanatory standards of the natural sciences".[53] But it is a familiar point in post-Quinean philosophy of science that we are entitled to whatever ontology we need for the best explanation of the observable phenomena: if the Marxist theory of ideology is, *in fact*, the best explanation of the socio-economic phenomena, and the Marxist theory requires an ontology of societies as self-maintaining systems, then that's the ontology of the social world we get.

Rosen's real objection, then, to the Marxist theory is that "there are alternative answers"[54] to why the many accept the rule of the few, even when it is not in their interests, i.e. the Society as Self-Maintaining System is not, in fact, part of the *best* explanation of the phenomenon. Strictly speaking, of course, showing that there are "alternative answers" won't suffice, since what we need to establish is that the alternatives are parts of *better* explanations for the phenomena. (Of course, Marxists too bear the burden of showing the theory of ideology is the *best* explanation.) Yet we needn't confront that issue, since it is not clear that Rosen actually adduces alternatives that are even *plausible* contenders. For example, Rosen suggests that the rule of the few might simply be the result of coordination problems confronting the many in overthrowing the few.[55] Even putting aside doubts about the claims of rational choice theory which undergird the analysis of coordination problems,[56] the real problem here is that coordination problems don't explain the relevant phenomenon. The coordination problem explanation of why the few rule the many is that the many can't coordinate their behavior to overthrow the few, but the *actual* phenomenon the Marxist theory explains is that the many don't even see the need to overthrow the few, indeed, don't even see that the few rule the many!

Perhaps we may save the coordination problem explanation by supplementing it with appeal to the phenomenon of "sour grapes": because the many can't overthrow the few, they end up believing that the few are *not* really dominating them, not really worth overthrowing. Rosen's general skepticism about the explanatory power of the "sour grapes" mechanism, however,[57] seems especially warranted here: where, one wonders, is the evidence that the dominated classes recognize

---

[51] Michael Rosen, *On Voluntary Servitude: False Consciousness and the Theory of Ideology* (Cambridge, Mass.: Harvard University Press, 1996) at 1.   [52] Id. at 260.

[53] Id. at 258–9.   [54] Id. at 259.   [55] Id. at 260–2.

[56] See Robert Paul Wolff, "Methodological Individualism and Marx: Some Remarks on Elster, Game Theory, and Other Things", *Canadian Journal of Philosophy* 20 (1990), 469–86.

[57] *On Voluntary Servitude*, 265–6.

themselves as dominated by the *few*, only to turn away from that and decide the grapes are sour?

At another point, Rosen suggests that perhaps the False Consciousness Thesis is true, but the Society as Self-Maintaining System Thesis false.[58] The difficulty, now, is to explain the former without recourse to the idea that it is "in the interests" of society for the many to suffer from false consciousness. Rosen complains throughout that Marx "gives no adequate suggestion regarding the mechanism by which" society's interests might bring about the truth of the False Consciousness Thesis.[59] While it is plainly true that Marx does not offer a detailed account of the mechanisms, it is equally clear that Rosen's treatment of the accounts Marx *does* offer are abrupt and uncharitable. So, for example, Marx famously proposed in *The Germany Ideology* that,

the class which is the ruling *material* force of a society is at the same time its ruling *intellectual* force. The class which has the means of material production at its disposal, has control at the same time over the means of mental production, so that thereby, generally speaking, the ideas of those who lack the means of mental production are subject to it.

To this Rosen retorts that Marx here embraces

a view of those who live under the domination of the ruling class as passive victims, taking their ideas from those who control the "means of mental production" like obedient chicks, with no critical reflection on their part as to whether the ideas are either true or in their own rational interests. This, it seems, is an almost paranoid view. Why should one suppose that the ruling class is capable of promoting its own interests effectively, forming its ideas in response to those interests, whereas the dominated class simply accept whatever is served up to them?[60]

Although this passage is heavy on rhetoric (Marx is a "paranoid") and thin on argument (what is the *evidence* for thinking most people aren't like "obedient chicks"?), what really matters is that Rosen fails to consider even the obvious answers to his last question. The best reason to suppose that the ruling class is, in fact, effective in promoting its own interests, and the dominated class is not, is precisely that ideas favorable to the interests of the ruling class typically dominate, and without being recognized as such!

In the United States, for example, a majority of the population favors abolition of the estate tax—what the ideologues of the ruling class now call a "death tax"—believing that it affects them, and that it results in the loss of family businesses and farms.[61] In fact, only 2 per cent of the population pays the estate tax, and there is no documented case of families losing their farms or businesses as a result of the tax's

---

[58] *On Voluntary Servitude*, 262–70. It is in this context that Rosen rejects "sour grapes".

[59] See, e.g., id. at 274.   [60] Id. at 182–3.

[61] "Focus on Forms Masks Estate Tax Confusion", *New York Times* (8 April 2001). As the economist Paul Krugman notes, a successful propaganda campaign resulted in the following bit of false consciousness by early 2003: "49 per cent of Americans believed that most families had to pay the estate tax, while only 33 per cent gave the right answer that only a few families had to pay." "The Tax-Cut Con", *New York Times Magazine* (14 September 2003), 59.

operation. Examples like this—in which the majority have factually inaccurate beliefs, that are in the interests of those with money and power—could, of course, be multiplied. Does this just happen by accident?

Rosen would still demand, no doubt, an explanation of why the ruling class is so good at identifying and promoting its interests, while the majority is not. But, again, there is an obvious answer: for isn't it generally quite easy to identify your short-term interests when the status quo is to your benefit? In such circumstances, you favor the status quo! In other words, if the status quo provides tangible benefits to the few—lots of money, prestige, and power—is it any surprise that the few are well-disposed to the status quo, and are particularly good at thinking of ways to tinker with the status quo (e.g. repeal the already minimal estate tax) to increase their money, prestige, and power? (The few can then promote their interests for exactly the reasons Marx identifies: they own the means of mental production.)[62]

By contrast, it is far trickier for the many to assess what is in their interest, precisely because it requires a counterfactual thought experiment, in addition to evaluating complex questions of socio-economic causation. More precisely, the many have to ascertain that (1) the status quo—the whole complex socio-economic order in which they find themselves—is not in their interests (this may be the easiest part); (2) there are alternatives to the status quo which would be more in their interest; and (3) it is worth the costs to make the transition to the alternatives—to give up on the bad situation one knows in order to make the leap into a (theoretically) better unknown. Obstacles to the already difficult task of making determinations (1) and (2)—let alone (3)—will be especially plentiful, precisely because the few are strongly, and effectively (given their control of the means of mental production), committed to the denial of (1) and (2). Since Rosen fails to consider any possible Marxian fleshing-out of the bare-bones explanation of ideological dominance in works like *The German Ideology*, his criticisms of the Marxist theory of ideology ultimately ring hollow.

So two features of the original Marxist project for developing a naturalistic account of society remain intact and promising: the qualitative predictions associated with the Marxian theory of developmental tendencies within capitalism are largely borne out once the time frame is expanded and Marx's giddy, Eurocentric optimism is abandoned; and the Marxian theory of ideology describes and explains a striking feature of the "ruling ideas" in all known societies (including, we might add, the self-proclaimed communist ones).

There remains a final worry about Cohen's argument, pertaining to the logical invalidity of the basic argument (propositions, 1–3, above): from the fact that history does not have a teleological structure, it doesn't follow that Marxists ought to turn to moral and political theory to bring about communism. Cohen says, recall, that since "capitalism does not produce its own gravedigger"—i.e. its downfall is *not*

---

[62] See, e.g., Edward Herman and Noam Chomsky, *Manufacturing Consent: The Political Economy of the Mass Media* (New York: Pantheon, 1988); Noam Chomsky, *Necessary Illusions: Thought Control in Democratic Societies* (Boston: South End Press, 1989); Ben Bagdikian, *The Media Monopoly* (Boston: Beacon, 1997); Robert McChesney, *Corporate Media and the Threat to Democracy* (New York: Seven Stories, 1997); Eric Alterman, *What Liberal Media?* (New York: Basic Books, 2003).

inevitable—"Socialists . . . must engage in more moral advocacy than used to be fashionable."[63] He makes the same basic point several times:

The disintegration of the characteristics [possessed by the classic proletariat] produces an intellectual need to philosophize, which is related to a political need to be clear as never before about values and principles, for the sake of socialist advocacy.[64]

The disintegration of the proletariat induces persons of Marxist formation to turn to normative political philosophy, and . . . the loss of confidence in a future unlimited abundance reinforces their tendency to take that turn.[65]

It is important to be clear here that what is at stake is the need for *moral and political philosophy*, not moral advocacy, *per se*: the claim is that we need to engage in a certain kind of systematic moral and political theorizing in order to undertake the required moral advocacy. (Most moral advocacy, needless to say, proceeds without the benefit of any systematic moral and political philosophy.)

In pitching the case for normative theory this way—i.e. in terms of its necessity for bringing about certain consequences (namely, the achievement of socialism, and therefore, justice)—Cohen appears to accept the fundamentally *pragmatic* premise of Marx's whole approach to philosophy. The clearest statement of this pragmatic premise comes in Marx's *Second Thesis on Feuerbach*:[66] "The dispute over the reality or non-reality of thinking which is isolated from practice is a purely *scholastic* question." In other words, philosophical questions—e.g. about whether or not thought corresponds to reality, or whether capitalism is just—are to be dismissed as "purely scholastic" unless they make a difference to practice, i.e. unless they have some impact on what we do and how we live. This is a particularly severe form of pragmatism, but it seems central to Marx's view of philosophy.

Now as Cohen notes, Marx believed that, "Devoting energy to the question, 'What is the right way to distribute?' is futile with respect to the present."[67]—that is, it is a purely "scholastic" question in the sense just noted. But Cohen retorts: "We can no longer believe the factual premises of those conclusions about the practical (ir)relevance of the study of norms."[68] The locution here is striking: "we can no longer believe" that the *study* of norms is practically irrelevant (norms may, of course, be practically relevant—the issue here concerns their theoretical study and philosophical articulation). But why *can't* we? Cohen never says. One suspects that this is more the expression of a pious hope than of the discovery of contrary evidence. As Cohen observes about Marx, no doubt correctly:

It was because he was so uncompromisingly pessimistic about the social consequences of anything less than limitless abundance that Marx needed to be so optimistic about the possibility of that abundance.[69]

Cohen, as we have seen, is not so optimistic, but it now appears that he simply substitutes a different kind of optimism, even less empirically grounded than Marx's: namely, optimism that theorizing about equality will help bring about

[63] *If You're an Egalitarian*, 112.   [64] Id. at 109.   [65] Id. at 117.
[66] *Marx-Engels Reader*, 144.   [67] *If You're an Egalitarian*, 115.   [68] Id.   [69] Id. at 114.

justice, even in the face of scarcity. But why anyone else should believe this is never explained.

Indeed, one might worry that Cohen's own elegant exercise in normative theory is counter-evidence to his own optimism. For Cohen argues that genuine egalitarians (at least those who are not welfarists) must give away their money. The argument is careful and often ingenious. But consider the reaction of a committed liberal egalitarian like Thomas Nagel:

> I have to admit that, although I am an adherent of the liberal conception of [justice and equality], I don't have an answer to Cohen's charge of moral incoherence. It is hard to render consistent the exemption of private choice from the motives that support redistributive public policies. I could sign a standing banker's order giving away everything I earn above the national average, for example, and it wouldn't kill me. I could even try to increase my income at the same time, knowing the excess would go to people who needed it more than I did. I'm not about to do anything of the kind, but the equality-friendly justifications I can think of for not doing so all strike me as rationalizations.[70]

If high-quality moral theory won't get high-quality moral philosophers to change their behavior, then it seems utopian, at best, and delusional, at worst, to think it will contribute anything to mass political action against injustice.

What, then is the Marxian alternative? On the Marxian view, what people need is not a theory of equality, or of justice, but rather the intellectual tools to understand—to render visible—the networks of socio-economic causation that circumscribe their lives and that *explain* the misery that is *antecedently* vivid to them. The background theory of agency here is essentially Humean, not Kantian, in structure: Marx takes for granted that people *desire* to relieve their misery; what they need are the *means*, which include understanding the *causes* of that misery. Moral theories won't motivate them to act; misery will. A theory that identifies the *causes* of that misery gives agents instrumental reasons to relieve that misery. "When reality is depicted," Marx remarked in an especially Quinean moment in *The German Ideology*, "philosophy as an independent branch of knowledge loses its medium of existence."[71] Philosophy, on this conception, is continuous with empirical science, whose task it is to illuminate the causal structure of the world, including the socio-economic world. Marx's lasting importance, I suspect, resides in his contribution to that project, not in marrying Marxish values to academic moral theory, theory whose impact is uncertain at best.

Nietzsche: From Psychology to Aestheticism

After four decades of postmodern and deconstructionist appropriations of Nietzsche, few philosophical readers—and even fewer outside philosophy—recognize Nietzsche as one of the great philosophical naturalists, at least on a par with Hume,[72] and perhaps to be preferred for his more thoroughly modern psychology. Both Hume and Nietzsche construct quasi-speculative theories of human nature to explain an array

---

[70] Thomas Nagel's review of Cohen, *Times Literary Supplement* (23 June 2000), 6.

[71] *The Marx-Engels Reader*, 155.

[72] The classic contemporary treatment of Hume as naturalist remains Barry Stroud, *Hume* (London: Routledge, 1977).

of human beliefs—philosophical, common-sensical, moral—precisely because they find that these beliefs do *not* admit of rational vindication. We must look beyond human reason—to certain natural facts and dispositions about human beings—to explain why humans hold these (unjustified) beliefs nonetheless. Thus, Hume argues that our belief in "causation" cannot be rationally justified, that is, justified on the basis of experience. Thus, to explain why humans nonetheless believe in causation, Hume posits a certain natural tendency or disposition in creatures like us to view instances of constant conjunction as instances of something much stronger: namely, the operation of a *necessary* cause-and-effect relationship.

Similarly, Nietzsche famously views morality as being without rational foundation. He commends the Sophists for having "the first *insight* into morality", namely that "every morality can be dialectically justified . . . [so that] all attempts to give reasons for morality are necessarily *sophistical*" (WP 428). He remarks that the attempt of all philosophers "to supply a *rational* foundation for morality . . . inspires laughter" (BGE 186), and dismisses the Kantian notion of "practical reason"—the type of "reason" that is supposed to guide us in moral matters—as "a special kind of reason for cases in which one need not bother about reason—that is, when morality, when the sublime 'thou shalt', raises its voice" (A 12). But like Hume, Nietzsche clearly recognizes that, notwithstanding the lack of rational justification, morality—in particular, the "ascetic" morality with which he is concerned in his most important work, *On the Genealogy of Morality*—continues to have a firm grip on the human mind. How are we to explain this fact? The *Genealogy*, and Nietzsche's mature philosophy generally, proposes a *naturalistic* explanation, i.e. an explanation that is continuous with both the results and methods of the sciences.

Now this is plainly not the Nietzsche of Derrida or Foucault, but it is the Nietzsche one actually meets in his books. It is the Nietzsche who says that psychology must be "recognized again as the queen of the sciences" since it is "now . . . the path to the fundamental problems" (BGE 32). It is the Nietzsche who calls on his readers to dispense with "the many vain and overly enthusiastic interpretations and connotations that have so far been scrawled and painted over the eternal basic text of *homo natura*" and to resist "with intrepid Oedipus eyes and sealed Odysseus ears . . . the siren songs of old metaphysical bird catchers who have been piping [at man] all too long, 'you are more, you are higher, you are of a different origin!' " (BGE 230). Instead, says this naturalistic Nietzsche, we must "stand before man . . . hardened in the discipline of science" (BGE 230) for it is "scientific *methods*" that "*are* what is essential, also what is most difficult, also what is for the longest time opposed by habits and laziness" (A 59).

This naturalistic Nietzsche is the one who throughout his corpus offers the following kind of two-stage causal explanation of human beliefs: a person's theoretical beliefs are best explained in terms of his moral beliefs; and his moral beliefs are best explained in terms of the psychological and physiological facts about the type of person he is. So Nietzsche says, "every great philosophy so far has been . . . the personal confession of its author and a kind of involuntary and unconscious memoir"; thus, to really grasp this philosophy, one must ask "at what morality does all this (does *he*) aim" (BGE 6)? But the "morality" that a philosopher embraces simply bears "decisive witness to *who he is*—i.e. who he *essentially* is—that is, to the "innermost drives of his nature" (BGE 6). "[M]oralities are . . . merely a sign language of the affects" (BGE 187), he says elsewhere. "Answers to the questions about the *value* of existence . . . may always be considered first of all as the symptoms of certain bodies" (GS P:2). "Moral judgments", he says are, "symptoms and sign languages which betray the process of physiological prosperity or failure" (WP 258). "[O]ur moral judgments and evaluations . . . are only images and fantasies based on a physiological process unknown to us" (D 119), so that "it is always necessary to draw forth . . . the *physio-logical* phenomenon behind the moral predispositions and prejudices" (D 542). A "morality of sympathy", he claims is "just another expression of . . . physiological overexcitability" (TI IX:37). *Ressentiment*—and the morality that grows out of it—he attributes to an "actual physiological cause" (GM I:15).

The general Nietzschean view is aptly captured in a preface to one of his earlier books that he added in 1886: "assuming that one is a person, one *necessarily* [*nothwendig*] has the philosophy that belongs to that person" (GS P:2). Or as he put it the following year, in his preface to the *Genealogy*: "our thoughts, values, every 'yes', 'no', 'if' and 'but' grow from us with the same inevitability as fruits borne on the tree—all related and each with an affinity to each, and evidence of one will, one health, one earth, one sun" (GM P:2). Nietzsche seeks to understand in naturalistic terms the *type* of "person" who would necessarily bear such ideas and values, just as one might come to understand things about a type of *tree* by knowing its fruits. And just as natural facts about the tree explain the fruit it bears, so too psychological and physiological facts about a person will explain the ideas and values he comes to bear.

I have dealt elsewhere with some of the specific objections to this reading of Nietzsche,[73] and I do not want to rehearse that debate here. But it is worth asking what the alternative "big picture" understanding of Nietzsche—the alternative to the naturalistic reading—is supposed to be? The most influential candidate must surely be Alexander Nehamas's elegant synthesis of postmodern and deconstruc-tionist interpretations in his 1985 book *Nietzsche: Life as Literature*.[74]

Nehamas attributes to Nietzsche a doctrine that Nehamas calls "aestheticism", according to which "Nietzsche . . . looks at [the world] as if it were a literary text. And he arrives at many of his views of human beings by generalizing to them ideas and prin-ciples that apply almost intuitively to the literary situation, to the creation and inter-pretation of literary texts and characters."[75] No one, of course, disputes that Nietzsche, reflecting no doubt his training as a philologist, often speaks metaphorically of the world as a "text" to be interpreted: let's call this Nietzsche's "text-talk". But the text-talk must be set against the background of Nietzsche's training in classical phi-lology, which was understood to be a *Wissenschaft* by nineteenth-century classicists like Nietzsche's teacher Friedrich Ritschl. And according to the canons of this *Wissenschaft*, as Nietzsche understood them, "reading well" means "reading facts

---

[73] See my *Nietzsche on Morality*, 11–26.

[74] The discussion that follows borrows from my lengthier critique of the Nehamas book in "Nietzsche and Aestheticism", *Journal of the History of Philosophy* 30 (1992): 275–90.

[75] *Nietzsche: Life as Literature*, 3. All further citations will be included in the body of the text.

without falsifying them by interpretation" (A 52). Nietzsche, it is important to remember, learned about the interpretation of texts from Ritschl, not Paul DeMan or Jacques Derrida.

Aestheticism, of course, claims something much stronger about the "textuality" of the world, namely, that interpretation of this particular text is like (a certain sort) of *literary* interpretation in two specific respects:

(1) the world and literary texts are essentially indeterminate, so that both admit of a plurality of *conflicting* interpretations; and

(2) the world and its occupants have features that we ordinarily associate with literary texts and literary characters.

One of the curious features of Nehamas's book is that it can adduce no textual support for either of these aestheticist doctrines. Nehamas either conflates examples of "text-talk" with evidence of aestheticism, or he simply misconstrues, mostly via selective quotation, the import of the texts he cites.[76] Let us look at just two examples of the problematic scholarship that underwrites Nehamas's anti-naturalist reading.

Nehamas (p. 62) invokes Nietzsche's talk of the "eternal basic text of *homo natura*" (BGE 230, quoted above) as evidence of aestheticism—the view, recall, that "texts can be interpreted equally well in vastly different and deeply incompatible ways" (3). But the talk of "text" in this passage is actually incompatible with aestheticism. For in this passage, as we have seen, Nietzsche asserts that prior claims to "knowledge" have been *superficial* precisely because they have ignored the "eternal basic text"—*ewigen Grundtext*—of man conceived as a natural organism. That this text is eternal *and* basic implies not that it "can be interpreted equally well in vastly different and deeply incompatible ways" but just the opposite: readings which do not treat man naturalistically *misread* the text—they "falsify" it. It is these misreadings, of course, that Nietzsche, ever the "good philologist", aims to correct.

Aestheticism also affects Nehamas's distinctive treatment of Nietzsche's ethical views, especially Nietzsche's conception of the "good life" or the ideal person. According to Nehamas, "Nietzsche's texts . . . do not describe . . . his ideal character" (232). (In fact, Nietzsche repeatedly describes his ideal person, and even says that he is doing so: e.g. EH II:2; cf. D 201, GS 55, BGE 287, WP 943. But we shall let this pass.) Rather than *describe* or *prescribe* the ideal type of person, Nietzsche, according to Nehamas, simply "produce[s] a perfect instance" of this ideal person (230), *namely, Nietzsche himself* "the character" that all his books "exemplify" and "constitute": "Nietzsche created a[n ideal] character out of himself" (233). Nietzsche creates himself as a literary character, according to Nehamas, by first writing all his books and then writing his last book, his "autobiography", *Ecce Homo*:

[T]his self-referential book [is one] in which Nietzsche can be said with equal justice to invent or to discover himself, and in which the character who speaks to us is the author who has created him and who is in turn a character created by or implicit in all the books that were written by the author who is writing this one (196).

---

[76] For a detailed catalogue of these problems, see my "Nietzsche and Aestheticism".

Let us put aside the threshold textual worry that there is nothing in *Ecce Homo* to suggest that this is how Nietzsche conceives of what he is doing.[77] On its own terms, the aestheticist reading of Nietzsche's ethical project has a bizarre implication. For since Nietzsche's having a view about the best kind of life depends on his having, in fact, completed all his works through *Ecce Homo* (so that he was properly exemplified in them), it would seem then that for Nietzsche to have had a view of the best kind of life *at any point* prior to *Ecce Homo* would require that he have *anticipated* writing the series of books culminating with *Ecce Homo* that he actually wrote! This might reasonably be construed as a *reductio* of the aestheticist reading of Nietzsche.

Neither the texts, then, nor the logic of the position, support aestheticism, the leading alternative to the naturalistic reading of Nietzsche. It is time, then, to finally bury the anti-naturalist readings of Nietzsche, especially now that there are many, more plausible naturalistic alternatives in hand.[78] Even allowing, however, that the naturalistic readings are more faithful to the texts, it is still reasonable to ask why philosophers should be interested in Nietzsche the naturalist? The simple answer is that Nietzsche is a penetrating moral psychologist, with only one real rival, namely, Freud. One example will have to suffice: Nietzsche's explanation in the *Genealogy* of the attraction of ascetic ideals, of ideals and moralities of self-denial.

Keep in mind, first, what a significant question is at stake here. Ascetic moralities, in Nietzsche's sense, are not rarities in human experience. Rather they are the dominant forms of moral evaluation globally: everywhere we look, it seems, we find moral prohibitions on pleasure, on sexuality, on self-regarding desires of all kinds. As Nietzsche puts it:

Such a monstrous method of valuation is not inscribed in the records of human history as an exception and curiosity: it is one of the most wide-spread and long-lived facts there are. Read from a distant planet, the majuscule script of our earthly existence would perhaps seduce the reader to the conclusion that the earth was the ascetic planet *par excellence*, an outpost of discontented, arrogant and nasty creatures who harboured a deep disgust for themselves, for the world, for all life and hurt themselves as much as possible out of pleasure in hurting:— probably their only pleasure. (GM III:11)

It is the central puzzle of Nietzsche's famed *Genealogy of Morality* to explain how such a state of affairs came to pass, how it is that Christianity, Judaism, Buddhism, Islam, Hinduism, and, most importantly, their distinctively ascetic moralities came to have such a profound hold upon the human mind.

Initially, at least, the appeal of the ascetic ideal seems paradoxical, and certainly hard to square with another familiar thesis of Nietzsche's concerning the prevalence of will to power. As he puts it in the *Genealogy*: "Every animal . . . instinctively strives

---

[77] On this point, see my "Nietzsche and Aestheticism", 288–9.

[78] See, e.g., Maudemarie Clark, "On Knowledge, Truth, and Value: Nietzsche's Debt to Schopenhauer and the Development of His Empiricism", in *Willing and Nothingness: Schopenhauer as Nietzsche's Educator*, ed. C. Janaway (Oxford: Oxford University Press, 1998); Ken Gemes, "Nietzsche's Critique of Truth", reprinted in *Nietzsche*, ed. J. Richardson and B. Leiter (Oxford: Oxford University Press, 2001); Richard Schacht, "Nietzsche's *Gay Science*, Or, How to Naturalize Cheerfully", in *Reading Nietzsche*, ed. R. Solomon and K. Higgins (New York: Oxford University Press, 1988).

for an optimum of favourable conditions in which fully to release his power and achieve his maximum feeling of power" (GM III:7). How could ascetic ideals, ideals demanding self-denial and self-flagellation, be understood to maximize "power"?

Yet just as Darwinian adaptationists assume that every biological phenomenon must be explained in terms of natural selection (no matter how unconducive to reproductive fitness it may appear initially)[79], so too Nietzsche assumes that whatever explains "life" must also explain these particular instances of life which *appear* hostile to it. " 'Life against life' ", Nietzsche says is a "self-contradiction" that "can only be *apparent*; it has to be a sort of provisional expression, an explanation, formula, adjustment, a psychological misunderstanding of something, the real nature of which was far from being understood" (GM III:13). "Life", of course, is rather vague, but we have already seen the explanatory constraint at issue: the doctrine of will to power. If, in fact, "every animal" strives to maximize the feelings of power, then even those "animals", like the majority of mortals who embrace the ascetic ideal, must fit within the same explanatory scheme. But how?

The crux of Nietzsche's explanation turns on three claims:

(1) Suffering is a central fact of the human condition.
(2) Meaningless suffering is unbearable and leads to "suicidal nihilism" (GM III:28).
(3) The ascetic ideal gives meaning to suffering, thereby seducing the majority of humans back to life, i.e. it maximizes their feeling of power within the constraints of their existential situation.

This, in schematic form, is the central argument of the Third Essay of Nietzsche's *Genealogy*. Let us explore each claim in turn.

(1) *Suffering is a central fact of the human condition.* Nietzsche takes over this idea from Schopenhauer, though his own account of the causes of this suffering is multifarious: sometimes Nietzsche attributes suffering to brute facts of physiology, other times to psychological and social factors. Yet whatever the precise cause, Nietzsche is clear that "the *majority* of mortals" suffer since they are "physiological casualties and . . . disgruntled" (GM III:1) (cf. GM III:13, where he again refers to "the whole herd of failures, the disgruntled, the under-privileged, the unfortunate, and all who suffer from themselves"). Nietzsche even sometimes invokes a more characteristically Schopenhauerian explanation for suffering, when he appeals to the fact that humans are endlessly striving and so are "unsatisfied and insatiable" (GM III:13). Indeed, even a kind of existential *angst* is said to be a source of suffering: man "*suffered* from the problem of what he meant", the problem of the "justification or explanation or affirmation" of his existence (GM III:28). In short: physiology, psychology, and society all conspire to produce a basic truth about the human situation: for the vast majority, *suffering* is the basic, continuing fact about their lives.

(2) *Meaningless suffering is unbearable and leads to "suicidal nihilism"* (GM III:28). The fundamental problem is not, Nietzsche thinks, suffering *per se*—"[S]uffering itself was

---

[79] Many evolutionary biologists are not, to be sure, adaptationists in this sense, since they think non-selectionist forces at work in evolution play a larger role than adapationists allow.

not [man's] problem"—but rather the persistent question: "Suffering for *what?*" (GM III:28). Indeed, we can go further: "Man, the bravest animal and most prone to suffer, does *not* deny suffering as such: he *wills* it, he even seeks it out, provided he is shown a *meaning* for it, a *purpose* of suffering. The meaninglessness of suffering, *not* the suffering, was the curse which has so far blanketed mankind" (GM III:28).

The "curse" is amplified by the fact that suffering also gives rise to the emotion of *ressentiment*, that festering hatred and vengefulness that Nietzsche first introduced in the context of explaining the slave revolt in morals (GM I). But why does suffering itself (for physiological or other reasons) give rise to *ressentiment?* The explanation constitutes Nietzsche's most important psychological insight:

[E]very sufferer instinctively looks for a cause for its distress; more exactly, for a culprit, even more precisely for a *guilty* culprit who is receptive to distress,—in short, for a living being upon whom he can release his emotions, actually or in effigy, on some pretext or other: because the release of emotions is the greatest attempt at relief, or should I say, at *anaesthetizing* on the part of the sufferer, his involuntarily longed-for narcotic against pain of any kind. (GM III:15)

Sufferers *instinctively* look for someone to blame because, more fundamentally (and more obviously), they *instinctively* want to relieve their suffering:[80] the *discharge* of their *ressentiment* would numb their suffering, but *ressentiment* can only be discharged when it has an object. As Nietzsche puts it in the same passage: " 'Someone or other must be to blame [*muss schuld daran sein*] that I feel ill'—this kind of conclusion is peculiar to all sick people, and in fact becomes more insistent, the more they remain in ignorance of the true reason." (GM III:15). Until he finds such a cause for his suffering, however, "that most dangerous and explosive material, *ressentiment*, continually piles up" in the sufferer (GM III:15).

So the psychological logic of Nietzsche's explanation works like this. First, sufferers want relief from their suffering. Second, discharge of strong emotions (like *ressentiment*) deadens suffering. Thus, as a result, sufferers seek someone to blame for their suffering, someone (or thing) upon whom to vent their *ressentiment*. The second point is crucial. "*Excess of feeling*", he says, is "the most effective anesthetic for dull, crippling, long-drawn-out pain" (GM III:19). All powerful emotions— Nietzsche names "anger, fear, voluptuousness, revenge, hope, triumph, despair, cruelty" (GM III:20)—"throw the human soul out of joint, plunging it into terror, frosts, fires and raptures to such an extent that it rids itself of all small and petty forms of lethargy, apathy and depression, as though hit by lightning" (GM III:20).

Now it should be clear why Nietzsche says (in GM III:28) that it is *meaningless* suffering that is the real problem for humankind: for only with a meaning attached can the sufferer discharge his emotions properly and deaden the pain, for it is the *meaning* that gives direction to the discharge of *ressentiment*, by identifying whom to blame.[81] In cases of meaningless suffering, by contrast, "*ressentiment* . . . piles up"

---

[80] That, too, is presumably an instinct to achieve the maximum feeling of power, i.e. through the cessation of suffering.

[81] There might, of course, be other ways to give meaning to suffering, but for the mass of humanity this is the primary way. (I am grateful to Sebastian Gardner for clarification on this issue.)

because the sufferer can find no *"guilty* culprit who is receptive to distress . . . upon whom [the sufferer] can release his emotions" (GM III:15). The ultimate consequence of such unrelieved suffering would be "suicidal nihilism" (GM III:28). The question, in turn, is how "to detonate this explosive material [*ressentiment*] without blowing up" the sufferer himself (GM III:15).

(3) *The ascetic ideal gives meaning to suffering, thereby seducing the majority of humans back to life.* The "genius" of those Nietzsche calls the "ascetic priests"—those teachers of the ascetic ideal that one finds in all major religions—is "the *alleviation* of suffering" (GM III:17). And their most important instrument is the ascetic ideal itself: for the ascetic ideal can give a meaning to suffering, and in so doing, prevent *ressentiment* from piling up to dangerous levels. Thus, Nietzsche says the ascetic priest is the *"direction-changer* of *ressentiment"* (GM III:15). How does the ascetic ideal bring this about?

Every sufferer, as we have seen, cries out for a culprit. The innovation of the ascetic priest is to provide a very accessible "culprit", namely, the sufferer himself! So the priest says: " 'Quite right, my sheep! Somebody must be to blame [for your suffering]: you yourself are this somebody, you yourself alone are to blame for it, *you yourself alone are to blame for yourself* " (GM III:15). In short, the sufferer *himself* is to be the object of his own *ressentiment*, since he is taught that he *himself* is the cause of his own suffering. As a result, the sufferer now has "a living being upon whom he can release his emotions" (GM III:15), namely, himself. He discharges his emotions against himself, in turn, by lacerating himself with feelings of guilt. Although the latter is, itself, a cause of additional suffering, this is now suffering *with a meaning*, hence bearable.

To see why this suffering is meaningful (hence bearable), we need to make *explicit*, in a way Nietzsche does not, the role of the ascetic ideal in this process. Such an ideal, according to Nietzsche, valorizes self-denial, and stigmatizes satisfaction of the rapacious and sensual desires. Yet human beings are fundamentally creatures of desire, who are "unsatisfied and insatiable" (GM III:13), who lust after power, cruelty, sexual gratification, and so forth. This means, of course, that humans stand almost continuously in violation of the ascetic ideal: all their basic instincts and inclinations are fundamentally anti-ascetic! The ascetic priests seize upon this fact in order to provide a meaning for human suffering: in a nutshell, one suffers, according to this explanation, as *punishment* for failure to live up to the ascetic ideal. As Nietzsche puts it:

Man, suffering from himself in some way, at all events physiologically, rather like an animal imprisoned in a cage, unclear as to why? what for? and yearning for reasons—reasons bring relief—, yearning for cures and narcotics as well, finally consults someone who knows hidden things too—and lo and behold! from this magician, the ascetic priest, he receives the *first* tip as to the "cause" of his suffering: he should look for it within *himself*, in *guilt*, in a piece of the past, he should understand his suffering itself as a *condition of punishment.* (GM III:20)

By setting up asceticism *as an ideal* by which most humans fall short, one can then reinterpret the basic existential fact of human suffering as "feelings of guilt, fear, punishment" (GM III:20): you suffer because you are guilty for betraying the (ascetic) commandments of your god, you suffer as punishment for your transgressions against this ideal, you suffer because *you* are a sinner, one who transgresses against the (ascetic) values laid down.

So the ascetic priest exploits a fact about our existential situation—namely, that most humans suffer[82]—by concocting a fictional explanation for this suffering: we suffer because we violate the ascetic ideal. Now our suffering has a meaning, and the suicidal nihilism which would result from meaningless suffering and undis-chargeable *ressentiment* is thwarted, since this *ressentiment* is now discharged against the agent himself in the form of powerful feelings of guilt, which then deaden the pain associated with the original suffering. Of course, by producing feelings of guilt, the priest's story about the ascetic ideal "brought new suffering with it, deeper, more internal, more poisonous suffering, suffering that gnawed away more intensely at life" (GM III:28). "But in spite of all that", Nietzsche quickly adds, "man was *saved*, he had a *meaning*" (GM III:28). And thus "from now on he could *will* something . . . the *will itself was saved*" (GM III:28), i.e. it was still possible for humans to retain their hold on life, to *will* to do things, since their suffering, at last, had a meaning.

We can now see, too, why Nietzsche thinks the ascetic ideal is part of the "favourable conditions in which [the majority of mortals can] fully . . . release [their] power and achieve [their] maximum feeling of power" (GM III:7). It is precisely because *"the ascetic ideal springs from the protective and healing instincts of a degenerating life* which uses every means to maintain itself and struggles for its existence" (GM III:13). The ascetic ideal makes it possible for the majority of suffer-ing mortals to escape "suicidal nihilism" and remain attached to life. And as Nietzsche tells us elsewhere, "will to exist at all, 'the drive to self-preservation' " is one of the "disguised" forms of the will to power, albeit its "lowest form" (WP 774). The maximum feeling of power available to most people is only this: not to despair so much that they give up on life altogether.

We need not, of course, accept Nietzsche's hypothesis that suicidal nihilism is inevitable: it suffices for the psychological importance of Nietzsche's insight that the ascetic ideal renders intelligible, and thus bearable, the brute fact of human suffer-ing. And must we even make explicit why understanding the appeal of ascetic ideals is especially imperative today? On one side, the industrialized West confronts the forces of Islamic fascism, whose hatred of sensuality in all its forms—from the sexual to the aesthetic—is one of the hallmarks of its ideology. On the other side, within the most powerful and dangerous of the Western powers, the United States, we find the same ascetic extremists in ideological ascendance, albeit attached to a somewhat different liturgy and cosmology. As Nietzsche says in the *Genealogy*, however, it is the "poison" and not "the Church" that should concern us (GM I:9). And the "poison" of asceticism is a feature of all the ascendant religious funda-mentalisms around the globe. If—to borrow the apt slogan of the Revolutionary

---

[82] Nietzsche, to be sure, does *not* distinguish between the genuinely existential causes of suffering—e.g. desire, physiological malady, bad conscience—and the contingent, social causes.

Association of the Women of Aghanistan—"Fundamentalism is the mortal enemy of all civilized humanity",[83] then so far Nietzsche is one of the few with a richly textured psychological story to explain the continuing appeal of this world-view.

Freud: From Science of the Mind to Kantian Rectitude

Freud's self-understanding and presentation was, *contra* Ricoeur, clearly a scientific one: psychoanalysis is supposed to be a science of the mind, on a par with the most successful natural sciences. The eminent philosopher of science Adolf Grünbaum made that point convincingly, nearly two decades ago, against Ricoeur and other Continental interpreters,[84] but Grünbaum didn't, as is well known, stop there. Grünbaum aimed to show that Freud's theory did not live up to its own scientistic ambitions, that, in particular, the "clinical data"—i.e. the evidence for the theory arising from the therapeutic context—on which Freud purportedly relied could not possibly be adequate to "confirm" his theory, because of the risk of "contamination": the patient's "cure" might simply be the product of suggestion by the analyst—in other words, the patient doesn't recover because he *really* wanted to sleep with his mother; he recovers because the analyst *suggested* that was the source of all his troubles.

Anti-Freudians with little understanding of philosophy of science—most notably, the literary critic Frederick Crews[85]—soon began regurgitating a crude version of the Grünbaum critique in the popular media.[86] They did so, needless to say, without ever mentioning the wide-ranging demolition of Grünbaum's original critique by other philosophers and Freud scholars.[87] As David Sachs, for example, noted:

Grünbaum nowhere discusses Freud's conviction that he had found practical applications and confirmations of his doctrines outside the sphere of clinical practices . . . [e.g.] psychotic manifestations, the vagaries of sexual orientation, jokes, taboos, religious practices and creeds, myths, folklore, so-called symptomatic actions, and sundry literary and biographical items.[88]

---

[83] http://rawa.fancymarketing.net/sep11-02.htm   [84] *The Foundations of Psychoanalysis*, op. cit.
[85] Crews began his anti-Freudian campaign before Grünbaum (see, e.g., the 1980 "Analysis Terminable", reprinted in Frederick Crews, *Skeptical Engagements* [New York: Oxford University Press, 1986]), but reached his widest audience as an unsubtle popularizer of the Grünbaum critique (see, e.g., the 1985 essay "The Future of an Illusion", from *The New Republic*, and also reprinted in id.).
[86] For a critique of Crews in particular, see Jonathan Lear, *Open Minded: Working Out the Logic of the Soul* (Cambridge, Mass.: Harvard University Press, 1998), 21–2. Lear, who does an admirable job debunking the Freud debunkers, at times succumbs, himself, to a kind of moralizing tendency, since he wants to argue that "psychoanalysis is crucial for a truly democratic culture to thrive." Id. at 19. This is, needless to say, an unFreudian concern, as Lear himself would no doubt acknowledge.
[87] See, e.g., Arthur Fine and Mickey Forbes, "Grünbaum on Freud: Three Grounds for Dissent", *Behavioral and Brain Sciences* 9 (1986): 237–8; Jim Hopkins, "Epistemology and Depth Psychology: Critical Notes on *The Foundations of Psychoanalysis*", in P. Clark and C. Wright (eds.), *Mind, Psychoanalysis and Science* (Oxford: Blackwell, 1988); David Sachs, "In Fairness to Freud", reprinted in J. Neu (ed.), *The Cambridge Companion to Freud* (Cambridge: Cambridge University Press, 1992); Richard Wollheim, "Desire, Belief, and Professor Grünbaum's Freud", in his *The Mind and Its Depths* (Cambridge, Mass.: Harvard University Press, 1993).
[88] "In Fairness to Freud", 317. Grünbaum also challenged whether Freud had adequately *confirmed* his causal claims. For example, to show that repressed homosexuality *causes* paranoia, ordinary canons of

Nor do Grünbaum or Crews acknowledge that there are experimental findings confirming aspects of Freud's theory.[89] In short, Grünbaum deprives Freud of the most powerful argument for the (approximate) truth of his theory: namely, its consilience, its ability to render intelligible a wide array of human phenomena. Freud effects an explanatory unification of this diverse range of phenomena—from the clinical to the cultural to the experimental—that are otherwise unexplained. Even the recent Darwinian fashion in social science has failed to produce a competitor that even compares to Freud's for consilience and simplicity.[90]

Even as the scholarly debate about the scientific status of Freud's theory has exhausted itself, a number of moral philosophers—John Deigh, Samuel Scheffler, Nancy Sherman, Michael Stocker, David Velleman, among others—have begun turning to Freud for a different reason: to understand the nature of morality and moral motivation.[91] Some, like Deigh, see in Freud the resources for a naturalistically respectable account of moral motivation that poses a *challenge* to the Kantian tradition in modern ethics.[92] Others, like Velleman, are drawn to Freud for a related reason— Freud locates moral motivation within a naturalistic conception of persons—but

confirmation would dictate that one adduce *not only* evidence of paranoids who were repressed homosexuals, but also evidence that where homosexuality was unrepressed, paranoia was absent. Of course, we make no such demand on the confirmation of folk-psychological claims—to confirm that John went to the refrigerator because he was hungry we don't need to show also that most people who aren't hungry don't go to the refrigerator—and since Freudian claims are on a simple continuum with these claims, it is not entirely clear why Grünbaum thinks other canons of confirmation apply. (On this point, I am indebted to Ken Gemes, though he is, for other reasons, less sympathetic to Freudian theses than I am.) In addition, this criticism neglects the enormous empirical literature supporting central Freudian causal posits: see the sources cited in the next note.

[89] A wonderful recent example is Henry E. Adams, Lester W. Wright, Jr., and Bethany A. Lohr, "Is Homophobia Associated with Homosexual Arousal?" *Journal of Abnormal Psychology* 105 (1996): 440–5, a study which reports experimental evidence confirming the familiar Freudian hypothesis about homophobia as a defense mechanism against homosexual desires. And for a splendid review of the enormous experimental literature supporting distinctively Freudian hypotheses, see Drew Westen, "The Scientific Legacy of Sigmund Freud: Toward a Psychodynamically Informed Psychological Science", *Psychological Bulletin* 124 (1998), 333–71. Westen identifies five tenets of Freudian psychoanalysis—for example, "much of mental life—including thoughts, feelings, and motives—is unconscious, which means that people can behave in ways or develop symptoms that are inexplicable to themselves" and "stable personality begins to form in childhood, and childhood experiences play an important role in personality development, particularly in shaping the ways people form later social relationships"—and then reviews an overwhelming body of experimental literature supporting all five. As Westen notes, the five "propositions were all once highly disputed in psychology and were exclusively associated with psychoanalysis" and "are indeed central to contemporary thinking among practicing psychodynamic psychologists and psychiatrists." Id. at 335.

[90] Freud's theory is tremendously parsimonious, simply extending the familiar apparatus of commonsense belief-desire psychology to the unconscious, a realm recognized long before Freud's systematic account of its contours.

[91] John Deigh, *The Sources of Moral Agency: Essays in Moral Psychology and Freudian Theory* (Cambridge: Cambridge University Press, 1996); Samuel Scheffler, *Human Morality* (New York: Oxford University Press, 1992), ch. 5; Nancy Sherman, "The Moral Perspective and the Psychoanalytic Quest", *Journal of the American Academy of Psychoanalysis* 23 (1995): 223–41; Nancy Sherman, "Emotional Agents", in *The Analytic Freud*, ed. M. Levine (London: Routledge, 2000); Michael Stocker with Elizabeth Hegman, *Valuing Emotions* (Cambridge: Cambridge University Press, 1996); Velleman, "A Rational Superego"; J. David Velleman, "Love as a Moral Emotion", *Ethics* 109 (1999): 338–47.

[92] See esp. "Freud, Naturalism, and Modern Moral Philosophy" in *The Sources of Moral Agency*.

then go on to argue, somewhat remarkably, that Freud's theory can complement, rather than undermine, Kant's. It is this moralizing interpretation of Freud—one that marries Freudian theory to Kantian rectitude—that is our concern here.

There is an obvious, threshold difficulty for the marriage of Freud to Kant, one which the moralizing interpreters certainly recognize. For Kant himself cannot, given his understanding of morality, even *hope* for a naturalistic account of *moral* motivation. For in the natural world, all motivation is heteronomous, that is, determined by something other than reason, and thus could not, *by definition*, be moral, since moral motivation is autonomous. Thus, for Kant, a naturalized account of "moral" motivation is a contradiction in terms.

Now the Kantian readers of Freud no doubt feel the pressure of modernity here, which demands that our story about moral motivation be reconciliable with some plausible scientific story about how the mind works.[93] Kant's anti-naturalistic posture, then, is just abandoned, and the question now becomes whether the Freudian account of moral motivation can be reconciled with *other* important features of Kant's view of morality (i.e. other than his view that moral motivation is necessarily *not* heteronomous). Let us allow the moralizers this move.

The difficulty for this reformulated project is well-put by Velleman:

In Freud's thoroughly naturalistic account, our obedience to moral requirements owes nothing to their meriting obedience; it's due entirely to incentives that appeal to our inborn drives. Freud thus explains the influence of morality in a way that tends to debunk its rational authority, whereas [Kant's] Categorical Imperative is supposed to carry all the authority of practical reason.[94]

Freud, recall, offers two famous accounts of the origin of moral conscience:[95] in one, conscience arises through the internalization (or "introjection") of the parental superegos as a way of resolving the Oedipal complex;[96] in the other, conscience arises as a result of the introjection of innate aggressive drives, whose taming is a necessary precondition for civilization.[97] Yet the two accounts are complementary once we recall that the superego—the locus of moral conscience—has a dual function for Freud, as the enforcer of moral standards and as the custodian of the "ego ideal" to which we aspire. As Deigh observes: "The [enforcement] operations of conscience [for Freud] owe their motivational force to [internalized] aggressive instincts; the operations of the ego ideal owe theirs to sexual drives",[98] namely, those

[93] This is, happily, becoming a more widely felt need among moral philosophers. For a different approach of this kind—bringing recent social psychology to bear, critically, on virtue ethics—see John M. Doris, *Lack of Character* (Cambridge: Cambridge University Press, 2002).

[94] "A Rational Superego", 530.

[95] I should note that I here follow John Deigh's reading, which treats Freud as having two different accounts of the origin of moral conscience, a reading rejected by Velleman in "A Rational Superego", 540, n. 29. My criticisms of Velleman, however, below, do not depend at all on my siding with Deigh on this issue.

[96] See Sigmund Freud, "The Dissection of the Psychical Personality", in *New Introductory Lectures on Psychoanalysis*, trans. J. Strachey (New York: Norton, 1965), 57.

[97] See Sigmund Freud, *Civilization and Its Discontents*, trans. J. Strachey (New York: Norton, 1961), esp. 78–9. This is the account that mirrors Nietzsche's in the Second Essay of *On the Genealogy of Morality*.

[98] Deigh, "Freud, Naturalism, and Modern Moral Philosophy", 127.

drives at issue in the resolution of the Oedipal complex. The upshot, then, is that "judgments of morality and value have motivational force that is traceable to these basic [aggressive and sexual] instincts".[99]

The difficulty from a Kantian standpoint is that the authority of morality on this account is *de facto*: it's just a brute fact about the aggressive and sexual instincts in creatures like us that they invest the superego with the capacity to move us to act. But for a Kantian, the motivational authority of the superego must be *justified*—it must be a *de jure* authority—not simply a brute fact: the superego must *deserve* obedience, not simply secure it in fact (i.e. in virtue of the facts about our instinctual make-up).

Yet even Freud, Velleman argues, must acknowledge this: for the superego, on Freud's account, is able to instill feelings of *guilt* in us when we transgress its commands, and feelings of guilt would not arise from disobeying a mere *de facto* authority. Consider: those who defied the Nazis in occupied Europe during World War II must surely have felt *fear* about the consequences of their disobedience, but they surely didn't feel *guilty*, because they didn't view Hitler's domination of them as *justified* or *legitimate*. So Freud, too, has to explain "how the authority [of the superego] to punish is recognized".[100]

The Freudian solution to this problem invokes the notion of the "ego ideal" that the superego maintains:

> The ego ideal provides the normative background against which the superego can be conceived as having authority. The superego's aggression is seen as premised on a normative judgment, to the effect that the ego has fallen short of the ideal. . . . The ego thinks that it is being criticized and punished for a failure to meet its own standards, the standards that it accepted as applicable to itself when it adopted an ideal.[101]

But why, then, does the ego accept the ego ideal—why, in short, does it *idealize* the superego, and thus invest the superego with *de jure* authority? As Velleman puts it: "What is needed is an explanation of how the ego comes to elevate someone or something to the status of an ideal, which can become the object of moral anxiety."[102]

Velleman finds the Freudian answer wanting. As Velleman explains, "the ego ideal [for Freud results from the] introjection of the parents as objects of admiration."[103] Since the child loves the parents, the child loves the ego ideal, and invests it with normative authority. But Velleman finds this unconvincing: the child's desire "to incorporate his father [as a way of *being like* the father] should hardly lead him to like or dislike himself according to whether he succeeds" unless it were the case that "wanting to resemble or be another person" were "sufficient for idealizing him".[104] Yet it is unclear why Velleman thinks *strong-enough* wanting isn't more than sufficient for idealization. If you *really* desire *to be like* X, some positive valence is attached to X; when you *become* X (when you manifest or embody Xness), why wouldn't the positive valence then attach to you? The child *loves* the father, meaning that a strong positive valence attaches to the father; the introjected father, namely the ego ideal,

---

[99] Deigh, "Freud, Naturalism, and Modern Moral Philosophy" Id.
[100] Velleman, "A Rational Superego", 539.   [101] Id. at 541–2.   [102] Id. at 548.
[103] Id.   [104] Id. at 549.

retains that positive valence, that "normative authority" which enables the superego to instill guilt for failure to live up to that ideal, the ideal of the father. Thus, Freud does have an explanation of the normative authority of the superego, but it is still one that would fail to satisfy a Kantian: the superego so conceived has no claim, as Velleman puts it, to "the authority of practical reason".[105] The superego is *perceived* as a *de jure* authority as a result of idealization, to be sure, but it may or may not have a justified claim to being one. The ego ideal, as far as Freud is concerned, could even endorse the values of utilitarianism!

Now Velleman, to be sure, has a Kantian account of the authority of the superego to offer, one that, he admits, "entails a fair amount of extrapolation from the Freudian texts".[106] This account is worth attending to, if only briefly, as an illustration of how the moralizing tendency leads interpreters far afield. According to Velleman, Freud needs an account of the ego as possessing "an independent faculty of normative judgment" which is able to engage in "evaluative reasoning about ideals", and thus is capable of deciding that the superego *merits* idealization and admiration for sound Kantian reasons.[107] Velleman adduces evidence that Freud himself acknowledges the ego's capacity for normative judgment. For example, Freud describes the ego as the seat of "reason and good sense"[108] and observes that "Small events in the child's life which make him feel dissatisfied afford him with provocation for beginning to criticize his parents, and for using, in order to support his critical attitude, the knowledge which he has acquired that other parents are in some respects preferable to them."[109] Velleman takes this as evidence that Freud acknowledged the existence of "an evaluative capacity that is independent of the received values preserved in [the child's] superego"[110] and that, therefore, "the ego possesses an independent faculty of judgment as to whom or what to admire."[111]

The difficulty for Velleman, however, is that the only "reason and good sense" required to do the evaluative work at issue here is *instrumental* in nature—the same capacity for instrumental reasoning that the Ego employs, to good effect, in mediating between the Id and the demands of reality, for example. Consider Freud's own example (suitably modernized) of the child's comparative judgment about the merits of parents, his and others. The child notices that his father forbids television, while another child's father permits it. The child *desires* to watch television. The child is *frustrated* by his father's prohibition and so concludes, "The other father is a better father." The Ego can do all the work here with no more than the resources of instrumental reason and the valuations it entails: the best *means* for realizing the child's desire to see television would be to have a father more like the other child's; ergo, the other father is "better", i.e. better at permitting the child to realize his desires.

Now an Ego capable only of instrumental reasoning is not going to be sufficient for Velleman's purposes: the suitably Kantian Ego has to be able to appreciate when the soon-to-be-introjected parent embodies the demands of practical reason—the

---

[105] Velleman, "A Rational Superego", 530.   [106] Id. at 551.   [107] Id.
[108] *New Introductory Lectures on Psychoanalysis* (95 in S.E. version).
[109] "Family Romances", S.E.: 9: 236–41, at 237.   [110] "A Rational Superego", 554.
[111] Id. at 555.

Categorical Imperative—not simply when it constitutes an effective means to desire-satisfaction. Velleman's *morally enriched* Ego is the only Ego capable of idealizing the superego in a way that guarantees its *actual*, not merely apparent, normative authority, as the following passage illustrates:

What the child experiences in being loved by his parents, and what he responds to in loving them, is their capacity to anticipate and provide for his needs, *often at the expense of their own interests* [emphasis added]. And this capacity of the parents is nothing other than their practical reason . . . by which their immediate self-gratification is subordinated to rational requirements embodied in another person. It's their capacity to take another person as an end. Hence the child's love for his parents doesn't merely project a superficial glow onto them; it registers the genuine value of their reason and good sense—what Kant would call their rational nature, or humanity—as manifested in their loving care.[112]

The fictional phenomenology of the child–parent relationship that undergirds this story is stark testimony to the distorting effects of the moralizing tendency on interpretation. Children surely do respond to the fact that parents "anticipate and provide for their needs", but what evidence is there that children—that is, children before the acquisition of a superego and its ego ideal—ever register the fact that the parents do so *"at the expense of their own interests"*? And what parents meet the child's needs because they "subordinate" their "self-gratification . . . to rational requirements embodied in another person"? As a former child, who is now a parent, I confess this strikes me as utterly fantastic. Of course, that should hardly be surprising: like the rest of Kant's extravagant moral psychology, this far-fetched account bears no relationship to what we know about motivation or emotions like love, from ordinary experience or from science.

Once we bury the clever, if unconvincing, moralistic reinvention of Freud, we can return to the Freud that matters, the one who shows us, as Jonathan Lear aptly puts it, that "humans . . . hav[e] depth", that they are "complex psychological organisms who generate layers of meaning which lie beneath the surface of their own understanding".[113] Like all the practitioners of the hermeneutics of suspicion, Freud shows us that we are not "transparent to ourselves".[114] If we are to make any progress in penetrating that opaqueness, then we still need to take seriously Freud's explanatory framework for doing so.

The Epistemology of the Hermeneutics of Suspicion

On the reading urged here, we should understand Marx, Nietzsche, and Freud as seeking a naturalistically respectable account of how we arrived at our current, conscious self-understandings. But arriving at such an understanding of the causal genesis of our conscious self-understandings is not—obviously, at least—equivalent to a "hermeneutics of suspicion", to an understanding that should make us regard them as "suspect". Why, to put it simply, is the correct naturalistic account of the genesis of our beliefs a reason to make us suspicious of those beliefs? It is useful,

---

[112] Id. at 557.   [113] *Open-Minded*, 27.   [114] Id.

I believe, to take a short, though perhaps surprising, detour through Anglo-American epistemology of the past forty years to see how and why the "naturalistic" turn of Marx, Nietzsche, and Freud remains philosophically important.

In 1963, in a remarkably brief paper,[115] Edmund Gettier convinced most philosophers that the received wisdom of millennia about the concept of knowledge was mistaken: "knowledge" was not simply a matter of having a justified, true belief, since one could adduce examples of beliefs that were both "justified" and "true" but which didn't seem to be cases of "knowledge".[116] The Gettier counter-examples to the "justified true belief" analysis of "knowledge" all had the form of the following example:

Suppose Smith and Jones apply for the same job. And suppose Smith is *justified* in believing both that (1) Jones will get the job, and (2) Jones has 10 coins in his pocket. Smith would then also be *justified* in believing that (3) the person who gets the job will have 10 coins in his pocket. In fact, Smith (not Jones) gets the job *and*, as it happens, he has 10 coins in his pocket. (3) turns out to be a justified true belief, but it doesn't seem that Smith "knows" (3). Of course, Smith *should* believe (3), but not for the reasons that he does. He has a true belief, but not knowledge.

The legacy of the Gettier counter-examples was a powerful one: a justified true belief isn't "knowledge" when the justification for the true belief isn't the *cause* of why the agent holds the belief. As Philip Kitcher put the point, in explaining the stimulus Gettier provided to the "naturalistic" turn in epistemology: "the epistemic status of a belief state depends on the etiology of the state."[117] Beliefs caused the "wrong" way suffer epistemically.

We can understand, now, the logic of the hermeneutics of suspicion as exploiting precisely this point about the epistemic status of belief: we *should* be suspicious of the epistemic status of beliefs that have the wrong causal etiology. That's the lesson of the Gettier counter-examples, and it is the lesson which underwrites the *suspicion* that Marx, Nietzsche, and Freud recommend by way of providing alternative causal trajectories to explain our beliefs. To be sure, beliefs with the wrong causal etiology might be *true*; but since they are no longer cases of knowledge, we have no reason to presume that to be the case. To the contrary, we now have reason to be *suspicious*—nothing more—of their veritistic properties. Examples abound:

(1) The U.S. President George W. Bush claimed to know that Saddam Hussein was a threat to the United States, who must be removed from power. If what *caused* him to believe that is that it would be in the interests of the U.S. ruling classes to have more reliable control over large Middle East oil reserves,[118] then

[115] Edmund N. Gettier III, "Is Justified True Belief Knowledge?" *Analysis* 23 (1963): 121–3.

[116] I prescind here from commenting on some of the more recent doubts raised about the Gettier style of argument. See esp. Jonathan Weinberg, Shaun Nichols, and Stephen P. Stich, "Normativity and Epistemic Intuitions", *Philosophical Topics* 29 (2001): 429–60.

[117] Philip Kitcher, "The Naturalists Return", *Philosophical Review* 100 (1992), 60.

[118] An alternative causal hypothesis, also in wide circulation, is that the Bush domestic policy agenda, involving yet another massive transfer of resources to the ruling classes, was only viable in a political environment in which the masses are suitably distracted by war.

we have a reason to re-evaluate the epistemic status of Bush's claims about Saddam.

(2) Hundreds of millions of religious fundamentalists, of all creeds, affirm the moral knowledge that sexual expression, outside the confines of properly sanctioned heterosexual marriage, is an abomination. If what *causes* them to believe this is a need to render intelligible and bearable their own miserable condition—their own sexual frustration, physical inadequacy, loneliness, sexual malfeasance, and so on—then we have reason to be skeptical about the epistemic status of their moral claims.

(3) Millions of people profess knowledge of the reality of God, claiming miracles witnessed or voices heard. If what really *causes* them to believe that they know of God's existence (and that they have had these experiences) is an unconscious, infantile wish for the protection of an all-powerful father-figure, then we have reason to wonder about the epistemic status of their belief in God's existence.

Beliefs arrived at the wrong way are *suspect*: that is the epistemological point exploited by the practitioners of the hermeneutics of suspicion. It is ironic, to be sure, that, in recent years, these practitioners should have fallen prey to moralizing readings, readings that, themselves, cry out for a suspicious interpretation—though that is a task for a different day. What bears emphasizing here is that—the fashions of academic moral and literary theory notwithstanding—the continuing importance of Marx, Nietzsche, and Freud stands (or falls) with their contribution to the causal explanation of the moral and social world we inhabit. The proper task for scholars is not the moralistic reinterpretation of these claims, but their development and evaluation within the actual naturalistic framework the practitioners of the hermeneutics of suspicion recommend.[119]

[119] I am grateful to an audience at the philosophy department at Birkbeck College, London for very helpful discussion of an earlier draft of this paper in the fall of 2002, and to Michael Rosen for detailed comments on this same version, comments that saved me from several errors. The treatment of Marx was greatly helped by discussion with G. A. Cohen during his visit to Austin in March 2003. For valuable comments on a later draft of the essay, I thank Stephen Bero, Sebastian Gardner, Joshua Knobe, Conor Roddy, Neil Sinhababu, and especially, John Deigh and Larry Sager. Finally, I am indebted to the members of the audience at the Philosophical Society at Oxford University at the end of May 2003 for their challenging questions.

4
Past the Linguistic Turn?

Timothy Williamson

The Linguistic Turn is the title of an influential anthology edited by Richard Rorty, published in 1967. In his introduction, Rorty explained:

The purpose of the present volume is to provide materials for reflection on the most recent philosophical revolution, that of linguistic philosophy. I shall mean by 'linguistic philosophy' the view that philosophical problems are problems which may be solved (or dissolved) either by reforming language, or by understanding more about the language we presently use. (1967: 3)

'The linguistic turn' has subsequently become a standard vague phrase for a diffuse event—some regard it as *the* event—in twentieth-century philosophy, one not confined to signed-up linguistic philosophers in Rorty's sense. For those who took the turn, language was somehow the central theme of philosophy. There is an increasingly widespread sense that the linguistic turn is past. In this essay I ask how far the turn has been, or should be, reversed.

1. A. J. Ayer, my predecessor but two in the Wykeham Chair of Logic at Oxford, was the first of its holders to take the linguistic turn.[1] In 1936, back from Vienna but not yet in the Chair, he announced an uncompromisingly formal version of linguistic philosophy:

[T]he philosopher, as an analyst, is not directly concerned with the physical properties of things. He is concerned only with the way in which we speak about them. In other words, the propositions of philosophy are not factual, but linguistic in character—that is, they do not describe the behaviour of physical, or even mental, objects; they express definitions, or the formal consequences of definitions. (1936: 61–2).

Ayer traced his views back ultimately to the empiricism of Berkeley and Hume (1936: 11). His contrast between definitions of words and descriptions of objects is, roughly, the linguistic analogue of Hume's contrast between relations of ideas and matters of fact. For an empiricist, the a priori methods of philosophy cannot provide us with knowledge of synthetic truths about matters of fact ('the behaviour of physical, or even mental, objects'); they yield only analytic truths about relations of ideas ('definitions, or the formal consequences of definitions'). A rather traditional empiricism later overshadowed the linguistic theme in Ayer's work.

---

[1] Ayer's immediate three predecessors were John Cook Wilson, H. H. Joachim, and H. H. Price.

Ayer was the predecessor of Michael Dummett in the Wykeham Chair. Dummett gave a classic articulation of the linguistic turn, attributing it to Frege:

Only with Frege was the proper object of philosophy finally established: namely, first, that the goal of philosophy is the analysis of the structure of *thought*; secondly, that the study of *thought* is to be sharply distinguished from the study of the psychological process of *thinking*; and, finally, that the only proper method for analysing thought consists in the analysis of *language* . . . [T]he acceptance of these three tenets is common to the entire analytical school. (1978: 458)

On this view, thought is essentially expressible (whether or not actually expressed) in a public language, which filters out the subjective noise, the merely psychological aspects of thinking, from the inter-subjective message, that which one thinks. Dummett's own corpus constitutes one of the most imposing monuments of analytic philosophy as so defined.

Elsewhere, Dummett makes it clear that he takes this concern with language to be what distinguishes 'analytical philosophy' from other schools (1993: 4). His account of its inception varies slightly. At one points, he says:

[A]nalytical philosophy was born when the 'linguistic turn' was taken. This was not, of course, taken uniformly by any group of philosophers at any one time: but the first clear example known to me occurs in Frege's *Die Grundlagen der Arithmetik* of 1884. (1993: 5)

Later, we read:

If we identify the linguistic turn as the starting-point of analytical philosophy proper, there can be no doubt that, to however great an extent Frege, Moore and Russell prepared the ground, the crucial step was taken by Wittgenstein in the *Tractatus Logico-Philosophicus* of 1922. (1993: 127)

Presumably, in Frege the linguistic turn was a fitful insight, in Wittgenstein, a systematic conception.

That 'analytical philosophers' in Dummett's sense coincide with those usually classified as such is not obvious. Some kind of linguistic turn occurred in much of what is usually called 'continental [supposedly non-analytic] philosophy'. It is not obvious that Jacques Derrida does not subscribe in his own way to Dummett's three tenets: if some stretching of terms is required, it is for the later Wittgenstein too. Conversely, Bertrand Russell did not subscribe to the three tenets, although often cited as a paradigm 'analytical philosopher'. Over the last twenty years, fewer and fewer of those who would accept the label 'analytic philosophy' for their work would also claim to take the linguistic turn (I am not one of those few). Even philosophers strongly influenced by Dummett, such as Gareth Evans, Christopher Peacocke, and John Campbell, no longer give language the central role that he describes. For Dummett, they belong to a tradition that has grown out of 'analytical philosophy' without themselves being 'analytical philosophers' (1993: 4–5). In effect, they aim to analyse thought directly without taking a diversion through the analysis of language.

The philosophy of mind has famously displaced the philosophy of language at the centre of much current debate. This is hardly a form of the linguistic turn, even granted the importance of Jerry Fodor's notion of a language of thought (the brain's computational code) in the philosophy of mind (Fodor, 1975). However, the notion of a *mental representation* is central to the new philosophy of mind. A concept is a mental representation in this sense, whether or not it corresponds to an expression in a language of thought. One might therefore classify both thought and language together under the more general category of representation, and argue that the linguistic turn was just the first phase of the *representational turn*, on which the goal of philosophy is the analysis (in a generous sense) of representation. For the classification to be appropriate, we need a generous sense of 'representation' too, correlative with a loose notion of *aboutness*. We think about things and talk about them. We represent how things are when we know or believe or assert that they are some way; we represent how things are to be when we intentionally bring it about or hope or ask someone to bring it about that they are that way. Things are or are not as they are represented to be. In both thought and language, questions of truth and falsity arise: even if there is some thinking or speaking neither truly nor falsely, there would be no thinking or speaking at all if there were no thinking or speaking truly or falsely.[2] On some views, perception involves non-conceptual representations of one's environment: they too raise the question of misrepresentation. As non-conceptual, they presumably fall outside Dummett's category of thought; they threaten even his first tenet, that the goal of philosophy is the analysis of the structure of thought. Nor is it clear how far contemporary philosophy of mind accepts his second tenet, for it does not always sharply distinguish the study of thought from the study of the psychological process of thinking. *Naturalists* hold that everything is part of the natural world, and should be studied as such; how should one study thought as part of the natural world if not by studying the psychological process of thinking?

We could have brought thought and language together as forms of representation in other words by saying that both are forms of *intentionality*. This terminology reminds us how little the representational turn is confined to what would ordinarily be called 'analytic philosophy'. The phenomenological tradition may constitute another form of the representational turn. In the hermeneutic study of interpretation and various shades of postmodernist discourse about discourse the representational turn takes a more specifically linguistic form.

Have we stretched our terms so far that it is vacuous to say that a piece of philosophy takes the representational turn? No. What language and thought have most obviously in common is that they are both manifestations of *mind*. If we reject idealism in all its forms, we take mind to constitute only a small fraction of reality. It is no platitude to claim that the goal of philosophy is to analyse manifestations of that small fraction. To put it very schematically, let *idealism about the subject-matter of philosophy* be the view that what philosophy studies is mind, in contrast to *ontological*

---

[2] That language and thought are representational in this sense does not imply that sentences or thoughts represent entities such as states of affairs; the representing might be done by constituent words or concepts. When Davidson denies that language is representational, he is denying that sentences as contrasted with singular terms represent objects of some kind (1990: 281, 304).

idealism, the view that what exists is mind. Although idealism about the subject-matter of philosophy does not entail ontological idealism, it is unclear why we should accept idealism about the subject-matter of philosophy if we reject ontological idealism. Of course, one might reject idealism about the subject-matter of philosophy while nevertheless holding that the correct method for philosophy is to study its not purely mental subject-matter by studying mental or linguistic representations of that subject-matter. This methodological claim will be considered later; for present purposes, we merely note how much weaker it is than those formulated by Ayer and Dummett.

The statement that mind constitutes only a small fraction of reality may be accused of violating Dummett's second tenet by confusing thought with the process of thinking. Almost everyone agrees that psychological events constitute only a small fraction of reality, but that is not yet to concede that thought in a non-psychologistic sense is similarly confined. John McDowell, for instance, argues:[3]

[T]here is no ontological gap between the sort of thing one can mean, or generally the sort of thing one can think, and the sort of thing that can be the case. When one thinks truly, what one thinks *is* what is the case. So since the world is everything that is the case . . . there is no gap between thought, as such, and the world. Of course thought can be distanced from the world by being false, but there is no distance from the world implicit in the very idea of thought. (1994: 27)

For McDowell, the sort of thing one can think is a conceptual content: the conceptual has no outer boundary beyond which lies unconceptualized reality. He denies the accusation of idealism on the grounds that he is not committed to any contentious thesis of mind-dependence.

The sort of thing that can be the case is that a certain object has a certain property. McDowell's claim is not that the object and the property *are* concepts; it is merely that we can in principle form concepts *of* them, with which to think that the object has the property. Indeed, we can in principle form many different concepts of them: we can think of the same object as Hesperus or as Phosphorus. In Fregean terms, different senses determine the same reference. McDowell admits 'an alignment of minds with the realm of sense, not with the realm of reference' (1994: 179). For objects, his claim that the conceptual is unbounded amounts to the claim that any object can be thought of. Likewise for the sort of thing that can be the case: the claim is, for example, that whenever an object has a property, it can be thought, of the object and the property, that the former has the latter. But, on a coherent and natural reading of 'the sort of thing that can be the case', such things are individuated coarsely, by the objects, properties, and relations that they involve. Thus, since Hesperus *is* Phosphorus, what is the case if Hesperus is bright *is* what is the case if Phosphorus is bright: the objects are the same, as are the properties. On this reading, McDowell's claim 'When one thinks truly, what one thinks *is* what is the case' is false,

---

[3] Although McDowell is sometimes classified as a 'post-analytic' philosopher, he finds his own way to accept Dummett's 'fundamental tenet of analytical philosophy', that 'philosophical questions about thought are to be approached through language' (1994: 125).

because what one thinks is individuated at the level of sense while what is the case is individuated at the level of reference. Although McDowell's claim is true on other readings, it is not clear that they will bear the weight that his argument puts on them.

McDowell's argument seems to require the premiss that everything (object, property, relation, state of affairs) is thinkable. That premiss is highly contentious. What reason have we to assume that reality does not contain *elusive objects*, incapable in principle of being individually thought of? Although we can think of them collectively—for example, as elusive objects—that is not to single out any one of them in thought. Can we be sure that ordinary material objects are not constituted of clouds of elusive sub-subatomic particles? We might know them by their collective effects while unable to think of any single one of them. Of course, McDowell does not intend the conceptual to be limited by the merely medical limitations of human beings, but the elusiveness might run deeper than that: the nature of the objects might preclude the kind of separable causal interaction with complex beings that isolating them in thought would require. In Fregean terminology again, a sense is a mode of presentation of a referent; a mode of presentation of something is a way of presenting it to a possible thinker, if not an actual one; for all that McDowell has shown, there may be necessary limitations on all possible thinkers.[4] We do not know whether there are elusive objects. It is unclear what would motivate the claim that there are none, if not some form of idealism. We should adopt no conception of philosophy that on methodological grounds excludes elusive objects.[5]

Suppose, for the sake of argument, that there are no elusive objects. That by itself would still not vindicate a restriction of philosophy to the conceptual, the realm of sense or thought. The practitioners of any discipline have thoughts and communicate them, but they are rarely studying those very thoughts: rather, they are studying what their thoughts are about. Most thoughts are not about thoughts. To make philosophy the study of thought is to insist that philosophers' thoughts should be about thoughts. It is not obvious why philosophers should accept that restriction.

Biology and physics are not studies of thought. In their most theoretical reaches, they merge into the philosophy of biology and the philosophy of physics. Why then should philosophers of biology and philosophers of physics study only thought? Sometimes they do study biologists' and physicists' thought, but sometimes they study what that thought is about, in an abstract and general manner. Why should such activities not count as philosophy?

There is a more central example. Much contemporary metaphysics is not primarily concerned with thought or language at all. Its goal is to discover what

[4] McDowell's invocation of humility (1994: 40) addresses contingent limitations rather than necessary ones.
[5] Mark Johnston (1993: 96–7) discusses 'the Enigmas, entities essentially undetectable by us'. He stipulates that they are collectively as well as individually undetectable; thus our elusive objects need not be his Enigmas. If we cannot have good evidence that there are no Enigmas, it may well be a waste of time to worry whether there are Enigmas. But it would not follow that it is a waste of time to worry whether there *can be* Enigmas. Their definition does not rule out knowledge of the possibility of such things, and knowledge of that possibility may itself be philosophically useful (indeed, Johnston uses it for his philosophical purposes).

fundamental kinds of things there are and what properties and relations they have, not how we represent them. It studies substances and essences, universals and particulars, space and time, possibility and necessity. Although nominalist or conceptualist reductions of all these matters have been attempted, such theories have no methodological priority and often turn out to do no justice to what they attempt to reduce.

The usual stories about the history of twentieth-century philosophy fail to fit much of the liveliest, exactest, and most creative achievements of the final third of that century: the revival of metaphysical theorizing, realist in spirit, often speculative, often commonsensical, associated with Saul Kripke, David Lewis, Kit Fine, Peter van Inwagen, David Armstrong, and many others: work that has, to cite just one example, made it anachronistic to dismiss essentialism as anachronistic.[6] On the traditional grand narrative schemes in the history of philosophy, this activity must be a throwback to pre-Kantian metaphysics. It ought not to be happening; but it is. Many of those who practise it happily acknowledge its continuity with traditional metaphysics; appeals to the authority of Kant, or history, ring hollow, for they are unbacked by any argument that has withstood the test of recent time.

One might try to see in contemporary metaphysics a Quinean breakdown of divisions between philosophy and the natural sciences. But if it is metaphysics naturalized, then so is the metaphysics of Aristotle, Descartes, and Leibniz. Broadly a priori argument retains a central role, as do the modal notions of possibility and necessity. Although empirical knowledge constrains the attribution of essential properties, results are more often reached through a subtle interplay of logic and the imagination. The crucial experiments are thought experiments.

Might the contrast between the new-old metaphysics and the representational turn be less stark than it appears to be? These metaphysicians firmly resist attempts to reconstrue their enterprise as the analysis of thought—unlike Sir Peter Strawson, who defined his 'descriptive metaphysics' as 'content to describe the actual structure of our thought about the world' (1959: 9). But perhaps one cannot reflect on thought or talk about reality without reflecting on reality itself, for the aboutness of thought and talk is intrinsic to it, and its very point. This idea has been emphasized by David Wiggins, Dummett's successor and my predecessor, author of some of the most distinguished essentialist metaphysics, in which considerations of logic and biology harmoniously combine. Wiggins writes: 'Let us forget once and for all the very idea of some knowledge of language or meaning that is not knowledge of the world itself' (Wiggins 2001: 12). In defining words—for example, natural kind terms—we must point at real specimens. What there is determines what there is for us to mean. In knowing what we mean, we know something about what there is. That may prompt us to wonder how far the analysis of thought or language could be pursued autonomously, with any kind of methodological priority.

Dummett claimed not that the traditional questions of metaphysics could not be answered but that the way to answer them was by the analysis of thought and

⁶ See, e.g., Kripke, 1980; French, Uehling, and Wettstein 1986; Fine, 1994 and 1995; and Wiggins, 2001.

language. For example, in order to determine whether there are numbers, one must determine whether number words such as '7' function semantically like proper names in the context of sentences uttered in mathematical discourse. But what is it so to function? Devil words such as 'Satan' appear to function semantically like proper names in the context of sentences uttered in devil-worshipping discourse, but one should not jump to the conclusion that there are devils. However enthusiastically devil-worshippers use 'Satan' as though it referred to something, that does not make it refer to something. Although empty names *appear* to function semantically like referring names in the context of sentences uttered by those who believe the names to refer, the appearances are deceptive. 'Satan' refers to something if and only if some sentence with 'Satan' in subject position (such as 'Satan is self-identical') expresses a truth, but the analysis of thought and language may not be the best way to discover whether any such sentence is indeed true.

Historians of philosophy on the grand scale will probably be too Whiggish or Hegelian to regard the linguistic or representational turn as merely a false turning from which philosophy is withdrawing now that it recognizes its mistake. We are supposed to go forward from it, not back. At the very least, we should learn from our mistakes, if only not to repeat them. But if the representational turn was a mistake, it was not a simple blunder; it went too deep for that.

2. It is time to get down to serious work. My aim in what follows is to explore these issues about the nature of philosophy in a microcosm. As a case study, I will consider the problem of vagueness, partly out of habit, but also because it appears to be a paradigm of a philosophical problem about thought and language. For vagueness is generally conceived as a feature of our representations of the world, not of the world itself. Admittedly, some philosophers find tempting the idea of mind-independently vague objects, such as Mount Everest, vague in their spatiotemporal boundaries and mereological composition, if not in their identity. That kind of vagueness is not my concern here. I will consider an example of a quite standard type, involving a vague predicate.[7]

Suppose that there was once plenty of water on the planet Mars; it was clearly not dry. Ages passed, and very gradually the water evaporated. Now Mars is clearly dry. No moment was clearly the first on which it was dry or the last on which it was not. For a long intermediate period it was neither clearly dry nor clearly not dry. Counting the water molecules would not have enabled us to determine whether it was dry; other measurements would have been equally inconclusive. We have no idea of any investigative procedure that would have resolved the issue. It was a borderline case. No urgent practical purpose compels us to decide whether Mars was dry then, but only a limited proportion of thought and talk in any human society is driven by urgent practical purposes. We should like to know the history of Mars. When necessary, we can always use words other than 'dry'. Nevertheless, we reflect

---

[7] On vagueness in general see Keefe and Smith, 1997 and Williamson, 1994. On vague objects see Williamson, 2003 and references therein.

on the difficulty of classifying Mars as dry or as not dry at those intermediate times, even given exact measurements. We may wonder whether it was either. We ask ourselves:

Was Mars always either dry or not dry?

Henceforth I will refer to that as *the original question*. More precisely, I will use that phrase to designate that interrogative sentence, as used in that context (which is not to deny that the word 'question' can also be applied to what interrogative sentences express rather than the sentences themselves).

The original question is at least proto-philosophical in character. It is prompted by an obstacle both hard to identify and hard to avoid that we encounter in applying our conceptual distinctions. It hints at a serious threat to the validity of our most fundamental forms of logical reasoning. Philosophers disagree about its answer, on philosophical grounds that will be explored below. A philosophical account of vagueness that did not tell us how to answer the original question would thereby be incomplete. Without an agreed definition of 'philosophy', we can hardly expect to *prove* that the original question or any other is a philosophical question; but when we discuss its answer, we find ourselves invoking recognizably philosophical considerations. Before we worry about the answer, let us examine the original question itself.

The question queries just the supposition that Mars was always either dry or not dry, which we could formalize as a theorem of classical logic, $\forall t(Dmt \lor \sim Dmt)$.[8] In words: for every time t, either Mars was dry at t or Mars was not dry at t. The question is composed of expressions that are not distinctively philosophical in character: 'Mars', 'always', 'either ... or ... ', 'not', 'was', and 'dry'. All of them occur in a recognizably unphilosophical question such as 'Was Mars always either uninhabited or not dry?', which someone might ask on judging that Mars is both uninhabited and dry and wondering whether there is a connection. Although philosophical issues can be raised *about* the words in both questions, it does not follow that merely in using those words one is in any way engaging in philosophy. One difference between the two questions is that it is not obviously futile to try to argue on a priori grounds that Mars was always either dry or not dry, whereas it is obviously futile to try to argue on a priori grounds that Mars was always either uninhabited or not dry.

The original question does not itself *ask* whether it is metaphysically necessary, or knowable a priori, or analytic, or logically true that Mars was always either dry or not dry. It simply asks whether Mars always *was* either dry or not dry. Expressions such as 'metaphysically necessary', 'knowable a priori', 'analytic', and 'logically true' do not occur in the original question; one can understand it without understanding any such philosophically distinctive terms. This is of course neither to deny nor to assert that it *is* metaphysically necessary, or knowable a priori, or analytic, or logically true that Mars was always either dry or not dry. For all that has been said,

[8] Classical logic is the standard logic of expressions such as 'every', 'either ... or ... ' and 'not' on the assumption that there is a mutually exclusive, jointly exhaustive dichotomy of sentences into the true and the false.

the proposition may be any combination of those things. But that is not what the original question asks.

In other circumstances, we could have answered the original question on philosophically uninteresting grounds. For instance, if there had never been liquid on Mars, then it would always have been dry, and therefore either dry or not dry. In order to pose a question which could not possibly be answered in that boring way, someone who already grasped one of those philosophically distinctive concepts might ask whether it is metaphysically necessary, or knowable a priori, or analytic, or logically true that Mars was always either dry or not dry. The philosophically distinctive expression might then fall under various kinds of suspicion, which would extend to the question in which it occurred. But the original question itself cannot be correctly answered in the boring way with respect to the originally envisaged circumstances. Its philosophical interest, however contingent, is actual.

We could generalize the original question in various ways. We might ask whether *everything* is always either dry or not dry. Then we might notice that discussing that question is quite similar to discussing whether everything is either old or not old, and so on. We might therefore ask whether for every property everything either has that property or lacks it. Such generalizing over properties might itself fall under various kinds of suspicion, which would extend to the question in which it occurred. Someone might even doubt whether there is such a property as dryness. But the original question itself does not attempt such generality. That it has the same kind of philosophical interest as many other questions does not imply that it has no philosophical interest. If that interest is obscured by problematic features of the apparatus with which we try to generalize it, we can refrain from generalizing it, and stick with the original question.[9]

What is the question about? 'About' is not a precise term. On the most straightforward interpretation, a sentence in a context is about whatever its constituents refer to in that context. Thus, taken at face value, the original question is about the planet Mars, the referent of 'Mars' in this context; perhaps it is also about dryness, the referent of 'dry', and the referents of other constituents too. Since the original question contains no metalinguistic expressions, it is not about the name 'Mars' or the adjective 'dry'. Evidently, the original question is not explicitly about words.

Is the original question implicitly about language? Someone might claim so on the grounds that it is equivalent to questions that are explicitly about language, such as these:

Is the sentence 'Mars was always either dry or not dry' true? (Does it express a truth as used in this context?)

Did Mars always belong either to the extension of the word 'dry' or to the anti-extension of 'dry' (as the word 'dry' is used in this context)?

But parallel reasoning would lead to the conclusion that the unphilosophical question 'Was Mars always either uninhabited or not dry?' and all everyday questions are

---

[9] See also Quine, 1970: 11.

also implicitly about language. Since they are not about language in any distinctive sense, the reasoning does not show that the original question is about language in any distinctive sense. Even if the equivalences did show that the original question was in some sense implicitly about language, they could be read in both directions: they would also show that the explicitly metalinguistic questions were in an equally good sense implicitly not about language.

The equivalences between the questions are in any case only as strong as the corresponding disquotational biconditionals:

(T1)   'Mars was always either dry or not dry' is true if and only if Mars was always either dry or not dry.

(T2a) For any time t, Mars belongs to the extension of 'dry' at t if and only if Mars is dry at t.

(T2b) For any time t, Mars belongs to the anti-extension of 'dry' at t if and only if Mars is not dry at t.

On the face of it, these biconditionals express at best contingent truths. For the word 'dry' could have meant *wet*, in which case Mars would have belonged to the extension of 'dry' when wet and to the anti-extension of 'dry' when dry: for *we* use the word 'dry' to mean *dry* even when we are talking *about* circumstances in which it would have meant something else, because we are not talking *in* those circumstances. Thus T2a, and T2b do not express necessary truths. Similarly, the sentence 'Mars was always either dry or not dry' could have failed to express a truth even though Mars always either dry or not dry, since 'always' could have meant *never*. Thus T1 does not express a necessary truth. We should not assume that a useful notion of aboutness would transfer across merely contingent biconditionals. Perhaps one could interpret T1, T2a, and T2b as expressing necessary truths by individuating linguistic expressions in some non-standard manner on which their semantic properties are essential to them; it is a delicate matter. Moreover, some theorists of vagueness have denied even the actual truth of biconditionals such as T1, T2a, and T2b; they might respond to the original question in one way and to the explicitly metalinguistic questions in another. Thus the questions are not pragmatically, dialectically, or methodologically equivalent within the context of debates on vagueness. For present purposes, we need not resolve the status of the disquotational biconditionals, because we have already seen that the sense in which they make the original question implicitly about words is too indiscriminate to be useful.

We can argue more directly that the original question is not implicitly about the word 'dry' by appeal to a translation test. For consider the translation of the original question into another language, such as Serbian:

Da li je Mars uvek bio suv ili nije bio suv?

The Serbian translation is not implicitly about the English word 'dry'. But since the questions in the two languages mean the same, what they are implicitly about should also be the same. Therefore, the original question is not implicitly about the word 'dry'. By similar reasoning, it is not about any word of English or any other language. Of course, given the informality of the notion of implicit aboutness, the argument is not fully rigorous. Nevertheless, the translation test emphasizes how far one would have to water down the notion of reference in order to reach a notion of implicit aboutness on which the original question would be implicitly about a word.

The translation test does not show that the original question is not implicitly about a *concept*, something like the meaning of a word rather than the word itself, for the English word 'dry' and its Serbian synonym 'suv' both express the concept *dry*. But what basis is there for the claim that the original question is implicitly about the concept *dry*? We might argue that the original question is in some sense equivalent to a metaconceptual question:

Did Mars always belong either to the extension of the concept *dry* or to the anti-extension of *dry*?

For we might apply the notions of extension and anti-extension to concepts by means of biconditionals similar to T2a and T2b respectively:

(TC2a)   For any time t, Mars belongs to the extension of *dry* at t if and only if Mars is dry at t.

(TC2b)   For any time t, Mars belongs to the anti-extension of *dry* at t if and only if Mars is not dry at t.

TC2a and TC2b have a better chance than T2a and T2b of expressing necessary truths, for the contingent relation between words and their meanings has no straightforward analogue for concepts. Concepts are individuated semantically: rather than merely having meanings, they *are* meanings, or something like them.[10] Nevertheless, the argument that the original question is implicitly about the concept *dry* in virtue of being equivalent to the metaconceptual question wildly overgeneralizes, just like the argument that the original question is implicitly about the word 'dry' in virtue of being equivalent to the metalinguistic question. For parallel reasoning would lead to the conclusion that the unphilosophical question 'Was Mars always either uninhabited or not dry?' is implicitly about the concept *dry*, and likewise for any other unphilosophical question. Since those questions are not about concepts in any distinctive sense, the original reasoning does not show that the original question is about concepts in any distinctive sense. Even if the equivalences did show that the original question was in some sense implicitly about thought, they can be read in both directions: they would also equally show that the explicitly metaconceptual questions were in an equally good sense implicitly not about thought.

---

[10] Even if a word retains its linguistic meaning, its reference may shift with the context of utterance ('I', 'now', 'here'). If 'dry' undergoes such contextual shifts, T2a and T2b may fail when interpreted as generalizations about utterances of 'dry' in contexts other than the theorist's own. It might be argued that concepts can also undergo contextual shifts in reference: you use the concept *I* to refer (in thought) to yourself but I use the same concept to refer to myself; at noon we use the concept *now* to think of noon but at midnight we use the same concept to refer to midnight; at the North Pole we use the concept *here* to refer to the North Pole but at the South Pole we use the same concept to refer to the South Pole. If so, TC2a and TC2b may also fail when interpreted as generalizations about uses of the concept *dry* in contexts other than the theorist's own.

A Fregean might argue: the original question is *explicitly* about the concept *dry*, because it contains the predicate '. . . is dry' (in the past tense), which refers to the concept *dry*. In that sense, the question 'Was Mars always either uninhabited or not dry?' would also be explicitly about the concept *dry*. However, the Fregean is not using the word 'concept' with its contemporary meaning, on which concepts are mental or semantic representations, in the realm of sense rather than reference. The Fregean referent of a predicate (a Fregean concept) is simply the function that maps everything to which the predicate applies to the true and everything else to the false: it could be treated as the extension of the predicate, except that it is a function rather than an object. If the predicate refers to the property of dryness or to the set of dry things, then the original question is about the property of dryness or the set of dry things, but that has no tendency to show that it is about thought. Similarly, the Fregean claim has no tendency to show that the question is about thought, for the Fregean concept is in the realm of reference, not in the realm of thought. Like the property and the set, it is no representation but that which is represented.

Representations do not always represent representations. To judge by its overt compositional structure, the original question in particular does not represent any representations. It is not a metalinguistic or metaconceptual question. We have encountered no reason to regard its overt structure as at all misleading in that respect. Our provisional conclusion must therefore be that the original question, although at least proto-philosophical, is not about thought or language in any distinctive sense. It does not support the representational turn.

3. If the original question, read literally, had too obvious an answer, either positive or negative, that would give us reason to suspect that someone who uttered it had some other meaning in mind, to which the overt compositional structure of the question might be a poor guide. But competent speakers of English may find themselves quite unsure how to answer the question, so we have no such reason for interpreting it non-literally.

The most straightforward reason for answering the original question positively is that 'Mars was always either dry or not dry' is a logical truth, a generalization over instances of the law of excluded middle ($P \lor \sim P$, 'It is either so or not so') for various times. In my view, that reasoning is sound. However, many think otherwise. They deny the validity of excluded middle for vague terms such as 'dry'.

The simplest way of opposing the law of excluded middle is to deny outright when Mars is a borderline case that it is either dry or not dry, and therefore to answer the original question in the negative. For instance, someone may hold that Mars was either dry or not dry at time t only if one can know (perhaps later) whether it was dry at t, given optimal conditions for answering the question (and no difference in the history of Mars): since one cannot know, even under such conditions, whether it was dry when the case was borderline, it is not either dry or not dry. One difficulty for this negative response to the original question is that it seems to imply that in a borderline case Mars is neither dry nor not dry: in other words, both not dry and not not dry. That is a contradiction, for 'not not dry' is the negation of 'not dry'.

Intuitionistic logic provides a subtler way to reject the law of excluded middle without denying any one of its instances. Intuitionists ground logic in states of increasing but incomplete information, rather than a once-for-all dichotomy of truth and falsity; they deny that anything can be both proved and refuted, but they do not assert that everything can be either proved or refuted. For intuitionists, the denial of an instance of excluded middle ($\sim(P \lor \sim P)$, 'It is not either so or not so') entails a contradiction ($\sim P \ \& \sim \sim P$, 'It is both not so and not not so'), just as it does in classical logic, and contradictions are as bad for them as for anyone else. Thus they cannot assert that Mars was once not either dry or not dry ($\exists t \sim (Dmt \lor \sim Dmt)$), for that would imply that a contradiction once obtained ($\exists t(\sim Dmt \ \& \sim \sim Dmt)$), 'Mars was once both not dry and not not dry'), which is intuitionistically inconsistent. However, although intuitionists insist that proving an existential claim in principle involves proving at least one instance of it, they allow that disproving a universal claim need not in principle involve disproving at least one instance of it. The claim that something lacks a property is intuitionistically stronger than the claim that not everything has that property. Thus one might assert that Mars was not always either dry or not dry ($\sim \forall t(Dmt \lor \sim Dmt)$), on the general grounds that there is no adequate procedure for sorting all the times into the two categories, without thereby committing oneself to the inconsistent existential assertion that it was once not either dry or not dry. Hilary Putnam once proposed the application of intuitionistic logic to the problem of vagueness for closely related reasons.[11] Thus one might use intuitionistic logic to answer the original question in the negative.

On closer inspection, this strategy looks less promising. For a paradigm borderline case is the worst case for the law of excluded middle with respect to a term such as 'dry' for which threats to the law other than from vagueness are not relevant, in the sense that both proponents and opponents of the law can agree that it holds in a paradigm borderline case only if it holds universally. In symbols, if τ is a time when Mars was a paradigm borderline case, then we have $(Dm\tau \lor \sim Dm\tau) \rightarrow \forall t(Dmt \lor \sim Dmt)$ ('If Mars was either dry or not dry at time τ, then Mars was always either dry or not dry'). But on this approach the law does not hold always hold in this case ($\sim \forall t(Dmt \lor \sim Dmt)$, 'Mars was not always either dry or not dry'), from which intuitionistic logic allows us to deduce that it does not hold in the paradigm borderline case ($\sim (Dm\tau \lor \sim Dm\tau)$, 'Mars was not either dry or not dry at τ'), which is a denial of a particular instance of the law, and therefore intuitionistically inconsistent (it entails $\sim Dm\tau \ \& \sim \sim Dm\tau$, 'Mars was both not dry and not not dry at τ'). Thus the intuitionistic approach forces one to deny that there are such paradigm borderline cases for vague terms. That denial is hard to reconcile with experience: after all, the notion of a borderline case is usually explained by examples.

The problems for the intuitionistic approach do not end there. One can show that the denial of the conjunction of any finite number of instances of the law of

---

[11] For intuitionist logic in general see Dummett, 1977. For its application to the problem of vagueness see Putnam, 1983 and, for discussion, Williamson, 1996; Chambers, 1998, and references therein.

excluded middle is intuitionistically inconsistent.[12] A universal generalization of the law over a finite domain is therefore intuitionistically false too. If time is infinitely divisible, the formula $\forall t(Dmt \lor \sim Dmt)$ generalizes the law over an infinite domain of moments of time, but that is not crucial to the phenomena of vagueness. We could just as well have asked the original question about a long finite series of moments at one-second intervals; it would have been equally problematic. The classical sorites paradox depends on just such a finite series: a heap of sand consists of only finitely many grains, but when they are carefully removed one by one, we have no idea how to answer the question 'When did there cease to be a heap?' It is intuitionistically inconsistent to deny that Mars was dry or not dry at each of those moments. Thus intuitionistic logic provides a poor basis for a negative answer to the original question.

Other theorists of vagueness refuse to answer the original question either positively or negatively. They refuse to assert that Mars was always either dry or not dry; they also refuse to assert that it was not always either dry or not dry.

A simple version of this approach classifies vague sentences (relative to contexts) as definitely true (T), definitely false (F), or indefinite (I); borderline sentences are classified as indefinite. The generalized truth-tables of a three-valued logic are used to calculate which of these values to assign to a complex sentence in terms of the values assigned to its constituent sentences. The negation of P, $\sim P$, is definitely true if P is definitely false, definitely false if P is definitely true and indefinite if P is indefinite:

P	$\sim P$
T	F
I	I
F	T

A conjunction $P \,\&\, Q$ ('P and Q') is definitely true if every conjunct is definitely true; it is definitely false if some conjunct is definitely false; otherwise it is indefinite. A disjunction $P \lor Q$ ('Either P or Q') is definitely true if some disjunct is definitely true; it is definitely false if every disjunct is definitely false; otherwise it is indefinite:

P	Q	$P \,\&\, Q$	$P \lor Q$
T	T	T	T
T	I	I	T
T	F	F	T
I	T	I	T
I	I	I	I
I	F	F	I
F	T	F	T
F	I	F	I
F	F	F	F

---

[12] One proves by mathematical induction on n that if A_n is the conjunction of n instances of excluded middle then $\sim A_n$ is intuitionistically inconsistent.

A universal generalization is treated like the conjunction of its instances: it is definitely true if every instance is definitely true; it is definitely false if some instance is definitely false; otherwise it is indefinite. An existential generalization is treated like the disjunction of its instances: it is definitely true if some instance is definitely true; it is definitely false if every instance is definitely false; otherwise it is indefinite. The three-valued tables generalize the familiar two-valued ones in the sense that one recovers the latter by reading 'T' as 'true', 'F' as 'false', and ignoring lines with 'I'.

Let us apply this three-valued approach to the original question. If Mars is definitely dry or definitely not dry at t, then Dmt is definitely true or definitely false, so the instance of excluded middle $Dmt \lor \sim Dmt$ is definitely true. But if Mars is neither definitely dry nor definitely not dry at t, then Dmt is indefinite, so $\sim Dmt$ is indefinite too by the table for negation, so $Dmt \lor \sim Dmt$ is classified as indefinite by the table for disjunction. Since Mars was once a borderline case, the universal generalization $\forall t(Dmt \lor \sim Dmt)$ has a mixture of definitely true and indefinite instances; hence it is classified as indefinite. Therefore its negation $\sim \forall t(Dmt \lor \sim Dmt)$ is also indefinite. Thus three-valued theoreticians who wish to assert only definite truths neither assert $\forall t(Dmt \lor \sim Dmt)$ nor assert $\sim \forall t(Dmt \lor \sim Dmt)$. They answer the original question neither positively nor negatively.

Three-valued logic replaces the classical dichotomy of truth and falsity by a three-way classification. Fuzzy logic goes further, replacing it by a continuum of degrees of truth between definite truth and definite falsity. According to proponents of fuzzy logic, vagueness should be understood in terms of this continuum of degrees of truth. For example, 'It is dark' may increase continuously in degree of truth as it gradually becomes dark. On the simplest version of the approach, degrees of truth are identified with real numbers in the interval from 0 to 1, with 1 as definite truth and 0 as definite falsity. The semantics of fuzzy logic provides rules for calculating the degree of truth of a complex sentence in terms of the degrees of truth of its constituent sentences. For example, the degrees of truth of a sentence and of its negation sum to exactly 1; the degree of truth of a disjunction is the maximum of the degrees of truth of its disjuncts; the degree of truth of a conjunction is the minimum of the degrees of truth of its conjuncts. For fuzzy logic, although the three-valued tables above are too coarse-grained to give complete information, they still give correct results if one classifies every sentence with an intermediate degree of truth, less than the maximum and more than the minimum, as indefinite.[13] Thus the same reasoning as before shows that fuzzy logicians should answer the original question neither positively nor negatively.

---

[13] This point does not generalize to the semantics of conditionals in fuzzy logic, given the standard rule that if the consequent is lower than the antecedent in degree of truth then the degree of truth of the conditional falls short of 1 by the amount by which the consequent falls short of the antecedent in degree of truth; otherwise the degree of truth of the conditional is 1. Thus if P has a higher degree of truth than Q but both are indefinite then $P \to Q$ is indefinite while $Q \to P$ is definitely true. Thus the information that the antecedent and consequent are indefinite does not determine whether the conditional is indefinite.

Although three-valued and fuzzy logicians reject both the answer 'Yes' and the answer 'No' to the original question, they do not reject the question itself. What they reject is the restriction of possible answers to 'Yes' and 'No'. They require a third answer, 'Indefinite', when the queried sentence takes the value I. More formally, consider the three-valued table for the sentence operator Δ, read as 'definitely' or 'it is definite that':

P	ΔP
T	T
I	F
F	F

Even for fuzzy logicians this table constitutes a complete semantics for Δ, since the only output values are T and F, which determine unique degrees of truth (1 and 0). A formula of the form $\sim\Delta P$ & $\sim\Delta\sim P$ ('It is neither definitely so nor definitely not so') characterizes a borderline case, for it is definitely true if P is indefinite and definitely false otherwise. In response to the question P?, answering 'Yes' is tantamount to asserting P, answering 'No' is tantamount to asserting $\sim P$, and answering 'Indefinite' is tantamount to asserting $\sim\Delta P$ & $\sim\Delta\sim P$. On the three-valued and fuzzy tables, exactly one of these three answers is correct (definitely true) in any given case; in particular, the correct answer to the original question is 'Indefinite'.

On the three-valued and fuzzy approaches, to answer 'Indefinite' to the question 'Is Mars dry?' is to say something about Mars, just as it is if one answers 'Yes' or 'No'. It is not a metalinguistic response. For Δ is no more a metalinguistic operator than $\sim$ is. They have the same kind of semantics, given by a many-valued truth-table. Just as the negation $\sim P$ is about whatever P is about, so are ΔP and $\sim\Delta P$ & $\sim\Delta\sim P$. Thus the answer 'Indefinite' to the original question involves no semantic ascent to a metalinguistic, metaconceptual, or metarepresentational level. It remains at the level of discourse about Mars.

The three-valued and fuzzy approaches have many suspect features. For instance, they treat any sentence of the form ΔP as perfectly precise, because it always counts as definitely true or definitely false, never as indefinite, whatever the status of P; thus $\Delta\Delta P \bigvee \Delta\sim\Delta P$ ('It is definite whether it is definitely so') is always definitely true. This result does not fit the intended interpretation of Δ. For 'Mars is definitely wet' is not perfectly precise. Just as no moment is clearly the last on which Mars was wet or the first on which it was not, so no moment is clearly the last on which it was definitely wet or the first on which it was not definitely wet. Just as it was sometimes unclear whether Mars is wet, so it was sometimes unclear whether it was definitely wet. This is one form of the notorious problem of higher-order vagueness: in other words, there are borderline cases of borderline cases, and borderline cases of borderline cases of borderline cases, and so on. The problem has never received an adequate treatment within the framework of three-valued or fuzzy logic, and it is far from obvious that it could.[14]

---

[14] See Williamson 1999b for an analysis of higher-order vagueness.

Some philosophers, often under the influence of the later Wittgenstein, deny the relevance of formal semantic theories to vague natural languages. They regard the attempt to give a systematic statement of the truth-conditions of English sentences in terms of the meanings of their constituents as vain. For them, the formalization of 'Mars was always either dry or not dry' as $\forall t(Dmt \vee \sim Dmt)$ is already suspect. This attitude suggests a premature and slightly facile pessimism. No doubt formal semantics has not described any natural language with perfect accuracy; what has not been shown is that it provides no deep insights into natural languages. In particular, it has not been shown that the main semantic effects of vagueness are not susceptible to systematic formal analysis. In any case, for present purposes the claim that there can be no systematic theory of vagueness is just one more theory of vagueness, although—unless it is self-refuting—not a systematic one; it does not even answer the original question. Even if that theory were true, the other theories of vagueness, however false, would still exist, and would still have been accepted by some intelligent and linguistically competent speakers.

This is no place to resolve the debate between opposing theories of vagueness. The present point is just that different theories support contrary answers to the original question. All these theories have their believers. Any answer to the original question, positive, negative or indefinite, is contentious. Of course, if everyone found their own answer obvious, but different people found different answers obvious, then we might suspect that they were interpreting the question in different ways, talking past each other. But that is not so: almost everyone who reflects on the original question finds it difficult and puzzling. Even when one has settled on an answer, one can see how intelligent and reasonable people could answer differently while understanding the meaning of the question in the same way. If it has an *obvious* answer, it is the answer 'Yes' dictated by classical logic, but those of us who accept that answer can usually imagine or remember the frame of mind in which one is led to doubt it. Thus the original question, read literally, has no obvious answer in any sense that would give us reason to suspect that someone who uttered it had some other reading in mind.

Without recourse to non-literal readings, some theorists postulate ambiguity in the original question. For example, some three-valued logicians claim that 'not' in English is ambiguous between the operators $\sim$ (strong negation) and $\sim\!\Delta$ (weak negation): although $\sim P$ and $\sim\!\Delta P$ have the same value if P is definitely true or definitely false, $\sim\!\Delta P$ is true while $\sim P$ is indefinite if P is indefinite. While $P \vee \sim P$ ('It is so or not so') can be indefinite, $P \vee \sim\!\Delta P$ ('It is so or not definitely so') is always definitely true. On this view, the original question queries $\forall t(Dmt \vee \sim Dmt)$ on one reading, $\forall t(Dmt \vee \sim\!\Delta Dmt)$ on another; the latter is definitely true (Mars was always either dry or not definitely dry) while the former is indefinite. Thus the correct answer to the original question depends on the reading of 'not'. It is 'Indefinite' if 'not' is read as strong negation, 'Yes' if 'not' is read as weak negation. The three-valued logician's reasoning here is undermined by higher-order vagueness, but that is not the present issue.

If 'not' were ambiguous in the way indicated, it would still not follow that the dispute over the original question is merely verbal. For even when we agree to consider it under the reading of 'not' as strong negation, which does not factorize in the manner of ~Δ, we yet find theories of vagueness in dispute over the correct answer. We have merely explained our terms in order to formulate more clearly a difficult question about Mars.

Still, it might be suggested, the dispute between different theories of vagueness is verbal in the sense that their rival semantics characterize different possible languages or conceptual schemes: our choice of which of them to speak or think would be pragmatic, based on considerations of usefulness rather than of truth.

To make sense of the pragmatic view, one must suppose that vague atomic senten-ces are classifiable according to both the bivalent scheme (as true or false) and the trivalent scheme (as definitely true, indefinite, or definitely false), and that the truth-tables of each scheme define intelligible connectives, although the connective defined by a trivalent table should be distinguished from the similar-looking connec-tive defined by the corresponding bivalent table. Definite truth implies truth, and def-inite falsity implies falsity, but indefiniteness does not discriminate between truth and falsity: although all borderline atomic sentences are indefinite, some are true and oth-ers false. As Mars dries, 'Mars is dry' is first false and definitely false, then false but indefinite, then true but indefinite, and finally true and definitely true. However, this attempted reconciliation of the contrasting theories does justice to neither side. For trivalent logicians, once we know that a sentence is indefinite, there is no further question of its truth or falsity to which we do not know the answer: the category of the indefinite was introduced in order not to postulate such a mystery. Similarly, for fuzzy logicians, once we know the intermediate degree of truth of a sentence, there is no further question of its truth or falsity to which we do not know the answer: intermediate degrees of truth were introduced in order not to postulate such a mys-tery. In formal terms, trivalent and fuzzy logics are undoubtedly less convenient than bivalent logic: the justification for introducing them was supposed to be the inapplic-ability of the bivalent scheme to vague sentences. If a bivalent vague language is even a possible option, then the trivalent and fuzzy accounts of vagueness are mis-taken. Conversely, from a bivalent perspective, the trivalent and fuzzy semantics do not fix possible meanings for the connectives, because they do not determine truth-conditions for the resultant complex sentences: for example, the trivalent table for ~ does not specify when ~P is true in the bivalent sense. It would therefore be a fundamental misunderstanding of the issue at stake between theories of vagueness to conceive it as one of a pragmatic choice of language.

We already speak the language of the original question; we understand those words and how they are put together; we possess the concepts that they express; we grasp what is being asked. That semantic knowledge may be necessary if we are to know the answer to the original question.[15] It is not sufficient, for it does not by itself

---

[15] Of course, monolingual speakers of another language might know whether Mars was always dry or not dry without ever hearing of the original question, which is an interrogative sentence of English; they use a synonymous sentence of their own language. They do not know whether the original English question has a positive answer. Someone might even have that knowledge without understanding the original question, because the knowledge can be passed along a chain of testimony; understanding of the original question is needed only at one end of the chain. These quibbles do not affect the argument.

put one in a position to arbitrate between conflicting theories of vagueness. For each of those theories has been endorsed by some competent speakers of English who fully grasp the question.

Competent speakers may of course fail to reflect adequately on their competence. Although the proponents of conflicting theories of vagueness presumably have reflected on their competence, their reflections may have contained mistakes. Perhaps reflection of sufficient length and depth on one's competence would lead one to the correct answer to the original question. But the capacity for such more or less philosophical reflection is not a precondition of semantic competence. Philosophers should resist the professional temptation to require all speakers to share their proclivities.

We can distinguish two levels of reflection, the logical and the metalogical. In response to the original question, logical reflection would involve reasoning with terms of the kind in which the question is phrased; the aim is to reach a conclusion that answers the question. For example, one might conclude by classical logic that Mars was always either dry or not dry; one might conclude by fuzzy logic that it is indefinite whether it was always one or the other. The logical level is not purely mechanical. When the reasoning is complex, one needs skill to select from the many permissible applications of the rules one sequence that leads to an answer to the question. When the reasoning is informal, one needs good judgement to select only moves that really are permissible applications of the rules. But one is still thinking about whatever the question was about. It is at the metalogical level of reflection that one starts to think about the semantics of the logical connectives and other expressions that one employed at the logical level. For example, at the metalogical level one may assert or deny that the sentence 'Mars was always either dry or not dry' is a logical truth. Only at the metalogical level can one be expected to articulate the rules that one was using at the previous level.

It must be possible to think logically without thinking metalogically, for otherwise by the same principle thinking metalogically would involve thinking metametalogically, and so *ad infinitum*: our thinking never goes all the way up such an infinite hierarchy. What can prompt ascent to the metalogical level are hard cases in which one feels unclear about the permissibility of a given move at the logical level. One's mastery of the language and possession of concepts leave one quite uncertain how to go on. In the case of the original question, a salient line of classical reasoning leads to a positive answer: it persuades some competent speakers while leaving others unconvinced. Even to discuss the contentious reasoning we must semantically ascend. We cannot hope to resolve the dispute undogmatically if we never leave the lower level.

4. The argument so far has reached two conclusions that at first sight are hard to reconcile with each other. First, the original question is not about thought or language. Second, to answer it adequately one must assess rival theories of vagueness in thought and language. How can that way of reaching an answer be appropriate to the original question? We might therefore find ourselves tempted back to the idea that somehow the original question was surreptitiously about thought or language.

On further reflection, the apparent conflict between the two conclusions is less surprising. Many non-philosophical questions that are not about thought or language cannot be resolved without inquiry into thought or language.

Suppose that a court of law must decide whether Smith killed Jones. The question is not who said or thought what. Nevertheless, the crucial arguments may be over whether to trust the witnesses' testimony. How is what they say now related to what they think now or thought then? How is what they think now or thought then related to what actually happened? Are they lying or sincere? Are their memories confused or clear? Those are questions about their thought and speech, their representations. They hold the key to whether Smith killed Jones, even though that question is not about representations. Of course, the questions about representations are not about them in isolation from what they represent: they are relevant because they concern the relation between the representations and what they represent.

The court must decide the issue on the evidence before it. In a criminal case, does the evidence put it beyond reasonable doubt that Smith killed Jones? In a civil case, does the evidence make it more probable than not? If the court is really deciding a question about testimonial evidence, is that not already a question about representations?[16] But the question about the evidence arises in virtue of its bearing on the primary question, whether Smith killed Jones. Indeed, the question about the evidence is exactly a question about its bearing on the primary question. So the point stands.

Historians are often in a similar position. They want to know what happened. The way to achieve that is largely by considering documents, representations of what happened—not in isolation, but in relation to what they represent. Most obviously, the historian wants to know whether the documents accurately represent what happened, but to answer that question one must in turn ask about their provenance: who produced them, when and why? Thus the history of the events of primary interest requires a history of representations of those events. Those histories typically overlap, for the production of a representation of some part of a complex human event is often another part of the same complex event.

Something analogous occurs in the methodology of the natural sciences. We wish to know the value of some physical quantity. We must devise apparatus to measure it. We may find ourselves in disputes over the functioning of different devices. Although the primary question was not about those measuring devices, we cannot answer it adequately without considering them. We need a theory about the relation between the value of the quantity and the representations of it that we record when we use our instruments. The scientific investigation of the physical quantity widens to include the scientific investigation of its interaction with our experimental equipment. After all, our apparatus is part of the same natural world as the primary topic of our enquiry.

---

[16] Non-testimonial evidence may be taken to include non-representational items such as a bloodied knife; this is what lawyers call 'real evidence'. For an argument that all evidence in an epistemologically central sense of the term is propositional see Williamson, 2000: 194–200. For example, the evidence in this sense might include the proposition that the bloodied knife was found at the scene of the crime, but not the knife itself.

These analogies make it less surprising that when we try to answer the original question, which is not a question about thought or language, our main task is to adjudicate between rival theories of vague thought and language. A theory of vagueness validates some deduction that concludes with an answer to the original question. That deduction uses but does not mention vague thought or language. It is formulated at the logical level, like the original question itself, not at the meta-logical level. But to justify trusting that deduction, rather than one that reaches another conclusion by other rules, one must assess the rival theories of vagueness.

That theories of vagueness conflict in their answers to the original question shows that they are not confined to claims about thought and talk. Theories such as epistemicism and supervaluationism which employ classical logic have 'Mars was always either dry or not dry' as a theorem, once they are formulated in a suitably expressive language. To reiterate, that theorem is not about thought or talk.

For three-valued and fuzzy approaches, the matter is only slightly more complicated. Their proponents assert:

(C)   It is indefinite whether Mars was always either dry or not dry.

On those approaches, C does not count as about thought or language. Strictly speaking, however, C does not follow from the three-valued or fuzzy theory of vagueness itself; for all the theory implies, there was never any liquid on Mars, in which case it would always have been either dry or not dry, even by three-valued or fuzzy standards, and it would not have been indefinite. The theory implies only a conditional theorem:

(P1)   If it was once indefinite whether Mars was dry then it is indefinite whether Mars was always either dry or not dry.

Three-valued or fuzzy theorists can combine P1 with what they regard as an empirical truth about Mars:

(P2)   It was once indefinite whether Mars was dry.

From P1 and P2 they use the rule of modus ponens (from 'If P then Q' and 'P' infer 'Q') to infer C, the answer to the original question. Although their theorem P1 does not answer the question by itself, it is no more about thought or language than C is. Their theories are just as committed as classical ones to making claims that are not about thought or language.

In order to give an adequately reflective answer to a simple, non-technical, non-metarepresentational question, we were forced to adjudicate between complex, technical, metarepresentational theories. This phenomenon seems to have been overlooked by those who complain about the 'arid' technical minuteness of much philosophy in the analytic tradition. A question may be easy to ask but hard to answer. Even if it is posed in dramatic and accessible terms, that does not entail that the reflections needed to select between rival answers are equally dramatic and accessible. Such contrasts are commonplace in other disciplines; it would have been amazing if they had not occurred in philosophy. Impatience with the long haul of technical reflection is a form of shallowness, often thinly disguised by histrionic advocacy of depth. Serious philosophy is always likely to bore those with short attention-spans.[17]

The rise of modern logic from Frege onwards has provided philosophers with conceptual instruments of unprecedented power and precision, enabling them to formulate hypotheses with more clarity and to determine their consequences with more reliability than ever before. Russell's theory of descriptions showed vividly how differences between the surface form of a sentence and its underlying logical form might mislead us as to its logical relations and thereby create philosophical illusions. The development of formal model-theoretic truth-conditional semantics by Tarski and others has provided a rigorous framework for thinking about the validity of our inferences. These theoretical advances have enormous intellectual interest in their own right. They may have made it tempting to suppose that all philosophical problems are problems of language: but they do not really provide serious evidence for that conjecture.

Many have been attracted to the idea that all philosophical problems are linguistic or conceptual for deeper philosophical reasons, which I can barely touch on here. For instance, if the method of philosophy is a priori reflection, how can it lead to substantive knowledge of the world? Those who find that question compelling may propose that it informs us of relations of ideas rather than matters of fact, or that its truths are analytic rather than synthetic, or that it presents rules of grammar disguised as descriptions, or that its aim is the analysis of thought or language. We have noted how poorly these claims fit the case of vagueness. We may suspect the presence of empiricist presuppositions in the background—or, as with Ayer, in the foreground. Not starting with such presuppositions, we should be open to the idea that thinking just as much as perceiving is a way of learning how things are. Although we do not fully understand *how* thinking can provide new knowledge, the cases of logic and mathematics constitute overwhelming evidence that it does so. The case of the original question, which is philosophical yet queries a theorem of classical logic, shows that we cannot segregate logic from philosophy and claim that a priori thinking illuminates the former but not the latter. In particular, conceptions of logic and mathematics as (unlike philosophy) somehow trivial or purely formal have not been vindicated by any clear account of 'trivial' or 'purely formal'. Whether a given formal system of logic or mathematics is consistent is itself a non-trivial question of logic or mathematics; we know from Gödel's second incompleteness theorem that the consistency of a system of elementary mathematics can only be decided in less elementary mathematics, unless the original system was inconsistent.

To deny that all philosophical questions are about thought or language is not to deny the obvious, that many are. We have also seen how in practice the attempt to answer a question which is not about thought or language can largely consist in thinking about thought and language. Some contemporary metaphysicians appear to believe that they can safely ignore formal semantics and the philosophy of language because their interest is in a largely extra-mental reality. They resemble an astronomer who thinks that he can safely ignore the physics of telescopes because

---

[17] Popularization has its place, in philosophy as in physics, but should not be confused with the primary activity.

his interest is in the extra-terrestrial universe. In delicate matters, his attitude makes him all the more likely to project features of his telescope confusedly onto the stars beyond. Similarly, the metaphysicians who most disdain language are the most likely to be its victims. Again, those who neglect logic in order to deduce their philosophy from natural science make frequent logical errors in their deductions; their philosophical conclusions are not logical consequences of their scientific premises.

Analytic philosophy at its best uses logical rigour and semantic sophistication to achieve a sharpness of philosophical vision unobtainable by other means. To sacrifice those gains would be to choose blurred vision. Fortunately, good vision is not restricted to looking at eyes.[18]

Bibliography

Ayer, A. J. 1936. *Language, Truth and Logic* (London: Victor Gollancz).

Chambers, T. 1998. 'On vagueness, *sorites*, and Putnam's "intuitionistic strategy" ' *Monist* 81: 343–8.

Davidson, D. 1990. 'The structure and content of truth' *Journal of Philosophy*: 278–328.

Dummett, M. A. E. 1977. *Elements of Intuitionism* (Oxford: Oxford University Press).

—— 1978. *Truth and Other Enigmas* (London: Duckworth).

—— 1993. *Origins of Analytical Philosophy* (London: Duckworth).

Fine, K. 1994. 'Essence and modality', in J. Tomberlin (ed.), *Philosophical Perspectives, 8, Logic and Language* (Atascadero, Calif.: Ridgeview).

—— 1995. 'Senses of essence', in W. Sinnott-Armstrong, D. Raffman, and N. Asher (eds.), *Modality, Morality, and Belief: Essays in Honor of Ruth Barcan Marcus* (Cambridge: Cambridge University Press).

Fodor, J. 1975. *The Language of Thought* (New York: Thomas Y. Crowell).

French, P. A., Uehling, T. E., and Wettstein, H. K. (eds.) 1986. *Midwest Studies in Philosophy XI: Studies in Essentialism* (Minneapolis: University of Minnesota Press).

Johnston, M. 1993. 'Objectivity refigured: pragmatism without verificationism', in J. Haldane and C. Wright (eds.), *Reality, Representation and Projection* (Oxford: Oxford University Press).

Keefe, R., and Smith, P. (eds.) 1997. *Vagueness: A Reader* (Cambridge, Mass.: MIT Press).

Kripke, S. A. 1980. *Naming and Necessity* (Oxford: Blackwell).

McDowell, J. H. 1994. *Mind and World* (Cambridge, Mass.: Harvard University Press).

Putnam, H. 1983. 'Vagueness and alternative logic', *Erkenntnis* 19: 297–314.

Quine, W. V. 1970. *Philosophy of Logic* (Englewood Cliffs, N. J.: Prentice-Hall).

Rorty, R. (ed.) 1967. *The Linguistic Turn: Recent Essays in Philosophical Method* (Chicago: University of Chicago Press).

Strawson, P. F. 1959. *Individuals: An Essay in Descriptive Metaphysics* (London: Methuen).

Wiggins, D. R. P. 2001. *Sameness and Substance Renewed* (Cambridge: Cambridge University Press).

Williamson, T. 1994. *Vagueness* (London: Routledge).

—— 1996. 'Putnam on the sorites paradox', *Philosophical Papers* 25: 47–56.

—— 1999a. 'Truthmakers and the converse Barcan formula', *Dialectica* 53: 253–70.

—— 1999b. 'On the structure of higher-order vagueness', *Mind* 108: 127–43.

—— 2003. 'Vagueness in reality', in M. Loux and D. Zimmerman (eds.), *The Oxford Handbook of Metaphysics* (Oxford: Oxford University Press).

[18] Thanks to Brian Leiter and discussion groups at Oxford University and the University of Texas at Austin for comments on earlier versions of this paper.

5

The Mind–Body Problem at Century's Turn

JAEGWON KIM

Through much of the twentieth century, especially during its second half, debates over the mind–body problem were shaped by physicalism, a philosophical world-view that has been inspired and fostered by an appreciation of the foundational posi-tion of physics among the sciences. The core of contemporary physicalism is the thesis that all things that exist in this world are bits of matter and structures aggreg-ated out of bits of matter, all behaving in accordance with laws of physics. This metaphysical thesis has a companion epistemological thesis, the claim that all phe-nomena of the world can be physically explained if they can be explained at all. When physicalism is accepted as a basic framework, the foremost metaphysical problem about the mind is where in the physical world our minds fit—in fact, whether minds have a place in such an austerely physical world at all. In this paper, I want to review the current state of the mind–body debate to see where we are now and how we got there, with particular attention to the question to what extent the hopes and promises of physicalism have been, or are likely to be, realized—that is, how much, and what kind of, physicalism we can, after fifty years of debate, reas-onably expect to have. This will not be a survey of the current scene in the mind–body debate; nor will I be offering a historical narrative of how we got where we are; it will be more like a "rational reconstruction", a story of how one could get there, "rationally" and "logically" (more or less), starting from a blank page on the mind–body problem. As we will see, the physicalist program does not succeed entirely, but it succeeds *nearly enough*—or so I will claim. Finally, I will discuss where the mind–body debate appears headed—or rather where I think it *ought* to be headed—as we look ahead at the dawn of a new century.

Cartesian Minds Eliminated

Let us begin with physicalism as an ontological thesis, the claim that the content of the world is wholly exhausted by matter. Material things are all the things that there are; there is nothing inside the spacetime world that isn't material, and there is noth-ing outside it either. The spacetime world is the whole world, and material things, bits of matter and complex structures made up of bits of matter, are the only inhab-itants of this world. This is the so-called "ontological physicalism".

But why should we accept ontological physicalism? Why can't there be things other than material things? Here we will focus on Cartesian ontological dualism, a leading antiphysicalist alternative, according to which there are two sorts of things in this world, material things in physical space and immaterial minds, or souls, outside space. I believe we can mount a persuasive argument against immaterial things, like Cartesian minds conceived as immaterial substances outside physical space; we can show that if there were such things, they would serve no useful purpose. More specifically, we will argue that not only could immaterial minds not causally inter-act with material things situated in space, a difficulty noted by some of Descartes's contemporary critics, but also that they could not causally interact with anything else, including other immaterial minds. Immaterial objects would be causally impo-tent and hence explanatorily useless; positing them would be entirely pointless.

Here is the argument.[1] To set up an analogy and a point of reference, let us begin with an example of physical causation. A rifle, call it A, is fired and this causes the death of a person, A^*. Another rifle, B, is fired at the same time (say, in A's vicinity—but this is unimportant), and this results in the death of another person, B^*. What makes it the case that the firing of A caused A^*'s death and the firing of B caused B^*'s death, and not the other way around—that is, A's firing causing B^*'s death and B's firing causing A^*'s death? What principle governs the "pairing" of the right cause with the right effect? There must be a relation R that grounds and explains the cause–effect pairings, a relation that holds between A's firing and A^*'s death and also between B's firing and B^*'s death, but not between A's firing and B^*'s death or between B's firing and A^*'s death. What is this R, the "pairing relation" as we might call it? We are not necessarily supposing at this point that there is a single such R for all cases of physical causation, only that some relation must ground the fact that a given cause is a cause of the particular effect that is caused by it.

For the present example, two ideas naturally come to mind. The first is the idea of a *causal chain*: there is a continuous causal chain between A's firing and A^*'s death, as there is between B's firing and B^*'s death, whereas no such chains exist between A's firing and B^*'s death or between B's firing and A^*'s death. In fact, with a high-speed motion picture camera, we could trace the bullet's movement from each rifle to its impact point on the target. The second idea is that each rifle when it fired was at a certain distance and in appropriate orientation in relation to the person it kills, but not to the person it does not kill. That is, *spatial relations* do the job of pairing causes with their effects.

A moment of reflection shows that the first idea will not work as an independent solution to the problem. A causal chain after all is a chain of causal relations, and inter-polating more cause–effect pairs will not solve the pairing problem. For obviously it begs the question: we would need to explain what pairing relations ground these inter-polated causal–effect pairs. Interpolating intermediate causal links only multiplies the problem. It seems to me that spatial relations, and more broadly spatiotemporal

[1] Here I will give only a brief sketch of the argument; for a fuller discussion see my "Lonely Souls: Substance Dualism and Causality", in *Soul, Body, and Survival*, ed. Kevin Corcoran (Ithaca, N.Y.: Cornell University Press, 2001). I first discussed the pairing problem in "Causation, Nomic Subsumption, and the Concept of Event", *Journal of Philosophy* 70 (1973): 217–36. My discussion was prompted by John Foster's "Psychophysical Causal Relations", *American Philosophical Quarterly* 1 (1968). Haskell Fain discusses a similar problem in "Some Problems of Causal Explanation", *Mind*, 72 (1963): 519–32.

relations, are the only possible way of generating pairing relations. Intuitively, space seems to have nice causal properties; for example, as the distance increases, causal influence diminishes, and it is often possible to set up barriers, at intermediate positions, to block or impede the propagation of causal influence. In any case, I can state my fundamental assumption in more general terms, and it is this: it is metaphysically possible for there to be two distinct physical objects, or events, a and b, with the same intrinsic properties and hence the same causal potential or powers; one of these, say a, causes a third object, c, to change in a certain way but object b has no causal influence on c. Now, the fact that a, but not b, causes c to change must be grounded in some fact about a, b, and c. Since a and b have the same intrinsic properties, it must be their relational properties with respect to c that provide the desired explanation of the different causal roles played by them. What relational properties or relations can do this job? It is plausible to think that it is the spatial relation between a and c, and that between b and c, that are responsible for the causal difference between a and b vis-à-vis c (a was in the right spatial relation to c; b was "too far away" from c to exert any influence on it). At least, there seems no other obvious candidate that comes to mind. Later I will give an explanation of what it is about spatial relations that enables them to do the job.

Now consider the possibility of immaterial souls, outside physical space, causally interacting with material objects in space. The following again should be a metaphysically possible situation: Two souls that have the same intrinsic properties[2] act in a certain way at the same time, and as a result a certain material object undergoes a change. Moreover, it is the action of one of the souls, not that of the other, that is the cause of the physical change. What makes it the case that this is so? What pairing relation pairs the first soul, but not the second soul, with the physical object? Since souls, as immaterial substances, are outside physical space, it is not possible to invoke spatial relations to do the pairing. What possible relations could provide causal pairings across the two domains, one of spatially located material things and the other of immaterial minds outside space?

Consider a variation on the foregoing example: there are two physical objects, a and b, with the same intrinsic properties, and an action of an immaterial soul causally affects one of them, say a, but not b. How can we explain this? Since a and b have identical intrinsic properties, they must have the same causal capacity ("passive" causal powers as well as "active" causal powers), and it would seem that the only way to make them discernible in a causal context is their spatial relations to other things. Doesn't that mean that any pairing relation that can do the job must be a spatial relation? If so, the pairing problem is unsolvable since the soul is not in space and cannot bear spatial relations to anything. The soul cannot be any "nearer" to, or "more properly oriented" toward, one physical object than another. Nor could we say that there was a causal barrier "between" the soul and one of the physical objects but not the other; for what could "between" mean as applied to something in space and something wholly outside it? And it is a total mystery what nonspatial

[2] If this assumption looks dubious to you, or if you are inclined to invoke the identity of intrinsic indiscernibles to dissipate the issue, the pairing problem can be generated without such special assumptions. These assumptions help present the problem in a simple and compelling way.

relations there could be that might help discern between two intrinsically indiscernible physical objects from the point of view of an immaterial soul.

According to Descartes, the pineal gland is where the soul and the body meet for mutual causal action. The soul of course cannot literally be *in* the pineal gland, though it was claimed to move the gland to and fro and thereby initiate the motion of animal spirits. One implicit assumption here is that *my* mind acts on *my* pineal gland, and *your* mind acts on *yours*. More generally, a person is a "union", as Descartes said, of an immaterial mind and a material body, and it might be said that this idea of union provides the needed pairing relation. That is, in our foregoing example, what distinguishes the two souls in their causal relationship to a physical object is that the first, not the second, forms a union with the object in space. This may well be an appropriate thing for the dualist to say, but it is hardly a solution to the problem on hand. The reason is that mind–body causation is implicitly but essentially involved in the notion of a union of a mind and a body. A mind is united with that body with which it is in "direct" causal relation, that is, without another body or mind serving as a causal intermediary. This pineal gland, not that one, counts as mine because my mind is in direct causal relations to it and only to it. It is difficult to see what other explanation is possible. Unless we understand mind–body causal relations, we do not understand the idea of mind–body union. And we do not understand mind–body causal relations unless we have a solution to the pairing problem for minds and bodies.

But could there be causal interactions among immaterial substances? Ruling out mind–body causal interaction does not in itself rule out the possibility of a causally autonomous domain of immaterial minds in which minds are in causal commerce with other minds. Perhaps, that is the picture of a purely spiritual afterlife offered by some religions and theologies. Is that a possibility? The pairing problem makes such an idea a dubious proposition. Again, any substance dualist who wants causation in the immaterial realm must allow the possibility of there being three mental substances, m_1, m_2, and m_3, such that m_1 and m_2 have the same intrinsic properties, and hence the same causal powers, and yet an action by m_1, but not the same action by m_2 at the same time, is causally responsible for a change in m_3. If such is a metaphysically possible situation, what pairing relation could pair m_1 with m_3, but not m_2 with m_3? If causation is to be possible within the mental domain, there must be an intelligible and motivated answer to this question. But what mental relations could serve this purpose? It is difficult to think of any.

Consider what space does for physical causation. In the kind of picture envisaged, where a physical thing or event causally acts on one of the two objects with identical intrinsic properties but not on the other, what distinguishes these two objects has to be their spatial locations. Space provides a principle of individuation of material objects. Pure qualities and causal powers do not. And what enables space to serve this role is the fact that physical objects occupying exactly the same location in space at the same time are one and the same object.[3] This is in effect the principle

---

[3] There is the familiar problem of a statue and the lump of clay of which it is made. Some claim that although these occupy the same region of space and coincide in many of their properties, they are distinct objects. I must set this problem aside.

of "impenetrability of matter", which can usefully be understood as an exclusion principle for space: material things exclude one another from spatial regions. This principle is what enables space to individuate material things with identical intrinsic properties. The same goes for causation in the mental domain. What is needed to solve the pairing problem for immaterial minds is a kind of mental coordinate system, a "mental space", in which these minds are each given a unique "location" at a time. Further, a principle of "impenetrability of minds" must hold in this mental coordinate system; that is, minds that occupy the same "location" in this space must be one and the same. I don't think we have any idea how a mental space of this kind could be constructed.[4] Moreover, even if we could develop such a space for immaterial minds, that would not be a complete solution to the pairing problem; to solve it for causal relations across the mental and the physical domains, we would need to somehow coordinate the two spaces, the mental and the physical, to yield unitary pairing relations across the domains. The complexity of the tasks involved should be evident.

We must conclude, then, that if there are Cartesian minds, they must be in total isolation from one another as well as from the material world. The arguments presented do not show that causal relations cannot hold within a single mental substance (even Leibniz, famous for disallowing causation between monads, allowed it within a single monad, as I understand it). However, what has been shown, I believe, is sufficient to defeat any rationale for substance dualism. If this is right, we have a causal argument for monistic physicalist ontology. Causality requires a space-like structure, and, as far as we know, the physical domain is the only domain with a structure of that kind.

The Collapse of Property Dualism

Nonreductive materialism, a form of property dualism, was the most influential position on the mind–body problem during the last three decades of the twentieth century and, although its once formidable armor has begun to show some serious cracks in recent years, it is still hanging on. This is a testimony to the powerful appeal its message has had for a wide range of audiences, including philosophers and nonphilosophers alike. The antireductive perspective has been a dominant force in other areas of philosophy as well—in particular, philosophy of science where acknowledgement of conceptual/theoretical disunity and incommensurability seems to have become *de rigueur*. It is no exaggeration to say that antireductionism has come to be entrenched as a pervasive trend in high culture, an intellectual fad and fashion, making "reductionism" and "reductionist" slightly derisive put-down epithets in the highbrow press. But philosophical positions cannot live on messages alone: they have to deliver the goods as advertised.

As it has turned out, nonreductive materialism could not deliver on mental causation—any better than Cartesian dualism could. It could not explain, on its own

---

[4] It won't help to try to bring souls into physical space and give them physical locations. For details see my "Lonely Souls: Causality and Substance Dualism".

terms, how mental phenomena, like belief, desire, feeling, and sensation, could causally affect the course of events in the physical world. Mind-to-body causation is fundamental if our mentality is to make a difference to what goes on in the world. If I want to have the slightest causal influence on anything outside me—to change a light bulb or start a war—I must first move my muscles and limbs; somehow, my belief and desire must cause the muscles in my arms and legs to contract. Mental causation is fundamental to our conception of mentality, and to our view of ourselves as agents and cognizers; any theory of mind that is not able to accommodate mental causation must be considered inadequate, or at best incomplete.

So how can a mental phenomenon, say, my desire for a drink of water, manage to cause my legs to move so as to transport my entire body to the kitchen? If mental phenomena are neural events in the brain, that would be no special mystery; I believe we know quite well the neurophysiology involved—how neural excitations in the motor cortex send electrochemical signals through the efferent nerve channels to the appropriate muscles causing them to contract, which in turn causes the limbs to move. According to property dualism, mental phenomena are distinct from neural phenomena, and it becomes a prima facie mystery by what mechanisms, or through what intervening links, these supposedly nonphysical phenomena can cause the muscles to contract. At least, this much seems undeniable: If my desire is to cause my legs to move, it must somehow make use of, or ride piggyback on, the causal chain from my motor cortex to the leg muscles. It just is not possible to believe that my desire might be able to act on my legs directly, through some form of telekinesis, or that there could be another causal path, independent of the neural/physical causal chain, that connects the desire and the leg movement. It seems then that if a neural event in the motor cortex is the ultimate physical cause of the leg movement, my desire must somehow cause that neural event. But how is that possible?

Much is known about the physicochemical processes involved in the firing of a bundle of neural fibers—how electrical potential builds up in a neuron until it reaches a critical point and then discharges. The rising of electric potential involves the movement of electrically charged molecules; if some nonphysical causal agent is to cause a neuron to fire, it must be able to causally influence the motion of molecules. I assume we know something about how molecular motions take place, what physical forces are involved in their causation, and how these forces affect their motion. Do we really have a conception of how some immaterial, nonphysical force might change the motion of even a single molecule, causing it to speed up or slow down, or change its direction? Will brain scientists ever look for nonphysical forces, or nonphysical phenomena, to explain some neural event if they are having difficulties identifying its physical cause? If they should decide to do that, how would they go about it? Where and how would they look for a nonphysical cause of a neural event? How would they identify one and measure its properties?

The answer of course is that brain scientists will not look outside the physical domain for explanations of neural phenomena. They will not think that it would be scientifically productive to look for nonphysical, immaterial forces to explain neural events. We expect the physical world to be causally self-contained and explanatorily self-sufficient. That is, we suppose that if a neural event—or more broadly, a physical event—has a cause, or an explanation, then it must have a physical cause and a physical explanation. This is the principle of *causal/explanatory closure of the physical domain*.

Some dualists may think that these considerations are question-begging in that it assumes the causal closure of the physical. There are excellent, even compelling, reasons for accepting the causal and explanatory self-sufficiency of the physical world, but rather than arguing this point, let me show you another way of generating the problem of mental causation for property dualists. Consider a mental event, say an occurrence of pain. We believe—in fact, we know—that pain occurs only because a certain neural state, call it Ψ, occurs. Ψ may differ from organism to organism, especially in organisms belonging to different biological species, but we do not think that there are sensations that float free from the brain, without being grounded in underlying neural processes. Assume that Ψ is the neural substrate of pain in you: if Ψ occurs, you will experience pain, and you will not experience pain unless Ψ occurs. Consider the claim that the pain caused your finger to twitch. Suppose, further, that neurophysiologists have discovered a causal chain from Ψ, the neural substrate of your pain, to the finger twitching, establishing Ψ as its sufficient physical cause. I believe the existence of such a causal chain is highly likely; we already know a lot about physical causal processes underlying many sensory events. This means that your finger twitching has two putative causes, one mental (your pain) and one physical (the pain's neural substrate Ψ). Given that your finger twitching, a physical event, has a full physical cause, how is a mental cause also possible? How could one and the same event have two distinct causal origins? Doesn't the physical cause threaten to preempt the supposed mental cause? This is the problem of *causal exclusion*, much discussed in recent years. Note that in developing this problem, we have used various highly plausible empirical assumptions about the neurophysiology of pain, but not the principle of physical causal closure.

It is clear that property dualism has no way to deal with these questions, and that, especially in view of physical causal closure, phenomena outside the physical domain must remain causally impotent, mere epiphenomena, at least with regard to physical phenomena. Nor is there any room for causality outside the physical world. In 1970, Donald Davidson's "Mental Events"[5] appeared, and this influential paper sparked the revival of the problem of mental causation, more than 300 years after the problem doomed Descartes's interactionist dualism. What has become increasingly evident over the past thirty years is that mental causation poses insuperable difficulties for all forms of mind–body dualism—for property dualisms no less than substance dualisms. Some philosophers are still gamely holding on, trying to somehow fashion an account of mental causation within the nonreductive scheme, but I believe that if we have learned anything from the three decades of debate, it is the

---

[5] In *Experience and Theory*, ed. Lawrence Foster *et al.* (Amherst, Mass.: University of Massachusetts Press, 1970); repr. in Davidson, *Essays on Actions and Events* (Oxford and New York: Oxford University Press, 1980).

simple point that unless we bring the supposed mental causes fully into the physical world, there is no hope of vindicating their status as causes, and that the reality of mental causation requires reduction of mentality to physical processes, or of minds to brains.

Physicalism at a Crossroads

Let us take stock of where we are. The first choice point we faced was where we had to choose between substance dualism, which posits both material bodies and immaterial minds, and ontological physicalism, which admits only material objects. Motivations for introducing entities other than material things vary—from supposed philosophical requirements in connection with certain issues—for example, the persistence of persons over time, the possible survival of bodily death, and the special directness of our knowledge of our own minds—to religious imperatives and mystical intimations. As we saw, however, immaterial minds, outside physical space, are causally cut off not only from physical objects and events but also from other minds as well. Each immaterial mind is a totally isolated entity, a terribly lonely thing to be! Its existence is inexplicable and its presence or absence can make no difference to anything else. That is, such things, if they existed, would do no work for us, and their existence would be causally and explanatorily otiose. Physicalism prides itself on being the simplest and most parsimonious ontology adequate to do the job of explaining what can be explained and leaving alone what cannot be explained. I believe this is sufficient ground for rejecting substance dualism of all kinds, or any ontology that acquiesces in immaterial, nonphysical things. Here physicalism, as noted, opts for an ontology that countenances only material things. There is just one kind of substance, and it is material substance. The physical world of spacetime is the whole world.[6]

Let us suppose then that at the first choice point we have opted for ontological physicalism. The next choice point we face concerns the properties of material things: Given that only material things exist, what kinds of properties do they, or can they, have? Specifically, can they have properties that are not physical? That is, can they have properties that are not dealt with in fundamental physics or reducible, in some broad but clear sense, to fundamental physical properties? As we saw, many thinkers have been attracted to an affirmative answer to this question, holding the view that complex physical systems can exhibit novel, "emergent" properties that are not reducible to the properties of their simpler constituents. Early emergentists thought that even such simple physicochemical properties as the transparency of water were emergent; now it is generally conceded that consciousness and mentality are the best, and perhaps the only, candidates for emergence. Emergentism, which is now showing some signs of a revival after having been moribund for much

---

[6] What of abstract things, like numbers, properties, propositions, and the like? I am here concerned only with the concrete world; I am setting aside the issue of Platonic objects, although some philosophers believe that Platonism is excluded by naturalism.

of the second half of the twentieth century, is a form of property dualism, the position that, in addition to physical properties, there are physically irreducible domains of emergent properties, of which mental properties are among the leading candidates. Other forms of antireductionism include Donald Davidson's "anomalous monism" and the early functionalism of Hilary Putnam and Jerry Fodor. Property dualism based on ontological physicalism is called nonreductive materialism (or physicalism). Emergentism, anomalous monism, and the Putnam–Fodor functionalism are the best-known examples of nonreductive materialism.[7]

What we have just seen is that this intermediate halfway house between the two poles of substance dualism and reductionist physicalism is a promissory note that cannot be redeemed. As we saw, property dualism is not able to explain how mental causation is possible; instead of saving mental causation, it ends up relegating mental phenomena to the status of epiphenomena. Nonreductive materialism has been motivated by a desire to save mentality as something distinctive and special, and something that we value. Instead of saving it, it helps us lose it by depriving it of causal powers. The important lesson we have learned from three decades of debate—since Davidson's "Mental Events" was published in 1970[8]—is this: the demands of causality do not tolerate duality of properties any more than duality of substances, and both Cartesian substance dualism and contemporary property dualism run aground on the rocks of mental causation.

So property dualism is out—at least, for now. Where do we go from here? If causality excludes dual realms of mental and physical properties, that means that there is only one secure causal domain, the domain of physical properties. What then happens to mental properties? One possibility is that mental properties are reducible to physical properties: if mental properties are reduced to physical properties, this would conserve and legitimize them as members of the physical domain, thereby safeguarding their causal status. But suppose that the mental fails to reduce: we would then be faced with the specter of epiphenomenalism, and we must find a way to live with causally impotent mental properties. This may very well push us over the edge into mental irrealism; for one might argue that epiphenomenalism is a fate no better than irrealism—that is, as Samuel Alexander urged, to deprive something of causal powers is to deprive it of existence.[9] This leads to eliminativism: mental properties are banished from our ontology as causally idle "danglers" with no purpose to serve. This is not an outcome that anyone can welcome; most philosophers—for example, Jerry Fodor as we will see below—take mental causation as wholly non-negotiable. The best outcome would have been a vindication of mental causation along the line of nonreductive materialism; that would have allowed us to retain mentality as something that is causally efficacious and yet autonomous vis-à-vis the physical domain.

[7] The qualifier "Putnam–Fodor" is needed because functionalism of the kind advocated by David Armstrong and David Lewis cannot be viewed as a form of property dualism.

[8] Donald Davidson, "Mental Events", in *Experience and Theory*, ed. Lawrence Foster and J. W. Swanson (Amherst, Mass.: University of Massachusetts Press, 1970).

[9] Samuel Alexander, *Space, Time and Deity* (London: Macmillan, 1927), vol. 2, 8.

But the best outcome, as we saw, cannot be had. The next best outcome, in fact our only hope at this point if mental causation is to be saved, is physical reductionism. Physical reduction would save causal efficacy for mentality, at the cost of its autonomy. Reductionism allows only one domain, the physical domain, but the mental may find a home in that domain. Some will say that the reductionist option is hardly distinguishable from eliminativism, that to reduce minds and consciousness to mere patterns of electrical activities in a network of soulless neurons is in effect to renounce them as a distinctive and valued aspect of our being. This reaction is understandable but inappropriate. There is an honest difference between elimination and reduction. Phlogiston was eliminated, not reduced; temperature and heat were reduced, not eliminated. Witches were eliminated, not reduced; the gene has been reduced, not eliminated. We have a tendency to read "nonphysical" when we see the word "mental", and think "nonmental" when we see the word "physical". This has the effect of making the idea of physical reduction of the mental a simple verbal contradiction, abetting the misguided idea that physical reduction of something we cherish as a mental item, like thought or feeling, would turn it into something other than what it is. But this would be the case only if by "physical" we meant "nonmental". We should not prejudge the issue of mind–body reduction by building irreducibility into the meanings of our words. When we consider the question whether the mental can be physically reduced, it is not necessary—even if this could be done—to begin with general definitions of mental and physical; rather, the substantive question that we are asking, or should be asking, is whether or not things like belief, desire, emotion, and sensation are reducible to physical properties and processes. We can understand this question and intelligently debate it, without subsuming these items under some general conception of what it is for something to be mental. If "mental" is understood to imply "nonphysical", it would then be an open question whether or not belief, desire, sensation, perception, and the rest are mental in that sense. And this question would replace the original question of their physical reducibility. We cannot evade or trivialize this question by a simple verbal ploy.

In any case, our best remaining option is reductionism. Does this mean that we are committed willy-nilly to reductionism? The answer is no: what we have established, if our considerations have been generally correct, is a *conditional* thesis "If mentality is to have causal influences in the physical domain—in fact, if it is to have any causal efficacy at all—it must be physically reducible." I have not argued for reductionism; rather, I have argued that mental causation requires reduction, and that anyone who believes in mental causation must be prepared to accept mind–body reduction. We may call this *conditional reductionism*; it is important to keep in mind that this is not reductionism *tout court*. Moreover, none of this says anything about the truth or plausibility of reductionism. Whether or not the mental can be reduced to a physical base is an independent question that must be settled on its own merits. Those of us who believe in mental causation should hope for a successful reduction. But again this is only a wish; it doesn't make reducibility real or reductionism true.

So we have finally come to the critical question: Can we physically reduce minds? Is mentality reducible in physical terms?

Can We Reduce Minds?

In raising this question about the reducibility of the mental, it is important not to think that the mental as a totality must be either all reducible or all irreducible. It may well be that parts of the mental are reducible while the rest is not. It may be that the physicalist project can be carried through for various subdomains of the mental but not for all, and that physicalism can be vindicated for much of the world but not for the whole world. I will argue that this is in fact the case, namely that much of the mental domain can be physicalized but not all of it. More specifically, my view is that the qualitative characters of conscious experience, what are now commonly called "qualia", are irreducible, but that we have reason to think that the rest, or much of it anyway, is reducible. I am of course not the first, or only, person to hold a view like this; David Chalmers and others have argued, quite plausibly in my opinion, for just such a position.[10]

Chalmers distinguishes between two classes of mental states, those he calls "psychological" and those he calls "phenomenal". Psychological states are states that "play the right sort of causal role in the production of behavior",[11] and include states like belief, desire, memory, and perception. I will call them "intentional/cognitive properties". Phenomenal states are states with a qualitative character—or, to use a phrase popularized by Thomas Nagel, states such that there is "something it is like" to be in those states—like pain, itch, the visual experience of yellow when you look at a field of sunflowers, and the tactile sensation you experience when you run your fingers over a smooth marble surface. On Chalmers's view, intentional/cognitive properties are physically reducible, whereas phenomenal properties, or "qualia", resist reduction.[12]

But what is it to "reduce" something? What needs to be done to accomplish a physical reduction of something mental? Consider the gene and how it has been reduced in molecular biology. The concept of a gene is the concept of a mechanism in an organism that encodes and transmits genetic information. That, I believe, was indeed the concept that Mendel, the founder of modern genetics, had in mind when he spoke of "genetic factors". Genetic factors were to be whatever mechanisms or processes in organisms that are causally responsible for the transmission of heritable characteristics. In short, the concept of a gene is defined in terms of a causal function, or causal role—in terms, that is, of the causal task that must be performed by whatever it is that is to qualify as a gene. As we will say, the concept of a gene is a "functional" concept, and the property of being a gene is a functional property

---

[10] David Chalmers, *The Conscious Mind* (New York: Oxford University Press, 1996). See esp. ch. 3.

[11] Id. at 11.

[12] Chalmers would put this in terms of reductive explanation, not reduction. However, his concept of reductive explanation closely corresponds to my notion of reduction; on the model of reduction to be explained shortly, reductive explanation is not separable from reduction.

defined by a "job description". A functional conception of the gene helps to define the empirical scientific research program: Identify the mechanisms—say, in pea plants or fruit flies or whatever—that perform the task of transmitting heritable characteristics. As I take it, research in molecular genetics has shown that it is the DNA molecules that perform this task—they are the genes we have been looking for. As we say, the DNA molecules are the "realizer" of the gene. Moreover, molecular genetics has an explanation of how DNA molecules manage to perform this complex causal work. When all this is in, we can say that the gene has been physically reduced, and that we now have a reductive explanation of how the process of heredity works at the molecular level. Notice that while, as far as we know, DNA molecules are the genes for terrestrial life, there is no reason to presume that they are the only possible physical mechanisms capable of performing the causal tasks associated with the concept of a gene. It might well be that in certain extraterrestrial organisms these tasks are performed not by DNA molecules but molecules of another kind, say XYZ; for them, XYZ molecules, not DNA molecules, would be the genes. This sort of "multiple realization" must be expected, but the phenomenon of multiple realization, whether actual or only nomologically possible, does not, as some philosophers used to assume, represent an impediment to reduction or reductive explanation.[13]

To summarize, then, reduction can be understood as consisting of three steps. The first is a conceptual step of interpreting, or reinterpreting, the property to be reduced as a functional property in terms of the causal work it is supposed to perform. Once this has been done, scientific work can begin in search of the "realizers" of the functional property—that is, the mechanisms or properties that actually perform the specified casual work—in the population of interest to us. The third step consists in developing an explanation at the lower, reductive level of how these mechanisms perform the assigned causal work. When the first step has been carried out and the property targeted for reduction has been functionalized, in an important sense the property has been shown to be "reducible"— it is now a matter of scientific research to find the realizers. Moreover, if anything has the targeted functionalized property, there has to be some lower-level physical realizer instantiated by it, and it must in principle be possible for scientific investigation to identify it. Even if we have not identified the actual realizer—perhaps we never will—it would make not much difference philosophically: we know that there is a lower-level physical realizer, even if we don't have a perspicuous description of it in an underlying theory, and we know the phenomenon involved to be reducible to its physical realizer, whatever it is. This means that as far as the metaphysical situation is concerned the functional definability of a property is the only issue that matters. That a property is functionalizable— that is, it can be defined in terms of causal role—is necessary and sufficient for

---

[13] On this issue see my "Multiple Realization and the Metaphysics of Reduction", reprinted in *Supervenience and Mind* (Cambridge: Cambridge University Press, 1993), and *Mind in a Physical World* (Cambridge, Mass.: MIT Press, 1998).

reducibility.[14] It is only when we want to claim that the property has been *reduced* (for a given system) that we need to have identified its physical realizer (for that system).

Our question about reduction of minds, therefore, comes to this: Are mental properties functionalizable? Can they be defined in terms of their causal work? The answer, as I have indicated, is yes and no. No for qualitative characters of experience, or "qualia", and yes, or probably yes, for the rest.

Why should we think that intentional/cognitive properties like believing, desiring, and intending are functionally definable, in terms of the work they do? I do not believe that anyone has produced full functional definitions for them, and it is perhaps unlikely that we will have such definitions any time soon.[15] However, there are various considerations that indicate that these properties are functional properties and should be characterizable in terms of the causal work they do in the overall economy of human behavior. Consider a population of creatures, or systems, that are functionally and behaviorally indistinguishable from us, and, in general, observationally indistinguishable from us. Exact indistinguishability or indiscernibility is unimportant; we may simply suppose that their behaviors are largely similar to ours. They interact with their physical environment, which we may suppose is pretty much like ours, and interact with one another, much the same way we do. In particular, they exhibit similar linguistic behavior; as far as we can tell, they use language as we do for expressive and communicative purposes. If all this is the case, it would be incoherent to withhold states like belief, desire, knowledge, action, and intention from these creatures. If, for example, we grant that these creatures are genuine language users, that alone would be sufficient to qualify them as creatures with thought, belief, understanding, intentionality, meaning, and the rest. A language user must be capable of making assertions, and when someone makes an assertion, he expresses a belief; thought, intentionality, and meaning follow. And if we grant agency to them (how could we not, given that they have thought and belief, and that their observable behavior is like ours?), we will be compelled to see them as creatures with desires, preferences, and intentions, and whose behavior and actions can be evaluated according to the norms of rationality. It seems to me that we cannot avoid thinking of intentional/cognitive states, like thought, belief, and desire as supervenient on behavior and other observable physical facts. We must accept creatures that are behaviorally and physically like us as creatures with a mentality similar to ours—with belief, desire, intentionality, and all the rest. This is one strong reason for thinking that such mental properties are definable and interpretable in terms of their roles in behavior causation.

Looking at the situation less globally, suppose that we are told to produce a device that perceives shapes and colors of medium-sized objects presented to it

---

[14] Some philosophers concede that functionalization is sufficient for reduction, but deny that it is necessary. See, in particular, Ned Block and Robert Stalnaker, "Conceptual Analysis, Dualism, and the Explanatory Gap", *Philosophical Review* 108 (1999): 1–46. I respond to Block and Stalnaker in *Physicalism, or Something Near Enough* (Princeton University Press, forthcoming), chs. 4 and 5.

[15] Perhaps the most comprehensive attempt at a functionalization of important mental concepts is found in David M. Armstrong's *A Materialist Theory of Mind* (New York: Humanities Press, 1968).

(perception), processes and stores the information so gained (belief, memory, knowledge), and uses it to guide its actions (agency). I believe we would know how to go about designing and manufacturing machines with such capabilities. That is because these states and processes, like belief, memory, and using information to guide action, are specifiable in terms of their causal roles, in terms of "job descriptions". A creature, or system, that has the capacity to do certain things in certain ways is ipso facto something that perceives, remembers, and appropriately behaves. I believe this is why mental talk comes so naturally to us in describing the activities and capacities of certain artifacts; we talk of a radar system "thinking" that a weather balloon is an approaching airliner, a chess playing computing program as "trying to figure out" how to respond to a check, and even a supermarket automatic door opener as "seeing" or "knowing" that a customer is approaching. Mental talk is even more natural and familiar for animals—not only dogs and cats, but also those farther removed from us, say, mollusks and insects and even amoebas; it is just as natural for artifacts, for similar reasons.

These are among the reasons for thinking that cognitive/intentional mental properties are closely tied, conceptually and semantically, to behavior. This does not mean that we are now, or ever will be, in a position to produce neat functional definitions for complex and multifaceted properties like belief, desire, and emotion. Logical behaviorists and functionalists have famously failed to deliver such definitions. But I believe that is not crucial. I think the following two facts are important in this context: first, partial analyses of these properties in terms of their causal work, even if complete analyses are not available, can get us going with the scientific projects of searching for the underlying physical/biological mechanisms. We don't have to know all the various things that belief does before we start work on uncovering its possible neural mechanisms; a partial list will be enough to start us off. The list will grow richer and more detailed, and this will set further conditions and constraints on the scientific work. Second, the fact is that even though a complete analysis of belief is not in and perhaps never will be, we don't think there is anything beyond causal work vis-à-vis observable behavior that is involved in belief. If there were, that would violate supervenience. As far as such psychological states are concerned, we are within the domain of behaviors and physical mechanisms involved in their production; they do not take us outside this domain.

Let us now turn to sensory states. Suppose we are given another engineering project. This time, we are to design a machine that responds to punctures and abrasions to its skin ("tissue damage") by taking evasive maneuvers to separate itself from the source of the damage ("escape behavior"); in addition, we are told to make this device experience pain when it suffers damage to its skin. That is, we are asked to design into the machine a "pain box" which, in addition to its causal work of triggering an appropriate motor response when it suffers damage, gives rise to a pain experience. We can, I am sure, easily design into a machine a device that will serve as a causal intermediary between the physical input and the behavior output, but making it experience pain is a totally different affair. I don't think we even know where to begin. What we miss, something that we need to know in order to design a pain-experiencing machine, is a connection between the causal work of the pain box on one hand and the fact that a sensation of pain arises in it when it is activated. Why pain rather than itch or tickle? The machine would try to flee when its skin is punctured even if we had, wittingly or unwittingly, designed itch or tickle into the box. What this shows is that we cannot distinguish pain from itch or other sensations by their causal work; our strong intuition is that even if pain is associated with scratching behavior (like itch) or squirming behavior (like tickle), as long as it is felt as pain—as long as it hurts—it is pain. Pain may be associated with certain causal tasks, but these tasks do not define pain. Pain as a sensory quale is not a functional property. In general, qualia are not functional properties.

Some philosophers have invoked the conceivability of "zombies" to show that qualia are not logically supervenient on physical/biological facts. Zombies are creatures that are physically and functionally (hence also behaviorally) indistinguishable from us but that have no inner experiences. The zombie hypothesis has been controversial; less controversial is the qualia inversion hypothesis, namely the possibility of creatures like us, perhaps other human beings, whose quality space is inverted with respect to ours—who, for example, when they look at mounds of lettuce, experience a color quale of the kind we experience when we look at ripe tomatoes, and who, when they look at ripe tomatoes, sense the color that we sense when we look at lettuce. Such spectrum-inverted people would be as adept as we are in picking tomatoes out of mounds of lettuce and obeying traffic signals, and in general they will do just as well as we do with tasks requiring discrimination of red from green. If this is the case, color qualia do not supervene on behavior; two perceivers who behave identically with respect to input applied to their sensory receptors can have different sensory experiences. If that is true, qualia are not functionally definable; they are not task-oriented properties.

So qualia are not functionalizable, and hence physically irreducible. Qualia, therefore, are the "mental residue" that cannot be accommodated within the physical domain. This means that global physicalism is untenable. It is not the case that all phenomena of the world are physical phenomena; nor is it the case that physical facts determine all the facts. There is a possible world that is like this world in all respects except for the fact that in that world qualia are distributed differently. I don't think we can show it to be otherwise.[16]

Living with the Mental Residue

So what do we do with this mental residue? If we have physicalist inclinations, we should try to minimize its impact on physicalism, as we will shortly attempt to do. If our sympathies run in the opposite direction, can we celebrate our victory? Hardly. For one thing, the mental residue encompasses only qualitative mental

---

[16] The current philosophical opinion on this issue is very much divided. There already is a large literature on the possibility—logical, conceptual, and metaphysical—of zombies or qualia inversion; see, e.g. Chalmers, *The Conscious Mind*; Ned Block and Robert Stalnaker, "Conceptual Analysis, Dualism, and the Explanatory Gap".

states, and does not touch the intentional/cognitive domain. And it is in this domain that our cognition and agency are situated. Second, we will do well to remember that our conditional physicalism still stands: If anything is to exercise causal powers in the physical domain, it must be an element in the physical domain or be reducible to it. This has two implications.

First, our mental residue, insofar as it resists physical reduction, remains epiphenomenal. It has no place in the causal structure of the world and no role in its evolution and development. Second, if we are right about the reducibility of cognitive/intentional mental states, we have vindicated their causal efficacy and thereby largely, if not completely, solved the problem of mental causation. Consider Fodor's oft-quoted lament over the possible loss of mental causal efficacy:

"if it isn't literally true that my wanting is causally responsible for my reaching, and my itching is causally responsible for my scratching, and my believing is causally responsible for saying . . ., if none of that is literally true, then practically everything I believe about anything is false and it's the end of the world."[17]

Three mental causes are on Fodor's wish list: wanting, itching, and believing. We have good news for Fodor—his world is not coming to end, at least not completely, because two items on his list, wanting and believing, turn out to be fully causally efficacious. Two out of three isn't bad! But what can we tell Fodor about itching? Should he care about itching, as much as about wanting and believing? At least we can say this: If we can save intentional/cognitive properties we can save our status as cognizers and agents. Saving itching isn't required for saving cognition or agency.

Actually, though, I believe we can go some distance toward saving qualia, although not all the way. We have earlier seen how two persons whose color spectra are inverted with respect to each other can exhibit the same discriminative behavior. Brief reflection shows that some important aspects of qualia are closely tied to behavior and therefore functionalizable. For an analogy, consider traffic lights: everywhere in the world, red means stop, green means go, and yellow means slow down. But that is only a convention, the result of a social arrangement; we could have adopted a system according to which red means go, green means slow down, and yellow means stop, or any of the remaining combinations. That would have made no difference to traffic management. What matters are the differences and similarities among colors, not their intrinsic qualities. In fact, we could have chosen shapes instead of colors, with circle meaning go, square meaning stop, and so on. Discrimination is what matters; qualities discriminated do not. I believe Moritz Schlick made the observation that what can be communicated about experiences is their form, not their content.

Suppose that we have already acknowledged that a given perceiver can experience a range of qualia. When we present to him a ripe tomato, we may not know what the intrinsic quality of his visual experience is—what color quale he is experiencing.

---

[17] Jerry Fodor, "Making Mind Matter More", repr. in *A Theory of Content and Other Essays* (Cambridge, Mass.: MIT Press, 1990), 156.

Similarly, when we present to him spinach leaves, we may not know what quale characterizes his visual experience. However, we can tell whether his color quale of the tomato is the same as, or different from, his color quale of the spinach leaves. When we present to him a bunch of lettuce leaves, we can tell whether the quale he is now experiencing is similar to, or different from, each of the two color qualia he has just experienced. That is, the intrinsic qualities associated with qualia are, or may be, undetectable but differences and similarities between qualia, within a single individual, are behaviorally detectable, and this opens a way for their behavioral functionalization.[18]

And intuitively that seems right. The fact that blue looks just *this* way to me, green looks *that* way, and so on, should make no difference to the primary cognitive function of my visual perception—its function in the generation of information about my physical environment of the sort that makes a difference to my survival and flourishing. Color-inverted persons, as long as they have the capacity to make the same discriminations, should do as well as we do in coping with the world. Intrinsic qualities of qualia are not functionalizable and irreducible, and hence causally impotent. They stay outside the physical domain, but they make no causal difference and we won't miss them. In contrast, the relational facts about qualia, in particular their similarities and differences, are detectable and functionalizable, and can enjoy causal powers as full members of the physical world. But there is a further question: Why are there such things as qualia? And why should there be qualia? Because we need them as place markers; without them there can be no qualia differences or similarities. Without content, there can be no form, no structure. You may now ask: Why are there just *these* qualia and not other possible ones? That remains a mystery; I do not believe that the present approach is capable of answering that question.

Where We Are with the Mind–Body Problem

I feel that the position I have been describing here is a plausible terminus for the mind–body debate. There are many issues that need to be sorted out in more detail and with greater care and precision; among them are the functional reducibility of cognitive/intentional states, the functionalizability of qualia differences and similarities, and a more precise understanding of the relation between reduction and conservation, and between reduction and elimination. But in spite of the further work required, I feel that the remaining work is for the most part a mopping-up operation, and that the important outlines of the position stand out with clarity and salience.

Let me briefly redescribe the position that has emerged. It begins by embracing ontological physicalism. Taking mental causation seriously, it also embraces conditional reductionism, the thesis that only physically reducible mental properties can

---

[18] For some interesting observations on these issues, see Sydney Shoemaker, "The Inverted Spectrum", *Journal of Philosophy* 74 (1981): 357–81. What I am saying here, I believe, is in line with Shoemaker's view that although "absent qualia" are not possible, qualia inversion is possible, or at least meaningful.

be causally efficacious. Are mental properties physically reducible? Yes and no: intentional/cognitive properties are reducible, but qualitative properties of consciousness, or "qualia", are not. In saving the causal efficacy of the former, we are saving cognition and agency. Moreover, we are not losing sensory experiences altogether: qualia similarities and differences can be saved. What we cannot save are their intrinsic qualities—the fact that yellow looks this way, that ammonia smells that way, and so on. But, I say, this isn't losing much, and when we think about it, we should have expected it all along.

The position is, as we might say, a slightly defective physicalism—physicalism manqué but not by much. I believe that is as much physicalism as we can have, and, more importantly, there seems no credible alternative to physicalism as a general worldview. Physicalism is not the whole truth, but it is *the truth near enough*, and *near enough* should be *good enough*.

Beyond the Mind–Body Problem: Self and Subjectivity

It is common to characterize consciousness, especially phenomenal consciousness, as something "subjective". In his well-known paper, "What Is It Like to Be a Bat?", Nagel quickly moves from his characterization of phenomenal consciousness in terms of "what it's like" to the "subjectivity" of consciousness:

But fundamentally an organism has conscious mental states if and only if there is something that it is like to be that organism—something it is like for the organism. . . . We may call this the subjective character of experience.[19]

Nagel then proceeds to connect subjectivity with the idea of a "point of view":

every subjective phenomenon is essentially connected with a single point of view, and it seems inevitable that an objective, physical theory will abandon that point of view.[20]

Nagel does not explain, at least not in this paper, in what sense phenomenal experience is "subjective", and in what sense, and why, a single "point of view" is associated with each subjective phenomenon—or indeed what a "point of view" really is. But this is pretty standard; we often see philosophers in this area bandy about expressions like "subjective", "point of view", "perspective", "what it's like", and others, without explanation, as though they have well-established meanings and their interrelationships are common knowledge. And, as is clear from the Nagel quotations above, these terms are standardly used, implicitly or explicitly, to contrast with "objective", "scientific", and "physical", and often a quick inference is made from something's being subjective to its physical irreducibility. Consider how Nagel's thought appears to run in the quoted passages: the transition from what-it's-like to subjectivity seems to be made almost by stipulation, and then the thought

---

[19] Thomas Nagel, "What Is It Like to Be a Bat?", in *The Nature of Mind*, ed. David Rosenthal (Oxford and New York: Oxford University Press, 1991), 422. Originally published in *Philosophical Review* 83 (1974): 435–50.   [20] Nagel, "What Is It Like to Be a Bat?", 423.

occurs to one that since all physical things must be objective, anything subjective, that is, anything that has a what-it's-like character, cannot be reduced to something physical or understood in objective scientific terms.[21] This is not in criticism of Nagel; I am merely pointing to the rather chaotic and confusing way in which these terms are often used, obfuscating whatever philosophical points that are being made.

Rather than belaboring this point, let us move on, supposing that phenomenal states are subjective, in some sense. But they are not the only states that have been, and can be, claimed to be subjective. Consider thoughts, beliefs, and other intentional/cognitive states. As we noted in an earlier section, it is now customary to distinguish these as constituting a class of mental states distinct from sensory or phenomenal states. Perhaps, some instances of these states, say instances of strong belief or nagging doubt, have phenomenal feels, or what-it's-like qualities; however, it is clear that phenomenal qualities are not necessary to these states, and that these states are not type-individuated in terms of their phenomenal qualities. It is not the case that your belief that there are horses in the field and my belief that there are horses in the field fall under the same belief-type because there is a shared phenomenal feel to them, in the way your pain and my pain are both instances of pain because there is a certain phenomenal quality common to them. In any case, states like belief and desire typically exhibit properties that are traditionally associated with subjectivity. For one, most philosophers would accept the thesis, often associated with Descartes, that our access to our own current thoughts is specially authoritative and privileged, even if it is not absolutely incorrigible or indubitable as Descartes claimed. In standard situations, you know "directly" what it is that you are thinking or what it is that you want—that is, without needing to make observations, acquire evidence, or making inferences. In a sense you don't have to "find out" what you think; it is almost as though in the very act of thinking you are in direct cognitive touch with the content of your thought—there is no further step you need to take to know what it is. Philosophers differ as to the exact character of such knowledge, and there is no need to claim that the knowledge involved is "incorrigible" or "indubitable" in an unconditional sense. How such knowledge is possible given the widely accepted content externalism—the view that contents of our thoughts are determined in part by factors outside us—has been much debated in the last decade or so. However, virtually all the disputants in this debate share the premise that our knowledge of our own propositional-attitudes states is privileged in a special way. It is not that the knowledge cannot be shared with third persons; rather, it is that the "directness" of such knowledge attaches only to the first person, not to the third person. And in that sense it seems perfectly appropriate to call thoughts and first-person knowledge of them "subjective".[22] As we saw, the prevailing view is that there is not, or need not be, any "what-it's-like" phenomenal qualities to beliefs,

---

[21] Nagel, at least in some places, seems to argue this way. For another example, see John R. Searle, *The Rediscovery of the Mind* (Cambridge, Mass.: MIT Press, 1992), ch. 5.

[22] This of course is a traditional sense in which phenomenal states too are thought to be subjective.

desires, and other propositional attitudes. It follows then that phenomenal qualities are not all that there is to subjectivity.

The point becomes clear when we consider an entity like Commander Data of the television series *Star Trek*: Data, an electromechanical device made up of computer chips, wires, plastic skins, and what have you, is largely isomorphic to us in functional/behavioral organization; that is, in terms of patterns of sensory input and behavioral output, he is like a normal—if a bit quirky—human being. And this includes speech behavior: he is a speaker of English, and when he utters the sentence "The starship has been hit" we interpret him to be expressing his belief that the starship has been hit. As we earlier noted, it would be incoherent to grant an entity the capacity for speech and at the same time deny it the capacity for beliefs and other cognitive/intentional states. And yet whether or not Data is capable of phenomenal consciousness—whether he can experience pains and sense the yellow of sunflowers—is in doubt; moreover, it is not at all clear how it could be determined that Data is, or is not, phenomenally conscious.[23] I don't believe there is anything incoherent in the idea that an entity like Data is possible—I doubt that the prevailing laws of nature preclude entities like Data.

Consider the fact that, like us, Data is able to utter and use "I"-sentences, like "I am on the bridge now" in appropriate circumstances, say, in response to the question "Commander Data, where are you?" There seems prima facie no reason to think that Data's use of "I" to refer to himself differs in any way from our use of "I" to refer to ourselves, and we seem compelled to grant him the fundamental capacity of a cognizer to refer to himself qua himself, in a specially direct and intimate way. Hector-Neri Castaneda and others have brought to light some highly significant and complex properties of propositions expressed by "I"-sentences.[24] Consider Descartes who expressed a famous belief by uttering an equally famous sentence, "I exist." We report his belief with the sentence "Descartes believes that he exists." What is the content of his belief, or the proposition that he reportedly believes? Clearly it is not the proposition that Descartes exists. Descartes did not claim that he proved beyond any doubt that Descartes existed. Whatever we may think of Descartes's "cogito" argument, we cannot take this proposition, that Descartes exists, to be the conclusion of his argument. Nor can we say that the conclusion is the proposition that *he* exists—there is no such proposition. There is a sense in which the proposition Descartes asserts when he utters, or thinks, "I exist" is inaccessible to the rest of us. It is not entirely ineffable since we have a way of indicating the proposition in question, as we have been doing; we do so indirectly, with circumlocutions, like "the proposition expressed by Descartes when he uttered the sentence 'I exist' ", "the proposition expressed by the subordinate clause in 'Descartes believes that he exists' ", and the like. The point rather is that this proposition cannot be a possible object of belief, or disbelief, or doubt, or any other

---

[23] For an interesting discussion of this issue see Ned Block, "The Harder Problem of Consciousness", *Journal of Philosophy* 96 (2002): 1–35.

[24] See the essays collected in Hector-Neri Castaneda, *The Phenomeno-Logic of the I*, ed. J. G. Hart and T. Kapitan (Bloomington: Indiana University Press, 1999).

propositional attitude on the part of anyone else. I can *refer to, think about,* and *talk about* Descartes's "I exist" proposition, but I cannot *think* it, *believe* it, *doubt* it, or *disbelieve* it; that is, it is a proposition toward which only Descartes, and no one else, can hold propositional attitudes. The same goes for all other propositions expressed by Descartes's "I"-sentences.

Therefore, these propositions, or "I"-propositions as we may call them, are essentially subjective, in a robust and intuitive sense of this term; they are unlike propositions expressed by sentences like "Socrates is wise" and "Horses are mammals" which can be shared objects of more than one thinker's propositional attitudes. It seems plausible to suppose that this difference springs from the special way, direct and unmediated, in which a thinker refers to himself qua self, not through an objective description or representation that is in principle available to the third person. What such direct self-reference (sometimes called "reflexive self-reference") consists in and what cognitive/intellectual capacities underwrite it are questions that remain to be fully explored. There is a large body of literature on some of these issues, much of it suggestive and important, by philosophers including Castaneda, Sydney Shoemaker, Elizabeth Anscombe, Gareth Evans, John Perry, Roderick Chisholm, and others.

These reflections suggest that some important issues concerning self and subjectivity do not go away when we are done with the mind–body problem; perhaps it is better to put the point by saying that a comprehensive treatment of the mind–body problem should explore subjectivity in all its manifestations. In our earlier traversal of the mind–body problem, consciousness was seen as the chief potential roadblock to achieving a full and satisfying physicalist worldview. As we saw with Nagel above, its supposed subjectivity is invoked as the fundamental reason for its physical irreducibility. Obviously we need a deeper understanding of what subjectivity is before we can properly assess such an argumentative strategy.

One reason—in fact, the principal reason—that we are interested in the mind-body problem is to better understand what we are—the kind of being that we are and what it is about our nature that should matter to us. If self-understanding broadly conceived is our goal, coming to terms with the mind–body problem narrowly conceived cannot be our final destination. In order to underscore the importance of subjectivity, let us briefly consider how subjectivity is essentially involved in another fundamental aspect of our being, namely agency. We earlier discussed mental causation. Clearly, the main reason for taking mental causation as a serious philosophical problem is that it is crucial to agency. To be agents in this world, our beliefs and desires must be able to move our limbs and thereby cause changes in the objects around us. Causation, however, is not all there is to agency; even if the problem of mental causation is fully resolved, there still remains the problem of subjectivity in agency.

One way to appreciate this is to notice a crucial difference between the perspective an agent must take toward her action and the perspective a third person may take toward the same action. When we deliberate about what to do, our beliefs about the world—in particular, an assessment of the probable consequences of various courses of action open to us—and our preferences in regard to these possible consequences play a critical role in shaping our deliberation and decision. As an agent in deliberation, I ask: Given that this is what I want and these are the beliefs I hold about the world, what *ought* I to do? What is the *best*, the *rational*, thing for me to do? Now consider the perspective of a third person, say my wife, observing me in the process of deliberation and decision. Assume that she has much the same information about my desires and beliefs. As an observer of this passing scene, the question she asks is this: Given that this is what he wants and this is what he believes about the world, what *will* he do? What is the likely outcome of his deliberation? She may also have information about my general character and my past record of decision-making in similar situations; she perhaps has access to my hidden motives and desires which are not evident to me. But notice that for the observer my beliefs and preferences serve as *evidence*, or epistemic ground, for her prediction, whereas for me, the agent, they function as *reason*, a normative ground, that rationalizes my decision and action.

It seems possible for a third person to "take" my point of view as an agent—to put herself in my position as an agent. I might go to my wife and ask for her advice on what I ought to do. So just as I ask "Given this is what I want and this is what I believe, what ought I to do?", she asks "Given that this is what he wants and this is what he believes, what ought he to do?" When a third person asks this question, she is taking an agent's stance, not a predictor's stance, toward my action.[25] That precisely is the difference between a friendly adviser and a fortune teller (or a social psychologist doing research on decision-making); a friend takes an agent's point of view in your behalf whereas a fortune teller takes a third-person predictor's perspective. Explanation of action by rationalization—that is, making sense of what a person does in terms of his "reasons"—consists fundamentally in the explainer's taking that person's point of view as an agent. I believe this to be the plausible intuitive core of the doctrine, much debated since over a century ago, that explanation in the human sciences must be grounded in an empathetic understanding of the agents involved, and that in this respect it is unlike explanation of natural phenomena based on causal/predictive laws.[26] It has been pretty common to regard the debate between the "causalists" and the "rationalizers" about action explanation as a dispute about whether the connection between reasons and actions (or decisions) is logical/conceptual or nomological/causal.[27] I believe this diagnosis is mistaken—at least, it is superficial and fails to get to the root of the issues. I believe the dispute arises fundamentally from the tension between the first-person/third-person

[25] This is perhaps related to, but not the same as, the "simulation" that has recently been much discussed, in the dispute between the simulationists and the theory theorists concerning vernacular psychology. A simulator puts himself in my shoes and asks what he *would* do ("What will I do?"); obviously he is asking the third-person predictor's question, not the agent's.
[26] This tradition goes back at least to the debate, in the second half of the nineteenth century, on the proper methodology of explanation and understanding in the "Geisteswissenschaften", in the works of J. G. Droysen, Wilhelm Dilthey, and others. More recent advocates of this view in analytic philosophy include William Dray in *Laws and Explanation in History* (Oxford: Oxford University Press, 1957) and Georg H. von Wright in *Explanation and Understanding* (Ithaca, New York: Cornell University Press, 1971).
[27] See Georg H. von Wright, *Explanation and Understanding*.

perspectives, and that the issues concern the contrast between the subjective and the objective. It is possible that the subjective/objective split manifests itself in a logical/causal distinction; but we should not confuse symptoms with explanatory grounds.

I believe that a proper understanding and resolution of the major issues concerning agency, freedom, and explanation of action requires a systematic and unified account of subjectivity. It isn't just that many of the well-known and much debated issues about these topics, topics that are so crucial to our understanding of our own nature, have their sources in the tension between the subjective and the objective;[28] new puzzles and apparent incoherencies, I believe, can be seen to arise when we keep pushing the subjective/objective tension to the limit. And, beyond agency, there are many issues concerning self and subjectivity for which we are badly in need of a unified account. One of them is the familiar problem of the identity and persistence of a self; this obviously is not the place to go into this problem, but I believe that any real progress in this area depends on a better understanding of subjectivity. Another issue is normativity. It has often been observed that cognitive/intentional states have an aspect of normativity in that they are subject to norms of rationality, coherence, and the like. I believe there is a real possibility that the normativity of the intentional arises out of its subjectivity. A unified theory of subjectivity could throw new light on the issues of normativity. Moreover, we must at some point revisit the mind–body problem with the general issue of subjectivity in mind. You may recall my earlier contention that there is reason for thinking that intentional/cognitive states, unlike phenomenal states, could be accommodated within a physicalist framework, via functional reduction. When this result is combined with the observation defended in this section that subjectivity is a characteristic of cognitive/intentional states no less than phenomenal states, it might appear that subjectivity as such is no barrier to physicalism, and that there is no special problem about explaining how subjectivity can arise in a wholly physical world. But I believe this conclusion is subject to reconsideration; the functional reducibility of cognitive/intentional states must, I think, be reconsidered in light of the subjectivity of these states. If subjectivity should turn out to be accommodatable in a physical world, we would like to know exactly how the accommodation works—or exactly how subjectivity arises in a purely physical system. For example, a mere claim of supervenience, that two worlds that are physically indiscernible must be indiscernible in the distribution of intentional/cognitive states, with all their subjectivity and normativity intact, cannot satisfy us. We should want an explanation of the "mechanism" of this supervenience.

It is not as though enough articles and books have not been written about self and subjectivity in recent years. It is rather that we are still lacking a common set of established concepts and a common set of problems formulated in terms of shared concepts. One gets the impression that philosophers writing on subjectivity are often talking past each other; and it is far from clear what all the problems that have

---

[28] An observation made by Nagel in *The View From Nowhere*.

been called "problems of subjectivity" have in common that makes them problems about subjectivity. The situation is rather like the situation involving discussions of consciousness about a couple of decades ago. One notable advance that the consciousness debate has made during the past dozen years is the fact that there now appears to be a rough consensus about what the central problems are and about the range of possible solutions, if not an agreement on the actual solutions. Discussion of subjectivity, in my view, has not reached this stage yet; we still don't have a shared problematic concerning subjectivity, and we don't have a clear idea as to what major alternative views are possible on the issues. What we now have is a confusing collection of issues that we associate with subjectivity. We seem to have no clear idea as to how, or even whether, they are connected with one another. What we need, as I said, is a unified theory or viewpoint that can introduce some intelligible order into this jumble of issues, ideas, and claims, all of them raised or invoked in the name of subjectivity. It is my hope that we will see in the near future serious attempts at constructing a systematic general account of subjectivity. I believe that if the ultimate ideal of philosophy is self-understanding—that is, an understanding of our nature and our place in the natural world—achieving an understanding of our subjectivity is one of the essential philosophical tasks.

6

The Representational Character of Experience

DAVID J. CHALMERS

1. Introduction

Consciousness and intentionality are perhaps the two central phenomena in the philosophy of mind. Human beings are conscious beings: there is something it is like to be us. Human beings are intentional beings: we represent what is going on in the world. Correspondingly, our specific mental states, such as perceptions and thoughts, very often have a phenomenal character: there is something it is like to be in them. And these mental states very often have intentional content: they serve to represent the world.

On the face of it, consciousness and intentionality are intimately connected. Our most important conscious mental states are intentional states: conscious experiences often inform us about the state of the world. And our most important intentional mental states are conscious states: there is often something it is like to represent the external world. It is natural to think that a satisfactory account of consciousness must respect its intentional structure, and that a satisfactory account of intentionality must respect its phenomenological character.

With this in mind, it is surprising that in the last few decades, the philosophical study of consciousness and intentionality has often proceeded in two independent streams. This was not always the case. In the work of philosophers from Descartes and Locke to Brentano and Husserl, consciousness and intentionality were typically analyzed in a single package. But in the second half of the twentieth century, the dominant tendency was to concentrate on one topic or the other, and to offer quite separate analyses of the two. On this approach, the connections between consciousness and intentionality receded into the background.

In the last few years, this has begun to change. The interface between consciousness and intentionality has received increasing attention on a number of fronts. This attention has focused on such topics as the representational content of perceptual experience, the higher-order representation of conscious states, and the phenomenology of thinking. Two distinct philosophical groups have begun to emerge. One group focuses on ways in which consciousness might be grounded in intentionality. The other group focuses on ways in which intentionality might be grounded in consciousness.

Grounding consciousness in intentionality   Those who take this approach typically try to analyze consciousness in terms of intentionality, without remainder. Some (such as

David Rosenthal and Peter Carruthers) analyze conscious states in terms of higher-order states that represent them. But perhaps the most popular approach (taken by Michael Tye and Fred Dretske, among others) focuses on the first-order intentional content of conscious states, and advocates *representationalism*, analyzing conscious states as a certain sort of first-order intentional state. This approach is often combined with the view that intentionality can be explained in physical terms, to motivate a physically acceptable explanation of consciousness.[1]

Grounding intentionality in consciousness   Those who take this approach argue that phenomenology plays a crucial role in grounding representational content. Some (such as John Searle) argue that consciousness is the ground of all true intentional content. Others (such as Terence Horgan and John Tienson, Colin McGinn, and Charles Siewert) argue that there is at least a distinctive and crucial sort of intentional content that accrues in virtue of the phenomenal character of mental states. These theorists do not typically offer reductive analysis of intentionality in terms of consciousness, but they typically hold that consciousness has a certain priority in the constitution of intentionality.[2]

My own sympathies lie more with the second group, but I think that the ideas of both groups deserve close attention. In particular, I think that there is significant promise in representationalism. Representationalism is often understood as taking a reductive view of consciousness, but this association is inessential. I think that the insights of representationalism cohere equally well with a view on which consciousness cannot be reduced to anything more basic than itself.

In what follows I proceed largely from first principles in analyzing aspects of the relationship between consciousness and intentionality, while leaning on the analyses of others along the way. I focus on the phenomenal character and the intentional content of perceptual states, canvassing various possible relations among them. I argue that there is a good case for a sort of representationalism, although this may not take the form that its advocates often suggest. By mapping out some landscape, I try to open up territory for different and promising forms of representationalism to be explored in the future. In particular, I argue for a nonreductive, narrow, and Fregean variety of representationalism, which contrasts strongly with more widely explored varieties. I conclude with some words about the fundamental relationship between consciousness and intentionality.

2. Phenomenal Properties and Representational Properties

Consciousness involves the instantiation of *phenomenal properties*. These properties characterize aspects of what it is like to be a subject (what it is like to be me right

---

[1] See Rosenthal (1997), Carruthers (2000), Tye (1995), and Dretske (1995). Others who take this sort of approach include Harman (1990) and Lycan (1996).

[2] See Searle (1990), Horgan and Tienson (2002), McGinn (1988), and Siewert (1998). Others who take this sort of approach include Strawson (1994) and Loar (2003).

now, for example, or what it is like to be a bat), or what it is like to be in a mental state (what it is like to see a certain shade of green, for example, or what it is like to feel a certain sharp pain). Whenever there is something it is like to be a subject, that subject has specific phenomenal properties. Whenever there is something it is like to be in a mental state, that state has specific phenomenal properties. For many purposes it does not make much difference whether one focuses on the phenomenal properties of subjects or of mental states (it is easy to translate between the two ways of talking), and in what follows I will move back and forth between them.

Intentionality involves the instantiation of *representational properties*. We can say that a *pure representational property* is the property of representing a certain intentional content (or the property of having a certain intentional content; I will usually not pay much attention to this grammatical distinction). Intuitively, this involves representing things as being a certain way in the world. A perceptual state might have the content that there is a green object in front of me, and a belief might have the content that javelinas live in the desert. We can be neutral on just what sort of content this is: it might involve a set of possible worlds, a complex of objects and properties, a complex of Fregean senses, or something else again. What is most important is that intentional contents have *conditions of satisfaction*: they are the sort of thing that can be satisfied or can fail to be satisfied by states of the world. As with phenomenal properties, we can regard representational properties as being instantiated by either subjects or by mental states.

An *impure representational property* is the property of representing a certain intentional content in a certain manner. This involves representing such-and-such as being the case in such-and-such a way. Here the "way" is a *manner of representation*, and involves a mental characterization of the state of representing. There are many different manners of representation. For example, one can represent a content perceptually, and one can represent a content doxastically (in belief): these correspond to different manners of representation. At a more fine-grained level, one can represent a content visually or auditorily. Manners of representation may also involve functional characterizations of the representing state. For example, one can represent a certain content in such a way that the content either is or is not available for verbal report.[3]

Whenever an impure representational property is instantiated, the corresponding pure representational property will also be instantiated (whenever a content is represented in a certain way, it is represented). And whenever a pure representational property is instantiated, numerous corresponding impure representational properties will be instantiated (whenever a content is represented, it is represented in certain ways).

I will take *representationalism* to be the thesis that phenomenal properties are identical to certain representational properties (or that they are equivalent to certain

---

[3] Manners of representation are closely related to what Crane (2003) calls "intentional modes". I do not use this way of speaking as it invites confusion with the quite distinct notion of modes of presentation (which are contents rather than psychological properties, used later in this article).

representational properties; see below). We can say that *pure representationalism* is the thesis that phenomenal properties are identical to pure representational properties, while *impure representationalism* is the thesis that phenomenal properties are identical to impure representational properties. In practice, almost all representationalists are impure representationalists, for reasons to be given shortly.

Some representationalists, such as Dretske and Tye, occasionally put their view by saying that phenomenal properties are identical to certain *represented* external properties, such as physical redness. As I am putting things, that would be a category mistake: phenomenal properties are by definition properties of subjects or of mental states, and physical redness is not (or need not be). I think that this is simply a terminological difference, however. For example, Dretske defines phenomenal properties ("qualia") as the properties we are directly aware of in perception, and concludes these are properties such as colors. This is quite compatible with the claim that phenomenal properties in my sense are representational properties, as long as one holds that one is directly aware of the represented property rather than the representational property. Once we make the relevant translation, I think that these representationalists' most important claims can be put in the terms used here without loss.

3. Relationships

What are the relationships between phenomenal and representational properties? Do phenomenal properties *entail* (pure or impure) representational properties, or vice versa? Are phenomenal properties *identical* to representational properties? Are phenomenal properties *reducible* to representational properties, or vice versa?

We can say that one property entails another property when it is necessarily the case that whatever has the first property has the second property. We can say that two properties are equivalent when each entails the other: that is, if it is necessarily the case that whatever has one of the properties has the other. I will take it in what follows that the equivalence of two properties suffices for them to be identical. Not much rests on this: if one thinks properties are finer-grained than this, one can simply replace talk of identity throughout this paper by talk of equivalence.

This approach yields the following more detailed characterization of representationalism. Representationalism (about a class of phenomenal properties) is the thesis that for every phenomenal property (in that class), there is some representational property such that necessarily, a mental state (or a subject) has that representational property if and only if it has that phenomenal property.

I will concentrate on the class of perceptual phenomenal properties, and in some places more specifically on the class of visual phenomenal properties. So in the first instance, I am interested in the relationship between visual phenomenal properties and (pure or impure) representational properties, though it is natural to hope that this relationship will generalize to other phenomenal properties. In what follows, I canvas various possible relations among these properties, one step at a time.

Do pure representational properties entail phenomenal properties?   That is, is it necessarily the case that any subject (mental state) that represents a certain content also has a certain phenomenal character? Here, it is most natural to answer 'no'. The reason is that it seems that most or all representational contents can be represented *unconsciously*, without any associated phenomenal character at all. There can be unconscious beliefs, and subconscious perception, and it seems that in principle these unconscious states can represent a very wide range of intentional contents. One could preserve the entailment thesis by denying that there are unconscious representational states, but that view is now almost universally rejected.

There are some weaker theses that may be left on the table here. First, one could hold that there are some special intentional contents (perhaps concerning phenomenal properties themselves, or intimately related to phenomenal properties) that cannot be represented unconsciously. If so, the corresponding pure representational properties would entail phenomenal properties. Second, one could hold (with Searle, 1990) that representing an intentional content requires that one have some corresponding conscious state at some time or other, or at least potentially. If so, there could be an entailment from pure representational properties to certain diachronic or dispositional phenomenal properties (the property of having certain phenomenal properties in the past or the future, or potentially), if not to phenomenal properties in the strict sense. Finally, one could hold that there is an entailment from certain *impure* representational properties to phenomenal properties. I will return to this possibility below.

Do phenomenal properties entail pure representational properties?   That is, is it necessarily the case that any subject with a certain phenomenal character thereby represents the world as being a certain way? Here the answer is quite plausibly 'yes', at least in the case of perceptual phenomenal properties. It seems intuitively clear that perceptual phenomenology, by its very nature, involves the representation of the external world. For example, my visual phenomenology right now involves the representation of a computer on a desk in front of me, with various books and papers scattered on the desk.

The claim that phenomenal experiences (in a given class) always have representational content is sometimes called *weak representationalism*. Weak representationalism (at least about visual experiences) is extremely plausible, and rarely denied.[4] A stronger thesis also seems plausible: that any two phenomenally identical states will share some aspect of their representational content. As Colin McGinn has put it, there is a strong intuition that something about representational content is *internal* to phenomenology. That is, given a specific phenomenology, it seems that if a mental state has this phenomenology, it must also have a certain specific representational content. If this is right, then phenomenal properties entail certain pure representational properties.

---

[4] Weak representationalism is characterized in roughly this way by Crane (2003), Levine (2003), and Lycan (2000). Even the views of such anti-representationalists as Block and Peacocke appear to be compatible with weak representationalism. For a recent denial of weak representationalism, see Travis (2004).

This line of thought has been developed into an argument at greatest length by Charles Siewert (1998). I will not recapitulate Siewert's extensive arguments here, but the basic idea is that visual experiences are *assessable for accuracy*, in virtue of their phenomenal character. For example, when I have a visual experience as of something X-shaped in front of me, this experience may be either accurate or inaccurate, depending on what is really in front of me. Further, it seems that any visual experience with the same phenomenal character would be assessàble for accuracy in the same sort of way: roughly, it would be correct if and only if there is an object with an appropriate shape in front of the subject. If this is right, then a phenomenal property (having an experience with the phenomenal character as of seeing something X-shaped) entails a pure representational property (roughly, representing that there is an object with a certain shape in the world).

Something similar plausibly applies to other visual experiences, such as experiences of position and of color, and to other perceptual experiences, such as auditory and tactile experiences. Siewert argues that this reasoning can be extended to the phenomenology and intentionality of thought, as well as perception, but this raises complications that I will not go into here. For now, what matters is that there is plausibly an entailment from perceptual phenomenal properties to pure representational properties.

A similar point can be made for subjects of experience, as well as for mental states. Terence Horgan and John Tienson (2002) have argued that necessarily, any two subjects that are phenomenal duplicates will share significant representational content.[5] Even a brain in a vat that has experiences that are phenomenally identical to mine will represent its environment as being in significant respects just as I represent my environment as being. This suggests that the phenomenal properties of a subject entail pure representational properties for that subject.

Just what sort of representational properties are entailed by phenomenal properties? Some tricky questions arise here. If phenomenal properties are intrinsic properties of an individual, then presumably the corresponding representational properties must be intrinsic too. One might reasonably wonder just how to characterize these properties, given the apparent extrinsicness of many representational properties. I will look more closely at these questions later. For now, I will take it that there is at least a strong prima facie case that phenomenal properties entail pure representational properties.

Are phenomenal properties identical to pure representational properties?   That is, for a given phenomenal property, is there some representational content that is represented if and only if that phenomenal property is instantiated? The answer to this question is plausibly 'no', for reasons given above: identity requires entailment, and it is plausible that phenomenal properties are not entailed by pure representational

---

[5] Loar (2003) makes a related argument from phenomenal duplicates, although his conception of phenomenal intentionality (unlike Horgan and Tienson's) is shorn of the connection to conditions of satisfaction.

properties. If any given representational content can be represented unconsciously, then pure representational properties cannot be identical to phenomenal properties, and pure representationalism is false.

The only hope for pure representationalism is to deny that any given representational content can be represented unconsciously. The pure representationalist might deny that unconscious representation is possible, or might hold that there are some special representational contents that cannot be represented unconsciously and can be represented only by a specific sort of phenomenal state.[6] If such contents exist, the property of representing one of them might be identical to a phenomenal property. In the absence of strong reasons for thinking that such contents exist, however, I will pass over this option in what follows.

Are phenomenal properties identical to impure representational properties?   We have seen that pure representational properties are plausibly entailed by phenomenal properties, but that the reverse is not the case, because of the possibility of unconscious representation. This rules out an identity between phenomenal properties and pure representational properties. However, it leaves open the possibility of an identity between phenomenal properties and *impure* representational properties, which require an appropriate manner of representation. If we stipulate the right manner of representation, the possibility of unconscious representation might be ruled out, removing at least one obstacle to an identity.

The obvious suggestion is to require a *phenomenal* manner of representation. Representational contents can be represented either phenomenally (as in conscious vision, for example) or nonphenomenally (as in unconscious thought). For a given content, we can define a corresponding impure representational property: the property of phenomenally representing that content. It is natural to wonder whether phenomenal properties might be identical to impure representational properties of this sort.

For a given phenomenal property, one can find a corresponding impure representational property of this sort. If the phenomenal property entails some representational properties (as at least perceptual phenomenal properties plausibly do), then it will entail some maximally specific representational property, involving a specific representational content. We can then define the impure representational property of phenomenally representing that content. The original phenomenal property will clearly entail this impure representational property. If the impure representational property itself entails the original phenomenal property, then the two properties are identical.

The only obstacle to this identification is the possibility that two distinct phenomenal properties might correspond to the same impure representational property. This will happen if two distinct phenomenal states can have exactly the same representational content. This would happen if a perceptual state and a nonperceptual state

---

[6] Something like pure representationalism is advocated by Lloyd (1991), who takes the first strategy, and by Thau (2002), who takes the second strategy.

(a visual experience and a conscious belief, for example) could phenomenally represent the same content. It would also happen if two perceptual experiences in different modalities (a visual experience and an auditory experience) could have the same content. Finally, it would happen if two phenomenally distinct perceptual experiences in the same modality (two visual experiences, for example) could have the same content.

It is not clear whether any of these cases can arise. But if they arise, there is a natural strategy for dealing with them: one can add more specificity to the manner of representation. Taking the first sort of case, one might argue that an experience of color and a belief about color could in principle have the same content, perhaps representing an object as having a certain specific shade of red. If this sort of case can arise, the perceptual phenomenal property will not be identical to the property of phenomenally representing the content in question. But one can handle the case by moving to a more specific impure representational property, such as the property of *perceptually* phenomenally representing the content in question.

Likewise, one might argue that a visual experience and an auditory experience might have the same content, perhaps representing that there is an object on one's left. In this case, it is far from clear that such states can have the same *specific* representational content, which is what is needed for a counterexample to equivalence. In most of the cases one might introduce, even if there is an equivalence in unspecific content (that there is an object on one's left), there is usually a difference in specific content (say, that there is a red spherical object on one's left, or that there is an object making a certain sound on one's left). So it is far from clear that this sort of case can arise. But if it can arise, one need only move once again to a more specific impure representational property, such as the property of *visually* (or auditorily) phenomenally representing the content in question.

Finally, one might argue that two phenomenally distinct visual experiences might have the same content. It is not easy to see how this could happen. Byrne (2001) has argued that this could not happen, on the grounds that any phenomenal difference between visual experiences is a difference in how things seem, and any difference between how things seem is a difference in representational content. Even if one resists this argument (on the grounds, perhaps, that it involves an equivocation on "how things seem"), it is not easy to come up with specific cases of phenomenally distinct visual experiences with the same content. When we conceive of phenomenally distinct visual experiences, it seems that we almost always conceive of experiences that differ in aspects of their representational content.

Peacocke (1983) has argued that there are such cases: for example, images of two trees at different distances might represent them as having the same height, while the images take up differently-sized portions of the visual field. But representationalists (e.g. Tye, 1995) have plausibly replied that these images differ in certain representational properties (such as their representation of distance, or of visual angle). Block (1990) has argued that subjects with phenomenally distinct color experiences in different environments might represent the same external colors. But one can argue, along lines developed later in this paper, that such experiences always differ in certain key aspects of their representational content. Other purported examples, involving cases of blurry vision, double images, and the like, have received reasonably plausible replies (e.g. Tye, 2003) from representationalists.

To my mind, the most plausible potential cases of phenomenally distinct visual experiences with the same representational content involve differences in attention. Shifts in attention clearly make a phenomenal difference to visual experiences. In typical cases, they also make a representational difference: for example, shifting attention to a word may lead one to represent the shapes of its letters with greater specificity. But there are cases that are less clear. For example, one might look at two red pinpoint lights against a black background, and shift attention from one to the other. Here it is not obvious that there is a representational difference between the cases. There are various suggestions one might make in response, however. One might argue that the position or color of the light to which one is attending is represented with greater specificity than that of the light to which one is not attending. Or one might argue that the light to which one is attending is represented as being more salient than the other light. Here it is not completely clear what sort of property "salience" is, but it is plausible that there is such a property (though it may be a relational property, relative to a subject at a time), and the suggestion that it is represented in attention seems reasonably apt to the phenomenology.

If there are any cases of phenomenally different visual experiences with the same representational content, one will have to build further differences into the manners of representation in impure representational states (so one might have the property of attentively representing a certain content, and so on). But it is not clear that such cases exist. My own view is that the claim that phenomenal differences between visual experiences always correspond to representational differences has some prima facie plausibility, and serves as a sort of null hypothesis that should be rejected only if there is strong evidence against it. If the view is correct, then visual phenomenal properties are identical to impure representational properties of the form involving the (visual) phenomenal representation of a certain content.

Is representationalism correct?   If what has gone before is correct, then there is a strong prima facie case for the truth of impure representationalism, at least about visual phenomenal properties. These properties are plausibly equivalent to certain impure representational properties. These impure representational properties have the character: *phenomenally representing such-and-such content*, or (if nonperceptual phenomenal states can have the same content) *perceptually phenomenally representing such-and-such content*, or (if experiences in a different perceptual modality can have the same content) *visually phenomenally representing such-and-such content*.

4. Reductive and Nonreductive Representationalism

I have argued that phenomenal properties are plausibly identical to certain impure representational properties. In the characterization of these impure representational properties, however, the concept of the *phenomenal* itself plays an important role. So the analysis I have given certainly does not offer any sort of reductive analysis of phenomenal properties in terms of nonphenomenal notions.

Here, it is useful to distinguish *reductive* from *nonreductive* representationalism. Representationalism is the thesis that phenomenal properties are identical to certain pure or impure representational properties. Reductive representationalism holds that phenomenal properties are identical to certain pure or impure representational properties that can be understood without appeal to phenomenal notions. Nonreductive representationalism holds that phenomenal properties are identical to certain pure or impure representational properties, where these cannot be understood without appeal to phenomenal notions.

In a little more detail: representationalism holds that any given phenomenal property is identical to the property of representing a certain content in a certain manner (or in the case of pure representationalism, to the property of representing a certain content). Here, the right-hand side invokes a number of notions: the notion of representation, the notion of a certain content, and the notion of a certain manner of representation. If all of these notions can be understood without appeal to phenomenal notions, then the right-hand side offers a reductive account of phenomenal properties. If any of these notions can only be understood in terms of phenomenal notions, then the right-hand side offers a nonreductive account of phenomenal properties.[7]

The analysis I have given above is clearly not a reductive analysis. The manner of representation invoked in this analysis makes explicit appeal to the notion of the phenomenal. It may also be, for all I have said so far, that the contents involved in characterizing the representational properties must themselves be understood in terms of phenomenal notions (for example, if they involve the attribution of phenomenal properties to objects, or if they involve the attribution of certain dispositions to cause phenomenal properties). And it might even be that the notion of representation cannot be understood in wholly nonphenomenal terms. The status of the last two claims is unclear, but certainly the first claim makes it clear that this is not a reductive analysis.

Proponents of reductive representationalism need to do three things. First, they need to argue that an account of representation can be given in nonphenomenal terms. Second, they need to argue that the relevant contents can be specified in a manner that is independent of phenomenal notions (this is a version of what Peacocke (1983) calls the "Adequacy Constraint"). And third, they need to argue that the appeal to a phenomenal manner of representation can be replaced by some nonphenomenally characterized manner of representation.

---

[7] One can also distinguish *epistemically* reductive representationalism from *metaphysically* reductive representationalism, depending on whether the identity between phenomenal properties and non-phenomenally-specified representational properties is held to be a priori (or conceptually true), or simply to be true. Epistemically reductive representationalism entails metaphysically reductive representationalism, but not vice versa. For example, Tye's representationalism is metaphysically but not epistemically reductive.

In practice, this is just what reductive representationalists (such as Tye, 1995 and Dretske, 1995) try to do.[8] They appeal to an independently motivated account of representation in causal, informational, and teleological terms. They argue that the relevant representational contents can be understood as involving the attributions of ordinary physical properties (such as surface reflectance properties, in the case of color experiences) to physical objects in the world, without any need for phenomenal notions. And they argue that the relevant manner of representation can be understood in wholly functional terms.

I will set aside the first two points for now, and focus on the third. For the reasons given earlier, it seems that a manner of representation is needed to distinguish phenomenal from nonphenomenal representation of a given content. At this point, Tye introduces the constraint that the representing state must be *poised* to play a certain role in the control of speech and action. This constraint is introduced precisely to distinguish phenomenal from nonphenomenal representation, in cases such as blindsight. Dretske's account is less explicit about how to handle unconscious representation, but at some places he appeals to the constraint that the representational states must play an appropriate role in the formation of beliefs.

These accounts involve broadly *functional* accounts of the manner of representation: they require that the relevant representational states play the right sort of functional role within the cognitive system. In effect, this functional constraint is offered as an account of the difference between phenomenal and nonphenomenal representations (of the content in question). To this extent, then, the accounts involve functionalism about the phenomenal/nonphenomenal distinction. We might say these accounts are a species of *functionalist representationalism*. They are not functionalist across the board (both Dretske and Tye lean on nonfunctionalist teleological accounts of what it is to represent the contents in question), but they involve functionalism about the crucial distinction between phenomenal and nonphenomenal representation of the relevant contents.

Functionalist representationalism might be seen as the result of *conjoining* the relatively neutral version of representationalism above with functionalism about the phenomenal/nonphenomenal distinction. If we grant that phenomenal properties are identical to the property of phenomenally representing a certain content, and if we grant that what it is to phenomenally represent a content is to represent the content with a state that plays an appropriate functional role, the result is just this sort of account. So if functionalism about the phenomenal/nonphenomenal distinction can be justified, then functionalist representationalism can be justified.

Conversely, however, if there is reason to doubt functionalism about the phenomenal/nonphenomenal distinction, then there is reason to doubt functionalist representationalism. And there are many reasons to doubt functionalism about the phenomenal/nonphenomenal distinction. While there is some reason to believe that phenomenality is *correlated* with certain functional properties (such as the

---

[8] Reductive representationalists include Clark (2000), Dretske (1995), Droege (2003), Harman (1990), Jackson (2003), Lycan (1996), and Tye (1995).

property of global availability), there are familiar reasons to doubt that it is reducible to these properties. For example, it seems coherent to suppose that any such functional property can be instantiated without any associated phenomenology at all. Many have argued that such a situation is metaphysically possible, and some (e.g. Block, 1979 and Searle, 1981) have even argued that it is nomologically possible. Others (e.g. Levine, 1983) have argued that there is an explanatory gap between a functional characterization of a state and a phenomenal characterization: there is no clear reason why the fact that a state plays a certain functional role should somehow make it the case that there is something it is like to be in that state.[9]

I will not try to adjudicate these arguments here. I will simply note that the functionalism in these varieties of representationalism is entirely optional. It is also worth noting that this functionalism is often largely unargued. Tye's defense consists mostly in noting that the functional criterion handles cases such as blindsight, but clearly this falls well short of establishing any sort of reduction; while Dretske is not explicit about the matter at all. In arguing for their views, both spend by far the greatest portion of their time arguing for representationalism, and the crucial functionalism is left mostly in the background.

This leaves the following situation: there are good arguments for representationalism, but these are not good arguments for reductive representationalism. There is good reason to believe that phenomenal properties are identical to impure representational properties involving the phenomenal representation of certain contents. Both the reductive and the nonreductive representationalist can accept this. The reductive representationalist must conjoin this with a reductive account of the phenomenal/nonphenomenal distinction. But there are familiar reasons to doubt that such an account is possible, and the arguments for representationalism give no special reason to think that such an account exists.[10]

For my part, I think that nonreductive representationalism is a much more plausible view.[11] This view articulates an internal connection between phenomenal properties and representational properties, without trying to reduce the phenomenal to a wholly nonphenomenal domain. At the very least, the nonreductive style of analysis above provides a reasonably neutral starting point for further representationalist analyses. Representationalists of many different stripes can agree that visual

[9] A teleological representationalist such as Dretske allows that any narrow functional property can be instantiated without phenomenology, as phenomenology requires the relevant sort of environment. However, the central anti-functionalist arguments (by Block, Searle, etc.) also tend to suggest that any given functional property could in principle be instantiated in any given environment, without phenomenology. So "teleofunctionalist" views are vulnerable to the same sort of arguments as functionalist views.

[10] Versions of this point are made by Chalmers (1996, p. 377), Kriegel (2002a), Vinueza (2000), and Warfield (1999). The point that representationalism on its own does not offer the prospect of closing the explanatory gap is also made in a slightly different way (focusing on the represented contents rather than the manner of representation) by Stoljar (forthcoming).

[11] To my knowledge, nonreductive representationalism has not been discussed explicitly as such in the literature, but Byrne (2001) notes the possibility of representationalism without reduction, and Crane (2003) and Levine (2003) indicate sympathy for this combination. The views suggested by Horgan and Tienson (2002), Searle (1983), and Siewert (1998) seem broadly compatible with the same combination.

phenomenal properties are equivalent to impure representational properties of the form: phenomenally (or visually phenomenally, or whatever) representing such-and-such a content.

The questions for further debate concern: (i) the specificity in the manner of representation (e.g. phenomenal, perceptual phenomenal, or visual phenomenal?); (ii) whether the phenomenal manner of representation can itself be reductively analyzed; and (iii) the nature of the represented contents. So far, I have addressed the first two questions. In what follows I will address the third.

5. Narrow and Wide Representationalism

It is widely believed that phenomenal properties depend only on the internal state of the subject. It is also widely believed (following the arguments of Putnam, 1975 and Burge, 1979) that most representational properties depend not only on the internal state of the subject, but also on the subject's environment. For example, it is widely accepted that if two physically identical subjects have relevantly different environments (e.g. an "Earth" environment containing H_2O, or a "Twin Earth" environment containing XYZ), the contents of their mental states may be relevantly different (e.g. one has beliefs about H_2O, while the other has beliefs about XYZ).

This poses a prima facie problem for representationalism. Let us say that a property is *narrow* when necessarily, for any individual who has the property, an intrinsic duplicate of that individual has the property (regardless of environment). Let us say that a property is *wide* when it is possible for an individual to have the property while an intrinsic duplicate lacks that property. Then the following three propositions form an inconsistent triad:

(i) phenomenal properties are equivalent to representational properties,
(ii) phenomenal properties are narrow,
(iii) representational properties are wide.

One can react to this inconsistent triad in three different ways: one could deny (i), (ii), or (iii). The first strategy leads to *anti-representationalism*. Block (1990) takes this strategy, in effect using the plausibility of (ii) and (iii) as an argument against representationalism.

The second strategy leads to *wide representationalism*, on which both phenomenal properties and the representational properties that they are equivalent to are taken to depend on a subject's environment. This strategy is taken by Dretske (1995), Tye (1995), and Lycan (1996), who in effect use the plausibility of (i) and (iii) to argue against the narrowness of phenomenal properties.

Both of these strategies have significant costs. The anti-representationalist strategy has trouble doing justice to the persistent intuition that phenomenal duplicates are deeply similar in certain representational respects. The wide representationalist strategy is even more counterintuitive, entailing that what it is like to be a subject depends constitutively on factors that may be far away from the subject and in the distant past. Some wide representationalists (especially Lycan, 2001) have tried to defend this view, but it has many odd consequences. To pick just one: a change in environment can often yield a gradual change from one wide representational content to another quite different content (e.g. from representing red to representing green), with a period of indeterminate representation of both contents (or divided reference) in the middle. But it is hard to know what an indeterminate phenomenal state involving both phenomenal red and phenomenal green could be like (striped? superimposed?), and it is hard to believe that a subject going through this change in environment would pass through such a state. Lycan suggests that there may be much less indeterminacy in perceptual representation than in cognitive representation, but it is hard to believe that indeterminacy can be eliminated entirely. If there is even a brief period of indeterminacy, then the puzzle arises.

I think that by far the best-motivated strategy is the third. This is the strategy of *narrow representationalism*, which holds that both phenomenal properties and the representational properties they are equivalent to depend only on a subject's internal state. The arguments by Putnam, Burge, and the like give good reason to think that *many* representational properties are wide, but they give little reason to think that *all* representational properties are wide. If we accept that some representational properties are narrow, the inconsistent triad disappears. The natural strategy is then to exploit narrow representational properties in developing a narrow representationalism.[12]

Narrow representational properties can most naturally be developed by an appeal to *narrow contents*: contents of the sort that, if they are represented by a subject, they are represented by any intrinsic duplicate of that subject (regardless of the environment). The arguments of Putnam and Burge suggest that many contents are wide: especially the contents of beliefs about natural kinds and about individuals, and those involving deference to a linguistic community. But these arguments are consistent with the view that many other contents are narrow.

For example, it is widely accepted that many logical and mathematical beliefs have narrow content. More generally, Horgan and Tienson (2002) have argued that the existence of rich narrow content is a consequence of the plausible view that phenomenal duplicates share rich representational content. And it is possible to hold on quite general grounds that all mental states have a sort of narrow content, in addition to any wide content they might have. On the latter sort of view, although two corresponding "water"-beliefs of subjects on Earth and Twin Earth may differ in that one is about H_2O and the other is about XYZ (wide content), the beliefs will also have significant narrow content in common, perhaps characterizing the relevant liquids in qualitative terms.

I have argued elsewhere (Chalmers, 2002) for a view of the latter sort, holding that the narrow content of beliefs can be understood as a sort of Fregean epistemic content. I think that this sort of account can naturally be extended to give an account of the narrow content of perceptual states. But first, it is useful to examine different ways of characterizing representational content.

---

[12] Versions of narrow representationalism are advocated by Rey (1998), Kriegel (2002b), and Levine (2003).

6. Russellian Representationalism

One natural way of characterizing the content of mental states involves objects and properties in the world. A belief, such as the belief that Hesperus is bright, can be regarded as composed of concepts (which I will regard here as mental items of some sort). One can naturally say that concepts have *extensions*: objects and properties that are picked out by these concepts. The extension of the concept *Hesperus* is the planet Venus, and the extension of the concept *bright* is the property of brightness. One can then characterize the content of a belief in terms of the extensions of the concepts that are involved in the belief. For example, a belief that Hesperus is bright might have the content: [*Venus, brightness*]. Contents of this sort, involving complexes of specific objects and/or properties in the world, may be thought of as Russellian contents (following Bertrand Russell, who thought all contents were like this).

Let us say that a Russellian representational property is the property of representing a certain Russellian content, or the property of representing a certain Russellian content in a certain way. Then *Russellian representationalism* holds that phenomenal properties are identical to Russellian representational properties. Most contemporary representationalists are Russellian representationalists.[13]

It is natural to think that perceptual experiences have Russellian content. They involve the attribution of properties to objects. For example, when I have a veridical experience of a green ball B, it is natural to think that I represent the ball as being green, and that my experience has an *object-involving* Russellian content roughly as follows: [*B, greenness*]. It is also natural to think that my experience has a sort of *existential* (or merely *property-involving*) Russellian content, to the effect that there is an object in front of me that is green.

To develop a Russellian representationalism, most Russellian representationalists invoke something like the property-involving Russellian content mentioned above, rather than an object-involving Russellian content. The reason is that it seems that phenomenology can be dissociated from the object-involving content. My visual experience when I look at a green ball has a certain object-involving content, but it seems that a phenomenally identical experience could lack that content, if I were looking at a different object, for example, or if I were hallucinating. (Some direct realists will deny this claim, but most contemporary representationalists accept it.) But in these cases, the property-involving content of the original experience is still plausibly present: my visual experience still represents that there is a green object in front of me.

To go into more detail, it is useful to focus on the case of phenomenal properties associated with colors (though I think the discussion that follows generalizes). Let us say that *phenomenal redness* is the phenomenal property typically associated in our community with seeing red things. (Phenomenal redness should be distinguished from ordinary redness: the first is a property of experiences or of subjects, the second is a property of objects in one's environment.) It is natural to think that

---

[13] Thompson (2003) also distinguishes Fregean and Russellian representationalism. McLaughlin (2003) uses "denotational intentionalism" for something like Russellian representationalism.

instances of phenomenal redness have the content that certain objects in the environment are *red*: that is, these have contents that attribute the property of redness.

This line of thought naturally leads to the most common Russellian representationalist view. This view holds that phenomenal redness is equivalent to the impure representational property of (visually) phenomenally representing a certain Russellian content involving the attribution of redness. Of course, for this view to be made more specific, one needs to specify just what sort of property redness is.[14]

Most commonly, Russellian representationalists of this sort take the view that redness is a physical property, such as a certain surface spectral reflectance. Then phenomenal redness is equivalent to a certain sort of attribution of this physical property to objects. Something analogous is usually said about other perceptual phenomenal properties: all are equivalent to representational properties involving the attribution of physical properties. The resulting view might be called *physical Russellian representationalism*. This strategy has the advantage of being reductive, at least where the content is concerned: there is no need to use phenomenal notions in characterizing the relevant contents.

Physical Russellian representationalism is plausibly a sort of wide representationalism. To have the relevant representational property, the subject must represent the relevant physical property, which plausibly requires that the subject has been inhabiting an appropriate environment. This leads to numerous counterintuitive consequences. For example, it seems possible that a subject might have experiences phenomenally identical to my experiences of redness, even though their experiences have been caused by objects that are not physically red (i.e. objects that have a different surface spectral reflectance); and it seems possible that these color experiences in such a subject might nevertheless be veridical. But physical Russellian representationalism must deny this possibility. I will not pursue this matter here, as it has been explored at length by others (e.g. Block, 1990; Shoemaker, 2002).

If we are interested in the prospects for narrow representationalism, it seems that other forms of Russellian representationalism are more compatible with this view. For example, *projectivism* about colors holds that colors are phenomenal properties, or perhaps that they are qualitative properties of a visual field. *Projectivist Russellian representationalism* holds that color experiences attribute these properties to objects, and that phenomenal color properties are equivalent to corresponding representational properties.[15] (One might embrace projectivist Russellian representationalism without embracing projectivism about colors, if one holds that the relevant contents do not involve attribution of colors.) This is most naturally seen as a sort of narrow and nonreductive representationalism: two intrinsic duplicates will share

[14] The distinctions that follow between physical, projectivist, primitivist, and dispositionalist versions of representationalism are also made by Stoljar (forthcoming). Stoljar calls the first of these the "physicalist" interpretation of representationalism, but I avoid this usage to avoid a natural confusion. Stoljar suggests that projectivism is not really a form of representationalism because it appeals directly to qualia; but once we acknowledge the possibility of nonreductive representationalism, this problem falls away.

[15] Boghossian and Velleman (1989) have a view that seems compatible with projectivist Russellian representationalism: they advocate projectivism about colors, and hold that properties of this sort are represented in color experience.

the relevant representational properties, given that they share their phenomenal properties.

A related view, *primitivism* about colors, holds that colors are certain primitive intrinsic properties that are not phenomenal properties or properties of a visual field, but that are nevertheless constitutively connected to such properties. On this view colors have an intrinsic "qualitative" nature that is revealed in some fashion by color experiences. *Primitivist Russellian representationalism* holds that color experiences attribute these primitive properties to objects, and that phenomenal color properties are equivalent to corresponding representational properties.[16] (One might embrace primitivist Russellian representationalism without embracing primitivism about colors, if one holds that the relevant contents do not involve attribution of colors.) This is again naturally seen as a sort of narrow representationalism, given that phenomenal duplicates represent the same primitive properties, and given that phenomenal properties are narrow. It is also plausibly seen as nonreductive, given that colors are taken to be irreducible properties that are constitutively tied to phenomenal properties.

There is a certain phenomenological plausibility in both projectivist and primitivist Russellian representationalism. Both involve the attribution of intrinsic properties to objects, properties with a qualitative nature that is closely connected to the qualities of experience itself. But these views seem to have the counterintuitive consequence that color experience is massively illusory. When we have an experience as of a red apple, it seems unlikely that the apple itself instantiates phenomenal redness, or that it instantiates a corresponding property of our visual field. It also seems unlikely that it instantiates a simple intrinsic property with a qualitative nature that is constitutively connected to the quality of my visual experience. Further: it seems plausible (as above) that subjects in different environments might have phenomenally red experiences that are caused by objects that share no relevant intrinsic properties, without either subject being in a privileged position with respect to veridicality. If both experiences attribute the same intrinsic properties, then both cannot be correct, so neither is correct. Generalizing, it seems that projectivist or primitivist representationalism leads to the consequence that all color experiences are illusory. Some have accepted this consequence, but it seems a high price to pay.[17]

Finally, *dispositionalism* about color holds that colors are dispositional properties, involving the disposition to cause certain sorts of experiences: for example, redness might be the disposition to cause phenomenally red experiences in a certain class of subjects in normal conditions. *Dispositionalist Russellian representationalism* holds that color experiences attribute these dispositional properties to objects, and that phenomenal color properties are equivalent to corresponding representational

[16] The "figurative projectivism" of Shoemaker (1990) is a sort of primitivism, while projectivism corresponds to his "literal projectivism". Advocates of (something like) primitivist Russellian representationalism include Maund (1995), Holman (2002), Jakab (2003), and Wright (2003), who are also primitivists about colors, and Thau (2002), who is not.

[17] Boghossian and Velleman, Holman, Jakab, Maund, and Wright all accept that color experiences are illusory. Thau is not explicit about the matter.

properties. As before, one might embrace dispositionalist Russellian representation-alism without embracing dispositionalism about colors, if one holds that the relev-ant contents attribute properties other than colors. This sort of view is most closely associated with Shoemaker (1994, 2001).

Dispositionalist representationalism characterizes the relevant representational contents in partly phenomenal terms, so it can easily be seen as a sort of nonreduct-ive representationalism. Shoemaker does not see it this way. He conjoins the basic view with the view that phenomenal properties are identical to certain neurophysi-ological properties, and so holds that the relevant dispositional properties can be identified nonphenomenally. So his version of the view is a sort of reductive repres-entationalism. But the reductive aspect of his view is largely independent of the representationalist aspect, and one might well embrace the basic shape of the rep-resentationalist view without embracing the reductive claim. If so, the result is a nonreductive version of representationalism.[18]

Dispositionalist representationalism can also easily be seen as a sort of narrow representationalism. It seems plausible to think that two intrinsic duplicates will share their representational contents: both will have phenomenally red experiences, attributing the disposition to cause red experiences to their objects. However (as Egan, forthcoming, and Thompson, 2003, have pointed out), it is not clear just how this dispositional property should be characterized. If it is the disposition to cause phenomenally red experiences in a specific subject (the subject of the experience), the phenomenally red experiences in different subjects will attribute *different* dispo-sitional properties to their objects, and will differ in the relevant content. This con-tent will not be narrow (the attributed properties will differ between duplicate subjects); and worse, the corresponding representational property will not be entailed by the phenomenal property. An appeal to dispositions to cause the experi-ence in a specific community has the same problem.

Partly to deal with this sort of problem, Shoemaker's version of dispositionalist representationalism appeals to the "higher-order" disposition to cause the experience in one or more sorts of creature in some circumstance; but this view has the consequence that illusory representation is impossible (every object will have the relevant disposition). Egan suggests that the experience attributes an *indexical* disposition: something like the disposition to cause phenomenally red experiences in *me*, where this disposition is attributed equally by both subjects; but it is not clear that this indexical disposition is a legitimate property, or that it could be shared by objects of veridical perception by different subjects in different environments. Alternatively, one might hold that one is attributing to *oneself* the property of being confronted by an object with the disposition to cause certain experiences in one; but it is counterintuitive to hold that experience involves the attribution of properties to oneself and not to an external object.

This is one difficulty with the view. Another difficulty is that it seems implausible for various reasons that colors are dispositions. It seems possible that in counterfactual

---

[18] Kriegel (2002b) and Levine (2003) embrace the basic shape of Shoemaker's dispositionalist repre-sentationalism, without Shoemaker's reductive claim.

circumstances, red objects might be disposed to cause phenomenally green experiences in normal observers, or in me. If this is right, redness is distinct from the disposition to cause phenomenally red experiences. It seems more compatible with our judgments about the cases that redness is an intrinsic property, such as surface spectral reflectance. But then the dispositional representationalist must say (as Shoemaker does) that the relevant contents attribute properties other than colors to objects. This is at least a counterintuitive thing to say.

We can sum up the problems for Russellian representationalism as follows. The following three claims are plausible: (i) color experiences attribute colors to objects; (ii) colors are intrinsic properties; and (iii) there can be veridical phenomenally identical color experiences (in different subjects) of objects with relevantly different intrinsic properties. But these claims entail that phenomenally identical color experiences can attribute different properties to objects. So these claims are inconsistent with Russellian representationalism about color experience.

Denying any of these claims has significant costs. It is possible that some of these costs might be worth paying, if Russellian representationalism were the only way to get a viable representationalism off the ground. But I think that one can avoid these costs entirely. The problems arise only if we assume that the relevant contents must be Russellian contents. If we appeal to a quite different sort of content, the problems may be avoided.

7. Fregean Content

Frege distinguished between the sense and the reference of linguistic expressions. The referent of an expression such as 'Hesperus' is the planet Venus, but its sense is a *mode of presentation* of that planet. Two distinct terms, such as 'Hesperus' and 'Phosphorus', may have the same referent but different senses. Something similar goes for a property term, such as 'bright'. Here one might say that the referent of the term is the property of brightness, while its sense is a mode of presentation of that property. Frege held that the sense of an expression determines the expression's referent, in some fashion.

One can make a similar distinction for mental states. A belief such as *Hesperus is bright* is composed of concepts, such as *Hesperus* and *bright*. The concepts can be said to have extensions: the planet Venus and the property of brightness, respectively. The concepts can also be said to have *modes of presentation* of those extensions. These modes of presentation can be thought of as an aspect of the content of the concepts. Two different concepts, such as *Hesperus* and *Phosphorus* may have the same extension but different modes of presentation. The belief as a whole may have a complex content that is composed of these modes of presentation.

What is a mode of presentation? Frege was not entirely clear on this. But one natural approach characterizes a mode of presentation as a *condition on extension*. The idea is that every concept is associated with some *condition*, such that an entity in the world must satisfy this condition to qualify as the extension of the concept. For example, the concept *Hesperus* might be associated with a condition something like: *the object usually visible at a certain point in the evening sky*. (Strictly speaking, the condition is *being the object* . . . , but I will usually use the simpler form.) In the actual world, Venus satisfies this condition, so Venus is the extension of *Hesperus*. The concept *Phosphorus* might be associated with a different condition (involving the morning sky). Venus also satisfies this condition, so Venus is the extension of *Phosphorus*. On this analysis, *Hesperus* and *Phosphorus* have the same extensions but different modes of presentation, just as desired.

We can think of these modes of presentation as the *Fregean contents* of concepts. We can also speak of the Fregean contents of entire thoughts, by composing the Fregean contents of the concepts involved. For example, the Fregean content of the thought *Hesperus is Phosphorus* might be something like the condition *the object usually visible at a certain point in the evening sky is usually visible at a certain point in the morning sky*. This is a condition on the state of the world, reflecting what it takes for the thought to be true: that is, it is a sort of truth-condition.

To determine the condition of extension associated with a concept or with a thought, one can consider different hypothetical possibilities concerning the way one's world might turn out to be, and determine what the concept's extension (or the thought's truth-value) would be under those possibilities. For example, if it turned out that star A was the bright object in the evening sky and a different star B was the bright object in the morning sky, we would say that *Hesperus* picks out A and *Phosphorus* picks out B, and we would say that *Hesperus is Phosphorus* is false. Formally, one can say that the Fregean content of a concept is a mapping from scenarios to extensions, and that the Fregean content of a thought is a mapping from scenarios to truth-values, where scenarios are maximal epistemic possibilities, or centered possible worlds. I have developed this sort of approach extensively elsewhere (e.g. Chalmers, 2002), but for the most part the informal understanding will suffice here.

(Note that modes of presentation are quite distinct from the manners of representation invoked earlier. Manners of representation are psychological features of an individual. By contrast, modes of presentation are a sort of *content*. Unlike manners of representation, modes of presentation have built-in conditions of satisfaction. Rather than being psychological entities, they are abstract entities to which psychological states may be related, by having them as their content.)

One can extend this approach to the content of perceptual experiences. Perceptual experiences attribute properties to objects: e.g. my visual experience might attribute greenness to a ball. And as with beliefs and concepts, we can hold that a perceptual experience involves some *modes of presentation* of these properties and objects. As before, these modes of presentation can be seen as conditions on extension. For example, there is a condition that an object must satisfy in order to be the object represented by my experience. The ball satisfies this condition, so it is the object represented by my experience. There is also a condition that a property must satisfy in order to be the property attributed by my experience. Greenness satisfies this condition, so greenness is the property represented by my experience.

What are the modes of presentation associated with a given perceptual experience? To determine these, one considers scenarios involving different ways the world might turn out, and consider what the objects and properties represented by the experience will then be. Take a visual experience as of a green sphere. At a very rough first approximation, one might say that for an object to be represented by an experience, it must cause the experience in the appropriate way. So the mode of presentation of the object will be something like: *the object that is causing this experience in the appropriate way.* Likewise, one might say that for a property (say, greenness) to be attributed by the experience, it must be the property that has usually caused that sort of color experience in normal conditions in the past. So the mode of presentation of the property will be something like: *the property that usually causes phenomenally green experiences in normal conditions.*[19]

Overall (if we abstract from all other features of the experience, such as its spatial features), the experience will be associated with a Fregean content along the lines: *the object causing this experience has the property that normally causes experiences of phenomenal greenness.* This is very roughly compatible with our intuitive judgments about cases. If it turns out that no object is causing the experience in the appropriate way (e.g. if we are hallucinating the object), then we will judge that the experience is not veridical. If it turns out that the object has a property that normally causes phenomenally red experiences, but is now causing a phenomenally green experience due to abnormal conditions, we will judge that the experience is not veridical. And so on.

(One could also make a case for dropping the "object causing this experience" aspect of the content, yielding a "pure existential" Fregean content along the lines of "there exists an object [at such-and-such location] with the property that usually causes experiences of phenomenal greenness". This turns on subtle issues about whether alleged cases of "veridical hallucination" (e.g. when one hallucinates a red square in front of one, and by coincidence there is a red square in front of one) should be classified as veridical or non-veridical. If veridical, one should go with the pure existential Fregean content. If non-veridical, one should go with the more complex causal Fregean content.)

One can formalize this approach to Fregean content by using the two-dimensional framework for analysing mental and linguistic content. I develop this sort of analysis in forthcoming work.[20] For present purposes, the informal understanding above will suffice.

8. Fregean Representationalism

This leads to a natural proposal. Let us say that a *Fregean representational property* is the property of having a certain Fregean content (in a certain way). Let us say that

---

[19] The suggestion that color experiences have dispositional modes of presentation of this sort that fix reference to intrinsic properties in the external world can be seen as analogous to a corresponding claim about color expressions: e.g. that "red" refers to an intrinsic property, with a mode of presentation that picks out whatever normally caused phenomenally red experiences.

[20] On this approach, the Fregean content of an experience can be analyzed as a primary or epistemic intension mapping epistemic possibilities to extensions. I develop this analysis in forthcoming work. In another work (Chalmers, forthcoming), I try to develop a more refined view of the Fregean content of experience in a way that respects some of the phenomenological insight of primitivism.

Fregean representationalism is the thesis that phenomenal properties are equivalent to certain (pure or impure) Fregean representational properties. Then one might use the Fregean contents of the sort described above to put forward a version of Fregean representationalism.[21]

For example, one might propose that phenomenal redness is equivalent to the property of having a certain Fregean content (in the appropriate phenomenal way), where this Fregean content involves a mode of presentation such as *the property that normally causes experiences of phenomenal redness*. On this view, the relevant representational content does not directly involve the property attributed by the experience. It may well be that the experience attributes the property of redness to an object, and that redness is a surface spectral reflectance property. This attributed property may enter into the Russellian content of the experience, but it does not enter into the Fregean content. Rather, the Fregean content involves a mode of presentation of this property.

Here it is highly plausible that two phenomenally identical experiences will have the same Fregean content. This will certainly be the case if the Fregean content of perceptual experiences works as above, by requiring a certain relation to the relevant phenomenal property. For example, any two phenomenally red experiences will involve the mode of presentation *the property that normally causes phenomenally red experiences*. Of course, this mode of presentation may pick out different properties in different environments, or in creatures with different perceptual systems. In me, it might pick out a certain surface spectral reflectance; in a subject in a different environment or with a different perceptual system, it might pick out a different property entirely. But this is just what one would expect.

This suggests that a phenomenal property entails the corresponding Fregean representational property. For example, phenomenal redness entails visually phenomenally attributing a property under the Fregean mode of presentation *the property that normally causes phenomenally red experiences*. As for the converse, it seems plausible that any mental state that visually phenomenally attributes a property under this mode of presentation will itself be phenomenally red. One might be able to replace "visually" with "perceptually", as it is implausible that a non-visual perceptual experience could attribute a property under this mode of presentation. It may well be that a *belief* could attribute a property under this mode of presentation, however, so one needs to at least specify a perceptual manner of presentation. As a result, it seems plausible that phenomenal redness is equivalent to the representational property of perceptually phenomenally representing the relevant Fregean content.

This view handles the central problems for Russellian representationalism straightforwardly. These views arose because Russellian representationalism is inconsistent with the plausible claims that (i) color experiences attribute colors to objects, (ii) color is an intrinsic property, and (iii) there can be veridical phenomenally identical experiences (in different subjects) of objects with relevantly different intrinsic properties. By contrast, Fregean representationalism is clearly compatible with these claims, for the reasons given above.

---

[21] Thompson (2003) also defends Fregean representationalism.

The view is plausibly a sort of narrow representationalism. I have argued elsewhere that the Fregean content of thoughts (understood appropriately) is always a sort of narrow content. It can equally be argued that the Fregean content of perception is a sort of narrow content. Given that the Fregean contents of a subject's experiences are determined by the subject's phenomenal properties, and that the phenomenal properties are intrinsic properties of a subject, this conclusion follows automatically. So as long as the relevant manners of representation are also narrow, the resulting Fregean representational properties will be narrow, and we will have a sort of narrow representationalism.

The view is also naturally seen as a sort of nonreductive representationalism, as phenomenal notions are used in specifying the relevant Fregean contents. If one holds that the relevant manners of representation are also phenomenally specified (as I do), the result is a *doubly nonreductive* representationalism, involving phenomenal elements in both the manner of representation and in the content.

It seems that this view has the potential to accommodate most of the problems mentioned so far. It is compatible with the narrowness of phenomenology, while also being compatible with the view that experience attributes intrinsic properties to objects. It is also compatible with our intuitions about the veridicality or nonveridicality of experiences in specific cases. Fregean content is defined in such a way that most of these intuitions are accommodated automatically. If one judges that a certain experience in a certain environment will be nonveridical, this requires only that the Fregean content of the experience should be a condition that maps this environment to "false". The overall Fregean content of the experience will be a condition that mirrors our judgments about the veridicality of an experience under arbitrary hypotheses about the state of the external world.

Of course, this means that the Fregean content may need to be refined beyond the very crude first characterization given above (involving *the property that normally causes phenomenally red experiences*). But this was only a rough approximation: the real content will be a condition (or mapping) that reflects our specific judgments about cases. So if there are cases that the crude characterization of the content misclassifies as veridical or nonveridical (as there certainly will be), one may want to refine the characterization, but in any case the problem concerns only the characterization, not the content. The general thesis that phenomenal properties are Fregean representational properties will be unthreatened by any such case.

This Fregean representationalism is closely related to Shoemaker's dispositional Russellian representationalism, discussed earlier. Both views give a key role to dispositional notions such as *normally causes phenomenally red experiences*. The difference is that where Shoemaker's view holds that color experiences attribute these dispositions to objects, my view holds that color experience attributes intrinsic properties (colors) to objects, with the dispositional notions serving as a mode of presentation of these intrinsic properties. That is, a dispositional relation to experience is used to *determine* the property attributed by the experience, but the property attributed is not itself dispositional. This avoids one major difficulty for Shoemaker's view: the claim that the primary properties attributed by color experiences are not colors.

The other major difficulty for Shoemaker's view was the problem of specifying the relevant dispositions. This problem is easily handled here. The mode of presentation will be something like *the property that normally causes phenomenally red experiences in me*, where the last part involves an indexical mode of presentation of oneself, one that different individuals can use to refer to themselves.[22] Indexical modes of presentation are already required for many other purposes in this sort of account of Fregean content, for example in specifying the Fregean content of indexical concepts such as *I* and *here*. Formally, they can be modeled using functions from centered possible worlds (worlds marked with an individual and a time) to extensions. So the Fregean content of *I* can be seen as a mapping that takes a centered world to the individual at the center of that world; and the Fregean content of a phenomenally red experience can be seen as a mapping that takes a centered world to whatever property normally causes red experiences in the individual at the center. While the notion of an indexical *property* is problematic, there is no such problem with the notion of an indexical mode of presentation. When a perceptual experience (embedded in an environment) has this sort of indexical mode of presentation, it will usually determine a perfectly objective property as its extension.

One might wonder whether this view is compatible with the oft-noted *transparency* of experiences. As I construe it, the central datum of transparency is that when we attempt to introspect the qualities of our experiences (e.g. phenomenal redness), we do so by attending to the qualities of external objects (e.g. redness). In effect, we look "through" the phenomenal property. But this is just what one would expect where modes of presentation are involved. When one introspects the content of a belief such as *Hesperus is bright*, one does so by thinking about Hesperus; one looks right through the mode of presentation. But nevertheless the mode of presentation exists, and one can become introspectively aware of it. The same goes for manners of representation, such as visualness. One looks "through" this manner of representation on introspecting an experience of phenomenal greenness, but the manner is nevertheless there, and one can obviously become introspectively aware of it. (This case shows especially clearly that there is no inference from the datum of transparency to the absence of introspective awareness.) So if phenomenal properties are associated with having certain modes of presentation of represented properties, under certain manners of representation, it is to be expected that these properties will be transparent.

One might object that the sort of modes of presentation I have been discussing over-intellectualize the contents of experience. When one attends to a red ball, one does not usually conceive of it as the cause of one's experience, or as possessing properties that normally cause that sort of experience. But this point is compatible with what I have said. The Fregean contents I have appealed to may very often be *nonconceptual* contents: to have a state with these contents, a subject need not deploy

---

[22] One might be tempted to replace *normally causes phenomenally red experiences in me* with *normally causes phenomenally red experiences in my community*. But this would have the odd consequence that someone who is spectrally inverted with respect to their community will have mostly illusory experiences.

a concept with those contents. So a subject's visual experience can have a mode of presentation along the lines of *the object causing this experience* without the subject deploying the concept of causation, or of the experience. It should be kept in mind that modes of presentation are fundamentally *conditions*, which can be seen as mappings from scenarios to extensions. The descriptive characterizations such as *the object causing this experience* are only rough ways of characterizing these conditions. Of course we have to use linguistic expressions and concepts to formulate these characterizations, but the conditions themselves may be entirely nonlinguistic and nonconceptual.

Further, it seems clear that there is some psychological reality to these modes of presentation. When a subject has a perceptual experience, the subject is usually capable of judging whether the experience is veridical or not, depending on further information about the state of the world. For example, if a rational subject discovers that there is no object causing the experience, the subject will conclude that the experience is nonveridical. Speaking broadly, one might think of this pattern of judgments as part of the *inferential role* of the experience. The Fregean content of an experience reflects this sort of inferential role directly. And it is plausible that the (rational) inferential role of an experience is grounded in some fashion in the representational content of the experience. So there is good reason to think that Fregean representational properties play an important psychological role.

I have outlined how this account works for the case of a simple color experience. I think the account can be generalized to other visual experiences, though some tricky issues arise. Thompson (2003) argues that one can handle spatial experiences in a similar way: these function by attributing properties (or relations) to objects, where these properties are picked out under a mode of presentation that characterized them as being those properties that stand in the relevant causal relation to spatial phenomenal properties. Other aspects of visual experience might be handled in a similar way.

It is natural to extend the account to other perceptual experiences, and to bodily sensations. It is easy enough to see how this will go: in every case, there will be a mode of presentation that picks out a property as something like the normal cause of the sort of experience in questions. Here, I will not try to address the issue of whether this extension would be appropriate. There are some difficult questions, not least about whether (for example) olfactory experiences or pain experiences can be veridical or nonveridical. I am inclined to say that *if* these experiences can be veridical or nonveridical, then an extension of the current approach will give a reasonable analysis of their content.

9. Summary

It may be useful to sum up the various distinctions that have been introduced, and to indicate where the view I have advocated falls.

Representationalism holds that phenomenal properties are equivalent to pure or impure representational properties: properties of representing a certain content (in a certain manner).

Pure representationalism holds that phenomenal properties are equivalent to pure representational properties: properties of representing a certain content. *Impure representationalism* holds that phenomenal properties are equivalent to impure representational properties: properties of representing a certain content in a certain manner.

Reductive representationalism holds that phenomenal properties are equivalent to representational properties that can be fully characterized in nonphenomenal terms. *Nonreductive representationalism* holds that phenomenal properties are equivalent to representational properties that cannot be fully characterized in nonphenomenal terms. Nonreductive representationalism might be nonreductive about the manner of representation, or about the representational content, or both.

Narrow representationalism holds that phenomenal properties are equivalent to narrow representational properties, depending only on a subject's intrinsic properties. *Wide representationalism* holds that phenomenal properties are equivalent to wide representational properties, depending partly on the subject's environment.

Russellian representationalism holds that phenomenal properties are equivalent to Russellian representational properties, with contents involving objects and/or properties in the world. (One can further distinguish *physical, projectivist, primitivist*, and *dispositionalist* Russellian representationalism, depending on what properties are held to be represented.) *Fregean representationalism* holds that phenomenal properties are equivalent to Fregean representational properties, with contents involving modes of presentation of objects and properties in the world.

The view I have advocated is a form of impure, nonreductive, narrow, Fregean representationalism. The view is in fact doubly nonreductive, with phenomenal elements involved in both the manner of representation and the representational content. In the case of a phenomenal color property, the associated manner of representation is required to be a perceptual phenomenal manner of representation. The associated representational content is a Fregean mode of presentation, one that picks out whatever property normally causes that sort of color experience in the subject. This view contrasts sharply with the most common versions of representationalism, which are reductive, wide, and Russellian.

10. Conclusion

I expect that the interface between consciousness and intentionality will be the central topic in the next decade of the philosophy of mind. I hope that the analysis I have given here helps to clarify some crucial issues in exploring this interface, and to open up some underexplored possibilities for making progress.

What of the issues mentioned at the start of the paper: is consciousness grounded in intentionality, or is intentionality grounded in consciousness? I have argued for a necessary equivalence between phenomenal and representational properties; but which of the phenomenal and the representational is more fundamental?

The nonreductive approach I have taken offers little prospect for grounding consciousness wholly in intentionality, where the latter is construed independently of consciousness. The representational analyses I have given all make unreduced appeal to phenomenal notions, and I think there is little hope of giving analyses that do without such notions altogether. So I think that a reduction of the phenomenal to the representational is not on the cards.

One might think that this approach offers more hope of grounding intentionality in consciousness. It is not implausible that there is something about consciousness, which by its very nature yields representation of the world. One might hold that at least with perceptual experiences, representational content accrues *in virtue* of the phenomenology. One might further hold that something similar holds for beliefs: their representational content accrues either in virtue of their phenomenal character, or in virtue of their connections to other beliefs and experiences whose content is grounded in phenomenal character.

Still, for this approach to provide a reductive grounding of the intentional, we would need to characterize the underlying phenomenal domain in non-intentional terms. And it is far from clear that this is possible. On the face of things, a characterization of my phenomenology that avoids intentional notions entirely would be quite inadequate. Rather, intentional content appears to be part and parcel of phenomenology: it is part of the essential nature of phenomenology that it is directed outward at a world. If so, we cannot reduce intentionality to something more fundamental; at best, we can locate its roots in the intentionality of the phenomenal.

I think, then, that the most attractive view is one on which neither consciousness nor intentionality is more fundamental than the other. Rather, consciousness and intentionality are intertwined, all the way down to the ground.[23]

References

Block, N. 1978. 'Troubles with functionalism', in (C. W. Savage, ed.) *Perception and Cognition: Issues in the Foundation of Psychology* (Minneapolis: University of Minnesota Press).

—— 1990. 'Inverted earth', *Philosophical Perspectives* 4: 53–79.

Boghossian, P., and Velleman, J. D. 1989. 'Color as a secondary quality', *Mind* 98: 81–103.

Burge, T. 1979. 'Individualism and the mental', *Midwest Studies in Philosophy* 4: 73–122.

Byrne, A. 2001. 'Intentionalism defended', *Philosophical Review* 110: 199–240.

Carruthers, P. 2000. *Phenomenal Consciousness: A Naturalistic Theory* (Cambridge: Cambridge University Press).

Chalmers, D. J. 1996. *The Conscious Mind: In Search of a Fundamental Theory* (Oxford: Oxford University Press).

---

[23] I have presented versions of this paper, starting in 2001, at MIT, Cornell, Rutgers, Brown, and at the 2002 NEH Summer Institute on Consciousness and Intentionality. I would like to thank audiences on all of these occasions for discussion. Thanks especially to all the participants in the NEH Institute for many valuable conversations, and to Torin Alter, Justin Fisher, Terry Horgan, Uriah Kriegel, Brian Leiter, David Pitt, Sydney Shoemaker, Susanna Siegel, Brad Thompson, Leora Weitzman, and Wayne Wright for comments on a draft of this paper. Brad Thompson's dissertation on phenomenal content explores many of the same issues as this paper, and I have had much valuable discussion with him. Finally, this work has been influenced by the work of others in various obvious ways, but it has been influenced by the work of Sydney Shoemaker and Charles Siewert in ways that may be deeper than the obvious.

Chalmers, D. J. 2002. 'The components of content' in (D. Chalmers, ed.) *Philosophy of Mind: Classical and Contemporary Readings* (Oxford: Oxford University Press).

—— (forthcoming). 'Perception and the Fall from Eden', in T. Gendler and J. Hawthorne, eds., *Perceptual Experience*.

Clark, A. 2000. *A Theory of Sentience* (Oxford: Oxford University Press).

Crane, T. 2003. 'The intentional structure of consciousness', in (Q. Smith and A. Jokic, eds.) *Consciousness: New Philosophical Perspectives* (Oxford: Oxford University Press).

Dennett, D. C. 1968. *Content and Consciousness* (London: Routledge).

Droege, P. 2003. *Caging the Beast: A Theory of Sensory Consciousness* (Amsterdam: John Benjamins).

Dretske, F. 1995. *Naturalizing the Mind* (Cambridge, Mass.: MIT Press).

Egan, A. (forthcoming). Appearance properties? [www.geocities.com.\egànàmit\papers.html]

Harman, G. 1990. 'The intrinsic quality of experience', *Philosophical Perspectives* 4: 31–52.

Holman, E. 2002. 'Color eliminativism and color experience', *Pacific Philosophical Quarterly* 83: 38–56.

Horgan, T., and Tienson, J. 2002. 'The intentionality of phenomenology and the phenomenology of intentionality', in (D. Chalmers, ed.) *Philosophy of Mind: Classical and Contemporary Readings* (Oxford: Oxford University Press).

Jackson, F. 2003. 'Mind and illusion', in (A. O'Hear, ed.) *Minds and Persons* (Cambridge: Cambridge University Press).

Kriegel, U. 2002*a*. 'PANIC theory and the prospects for a representational theory of phenomenal consciousness', *Philosophical Psychology* 15: 55–64.

—— 2002*b*. 'Phenomenal content', *Erkenntnis* 57: 175–98.

Levine, J. 2003. 'Experience and representation', in (Q. Smith and A. Jokic, eds.) *Consciousness: New Philosophical Perspectives* (Oxford: Oxford University Press).

Lloyd, D. 1991. 'Leaping to conclusions: connectionism, consciousness, and the computational mind', in (T. Horgan and J. Tienson, eds.) *Connectionism and the Philosophy of Mind* (London: Kluwer).

Loar, B. 2003. 'Phenomenal intentionality as the basis of mental content', In (Hahn and B. Ramberg, eds.) *Reflections and Replies* (Cambridge, Mass.: MIT Press).

Lycan, W. G. 1996. *Consciousness and Experience* (Cambridge, Mass.: MIT Press).

—— 2001. 'The case for phenomenal externalism', *Philosophical Perspectives* 15: 17–35.

Maund, J. B. 1995. *Colours: Their Nature and Representation* (Cambridge: Cambridge University Press).

McGinn, C. 1988. 'Consciousness and content', Proceedings of the British Academy 74: 219–39; repr. in *The Problem of Consciousness* (Oxford: Blackwell, 1991).

McLaughlin, B. 2003. 'Color, consciousness, and color consciousness', in (Q. Smith and A. Jokic, eds.) *Consciousness: New Philosophical Essays* (Oxford: Oxford University Press).

Peacocke, C. 1983. *Sense and Content: Experience, Thought, and their Relations* (Oxford: Oxford University Press).

Putnam, H. 1975. 'The meaning of "meaning" ', in *Mind, Language, and Reality* (Cambridge: Cambridge University Press).

Rey, G. 1998. 'A narrow representationalist account of qualitative experience', *Philosophical Perspectives* 12: 435–58.

Rosenthal, D. M. 1997. 'A theory of consciousness', in (N. Block, O. Flanagan, and G. Güzeldere, eds.) *The Nature of Consciousness* (Cambridge, Mass.: MIT Press).

Searle, J. R. 1980. 'Minds, brains and programs', *Behavioral and Brain Sciences* 3: 417–24.

—— 1983. *Intentionality* (Cambridge: Cambridge University Press).

—— 1990. 'Consciousness, explanatory inversion and cognitive science', *Behavioral and Brain Sciences* 13: 585–642.

Shoemaker, S. 1990. 'Qualities and qualia: What's in the mind?' *Philosophy and Phenomenological Research Supplement* 50: 109–31.

—— 1994. 'Phenomenal character', *Nous* 28: 1–38.

—— 2001. 'Introspection and phenomenal character', *Philosophical Topics*: repr. in (D. Chalmers, ed.) *Philosophy of Mind: Classical and Contemporary Readings* (Oxford: Oxford University Press).

Siewert, C. 1998. *The Significance of Consciousness* (Princeton: Princeton University Press).

Stoljar, D. (forthcoming) Consequences of intentionalism [humanities.vcsc.edu\NEH\Stoljar.htm].

Strawson, G. 1994. *Mental Reality* (Cambridge, Mass.: MIT Press).

Thau, M. 2002. *Consciousness and Cognition* (Oxford: Oxford University Press).

Thompson, B. 2003. *The Nature of Phenomenal Content*. Ph.D. dissertation, University of Arizona.

Travis, C. 2004. 'The silence of the senses', *Mind* 113: 57–94.

Tye, M. 1995. *Ten Problems of Consciousness: A Representational Theory of the Phenomenal Mind* (Cambridge, Mass.: MIT Press).

—— 2003. 'Blurry images, double vision, and other oddities: New problems for representationalism?' in (Q. Smith and A. Jokic, eds.) *Consciousness: New Philosophical Perspectives* (Oxford: Oxford University Press).

Vinueza, A. 2000. 'Sensations and the language of thought', *Philosophical Psychology* 13: 373–92.

Warfield, T. 1999. 'Against representational theories of consciousness', *Journal of Consciousness Studies* 6: 66–9.

Wright, W. 2003. 'Projectivist representationalism and color', *Philosophical Psychology*.

The Need for Social Epistemology

ALVIN GOLDMAN

Epistemology is one of the oldest fields of philosophy. Plato, for example, devoted several dialogues, or portions thereof, to epistemology, including *Meno*, *Phaedo*, *Republic*, and *Theaetetus*. Epistemology is as lively a subject today as in many periods, though its intricacies are not widely known outside academic philosophy. Much of today's epistemology, like the epistemology of yesteryear, is focused on skepticism. But there is also a novel development in epistemology, the emergence of social epistemology. This paper's aim is to sketch the contours of social epistemology and to show why its rapid and extensive growth is to be encouraged.

Two types of sources or pressures are pushing epistemology down the social path. One source is a purely internal dialectic. Epistemologists have already identified a variety of reasons internal to the field for highlighting the social dimension, and such reasons are easily multiplied and elaborated. A second source is external. Arguments originating in other academic disciplines or outside the academy entirely create a demand for social theories of knowledge. We live in an information age, and questions about knowledge and information continually arise in far-flung sectors of social, political, and economic life. Epistemology is the natural place to seek at least the conceptual basis of such a theory, and perhaps more than a conceptual basis. Some epistemologists might resist pressures from extra-philosophical quarters to tackle concerns arising there. Epistemology, they might say, should stick to its distinctive agenda or "problematic". I don't agree with this stance, but I shall not try to settle this dispute in detail. I shall merely present an assortment of considerations, some from the internal perspective and others from the external perspective. If either type of reason is well founded, there are ample reasons why the social wing of epistemology should be expanded in the years ahead.

Justification, Rationality, and Relativism

The status of testimony   What am I justified in believing? Which types of evidence or indicators can I justifiably rely upon in forming my beliefs? Can I trust vision when it "tells" me that the magician just pulled a rabbit out of a hat? Am I justified in trusting memory when it "tells" me that I paid my telephone bill last week? Am I justified in trusting mathematical intuition when it yields up some arithmetic or set-theoretic proposition? These are typical examples that a theory of justification should address. Nothing concerning the social domain, however, appears on the foregoing list. The preceding items concern a person's belief entitlements based on his own psychological states or processes, with no reference to other individuals or groups. An element of the social enters the picture when a different question is posed: Am I justified in trusting another *person* when I hear her make an assertion? May I justifiably rely on her testimony and believe what she asserts?

The problem of testimony has recently become a leading item on the agenda of mainstream epistemology. It constitutes an "internal" reason for epistemology to explore the social dimension. A brief review of the two main positions on the problem of testimony will get us started. A first position is that the testimony of others lacks the same fundamental epistemic status as perception, memory, or inductive inference. The latter sources of belief are justificationally *basic* in the sense that they confer (or transmit) prima facie justifiedness even if one has no independent justification for regarding the sources as reliable. Even if you cannot non-circularly support the reliability of your memory, you are entitled to rely on it unless you have specific evidence that undercuts what you ostensibly remember. You are not, however, analogously entitled to rely on testimony without independent support. Trust in the statements of others is warranted only if you first establish their reliability by means of basic sources like perception, memory, and induction. If you compare a given speaker's statements with the facts by yourself observing and remembering those facts, and if you thereby determine that the speaker has generally been reliable (accurate) in the past, then you can inductively infer that a new statement by the same speaker is also likely to be true, and you are justified in believing it. But this requires an inductive inference from beliefs that are justified by independent sources (perception and memory). Thus, the justificational status of testimony beliefs is not fundamental, but must be derived from other sources. This position is called *reductionism*, and was endorsed by David Hume.

In contrast to reductionism, some historical epistemologists and many recent ones have defended an *anti-reductionist* position (Reid, 1983; Sosa, 1991; Coady, 1992; Burge, 1993; Fricker, 1995). According to this view, a hearer has prima facie or default justification for believing what another person asserts quite independently of anything the hearer otherwise knows or believes about the speaker's competence or sincerity. In the absence of countervailing evidence, one is entitled to trust another person in the same fundamental way that one is prima facie justified in trusting perception or memory. On this view, there is a certain epistemic "autonomy" about the belief-worthiness of other people's statements. This gives the social or communicative basis for belief a special and fundamental authority, in contrast with the reductionist position.

Interpersonal comparisons of credibility   A next question that naturally arises is how to *weight* the credibility of other speakers? How much should one trust others in comparison with oneself, i.e. one's own unaided faculties? This is not settled by the anti-reductionist postulate that automatically confers *some* prima facie credibility on the testimony of others. Richard Foley (1994; 2001) gives this question some attention. He starts from a principle of self-trust, the principle that I must necessarily trust myself. But given the similarity between my own intellectual faculties and those of others, it would be inconsistent of me (in a weak sense, at least) not to place intellectual trust in them as well. Thus, trust in myself "radiates outwards" toward others (2001: 106). Foley thus accepts a modest form of epistemic universalism. However, it does not settle the problem of weighting. When I find my opinions in conflict with those of others, should I retract my opinions or reduce their strength? Under what conditions and to what degree? Some psychological studies suggest that people are all too prone to be influenced by the opinions of others (cf. Asch, 1956). But what is the *proper* degree of influence? Philip Kitcher (1993: 306–28) addresses a problem in this vicinity that faces the working scientist. Under what circumstances should the scientist borrow or rely on the investigations of others rather than doing the research herself? For both theoretical and practical reasons, these are important questions for social epistemology to address, and it has only begun to explore them.

The problem of interpersonal comparisons of trustworthiness is not restricted to self versus other. It arises equally for two or more others. Suppose I grant that on a certain technical subject I have minimal intellectual authority. I haven't investigated the evidence that bears on the issue, and I lack the formal training that would enable me to assess the force of this evidence even if I possessed it. I encounter two other people, however, who both claim expertise on this subject but disagree with one another. Which one should I trust? Or how much should I trust one in comparison with the other? This is an example of what I call the *novice/two-expert* problem (Goldman, 2001*a*); it is an instance of the general problem of comparing the expertise of others.

Weighing the judgments of experts is a practical problem we regularly encounter in daily life. We don't have to be epistemologists to feel its pinch. A patient may need to assess the relative credibility of two physicians offering conflicting assessments of his medical condition. A consumer may be confronted with conflicting expert opinions about the safety or risks associated with various foods, materials, or over-the-counter medicines. A parent may sift through "expert" opinions about the effects of this or that system of raising and educating children. A juror may have the task of deciding which of two experts, one for each party in a lawsuit, deserves greater credence. How should all these intellectual tasks be performed? These are examples of the "external", practical problems that invite contributions from epistemology. Surely the aid of epistemology—the social side of epistemology—would be welcome in all of these cases.

One simple solution to many of these problems might be: go with the numbers. If most experts agree on viewpoint V, the novice should also accept V, or give it greater credence than not-V. If the novice can determine which of two experts sides with the majority, or plurality, opinion on a target issue, preference should be given to that expert. But is this solution correct? Should the more popular opinion always receive increased weight? I have argued in the negative (Goldman, 2001*a*: sect. 4). Agreement, even among experts, does not always provide grounds for raising your degree of credence on a given subject beyond the level of credence derived from a single opinion-holder. An illustration will indicate why. Suppose you hear a certain proposition defended by a very persuasive speaker. You therefore assign a degree of credence of 0.90 to that proposition. You then learn that an additional thousand people agree with that speaker. Does this new fact justify raising your credence? Not necessarily. Suppose you know that the speaker is a guru and that the extra thousand believers are blind followers who automatically agree with everything he says without consulting other evidence. In light of that information, you are not justified in letting the new numbers affect your assessment.[1] If this analysis is right, it illustrates how social epistemology can be of help in guiding people's judgments in the context of choosing among experts.

A social analysis of justification?   I turn now to a different approach to justification and social epistemology. Testimony and the assessment of expertise constitute a small part of the overall subject of justification. Although they introduce a social component into the theory of justified belief, this social component is fairly limited. By contrast, the approach to justification I shall now present, though not endorse, is socially much more ambitious. It claims that social factors lie at the very heart of the justification concept. According to this approach, being justified is constituted by standing in an appropriate relation to members of one's community. In other words, a proper analysis of "S is justified in believing p" must advert to a relation between believer and community. This kind of view is to be found in the writings of Ludwig Wittgenstein (1969), Wilfrid Sellars (1956), and several of Sellars' intellectual heirs. The underlying motif of these writings is that the justifiedness of a belief (or assertion) arises from the *social practice* of giving and acknowledging reasons.

One such heir of Sellars is David Annis, who offers what he calls a "contextualist" approach to epistemic justification (Annis, 1978). The basic idea of Annis's theory is that a belief in p is justified if and only if the believer can meet the objections to p lodged by members of his community. Justification is to be relativized to an "issue-context", which determines the appropriate objector-group for the evaluation in question. If Jones believes that polio is caused by a virus, we might consider this belief justified relative to a context in which the objector group is non-medically trained people, or relative to the context of an M.D. examination in which the relevant group are qualified medical examiners. Against this background, Annis offers the following analysis:

For S to be justified in believing h relative to the issue-context, S must be able to meet all current objections . . . which express a real doubt of the qualified objector-group where the objectors are critical truth-seekers. (1978: 215)

He adds to this analysis the following:

To determine whether S is justified in believing h we must consider the actual standards of justification of the community of people to which he belongs. More specifically, we determine whether S is justified in believing h by specifying an issue-context raised within a community of people G with certain social practices and norms of justification. . . . To be justified in believing h, S must be able to meet their objections in a way that satisfies their practices and norms. (1978: 215)

---

[1] A probabilistic analysis of this situation is offered in Goldman 2001a, sect. 4.

Clearly, on this approach to justification, the status of epistemic justifiedness is thoroughly saturated with the social. It's not merely that one source of justification, e.g. testimony, has a social character; rather, epistemic justification is social through and through.

Although this approach can hardly be faulted for insufficient sociality, there are problems at several levels. First, at the level of detail, the account seems too weak, because it makes a belief's justifiedness hinge on the *actual* objections raised by members of a contextually selected community. The vast majority of a person's beliefs, however, encounter no objections from anyone. People go around with innumerable beliefs, most of which receive no verbal expression. These certainly elicit no objections. Of the ones that are verbally expressed, only a fraction strike listeners as worth the trouble of comment. Thus, only a small fraction of one's beliefs are the targets of actually lodged objections. The rest, which face no objections, vacuously pass Annis's requirements. That makes the conditions of the analysis too easy to meet. Unjustified beliefs are not declared unjustified by the analysis because there are no objections that the believer is unable to answer.

To avoid this problem, the social approach to justification can revise its analysis by invoking objections that *could* be lodged, as opposed to objections that are *actually* lodged. On this version of the theory, we should now focus on a different problem for the approach, i.e. that it imposes too strong a requirement on justified belief. The ability to respond to objections is a capacity that requires a kind of reflective command of one's reasons for belief that it is wrong to demand of all justified believers. Many of our sophisticated beliefs depend on a complex web of inferences that it is difficult to marshall or reconstruct, especially when one is verbally confronted with objections. Other beliefs of ours, viz. perceptual beliefs, depend for their justification on the ways in which we are appeared to. But it is difficult to say just what these ways are. In general, then, it is hard to fill in all mentally suppressed premises, to describe all perceptual appearances, or to specify the cognitive operations that are responsible for one's beliefs. But these are just the sorts of conditions that *make* a belief justified (or unjustified). Thus, it is an excessively stringent requirement on a justified belief for a believer to be able to supply—in a sociolinguistic interchange—all factors that would (correctly) resolve all possible objections.

Still a different problem for this kind of approach is the vagueness and relativity of the relevant epistemic community. A believer can be considered a member of indefinitely many epistemic communities. A belief of his might be considered obvious and uncontroversial in one of these communities but highly suspect in another of the communities. Are judgments of justification so contextual or relative that they can be made with respect to any selected one of these communities? In a different vein, is it really required that judgments of justification be relativized to one of the *believer's* communities? Can't an evaluator assess a belief by appeal to his own standards, not by those of one of the believer's communities?[2] Can't we legitimately

---

[2] Restricting criteria of justifiedness to the standards of the believer's community corresponds roughly to what I call (in Goldman, 1988) "weak" justifiedness. This is contrasted with "strong" justifiedness, which is not so restricted.

say of someone living in ancient times, whose community accepted the evidence of birds' entrails, that someone's beliefs based on such evidence were unjustified? Relativizing exclusively to a believer's community seems misguided.

These are among the reasons why I do not personally accept the approach in question. But insofar as others find it acceptable, it is a further example of the appeal of the social in epistemology.

Rorty and social epistemology   A more prominent intellectual heir of Sellars is Richard Rorty. Rorty offers a variety of reflections on truth and justification with a social slant. Although he frequently disclaims the business of advancing epistemological theories, what he says sometimes *looks* like an epistemological theory and is often taken as such. So, let us look at some relevant passages and see whether they might be transformed into a version of social epistemology.

In *Philosophy and the Mirror of Nature* Rorty proposes that we should explain "rationality and epistemic authority by reference to what society lets us say" (Rorty, 1979: 174). Since he often uses "rationality" and "justification" interchangeably, I shall interpret this remark as a sketch of a theory of justifiedness. Under one interpretation the theory approximates that of Annis. A belief or assertion of S is justified just in case S's community would let him hold that belief or make that assertion. Presumably, his society "lets" him say it not merely in the sense of giving him freedom of speech, but rather in approving of his holding or saying it in virtue of the society's epistemic norms. S's belief is justified just in case it is permitted by the epistemic norms of S's society (here we waive the problem of *which* society this might be).

Now, this theory is social because the *source* of the relevant norms is the believer's community. The belief is governed by the norms of that community, whatever the *content* of the norms. The distinction between source and content is worth pausing over. Just because a social entity ("society") is the source of the norms, this does not mean that the contents of the norms concern purely social matters. The contents of the norms are thus far unconstrained. The norms might permit a person to hold beliefs in virtue of things he perceives, things he remembers, or the reasonings he (mentally) undergoes. These kinds of norms do not advert to any other people or any community; so the *contents* of these norms seem to be asocial, even if their *source* is social. Thus, the above-quoted passage from Rorty is consistent with a theory of justification that is social in the sense that pertinent norms have a social source, but not necessarily a social content.

In other work, however, Rorty gestures toward a rather different kind of theory, one that seems to endorse social contents, indeed exclusively social contents. Here is one passage that apparently expresses this idea:

Let me sum up by offering a third and final characterization of pragmatism: it is the doctrine that *there are no constraints on inquiry save conversational ones*—no wholesale constraints derived from the nature of objects, or of the mind, or of language, but only those retail constraints provided by the remarks of our fellow inquirers. . . .

I prefer this third way of characterizing pragmatism because it seems to me to focus on a fundamental choice which confronts the reflective mind: that between accepting the contingent character of starting-points, and attempting to evade this contingency. To accept the contingency of starting-points is to accept our inheritance from, and our conversation with, our fellow-humans as *our only source of guidance*. (1980/2003: 197; italics added)

This passage suggests a decidedly heterodox approach to justification, viz. that other people's talk is the *only* justification-conferring factor. Unlike the view that conversation (testimony) is one among many bases of justification, it implies that neither perception, nor memory, nor any sort of reasoning can promote or defeat the justifiedness of a belief. Only what other people say can perform this job. One oddity about this view is that knowing what others say depends essentially on perception. How is someone's belief supposed to be guided or constrained by conversation with others unless they are epistemically entitled to believe that a conversational partner has said thus-and-so? But how could they be so entitled unless perception confers this entitlement? The theory of justification suggested in the foregoing passage implicitly denies perceptual entitlement, so how can an inquirer legitimately exploit any conversational episodes?

It is far from clear, however, that Rorty means to advance any theory of justification at all. In some writings, such as "Solidarity or Objectivity?" (Rorty, 1991), he abjures such an aim. First, here is what he says about his philosophical opponents, whom he calls "realists":

[T]hey must construct a metaphysics which has room for a special relation between beliefs and objects which will differentiate true from false beliefs. They also must argue that there are procedures of justification of belief which are natural and not merely local. So they must construct an epistemology which has room for a kind of justification which is not merely social but natural, springing from human nature itself, and made possible by a link between that part of nature and the rest of nature. On their view, the various procedures which are thought of as providing rational justification by one or another culture may or may not really *be* rational. For to be truly rational, procedures of justification *must* lead to truth, to correspondence to reality, to the intrinsic nature of things. (1991: 22)

The aim of realism, says Rorty, is "objectivity", where objectivity involves, among other things, the attainment of true belief in the correspondence sense of "truth". Opposed to realism, in this sense, is Rorty's own view which he calls "pragmatism", and pragmatism takes as its aim "solidarity".

For pragmatists, the desire for objectivity is not the desire to escape the limitations of one's community, but simply the desire for as much *intersubjective agreement* as possible. (1991: 23; italics added)

This sounds like a kind of social epistemology, where the social element consists in simple agreement. But Rorty denies that what pragmatism offers is a species of epistemology. He makes this clear in the course of denying that he is a relativist.

But a pragmatist does not have a theory of truth, much less a relativistic one. As a partisan of solidarity, his account of the value of cooperative human inquiry has only an ethical base, not an epistemological or metaphysical one. Not having *any* epistemology, *a fortiori* he does not have a relativistic one. (1991: 24; italics in the original)

If Rorty qua pragmatist has no epistemological theory, his view cannot be considered a variety of social epistemology.

In any case, why would intersubjective agreement be a valuable end-state or desideratum around which an epistemology might be built? Intersubjective agreement, as noted earlier, can be the product of blind or dull conformity. It can result from one intellectually "blind" person leading others who are equally blind. Arguably, the fruit of intersubjective agreement is amity and social harmony. These are genuine political goods, and perhaps moral goods as well. But are they epistemological goods? I don't think so. Nor does Rorty claim that they are, since he sees pragmatism as offering no epistemological theory at all. If we take him at his word, he does not offer a distinctive variant of social epistemology.

Epistemic diversity and relativism   Although Rorty distances himself from the "relativism" label, sociologists of knowledge typically welcome it. Barry Barnes and David Bloor (1982) explicitly advance a relativistic sociology of knowledge. They focus on the fact that different communities or cultures have different standards of justification or rationality, and they reject the idea that justification or rationality has a universal essence, independent of what is created by particular communities or cultures.

For the relativist there is no sense attached to the idea that some standards or beliefs are really rational as distinct from merely locally accepted as such. . . . [T]here are no context-free or super-cultural norms of rationality. (1982: 27)

The idea is that because all standards arise from a local culture, there is no possibility of transcending all cultures to find some super-cultural, or universal, standards for rationality.[3]

Critics of relativism will want to look carefully at the inference from cross-cultural diversity in epistemic norms to the impossibility of norm objectivity. How might this inference be resisted? Here is one line of thought I have developed (Goldman, 1992a; 1999b, sect. 4). Cultural or communal differences in epistemic norms do not result primarily from divergence in epistemic values but rather from divergence in beliefs about which practices would realize those values. In particular, true belief is a widely shared value and desideratum across cultures (Goldman, 1999a: 3–4, 30–3). Where cultures differ is in the practices they regard as good means or methods of getting true belief. Some ancient cultures thought that looking at bird entrails was a reliable means to true belief about future battles, but no contemporary culture thinks this. Some medieval cultures thought that trial by ordeal was a sound, i.e. truth-conducive, method of determining guilt, but no contemporary culture thinks this. A relevant ancient culture would have said that certain beliefs about future battles were justified if they appropriately exploited information about bird entrails, and the relevant medieval culture would have said that certain beliefs about guilt were justified if there was an appropriate outcome of a trial by ordeal;

---

[3] One philosopher who defends epistemic relativism in something like the spirit of Barnes and Bloor is Stephen Stich; see Stich (1990) and Weinberg, Nichols, and Stich (2001). However, the evidence adduced in Weinberg et al. (2001) specifically concerns cultural diversity in intuitions about *knowledge*, and it is questionable whether these intuitions result from diversity in epistemic norms of justification or rationality.

but no contemporary culture would agree with these judgments of justifiedness.[4] So diversity in epistemic norms and epistemic standards of justification are traceable to divergences in beliefs about truth-conducive methods. Turning to the prospect of objectivity in justification-ascribing standards, one might say that a standard of justification is objectively correct if it ascribes justification to beliefs that are caused by some method M only if method M is *objectively* truth-conducive (reliable). Thus, there is a conception of objective justifiedness independent of particular cultures or communities.

Because I do not think that cultural diversity has such radical implications for epistemology as relativists claim, I do not regard it as quite so critical a move in the argument for social epistemology. Nonetheless, it represents yet another possible route for the development of social epistemology.

Knowledge and Socially-Based Skepticism

Although I began this discussion with the topic of justification, knowledge is arguably the central topic of epistemology: What *is* knowledge? How can it be obtained? Are there inherent difficulties in attaining knowledge? Much of epistemology is concerned with problems that generate the threat of skepticism: the prospect that there is little if anything that people can know.

According to standard epistemological treatments, knowledge consists in justified true belief plus some additional condition.[5] The truth component of knowledge implies that a person doesn't know a proposition p unless p is true. Nobody knows that Charles de Gaulle was the first president of the United States because it is false that Charles de Gaulle was the first president of the United States. The truth condition is not usually viewed as a skeptical threat. False propositions can't be known, but there are plenty of true propositions that seem (in principle) knowable. The "additional condition" required of knowledge, however, may be a sticking point. According to some epistemologists, the additional condition is the requirement that a knower be able to exclude all possibilities contrary to what he knows. If he is to know that he's holding a glass in his hand, he must be able to exclude the contrary possibility that he is merely a bodiless brain floating in a vat that possesses no hand and holds no glass but has experiences as if he has a hand holding a glass. Nobody is in an evidential position to exclude this brain-in-a-vat possibility, because their experience is perfectly compatible with it. Hence, they cannot know the glass-in-the-hand proposition, nor, for analogous reasons, any other ordinary proposition. Here is a genuine skeptical threat to knowledge.[6]

---

[4] Actually, there may be different senses of "justification" (Goldman, 1988). A "weak" sense may take into account the subject's social context. But there is also a "strong" sense of justification that does not do this. Judgments of justification in this strong sense are what I have in mind in this passage.

[5] The need for an additional condition was established by Edmund Gettier (1963).

[6] The standard way of formulating this skeptical threat is not via an "exclusion" principle, as I have formulated it, but via a related "closure" principle (Nozick, 1981; DeRose, 1995). I use the exclusion principle in the interest of simplicity. The differences are unimportant here, because I shall not be exploring this problem in any detail.

This skeptical threat, however, has nothing to do with the social dimensions of knowledge. Are there other kinds of skeptical threats that are associated with social dimensions of knowledge? Different kinds of skepticism about knowledge can readily be found or constructed (perhaps with a little embellishment) in the social studies of knowledge (SSK) literature. The first kind of skepticism I shall mention is associated with a rejection of truth as standardly understood in the philosophical literature. In many works within SSK, one finds the claim, either explicit or implied, that truth is merely socially prevalent belief. Here is an explicit statement of the idea by Steven Shapin:

> I want to argue the adequacy and legitimacy of a thoroughgoing social conception of truth. What counts for any community as true knowledge is a collective good and a collective accomplishment. That good is always in others' hands, and the fate of any particular claim that something "is the case" is never determined by the individual making the claim. This is a sense in which one may say that truth is a matter of collective judgment and that it is stabilized by the collective actions which use it as a standard for judging other claims. In short, truth is a social institution and is, therefore, a fit and proper topic for the sociologist's investigation. (1994: 5–6)

What Shapin seems to be proposing is that we abandon the standard notion of truth and substitute for it the notion of "collective judgment".[7] Why that should be done is unclear. He may be right that *sociologists* need nothing more for *their* investigations than the notion of collective judgment. They don't need to assess the truth values of the statements of the people they study. But that does not mean that the ordinary truth-concept should be abandoned for all purposes—including the purposes of evaluating what sociologists themselves say.

Two other theses typical of the SSK literature might lead to a more standard form of knowledge-skepticism. Closely related to the "no-counterpossibilities" account of knowledge mentioned earlier is a counterfactual approach to knowledge. Robert Nozick formulates the crucial condition as follows: "If p weren't true, S wouldn't believe that p" (1981: 172). Now assume that for a large number of cases, satisfaction of this condition depends on the subject's *causal access* to the target subject-matter. If S has a proper causal relationship to a fruit bowl and is paying attention, he will not only believe truly that there is an orange in the fruit bowl when there is one, but if, counterfactually, there were no orange in the fruit bowl, he wouldn't believe that there is. S thereby satisfies the counterfactual condition. However, if S stands in no such causal relationship to the fruit bowl—for example, if it is located on a distant planet, or simply in a locked room—then he would not be able to *know* there is an orange in the fruit bowl.

Now according to an influential work in the SSK literature, sociology of science establishes that physical scientists do not stand in an appropriate causal relationship

---

[7] Shapin is somewhat ambiguous about his intentions. He acknowledges that "communities making truth-judgments mean to distinguish statements or beliefs which correspond to reality from those which do not" (1994: 4), and he doesn't unequivocally reject a 'materialist' sense of truth that might make sense of this correspondence. But other sociologists and historians of science go further, accepting the account of truth quoted in the text as the only legitimate notion of truth.

to the physical subject-matter they purport to study. The work in question is Bruno Latour and Steve Woolgar's *Laboratory Life: The Construction of Scientific Facts* (1979/1986). The relevant claim of Latour and Woolgar is expressed in the following passage:

We do not use the notion of reality to account for the stabilization of a statement . . . because this reality is formed as a consequence of this stabilization.

We do not wish to say that facts do not exist nor that there is no such thing as reality. . . . Our point is that "out-there-ness" is the *consequence* of scientific work rather than its *cause*. (1979/1986: 182)

Philip Kitcher (1993) interprets this passage as saying that scientists' beliefs are not causally affected by interactions with the ostensible subject of their study.

[T]he fact that TRF [thyrotropin releasing factor] has a certain structure does not play a causal role in the genesis of the belief that it has that structure; rather, because we believe, as the result of a complex social process, that TRF has that structure the fact that TRF has that structure is *constructed*. The thesis of the social construction of facts is thus the claim that the acceptance of statements as firm parts of consensus practice is to be explained in a particular fashion, a fashion that makes no reference to the constraining power of stimuli from external, asocial nature. . . .

To defend the thesis of the construction of facts, as I have interpreted it, one would have to show that the encounters with nature that occurred during the genesis of belief about TRF played no role. *However those encounters had turned out the end result would have been the same.* (1993: 165–6)

On Kitcher's interpretation, Latour and Woolgar are claiming that scientists' beliefs are not causally influenced by the underlying structure of reality, their beliefs do not vary counterfactually as a function of different states of nature. If they were right, if only social processes causally account for scientists' beliefs, then there would indeed be a skeptical threat to scientific knowledge.

As Kitcher argues, however, this is a most implausible scenario. He describes an "ideal" experiment to test Latour and Woolgar's hypothesis. Take a large number of populations of scientists, start each in the same state as the community of molecular endocrinologists actually started in, and expose each population to different inputs from nature (perhaps by having them run their assays on different substances). How much variation in beliefs do you get? Although the experiment cannot be performed, we surely know in advance how it would turn out. Surely there would be *some* variation in the beliefs of some of these populations, contrary to what Latour and Woolgar's claim implies (Kitcher 1993: 166–7).

I offer a slightly different diagnosis of the Latour–Woolgar line of argumentation, but I agree with Kitcher in finding it quite weak (Goldman 1999a: 14–16). What Latour and Woolgar fail to appreciate is the compatibility between their social explanations of scientists' beliefs and nature-based explanations of these beliefs. Sociologists of science are not wrong to claim that interpersonal discourse dramatically influences scientists' conclusions. What they fail to recognize is that such social causes do not exclude nature-based causes as well. Thus, there can be no inference from the existence of social causes to the non-existence of nature-based causes. Why is there no rivalry between the two families of causes? Because underlying facts of nature can influence beliefs via a causal chain of influences that include interpersonal communication. The structures of the molecules being studied cause readings on scientific instruments, which cause perceptual beliefs in the heads of scientists, which in turn cause discourse on theoretical matters, which generates still further (theoretical) beliefs. Thus, one cannot infer from the fact that beliefs are mediated by interpersonal discourse that scientists *lack* any causal access to nature. Scientific knowledge of nature is not endangered by these types of studies in the sociology of science.

A final way by which SSK might generate a skeptical threat involves still another tweaking of the analysis of knowledge. According to a reliabilist theory of knowledge, S knows that p only if S has a belief in p which is caused by a generally reliable process of belief formation, where a reliable process is one that usually generates truths (Goldman, 1986: ch. 3). If it can be shown that the processes of scientific belief formation are unreliable, that would pose a significant threat to scientific knowledge. One line of argument is especially relevant to social epistemology. This argument has two premises: first, science is a social process, and second, social processes inevitably create bias and distortion that make reliability impossible. This is precisely a line of argument that certain segments have SSK have pursued. In particular, they have tried to show how scientific work is often influenced by political agendas, and how professional interests deriving from social networks shape the course of science. They also claim that evidential gaps associated with the "underdetermination" of theory are often filled by sociopolitical factors.

The influence of political agendas is illustrated by Donald Mackenzie's (1981) study of the history of statistics. According to Mackenzie, Galton and Pearson developed certain concepts of statistics because they were driven by a social program of eugenics, intended to improve the genetic composition of the human race by promoting the fertility of "better types". Other sociologists of science emphasize that scientists are not driven by purely cognitive interests, but by professional desires to receive credit from their peers and expand their research programs. This means they must create alliances and engage in other "political" activities not traditionally associated with purely epistemic pursuits (Shapin and Schaffer, 1985; Latour, 1987). Noting the existence of logical gaps between scientific theory and evidence, Sandra Harding writes that "any theory can always be retained as long as its defenders hold enough institutional power to explain away potential threats to it" (1992: 582).

One type of response to these ideas is to challenge some of their specifics. "Underdetermination" of theory by evidence merely means that evidence does not *logically* require a unique choice of theory. But deductive relationships do not exhaust evidential relationships; factors above and beyond deducibility can be and are brought into play. At a minimum, then, it is far from clear that logical gaps between theory and evidence are usually filled by motives, interests or institutional power (Laudan, 1990; Slezak, 1991). In the case of intrusions from political agendas, as in the history of statistics example, it is noteworthy that Mackenzie himself cites this as a case of *good* science, i.e. a genuine advance in knowledge. Thus, even the intrusion of interests or political agendas does not inevitably deflect science from truth attainment (I return to this point below). As concerns the attempt to view science through the lens of political or military battle, I submit that political and military analogies can fruitfully be replaced by epistemic models (Goldman, 1999: 225–30).

Going beyond such specific responses, it is desirable to raise the analysis above the level of isolated examples, which may or may not be representative of the general course of science. It also seems advisable to frame the general issue in *comparative* terms. Does the social dimension of science make science epistemically *better* or *worse* than it would be as a purely individual enterprise? Does its social dimension on the whole tilt it toward greater or less reliability? There is much to be said for the thesis that social factors increase, rather than decrease, reliability, that they tend to mute the impact of bias rather than amplify it.

An obvious fact about sociality is that multiple agents are involved, who will typically have non-identical interests and often have distinct abilities and types of training. Non-identity of interests yields a partly competitive relationship which can and does result in mutual correction. Where biases do exist, they can be identified and rectified by others. A principal theme of Miriam Solomon's (1992) work is that a properly distributed set of biases can actually have salutary effects. Cooperation is another element in sociality that constitutes a positive force for reliability. Scientists can build on the work of others rather than rely exclusively on their own talents (Kitcher, 1993: ch. 8). They can pool their expertise and exploit the advantages of multiple disciplinary specialties (Thagard, 1997). Science can be an especially effective community for knowledge production, says Helen Longino (2002), if it conforms to norms requiring publicly recognized forums for the criticism of evidence and methods plus actual "uptake" or responsiveness to these criticisms.

A full development of these themes would require more than the typical exchanges between SSK practitioners and their critics, which often consist in igniting assorted skeptical fires or trying to stamp them out. The sort of epistemological effort I foresee—featuring a confluence of efforts between philosophers and social scientists—would involve the construction of a cognitive-descriptive theory of science that accords a proper role to the social components.

Veritistic Social Epistemology

Veritistic value   There is one fundamental difference, however, between social scientists and philosophers when it comes to social epistemology. As Shapin indicates, sociology of knowledge is really interested in *beliefs* of agents or groups of agents, irrespective of their epistemic properties. Social scientists are either unconcerned with or downright suspicious of epistemic properties like truth and falsity, rationality and irrationality, etc. By contrast, these epistemic properties are precisely what interest epistemologists. Epistemologists don't always agree on which epistemic properties are of primary interest, but I shall concentrate on the *truth-values* of belief-states and credal states more generally.[8] There is nothing idiosyncratic about this theme. Epistemologists of many persuasions (not just reliabilists about know-ledge or justification) start from the assumption that the "aim" of belief is truth, and that epistemic agents value truth acquisition and the avoidance of error.[9] True belief is not valued only for intrinsic reasons, but also for its instrumental value, inasmuch as true belief is demonstrably useful for attaining practical goals, at least in an important class of cases (Goldman 1999a: 73–4). There is a dimension of value, then, on which true belief is superior to both false belief and ignorance (failure to believe a truth). I call this dimension *veritistic value*. The idea is generalized to degrees of belief, so that higher degrees of belief in a particular truth have more veritistic value than lower degrees of belief in the same truth. Social epistemology that concentrates on veritistic value I call *veritistic social epistemology*.

Social practices and their veritistic consequences   What is "social" about veritistic social epistemology (VSE)? The believing agents discussed are principally individuals, and *qua* believers they are not a locus of sociality.[10] The social dimension enters with the social practices that cause an agent to have this or that belief (or degree of belief). A social practice can be a relatively simple relationship between speakers and hear-ers, or it can be a more complex technological or institutional structure that has an impact on opportunities for speech and/or speech reception. Internet technology, for example, makes it easy for speakers to disseminate their messages to a wide audi-ence, and makes it relatively easy for interested receivers to access messages others have sent. A journal also disseminates messages, but journal editors and referees play important filtering roles. Not every aspiring sender will have his/her submitted message disseminated over that medium. The principal question for VSE is which social practices have which veritistic properties. Which ones promote a relatively high ratio of true belief and which ones are more error-prone? Complicating the picture is the matter of interest. Not all truths are of equal interest to participating agents, so interest should play some role in the veritistic assessment of social prac-tices. How interest fits into the picture will be addressed below.

Earlier I alluded to the prospect of epistemologists and social scientists collaborat-ing in the construction of a descriptive theory of science. Can this really be done, if veritistic properties are supposed to be included in the theory? Science is undoubt-edly one of the toughest and most controversial social enterprises where one might aspire to produce such a theory. Let us therefore look first at a more manageable domain, and see whether this type of project is feasible. We might consider certain

---

[8] This continues the theme pursued in *Knowledge in a Social World* (Goldman, 1999a).

[9] For a list of non-reliabilist epistemologists who emphasize the value of true belief, see (Goldman 2001b: sect. 2)

[10] This claim might be challenged by "anti-individualists" in the philosophy of mind (Burge, 1979), who hold that belief contents are partly fixed by the social context. The topic of the contents of propositional attitudes, however, is tangential to the present discussion. The claim in the text concerns only believers as subjects, not the contents of their belief states.

practices of a legal system and inquire about their veritistic properties. More cautiously, let us ask whether it is even possible, or feasible, to make such a veritistic inquiry.

Many criminal prosecutions in the United States, including prosecutions of capital cases, feature witness evidence from jailhouse snitches. These are prisoners who have been in jail with the defendant and testify about confessions that they allegedly heard the defendant make. Frequently, these jailhouse snitches receive favorable treatment from the penal system in exchange for their testimony. As it happens, quite a few prisoners on death row in America have wound up there partly as a result of testimony by jailhouse snitches. A legal system's practice of allowing testimony from such witnesses, and simultaneously offering them favorable treatment, is an example of a social practice, one that is relevant for epistemological purposes because their testimony ultimately influences the *beliefs* (and hence decisions) of jurors. Clearly, one wants to inquire into the veritistic properties of such a practice. How does it, on the whole, affect the accuracy of jurors' beliefs (and decisions)?

It might seem impossible, or somehow circular, to assess the veritistic properties of any such practice. How can we decide when jurors have erred in believing the testimony of jailhouse snitches unless we have some independent way of determining the truth-values of the propositions asserting that such-and-such defendants were guilty or innocent? Indeed, we must rely on some method or practice of forming beliefs in order to make this determination. But there is nothing objectionable or circular about this. Of course, any method of determining a practice's veritistic propensities will only be as good as the veritistic properties of that method itself. But it doesn't follow that we cannot or should not apply determination methods that we believe, and have good reason to believe, to be highly reliable. In the case of determining a legal system's prior errors, some investigative bodies in America have used DNA evidence (unavailable at the original trials) to determine the innocence of death-row inmates. Almost everybody agrees that proper use of DNA evidence is an extremely reliable method.

Science   Returning to science, we certainly cannot expect to identify comparably simple methods for evaluating the veritistic properties of science (or particular branches of science). But a research program with two components should be helpful. First, we need descriptive models of what transpires in the formation and transformation of scientific beliefs. These models must somehow integrate the mental processes of scientific reasoning, the motivational impetus of personal ambition, and the methodological constraints of a scientific community or culture. Second, these models must be analyzed for their veritistic implications. In very rough terms the construction of descriptive models is the province of social science, whereas veritistic-evaluative analysis is the province of epistemology. In fact, this division of labor should not be strict, in part because the descriptive models must lend themselves to veritistic analysis. Hence, people constructing the descriptive models should already have veritistic analysis in mind to guide them in choosing pertinent models, and this may require familiarity with the second component of the research program.[11]

Economists William Brock and Steven Durlauf (1999) have produced an example of the kind of social model of scientific theory choice that I have in mind for the first component. Their model incorporates a relatively simple "social factor" in the form of a conformity effect, but this effect is capable of accounting for rapid consensus formation after a period of extended disagreement. Their model is not tailored, however, to veritistic analysis. Both Kitcher (1990; 1993: ch. 8) and Shaked and I (Goldman and Shaked, 1991; Goldman, 1999a: chs. 4, 8) have produced models of scientific activity with explicit veritistic intent.[12] Goldman and Shaked (1991) present a simple model of how scientists choose which experiments to perform and how their choice affects veritistic outcomes. Researchers choose experiments with an eye to their potential impact on scientific peers. Peers are assumed to give credit to experimentalists when their experiments generate findings that lead peers to change their degrees of belief about the hypotheses of interest. We first prove a result about the (objectively) expected increases in truth possession that result from Bayesian reasoning with accurate likelihoods. We then go on to show that, when this Bayesian reasoning condition is met (and known to be met), *credit*-driven scientists will make almost as good experimental choices—good from a veritistic perspective— as *truth*-motivated scientists. Thus, even if scientists are motivationally "sullied" (in Kitcher's phrase), the veritistic consequences of their research can approximate those of motivationally "pure" scientists.

Information science   Don Fallis (2000) has applied the central ideas and mathematical results of the Goldman–Shaked work to issues in information science, especially to the problem of verifying information on the Internet. For users to acquire knowledge from the Internet, Fallis points out, it isn't enough that content is readily available. Unless the content's veracity can be established, veritistic value may not increase. Since almost anyone can publish almost anything on the Internet, it contains a lot of inaccurate content and it is difficult to distinguish the accurate from the inaccurate. In the field of library and information science (LIS) the predominant strategy for addressing the verifiability problem is to supply Internet users with ways to evaluate web sites for veracity. These are features, or lists of features, that are supposed to indicate whether or not a web site is likely to contain accurate information. For example, users might be advised to look for a statement of sponsorship, a seal of approval from a service that evaluates web sites on this topic, etc.

[11] Another reason why this division should not be taken too seriously is that some academics double as philosophers of science and cognitive scientists, and they can make major contributions to the first component of the project even though they are partly philosophers. An example is Paul Thagard (1992), whose computational model of scientific reasoning is an interesting model of its kind.
[12] My own model of scientific activity might be called a "mini-model" because of its very limited scope and its admittedly simplified assumptions. Nonetheless, it illustrates what can be done in a veritistic vein.

Fallis indicates that the Goldman–Shaked framework provides a way of measuring the impact of an accuracy indicator on knowledge acquisition, or veritistic value. Here is Fallis's summary of the important factors according to this framework:

First, the amount of knowledge acquisition depends on the reliability of the indicator. Unless the presence of the indicator on a web page is correlated with the information on that page being accurate, the indicator is no more likely to lead an Internet user to true beliefs than to false beliefs. Second, the amount of knowledge acquisition depends on an Internet user's estimate of the reliability of the indicator. Even if the indicator is very reliable, an Internet user will fail to acquire knowledge if this user puts little or no faith in the indicator. Also, if an Internet user puts too much faith in the indicator, this user is likely to fall into error. Third, the amount of knowledge acquisition depends on the cost-effectiveness of checking for the presence of the indicator on a web page. Even if the indicator is very reliable and an Internet user has the right amount of confidence in the indicator, the indicator is not going to help this user acquire knowledge if this user does not think it is worth checking for the presence of the indicator. Goldman's theory of knowledge acquisition provides a way to formalize these factors and to determine the impact of an indicator on knowledge acquisition. (2000: 307)

There is no room here to give a full reconstruction of Fallis's application of the Goldman–Shaked results to Internet verifiability. The foregoing summary, however, highlights the salient ingredients in his demonstration of how to construct a veritistic analysis of one family of Internet practices, i.e. making veracity indicators available on web sites.

Evidence law   A core objective of legal adjudication is accuracy of judgment, where "judgment" refers to a decision by a trier of fact in a legal dispute. In the usual case, the judgment of a trier of fact is a function of the trier's *beliefs* about matters of fact. Hence, to maximize a legal system's judgmental accuracy, it should maximize the accuracy of the trier's beliefs concerning the fundamental factual issues before the court (which, together with the applicable law, fix the guilt or innocence, the liability or non-liability, of the defendant). Now a trial is a highly social affair, in the sense that it involves many players who make various contributions to the outcome—parties to the suit, attorneys, judges, and witnesses. There are very different traditions for the conduct of trials. These include the Anglo-American, or "common-law", system and the Continental, or "civil-law", system. In the common-law system the judge plays a relatively passive role, whereas in the civil-law system the judge, or panel of judges, plays a very active role. A good application of veritistic social epistemology is to ask which of these systems, on the whole, is better at getting the (legal) truth. I have addressed this question—with respect to selected features of the two systems—in *Knowledge in a Social World* (ch. 9). The relative merits of the two overarching systems, however, are not the only possible focus of veritistic analysis. In the study of evidence law within the common-law tradition, great attention is paid to each specific rule of the system. What are the veritistic consequences of each such rule or family of rules?[13] For example, does the hearsay

---

[13] I do not mean that the study of individual rules of evidence focuses exclusively on truth propensities; that is certainly not so. But that is the type of question of relevance here.

doctrine of the American system, which involves a central exclusion of hearsay evidence supplemented by a multitude of exceptions, really serve the interest of maximizing truth?

Brian Leiter (2001) has a keen appreciation of the relationship between evidence scholarship in academic law and veritistic social epistemology. The kinds of questions I have just been identifying, he indicates, are already a staple of much evidence scholarship. In fact, "many evidence scholars, though philosophically innocent, are practitioners of the social epistemology of evidence law" (2001: 322). Here is a clear instance in which studies external to mainstream epistemology invite attention from social epistemology. This does not mean, of course, that philosopher-epistemologists are compelled to devote their attention to this specific domain of application. But it seems probable that people studying social epistemology in general could have useful things to say in this application area, just as ethical theorists (or ethical theory) can contribute to the study of specific problems in bio-ethics, environmental ethics, business ethics, and so forth.

Leiter highlights another important feature of veritistic social epistemology, namely, that it is not a purely *a priori* or conceptual enterprise, but one that must rely, in part, on empirical research. One example that he cites involves empirical evidence about the value of demeanor evidence in the law. A pertinent article in this connection is by Guy Wellborn.

The importance of demeanor as an indicator of credibility is commonly cited as a premise of the general requirement of live testimony, the hearsay rule, and the right of confrontation. . . . The opportunity of the trier of fact to observe the demeanor of witnesses is a principal basis for the deference accorded by reviewing courts to factual determinations of trial courts and hearing officers. (Wellborn, 1991: 1077)

However, Wellborn contends, experimental evidence indicates that "ordinary observers do not benefit from the opportunity to observe nonverbal behavior in judging whether someone is lying" (1991: 1088). Many psychological studies indicate that people aren't terribly good at detecting liars. This does not mean, says Wellborn, that we should eliminate live testimony, nor that we should eliminate the hearsay rule. It does suggest, however, that appellate courts should give less deference to the factual findings of trial courts, at least as they bear on witness credibility. In fact, "a transcript is actually as good a basis for a credibility determination as live testimony" (1991: 1095). Wellborn acknowledges that one should not generalize too quickly from laboratory results to the rules of evidence as they apply at trial. Nonetheless, agreeing with Wellborn, Leiter concludes that veritistic social epistemology should work in tandem with empirical research, and I wholeheartedly concur.

Knowledge and democracy   Many writers on democracy have maintained that a successful democracy requires an informed citizenry. This is particularly clear on the *epistemic approach* to democracy (Cohen, 1986; Estlund, 1990, 1993). The epistemic approach is rooted in the assumption that there is an independent standard of correctness for decisions, outcomes, or electoral choices, and that democracy is to be recommended because it is comparatively good at tracking the truth about what the correct decisions or electoral choices are. According to Rousseau (1762/1973) what makes outcomes or electoral choices correct is that they embody the "general will" or the "common good". Thus, a democracy will be effective if citizens know what the general will or common good is. The argument in favor of democracy is further enhanced by appeal to the Condorcet jury theorem. In its standard form, the jury theorem says this: If each member of a jury is epistemically competent in the sense of being more likely to be right than wrong, then a majority of the jury is also epistemically competent in the sense of being more likely to be right than wrong; and the probability that the right outcome is supported by a majority of the jury is a swiftly increasing function of the size of the jury, converging to 1.0 as the size of the jury tends to infinity. Extrapolating from juries to electorates generally, this result constitutes "the jewel in the crown of epistemic democrats, many of whom offer it as powerful evidence of the truth-tracking merits of majority rule" (List and Goodin, 2001: 283).

Chapter 10 of *Knowledge in a Social World* (Goldman, 1999a) in effect generalizes the idea of voter competence in classical epistemic democracy frameworks.[14] Classical frameworks (like that of Rousseau and Condorcet) assume that whenever voters have an electoral choice, there exists a unique choice that is correct for all voters (independently of the actual outcome of the voting process). Chapter 10 makes the much weaker assumption that for each voter there exists a voter-specific correct candidate. This does not assume that some one candidate is best for all voters. A given candidate is correct for voter V just in case that candidate, if elected, would produce the best outcomes relative to V's preferences. If another voter has different preferences, a different candidate may be best for them. Chapter 10 goes on to argue that democracy "succeeds" (in a binary choice situation) only if a majority of voters get their best candidate. Furthermore, achieving that outcome depends not only on having a majority-rule voting system but also on voters having "core voter knowledge", that is, voters having knowledge (or a high degree of belief in the truth) about which candidate is best for them. If voters have incorrect beliefs about which candidate is best for them, they will vote for the "wrong" candidate, and despite a democratic voting rule, there will be no guarantee of a democratically "successful" outcome.

In this fashion it is shown how democracy depends on core voter knowledge, where "knowledge" is understood as true belief. An associated question that naturally arises for democratic theory is how voters can get the core voter knowledge that is needed to ensure, or make probable, democratically successful outcomes. This problem belongs on the agenda of veritistic social epistemology. How is electoral information to be disseminated or elicited so as to enhance the likelihood that voters will get core voter knowledge as opposed to core voter error? In the nature of

---

[14] I thank Christian List (personal communication) for suggesting this helpful way of viewing the proposals of ch. 10 of *Knowledge in a Social World*.

the case, it is in the interest of each candidate that as many voters as possible *believe* that he or she is their best candidate, whether such a belief would be true or false. Thus, each candidate seeks to persuade voters that he or she is best for them even when this would be a "deception". How is the system to deal with this—without, of course, violating suitable provisions for freedom of speech? What institutional arrangements for enhancing politically relevant knowledge should be in place to promote the likelihood of democratically successful outcomes? This is an important epistemological problem for all democracies.

Knowledge in organizations   As we have just seen, voters in a democracy have a special need for electorally relevant knowledge. This is but a special case of a general problem within organizations. The general problem, for organizations of all types, is to get information to those with a need to know. Two illustrations of the problem surround the events of September 11, 2001. In the months before September 11, each of two suspected members of an international terrorist group was known by some field agent of the FBI to be taking flight-training lessons in the U.S., and agents tried to alert appropriate superiors in each case. Nonetheless, this knowledge did not make its way to suitably high-level officials in the F.B.I. No high-level official learned that two such individuals were both getting flight-training lessons. Thus, there was a major organizational problem in amalgamating disparate pieces of information and conveying the amalgam to appropriate decision-makers. A second example concerned people in the upper reaches of the World Trade Center's south tower on the morning of the attack, where some 300 survived the initial impact. There was an open staircase used by at least 18 to flee while at least 200 others, unaware of that exit, made their way to a locked rooftop door. Meanwhile, the Emergency Broadcast System lay dormant.

These examples typify problems that can be construed as challenges to veritistic social epistemology, understood as an inquiry into both *conceptual* questions and *design* questions concerning social knowledge. The conceptual question is to explain, in general terms, what counts as good knowledge dissemination in an organization. A simple answer to this question was hinted at earlier: the members of an organization or a collective who should know the answer to a question are those who *need* to have an answer to it. An organization or collective has good social-epistemic structure if its knowledge flow meets this desideratum. But what determines whether the answer to a certain question "needs" to be known by a given member? What is the relevant sense of "need"? What determines who needs to know what?

When the problem concerns a loose or random collection of individuals, the relevant need is presumably a function of each agent's own interests. This applies to the occupants of the south tower. When the problem concerns an organization, like the FBI, the relevant need is fixed, presumably, by the organization's mission and by the division of labor that determines who makes critical organizational decisions. In either case, however, we still must settle what is meant by "interest". Interests cannot be restricted to "active" interests, i.e. issues to which the organization, or some leaders thereof, are actively attending. "Interest" must be understood in a dispositional sense. In that sense, the FBI had an interest in knowing (or having relevant high-level officials know) whether or not several potential terrorists were taking flight-training lessons in the U.S., even if no high-level official was actively entertaining that question.

The design question that confronts veritistic social epistemology is how to achieve appropriate distributions of knowledge for specified missions, tasks, or contexts.[15] Although the suitability of information-flow structures may vary from task to task, the intellectual content of the field need not be entirely fragmented. On the contrary, what is needed in the first instance is a theoretical framework that subsumes diverse types of design problems. In devising such a framework, tools like deductive logic and probability theory will not suffice. Some sort of systems theory or network theory is needed, using the kinds of tools found, for example, in distributed artificial intelligence and information science. If this is right, social epistemology should be a collaborative enterprise featuring members of these disciplines along with philosophical epistemologists. Innumerable knowledge problems in the public sphere create a climate that should be highly receptive to work in this territory, and it would be hardly surprising if epistemologists were induced to participate more actively in this sort of project.

Does Social Epistemology Need a Uniform Criterion of Value?

The simple measure of veritistic value proposed in *Knowledge in a Social World* is not satisfactory for all purposes. One thing it fails to do, as emphasized by Philip Kitcher (2002*a*), is present any method for the weighting of interests, so as to say which questions or issues are more *important* or *significant* than others. This raises questions for veritistic social epistemology in two ways. First, we sometimes wish to compare the significance of two states of knowledge. Is knowing p more significant than knowing q? Surely in matters of scientific knowledge, not all knowledge is equal. Certain scientific discoveries are more important and notable than others. Nobel Prizes are awarded to those who find solutions to the more significant questions. Second, we frequently want to assess a social practice in terms of its instrumental epistemic value. How can we do this unless we can assess the significance of the complex states of knowledge that each practice generates? If practice Π_1 generates knowledge of propositions P, Q, and R while practice Π_2 generates knowledge of propositions S, T, and U, which is the superior practice? This seems to hinge on the relative significance of the listed propositions.

Difficult though these problems may be, there is a potentially more serious challenge to the concept of veritistic value. In arguing that true belief has more veritistic value than ignorance one standardly takes the vantage point of the believing

---

[15] As the question itself signals, I presume that veritistic social epistemology does not have an exclusively *descriptive* mission. Another mission is to make recommendations for the design of knowledge networks that would promote veritistic ends.

subject. But in social epistemology, at any rate, a wider perspective is often appropriate, one that takes into account other agents' interests as well. And other agents sometimes prefer that a subject be ignorant of a certain truth rather than know it. This happens precisely when the proposition concerns a *private* matter. You may want me to be *ignorant* or *uninformed* of the books you read, the websites you visit, and your sexual proclivities. From your perspective, my knowing these things would be worse than my being ignorant of them.

This is not a direct challenge, of course, to the concept of veritistic value. It simply calls attention to the fact that evaluations of truth-possessional states are not always of the purely veritistic kind. For some purposes we might evaluate ignorance (or even error) as preferable to knowledge. The next point is that social epistemology can live with this observation. It need not be keyed exclusively to veritistic value. Veritistic value is arguably the *default* value with which epistemology should operate, but epistemology can also depart from this dimension of value.

An analogy may be useful here (Goldman, 2002b). The field of civil engineering studies, among other things, the structural properties of bridges. It is mainly concerned with how to build sturdier and more stress-resistant bridges (and other such structures). Sturdiness is the default value that guides the design choices of the civil engineer. However, sturdiness is not always the operative value. Consider a small, poor country with a militaristic neighbor. The neighbor has a fleet of tanks with which it might invade its sometime enemy. The little country needs a bridge built across a certain river, near its border with the longtime enemy. The bridge would normally carry light commercial traffic, but the little country also foresees the possibility of a tank invasion by the enemy. So it does not want a maximally sturdy bridge, one that would help the enemy transport tanks. On the contrary, it prefers a bridge that would collapse under the weight of a tank or two. It wants a civil engineer to design and build a bridge to this specificiation. Obviously, that's something that a good civil engineer can do. It's as much within the province of civil engineering to design and build a bridge to this specification as to design and build a bridge that maximizes sturdiness. Sturdiness may be the default criterion in bridge building, but it need not be the invariant criterion.

Apply this analogy now to social epistemology. The default criterion of value for social epistemology, I submit, is veritistic value, a conception of value in which, by definition, knowledge is preferable to ignorance and both are preferable to error. When designing a system of legal adjudication, veritistic value is the prime value to be considered.[16] But for other applications, social epistemology need not always adhere to the criterion of veritistic value. When incorporating considerations of privacy, for example, it will definitely have to depart from this default value.

What would happen, under this proposal, to the unified mission of social epistemology? We could no longer say that social epistemology has the mission of evaluating social practices in terms of their *veritistic* consequences, since veritistic

[16] I say "prime" value at work because legal adjudication practices must also be constrained by other values, such as the non-violation of the rights of the accused.

consequences would no longer be the be-all and end-all of social epistemological investigation. But that is all right. Social epistemology would still have an identifiable field of study; it would simply be more flexible and diverse than its purely veritistic cousin. Let us use the term *truth-possession profile* (TPP) to designate a profile or distribution of states of various individuals that include both their doxastic (psychological) states, and the truth-values of the propositional contents of those states. What would still be common to social epistemology is its interest in tracing causal connections between various social practices and resulting TPPs. This would be perfectly analogous to the subject of civil engineering, which examines causal relationships between various design structures and performance properties of such structures—how such structures would react under hypothetical stresses. Social epistemology would not recommend social practices unconditionally; it would recommend them only hypothetically, relative to certain assumed evaluations of the envisioned TPPs. It would not be the business of social epistemology *per se* to make TPP evaluations. That would be society's responsibility, and in the end the province of ethics or political philosophy. Veritistic considerations could undoubtedly enter the picture, but they would not necessarily be decisive. Nonetheless, social epistemology would have an important, and relatively homogeneous, field of study. Notice that this proposal for a looser or "extended" conception of social epistemology only defers the problem of importance, or significance, which was raised earlier. It is relevant to that problem, however, because we can now say that providing an invariant measure of importance, or significance, need not be the task of social epistemology alone. The task may ultimately be assigned to moral theory.[17] The work of social epistemology under the current conception can proceed even if we do not yet have a general solution to the problem of significance.

Conclusion

There are, then, many important reasons why social epistemology is a field ripe for development and a pressing one at that. From an internal point of view there are parts of epistemology's traditional agenda that cannot be completed without proper attention to the social dimension of justification and knowledge. There are also questions about the nature of epistemic value that cannot be adequately answered without reflection on the social contexts of knowing.[18]

From an external point of view there are reasons why people outside of philosophy should be interested in social epistemology. First, it intersects and sometimes substantially overlaps with inquiries in a variety of academic disciplines, including the social studies of science, information science, legal theory, democratic theory, and organization theory. Second, it brings classic philosophical concerns into direct contact with issues of immediate political and social import. Whether it be the

---

[17] *Perhaps* importance or significance can be explained in purely epistemic terms. I don't mean to take a position on this matter here.

[18] For a very valuable treatment of this topic, see Kitcher (2002*b*).

problem of choosing among experts or the problem of securing appropriate media coverage of electoral politics, there are pressing practical problems that can and should be addressed from a social epistemological perspective. People outside of philosophy tend to think of epistemology as abstract, impractical, and remote from the real world. But this need not be so. There are problems of real social institutions that cannot be responsibly tackled without an infusion of ideas from social epistemology. Many scholars within the humanities assume that only 'Continental' thinkers like Foucault or Latour approach epistemology in a manner that interfaces with real institutional problems. But that impression need not persist if the project of social epistemology as described here is actively pursued. This project preserves continuity with traditional epistemology in retaining such classical concepts as truth, justification, and knowledge but also opens the door to a broad range of practical and theoretical problems that confront us daily in society and stare us in the face as academic humanists or social scientists. While some epistemologists might agree that the field merits attention, they may not see it as their proper province. They may prefer to relegate it to others. In this paper I have tried to show, among other things, why the special expertise of epistemologists, at least the expertise of analytically inclined philosophers, is badly needed here. Philosophical expertise may not suffice for this job (which is why I envision an interdisciplinary project), but it cannot be satisfactorily pursued without major guidance and contributions from epistemologico-philosophers. These are the reasons why the diet of future philosophy ought to include generous servings of social epistemology.[19]

Bibliography

Annis, David (1978). "A Contextualist Theory of Epistemic Justification", *American Philosophical Quarterly* 15: 213–19.

Asch, Solomon (1956). "Studies of Independence and Conformity: A Minority of One against a Unanimous Majority", *Psychological Monographs* 70: 9.

Barnes, Barry, and Bloor, David (1982). "Relativism, Rationalism, and the Sociology of Knowledge", in M. Hollis and S. Lukes (eds.), *Rationality and Relativism* (Cambridge, MA: MIT Press).

Brock, William, and Durlauf, Steven (1999). "A Formal Model of Theory Choice in Science", *Economic Theory* 14: 113–30.

Burge, Tyler (1979). "Individualism and the Mental", in P. French, T. Uehling, Jr., and H. Wettstein (eds.), *Midwest Studies in Philosophy, 4, Studies in Metaphysics* (Minneapolis: University of Minnesota Press), 73–121.

—— (1993). "Content Preservation", *Philosophical Review* 102: 457–88.

Coady, C. A. J. (1992). *Testimony* (Oxford: Oxford University Press).

Cohen, Joshua (1986). "An Epistemic Conception of Democracy", *Ethics* 97, 1: 26–38.

DeRose, Keith (1995). "Solving the Skeptical Problem", *Philosophical Review* 104: 1–52.

Estlund, David (1990). "Democracy without Preference", *Philosophical Review* 49: 397–424.

[19] Thanks to the volume editor, Brian Leiter, for many extremely helpful suggestions, including ones for the concluding section.

Estlund, David (1993). "Making Truth Safe for Democracy", in D. Copp, J. Hampton, and J. Roemer (eds.), *The Idea of Democracy* (New York: Cambridge University Press), 71–100.

Fallis, Don (2000). "Veritistic Social Epistemology and Information Science", *Social Epistemology* 14: 305–16.

Foley, Richard (1994). "Egoism in Epistemology", in F. Schmitt (ed.), *Socializing Epistemology* (Lanham, MD: Rowman & Littlefield), 53–73.

—— (2001). *Intellectual Trust in Oneself and Others* (Cambridge: Cambridge University Press).

Fricker, Elizabeth (1995). "Telling and Trusting: Reductionism and Anti-Reductionism in the Epistemology of Testimony", *Mind* 104: 393–411.

Gettier, Edmund (1963). "Is Justified True Belief Knowledge?" *Analysis* 23: 121–3.

Goldman, Alvin (1986). *Epistemology and Cognition* (Cambridge, MA: Harvard University Press).

—— (1988). "Strong and Weak Justification", in J. Tomberlin (ed.), *Philosophical Perspectives, vol. 2: Epistemology* (Atascadero, CA: Ridgeview), repr. in Goldman (1992b).

—— (1992a). "Epistemic Folkways and Scientific Epistemology", in Goldman (1992b).

—— (1992b). *Liaisons: Philosophy Meets the Cognitive and Social Sciences.* (Cambridge, MA: MIT Press).

—— (1999a). *Knowledge in a Social World* (Oxford: Oxford University Press).

—— (1999b). "A Priori Warrant and Naturalistic Epistemology", in J. Tomberlin (ed.), *Philosophical Perspectives, vol. 13: Epistemology* (Malden, MA: Blackwell), repr. in Goldman (2002a).

—— (2001a). "Experts: Which Ones Should You Trust?" *Philosophy and Phenomenological Research* 63: 85–110, repr. in Goldman (2002a).

—— (2001b). "The Unity of the Epistemic Virtues", in A. Fairweather and L. Zagzebski (eds.), *Virtue Epistemology* (New York: Oxford University Press), repr. in Goldman (2002a).

—— (2002a). *Pathways to Knowledge: Private and Public* (New York: Oxford University Press).

—— (2002b). "Reply to Commentators", *Philosophy and Phenomenological Research* 64: 215–27.

—— and Shaked, Moshe (1991). "An Economic Model of Scientific Activity and Truth Acquisition", *Philosophical Studies* 63: 31–55, repr. in Goldman (1992b).

Harding, Sandra (1992). "After the Neutral Ideal: Science, Politics, and 'Strong Objectivity' ", *Social Research* 59: 567–87.

Kitcher, Philip (1990). "The Division of Cognitive Labor", *Journal of Philosophy* 87: 5–22.

—— (1993). *The Advancement of Science* (New York: Oxford University Press).

—— (2002a). "Veritistic Value and the Project of Social Epistemology", *Philosophy and Phenomenological Research* 64: 191–198.

—— (2002b). *Science, Truth, and Democracy* (New York: Oxford University Press).

Latour, Bruno (1987). *Science in Action* (Cambridge, MA: Harvard University Press).

—— and Woolgar, Steve (1979/1986). *Laboratory Life: The Construction of Scientific Facts* (Princeton: Princeton University Press).

Laudan, Larry (1990). "Demystifying Underdetermination", in C. W. Savage (ed.), *Minnesota Studies in Philosophy of Science*, vol. xiv (Minneapolis: University of Minnesota Press).

Leiter, Brian (2001). "Prospects and Problems for the Social Epistemology of Evidence Law", *Philosophical Topics* 29: 319–32.

List, Christian, and Goodin, Robert (2001). "Epistemic Democracy: Generalizing the Condorcet Jury Theorem", *Journal of Political Philosophy* 9: 277–306.

Longino, Helen (2002). *The Fate of Knowledge* (Princeton: Princeton University Press).

Mackenzie, Donald (1981). *Statistics in Britain: 1965–1930, The Social Construction of Scientific Knowledge* (Edinburgh: Edinburgh University Press).

Nozick, Robert (1981). *Philosophical Explanations* (Cambridge, MA: Harvard University Press).

Reid, Thomas (1983). *Inquiry and Essays*, R. Beanblossom and K. Lehrer (eds.), (Indianapolis: Hackett).

Rorty, Richard (1979). *Philosophy and the Mirror of Nature* (Princeton: Princeton University Press).

—— (1991). *Objectivity, Relativism, and Truth* (Cambridge: Cambridge University Press).

Rousseau, Jean-Jacques (1762/1973). *The Social Contract*. In G. Cole, trans., *The Social Contract and Discourses* (London: Everyman/Dent).

Sellars, Wilfrid (1956). "Empiricism and the Philosophy of Mind", in H. Feigl and M. Scriven (eds.), *Minnesota Studies in Philosophy of Science*, I (Minneapolis: University of Minnesota Press).

Shapin, Steven (1994). *A Social History of Truth* (Chicago: University of Chicago Press).

—— and Schaffer, Simon (1985). *Leviathan and the Air Pump: Hobbes, Boyle, and the Experimental Life* (Princeton: Princeton University Press).

Slezak, Peter (1991). "Bloor's Bluff: Behaviorism and the Strong Programme", *International Studies in the Philosophy of Science* 5: 241–56.

Solomon, Miriam (1992). "Scientific Rationality and Human Reasoning", *Philosophy of Science* 59: 439–55.

Sosa, Ernest (1991). "Testimony and Coherence", in *Knowledge in Perspective*. (Cambridge: Cambridge University Press).

Stich, Stephen (1990). *The Fragmentation of Reason* (Cambridge, MA: MIT Press).

Thagard, Paul (1992). *Conceptual Revolutions* (Princeton: Princeton University Press).

Thagard, Paul (1997). "Collaborative Knowledge", *Nous* 31: 242–61.

Weinberg, Jonathan, Nichols, Shaun, and Stich, Stephen (2001). "Normativity and Epistemic Intuitions", *Philosophical Topics* 29: 429–60.

Wellborn, Olin Guy III (1991). "Demeanor", *Cornell Law Review* 76: 1075–105.

Wittgenstein, Ludwig (1969). *On Certainty*, G. E. M. Anscombe and G. H. von Wright (eds.) (New York: Harper).

8

The Ends of the Sciences[1]

PHILIP KITCHER

I. The agenda for twentieth-century philosophy of science was set in the 1920s in Vienna and Berlin, as a group of thinkers who were to transform the character of English-language philosophy responded to the contrast they perceived between the grand achievements of physical inquiry and the inconclusive meanderings of many discussions in philosophy and in the human sciences. Their original ambition was to fashion a scalpel that could be used in intellectual surgery, to slice away statements that transcended the bounds of meaningful discourse or that could not be accepted with intellectual integrity. By the 1940s, however, it had become evident that no such instrument was available; proposed criteria that eliminated metaphysics had an unfortunate tendency to stigmatize huge chunks of revered science, while those that respected scientific accomplishments tolerated the most vapid metaphysical formulae.[2] Convinced of an important difference between science and other areas of inquiry, mid-century logical empiricists posed the questions that have dominated philosophy of science ever since: what is the logic of confirmation? what is a scientific theory? what are the characteristics of scientific explanation?[3] Even in the absence of a criterion of significance, one might hope that answers to these questions would help the reform of inquiry that had been the original Viennese dream.

I've rehearsed a familiar story to introduce an explanation of how some rather obvious issues about the sciences were hidden, so that they could only surface in odd and distorted ways in philosophical discussions. Many thinkers, including those in traditions that positivists and empiricists have viewed as misguided, have come to the sciences with a very different set of concerns. Viewing the natural sciences as a social institution, one of considerable prestige, they've asked about the effects of this institution: are those effects always beneficial?[4] From the perspective of the logical empiricist tradition, questions like this are off the table from the beginning, not solely (although partly) because issues about values are (at least in the early stages of the positivist movement) regarded as meaningless, but also because the sciences serve as the standard of what is to be promoted in inquiry generally. Further, the

---

[1] Many thanks to Brian Leiter for his helpful comments on an earlier draft of this essay.

[2] For a classic attempt to formulate the criterion and to motivate it, see A. J. Ayer, *Language, Truth, and Logic* (New York: Dover, 1952).

[3] See C. G. Hempel, "Problems and Changes in the Empiricist Criterion of Cognitive Significance", repr. in his *Aspects of Scientific Explanation* (New York: Free Press, 1965).

[4] See, e.g., many of the writings of Michel Foucault (especially those collected in *Power/Knowledge* (New York: Pantheon, 1980), Herbert Marcuse, *One-Dimensional Man* (Boston: Beacon, 1964), and Max Horkheimer and Theodor Adorno, *Dialectic of Enlightenment* (New York: Continuum, 1994).

social embedding of the sciences is to be ignored for philosophical purposes. The task of the philosopher is different, one of understanding the characteristics of scientific reasoning, of fathoming important metascientific concepts (*theory*, *explanation*, and so forth), and for such purposes *logical reconstructions* that ignore historical and social details are appropriate. Although twentieth-century philosophers of science, early and late, were often able to clarify significant theoretical disputes in physics, and although the late twentieth century witnessed a similar flowering of work in biology and psychology, the general thrust of the philosophy of science, from 1930 to 2001, could be summed up in a simple program: Science is great, and if we can find out how it works we can improve other discussions enormously.

The power of that program ensured that some dissenting voices were unheard, while others were assimilated to the idioms that the program allowed. Critiques of technology (and of "the technological society") are completely disreputable for those academic philosophers who know that they exist. Challenges to the logical empiricist program, even the quite sweeping challenges of Kuhn, Feyerabend, and the social constructivists whom they inspired, are routinely placed within the epistemological framework of the empiricist project. Historicists (Kuhn, Feyerabend, Toulmin, and others) are taken to advance arguments about the possibility of a general account of evidence that will be adequate to the ways in which scientific claims are actually accepted; social constructivists are viewed as presenting more general (and less subtle) forms of skepticism. Insofar as the critical movements have an epistemological thrust, these are perfectly acceptable ways of framing the objections. Yet something has been lost. In Kuhn's scattered and tentative remarks about progress (both in the sciences and elsewhere), and even more evidently in the later writings of Feyerabend and in some feminists, there are attempts to raise issues about the value of scientific research.[5] The dominant philosophical program is attacked in ways that its official defenses fail to acknowledge. Indeed, because of the influence of the program, the authors of the critiques often formulate their arguments in the epistemological idiom it allows, misrepresenting their own insights.

I cast the program as a crude slogan whose first three words—"Science is great"— invite philosophical scrutiny. First, are the sciences One or many? In recent years, one of the most exciting and valuable developments within philosophy of science has consisted in posing this question in a variety of ways, and writers like Nancy Cartwright, John Dupré, and Peter Galison have illuminated the diversity of diversities of the endeavors we pick out as natural sciences.[6] Second, in what, if anything, does the greatness of the sciences consist? As several generations of post-Kuhnian

---

[5] See Kuhn's *The Structure of Scientific Revolutions* (Chicago: University of Chicago Press, 1962), and several of the essays in *The Essential Tension* (Chicago: University of Chicago Press, 1977); Feyerabend's *Science in a Free Society* (London: New Left Books, 1978) and *Farewell to Reason* (London: Verso, 1987); Helen Longino, *Science as Social Knowledge* (Princeton: Princeton University Press, 1990); and Sandra Harding, *Whose Science? Whose Knowledge?* (Ithaca, NY: Cornell University Press, 1991).

[6] Nancy Cartwright, *The Dappled World* (Cambridge: Cambridge University Press, 1999), John Dupré, *The Disorder of Things* (Cambridge, MA.: Harvard University Press, 1993), and Peter Galison *Image and Logic* (Chicago: University of Chicago Press, 1998). As these authors have often noted, their views were shaped by conversations at Stanford, by interactions with and writings of Ian Hacking and Patrick Suppes.

historians and sociologists have made clear, the sciences profoundly affect and are affected by the societies within which scientific work is done, and it's surely appropriate to try to understand how what they contribute is (or is not) valuable. The dominant tradition thus ignored a second Aristotelian question: What are the ends of the sciences and are our actual practices well-adapted to promoting them? I hope to show why this question is important and how it can be addressed.

II. It will help to start slowly, and to examine the various ways in which considerations of value might enter into the practice of a science. When the value-freedom of Science[7] is touted as a virtue (as it often is), writers typically have something quite sensible in mind. They are envisaging a contrast between two ways of reacting to a body of evidence, comparing the sober judge who doesn't allow personal preferences to interfere with the credulous wishful thinker. Whether that contrast shows that *all* judgments of value are inappropriate to the acceptance of hypotheses is an interesting question, but we don't need to take a stand on that issue to recognize how far short this falls from the ideal of Science as a value-free zone. Accepting claims in the light of the evidence is something that scientists, as well as judges, historians, art dealers, and automobile mechanics, do, but this is only one context of scientific activity.[8] Once we recognize that scientific work is done in a social setting, one that includes institutions (universities, independent laboratories, corporations), complex exchanges of information and supplies, technological products and applications to policies that affect the lives of billions, we can appreciate many kinds of occasions on which scientific decisions are made.[9]

Classical logical empiricism operated with a tidy pair of contexts—discovery and justification, the former to be relegated to psychology, sociology, and history, the latter to serve as the province of philosophy. I'll double the number of contexts, and consider four. First, there's the context in which people (and I'm purposefully vague here) decide which questions should be addressed; call this the *context of anticipation*. Next, there's the context in which people figure out how to pursue inquiry into those questions, the *context of pursuit*. Third, comes my analog of the empiricist's favorite, occasions on which the evidence has been obtained and statements (formulas, images, instruments) are accepted or rejected, the *context of resolution*. Finally, there are decisions about how to translate the results of the context of resolution into practical ventures or policies, the *context of application*. It would surely be crazy to deny that judgments of value play

[7] Here and in what follows, I'll sometimes capitalize 'Science' to indicate the view that the sciences are part of a single enterprise with common features. So in sentences in which the capitalized form occurs, the implication is that all scientific disciplines can be treated alike.

[8] Although constructivist critics of logical empiricism sometimes charge that philosophers divorce scientific reasoning from natural rationality, the idea that decisions in science are continuous with those in everyday life has been a commonplace for decades.

[9] One valuable consequence of social constructivist studies has been the stimulus to consider problems of social epistemology. These problems concern the ways in which interactions among individuals, or social arrangements, promote or retard the acquisition of knowledge. See David Hull, *Science as a Process* (Chicago: Univesity of Chicago Press, 1988); Helen Longino, *Science as Social Knowledge*; Alvin Goldman, *Knowledge in a Social World* (New York: Oxford University Press, 1999); and my book *The Advancement of Science* (New York: Oxford University Press, 1993).

a role in the first, second, and fourth contexts: we direct research towards urgent needs, focusing on the AIDS virus or on methods for detecting bioterrorism, we honor constraints on the types of experiments that can be performed, banning deliberate infection of people without their consent, and we (sometimes) try to use existing knowledge to address issues of practical concern. Yet, once we've embedded the context of resolution within my four-part scheme, we can no longer assume that it lies beyond the reach of value judgment.

Here's why. When the practice of the sciences is socially embedded in the ways I've suggested, then we should think of it as a four-stage process (in which, I should concede, the neatness of my division into separate contexts is sometimes blurred).[10] That process is aimed towards particular ends, the ends of the sciences. We can't determine that one particular phase in the process should take a certain form without looking at the ways in which the design of that phase is integrated with the design of others.[11] From this perspective, the approach of logical empiricism must appear myopic. Cutting off the context of justification (roughly my context of resolution) from the surrounding occasions of scientific decision, philosophers of science have believed they could identify the methods governing that context in isolation. Suppose, however, that the methods so generated were to fail to accord with the promotion of the ends of the sciences, at least when embedded within all the reasonable variants of the other contexts that we can devise. It would be futile to insist that those methods must be appropriate, for the only standard by which they can be appraised is that of advancing the ends of the sciences.[12] Hence, we should remain open to the possibility that a broader investigation of the four contexts might revise the epistemological conclusions drawn by logical empiricists, and even to the chance that value judgments might invade here too.

I hope it's now evident that the neglected question—What are the ends of the sciences?—has considerable philosophical importance. Answers to the question are often tacitly assumed, subsequently framing the treatment of other issues. Thus one obvious way of isolating the logical empiricists' preferred context is to declare that the sciences aim at the provision of truth (or, perhaps, knowledge) and then to focus on how one might best arrive at true beliefs in areas that seem to pose specific challenges (universal generalizations, judgments about unobservables). Defenders of the dominant tradition are likely to maintain that my four-phase process simply muddles up things that ought to be separated. Science is one thing, technology another, and we can investigate the methods of the sciences by seeing how and when evidence statements support (or undermine) hypotheses, leaving to one side the issue of how and whether our new hypotheses might be applied. In what

[10] In considering research options, for example, one can't ignore questions about the existence of efficient means that honor moral constraints.

[11] This is one of the morals of the literature on optimization problems in economics and in evolutionary ecology.

[12] Effectively, I'm opposing "deontological" accounts of rationality, views that take being rational to be a virtue independently of the consequences. If a method were shown to be inept for attaining the goals we set for ourselves, it would be empty to declare it "cognitively virtuous" or to view following it as a "cognitive duty".

follows, I'll try to explain why I resist any such simple separation. For the moment, however, I should note that, outside philosophical circles, there's often a quite opposite emphasis. When policymakers consider the contributions of the sciences, they are apt to draw up lists of the practical benefits that scientific inquiry will provide; indeed, even those most sympathetic to "pure" or "basic" research are only able to sneak in references to the pursuit of truth for its own sake, almost as an afterthought;[13] the major case for "basic" research is its promise to deliver practical benefits down the road, in ways that are currently unforeseeable.

The opposition of the last paragraph exemplifies the unsatisfactory ways in which neglect of the question of ends skews the discussion. One view takes the context of resolution as constitutive of science (or *pure* science) and starts from the assumption that the aim is to disclose truth. The other focuses on the context of application and construes the ends of the sciences in terms of practical benefits (often presented as a list—improved crops, treatments for disease, defensive weapons, labor-saving devices, and so forth). Such extreme pragmatism is likely to strike philosophers as crude, but I want to argue that the "purist" position at the opposite pole is equally unsophisticated.

III. Although philosophers sometimes make casual claims that science aims at truth, that slogan typically figures in the writings of those who want to dispute it. A large body of anti-realist literature attacks the thesis that the sciences can provide us with theories that are literally true, sometimes on the basis of differentiating truth from a more limited notion (such as empirical adequacy), sometimes on the grounds that truth (as conceived by realists) is a problematic notion.[14] My concerns are orthogonal to these. Not even a card-carrying realist ought to accept the slogan. For, to recapitulate an important Popperian insight, the injunction "Seek truth!" is plainly incomplete.[15] Once one has framed a question, then the goal of finding a true answer is a sensible one. Before that, the directive invites those addressed to ask exactly what truth they should be seeking.

If truth figures in the ends of science, that's because some types of truth are worth finding. Which ones? Some scientists (and, less frequently, philosophers) betray odd ambitions, conceiving the goal of inquiry as the provision of a *complete* true account of the universe.[16] It's far from obvious that the idea of a complete true account is coherent, but, even it is, I doubt very much if any of us wants it or sees it as an appropriate aim for some idealization of beings like us. For any given region of

[13] See Vanevar Bush, *Science: The Endless Frontier* (Washington, DC: NSF, 1990). I discuss Bush's view of the goals of science in ch. 11 of *Science, Truth, and Democracy* (New York: Oxford University Press, 2001).

[14] See Bas van Fraassen, *The Scientific Image* (Oxford: Oxford University Press, 1980); Larry Laudan, *Science and Values* (Berkeley: University of California Press, 1984); and Steven Shapin, *A Social Theory of Truth* (Chicago: University of Chicago Press, 1994).

[15] Compare Popper's critique of the command "Observe!" (*Conjectures and Refutations*, New York: Harper Torchbooks, 1965, 46–7).

[16] The position is most prominent in the writings of eminent scientists; see, e.g., Steven Weinberg, *Dreams of a Final Theory* (New York: Vintage, 1994) and E. O. Wilson, *Consilience* (Cambridge, MA: Harvard University Press, 1998). Among philosophers, again, the view is most notable in critical writings. See, e.g., Hilary Putnam, *The Many Faces of Realism* (La Salle, IL: Open Court, 1987).

space-time, even regions that are quite small, one can frame indefinitely many languages that will express infinitely many distinct truths about that region; virtually all of those truths wouldn't be worth knowing. The sciences aim at the *significant* truths, where significance is a value-laden notion.

Partisans of the dominant philosophical tradition rarely view this as a threat to their views, perhaps because they understand the values in question to be cognitive or epistemic. They endeavor to preserve the ideal of a pure science, yearning for truth, by declaring that the kinds of truths that matter are those that play a distinctive role in understanding nature. It's as though human beings, as cognitive agents, as inquirers, are set an agenda by nature, and the end of Science is to find true answers to the questions on the agenda.[17] But that is just metaphor. We need a more careful specification of just what these distinctive types of truth are.

One obvious proposal is that we want to identify the correct laws of nature. Philosophers in the logical empiricist tradition have lavished effort on attempting to provide a characterization of natural laws, one that will distinguish laws from accidental generalizations.[18] I'm skeptical about the prospects for success, but, quite independently of that, it's worth asking just why fathoming the laws of nature is particularly valuable—what makes this a worthy end? Natural philosophers of the Renaissance and Early Modern Period could have answered the question, seeing the laws as instituted by the divine creator and human knowledge of the laws as a humble and pious appreciation of the creator's beneficent design.[19] I doubt that the answer appeals to many contemporary philosophers of science. What rival answer can a secular perspective yield?

Earlier, I characterized the significant truths as playing a special role in understanding nature. Unlike prediction and intervention, activities that tilt the sciences towards practical matters, understanding can be conceived as a pure goal, an end that is intrinsically worth pursuing. Suppose that we achieve understanding by seeing the phenomena as consequences of general regularities, take the laws to be statements of these regularities (or the most fundamental such regularities). We then have an answer to the question: we seek the laws of nature because we want understanding. Insofar as the logical empiricist tradition has a tacit view of the ends of the sciences, this strikes me as the major candidate.

Yet that view is riddled with obvious difficulties. First, it supposes that there's some general project of understanding nature. Second, it adopts a very specific account of

---

[17] In effect, the idea of an objective agenda for Science (with a capital 'S'), is accepted by Wesley Salmon in *Scientific Explanation and the Causal Structure of the World* (Princeton: Princeton University Press, 1984), and by me in *The Advancement of Science*. It lurks behind the writings of those who emphasize the discovery of laws of nature and natural kinds, as well as those who envisage "final theories". In various places, perhaps most explicitly in the Introduction to *Consequences of Pragmatism* (Minneapolis: University of Minnesota Press, 1982), Richard Rorty criticizes the view of "nature's agenda". I discuss these issues at greater length in *Science, Truth, and Democracy*.

[18] In part, this grew out of an attempt to honor Humean scruples, to view causation as the shadow of explanation, and laws as crucial to explanation. The emphasis is very clear in the writings of Ernest Nagel (*The Structure of Science*, New York: Harcourt Brace, 1961) and C. G. Hempel (*Aspects of Scientific Explanation*).

[19] See E. A. Burtt, *The Metaphysical Foundations of Modern Physical Science* (London: Routledge & Kegan Paul, 1967).

explanation, one that takes explanation to consist in lawful subsumption.[20] Third, it assumes that there's some manageable collection of laws that can be appreciated by human beings (or by recognizable idealizations of ourselves) and that will make possible the general project.

All three theses are vulnerable to criticism. The last would clearly be sustained if there were a genuine possibility of unified science, if the sciences formed a tidy hierarchy with higher levels reducing to lower levels and ultimately to physics at the base. In the light of investigations in the philosophy of biology and the philosophy of psychology during the past three decades, that picture is no longer tenable.[21] The issues are particularly clear in the case of the relations between genetics and molecular biology, because in this instance both the classical account of heredity (developed by T. H. Morgan and his successors) and the allegedly reducing theory are extremely well articulated. Although there's no doubt that increased knowledge of the chemical reactions among biologically significant molecules has advanced our understanding of many aspects of genetics, it's not true that *every* significant genetic generalization can be derived and explained within molecular biology. Consider, for example, the principle that genes on different chromosomes assort independently at meiosis. In the first place, this isn't derivable from principles of molecular biology, since there is no way of singling out, within the language of molecular biology just those segments of nucleic acid that count as genes. Secondly, even if this obstacle could be overcome, the explanation of independent assortment is that, at meiosis, homologous chromosomes are paired and (after exchange of genetic material between homologues) one member of each pair is passed on to a gamete; to understand independent assortment is to recognize the general form of this pairing and selection process, and that understanding doesn't depend on facts about what chromosomes are made of.[22]

Now although it would suffice to buttress the third thesis, the unity-of-science picture isn't necessary for it; the thesis would be sustained if one could retreat to the claim that the sciences fall into a finite number of clusters, each of which can be subsumed under a finite number of basic laws. So long as we focus on the areas of inquiry already marked out, our various subdisciplines within the physical and social sciences, then we might hope that the retreat would succeed—although even here the difficulty of finding candidates for basic laws in biology, psychology, economics, and sociology might give us pause. But more than that is needed. If the uncovering of laws is to be the key to a complete account of nature, then it must extend beyond

---

[20] From the 1940s until the end of the 1960s philosophers of science had reached a virtual consensus on the *covering-law model* of scientific explanation, most thoroughly articulated by C. G. Hempel in his "Aspects of Scientific Explanation". According to that model, explanations are arguments in which a description of the phenomenon to be explained is derived (deductively or inductively) from a set of premises that must include at least one general law.

[21] See Jerry Fodor, "Special Sciences" (*Synthese*, 28, 1974, 77–115); Alan Garfinkel *Forms of Explanation* (New Haven, CT: Yale University Press, 1981); and my essay "1953 and all that. A Tale of two Sciences" (*Philosophical Review* 93, 1984, 335–73).

[22] For more detailed versions of these arguments, see my articles "1953 and all that. A Tale of Two Sciences", and "The Hegemony of Molecular Biology" (*Biology and Philosophy*, 14, 1999, 195–210).

the areas of inquiry that have so far emerged in the actual history of the sciences to cover *all* the phenomena, whether or not they have yet figured in our conceptualization of nature. Once the unity-of-science picture has been discarded, there's no basis for thinking that the clusters of laws (even assuming we can always find them) won't proliferate indefinitely.[23]

Second, it's far from evident that laws are always required for scientific explanation. From the 1940s on, critics of the covering-law models of explanation have emphasized the existence of disciplines—history is a prime example—in which understanding seems to be generated without appeal to laws. The standard rejoinder to such objections has been to claim that the answers actually given to explanation-seeking questions are stripped-down versions of "ideal explanations"; the historian (say) formulates an "explanation sketch" that abstracts from the "ideal" in ways that are suited to the needs of the intended audience. But there are many areas in which explanations are given without any ability to formulate laws that would subsume the phenomena— most of biology, geology, psychology, and the social sciences—and the reiteration of claims that such laws must exist and stand behind the "explanation sketches" has come to look like an *idée fixe* drawn from overemphasis on small parts of physics. If actual people achieve actual understanding of the events of history, the facts of inheritance and the eruption of volcanoes without recognizing pertinent laws of nature, then maybe the laws don't matter to the worthwhile goal of understanding.[24]

The most fundamental problem for the view, however, lies in the idea of some general project of understanding nature. For this recapitulates the difficulty with which we began; the problem exposed by taking seriously the injunction "Seek truth!" has a parallel generated by reflecting on the analogous command "Understand nature!". To understand, I suggest, is to be in a position to answer questions that had previously arisen for one. The thought of a device that would answer all possible questions is as foolish as the idea of an account of nature that is both true and complete. Moreover, for any true statement one cares to select, it will be possible to devise questions with respect to which that statement is part of an adequate answer. Hence the notion that statements can be identified as significant on the grounds that they play a valuable explanatory role is powerless to make any distinctions whatsoever. Nor can one suggest that some statements (the laws, say) play a role in answering more questions than others; for it turns out that the set of questions for which some arbitrarily chosen true statement is needed as part of the answer has the same cardinality as the set of questions for which your favorite law is needed as part of the answer.[25]

None of this affects the sensible proposal that understanding is a worthwhile thing, and that the sciences aim to provide it. They show only that the proposal

---

[23] This challenged is deepened by Cartwright's arguments in *The Dappled World*. See also *Science, Truth, and Democracy*, chs. 6 and 7.

[24] This perspective was already offered in the late 1950s and 1960s by Michael Scriven (see, e.g., "Explanations, Predictions, and Laws" in *Minnesota Studies in the Philosophy of Science*, vol. III (Minneapolis: University of Minnesota Press, 1962). For a thorough review of the career of the covering-law model of explanation, see Wesley Salmon, *Four Decades of Scientific Explanation* (Minneapolis: University of Minnesota Press, 1990).   [25] See *Science, Truth, and Democracy*, ch. 6.

needs to be liberated from the over-ambitious commitment to understanding "everything". The resolute efforts to ban talk of values from the philosophy of science have obscured the fact that *certain types* of questions arise for us, and we seek explanations that answer these types of questions. Some of those questions endure through long periods of history. Like our predecessors in the ancient world, we still want to know how ordinary things are made up of component parts and how the behavior of the component parts affects the properties we detect; that's why we seek ever-deeper theories of matter, and why a misnamed "Theory of Everything" would be worth having (it would be a systematic account of a large number of phenomena that strike beings with our perceptual and cognitive capacities as salient). Other questions disappear. I suspect that nobody today seeks to understand why there's a common constancy in the behavior of fire and earth, the one moving up and the other down, although Aristotelians once built an influential account of nature on attempts to answer that kind of question; a few people continue to ask how the living world manifests the design of a creator, despite the fact that that's a dead issue for most. Finally, of course, new questions emerge. The biologists who want to understand how cells differentiate in the early life of an embryo pose questions about gene activation that wouldn't have occurred to their predecessors.

Properly understood, the view that the sciences aim at truth comes to this. One of the ends of the sciences is to provide us with true answers to questions that matter to us for their own sake. Thoughtful and perceptive people throughout history have sometimes entertained a question not because the answer would enable them to do something practical, something they couldn't have managed without it, but simply because the question itself fascinated them.[26] When we view a completely pragmatic account of the sciences as inadequate, I think we're responding to this (almost?) universal human sense of curiosity. Our aim isn't to give an account of nature that is both true and complete, or to fashion an explanatory device that could be used on any natural phenomenon, but simply to answer the questions that matter to us. If we prize generality and give a special name to some statements of regularity (those we pick out as "laws"), that reflects the fact that *when we can get it* the ability to address at once a lot of questions that concern us is a good thing. But we shouldn't assume that such statements of regularity will always be available, or that sciences that fail to supply them are second-rate, or that the questions we answer without appeal to them are any less important than others.

Truth, so understood is *one* end.[27] Plainly, however, it isn't our only concern. For there are questions to which we want true answers because those answers could be used in practical projects that are important to us. A biologist might be curious about the structure of the coat proteins in the anthrax bacterium, but the more obvious relevance of questions in this area is that answers might provide clues to fashioning quick and accurate diagnostic tests, novel antibiotics, or vaccines. As my

[26] Think of the long-standing interest in the motions of heavenly bodies, and our curiosity about human origins.

[27] For defense of truth as an end, and of a modest realism, see my "Real Realism: The Galilean Strategy" (*Philosophical Review*, 110, 2001, 151–97).

last example suggests, the questions of practical concern are even more obviously—and perhaps more rapidly—variable across history than those that arouse our disinterested curiosity. They bring home the point that an account of the ends of the sciences must be understood in terms of the interests of a particular group of people at a particular stage of inquiry. If the dominant philosophical tradition has slighted the practical import of the sciences, that is, I suspect, because the Search for Truth has been viewed as something constant across history and culture, something that overrode the ephemeral concerns of groups who faced highly specific challenges. On the account I've started to develop, the search for truth is directed towards answering questions that matter for their own sake, and the class of such questions is, like the set of practically urgent questions, historically variable. There is, then, no basis for a contrast between the enduring aim of pure science and the transient goals pursued in our practical ventures. Both sorts of ends must be understood in relation to the situation and needs of a group of people. Each must be balanced against the other.

We now have the beginnings of an account of the ends of the sciences, and of the standard against which the four-part process of Section II should be appraised. Relative to a particular group, the sciences aim to provide true answers to questions that matter to that group, where the sources of the mattering may be curiosity or relevance to a practical venture (or, as we'll see, sometimes a mixture of the two). This is only the beginning, for there are obvious issues that need to be clarified.

IV. Here are some obvious worries. First, I've characterized ends by reference to particular groups. But groups aren't typically homogeneous. You may be fascinated by issues about the evolution of hominids, while I'm worried about finding a cure for Alzheimer's disease; many others who belong to our society may be interested in neither of these. In what sense, then, can we think of aims for an entire group? Second, what matters to people (or what they take to matter to them) is sometimes quite a casual business, sometimes the product of ignorance. Should we treat equally the superficial concerns of the outsider who reads a popular article that excites his curiosity and the informed perspective of the researcher who understands how the answer to a recondite question will resolve a number of puzzles in her field? How do we distinguish genuine interests from superficial preferences? Third, what kinds of groups make sense for my relativization of the ends of the sciences? Is it the case that we should focus just on the societies in which scientific inquiry is practiced and attend only to the attitudes of the group members?

I'm going to respond to these legitimate questions by presenting a view of how deliberation would proceed in the context of anticipation if it were governed by a desire to promote the ends of the sciences. Let's imagine, then, that we start with a society within which scientific inquiry is practiced. The members of this society, including the scientists who will undertake research, have a variety of concerns, some of them the product of lengthy experience and reflection, others formed quite quickly. One way to answer the three questions would be to offer a simple procedure for them to sort out what kinds of science should be done. They are to come together and vote for pursuit of questions, each awarding highest marks to the questions he takes to matter most. If this is to accord with promoting the ends of the sciences then we can read off answers to the questions: the aims of the group are just a weighted average of the preferences of the members, all preferences (however formed) count equally, and only the members of the society are represented. I think all three answers are wrong.

My suggestion constitutes vulgar democracy, and it's inadequate not because of the democracy but in virtue of the vulgarity. The suggestion is worth making as a simple way of showing how specifying the ideal form of a deliberative process in the context of anticipation will yield answers to the questions. We can do better.[28]

Start from some obvious points. In planning our own lives each of us is often torn among a variety of projects that seem to us worthwhile. The general problem of balancing one form of activity is thoroughly familiar, and academics will immediately recognize the special version in which practical ventures contend with time-consuming intellectual work. Although we sometimes give weight to one way of spending time on the grounds that it will enhance other enterprises in which we take an interest, there are plainly cases in which we identify two quite different sources of value and are unwilling to slight either completely.[29] Moreover, we know that we sometimes make our apportioning decisions well, and sometimes make them badly. Over the course of our lives we develop strategies for avoiding the kinds of mistakes to which we are most susceptible.

Similarly, in joint decision-making with friends and family, we rarely undertake courses of action that have been successful in gaining a majority of votes, cast without prior discussion. An outcome that represents the collective will should be based on genuine appreciation of the possibilities, on recognition of the felt needs of others, and on a determination to avoid options that some would find unacceptable. Except when any effective action must be undertaken quickly, it's worth taking time to explore what others know and what others want. If voting ever occurs, it's as a matter of last resort, when attempts to produce consensus have failed.

Let's reflect these elementary points in outlining a process of ideal deliberation for the context of anticipation. Imagine a society within which scientific inquiry is practiced. That society is likely to contain many different views about how the various sciences should be extended; some, maybe most, of these perspectives may be sadly handicapped by ignorance of the state of the various sciences. Suppose, however, that representatives of the diverse perspectives come together, and that, at the first phase of the discussion, they gain a sense of what has so far been accomplished and of the directions along which research might continue. Those who have been addressing the technical questions of particular fields explain why they regard

---

[28] The account that follows is indebted to ideas of John Rawls (*A Theory of Justice*, Cambridge, MA: Harvard University Press, 1971) and to Amy Gutmann and Dennis Thompson (*Democracy and Disagreement*, Cambridge, MA: Harvard University Press, 1996). I elaborate it in more detail in ch. 10 of *Science, Truth, and Democracy*.

[29] For a valuable discussion of balancing different kinds of goals in personal decisions, see Thomas Hurka, *Perfectionism* (New York: Oxford University Press, 1993). The general problem of incommensurable goods is also discussed in an illuminating way by John Broome in *Weighing Goods* (Oxford: Blackwell, 1991).

certain findings, particular products, and broader questions, yet unanswered, to be significant. Sometimes they cite the intrinsic interest of answering a question; on other occasions, they relate how the answer has practical potential; on yet others, perhaps a majority, they mention both kinds of factors. At the end of this explanatory period, all the participants in the deliberation have a picture of how the various fields of science are currently constituted, in the sense of seeing how significance is taken to accrue to the individual projects on which researchers have been engaged.[30]

The next step is for them to arrive at a responsible account of the options that are available. We can imagine that the deliberators express their preferences about what kinds of inquiry are most important. In some instances, they may just articulate valuations with which they entered the deliberation; in others, the views set forth may reflect their newly achieved awareness of the current state of the sciences. As each listens to the attitudes of others, preferences are further modified, since each wishes to accommodate the others insofar as is possible and hopes to avoid outcomes that leave some participants completely unsatisfied. The process is further informed by the judgments of expert witnesses about the chances for success along various avenues of research. The pertinent experts are selected by following chains of deference: all participants initially defer to the community of scientists; within this community there's deference to fields, subfields, and ultimately to individuals. Where this process generates serious disagreement, the chains bifurcate, and those picked as "experts" may offer rival estimates. If there's no way to resolve the difference that generates the competing groups of "experts", then all the "expert" estimates are presented to the participants, together with whatever information is available about the past records of those whose expertise is sought.[31]

I've supposed that the deliberators respond to the others' concerns, that they're committed to an outcome that will not ignore the interests of any. But I don't think that *only* other deliberators should figure in their reflections. Each knows that two kinds of people who aren't represented will be affected by their decisions, the members of future generations and their own contemporaries in other societies. Their adjustment of preferences must also be informed by the ideal of doing what they can to meet what they identify as the needs of members of these other groups.

The deliberators know that the future course of inquiry is constrained by the resources available in their society. One can either suppose that the limit is externally imposed or that they have the option of deciding how to balance the costs of research against those of other societal projects. Their task is to arrive at a specification of projects that honors the constraint and reflects their collective priorities. Ideally the collective will is manifested in a consensus position, informed in the ways I've just outlined. A second best would be for each participant to find acceptable a set of specifications of projects and for the intersection of these sets to be nonempty. The third option is for the specification to be given by majority vote. That serves as a last resort for expressing the collective will.

[30] In the terms of ch. 6 of *Science, Truth, and Democracy*, they reconstruct the *significance graphs* for the fields of science, representations that show how significance flows to quite recherché questions.

[31] Here, I finesse some tricky issues. See ch. 10 of *Science, Truth, and Democracy*.

I've implicitly answered all the questions posed at the beginning of this section. Group aims are to be understood as what would be chosen in an ideal process of deliberation. The preferences of the deliberators are to be informed and adjusted in light of their recognition of the preferences of others. Finally, the deliberators are supposed to take into account the needs of other people, contemporaries in other societies, and members of future generations. The ends of the sciences, for a group at a time, are constituted by the set of projects and priorities that would emerge from an ideal process with these characteristics. So if we were to take the proper ends of contemporary science to include an integrated theory of the fundamental forces, a full account of the process of cellular differentiation, a complete specification of the causes of major climatic change, a vaccine against HIV, and a detailed account of hominid evolution, we'd be committing ourselves to the view that an ideal discussion of the sort I have described would culminate with a decision (ideally a consensus) to pursue these projects.

There's an obvious objection. I framed the decision that the deliberators must make by giving them a budget; it was assumed that they couldn't adopt the inclusive strategy of responding to everyone's wishes (raw, or modified through the initial provision of information about the state of the sciences). One could hope to find an ideal that might appear more objective by relaxing the constraint, supposing that the ends for a single generation comprised the total set of their projects (perhaps after scientific tutoring), and that the ends of the sciences (period) consist of those projects that would emerge in the limit of an indefinite iteration of the choice of courses of inquiry. The aim would be, in effect, to adjust the view that the aim of the sciences is the complete true account of nature by taking it to be the complete true view of those parts of nature which would be salient to human beings in the indefinite limit of scientific research.

I reject this approach to the issues because it doesn't take seriously either our human limitations in pursuing knowledge or the ways in which our needs and priorities evolve in the course of inquiry. Questions of relative value arise for us precisely because the space of what might be done is so much larger than what we can actually accomplish. Our choices today have important effects on the problems that will confront us tomorrow; thus the ideal process I've described would go very differently at future times than the alleged rival, since urgent needs are frequently unanticipated. As with the flawed programs from which it descends, the rival suggestion tries to accommodate all possibilities—not all possible truths or all explanations, this time, but the satisfaction of all possible needs. But human needs arise in an environment, and, in many instances, that environment is shaped by the particular course that inquiry has taken. Thus we do better, I believe, to adopt the version of ideal deliberation I've proposed, an account that sees the ends of the sciences as subject to an analogue of Darwinian selection, rather than embracing the alternative.

V. Let me now suggest how my suggestions about the ends of the sciences bear on the four-stage process envisaged in Section II. To a first approximation, the practice of science in a group goes well when that practice is carried out in ways that are likely to promote the ends of the sciences. This means that the context of anticipation will have to involve procedures that are likely to specify projects that would be favored in an ideal deliberation of the type just described, that the context of pursuit will generate lines of investigation that are efficient ways of undertaking those projects (subject to the moral constraints that the group imposes), that the context of resolution will have to set standards for the acceptance and rejection of statements that best accord with the attainment of the epistemic goals, and that the context of application must employ procedures for translating the results of inquiries that best fit the practical goals. Because there may be important changes during the period in which inquiries are undertaken, the goals that are important in these last two contexts must be those that would result from an ideal deliberation taken at these stages (which may be different from those that would have resulted earlier). A practice of science that goes well in this sense will be said to be *well-ordered*.

How does one design a well-ordered science? Surely not by supposing that the actual procedures for setting scientific priorities should literally recapitulate the stages of my envisaged ideal discussion. That would be impossibly cumbersome. Rather, we should want mechanisms that deliver some approximation to what would be achieved without the enormous expense of time and energy that a literal recapitulation would require; we should distinguish well-ordered science as an ideal from a means of attaining (or approximating) that ideal. So we might think of analyzing the four-stage process as an optimization problem. We imagine a broad class of representative situations in which the practice of science might be undertaken, consider an array of strategies for coping, and try to find the best way of mimicking the ideal outcomes. But this is over-ambitious, if not downright mad. Without enormously more knowledge than we are ever likely to have, there's no serious way of specifying a representative set of scientific predicaments, or of generating plausible strategies, or of deciding when a particular choice would mimic the ideal.

Yet the notion of well-ordered science is useful for appraising the scientific practices that actually exist, in that it can enable us to appreciate certain obvious pitfalls. Let me survey some examples, and the neglected philosophical problems to which they give rise. I'll start with the easiest cases.

During recent decades, it's become a commonplace that certain types of research can't be tolerated. We might hope to be able to settle issues about the causes of a disease by selectively exposing people to potential pathogens, or to resolve problems of nature and nurture by separating children from their families and rearing some of them in bizarre environments, but all scientific communities now acknowledge moral constraints that forbid such experiments. Communities also frown on scientific piracy, attempts to acquire without consent the data obtained by others, although they also recognize that scientists have obligations to share their findings. Issues like these exhaust what many authors think of as the domain of value questions about the sciences. As this essay has already indicated, and as we'll see in more detail shortly, I think that vision is too narrow. Nonetheless, deciding what methods of inquiry can be allowed is part of the evaluation of the sciences, and the examples I've given reveal that some of the decisions are relatively straightforward.

Only some, however. The two kinds of examples have more subtle relatives. Much contemporary research employs sentient animals, sometimes submitting them to unusual pain, sometimes bringing into existence creatures whose lives will be short and unpleasant. A total ban on experiments that inflict suffering on animals would inhibit many lines of inquiry that have great potential for alleviating human agony and misery; a completely tolerant attitude towards animal suffering would permit experiments that pursue ends that seem trivial. Where are lines to be drawn? When conclusions are announced with statistical estimators (confidence intervals), how much more animal pain should we be willing to inflict to make those estimators more precise? Similarly, in the second case, we're likely to frown on piracy when those who have important information act swiftly to release it to their colleagues. But there are envisageable cases (even perhaps actual cases) in which the information is urgently needed and in which a pathologically doubtful investigator feels the need for further trials. Under these circumstances, is it always wrong for others to seek to tease the findings out of subordinates in the lab, or to find ways of looking at a crucial photograph?

The scenarios raised in the last paragraph suggest a more general problem. It's natural to distinguish some contexts in which our everyday moral judgments are suspended. War and politics are obvious instances of arenas in which insisting on the principles we apply to private transactions appears futile. Are there occasions in which scientific research is exempted from our quotidian moral constraints? If so, what are the distinguishing marks of such occasions?

Turn now to the context of resolution. This, of course, is the home territory of the dominant tradition in the philosophy of science, and it's reasonable to believe that that tradition will have much to teach us about the practice of well-ordered science. Here's an obvious thought: statements should be accepted in the context of resolution just in case they are adequately supported by the evidence that's then available; twentieth-century philosophy of science has had much to say about what 'adequately supported' means.[32] True enough. But my use of the passive elides an important difficulty. *Who* are the people doing the accepting and rejecting? Almost without exception, philosophers have written about the decision-making of individuals. If they've thought of a community of scientists, that community has been envisaged as a large-scale individual. Once we take explicit note of the social character of inquiry, however, it's a serious issue whether we want complete homogeneity in outcome. Imagine, as a crude simplification, that the society divides into two groups, insiders and outsiders. Assume further that the pursuit of inquiries has issued in findings that bear positively to some degree on a particular proposition. Is it the case that, whatever that degree may be, we want the population to be in one of two states: everybody accepts the proposition, or everybody does not accept it? For there are other possibilities. (1) All the insiders accept and outsiders remain agnostic; (2) Some of the insiders accept, some remain agnostic; outsiders follow the majority;

---

[32] See, for three important examples, Rudolf Carnap, *Logical Foundations of Probability* (Chicago: University of Chicago Press, 1951); Wesley Salmon, *Foundations of Scientific Inference* (Pittsburgh: University of Pittsburgh Press, 1965); and John Earman, *Bayes or Bust?* (Cambridge, MA.: MIT Press, 1992).

(3) Some of the insiders accept, some remain agnostic; outsiders follow roughly the same distribution. I think we can envisage different examples in which different outcomes are most desirable.

Sometimes cognitive diversity is a good thing. It helps the community in its ongoing research if individual investigators are inclined to pursue an important problem from a different point of view.[33] But cognitive diversity may actually interfere with the projects of the community, including the enterprise of well-ordered science. If a minority position within the scientific community resonates with deeply held beliefs in the broader community, the outsiders may appeal to that minority opinion to prevent the spread of important scientific ideas.[34] (Think of opposition to evolution and to sex education.)

For reasons eloquently articulated by Mill, it's important for communities to contain challenges to received opinion.[35] Equally, a community that constantly subjects all parts of its corpus of beliefs to severe critiques is unlikely to fare forward far. How then is the balance to be struck? This is a large issue in social epistemology, and one that lies beyond the reach of the individualistic philosophy of science of the dominant tradition. That issue becomes even more complex when we recognize that the ways in which knowledge passes from the insiders to the outsiders can have various kinds of social consequences. Any serious attempt to address it will be up to its neck in judgments of value. Nevertheless, the more general approach I've proposed can take over important insights of the dominant philosophical tradition. For it seems hard to deny that there are occasions—possibly a large number of them— on which it will be desirable for individual people to abide by the epistemic standards that twentieth-century philosophers of science worked so hard to elaborate.[36]

I now confront the hardest cases, the contexts of anticipation and of application, where similar considerations are relevant. In both instances, the aim is to understand how we might fall short of well-ordered science, by identifying projects or making applications that don't conform to the collective will. There are obvious dangers. We may be too close to the situation of vulgar democracy, so that the scientific ventures actually pursued only reflect the raw preferences of the members of our societies, untutored in the way that my ideal deliberative process embodies. Or the sciences may be dominated by the interests of scientists, by refined curiosity about phenomena with which they have engaged intensely for their working lives, and the urgent practical concerns of ordinary citizens may be slighted. Or the sciences may respond to the needs of some groups within the society and marginalize the concerns of others. Or the sciences may be (or be becoming) subject to the influence of capitalist entrepreneurs who are more interested in immediate profits than with goals that either scientists or appropriately informed citizens would set.

---

[33] See my "The Division of Cognitive Labor" (*Journal of Philosophy*, 87, 1990, 5–22), and ch. 8 of *The Advancement of Science*.

[34] I develop these points in "An Argument about Free Inquiry" (*Noûs*, 31, 1997, 279–306), and in ch. 8 of *Science, Truth, and Democracy*.   [35] See J. S. Mill, *On Liberty*, sect. II.

[36] Obvious examples are instances in which researchers are assessing the safety of drugs and jurors are considering the innocence of the accused.

Or the sciences may not adequately reflect the needs of future generations. Or they may be insensitive to the plight of those who lie beyond the borders within which the research is done.

These possibilities raise increasingly difficult questions. It seems to me relatively obvious that most citizens of societies that invest heavily in scientific research have very little understanding of the reasons why virtually any researcher pursues the questions she does. If we imagine a world in which the citizenry take the trouble to look at lists of the projects pursued by scientists, they would wonder why energy, money, and talent are devoted to these things. Often, however, there's an intricate web of linkages between the issue that a researcher selects and matters that out-siders could view as important. Although general scientific publications (such as *Nature* and *Science*) do devote a few pages to brief articles explaining the significance of new findings (for scientists in adjacent fields), a more general depiction of the ways in which significance flows to recherché enterprises—the construction of *significance graphs*—is at best a haphazard part of our scientific education. If we began to take seriously the idea that the ability to understand significance graphs is one of the most important outcomes of elementary education in science—as necessary for citizens as an ability to work scientific problems or to understand what is often thought of as "scientific method"—then we would have to rethink parts of the basic curriculum. Unless we take that idea seriously, then there will continue to be a mismatch between the subtle questions appreciated by the scientific elect and the understanding of outsiders, and the research community will have genuine con-cerns that the Philistines might interfere with important work. A natural response, common in recent decades, is that lines of inquiry are advertised without regard for their true benefits, so that worthy ventures are begun in a condition of public false consciousness, a condition that sometimes distorts their further elaboration.

If "basic research" is to thrive in a well-ordered science, that will be because a tutored public understands the significance of trying to answer questions that may have no direct bearing on their practical concerns. The arguments for such research are of two main types. One emphasizes the future practical benefits of addressing general questions: in the usual metaphor, we should invest in the scientific equivalent of "seed corn".[37] That line of defense should receive more scrutiny from historians and philosophers of science than it typically does. Although it's fair to point out occa-sions on which an indirect approach to issues of practical importance was immensely fecund—as in early twentieth-century genetics with the investigation of heredity in tractable organisms like fruit flies—we would do well to balance telling anecdotes with a more systematic survey. The second line of argument insists that some ques-tions deserve answering for their own sake. Here there are deep and difficult philo-sophical questions, issues about the intrinsic value of understanding particular kinds of things, about how to balance our natural curiosity against the urgent demands on us. At first blush, at least, the polar positions are both uninviting; neither a world in which all our efforts are directed at addressing mundane needs nor a world in which

---

[37] See Vannevar Bush, *Science: The Endless Frontier*.

research cares nothing for the practical plight of millions seems a better choice than a more balanced agenda. My ideal of well-ordered science rests on the thought that an appropriate balance is one that would be struck in a certain type of deliberation. Since we can't actually bring about that deliberation, it's a significant philosophical problem, I suggest, to try to identify the range of considerations that might be relevant and to try to formulate ways in which the deliberation might go.

Turn now to the second potential pitfall, the possible marginalization of some interests within scientific practice. Denunciations of scientific research as the province of pale males may make a serious point about lack of opportunities for rewarding positions, but the claims made by feminists are sometimes much stronger. I distinguish three questions: (1) Do women and people of color have an equal opportunity to participate in scientific research? (2) Are the methods and conclusions of the sciences biased by male prejudices? (3) Do the lines of research undertaken slight the concerns of women and people of color? (1) Raises the serious point already mentioned, and (2) should receive an affirmative answer in some instances, for there have been clear examples of research in which distortions were introduced by the prior views of male investigators (the study of primate social behavior is one case);[38] but I see no basis for arguing, as is sometimes attempted, that there are general problems in a scientific pretense to objectivity or that the ideal of detached judgments about nature represents a psychological feature of males.[39] The inchoate metaphysics and epistemology of some strands in contemporary feminism[40] are best viewed, I believe, as attempts to express moral and social concerns within the only licensed idiom; without serious attention to the question of the ends of science, it's not been possible to point out that the agenda-setting that underlies our scientific practices may be quite at odds with the results of an ideal deliberation among a fully representative group of citizens. That possibility can't be simply read off the underenrollment of women and minorities in the sciences, but the serious point raised in question (1) surely makes the possibility worth investigating.

I've posed the issue of under-representation by citing the concerns of some contemporary feminists, because some important recent literature about the practice of

[38] In this case, male primatologists tended to focus on the noisy agonistic displays involving adult males. When female observers began to look at primate social interactions, they discovered interesting social strategies that had previously been missed—apparently subordinate males cultivating friendships with particular females, females finding clever ways to exercise choice. See, e.g., Shirley Strum, *Almost Human* (New York: Random House, 1987).

[39] I've attempted to respond to a broad spectrum of worries about scientific objectivity, first in *The Advancement of Science*, and more recently in *Science, Truth, and Democracy* and "Real Realism". My arguments are intended to buttress the idea that our investigations aim at, and sometimes achieve, truth in the sense of correspondence to a mind-independent world. If those arguments are cogent, then the specific criticism that the ideal of detached judgment embodies peculiarities of male psychology seems to collapse; for there are plenty of occasions on which it matters greatly to all sorts of people, male and female, rich and poor alike, that we come to believe the truth in the correspondence sense.

[40] See Sandra Harding, *Whose Justice? Whose Knowledge?*; the position advanced by Helen Longino in *Science as Social Knowledge* is much more sophisticated, and begins to address the value-theoretic issues on their own terms.

science has issued from those concerns. Yet the potential problem of lapses from well-ordered science is much more general. Even when we focus just on our own society, the allocation of funds for medical research attends to the needs of some groups and leaves others out of account; people from communities at risk for rare diseases sometimes complain that their concerns go unmet. At the beginning of the twenty-first century, however, the problem is becoming broader and more troubling. The affluent democracies have been used to a system of patronage for the sciences in which, in a rough and approximate way, decisions about pursuing some areas of inquiry (medicine being an obvious case) have been made by bodies who are responsive to the citizenry. I doubt very much that efforts by elected representatives to shape the kinds of research pursued by biomedical scientists funded by the NIH conform to the outcome of an ideal deliberation, but it seems overwhelmingly probable that the increasing role of privately funded ventures in biotechnology will make the existing gaps much wider. The reasons for this judgment are simple. The entrepreneurs who view biotechnology as fertile terrain are interested in relative quick profits; the best way to reach their goals is to try to satisfy whatever preferences people with the ability to pay can be persuaded to adopt. The co-opting of scientific talent that results need have—and probably will have—very little to do with the concerns that the full population would feel after appropriate tutoring. Plainly empirical investigation is needed here, but, on the face of it, this doesn't look like a case in which the invisible hand is going to guide a free market to the pertinent social good. Both the general public and the scientific community (particularly those in the biological sciences) should be worried, I believe, that coming decades will bring a pronounced departure from well-ordered science.

One common concern about well-ordered science, perhaps inspired by reflection on the trends discussed in the last paragraph, is that it's a utopian fantasy, the sort of thing that might figure in philosophical discussions but that has little place in a realistic account of the sciences.[41] It's important to recognize here (as I've already suggested above) that there's a difference between *specifying an ideal* (something at which the sciences should aim) and *identifying procedures for attaining or approximating that ideal*. The philosophical task is the former; the latter can only be undertaken by *combining* a clear understanding of the ideal with a vast amount of empirical information. Now it may well turn out that actual deliberations about the ends of the sciences are always infected by special interests, ideological presuppositions, and by the inequalities of power in a broader society. That fact in no way derogates from the importance of the ideal. What it means, of course, is that it will be difficult to work towards it—perhaps even that broader political changes will be required if anything like the ideal is to be realized. But to scoff at philosophical attempts to articulate ideals would be a serious mistake. Without some understanding of where one wants to go, an attempt to do better than the *status quo* will be a leap in the dark. I don't claim that the philosophical study of the ends of the sciences is

---

[41] This attitude seems to me to be expressed in Dick Lewontin's discussion of *Science, Truth, and Democracy* (*New York Review of Books*, May 9, 2002).

sufficient to provide a blueprint for doing things better, but I do hold that it is *necessary*.[42]

The last two problems (the problems of considering the needs of future generations and of distant people) are the most difficult. We can imagine a process of ideal deliberation in which the parties are exquisitely attuned to the possibilities and to one another's concerns. Yet the outcome might not yield an appropriate view of the ends of the sciences. Perhaps our deliberators are too insensitive to the potential challenges that will face future generations; or maybe they emphasize the long-term problems and slight urgent questions for their own society; they may ignore the plight of outsiders; or perhaps their sensitivity to that plight may be so great that they ignore other needs. There are large philosophical questions about how to strike a proper balance here. I'll illustrate the difficulty by looking at a concrete case.

Currently, the large majority of the research done in the biomedical sciences focuses on diseases that afflict people in affluent societies. (Officially, at least; a more careful look at what scientists actually do might disclose, however, that there are attempts to pursue more "basic" questions in biology, questions whose immediate significance wouldn't be apparent to the broader public but that might eventually bear on a variety of diseases.) Yet a look at the statistical data on death and disability worldwide reveals that the diseases that cause most human suffering receive only a tiny proportion of the research effort.[43] Nor can the imbalance be explained on the grounds that contemporary biomedicine has little to offer by way of strategies for tackling the infectious diseases that bring misery to millions. On the contrary, the tools for sequencing genomes lend themselves to thorough analyses of the relevant pathogens, and to possibilities for the design of effective vaccines. Here's a rough outline of a method: sequence the genome of the infectious agent; use the known computer programs to identify genes; seek out genes that encode proteins likely to appear on the surface of the pathogen; manufacture benign micro-organisms in which some selection of these proteins is exposed; test to see if injecting these micro-organisms into non-human animals is sufficient to produce antibodies to the pathogen. I should concede that this *is* rough, but, in comparison with many of the methods used to try to attack the major diseases of the affluent world, there's a more systematic way to proceed in this case and, I think, a higher chance that a direct biomedical assault will prove successful.

It's not hard to see that current neglect of infectious diseases represents a lapse from well-ordered science. The tricky philosophical issue is to provide a framework

[42] Lewontin's discussion of my views is somewhat peculiar, since he seems at times to appreciate the distinction between specifying an ideal and identifying procedures for realizing it, and yet chides me for not taking seriously the features of real-world deliberation. My response, in a nutshell, is that those features need to be taken seriously in our attempts to realize the ideal, and that, without a specification of the ideal, any reaction to the problematic features Lewontin notes is likely to be blind. Perhaps the most charitable reading of his discussion is that he thinks the problems are hopeless (or hopeless without radical political change); even so, I'd reply that political theory generally retains its importance in giving direction to our practical efforts, that political theorizing about the sciences is long overdue, and that the kind of discussion I attempt to provide may inspire attempts to do better, both theoretically and practically.

[43] For data see the *Full Report: World Health Report* (WHO, Geneva), for 1995 and for other recent years.

in which the concerns of large numbers of distant people are balanced against the interests of those who support and carry out the research. (In labelling the issue as tricky, I assume that the simplest answer—count all equally—shouldn't be accepted without discussion.)[44] But there's a different way to look at the same example. We live in a world in which the environments of pathogens have changed remarkably, allowing them unprecedented opportunities for finding their ways to new populations. Hence the failure to attack infectious disease has implications not only for the welfare of faraway contemporaries but also for future members of our own societies. The decision to concentrate on the major diseases of affluent societies can thus be viewed as a slighting of the interests of future generations.

VI. I began with the vision of the philosophy of science which the current philosophical community has inherited from some remarkable thinkers of the early twentieth century. Their questions should still hold our interest, and philosophy should continue to refine the answers that more than five decades of sustained effort have generated. But I hope for a broadening of the subject, a movement that will embrace the issues in social epistemology and methodology that surfaced briefly above and one that will confront directly the value-theoretic questions that appear to be more urgent for our times (and, I'd suggest, are likely to continue to be more urgent) than the matters of logic and metascientific analysis to which we're accustomed.

My case for that broadening rests on a conclusion about the ends of the sciences, the view that there's no general goal of inquiry in all contexts and at all times but that the sciences aim to find true answers to those questions that would strike particular groups as significant if they worked out their collective will in an ideal deliberation. If that view were accepted, then philosophers would need to address systematically the value of pure knowledge and to compare that with other values; they would need to work out the balancing of competing sources of value in the kinds of cases that were sketched in the last section; and philosophers of science would need to look carefully at the actual practice of inquiry in various fields and to construct a clear picture of the ways in which significance flows (or, maybe, in some cases fails to flow) to the investigations that are undertaken. I'm painfully aware that much of this essay contains gestures towards detailed accounts that are, as yet, undone.

The philosophical agenda I've outlined wouldn't be relevant if one could resist my conclusion about the ends of the sciences. The more limited path of resistance agrees that there's no context-independent specification of these ends, but disputes my view that the ends coincide with the results of the deliberative process described above. Philosophers who agree that the ends of the sciences are always relative to the concerns of a group should focus on the task of providing a context-dependent account that improves on mine. A much more radical opposition would insist that the retreat from a context-independent specification of the ends of the sciences was

---

[44] That issue has, of course, surfaced in discussions of world hunger. See Peter Singer, "Famine, Affluence, and Morality" (*Philosophy and Public Affairs*, Spring 1972), and Peter Unger, *Living High and Letting Die* (New York: Oxford University Press, 1996).

a mistake. Perhaps philosophy of science can remain closer to business as usual if one can resurrect the ideal of scientific inquiry as a search for truth and other unworrying cognitive desiderata. Even here, however, questions about the extent to which the supposedly constitutive cognitive goods take priority over other values will continue to arise. Further, anyone who opposes my plea for broadening on these grounds will have to face up to the apparent difficulties that beset context-independent proposals. At the very least, there's some serious work to be done, if the philosophy of science is to return to the value-free world of old Vienna.

9

From Causation to Explanation and Back[1]

NANCY CARTWRIGHT

1. Introduction

The dominant topics in general philosophy of science during the second half of the twentieth century were surely *the nature of scientific theory, realism*, and *explanation*. The discussion of *the nature of theory* today is still very much in the same terms as that of fifty years ago although the central paradigm has changed. The standard view, to which I will return below, used to be that a theory is a deductive system formulated in a formal language.[2] Nowadays it is probably the "semantic view" that dominates: theory is a set of models and any language will do for describing exactly what the models are like.[3] Nevertheless the basic presumptions are the same. We ask the same question: "What is a scientific theory and what makes for a good one", and in asking it we presume both that it is a worthwhile question and that it has an answer—that there is some form shared across the sciences that a good theory should take. The methods of adjudication remain the same too: internal coherence and goodness of fit both with the evidence and with what we deem to be our other best scientific theories, where the principal examples now, as then, are drawn from physics.

The nature of *realism* debates has shifted more. Under the influence of the Logical Positivists, for a long time Anglophone philosophy of science eschewed metaphysics. We did not talk about the truth of scientific theories nor about the reality of scientific entities but rather about scientific progress or the accumulation of scientific knowledge. The presumption was that whatever it is we are looking for when we evaluate a scientific theory, the characterization must be internal to our own activities; it should not depend on reference to relations between theory and the world. So we discussed how effective theories are at problem solving (Laudan, 1996), or whether they produce from within themselves, relying on their own heuristics, corrections that yield new predictions and applications (Lakatos, 1970).

Nowadays we have forsaken our Positivist prohibitions and talk wantonly of truth, near truth, resemblance to the truth, aiming for the truth, getting the structure right, getting the theoretical content right, true predictions and, within the semantic view of theories, of resemblances or isomorphisms between models

[1] Work on this paper was conducted under the AHRB project "Causality: Metaphysics and Methods". I would especially like to thank Jordi Cat, Roman Frigg, Julian Reiss, and Christoph Schmidt-Petri for their help.
[2] The most extensive and substantive treatment can be found in: Carnap (1956) and Hempel (1966).
[3] Early references include: Suppes (1967); classical references include: Suppe (1989) and Giere (1988).

and the world. Recent versions of the semantic view may seem more guarded (van Fraassen, 2002). They talk not of isomorphisms or resemblances between models and reality but instead, between models and other models, usually data models or models of the phenomena. Nevertheless there is the tacit assumption that these latter are themselves supposed to be accurate, true, true enough, or what have you. The language and the issues of the debates of the 1960s and 1970s have been entirely replaced.

Still, it is in the third area, that of *explanation*, that discussion has shifted most, for here the topic itself has changed. We no longer talk about explanation; its place has been taken by *causation*. We do of course still discuss explanation itself, but it is not at the core of the field. Probably it appears most centrally as a tool in the realism debates. We are entitled, many suppose, to regard as true, the *best explanation* of a given body of phenomena; this behooves us to provide an account of what a good explanation is. This situation is a real change. For three decades every undergraduate course in philosophy of science started out from the Deductive-Nomological account of explanation. Nowadays, large numbers of philosophers of science do not engage with the topic at all.

This essay will be concerned with this dramatic shift. I shall trace the gradual transformation of *explanation* into *causation*, and outline where I think we are now and where we could profitably be heading.

2. From Causation to Explanation

Carl Gustav Hempel's *Deductive-Nomological* account of explanation (Hempel, 1966) dominated work in philosophy of science for thirty years, and it still influences a number of related issues today. We should begin with a puzzle. Why was explanation thought to be such an important matter? Explaining is after all only one of a great many activities that the sciences engage in. Theories are used to explain, but they are also very importantly used to effect changes in the world. Yet theory application and use has never been a central topic. We also expect our theories to be well-confirmed if we are to rely on them, but during the last half-century confirmation certainly took a backseat to explanation. Scientists also approximate, they classify, they build models, they borrow methods and ideas and techniques from elsewhere, they measure and they experiment. Each of these activities needs a philosophical treatment—when is it done well, when badly and how can we tell; and each has its own philosophical problems. Why did explanation stand out?

I want to focus on one particular function that explanation served that gave it a special status. For decades explanation stood in lieu of causation—causation, which is critical if we are to account for how science can change the world. This role is particularly notable because the situation is now reversed; for better or for worse we now tackle questions about both the methods and the metaphysics of causation directly.

David Hume taught that talk of causation was metaphysics and should be consigned to the flames. The Logical Positivists similarly scorned metaphysics, and for the most part for them too this included causation. But Rudolf Carnap had a way to salvage some important metaphysical concepts (Carnap, 1928). He urged that there are many concepts that appear to be in the "material mode" but that would in fact be more perspicuously expressed in the "formal mode"; that is, there are many concepts that seem to be directly about the world but that are really instead about our own theories and descriptions of it.

Various concepts of causation came to be treated in just this way. Kepler's laws hold on account of Newton's. This fact is a central part of the argument for believing in Newton's laws. But how can one law be responsible for the obtaining of a second? We also regularly cite one event as the cause of another. Hempel's well-known example is the drop in temperature that caused the radiator to crack (Hempel, 1942). But, following Hume, what can this amount to over and above spatio-temporal connection and regular association between the two event types?

Explanation is the answer. Newton's laws explain Kepler's and the drop in temperature explains the cracking of the radiator. In both cases it is the same notion of *explanation* that does the job, and it is a notion that refers entirely to relations within language. The fact to be explained is deducible from a set of well-confirmed law claims and initial conditions, where the specific factors cited in explanation are factors that we find particularly salient among these. That is the famous *Deductive-Nomological* (D-N) account of explanation I mentioned above. It is important to bear in mind here that for the Positivists and their followers, explanation was not a mark in language of a relation that holds in the world but rather that the explanatory relation in language *is* the relation that holds; we only mistakenly project it onto the world.

3. From Explanation to Causation

The Deductive-Nomological model was recognized from the start as too restrictive. Insistence on deduction from strict laws would rule out a large number of explanations that we have high confidence in. Hempel added the *Inductive-Statistical* (I-S) model (Hempel, 1962): explanations may cite law claims and individual features from which it follows that the facts to be explained are highly probable even if they do not follow deductively. The underlying idea in both cases is that the factors offered in explanation (*the explanans*) should provide good reason to expect that facts to be explained should occur (*the explanandum*). This harkens back to Hume's account (Hume, 1997) in which the idea of causation is a copy, not of an impression of a relation in the external world, but rather a copy of an impression of our own feeling of expectation that the effect will occur when we observe the cause. For Hume this feeling of expectation results from our repeated experience of the cause being followed by the effect. For advocates of the D-N and I-S models, the expectation must be rational, not habitual—it must be justified under well-confirmed law claims.

The two models suffered a series of setbacks having to do with this very idea that the *explanans* should make it rational to expect the *explanandum*. First is Michael

Scriven's example of syphilis and paresis (Scriven, 1959). Paresis, Scriven maintained, is a last stage of syphilis; only those with syphilis suffer from it. On the other hand, it is not all that common even among syphilitics: syphilis does not make paresis probable. Yet, for those who do get paresis, there is no doubt that their syphilis explains it. Scriven's example is backed up by Richard Jeffrey's argument that a chance set-up explains all its outcomes equally, whether they are high probability or low probability outcomes (Jeffrey, 1971). If the chance set-up is genuinely probabilistic, citing the chance set-up and the probability distribution that characterizes it explains any outcome that occurs and nothing else can be said by way of explanation of any of them.

The natural response in this case is to amend the requirements for I-S explanation. The *explanans* need not render the *explanandum* probable; it need only raise the probability. But that will not do either, as Wesley Salmon's example of probability-lowering explanations makes clear (Salmon, 1971, 62–5). Salmon considered a case in which exactly one of two radioactive elements is randomly inserted into a box. Imagine that the strongly radioactive element has a probability of 0.9 of producing the decay product β; the weak element produces β with probability 0.1. The probability of β when the weak element is in the box is thus far lower than that when it is not (since when the weak element is not in the box, the strong one is). Yet if a β particle occurs when the weak element is in the box, it is undoubtedly the presence of the weak element that explains it, and this despite the fact that the weak element lowers rather than raises the probability of β.

Salmon's proposal was that the *explanans* should be *statistically relevant* to the *explanandum*—the probability of the *explanandum* should be different when the *explanans* obtains from when it does not. But that does not work either, as we can see by amending Salmon's set-up slightly: Use two structurally different radioactive elements that are equally strong in producing β. Whichever element is in the box when a β particle occurs will explain that occurrence even though the probability of a β particle is the same with both elements.

Why does the cause—a genuine positive cause—counterintuitively lower the probability of the effect in Salmon's set-up? Because the presence of the weak cause is correlated with the absence of an even stronger cause. This suggests following the strategy common in the social sciences: Stratify the background population. That is, divide the population of trials into subgroups. One contains all the trials on which the strong element is present; the other, those in which it is absent. In a population of trials in which the strong element is present in every case, introducing the weak element will increase the probability of a β particle, and the same is true in a population in which the stronger element is universally absent. Following this line of thought, the natural proposal is to insist that the *explanans* increase the probability of the *explanandum* in any population that is homogeneous with respect to all 'other' possible causes of the *explanandum*. Formally, demand an increase in the *partial conditional probability*.

This move is also suggested by what is called *Simpson's paradox* (Cartwright, 1979). Take any fact about the conditional probability of one factor, say A, on another, B.

B may increase the probability of A or decrease it or leave it unchanged. Consider a third factor, C, which is probabilistically dependent on both. Then, depending on how the numbers work out, if we stratify on ±C, the original relations between A and B can be shifted in any way at all: B may increase the probability of A in both the +C and −C subpopulations, or decrease it, or leave it unchanged. A standard example is the Berkeley graduate school, which appeared to be discriminating against women: The probability of admission for women was lower than the probability of admission for men. But, department by department, this turned out not to be the case. What was happening was that women were applying to the departments that were more difficult to get into. The 'true' relation between admission and sex is revealed by stratifying on departments.

The move to demand increase in probability conditional on a fixed arrangement of all other possible causal factors was widely adopted (Cartwright, 1979; Skyrms, 1980; Eells, 1991). This brought the standard account of explanation into parallel with Patrick Suppes's probabilistic theory of causality (Suppes, 1970), which was published one year before Salmon's influential paper on probability-lowering explanations. Suppes's probabilistic theory proceeded by two steps. One factor, C, is a prima facie cause of a second, E, if C raises the probability of E. A prima facie cause is a real cause if and only if C continues to raise the *conditional* probability of E in subpopulations that are homogeneous with respect to all other causes of E.

One problem for Suppes's account is a problem shared by all accounts that rely on stratification: It cannot deal adequately with cases of purely probabilistic causes where the causes produce their effects in tandem. Consider a purely probabilistic cause that produces a side effect in correlation with an intended effect. In the population that is homogeneous with respect to the presence of the joint cause, the side effect will increase the probability of the effect even though it does not cause it. (This does not happen for deterministic causes because, in the presence of the cause, both the effect and the side effect will have probability one.) Increase in the conditional probability of one factor on another thus cannot be a sufficient condition for the one factor to cause the other in cases where causes may produce their effects probabilistically.

Other problems arise for Suppes from the fact that he takes the two steps separately. Causes may not raise the probability of their effects in a given population for at least two kinds of reasons. First, background correlations may conceal the expected increase in probability, as we see from the amended version of Salmon's set-up in which the two radioactive elements are equally strong, so the conditional probability of a β particle is the same no matter which element is in the box.

Second, a single cause may itself have different capacities with respect to the same effect and these capacities may balance out. Gerhard Hesslow's case of birth control pills and thrombosis is the standard example here (Hesslow, 1976). Birth control pills do have a positive capacity to produce thrombosis. They also of course inhibit pregnancy and pregnancy can also cause thrombosis. Depending on the strengths of these various capacities, birth control pills may have no overall effect on the rate of thrombosis: Thrombosis may be equally probable both with and without birth control pills. Cases like this are likely to be common in the social and medical sciences. Consider a cause that produces a deleterious effect. If we want the cause for some other reason, or the cause is difficult or expensive to eliminate, we often try hard to enhance the cause's opposite operations in order to cancel out the unwanted effect. For these kinds of reasons there was a tendency not to adopt Suppes's two-stage definition but rather to move directly to partial conditional probabilities: C explains E just in case C raises the (partial) conditional probability of E in populations homogeneous with respect to all other factors that can cause E.

By this time the switch-over from explanation to causation was complete. Not only was the account in terms of partial conditional probabilities often explicitly offered as an account of probabilistic causality, but it is difficult to see how it could be thought of in any other way. What after all could defend this particular, very peculiar, choice of probabilistic relation as a mark of *explanation* other than the assumption that the explanations at stake involve *causal* factors?

I have explained that under the influence of Hume and the Positivists, philosophers and scientists alike have been eager to rid science of the concept of causality. One standard strategy has been to "reduce it away"; that is, to eliminate all use of causal notions and define causation purely in terms of regular association plus, perhaps, some other non-causal concepts, like temporal succession and spatio-temporal contiguity. Nowadays the demand for absolutely regular association has given way. In a move that parallels Hempel's introduction of the I-S model for explanation, purely probabilistic associations are allowed as well. Could we then turn the account I have just described into a reductive definition of causation, albeit a probabilistic one?

The answer is "No". The formula involving partial conditional probability cannot serve as a reductive account of causal relevance in terms of probabilistic association because, as it stands, we must condition on other *causal* factors. If we leave out any factors that are causal, we can certainly get mistaken results, as in the example of the Berkeley graduate school. Exactly the same is true if we include too many. Consider a population that is homogeneous with respect to a given disease. We might, for instance, be studying such a population unintentionally, perhaps even without recognizing it, if we are using records from a given hospital. Imagine the disease has two causes, A and B. In that population the absence of A will increase the probability of B, even though not-A does not cause B; and this will be the case even if we focus on a subpopulation that is homogeneous with respect to all the real causes of B.

So, what of the Humean program of reducing causation away? The formula in terms of partial conditional probabilities has real problems. Many come out immediately when we try to explain what is meant by the expression 'all other causes'. For instance, in testing C *causes* E, we must not for any particular individual case include any cause of E, say D, that occurs in the causal "chain" between C and E. That is because, once D is given, whether C obtains or not will no longer make any difference to the probability of E. On the other hand, if we do not insist that the test population be homogeneous with respect to D in individual cases where D occurs on its own, not as a part of the process by which C produces E, then Simpson's paradox problems may readily arise. Despite these real problems, this formula is the best on offer so far if we are looking for some one probabilistic relation between causation and probabilistic association. For Humeans then the question for future work is clear: How do we improve on this formula and make explicit what it means without invoking causal notions?

The admission that we are after all looking for a theory of *causal* explanation provides some progress on another of the central difficulties that the D-N and I-S models were thought to face—the problem of explanatory symmetry. The problem is especially visible for law claims expressed in functional form, where we can rewrite the equations to make any one of the variables appear as the dependent, or *explanandum*, variable. The canonical example is due to Sylvan Bromberger.[4] When the line of sight of the sun across the top of a flagpole is at an angle θ with the ground, the height of the flagpole (h) and the length (l) of the shadow it casts are related thus: $l = h \sin \theta$. Under the D-N model, we can thus explain why the length takes a given value by citing this law and the height of the pole. That sounds fine. But we can equally use the equation and the length of the shadow to explain the height of the flagpole, which seems entirely inappropriate in all but the most special of historical situations.

If we turn away from the D-N model, however, and call not for mere deductivity from law, but rather demand that explanations in science cite factors that are causally relevant, the problem does not appear. Causal-law claims come with the asymmetry between cause and effect built in. When the causal-law claims are expressed in the form of equations or, following John Stuart Mill or John Mackie,[5] as logical equivalences, the asymmetry is often expressed by writing the effect on the left-hand side and the cause on the right. Nowadays sometimes even a special symbol is inserted to signify both functional equality and causality from right to left.

The identification of explanatory relevance with causal relevance opens a line of attack alternative to the probabilistic accounts growing out of the D-N and I-S models. As a rule of thumb it is fair to say that a controlled experiment is the best way to test a causal claim. Perhaps we can read off a characterization of causal relevance from an appropriate account of exactly how a controlled experiment should be constructed. This is, for instance, the strategy for characterizing causal/explanatory relevance championed by James Woodward (Woodward, 1997. See also, Holland, 1986; Hausman, 1998; Cartwright, forthcoming) as well as by a number of social scientists. Accounts of this kind are often called *manipulation* or *agency accounts* (cf. Menzies and Price, 1993).

Sometimes manipulation accounts make the strong claim that a causal connection exists only where *we* can manipulate the cause to bring about the effect. This echoes one of Hume's suggestions that our idea of causation could come from our own experience of making things happen in ourselves. As a reductive account of causation, this is a non-starter: The relevant sense of 'manipulation' is that we make the cause vary; but 'making' is itself a causal concept.

---

[4] A presentation of this example can be found in van Fraassen (1980).
[5] Mackie (1972). For instance, $E = (C_1 + A_1) \text{ v } (C_2 + A_2) \text{ v} \ldots \text{ v } (C_n + A_n)$, where C_i is a salient factor we would normally cite as a cause and A_i is an auxiliary often left unmentioned.

But what if we do not add the additional demand that manipulation be done by us? What if we leave out all mention of what makes the cause vary and insist only that it vary in the way necessary for a good experiment? Again, as a reductive account of causation, this is a non-starter. The basic idea of the controlled experiment is to look for variation in the effect as the cause varies by itself; that is, while all other sources of variation in the effect remain constant. Usually of courses we do not know what all these other possible sources are. The standard strategy in that case is to randomize. We assign individuals randomly to be in either the "treatment" or in the "control" group. This makes things even worse for the hopes to read off a reductive account of causality from our best experimental procedures. What makes a good experiment, an experiment able to deliver sound conclusions? In the first place, *all the other causes of variation in the effect* must have the same distribution in both the treatment and the control group. In the second, the value that the cause under test takes for each individual in the experiment *must not be caused by any other factors that can influence the effect*. Again, it is difficult to see any way to express these two italicized clauses without the use of causal concepts. Also like the probabilistic account, characterizations in terms of controlled experiments are limited to the kinds of causal systems they can cover and the kinds of causal questions they can answer, as I shall discuss in Section 6. Nevertheless, probabilistic and manipulation accounts are the two primary strategies employed in philosophy of science at this time to characterize general explanatory relevance.

4. The Narrowing of the Project

The original concern in providing a model of explanation was about explanatory *relevance* of one kind of factor for another. This was clear from Hempel's presentation in his universally used text, *The Philosophy of the Natural Sciences*. As an example, Hempel cites a historical episode (Hempel, 1966). The astronomer Francesco Sizi claimed, against his contemporary Galileo, that there could not be satellites circling around Jupiter and offered the following argument: "There are seven windows in the head, two nostrils, two ears, two eyes and a mouth; so in the heavens there are two favourable stars, two unpropitious, two luminaries, and Mercury alone undecided and indifferent. From which [. . .] we gather that the number of planets is necessarily seven." These features, Hempel complains, do not have the right kind of relation to the planets; they are not the kind of features that *could* explain their arrangement. This echoes the earlier concerns of many of the Positivists about pseudo-sciences. Factors cited in, say, Freudian theory or Marx's theory of history do not have the right kind of internal development nor the right kind of relation to *explananda* to count as genuinely explanatory.

This underlying assumption about the point of the project can be seen at each step in the development just described, and it is still there in the probabilistic theory of causality that we now have. The theory is a theory of what *kinds* of factors can cause what other *kinds*, not a theory of what actually causes what on any single occasion. That is, it is not a theory of singular causation, a theory of what among all possible causes actually brought about the effect in any given case. This becomes especially apparent in cases of overdetermination. Two factors occur, each of a kind that is causally relevant to the effect. On any such occasion there may be a fact of the matter about which factor produced the effect; but the criteria for determining this are not provided in any of the accounts of explanation described in Section 3.

This situation is odd because one of the original exemplars of scientific explanation that Hempel offered was of a case of singular causation: The drop in temperature explains the cracked radiator. Once causation has been readmitted as a legitimate object of study, however, questions about singular causation can be addressed directly in philosophy of science. There are currently a number of tools available for doing so: counterfactuals (Lewis, 1973, 1986, 2000), causal processes (Salmon, 1984; Dowe, 1992a, 1992b), agency accounts (Menzies and Price, 1993; Woodward, 1997) and single-case probabilities (Humphreys, 1989; Eells, 1991).

The gap between explanatory relevance and actual explanation in a single case raises a number of challenges that we now face:

(1) Each of the accounts of singular causation on offer has its own internal problems, as do the accounts of explanatory relevance.

(2) There is currently no clear fit between the general accounts of explanatory or causal relevance and accounts of singular causation. For example, must all factors cited in a singular explanation be factors that meet some appropriate criterion for general explanatory or causal relevance in science? Donald Davidson has insisted that the answer is 'yes' (Davidson, 1967). But there are few accounts that offer explicit links between the two levels based on either this answer or any other.

(3) We have no criteria for adjudicating among the various accounts, either of singular explanation or of general explanatory relevance. Which is best? In Section 6 I will return to this question and offer some proposals about promising directions for future work.

Surprisingly the second major exemplar from Hempel has also been left behind in the developments surrounding explanatory relevance over the last half-century. In the original we looked for a model of explanation that could account for how one set of laws can be explained by another more general, more encompassing set; for instance, how Newton's laws explain Kepler's. Accounts that equate explanatory relevance to causal relevance will clearly not do this job. But it is a job that we still want to be able to do. After all, one of the justifications often cited for accepting Newton's laws is that they explain more concrete laws such as Kepler's.[6] This is often called *inference to the best explanation*: We infer that Newton's laws are (probably) true because they provide the best way to explain why Kepler's laws obtain.[7] Is the original D-N model sufficient to handle these kinds of explanations or must better models now be developed?

---

[6] Perhaps we should not altogether abandon the idea that explanation even in these cases has something to do with causation since, at least from the time of Copernicus, explanation of laws has often had a causal connotation.

[7] For an introduction, as well as a comprehensive survey of inference to the best explanation, see Lipton (1991).

The question becomes especially pressing if we wish to use inference to the best explanation as a reason to believe in the more general, more encompassing theory.

5. Whence Explanation: Understanding

One might think that explanation had to do with answering questions, relieving puzzles, supplying missing information, or providing understanding. This was the point of Sylvan Bromberger's well-known paper on explanations as answers to *why questions* (Bromberger, 1966). But it was not the presumption of the work described in Section 2. Explanation in the tradition described there is an objective matter independent of what we know, what we can grasp, or what helps us to understand. This odd feature of the tradition is part of the reason for the claim that the models of explanation on offer served as formal-mode surrogates for the material-mode concept of *causation*.

Bas van Fraassen famously rejected the idea that there is any such objective notion of causation (van Fraassen, 1980). He stressed instead that explanation is a pragmatic matter, and in particular a correct explanation will be highly sensitive to the form of the question asked. Following the work of Bromberger and van Fraassen there has been a spate of work on *why questions* and the pragmatics of explanation (for instance, Gardenfors (1980), Achinstein (1984), Sintonen (1984), Richardson (1995)).

But little of this work is of help with a problem about understanding that still plagues the philosophy of science. Scientists across both the natural and the social sciences regularly construct models that are highly artificial, seriously oversimplified, or blatantly false to the situation being modeled. Nevertheless, they claim, the models provide *understanding* of the target phenomenon. James Clerk Maxwell provided mechanical models that could account for various electromagnetic properties of the ether. He could not persuade himself fully that any one of these models might literally describe the inner working of the ether. Still he thought that such mechanical models were essential to a proper understanding of electromagnetism (Cat, 2001). George Fitzgerald did the same, and he even constructed real physical models, not just paper and pencil ones, ensuring that the gears worked properly and the strings would not get tangled up (see Hunt, 1991).

Economists regularly produce models that describe not real economies but small 'analogue' economies that bear little resemblance to the real economy of interest. Then they study the analogue economies of their models, they manipulate them, they derive results about them. The results are not accurate predictions about the real economy, even if we restrict attention to a narrow range of intended targeted issues. What is gained from these models? *Understanding*, we are told.

A different kind of case is in the models of game theory, for instance models that suppose that individuals are playing the prisoner's dilemma game. A lot of theoretical effort has gone into modeling the possible constellations of this one game—one-shot, finitely iterated, indefinitely iterated, with two or N players, rational, boundedly rational, with common knowledge of rationality or not, etc. (Kreps *et al.*, 1982). Some of these set-ups have even been 'tested' empirically (Roth, 1988; Cooper *et al.*, 1996).

But little detailed work has been done on what social situations these models could plausibly represent.

Also consider from evolutionary game theory the model of choice of neighborhood in which Schelling (1971) assumes that people have a preference to live in a neighborhood in which the majority of the dwellers are of the same kind as themselves, but without having a preference for a totally segregated environment. However, if everybody chooses the neighborhood in this way we end up with totally segregated neighborhoods in the model. The model is supposed to help us understand how segregation is possible without overt intention. But how does it do that since what it describes is not a real process that goes on in the way described in any of the real populations for which we might wish to understand neighborhood segregation?

The social contract is an example from political theory. The story is of people living in a 'state of Nature', a state without government. Because of this, it is supposed, each person is prey to each other. To avoid the terrible dangers, they all agree to submit to and obey a governing authority that will police them and provide safe social institutions. This is supposed to help us understand something. Presumably not how we actually came to have governments. Perhaps it helps explain the normative force of government—why we ought to obey it. But we never really started in a state of nature and never really agreed to a social contract. So how does the fable of the social contract help us either to understand or to legitimize government and its restrictions?

These are all different cases, and only a tiny sample. Perhaps they will each require a different account of understanding; perhaps we can find a single account that will cover them all. Perhaps many of the claims to understanding are misplaced. But the need for a philosophical treatment is pressing. When does a false model provide understanding? What kind of understanding is involved? And what practically are we able to do with the understanding that we acquire from a blatantly false model? These are crucial questions about an important and widespread scientific practice—and a practice that frequently informs policy—for which we currently have no good answers.

We should recognize that work on these questions may also improve our accounts in other areas. For instance, the standard account of how we use models to understand the world is that we do so by deriving predictions from the models about the target situations in the world; and we do that by looking at all the deductive consequences of the assumptions of the models, where some accounts allow for some corrections or emendations to the deductive consequences based on facts about the specific situation modeled (Giere, 1999). Mary Morgan, by contrast, argues that we gain understanding from *doing thing* with models (Morgan, 1999). In a simple economics model we leave the demand curve fixed and we move the supply curve. What happens to the price? Predictions from our simple model about *the kinds of effects* that result from this kind of change may be relatively accurate even if no prediction about the level of the price itself will be.

How do we know what we should and should not do to a model? Morgan argues that an essential ingredient in a model besides the formal structure we usually talk about is a *story*. The story of the model suggests and constrains how we can manipulate the model and what we can conclude from our manipulations. Even in the case where we intend to do nothing more than look at the deductive consequences of a model, something like the story will be necessary—we do not after all expect all the deductive consequences of a simple or blatantly false model to be of use or we would be immediately stopped in our tracks. But exactly what is a story and how are we to judge which stories are acceptable; and what relation does the story have to existing theory? Following up Morgan's ideas will require new work both on the structure of models and on the nature and use of theory.

6. Whence Explanation: Causation

We have seen a number of accounts of causal-explanatory relevance and I noted that there are also a variety of different accounts of singular causal explanation on offer. Which is the correct one? I shall suggest that probably they all are—each for a different kind of causal relation.

Begin with Suppes's theory of probabilistic causality. Suppes's definitions form the basis for powerful new methods for causal inference, developed by Wolfgang Spohn (Spohn, 1980), by Judea Pearl (Pearl, 1999), and by Peter Spirtes, Clark Glymour, and Richard Scheines (Spirtes et al., 1993), called *Bayes-nets methods*. These methods suppose, as does Suppes, that all causes are prima facie causes—i.e. a cause always increases the probability of its effects. Real causes are those that continue to increase the probability of their effects in populations that are homogeneous with respect to an appropriately chosen set of other causes. The methods also assume a *minimality* condition, which asserts that no more causal structure obtains relative to a given probability distribution than what is necessary to guarantee that causes increase the probability of their effects in the two ways presupposed.

The methods provide a way of making causal inferences from facts about probabilities and any antecedent causal knowledge available by exploiting these three constraints. Imagine, for example, a single effect E with two possible causes, C_1 and C_2. There are four possibilities: C_1 is a cause of E and so is C_2; C_1 is and C_2 is not; C_2 is and C_1 is not; and neither are causes of E. C_1 is a genuine cause just in case it raises the probability of E and it continues to do so conditioning on C_2, *if* C_2 is a genuine cause. C_2 is a genuine cause if it raises the probability of E and continues to do so conditioning on C_1, *if* C_1 is a genuine cause. Bayes-nets programs compute all the possible causal arrangements consistent with these assumptions and they do so entirely reliably. Supposing that the three basic assumptions about causation are satisfied, it can be proven that the methods will never yield a false causal conclusion, although in many cases no conclusion at all will be available or, more usually, a large disjunction of causal conclusions.

We have seen, however, that Suppes's conditions are violated in a number of cases. What then are we to make of Bayes-nets methods? Are they no good after all? Clearly that conclusion would be a mistake, for the proof referred to shows us exactly what kinds of causal systems the methods can be applied to: those satisfying the three conditions specified.

What do we do when we have a different kind of system? Consider the situation in which we hypothesize that a particular cause behaves like Hesslow's birth control pills—it does not increase the probability of its effect because it operates in different ways both to produce the effect and to prevent it. In this case we try to stop all the other ways the cause can operate and then look for an increase in probability or an increase in level of the effect due to the hypothesized mode of operation. Often we can do this by physically blocking the causal process by which the other operations are carried; often by conditioning on some factor that occurs in each alternative causal process. What about situations in which we suspect that one factor, A, increases the probability of another, B, not because A causes B but because B is a side effect of A from some common probabilistic cause? One standard thing to do in this case is to manipulate A while keeping fixed all the other causes of B. If B does not change in the appropriate ways, we conclude that A is not a cause.

Turn next to manipulation accounts, which are currently our major alternative strategy for characterizing causal/explanatory relevance. This strategy is not universally applicable, however, anymore than our best attempts at a probabilistic account. In vast numbers of causal systems, from the human circulatory system to an automobile carburetor, causes are locked together by the design of the system and cannot vary separately in the requisite ways. Very often a single cause cannot be changed on its own without varying others as well and very often it cannot be changed without interfering with the very process by which it or some other cause produces its effect.

There are also a variety of specific causal hypotheses that we would not test in this way even were the appropriate manipulations available. Consider a claim of the form, "A is a standing condition, just awaiting a trigger to produce B": for example, "The run-down condition of famine victims is a standing condition just awaiting a trigger to produce a fatal disease"; or, "The dryness arising from the drought is a standing condition just awaiting a trigger to produce a forest fire." In this case we do not manipulate A and look for a variation in B. Rather, we keep A fixed and vary the presence or absence of a variety of appropriate triggers to see if B generally results when the trigger occurs.

The lesson to be learned from these brief considerations is that there are different kinds of causal systems and different ways in which a cause can operate within them; and different methods for testing are appropriate for different specific kinds of causal hypotheses relative to different sets of background assumptions about the system in which the putative causal relation is imbedded.

This is the conclusion that we are beginning to draw. For instance, Laurie Paul (Paul, 1988), Judea Pearl (Pearl, 2000), and Christopher Hitchcock (Hitchcock, 2003) all describe a variety of different kinds of singular causal relations that can obtain—such as hasteners, delayers, sustainers, contributors. They offer different counterfactual tests for each of the different kinds of relationship.

At the level of general causal relevance, I am a strong advocate of causal diversity. We need, I believe, a background model of the kind of causal system we are dealing with and of the way by which the putative cause is supposed to operate before we can devise a test, or a characterization, for it. This means that settling matters of causal relevance requires either a lot of antecedent knowledge or a reasonable success at bootstrapping. This makes causal testing difficult, but not impossible. To proceed, however, we need far better accounts of the kinds of causal systems we may encounter and the variety of ways that a cause may operate within them.[8]

We are used to thinking of *causation* as a single monolithic concept: Causal relations all have one single feature in common that distinguishes them from mere association; and there is one single canonical mark of that feature. But we have a vast new project in philosophy of science once we recognize that there are a great variety of causal relations and a great variety of causal systems, and each may have its own way of testing. As Christopher Hitchcock advises, "The goal of a philosophical account of causation should not be to capture *the* causal relation, but rather to capture the many ways in which the events of the world can be bound together" (Hitchcock, 2003).

References

Achinstein, Peter (1984), "The Pragmatic Character of Explanation", *PSA* ii: 275–92, repr. in D. Ruben (ed.) (1993): 326–44.

Alexander, Jason, and Brian Skyrms (1999), "Bargaining with Neighbors: Is Justice Contagious?", *Journal of Philosophy* 96: 588–98.

Bromberger, Sylvain (1966), "Why Questions", in R. Colodny (ed.): *Mind and Cosmos* (Pittsburgh: Pittsburgh University Press: 86–111).

Carnap, Rudolf (1928), *Der Logische Aufbau der Welt*, Berlin: Weltkreis-Verlag; trans. R. George, *The Logical Structure of the World* (Berkeley, CA: University of California, Press, 1967).

—— (1956), "The Methodological Character of Theoretical Terms" in Herbert Feigl and Michaal Scriven (eds.): *Minnesota Studies in the Philosophy of Science* (1, Minneapolis: University of Minnesota Press).

Cartwright, Nancy (forthcoming), "On Herbert Simon: How to Get Causes from Probabilities", Causality Technical Reports, London School of Economics.

—— (1979), "Causal Laws & Effective Strategies", *Noûs* 13: 419–37.

—— (2001), "Measuring Causes: Invariance, Modularity and the Causal Markov Condition", *Measurement in Physics and Economics Discussion Paper Series, DP MEAS 10/00*, Centre for Philosophy of Natural and Social Science, London School of Economics.

Cat, Jordi (2001), "On Understanding: Maxwell on the Methods of Illustration and Scientific Metaphor", *Studies in the History and Philosophy of Modern Physics* 32: 395–441.

Collins, John, Ned Hall, and Laurie Paul (eds.) (2001), *Causation and Counterfactuals* (Cambridge, MA: MIT Press).

Cooper, Russell, Doughlas V. DeJong, and Thomas W. Ross (1996), "Cooperation without Reputation: Experimental Evidence from Prisoner's Dilemma Games", *Games and Economic Behavior* 12: 187–218.

Davidson, Donald (1963), "Causal Relations", *Journal of Philosophy* 64: 691–703.

Dowe, Phil (1992a), "An Empiricist Defence of the Causal Account of Explanation", *International Studies in the Philosophy of Science* 6: 123–8.

---

[8] This need is the basis for the three-year project "Causality: Metaphysics and Methods" now underway at LSE, funded by the British Arts and Humanities Research Board.

Dowe, Phil (1992b), "Wesley Salmon's Process Theory of Causality and the Conserved Quantity Theory", *Philosophy of Science* 59: 195–216.

Eells, Ellery (1991), *Probabilistic Causality* (Cambridge: Cambridge University Press).

Feigl, Herbert, and Grover Maxwell (eds.) (1962), *Minnesota Studies in the Philosophy of Science, III. Scientific Explanation, Space, and Time* (Minneapolis: University of Minnesota Press).

Gardenfors, Peter (1980), "A Pragmatic Approach to Explanations", *Philosophy of Science* 47: 404–23.

Giere, Ronald (1988), *Explaining Science* (Chicago: University of Chicago Press).

—— (1999), *Science Without Laws* (Chicago: University of Chicago Press).

Hausman, Daniel M. (1998), *Causal Asymmetries* (Cambridge: Cambridge University Press).

Hempel, Carl G. (1942), "The Function of General Laws in History", *Journal of Philosophy* 39: 35–48, repr. in Hempel (1965): 231–43.

—— (1962), "Deductive-Nomological Explanation vs. Statistical Explanation", in Feigl *et al.* (1962): 98–169.

—— (1965), *Aspects of Scientific Explanation and other Essays in the Philosophy of Science* (New York: Free Press).

—— (1966), *Philosophy of Natural Science* (Englewood Cliffs, NJ: Prentice Hall), 48.

—— and Paul Oppenheim (1948), "Studies in the Logic of Explanation", *Philosophy of Science* 15: 135–75, repr. in Hempel (1965): 245–95.

Hesslow, G (1976), "Discussion: Two Notes on the Probabilistic Approach to Causality", *Philosophy of Science* 43: 290–2.

Hitchcock, Christoph (2003), "Of Humean Bondage", *British Journal for the Philosophy of Science.*

Holland, Paul (1986), "Statistics and Causal Inference", *Journal of the American Statistical Association* 81: 945–60.

Hoover, Kevin D. (2001), *Causality in Macroeconomics* (Cambridge: Cambridge University Press).

Hume, David (1999), *Enquiries Concerning Human Understanding and Concerning the Principles of Morals* (Oxford: Oxford University Press), Sections 4–7.

Humphreys, Paul (1989), *The Chances of Explanation* (Princeton: Princeton University Press).

Hunt, Bruce J. (1991), *The Maxwellians* (Ithaca: Cornell University Press).

Jeffrey, Richard (1971), "Statistical Explanation vs. Statistical Inference", in Salmon *et al.*, 19–28.

D. Kreps, P. Milgrom, J. Roberts, and R. Wilson (1982), "Rational Cooperation in the Finitely Repeated Prisoner's Dilemma", *Journal of Economic Theory* 17: 245–52.

Lakatos, Imre (1970), "Falsification and the Methodology of Scientific Research Programmes", in Imre Lakatos and Alan Musgrave: *Criticism and the Growth of Knowledge* (Cambridge: Cambridge University Press), 91–196.

Laudan, Larry (1996), *Beyond Positivism and Relativism. Theory Method and Evidence* (Boulder: Westview Press), Part 3.

Lewis, David (1973), "Causation", *Journal of Philosophy* 70: 556–67.

—— (1986), "Postscript to 'Causation'", in his *Philosophical Papers*, II (Oxford: Oxford University Press), 173–213.

—— (2000), "Causation as Influence", *Journal of Philosophy* 97: 182–97.

Lipton, Peter (1991), *Inference to the Best Explanation* (New York: Routledge).

Mackie, John L. (1972), *The Cement of the Universe* (Oxford: Clarendon Press).

Menzies, Peter, and Huw Price (1993): "Causation as a Secondary Quality", *British Journal for the Philosophy of Science* 44: 187–203.

Morgan, Mary S. (1999), "Learning from Models", in *Morgan and Morrison* (1999) (eds.): 347–88.

—— and Margaret Morrison (eds.) (1999), *Models as Mediators* (Cambridge: Cambridge University Press).

Pearl, Judea (2000), *Causality: Models, Reasoning and Inference* (Cambridge: Cambridge University Press).

Paul, Laurie A. (1998), "Keeping Track of the Time: Emending the Counterfactual Account of Causation", *Analysis* 58: 191–8.

Richardson, Alan (1995), "Explanation: Pragmatics and Asymmetry", *Philosophical Studies* 80: 109–29.

Roth, Alvin E. (1988), "Laboratory Experimentation in Economics: A Methodological Overview", *The Economic Journal* 98: 974–1031.

Ruben, David (ed.) (1993), *Explanation* (Oxford: Oxford University Press).

Salmon, Wesley (1971), "Statistical Explanation", in Salmon *et al.*, 29–88.

—— (1984), *Scientific Explanation and the Causal Structure of the World* (Princeton: Princeton University Press).

Salmon, Wesley, Richard Jeffrey, and James Greeno (eds.) (1971), *Statistical Explanation and Statistical Relevance* (Pittsburgh: Pittsburgh University Press).

Skyrms, Brian (1980), *Causal Necessity* (New Haven: Yale University Press).

—— (1996), *Evolution of the Social Contract* (Cambridge: Cambridge University Press).

Schelling, Thomas C. (1971), "Dynamic Models of Segregation", *Journal of Mathematical Sociology* 1: 143–86.

Scriven, Michael (1959), "Explanation and Prediction in Evolutionary Theory", *Science* 130: 477–82.

Sintonen, Matti (1984), "The Pragmatics of Scientific Explanation", *Acta Philosophica Fennica*, 37.

Spirtes, Peter, Clark Glymour, and Richard Scheines (1993), *Causation, Prediction and Search* (New York: Springer).

Spohn, Wolfgang (1980), "Stochastic Independence, Causal Independence, and Shieldability", *Journal of Philosophical Logic*, 9: 73–99.

Suppe, Frederick (1989), *The Semantic Conception of Theories and Scientific Realism* (Chicago University Press).

Suppes, Patrick(1967), "What Is a Scientific Theory?" in Sidney Morgenbesser (ed.): *Philosophy of Science Today* (New York: New York Basic Books).

—— (1970), *A Probabilistic Theory of Causality* (Amsterdam: North-Holland).

Van Fraassen, Bas (1980), *The Scientific Image* (Oxford: Clarendon Press).

—— (2002), *The Empirical Stance* (New Haven: Yale University Press).

Woodward, James (1997), "Explanation, Invariance, and Intervention", *PSA* 1996, ii: S26–41.

10

Normative Ethics: Back to the Future

Thomas Hurka

The course of normative ethics in the twentieth century was a roller-coaster ride, from a period of skilled and confident theorizing in the first third of the century, through a virtual disappearance in the face of various forms of skepticism in the middle third, to a partial revival, though shadowed by remnants of that skepticism, in the final third. The ideal future of normative ethics therefore lies in its past. It must entirely shed its traces of mid-century skepticism if it is to return to the levels of insight provided by G. E. Moore, Hastings Rashdall, J. M. E. McTaggart, W. D. Ross, C. D. Broad, and other early twentieth-century moral theorists.

These theorists shared several fundamental assumptions about ethics, many derived from late nineteenth-century philosophers such as Henry Sidgwick. They were all moral realists, believing that moral judgements are objectively true or false. More importantly, they were non-naturalist realists, believing, as anti-realists also can, that moral judgements form a separate category of judgements, neither reducible to nor derivable from other judgements. For them the property of goodness is not identical to any physical or natural property, and no "ought" can be derived from an "is". They therefore accepted a realist version of the autonomy of ethics: at the level of fundamental principles, moral judgements are independent of all other judgements.

These theorists also shared the general normative project of systematizing common-sense morality, or finding more abstract principles that can unify and explain our particular judgements about good and right. This project was not unique to them, but their approach to it was distinctively shaped by their belief in the autonomy of ethics.

First, they trusted intuitive judgements as at least a reliable starting-point for moral inquiry. Precisely because they denied that moral claims can be derived from other claims, they thought direct intuitive insights, either their own or those of common sense, were the best available entree to the moral realm. They did not see these insights as infallible; they recognized that our intuitions can be distorted by self-interest and other factors. Nor did they think the disorganized and even conflicting collection of judgements that make up common-sense morality was in that form acceptable. This was their prime motive for theorizing common sense: only if its judgements could be systematized by a few fundamental principles would they be properly scientific. But one test of these principles was their consistency with every-day moral beliefs, and another was their own intuitive appeal. Many of these theorists considered intuitions about general principles more reliable than ones about particular cases, but at all levels of generality they thought the only route to moral knowledge was by some kind of intuitive insight.

Second, and because of their confidence in intuitive judgements, these theorists were in principle open to the whole range of moral views accepted in Western culture.[1] In practice their openness often had a limitation. Many of them were consequentialists, believing that what is right is always what will produce the most good, and as a result they did not say much about non-consequentialist views. Even Ross, who defended non-consequentialism, described more its general structure than its details. But Moore, Rashdall, and the others did collectively address a huge variety of views about the good: not only that pleasure is good, but also views valuing knowledge, aesthetic contemplation, virtue, love, and more. Theirs was a golden age of value theory, in part because its theorists defended so many views about what is intrinsically worth pursuing. In addition, they were prepared to explore the details of these views. They did not rest with general claims about their preferred values but produced subtle analyses of the elements of aesthetic contemplation (Moore), the specific character of love (McTaggart), and the forms of virtue and their comparative values (Ross).[2]

Finally, the analyses these theorists produced were what I will call structural rather than foundational. They described the underlying structure of common-sense judgements and in that sense unified and explained them. But they did not try to ground those judgements in others that concern a more fundamental topic and can therefore justify them to someone who does not initially accept them. Their analyses stayed within a circle of common-sense concepts rather than connecting them to others, either moral or non-moral, that they saw as more secure. For example, Sidgwick grounded utilitarianism in the principles that one should not prefer a lesser good at one time to a greater good at another or a lesser good for one person to a greater good for another. These principles make explicit two forms of impartiality central to utilitarian thinking; they also help to unify utilitarian claims. But they use similar concepts to those claims rather than relating them to others that are more fundamental.[3] The same holds for Moore's formulation of the retributive theory of punishment in terms of his principle of organic unities, which says the value of a whole need not equal the sum of the values of its parts. In the case of punishment, Moore argues, a person's having a vicious character is bad, as is his suffering pain, but the combination of a vicious character and pain in the same life is good as a combination, and sufficiently good that inflicting the pain makes the overall situation better.[4] This analysis again uncovers the structure of retributive claims and unifies them with others that involve organic unities. It also has important implications, for example, that while deserved punishment is good as deserved it is bad as involving pain, so the morally best response to it mixes satisfaction that justice is being done with regret at the infliction of pain. But the analysis does not

[1] They should also have been open to ideas accepted in other cultures, but tended to believe, like many in their time, in the higher moral development of the West.

[2] G. E. Moore, *Principia Ethica* (Cambridge: Cambridge University Press, 1903), 189–202; J. M. E. McTaggart, *The Nature of Existence*, vol. 2 (Cambridge: Cambridge University Press, 1927), 147–61, 436–9; W. D. Ross, *The Right and the Good* (Oxford: Clarendon Press, 1930), 155–73.

[3] Henry Sidgwick, *The Methods of Ethics*, 7th edn. (London: Macmillan, 1907), 379–84.

[4] Moore, *Principia Ethica*, 214–16.

ground retributivism in some other, less contentious claim and will not persuade someone initially hostile to retributivism. Or consider Broad's treatment of what he calls self-referential altruism. This view holds, contrary to Sidgwick, that our duty to others is not to treat them impartially but to care more about those who are in various ways closer to us, such as our family, friends, and compatriots. Broad's analysis unifies a variety of common-sense claims about the demands of loyalty and invites further inquiry about exactly which relations make for closeness of the relevant kind. But it does not justify self-referentiality in other terms; instead, it assumes self-referentiality, saying that each person should care more about his family and friends because he should in general care more about those who stand in special relations to him.[5]

These theorists were aware of more ambitious normative projects: many of their contemporaries proposed deriving moral claims from associationist psychology, Darwinian biology, or Idealist metaphysics. But Sidgwick, Moore, and the others gave both general arguments against this kind of derivation and specific critiques of their contemporaries' views. For them the foundational approach to ethics was illusory and structural analysis the only profitable route to pursue. They did not address every important topic in ethics or leave nothing to be said about those they did discuss. But methodologically they provided a model for how normative inquiry should proceed. And then, in the middle decades of the century, normative ethics virtually disappeared from philosophy.

One cause of this disappearance was the replacement of the moral realism that had dominated the earlier period by crude versions of expressivist anti-realism, which held that moral judgements are not true or false but only express simple pro- or con-attitudes, and which understood normative argument as an attempt to transmit these attitudes to others by a kind of emotional contagion.[6] Another cause was a general conception of philosophy as a second-order discipline, which analyzes the logic or language of first-order disciplines but does not participate in them itself. Just as philosophy of science analyzes the logic of scientific confirmation but does not itself make scientific claims, so philosophical ethics should study the language of morals but leave substantive moralizing to preachers and poets.

Over time, however, the influence of these causes faded and the intrinsic interest of normative questions, both theoretical and particular, was able to reassert itself. The result was a revival of normative philosophizing in the last third of the century, stimulated especially by the 1971 publication of John Rawls's A Theory of Justice.[7] Since then normative ethics has been a prominent part of the discipline and has produced much valuable work. But its revival has been only partial, held back by remnants of the mid-century's two dominant general attitudes to philosophy.

[5] C. D. Broad, "Self and Others", in Broad's Critical Essays in Moral Philosophy (London: George Allen & Unwin, 1971).

[6] See A. J. Ayer, Language, Truth, and Logic (London: Gollancz, 1936), ch. 6; and Charles L. Stevenson, Ethics and Language (New Haven: Yale University Press, 1944).

[7] John Rawls, A Theory of Justice (Cambridge, MA: Harvard University Press, 1971).

The first of these was the technical, scientizing attitude of logical positivism and successor views such as W. V. O. Quine's naturalism. This attitude was hostile to common sense and philosophies that take it seriously, holding that the everyday view of the world is riddled with errors. In the linguistic terms that were popular in this period, it held that ordinary language is inadequate for understanding reality and needs to be replaced by a more scientific language, such as first-order logic. The second attitude, which arose in reaction to the first, informed the ordinary-language philosophy of Ludwig Wittgenstein, J. L. Austin, and others. It had a high regard for common sense, which it took to be the repository of centuries of human learning. But it was resolutely anti-technical and anti-theoretical. It is a mistake, its partisans held, to think that whenever a single word applies to a set of objects there must be some single property they share; there may be only a loose set of "family resemblances". The attempt to capture that property in an abstract principle does not deepen the insights of common sense but gets them entirely wrong.

Even apart from any general skepticism about philosophical ethics, this pair of attitudes left little room for the earlier project of systematizing common-sense morality. On one side was a view friendly to abstract principles but hostile to common sense; on the other was a view friendly to common sense but hostile to abstract principles. And these two views have continued to influence normative ethics since its re-emergence.

For its part, the scientizing attitude has encouraged philosophers to reject many common-sense moral views as confused or in some other way unacceptable. The result, especially early in the normative revival, was that theoretical ethics considered only a small number of options: utilitarianism, Kantian deontology, and little else. Ideas about desert, natural rights, and virtue were commonly if not universally set aside or analyzed in other, allegedly less suspect terms; either way, the distinctive approaches to ethics they express were ignored. Another object of skepticism was the topic most discussed at the start of the century: intrinsic value. Many philosophers found the idea that there are goods a person should pursue for herself other than pleasure or the satisfaction of her desires deeply problematic, and they were equally hostile to proposed goods that span people's lives, such as distributions proportioned to their merits, or that lie outside them, such as complex ecosystems. This meant that consequentialism, which in the earlier part of the century had encompassed a wide variety of positions, was in the later period mostly equated with simple-minded versions of utilitarianism. This again cut philosophical ethics off from everyday moral thought. Just as many non-philosophers use desert and rights as basic moral concepts, so many think there are goods worth pursuing other than pleasure or satisfaction. If a person is compassionate or generous, that in itself makes her life better; likewise if she has deep personal relationships or accomplishes difficult goals. (Consider the longtime recruiting slogan of the U. S. armed forces: "Be all that you can be". It clearly appealed to widespread views about the intrinsic value of developing one's talents.) In rejecting all such views philosophers were again rejecting much of their culture's moral life.

In some cases the grounds of this rejection were conceptual, with philosophers urging, for example, that claims about intrinsic value are simply unintelligible. These particular arguments had little merit. If morality can tell people to pursue others' happiness regardless of whether this will satisfy their own desires, as most philosophers allow, why can it not also tell them to pursue knowledge? And if the worry was that claims about intrinsic value presuppose a suspect realism, that too was groundless. Even if moral realism is problematic, as is by no means clear,[8] claims about value can always be understood in an expressivist way. In fact, sophisticated versions of expressivism allow virtually any moral view to be accommodated in a scientizing or naturalistic picture of the world. These versions take the attitudes expressed by moral judgements to have the logical form of categorical imperatives, so they are directed at acts or states of a person in a way that is not conditional on that person's having any attitudes. Consider the judgement that malice is evil. According to sophisticated expressivism, someone who makes this judgement expresses a negative attitude to all malice, whatever the malicious person's attitude to malice. If she contemplates malice in someone who has no negative attitude to malice, her own attitude to the malice is negative; if she contemplates a possible world in which she herself has no negative attitude to malice and is malicious, her attitude (from this world) to her malice is negative.[9] As so formulated, expressivism makes virtually no difference to the study of normative questions. Both realists and expressivists can accept almost any substantive moral view and argue for it in the same way: by appealing to intuitive judgements, formulating abstract principles, and so on. The realists will interpret the judgements as providing insights into moral truth, the expressivists as expressing attitudes they hope others do or can come to share. But viewed on their own, their moral positions will be indistinguishable.

In other cases the grounds for rejecting common-sense views were normative: that people must be free to determine the content of their own good, as desire theories allow, or that all goods are, substantively, goods of individuals. But these arguments were often accompanied by a general sense that the views they targeted were too extravagant to be taken seriously. It is part of the self-image of scientizing philosophers to be tough-minded debunkers of confused folk beliefs, and in ethics this meant rejecting all views with more than a very austere content.[10] But it is again hard to see a persuasive rationale for this approach. Whether moral judgements report a distinctive kind of truth or merely express attitudes, why should their content be limited in this way? Whatever the merits of conceptual parsimony in other domains, it is hard to find one here.[11]

---

[8] For a recent defence of realism see Thomas Nagel, *The View From Nowhere* (New York: Oxford University Press, 1986), ch. 8.

[9] This point is made in recent defences of expressivism such as Allan Gibbard, *Wise Choices, Apt Feelings: A Theory of Normative Judgment* (Cambridge, MA: Harvard University Press, 1990); and Simon Blackburn, *Ruling Passions: A Theory of Practical Reasoning* (Oxford: Clarendon Press, 1998).

[10] Compare Bernard Williams's claim that utilitarianism's popularity rests on its being a *"minimum commitment* morality"; see his *Morality: An Introduction to Ethics* (New York: Harper & Row, 1972), 91.

[11] Note that austerity is not just a matter of theoretical simplicity. Robert Nozick's view that all values are instances of "organic unity" (see his *Philosophical Explanations* [Cambridge, MA: Harvard

Relatedly, and especially when ethics was first re-emerging, philosophers tended to confine their attention to structurally simple views rather than recognizing the complexities their predecessors had noted. Whereas Broad had analyzed the structure of self-referential altruism, several prominent works took the main views needing discussion to hold that people should either care only about their own good or care impartially about the good of all.[12] And a common form of argument assumed that if a moral factor such as the difference between killing and allowing to die makes no difference in one context, it cannot make a difference in any context.[13] But the point of Moore's doctrine of organic unities had been precisely that the difference a factor makes can vary from context to context, depending on what other factors it is combined with.

These scientizing influences have been countered but also complemented by those of the anti-theoretical, Wittgensteinian attitude. Its adherents are not debunkers; they are open to many common-sense moral views, especially about the virtues and vices. But they deny that these views can be systematized or captured in abstract principles. Many cite Aristotle's remark that in ethics one should not seek more precision than the subject-matter allows,[14] which they take to imply that theorizing about ethics is fundamentally misguided. The most extreme formulation of their view holds that moral knowledge always concerns particular acts in all their specificity; it does not generalize to other acts, cannot be codified in general principles, and is a matter only of trained moral insight.[15] People with the right moral character can "see" what is right, just, or virtuous in a given situation, but they cannot express that vision in other terms or communicate it to those who lack it.

In my view an anti-theoretical position is properly open only to those who have made a serious effort to theorize a given domain and found that it cannot succeed. Anti-theorists who do not make this effort are simply being lazy, like Wittgenstein himself. His central example of a concept that cannot be given a unifying analysis was that of a game,[16] but in one of the great underappreciated books of the twentieth century Bernard Suits gives perfectly persuasive necessary and sufficient conditions for something's being a game. (Roughly: in playing a game one pursues a goal that can be described independently of the game, such as directing a ball into a hole in the ground, while willingly accepting rules that forbid the most efficient

University Press, 1981], 415–28) is theoretically simple but would be rejected by scientizers as hopelessly extravagant.

[12] See, e.g. Thomas Nagel, *The Possibility of Altruism* (Oxford: Clarendon Press, 1970).

[13] For the most famous illustration of this argument see James Rachels, "Active and Passive Euthanasia", *New England Journal of Medicine* 292 (Jan. 9, 1975): 78–80.

[14] Aristotle, *Nicomachean Ethics*, trans. W. D. Ross and J. O. Urmson, in *The Complete Works of Aristotle*, ed. Jonathan Barnes (Princeton, NJ: Princeton University Press, 1984), 1094b12–28. Note that, despite this remark, Aristotle gives a mathematical formula for distributive justice at *Nicomachean Ethics* 1131a30–b16, saying that justice requires the ratio of person A's award to B's to equal the ratio of A's merits to B's. He is nothing like the consistent anti-theorist some of his contemporary admirers take him to be.

[15] See, e.g. John McDowell, "Virtue and Reason", *The Monist* 62 (1979): 331–50; and Jonathan Dancy, *Moral Reasons* (Oxford: Blackwell, 1993), chs. 4–6.

[16] Ludwig Wittgenstein, *Philosophical Investigations*, trans. G. E. M. Anscombe (Oxford: Basil Blackwell, 1972), sec. 66.

means to that goal, such as placing the ball in the hole by hand.) With an exemplary lightness of touch, Suits mentions Wittgenstein only once:

'Don't say,' Wittgenstein admonishes us, ' "there must be something common or they would not be called 'games' "'—but *look and see* whether there is anything common to all.' This is unexceptionable advice. Unfortunately, Wittgenstein himself did not follow it. He looked, to be sure, but because he had decided beforehand that games are indefinable, his look was fleeting, and he saw very little.[17]

Similarly, ethical anti-theorists have decided beforehand that there can be no unifying account of, say, the human good and therefore do not try seriously to construct one. More specifically, they typically consider only simple-minded ethical analyses and take the failure of those to demonstrate the impossibility of all analyses. But, for example, the fact that not all pleasure is good, because sadistic pleasure is bad, does not refute all general theories of the value of pleasure. An only slightly complex theory can say that sadistic pleasure, while good as pleasure, is bad as sadistic, and more bad than it is good; a more complex theory can say that when pleasure is sadistic it loses its goodness as pleasure. Far from abandoning generality, these analyses use it to illuminate values in a way anti-theorists never could.

Despite their differences, scientizers and anti-theorists share a common assumption: that any acceptable moral theory must be simple in its content and form. Believing in theory, the scientizers confine their attention to simple views; finding those views unacceptable, anti-theorists abandon theory. But both are hostile to the systematic analysis of complex moral views that had been the hallmark of the earlier period. Consider, for example, the topic of how different moral considerations weigh against each other. Scientizers are suspicious of such weighing, especially if it rests on intuitive judgements. They want a mechanical and even empirically implementable procedure for weighing values, as there would be if all values reduced to a single one.[18] By contrast, anti-theorists embrace a plurality of values but insist they are "incommensurable", which they take to imply that nothing systematic can be said about how they compare.[19] The early twentieth-century theorists avoided both these extremes. While recognizing that different values cannot be weighed precisely, they insisted that we can make rough comparative judgements about them, such as that an instance of one good is much, moderately, or only a little better than an instance of another. They also pursued structural questions, such as whether the complete absence of one good, say, knowledge, can always be compensated for by a sufficient quantity of another. Theirs was the intermediate approach of partly theorizing the partly theorizable, but it is excluded by both the scientizing and anti-theoretical attitudes.

[17] Bernard Suits, *The Grasshopper: Games, Life and Utopia* (Toronto: University of Toronto Press, 1978), p. x. Note that Suits's analysis of games is structural; once it is in hand, Wittgenstein's fussing about the differences between games that use boards and cards or that are and are not amusing is embarrassingly superficial.

[18] Rawls expresses a moderate version of this view in *A Theory of Justice*, saying that pluralist views that weigh principles intuitively are less satisfactory than ones that give some principles lexical priority over others, so the former's demands always take precedence over the latter's (40–5).

[19] See, e.g. Martha C. Nussbaum, *The Fragility of Goodness: Luck and Ethics in Greek Tragedy and Philosophy* (Cambridge: Cambridge University Press, 1986), 107–17, 294–8; and Michael Stocker, *Plural and Conflicting Values* (Oxford: Clarendon Press, 1990), chs. 7–8.

Among some ethicists the influence of these attitudes is now fading.[20] In the last decade or so there has been more sympathy for views that would earlier have been rejected as extravagant, such as perfectionist accounts of each person's good,[21] as well as detailed explorations of non-personal goods such as equality[22] and desert.[23] There has also been greater awareness of the complexity moral views can have; thus, the point that a factor's importance can depend on its relations to other factors has been made and is widely accepted.[24] Scientizing and anti-theoretical attitudes have by no means disappeared. Some philosophers still reject any normative claims not derived from desires; others still look askance at all formal analysis. But the two attitudes are becoming less dominant, and as they recede, ethics is coming to theorize a wider range of views. But there is another, more indirect effect of the scientizing attitude that continues to retard moral study.

Because they are skeptical of appeals to moral intuition, scientizers are dissatisfied with what I have called structural analyses, ones that relate a moral view to principles that are more abstract but use similar concepts. To them these principles appeal to the same basic intuitions as the original view and so cannot properly justify it. There are many illustrations of this dissatisfaction.

In a recent book on desert, George Sher says that Moore's defence of retributivism in terms of his principle of organic unities is "inconclusive", since it "merely restates what the retributivist needs to explain". Though intuitive appeals like Moore's are not worthless, they are at best a "prologue" that should lead to "independent justifications of our beliefs about desert".[25] Similarly, Rawls allows that a pluralist view that weighs its values intuitively can describe the structure of its comparative judgements, for example, on indifference graphs, but adds that since these graphs give no "constructive criteria" establishing the judgements' reasonableness, what results is "but half a conception".[26] Or consider non-consequentialism. A great contribution of recent ethics has been to show that non-consequentialist views have a self-referential or "agent-relative" structure. When they forbid, for example, killing, they tell each person to be especially concerned that *he* does not kill, even if the result is a somewhat greater number of killings by other people.[27] But rather than being seen to support

[20] In philosophy generally the scientizing attitude remains very strong; in fact, successor views to Quine's naturalism are now the dominant methodological views in the discipline. The anti-theoretical attitude lost its position in general philosophy decades ago and now survives almost solely in ethics.

[21] See, e.g. Derek Parfit, *Reasons and Persons* (Oxford: Clarendon Press, 1984), 493–502; Thomas Hurka, *Perfectionism* (New York: Oxford University Press, 1993); and George Sher, *Beyond Neutrality: Perfectionism and Politics* (Cambridge: Cambridge University Press, 1997), ch. 9.

[22] Derek Parfit, "Equality or Priority?", The Lindley Lecture (Lawrence, KS: University of Kansas Press, 1995); and Larry S. Temkin, *Inequality* (New York: Oxford University Press, 1993).

[23] See, e.g. George Sher, *Desert* (Princeton, NJ: Princeton University Press, 1987); and Shelly Kagan, "Equality and Desert", in Louis P. Pojman and Owen McLeod (eds.), *What Do We Deserve? Readings on Justice and Desert* (New York: Oxford University Press, 1999), 298–314.

[24] Shelly Kagan, "The Additive Fallacy", *Ethics* 99 (1988): 5–31; and F. M. Kamm, *Morality/Mortality*, vol. II: *Rights, Duties, and Status* (New York: Oxford University Press, 1996), ch. 2.

[25] Sher, *Desert*, 72, 19.   [26] Rawls, *A Theory of Justice*, 39, 41.

[27] Bernard Williams, "A Critique of Utilitarianism", in J. J. C. Smart and Bernard Williams, *Utilitarianism For and Against* (Cambridge: Cambridge University Press, 1973), 99; Parfit, *Reasons and Persons*, 143–8; Nagel, *The View From Nowhere*, 152–6, 175–85.

non-consequentialism, by clarifying its structure, this analysis has been taken to generate objections against it. How can it be rational, some have asked, to avoid one act of killing if the result is more killings overall? If killing is bad, should we not try to minimize killing by everyone?[28] Here it is not taken to be a sufficient answer to point to the intuitive appeal of an agent-relative prohibition against killing or even of the abstract structure it embodies. What is demanded is a justification of agent-relativity of some deeper, more philosophical kind.

This dissatisfaction has led many contemporary philosophers to search for foundational justifications of moral views, ones that relate them to other concepts they see as somehow more secure. These justifications have taken many forms. In some the foundational principles appealed to are still moral. Thus, a prominent justification of retributivism appeals to ideas about fairness, saying it is unfair if the majority of people have restrained their self-interest by obeying the law but a criminal has not. He has gained the benefit of others' restraint without paying a similar cost himself, and punishing him removes that imbalance.[29] Here the proposed foundational claim is at a coordinate level to those being justified; fairness is not a more abstract concept than desert. But other justifications start from very abstract principles, for example, that everyone should be treated with equal respect and concern[30] or that those acts are wrong that are forbidden by rules no one could reasonably reject.[31] They then claim that the best interpretation of these principles, guided by normative views but not by ones directly favouring a given moral position, can support that position and therefore justify it philosophically. The grand exemplar of this approach is Rawls, who says the correct principles of justice are those that would be chosen by rational contractors in a specified initial position. Rawls's general contractarian claim is best understood as a moral one, and moral judgements also guide his specification of his initial position. But since these judgements do not directly concern the principles the contractors choose among, the contract provides an "Archimedean point" for justifying specific claims about justice.[32]

These last analyses shade into ones that are more explicitly ambitious, claiming to derive specific moral views from the logic of moral language or the definition or purpose of morality. R. M. Hare claims that the language of morals, properly understood, allows only utilitarianism as a fundamental moral view; all other views misuse the language.[33] More vaguely, others claim that since the purpose of morality is to satisfy human wants and needs, any acceptable principles must concern wants

---

[28] Samuel Scheffler, *The Rejection of Consequentialism: A Philosophical Examination of the Considerations Underlying Rival Moral Conceptions* (Oxford: Clarendon Press, 1982), ch. 4; and Shelly Kagan, *The Limits of Morality* (Oxford: Clarendon Press, 1989).

[29] Herbert Morris, "Persons and Punishment", *The Monist* 52 (1968): 475–501; and Sher, *Desert*, ch. 5.

[30] Ronald Dworkin, "Liberalism", in Stuart Hampshire (ed.), *Public and Private Morality* (Cambridge: Cambridge University Press, 1977), 113–43.

[31] T. M. Scanlon, *What We Owe to Each Other* (Cambridge, MA: Harvard University Press, 1998).

[32] Rawls, *A Theory of Justice*, 261. In later work Rawls has abandoned this strong "Archimedean" claim about his contractarian argument, but still holds that connecting his liberal-egalitarian political views to contractarian ideas gives them a kind of justification they would not have if defended just by direct intuition.

[33] R. M. Hare, *Moral Thinking: Its Levels, Method, and Point* (Oxford: Clarendon Press, 1981).

and needs.[34] This seems to rule out perfectionist views of the good by definitional fiat, and certainly rules out goods not located within people's lives, such as distributions proportioned to their merits and the existence of ecosystems.

Yet another approach appeals to metaphysical facts, especially about the person, that it says an acceptable moral view must reflect. Rawls says that utilitarianism fails to take seriously "the separateness of persons", and that doing so leads to a more egalitarian view like his own;[35] Robert Nozick says the same facts about separateness support agent-relative prohibitions against using some as means to benefit others.[36] In a similar vein, Samuel Scheffler argues that what he calls "the independence of the personal point of view" justifies agent-relative permissions. Apart from its deontological prohibitions, common-sense morality does not require people always to produce the most good impartially calculated. It permits them to give somewhat more weight to their own interests and therefore, within limits, to fall short of doing what is impersonally best. This permission can be justified, Scheffler argues, by noting that people do not rank outcomes only from an impersonal standpoint but also, and independently, in terms of their own preferences and values.[37]

Yet another foundational approach tries to demonstrate the rationality of certain moral principles, so that failing to act on them is a species of irrationality. The most clear-headed such argument, that of David Gauthier, claims that accepting certain moral constraints is in each person's self-interest, where self-interest is understood austerely, as involving the satisfaction of her pre-existing desires.[38] A more high-minded view understands self-interest as involving an ideal of "flourishing" that may or may not be what a person actually wants. Here the justification of morality is that flourishing involves the moral virtues as essential components, and these virtues require one to act morally.[39] An especially grand form of argument, proposed by Alan Gewirth and Christine Korsgaard, tries to derive moral demands from the presuppositions of rational agency. The beliefs implicit in any rational action, it claims, commit one logically to certain moral principles, typically Kantian ones, so failing to act on those principles involves logical inconsistency.[40]

Despite their differences, these arguments share the general project of trying to ground moral views in something more than direct intuition, through what I have called foundational analyses. Now, the difference between these and structural analyses is only one of degree, not of kind. It turns on whether the concepts an

---

[34] See, e.g. Philippa Foot, "Moral Beliefs", *Proceedings of the Aristotelian Society* 59 (1958–9): 83–104; G. J. Warnock, *Contemporary Moral Philosophy* (London: Macmillan, 1967), chs. 5 and 6; and Warnock, *The Object of Morality* (London: Methuen, 1971).   [35] Rawls, *A Theory of Justice*, 27, 187.

[36] Robert Nozick, *Anarchy, State, and Utopia* (New York: Basic Books, 1974), 32–3.

[37] Scheffler, *The Rejection of Consequentialism*, ch. 3; for another version of metaphysical foundationalism see David O. Brink, "Self-Love and Altruism", *Social Philosophy and Policy* 14/1 (Winter 1997): 122–57.

[38] David Gauthier, *Morals By Agreement* (Oxford: Clarendon Press, 1986). Because of its austerity, this argument cannot justify all the moral constraints most people find intuitively compelling.

[39] G. E. M. Anscombe, "Modern Moral Philosophy", *Philosophy* 33 (1958): 1–19; and Rosalind Hursthouse, "Virtue Theory and Abortion", *Philosophy and Public Affairs* 20 (1991): 223–46.

[40] Alan Gewirth, *Reason and Morality* (Chicago: University of Chicago Press, 1978); and Christine M. Korsgaard, *The Sources of Normativity* (Cambridge: Cambridge University Press, 1996).

analysis uses are similar to those in the view it is analyzing, and similarity admits of degrees. There can even be analyses that straddle the structural-foundational divide, so they are neither clearly the one nor clearly the other. But a difference of degree is still a difference, and other analyses do clearly fit one model rather than the other. Thus, Rawls's and Hare's arguments are clearly foundational, while Moore's and Broad's are structural. There can also be similarities in how the two types of analysis are defended. Structural analyses cannot argue just from particular intuitive judgements to principles that fit them; if the principles are to explain the judgements, they must be independently plausible. Conversely, foundational analyses need not argue just from the general to the particular. They can and often do take the fact that an abstract idea coheres with and can explain particular judgements to be important evidence for it, as Rawls, for example, does. Both approaches can therefore use coherentist reasoning, treating all parts of a moral theory as justified by their relations to other parts and none as immune to revision or the source of all others' warrant.[41] But even when they share this coherentism the two approaches differ in the type of moral theory they generate and, more specifically, in the type of moral explanation they give. Structural analyses assume that a concrete moral view can be explained by principles that express similar ideas in a more abstract way, using similar concepts at a higher level of generality; those who demand foundational analyses require a genuine explanation to relate the view to ideas that are different and more fundamental, because they concern some more fundamental topic.

It would be impressive if any of these foundational arguments succeeded, but in my view critical discussion has repeatedly shown that they do not. It would be going too far to state categorically that no such argument will ever succeed; each must be assessed on its merits. But time and again it turns out that to yield the specific views they are meant to justify, they must tacitly appeal to the very intuitive judgements they are meant to supplant. Let me give a few illustrations.

Arguments from metaphysical facts about the person need not violate the autonomy of ethics if they make the general moral claim that the correct normative principles for a thing must reflect that thing's nature.[42] But in most cases the facts they start from either are not specific enough to support the particular moral views they are intended to or, if they are redescribed to do so, presuppose those views or something very close to them. For example, it is undeniable that persons are separate, in the sense that there are connections between states within a life that do not hold across lives. But many moral views reflect this fact other than the egalitarian ones it is usually taken to support. Consider a pluralist view that compares goods such as knowledge and achievement in a way that favours balance or well-roundedness within lives but not across them. It treats lives as morally significant units but has no distributive implications whatever. And even if separateness does have distributive

---

[41] Because of this, analyses that I call foundational need not involve foundationalism in the sense used in epistemology, where it connotes the view that some beliefs are self-justifying and the source of justification of all other beliefs. Analyses that appeal to the language of morals or defend the rationality of morality involve something like this epistemic foundationalism, but others such as Rawls's do not. The latter are foundationalist only in my sense, which concerns explanation rather than justification.

[42] Rawls, *A Theory of Justice*, 29.

implications, why must they be egalitarian? What is wrong in this respect with a desert principle requiring people's degrees of happiness to be proportioned to their degrees of virtue, or even with an anti-egalitarian principle like Nietzsche's that directs everyone to promote the excellence of the few most excellent individuals? Of course, one can redescribe the separateness of persons so it does support only egalitarian views, for example, by saying that unit gains in less happy lives count for more than similar gains in happier ones. But then egalitarianism is being built into the supposedly metaphysical facts, which no longer give it independent support. A similar point applies to Scheffler's justification of agent-relative permissions. The fact that people have a personal ranking of outcomes that can differ from the impersonal one seems perfectly well captured by a view that combines each person's personal ranking with the impersonal one, say by averaging them, and then requires him to maximize the resulting combined value. To support permissions in particular over this alternative, the metaphysical facts must be redescribed so they favour giving each person with an independent point of view the further independence to decide which point of view he will act from on particular occasions. But then the redescription again assumes something very close to the conclusion it is meant to justify.[43]

A similar difficulty faces arguments from abstract moral principles such as ones about equal respect or rational agreement. In some cases these principles will be widely accepted, but only because they are open to different interpretations that support very different substantive views; in other cases they do favour one view, but have contentious features that cannot be independently justified.[44] The former is true of arguments from equal respect. Their foundational principles are unexceptionable if they say only that a moral view must give all people equal standing, but this claim has no substantive implications. In particular, it does not imply that people should have, even initially, equal resources or happiness; it is perfectly satisfied by views that give people equal rights to acquire resources (which they may then exercise very unequally) or say they should receive different rewards according to their different deserts. The abstract claim does not even distinguish between consequentialist and deontological views, each of which interprets respect in its own way.[45] The contrary problem arises at many points in Rawls's contractarian argument. Its basic design excludes perfectionist, entitlement, and many other views—so it is hardly a neutral device—and even views it initially allows, such as utilitarianism, are eventually excluded by stipulations that have no persuasive

---

[43] In addition, most appeals to a metaphysical fact assume a certain valuation of it; thus, Scheffler assumes that the independence of the personal point of view is not simply regrettable, as strict impartialists might hold, but has positive worth. This is another point where these appeals come close to assuming what they are meant to explain.

[44] I think most philosophers would now agree that a similar dilemma faces arguments from the language of morals or the definition of morality. Most would say its having substantive moral implications actually counts against a view on these topics; an adequate view should allow the disagreements that obviously exist by remaining neutral on substantive moral questions.

[45] Consequentialist views say that respect for a person involves promoting her good, deontological views that it involves, more centrally, not sacrificing her good. This is a fundamental difference, but cannot be resolved by reflecting on the true meaning of "respect".

contractarian rationale. Or consider the suggestion that agent-relative prohibitions are justified because, by making persons "inviolable", they give them higher moral status than they would otherwise have.[46] It may be true that these prohibitions give each person higher status by denying that she may legitimately be sacrificed whenever this will give greater benefits to other people. But they also give her lower status by denying that other people may be sacrificed to give benefits to her, and there is no independent way of saying whether the gain or loss here is greater.[47]

These abstract arguments share a further difficulty with some that try to ground a moral view in another of a coordinate degree of abstractness, such as the fairness justification of retributivism. These latter arguments are difficult to generalize about and may sometimes prove illuminating. But consider the claim of the fairness justification that punishment removes an imbalance whereby some people have benefited from others' restraint without paying a similar cost themselves. If cost is understood in a standard way, say in terms of pleasure and pain, this claim does not yield the right results about particular punishments: many crimes that intuitively call for severe punishments, such as murder, are not ones people pay a high cost in avoiding, since they are not ones they are strongly tempted to commit. So the justification must revise its understanding of cost, and in doing so make some finely balanced claims about the relative positions of criminals and law-abiding citizens. And we can then ask whether those claims really are explanatory of retributivism. On one side is a simple judgement many find intuitively compelling, about the intrinsic appropriateness of punishing the guilty; on the other are some precarious claims about the balance of costs and benefits. Is it really an advance to relate the former to the latter? I am not suggesting that everyone must accept retributivism; many may on reflection reject it. But their reflection will be most productive if it considers retributivism in its own right rather than detouring through a view that seems too convoluted to underlie it.[48] A similar point applies to more abstract arguments. Rawls tries to ground his egalitarian claim that it is most important to improve the condition of the worst-off by arguing that his contractors will not know the probabilities of their occupying different positions in society and, lacking that knowledge, will prefer those principles whose worst outcome for them is least bad. Critics have questioned whether either of these stipulations is reasonable, in my view persuasively. But even if they are reasonable, how much is gained by relating an egalitarianism many find compelling in itself to these finely balanced claims about rational choice?

It was not with pleasure that the early twentieth-century theorists said, as they often did, that the resolution of a fundamental moral issue comes down to each person's intuitive judgement about the question when it is clearly framed. They would have been delighted if more satisfying justifications were available. But if they are

---

[46] Kamm, *Morality/Mortality*, vol. II, ch. 10.

[47] Kagan, "Replies to My Critics", *Philosophy and Phenomenological Research* 51 (1991): 919–20.

[48] In his version of the fairness justification Sher equates the cost a criminal avoids with the strength of the moral prohibition he violates (*Desert*, 81–2), but this brings the justification very close to the Moorean formulation it is meant to improve upon.

not available, the widespread search for foundational analyses in recent ethics has been quixotic. This is not a decisive objection; many philosophical projects are quixotic, and the discipline still learns from their failure. But in this case the pursuit of grand justifications has in several ways skewed the field's priorities.

First, it has helped keep the focus of normative ethics narrow; as well as rejecting moral views for being extravagant, philosophers can dismiss them for lacking deep foundations. In some cases this dismissal has not had such chilling effects. Thus, the charge of some that agent-relative prohibitions are irrational has not stopped others from exploring their details. But, in another case, the novel entitlement theory of justice described by Robert Nozick has received less constructive discussion than it deserves in part because of the complaint that Nozick's treatment leaves it "without foundations".[49] This might be a reasonable complaint if competing views did have such foundations; it is not when they do not.

Second, the search for foundations has diverted philosophers' attention from the details of moral views. Faced with a set of ideas about value or duty, a theorist can go in either of two directions. She can look into the view, to discover its structure and the way it generates specific claims, or she can try to connect it to larger ideas about, say, the nature of morality or the status of persons as free and rational. And the more she does of the latter the less she will do of the former. In fact, a climate of foundational inquiry can lead even theorists sympathetic to a given view to spend more time answering others' abstract objections to it than examining its specific contents. But in ethics as in many fields, God (or the devil) dwells in the details. Our common-sense ideas about any moral topic are at best loosely organized and demand systematization. Sometimes this task cannot be completed: the ideas turn out to conflict, and we can only retain some by abandoning others. But at other times theorizing a view can show it has hidden strengths. For example, what seemed at first a loose collection of judgements can turn out to have a sophisticated under-lying structure, even a mathematical one, that everyday moralists follow though they are unaware of doing so. Or the view can have a surprising unity. It may include, say, a pair of plausible intuitive judgements that look independent, so we can wonder whether they are even consistent. But then analysis reveals that, perhaps given a third plausible judgement, the two entail each other, so the view has an impressive internal integrity. Or the view can be surprisingly related to several oth-ers, all of which turn out to instantiate the same more abstract idea. Or, examined closely, it can generate fascinating new questions and offer intuitively satisfying answers to them—sometimes just one answer, sometimes a set of competing ones. Any of these developments counts in favour of a view's acceptability, as internal con-tradictions count against it. But none will emerge if philosophers are busy batting around abstract conditions and chasing foundational dreams.

In fact, the search for moral foundations can lead to high-minded distortions of the moral phenomena. Consider the increasingly popular view that most desires are for objects thought of as good or as somehow supported by reasons. It has led one

---

[49] Nagel, "Libertarianism Without Foundations", *Yale Law Journal* 85 (1975): 136–49.

writer to say that thirst involves a recognition that we have reason to drink,[50] but surely no one actually gets thirsty in this highly intellectualized way. As Plato said, what we want when we are thirsty is not a good drink, but just a drink.[51] And even Plato was too restrictive in limiting this type of desire to the bodily appetites. Anything we can desire on the basis of an evaluative judgement we can also desire apart from such judgements; as well as pursuing knowledge because we believe it is intrinsically good, we can pursue it from simple curiosity. Moore, Rashdall, and Ross recognized this, holding that alongside forms of virtue directed at the right and the good as such are forms that involve no evaluative thoughts, such as simple compassion.[52]

Other distortions are more disturbing. A persistent temptation for foundational views, especially ones that affirm the rationality of morality, is to ground moral requirements in facts about the self: in how acting on them promotes the agent's self-interest or flourishing or relates to a "practical identity" or conception she has of herself as a specific type of person.[53] But if they take this line, these views imply that my ultimate reason for benefiting another person, say, by relieving his pain, concerns how this will affect my life. And this is not the right ultimate reason, which concerns how my action will affect the other's life: my fundamental reason to help him is to help *him*. In a trivial sense morality has to concern me, since it has to tell me how to act. But it does not follow that the ground of its requirements must always be located in me, and views that place it always there are in that respect distortions. This is reflected in the fact that people who were motivated by what these views say are their ultimate reasons—people whose ultimate motive for helping another was to promote their own flourishing or to live up to their own practical identity—would be acting in an objectionably narcissistic way. It is not admirable but morally self-indulgent to relieve another's pain primarily from concern to be a virtuous reliever of pain.[54] Now, a moral view can say that people will only act successfully on their ultimate reasons if they do not try consciously to do so. Thus, consequentialist views often say that people will only produce the best consequences if they do not aim at those consequences directly but instead follow certain simple rules. But it would be very odd for the foundational views I am discussing to make this type of claim. That would involve their saying that acting on what they say are our ultimate reasons is objectionable in itself, and not just because of its effects, and surely a moral view cannot so directly condemn its own acceptance. That is a sign that something has gone deeply wrong—that the search for philosophical foundations has led theorists to place the source of our reasons where it intuitively cannot be.

It is in fact striking how many strands in contemporary ethics, of Kantian, Aristotelian, and other inspirations, approach the subject in an essentially self-centred

[50] Scanlon, *What We Owe to Each Other*, 38.

[51] Plato, *Republic*, trans. G. M. A. Grube (Indianapolis: Hackett, 1974), 438a–39b.

[52] Moore, *Principia Ethica*, 179; Hastings Rashdall, *The Theory of Good and Evil* (London: Oxford University Press, 1907), vol. 1, 119–24; Ross, *The Right and the Good*, 160–3, 170–3.

[53] For the latter view, see Korsgaard, *The Sources of Normativity*.

[54] On moral self-indulgence see Bernard Williams, "Utilitarianism and Moral Self-Indulgence", in his *Moral Luck: Philosophical Papers 1973–80* (Cambridge: Cambridge University Press, 1981), 40–53.

way. They see the fundamental task of the moral agent as being to reflect on her own desires, or care about her own flourishing or integrity, or give moral laws to herself and so achieve her own autonomy. On all these views the agent's fundamental orientation is toward herself. There are, of course, exceptions; Thomas Nagel says very clearly that another person's pain by itself gives me reason to relieve it.[55] But a great deal of currently influential writing seems to assume that moral reasons must be not only trivially but also substantively about the self. The causes of this are partly philosophical: disbelief that there could be underivative other-regarding reasons and distrust of the intuitions that say there are. But there may also be social causes. May the self-centredness of so much contemporary ethical theorizing be the predictable product of a narcissistic age, offering moral foundations for the me-generation?

Finally, there is an issue of philosophical style. The early twentieth-century theorists wrote about ethics simply, directly, and even (one thinks, for example, of Rashdall) with wit. But much contemporary ethical writing has a tone of high intellectual earnestness. Sidgwick thought the progress of ethics had been impeded by the desire to edify; today the greater danger is the desire to be philosophically profound. At the very least, the pursuit of grand foundational projects does not encourage an engaging lightness of touch.

Any assessment of the current state of ethics must address the mixed influence of Rawls. A Theory of Justice is a great book, with many novel ideas and an original proposal for uniting them. And in a lecture given shortly after that book's publication, Rawls made methodological recommendations similar to those of this essay: that at least for now philosophers should set aside questions of moral truth and examine the structures of the moral views people actually hold.[56] But these recommendations have had much less influence than Rawls's practice or what was taken to be his practice in A Theory of Justice. Many even of those who do not think that book's contractarian argument succeeds think it is the right type of argument, aiming to justify a moral view not by direct intuitions but by something more philosophically ambitious. And Rawls's later work has reinforced this tendency, with its emphasis on grand abstractions such as persons' "higher-order interest" in forming, revising, and pursuing a conception of the good and the ideal of "public reason". Rawls's writing in moral philosophy has had many effects, but one has been to encourage a style of argumentation that is more high-flown than it is productive.

How, then, should normative ethics proceed? I take it that on most views its starting-point is the moral judgements people actually make. And it is worth emphasizing that people do make these judgements. Despite the claims of some cultural analysts, categorical moral evaluations are not disappearing in the face of moral relativism. No one says that rape, racism, and genocide are morally all right for you if you believe they are all right; everyone simply condemns them as wrong. (Though some describe

---

[55] Nagel, The View From Nowhere, pp. 156–62.

[56] Rawls, "The Independence of Moral Theory", Proceedings of the American Philosophical Association 48 (1974–5): 5–22. But Rawls includes in the "structure" of a moral view an associated "conception of the person", which sounds more foundational than the more purely mathematical analysis of structure I have been urging.

themselves as relativists, their moral practice repeatedly belies that claim.) And though the content of these judgements may change somewhat over time, their core remains the same. There is less concern today than fifty or a 100 years ago with the ethics of consensual sexual activity, and more with discrimination and intolerance. But the central moral prohibitions against coercion and wilful harm remain essentially unchanged, as do the central recommendations of compassion and fidelity. There are metaethical questions about how these prohibitions and recommendations are to be understood: in a realist way, as making claims that can be true or false, or as merely expressing attitudes. But these questions do not affect, except at the margins, either the content of these judgements or their importance. Whatever metaethics decides, the practice of making moral judgements will continue essentially as before.

In their initial form, however, these judgements require philosophical analysis, both to understand and to assess them. In my view this analysis is best done by addressing them in their own right, by seeking to identify more abstract principles that, while using similar concepts, can organize and explain them, and by investigating their details. In fact, these two tasks often go together, since trying to describe a view's structure comprehensively can force one to address specific issues one might otherwise not have thought of. Much valuable work of this kind has been done in recent ethics. The clear description of agent-relative prohibitions and permissions, which require us to care especially that *we* do not kill and allow us to give more weight to *our* interests, is, when separated from bogus demands for deep justifications, an immense contribution to our understanding of common-sense and deontological views. Other writers have shown how, in formulating their prohibitions, these views can use either or both of the distinctions between harms one causes and those one merely allows, and between harms one intends as an end or means and those one merely foresees; they have also discussed how these two distinctions might combine with each other. This is not a topic where a completely satisfactory analysis has yet emerged. Perhaps that analysis requires a more subtle application of the principle of organic unities than has yet been considered; perhaps it is simply not possible. Even so, the identification of the two distinctions has greatly improved our understanding of this family of views.[57] There have also been subtle suggestions about how a deontological view can weigh its prohibitions against the overall good an action will cause without aggregating that good in a simple additive way. Thus, the view can make it permissible to kill one innocent person to save some large number of other people from being killed or otherwise seriously harmed, but not to save any number of people from mild headaches.[58]

---

[57] See, e.g. Philippa Foot, "The Problem of Abortion and the Doctrine of Double Effect", in her *Virtues and Vices* (Berkeley, CA: University of California Press, 1973), 19–32; Judith Jarvis Thomson, "Killing, Letting Die, and the Trolley Problem", *The Monist* 59 (1976): 204–17; Warren S. Quinn, "Actions, Intentions, and Consequences: The Doctrine of Doing and Allowing", *Philosophical Review* 98 (1989): 287–312; Quinn, "Actions, Intentions, and Consequences: The Doctrine of Double Effect", *Philosophy and Public Affairs* 18 (1989), 334–51; Jeff McMahan, "Killing, Letting Die, and Withdrawing Aid", *Ethics* 103 (1993): 250–79; Kamm, *Morality/Mortality, vol. II*, chs. 1–7.

[58] Samantha Brennan, "Thresholds for Rights", *Southern Journal of Philosophy* 33 (1995): 143–68; Kamm, *Morality/Mortality*, vol. I: *Death and Whom to Save from It* (New York: Oxford University Press, 1993), chs. 8–10; and Scanlon, *What We Owe to Each Other*, 229–41.

There have been similar insights into views about the good. Thus, it has been shown that these views need not require everyone to maximize the good. They can instead require agents only to aim at outcomes that in one of several senses are "good enough"; this identification of "satisficing" consequentialism has again widened the range of moral views philosophers can consider.[59] There have also been discussions about whether the onerousness of one person's duty to pursue good outcomes should be affected by other people's failure to fulfil their duty, and if not, why not.[60] And there have been illuminating analyses of particular values, such as a distinction between two kinds of broadly egalitarian view[61] and a searching examination of the complexities of one of them,[62] as well as the beginning of a sophisticated structural analysis of judgements about desert.[63] There remain many moral views that have not received the structural analysis they deserve, but on others significant progress has been made.

In some cases this analysis will contribute significantly to assessing the views. Thus, it may be that while one of two competing views resists structural analysis, because it contains ineliminably contradictory elements, another can be beautifully unified by an attractive general principle. This result supports the second view against the first. But in other cases even complete analysis may leave us with difficult judgements to make. If each of two views can be successfully unified, the choice between them comes down to an overall intuitive assessment that we may find difficult to make and that different people may make differently. Here there may be neither intuitive certainty for one person nor agreement among persons. This may also be the result in the more likely case where each view can be unified to a considerable degree but not entirely, so there is a plausible general principle that captures many of the intuitive judgements associated with it but requires others to be abandoned. But this is just the situation we face if, as I have argued, there are no magic-bullet arguments in normative ethics and intuitive judgements of some kind are all we have to go on. We can play such judgements off against each other, including judgements at different levels of generality. If we think some judgements are more likely to be distorted we can give them less weight, though if we do the correction will always come from other intuitive judgements. And if we think some judgements are especially reliable, we can place more trust in them. This methodology leaves philosophical analysis only some comparatively modest tasks: to clarify the issues our judgements must address and to help us understand the views that resolve them differently. But those are not insignificant tasks; on the contrary, and unlike the high flights of foundational analysis, they can actually yield results.

The main themes of this essay were anticipated by Friedrich Nietzsche. In *Beyond Good and Evil* he urged moral philosophers to own up

---

[59] Michael Slote, *Common-Sense Morality and Consequentialism* (London: Routledge & Kegan Paul, 1985), ch. 3; and *Beyond Optimizing: A Study of Rational Choice* (Cambridge, MA: Harvard University Press, 1989), chs. 1–2.

[60] Liam B. Murphy, *Moral Demands in Nonideal Theory* (New York: Oxford University Press, 2000); Brad Hooker, *Ideal Code/Real World* (Oxford: Clarendon Press, 2000).

[61] Parfit, "Equality or Priority?"   [62] Temkin, *Inequality*.   [63] Kagan, "Equality and Desert".

to what alone is justified so far: to collect material, to conceptualize and arrange a vast realm of subtle feelings of value and differences of value which are alive, grow, beget and perish . . . all to prepare a *typology* of morals.

To be sure, so far no one has been so modest. With a stiff seriousness that inspires laughter, all our philosophers demanded something far more exalted, presumptuous, and solemn from themselves as soon as they approached the study of morality: they wanted to supply a *rational foundation* for morality—and every philosopher so far has believed that he has provided such a foundation. . . . How remote from their clumsy pride was that task which they considered insignificant and left in dust and must—the task of description—although the subtlest fingers and senses can scarcely be subtle enough for it.[64]

Subtle fingers and senses, yes: normative ethics will do best if it does more of the work Nietzsche recommends and less of the kind that would have him rolling on the floor.

[64] Friedrich Nietzsche, *Beyond Good and Evil*, trans. Walter Kaufmann (New York: Vintage, 1966), sec. 186.

II

Toward an Ethics that Inhabits the World

PETER RAILTON

Looking Backward—An Introduction

The real world seems a long way from our moral ideals, and the challenge of making the world a better place is, of course, of the first importance. However, this should not be thought of as the only way in which reality and morality ought to be brought closer to each other. For surely our moral thinking has much to learn from the real world. Moral ideals would be arbitrary, perhaps even dangerous, if they owed nothing to a firm grasp of actual life and its possibilities. Indeed, the century just past—perhaps even the millennium just past—may hold as many tragedies born from fantasies of purity, virtue, or morality as from outright malice or shrewd self-interest. As Hobbes commented centuries ago, people mistaking their moral or religious "enthusiasms" for reality may cause more mischief than those better attuned to the actual world and their own interests in it.[1] Certainly, when it comes to mundane, daily questions of how to act or feel, convincing answers will never be found if we resort to formulae or rules with no resonance in actual human psychology, society, or history.

Setting the question of realism to the side for a moment, no one would dispute that twentieth-century philosophy has provided great insight into moral ideas, and has impressively articulated moral theory. On the side of *normative moral theory*—the attempt to give a coherent account of the structure and basic principles underlying actual moral judgments—utilitarianism and rational choice theory were greatly developed, while at the same time a serious alternative approach emerged in the contractarianism of John Rawls[2]. In general, the distinction between consequentialist and deontological approaches was clarified, and discussion of a possible third approach, virtue theory, was revived. And on the side of *meta-ethics*—higher-order theorizing about the nature and status of morality—twentieth-century ethical thought confronted questions of language, mind, and metaphysics to an extent quite unprecedented in nineteenth-century ethics. From Moore's influential *Principia Ethica* in 1903 right up to the final moments of the century, moral philosophers never ceased for long struggling with questions about the meaning or potential objectivity of moral claims.[3] As a result, the landscape of possible positions

---

[1] For discussion, see Albert O. Hirschman, *The Passions and the Interests: Political Arguments for Capitalism Before Its Triumph* (Princeton: Princeton University Press, 1977) esp. Pt. I.

[2] Rawls's seminal work is *A Theory of Justice* (Cambridge, Mass.: Harvard University Press, 1971).

[3] G. E. Moore, *Principia Ethica* (Cambridge: Cambridge University Press, 1903). For an idea of the continuing vitality of Moore's thought, see the Centenary Symposium in *Ethics*, 113 (2003): 465–677.

concerning the nature and status of morality, as well as the problems and prospects associated with these various positions, came to be mapped out with great care and insight. Disputes about *which* position to occupy did not go away. They persisted, even grew, as the century ended, providing yet more stimulus to the complex task of mapping the terrain. The result has been a quite substantial body of knowledge, and confusions that had inhibited the development of a coherent or defensible conception of ethics and its place in the world were removed piece by piece. Worries that moral concepts by their nature presupposed some extraordinary metaphysical domain of Moral Truth, or the existence of a Divine Order, were mitigated.[4] A variety of interpretations of moral concepts promised to reconcile the unquestionably "subjective" dimension of morality with its "objective" purport, by suggesting how evidence and reasoning might be brought to bear in moral thought and judgment in a world without marvels.

All this might sound like progress enough for one century. But it also sounds like *preparatory* work, clearing theoretical obstacles or embarrassments away, to make possible a flourishing of substantive moral thought.

And now it must be said that in this respect many have felt a keen sense of disappointment with twentieth-century ethics—a prologue without a play. To be sure, substantive progress did take place in the domain of substantive morality. Social, political, and cultural movements—against colonialism, totalitarianism, and racism, and on behalf of social democracy, civil rights, gender equality, and the protection of animals and the environment—brought profound changes in moral thought and feeling that many would vigorously defend as genuine progress. However, this progress and its sources were at considerable remove from the often delicate philosophical debates concerning normative theory and meta-ethics. Perhaps the deliberations of philosophers have always been somewhat closeted, and perhaps

---

[4] The initial, fundamental work suggesting the moral issues could be discussed in non-religious, non-metaphysical terms was accomplished by giants of early modern philosophy: Hobbes, Locke, Hume, Rousseau, Kant, Bentham, and Mill. With Moore's *Principia Ethica* and W. D. Prichard's famous essay, "Does Moral Philosophy Rest Upon a Mistake?", *Mind*, 12 (1912): 21–37, a further advance was made. Traditional moral philosophy tended to run together questions of meaning and questions of substance. Moore persuaded the preponderance of moral philosophers that moral *concepts* are by their nature distinct from religious, metaphysical, or even psychological concepts. Moore's criterion, the "open question test", showed that even the writings of the great religious philosophers revealed that we could *understand* a question such as "Why is that which God commands necessarily good?", since they spent so much intellectual energy trying to answer it convincingly. Such effort would hardly have been expended if this question *meant* no more than "Why is that which is necessarily good necessarily good?" Moral philosophy therefore could participate in a division of intellectual labor, in which the *analysis* of distinctively moral concepts and forms of moral argument, was distinguished from *substantive* theorizing—whether scientific, metaphysical, or religious—about the way the world works and whether this does or does not permit moral concepts to have geniune application. Critics dismissed this "linguistic turn" as trivializing moral philosophy or making it into a word game. Instead, analytic moral philosophy proved remarkably fruitful. Even so, the analysis of moral meanings—difficult as that task is—still does not settle the question whether our moral thinking and practice is well-grounded or erroneous. J. L. Mackie has argued that our moral thought is massively in error, and must be replaced by something more practical (see his *Inventing Ethics* [London: Penguin, 1971]). As we will see below, many questions arise about whether human psychology and society could possibly fit the conditions of application for moral concepts.

specialization in academic disciplines inevitably heightens the theory–practice gap, but the case in twentieth-century analytic ethics looks noticeably extreme. If it is unclear what social benefits have arisen from high-level twentieth-century moral theory, it is perhaps equally unclear what philosophical benefits could remain from its continued relative isolation.

Normative moral theory strikes some observers as having become increasingly unrealistic, addicted to imaginary examples owing to an exaggerated sense of the need for systematicity; meanwhile, the meta-level preoccupations of analytic moral philosophy seem to have grown desperately removed from any questions of *practical* reason and to have pushed serious engagement with moral practice, or with actual psychology, politics, or history, to the periphery of the discipline. *Applied ethics* may be a flourishing industry, but in its most public manifestations it has tended to operate on its own, intellectually and institutionally fairly independent of "hard core" philosophical ethics, and the *moral psychology* found in philosophical ethics is often remarkably aprioristic and limited in its contact with empirical evidence.

Looking Forward—A Tension?

This harsh appraisal of the state of ethics, always something of a caricature, is becoming increasingly out of date as we enter a new century. How fully the successes of twentieth-century moral philosophy can be put to better use will depend upon how certain tensions within the current debates and dynamics of moral philosophy are dealt with. In this brief essay, I will focus on only one.[5]

The principal tension I have in mind can perhaps be described with the help of an alleged dualism. This dualism is hardly new. And one need not think—indeed, I do not—that this dualism is ultimate. It may be that the dualism itself calls for rejection, rather than choosing a side. But history attests that it is enormously difficult for disciplines to escape this dualism, or to avoid repeatedly falling back into it.

A social theorist of the turn of the twentieth century would be familiar with the dualism in the form of distinguishing *explanation* from *understanding*. A social theorist, the thinking went, might be concerned to explain a phenomenon, citing causes, general principles, quantitative evidence of actual behavior. Or, a social theorist might be concerned to understand the lived world of those participating in this phenomenon, seeking its meaning for them, recovering the "qualitative character" of their lived experience. The first sort of task is obedient to norms of empirical science: third-party objectivity, nomological principles, the construction of general theories—the *nomothetic ideal* of "causal adequacy". The explanation one gives might be unrecognizable to those immersed in the practice—e.g. a functional interpretation of religion, an economic interpretation of marriage practices, a Darwinian interpretation of sexual conduct. The second sort of task is obedient to norms of mutual comprehension: first-person perspective, interpretive principles

---

[5] Left out, therefore, will be many important trends and tensions. Among those are questions about gender and ethics, wide-ranging debates over the nature and relations of community, equality, rights, and liberalism, and the character of moral judgments and sentiments, among many others.

of charity and phenomenological coherence, an emphasis on particularity—the *interpretive or hermeneutic ideal* of "meaning adequacy". One's account should both make others *recognizable* as individuals, and be a rendering of their world that would in principle be recognizable *to* them. Scholars, according to this dualistic line of thought, face a clear choice of goal and method.

These days, moral philosophers often speak as though we face a similar choice. Ethics should either give up the outdated, quasi-Intuitionistic pretense of being a special non-natural domain, and become more integrated into the nomothetic sciences—"naturalized" in terms of a scientific psychology, evolutionary history, etc.—or it should turn away from such inappropriate "science-aping" ambitions, and try to work with—rather than reduce or replace—our moral concepts and the lived character of lived moral experience. Defenders of the first approach tend to reject the idea of the *autonomy* of moral philosophy, while defenders of the second approach tend to be skeptical of the idea of moral *theory*.

It sometimes looks as if contemporary moral philosophy is shaping up for a fight along just this line. Theory or anti-theory? Reductionist scientism or autonomist intuitionism? Naturalism or non-naturalism? Causes or reasons? Functions or meanings?

Nonetheless, it would be a shame to repeat a drama from which significant areas of social science have successfully extracted themselves (though not without continuing difficulty, and never completely). And it would in particular be a shame for moral philosophers to dichotomize reason and cause now that philosophy of mind has done so much to show their essential connections.[6] Let us take a calming breath and ask: How could any explanation of a human phenomenon be *causally adequate* if it failed to give us an account that accurately rendered the *lived experience* or *subjectivity* of those immersed in a practice?—such experience is surely among the primary data to be accounted for. And how could an understanding of human action be *meaning adequate* if it failed to locate those ideas, images, or motives that actually played a role in bringing about the behavior and its effects? We cannot impute "objective functions" without subjective mediation; but neither can we take the self-narration of agents as authoritative concerning the meanings of, or reasons for, their conduct. Once we acknowledge that, in creatures such as humans, meanings and self-understandings are active factors in organizing such elementary components of life as the perceptions they have, the choices they make, the social alliances they form, the conflicts they create, we may lose our taste for ejecting either constraints of causal genuineness or constraints of interpretive coherence from the practice of philosophical ethics.

[6] Once again, the fundamental work suggesting that normative, reason-based explanations of acts can be reconciled with empirical, causal explanations of actions was done in the early modern period of philosophy—at a time when psychology had yet to emerge as a distinct science. The behaviorist scientific psychologies of the middle decades of the twentieth century cast this reconciliation in doubt. But behaviorism collapsed of its own accord—proving unable to give empirically adequate explanations of a large range of human and animal phenomena. The re-emergence of *cognitive* psychology in the latter decades of the century coincided with a philosophical rebirth of the early modern idea that intentional, rational explanations could be analyzed in terms of such notions as causation by beliefs and desires. See Donald Davidson's highly influential essays "Actions, Reasons, and Causes" and "Mental Events" (reprinted in his collection *Essays on Actions and Events* [Oxford: Oxford University Press, 1980]).

Some Hopeful Signs

Can we hope, then, that ethics will escape a polemical dichotomizing? I see some hopeful signs.

Bernard Williams,[7] one of the most influential contributors to analytic moral philosophy in the late twentieth century, has become strongly associated with the "anti-theory" camp, and he writes that ethics should "remind us of detail rather than bludgeon us with theory":

[Contemporary moral philosophy] typically lacks an account of why the project of articulating moral *theories* makes any sense at all. As many writers have pointed out, it bears little relation to the psychology of people's ethical lives, and inasmuch as it claims that turning morality into a theory makes it more rational, there is a pressing question of what concept of rationality is being invoked. To a limited extent, there may be an answer to that question, inasmuch as some ethical questions, such as those raised by medical ethics, are public questions, closely tied to politics and the law. . . . [But] many important ethical issues are not of this kind at all. Morality has always been connected not only with law and politics, but also with the meaning of an individual's life and his or her relations to other people. In these connections, the authority of theory over moral life remains quite opaque.[8]

Williams asks that ethics be more open to the role of literature and the imagination in moral philosophy, not because these are instrumental, "convenient sources of psychological information", but because:

. . . imaginative writing can powerfully evoke the strength of ethical considerations in giving sense to someone's life or to a passage of it, and, equally, present the possible complexity, ambivalence and ultimate insecurity of those considerations.[9]

So, does Williams conclude that good ethics should abandon theoretical ambitions and turn to literature and phenomenology, at least insofar as it deals with personal life rather than public policy?

There is another strand in his remarks. He begins his essay expressing a hope that philosophy can get beyond the twentieth-century *Kulturkampf* of "analytic" vs. "continental" philosophy, and that the *methods* of analytic philosophy can be divorced from a proprietary, artificially-narrowed conception of the proper goals or domain of philosophy, and put in the service of a more adequate general conception of the goal of understanding ethics and its place in human life—truer to "the psychology of people's actual lives", as he put it. Moreover, to advocate the role of literature in moral thought may be to take seriously the imagination, rather than encourage us in the direction of the imaginary. Again, the key for Williams seems to be a kind of *fidelity* to real life:

Good literature stands against the isolation of moral considerations from the psychological and social forces that both empower and threaten them. . . . [The] isolation of moral

---

[7] This essay was written before his death in 2003.
[8] Bernard Williams, "Contemporary Philosophy: A Second Look", in N. Bunnin and E. P. Tsui-James (eds.), *The Blackwell Companion to Philosophy* (Oxford: Blackwell, 1996), 36.   [9] Ibid., 37.

considerations from the rest of experience is an illusion very much fostered by moral philosophy itself; indeed, without that illusion some forms of moral philosophy could not exist at all.[10]

The methodological scruples of analytic philosophy can be put to good use, according to Williams, to the extent that they encourage us toward "argumentative accuracy" and "unfanatical truthfulness"[11]—valid reasoning in accord with norms capable of some objective vindication, straining toward conclusions that would stand the scrutiny of evidence beyond self-satisfaction.

Williams thus embraces considerations that would appear to favor, in the name of faithfulness to "the psychology of people's actual lives", a closer integration of our best philosophical methods—analytic *and* phenomenological—with the evidence and empirical discipline of natural and social science. How could we, as philosophers, offer a "theory of rational action" or "theory of moral perception" intended to be adequate for *understanding* actual life that took no account of the best-developed empirical *explanations* of human motivation, cognition, and perception? It is all very well for a philosopher to say, with assurance, that "our concept of a free act is such-and-such"; it is quite another thing to say, with equal assurance, that this sort of act *actually* has a central role in human moral life. The latter claim is a claim about—among other things—*what causes what*, and concepts alone lack the authority to decide such matters. Conceptual necessity does not dictate any actual sequence of events.

Morality in the World

Indeed, a proper understanding of our moral concepts may enable us to strengthen this claim on behalf of integrating explanation with understanding. At least since Moore, it has been recognized that moral judgments *supervene* on non-moral facts in at least the following sense: two situations cannot be identical in all their non-moral characteristics and yet merit different moral evaluations. Consider a simpler example. The *average weight in a population* can be changed by adding or subtracting individual members, or by changing individual weights. What we cannot do is to change the population average simply by altering "average weight" of the population, without affecting any individuals. Someone would display failure to master the concept of "average weight" if he thought he could save the time and trouble of changing any individual members by changing the population average directly. Similarly, someone would display failure to master the concept of "morally wrong" if, after deciding that breaking a contract without compensation would be morally wrong, he thought he could save time and money by adding moral rightness to the act directly, without changing it in any other respect. Moral concepts are not a world unto themselves, but are linked by their very nature to what transpires in life more widely. Because the link belongs to moral concepts rather to any particular substantive moral theory, it is a priori, and should be a point of convergence rather than contention for "naturalist" and "non-naturalist" approaches to ethics.

[10] Bernard Williams, "Contemporary Philosophy", 37.   [11] Ibid.

Let us call this point of convergence *compatibilism*, borrowing a term from debates over free will and determinism. Compatibilists believe that free will does not require human exemption from the causal order—if we act freely, we do so via causal processes of the usual sort. Similarly, the moral compatibilist believes that moral life does not require human exemption from the laws of nature—if we act rightly or wrongly, for the good or the bad, we do so *within* the natural world we inhabit as empirical beings. If we are to be compatibilists, then any account of the domain of moral thought and practice must be compatible with what we know of the domain of human psychology, biology, and circumstance upon which it supervenes. How might taking the idea of compatibilism seriously matter to the course of ethics in the next few years? Let us consider some examples, each as open-ended as the state of empirical science itself.

Virtue Theory and Psychological Realism

Dissatisfaction with the limited conception of moral action available to duty-based approaches to moral practice, and with the relative impoverishment of prevalent philosophical treatments of the role of emotion and motivation in moral thought, helped stimulate a revival of interest in virtue theories toward the end of twentieth century. Virtue theory had been influential in moral philosophy from ancient times into the early modern period, but it nonetheless suffered neglect in the twentieth century, partly because of incompletely-formulated doubts about whether such theories could really "add" anything to a proper account of moral obligation. It was felt that moral virtue either was a matter of *possessing* "non-cognitive" motivations or feelings not under conscientious voluntary control—"being brave", say—, and therefore outside the scope of a properly moral "ought", or it was a matter of *striving conscientiously toward* developing such valuable motivations or feelings or acting in accord with them—"trying to be brave" or "trying to act bravely", say—, in which case a theory of obligation could already incorporate it.

Critics, however, argued that such dismissive reactions to virtue theory drew upon an artificially dichotomized moral psychology, particularly in distinguishing between "cognitive" aspects (thought and perception) and "non-cognitive" aspects (motivation and feeling). Instead, it was claimed, moral conduct often flowed from an evaluatively-rich perception of situations, directly engaging feelings and motives that were themselves implicitly judgmental. *Moral disapproval* or *outrage*, say, were not a brute feelings of anger or dislike, but multi-layered emotional responses embodying representations of a situation as contrary to what is good or right, and thus *meriting* a certain response. Moreover, such responses structured perception of situations in ways that presented the agent with certain courses of action as *called for*. In this way, perception, cognition, feeling, and motivation could be integrated within a moral personality, though not by way of "dutifulness". Morally worthy conduct thus need not insert a notion of "obligation" or "moral law" between us and our acts, or between us and our friends or personal ties—rich emotions like love or friendship could enter figure directly in moral motivation. And the Aristotelian idea that ethics is properly an account of the conditions for leading a good life gained new plausibility.

Virtue theory owed some of its considerable appeal to the thought that it prom-ised a more realistic and "liveable" moral psychology than orthodox duty-based accounts of moral action, and seemed phenomenologically truer to the lived char-acter of personal relationships than "non-cognitivism". But can we accept a moral psychology as realistic or liveable or true-to-life without heeding what we know of actual human psychology? And here, the verdict on virtue has been mixed.

In the aftermath of behaviorism, cognitive psychology underwent an explosive development. Experiments revealed many ways in which "cognitive set" influenced perception, motivation, and feeling. Yet familiar ideas of virtue are more than accounts of moral perception. They also give a central role to the idea that virtues are long-lasting, dispositional "character traits" that yield a relatively consistent pat-tern of individual behavior across a broad range of circumstances. Honest or gener-ous individuals could be counted on to behave in consistently honest or brave ways, despite considerable variations in the circumstances they encountered. Those lack-ing such virtues could be expected to be less reliable.

Yet when personality psychologists set out to map and measure these character traits, they failed to come up with the patterns of intrapersonal cross-situational consistency and interpersonal characterological variation that virtue theory would lead one to expect. Individual behavior did show patterns that suggested relatively stable sets of underlying dispositions, but the dispositions seemed to be highly sensitive to relatively minor variations in the "mode of presentation" of otherwise similar circumstances. Some situations appeared to "cue" generous or honest behav-ior in the great majority of people, others to "cue" indifferent, compliant, ungener-ous, even devious behavior. The same individuals who displayed remarkable willingness to sacrifice or take on risk to help another in one kind of circumstance would display peremptory neglect of the suffering of another in a slightly varied circumstance. A picture began to emerge of humans as possessing fairly similar underlying behavioral repertoires, with situations possessing fairly uniform "cuing" effects on different elements of these repertoires, so that consistency owed more to context than "character".[12]

Philosophers have begun to notice this literature in cognitive social psychology, and to launch a corresponding critique of virtue theory.[13] Defenders of virtue theory have marshalled forces in response.[14] But a battle may prove unnecessary.

[12] For an overview, see Lee Ross and Richard Nisbett, *The Person and the Situation* (Philadelphia: Temple University Press, 1991), esp. ch. 4. Stabilities in personal character seemed to lie in other dimen-sions, e.g. introversion vs. extraversion positive vs. negative emotionality, etc.

[13] See Gilbert Harman, "Moral Philosophy Meets Social Psychology: Virtue Ethics and the Fundamental Attribution Error", *Proceedings of the Aristotelian Society* 99 (1999): 315–31 and John Doris, *Lack of Character: Personality and Moral Behavior* (Cambridge: Cambridge University Press, 2002).

[14] Some objections were already anticipated in Owen Flanagan, *Varieties of Moral Personality: Ethics and Psychological Realism* (Cambridge, MA: Harvard University Press, 1991) and Joel Kupperman, *Character* (Oxford: Oxford University Press, 1991). See also: Nafsika Athanassoulis, "A Response to Harman: Virtue Ethics and Character Traits", *Proceedings of the Aristotelian Society* 100 (2000): 215–21 and Harman's reply,

Virtue theorists have been vindicated, it seems, in many of their claims about the integrated character of human perception, cognition, affect, and motivation.[15] These insights can be put to good use not only giving a more "life like" account of the lived character of experience, but in improving our understanding of the various ways in which individuals can achieve more or less success in managing their responses to situational cues. This way of achieving greater behavioral consistency might differ in some causal details from classical virtue theory, but it might enable us to see moral training and development in similar ways, and to give a central role in moral life to "non-dutiful" considerations that cohere with a number of the themes of ancient ethics, and that might enable us to understand better how a moral existence could also be a humanly enjoyable life.

For example, a famous, early experiment on "deferred gratification" showed that children who deployed certain cognitive strategies were better able to accomplish the motivational task of deferring gratification in response to a tempting situation. They manifested a *skill* that integrated cognitive, emotional, and motivational elements. A long-term, longitudinal study showed that those possessing this skill showed greater success in many areas of school and life, and were more likely to avoid various kinds of moral and personal dysfunction.[16] Can such skills be acquired? Therapeutic work has shown the power of cognitive strategies, combined with training and experience, to help modulate emotions appropriately and give people greater control in their lives.[17] Aristotle did not think of courage as "ridding oneself of fear" or even of "toning fear down" and insulating oneself from its effects. Rather, he saw it as a skilled, intelligent ability to *use* fear in ways proportionate to actual risk—when confronting novel situations, to be able to marshal the experience and knowledge necessary to "fear the right things, for the right end, in the right way, at the right time", with appropriate effects on attention, perception, and action.[18] Making an excellent sea captain is less a matter of finding (or becoming) someone with "nerves of steel" than of training, education, and experience that enables someone of quite ordinary "nerve" to be better at identifying, assessing, anticipating, thinking through situations of risk, attuned by fear to real danger, but not distracted by fear into thoughtless responses.

Cognitive strategies and individual development clearly are not sufficient, however. Recognition that quite ordinary people can act virtuously must be coupled,

"The Nonexistence of Character Traits", *Proceedings of the Aristotelian Society* 100 (2000): 223–6. For a positive discussion of virtue ethics, see Rosalind Hursthouse, *On Virtue Ethics* (New York: Oxford University Press, 1999).

[15] For examples, see: Bernard Weiner (ed.), *Cognitive Views of Human Motivation* (New York: Academic Press, 1974) and R. S. Lazarus, "Cognition and Motivation in Emotion", *American Psychologist* 46 (1991): 352–67. For a general overview, see Daniel Goleman, *Emotional Intelligence* (New York: Bantam, 1995).

[16] Yuichi Shoda, Walter Mischel, and Philip K. Peake, "Predicting Adolescent Cognitive and Self-Regulatory Competencies from Preschool Delay of Gratification", *Developmental Psychology* 26 (1990): 978–86.

[17] For discussion, see R. E. McMullin, *Handbook of Cognitive Therapy Techniques* (New York: Norton, 1986). We would err in psychological realism, however, to ignore the role of the unconscious. See, e.g., Howard Shervin *et al.*, *Conscious and Unconscious Processes* (New York: Guilford, 1996).

[18] See *Nichomachean Ethics*, 1115b17–19.

regrettably, with recognition that ordinary people can also act viciously. The notorious, large-scale atrocities of the twentieth century were often carried out in large measure by ordinary, capable people, people of no special moral depravity. In the right circumstances—which is to say, the wrong circumstances—your charming neighbor who loves her cat and raises roses, or the dedicated sports coach at the local high school, or the respectable banker whom you've trusted for years with your deposits, . . . all these "good people" can become agents of, or active collaborators with, regimes of ruthless dislocation, organized cruelty, even systematic disappearance and murder. If we are not to live in bad faith with history, we all need to face the uncomfortable truth that this generalization applies even to ourselves. Those who failed to carry out these horrifying schemes were often moved more by what they felt to be weakness or squeamishness than by reflection on moral principle, while those who more actively resisted authorities, protected victims, or joined resistance organizations typically drew upon sources of peer, community, or religious support and recognition. The social and institutional setting in which individuals acted seems to have played the central role in either inhibiting or encouraging tragic forms of social exclusion, collaboration, and violence.[19]

Philosophical ethics may have taken a turn toward notions of individual character and moral particularism, yet these notions seem deeply inadequate to helping us understand, let alone help with, some of the greatest moral trauma and challenges of modern society. Whether the issue is averting spiraling social violence, or building communities capable of supporting cooperation and mutual aid in pluralistic or multi-ethnic settings, or encouraging suitable conduct across social boundaries, modern moral thought needs to take to heart what sociologists, anthropologists, and psychologists can tell us about the *contexts* that encourage ordinary humans to behave humanely or inhumanely toward others. The very same facts that seem so threatening to essentially "characterological" approaches to morality can also provide the grounds for "contextualist" and "interactionist" approaches.

Contextualism is not a newcomer to ethics. Ancient Greek moral philosophy treated actual participation in properly-structured communities and relationships—not merely a notional presence in an imagined Kingdom of Ends—as essential to the moral development of individuals. Moreover, cross-cultural or comparative ethics

---

[19] The literature on the Holocaust is, of course, central to these remarks. Recent debates have paid special attention to the social contexts in which Jews and others were protected or actively persecuted by local populations. See Jan T. Gross, *Neighbors: The Destruction of the Jewish Community in Jedwabne, Poland* (Princeton: Princeton University Press, 2001); Tzvetan Todorov, *The Fragility of Goodness: Why Bulgaria's Jews Survived the Holocaust*, trans. A. Denner (Princeton: Princeton University Press, 2001); Helen Fein, *Accounting for Genocide: National Responses to Jewish Victimization during the Holocaust* (New York: Free Press, 1979); Christopher Browning, *Ordinary Men: Reserve Police Battalion 101 and the Final Solution in Poland* (New York: HarperCollins, 1992). See also the experimental literature, in which the Milgram and Zimbardo Stanford Prison experiments are among the most infamous examples. See Stanley Milgram, *Obedience to Authority* (New York: Harper & Row, 1974) and P. G. Zimbardo, "The Psychological Power and Pathology of Imprisonment", in O. Milton and R. G. Wahler (eds.), *Behavior Disorders: Perspectives and Trends* (Philadelphia: Lippincott, 1973); and T. Blass (ed.), *Obedience to Authority: Current Perspectives on the Milgram Paradigm* (Mahwah, NJ: Erlbaum, 2000). For an overview of relevant historical and psychological research, see Roy F. Baumeister, *Evil: Inside Human Violence and Cruelty* (New York: W. H. Freeman, 1997).

suggests that in the Buddhist and Confucian strands of Chinese moral tradition alike, prominence is given to the role of context in shaping response, and, therefore, a central moral task becomes shaping or selecting the kinds of social settings we will inhabit or create.

More recently, social psychologists and educators concerned with the special problems of social exclusion and prejudice found in multicultural societies have compared the effects on attitudes, behaviors, and success of conditions that repeatedly call for competition and self-reliance, versus conditions that repeatedly call for mutual-dependence, joint activity. The former conditions tend to augment rather than reduce attitudes of exclusion and mutual distrust, and to increase underperformance by non-dominant groups; the latter tend to reduce exclusivity and distrust, while diminishing performance differentials.[20] Are the latter sorts of conditions "manipulative" or "artifical" in a way the former are not? Humans appear to have a range of responses equipping them for situations of group dependence and joint tasks as well as a range of responses equipping them for competition and dominance— is either one more "natural"? And is it objectionably "anti-individualistic" to seek to bring about social practices or structures in which individuals are less likely to regard others *or even themselves* in ethnic-identifying or stigmatizing ways?

Here, then, is a first hope: that those inspired by the great Aristotelian tradition in ethics, and those inspired by, or participating in, the exciting trajectory of contemporary psychology, will see each other as natural allies rather than rivals. No one in the history of ethics has taken the anatomy of the *psyche*, the nature of the *organism*, or the role of social context in constituting individual excellence more seriously than Aristotle himself—author not only of works on ethics, but on biology, the soul, and politics. To be sure, no single person today can, as Aristotle did, bring together mastery of the state of knowledge in ethics and psychology. Perhaps, then, a Neo-Aristotelian Community of philosophers and psychologists might emerge, capable of promoting a better understanding of the interplay of cognition, motivation, affect, and circumstance in creating the conditions for human lives both good and morally good.

To this pious hope, I would join another: that the understanding of social context be extended to embrace a genuinely *comparative* approach. It is easy, practicing philosophy and social psychology in the dominant academic circles of the contemporary world, to imagine that one is speaking with pure generality about "the human mind" or "emotion" or "intuitive moral judgment" when in fact one has under one's eyes only a fraction of the world's population and history. A wider perspective might reveal both deep variation in some dimensions, and surprising similarities in others. How could we know without further study? And how can we as theorists fully understand or evaluate *our own* responses if we cannot see how or why they might themselves be contextually-dependent?[21]

---

[20] See Rupert Brown, *Prejudice: Its Social Psychology* (Oxford: Blackwell, 1995); U. Neisser, *et al.*, "Intelligence: Knowns and Unknowns", *American Psychologist* 51 (1996): 77–101; and Claude Steele, "A Threat in the Air: How Stereotypes Shape Intellectual Identity and Performance", *American Psychologist* 52 (1997): 613–29.

[21] One important comparative dimension is clearly cross-cultural. For some examples, see J. W. Berry *et al.*, *Cross-Cultural Psychology: Research and Applications* (Cambridge: Cambridge University Press, 1992)

Reason and Imagination

What does it take to get someone to listen to reason? Consider someone engaged in a risky activity—smoking, drug-taking, roller-blading without a helmet, excessive dieting, etc. We might give such a person good arguments and good evidence. And such a person might be excellent at logic, and under no illusions about the reliability of the relevant statistics. Yet these might not alter behavior without enlisting the help of the imagination, which might—in response, say, to the suffering of an acquaintance, or a vivid portrayal in fiction or film—furnish the individual with a personal sense of "what it would really be like" to suffer the associated disabilities. Is this imagined experience, if accurate, a less "objective" way of understanding the risk than he or she had beforehand? In one sense, yes—it presents the disability from the perspective of an individual living with it; in another sense, no—it is *relevant*, *true-to-life*, and (unlike the statistical evidence) *equilibrated* with current, experience of the costs of quitting the risky activity. It permits one to juxtapose experience *now* with experience *then*, rather than experience *now* with non-experiential evidence concerning *then*.

A contemporary cognitive scientist might say that the individual now is a "better simulator" of the risks he or she is courting. And better simulations are just the sort of thing that competent decision-making needs, whether one is modeling climate change or life changes. In deciding about a risky activity, one is considering a decision to which the relative character of lived experience is immediately relevant, and we should be suspicious of any epistemic disqualification of "merely subjective" evidence. Vivid, personal imaging may be a poor guide when it is *unrepresentative*, but merely statistical evidence is by its nature *unrepresentative* of the felt quality of experience.[22] Experiential simulation thus may have more than a "heuristic" function. When, as often is the case, we need to have a good, representative sense of "What it would be like" were we to make a certain choice, we need an answer part of which is in the form "It would be like *this*", where a bit of experience is the object.

and Joel Marks and Roger Ames (eds.), *Emotions in Asian Thought: A Dialogue in Comparative Philosophy* (Albany: State University of New York Press, 1995). Another important comparative dimension is historical. See, e.g., the discussion of ancient notions of happiness or emotion in Julia Anna's *The Morality of Happiness* (New York: Oxford University Press, 1993), J. C. B. Gosling and C. C. W. Taylor, *The Greeks on Pleasure* (Oxford: Clarenon Press, 1982), and J. M. Cooper, *Reason and Emotion: Essays on Ancient Moral Psychology and Ethical Theory* (Princeton: Princeton University Press, 1999), or the discussion of love and pain in Georges Duby, *Love and Marriage in the Middle Ages*, trans. by Jane Dunnett (Chicago: University of Chicago Press, 1988). Recent revival of interest in evolutionary approaches to moral psychology also provide an avenue of understanding that crosses social or historical boundaries, see for example Jerome Barkow, Leda Cosmides, and John Tooby (eds.), *The Adapted Mind: Evolutionary Psychology and the Generation of Culture* (New York: Oxford University Press, 1992).

[22] Must the representations of the imagination be imagistic, i.e. non-propositional? Talk of conveying "what it's like" may suggest this, though some philosophers would contend that propositional representations may accomplish this. In any event, the point being made here about the imagination is independent of whether it is imagistic. What matters is that familiar forms of third-personal quantitative information, whatever their virtues, are not sufficient to represent first-personal "what it would be like"-ness.

Deliberative simulation appears to redeploy our own, current experiential capacities as a "test bed" for running hypothetical scenarios.[23] This sort of thing we commonly call "imagining", and we can see how an anemic imagination will yield unrepresentative results, just as weak or erratic senses will yield unrepresentative perceptions. If you like, imagination is part of an extended but essential sort of "perception" or perceptiveness. The imagination helps us *envisage*—and not merely verbally describe—now-absent, but real or potentially real, situations. We cannot see the future or the distant past, the path not taken or the internal life of another. This could pose an enormous obstacle to balanced deliberation, for it tends to favor the short-term and personal over the long-term and impersonal. More generally, it tends to favor the actual, "the way things are", over the possible, "the way things might be". Imagination can help correct this imbalance and add perspective and objectivity to our thought and action—*if* it is both sufficiently rich and sufficiently inventive.

Perception itself is rich in part because it is so much more than a passive registration of impressions. Instead, it is an active, cognitively and affectively rich mental activity that mobilizes stereotypes, ideas, expectations, narrative proto-forms, and emotions to yield structured and meaningful experience from the flux of sensation. To richly "envisage" absent possibilities or the future, and help balance active perception, we must draw upon all these cognitive and affective capacities, and more.

Proper attunement to prudential considerations, including the mobilization of effective prudential motivation—not just "I wish I could quit smoking" but "I *want* to stop smoking" (and will be actively frustrated and angry with myself if I can't)— appears from psychological observation and research to draw directly upon this capacity to "envisage" or "think through" absent outcomes and feelings by empathetically simulating one's own possible future self.[24] Proper attunement to moral considerations, including effective moral motivation—not just "I wish I could help" but "I *want* to help"—has similarly come to be seen by psychologists as deploying empathetic simulation of the states of others more than abstract principles.[25] Pioneers in understanding this phenomenon were David Hume and Adam Smith, who attempted to explain the possibility of moral knowledge and corresponding motivation via a mechanism they called "sympathy", in which each of us internally reflects and models the condition of others—by a complex process of resonance and

---

[23] Recent work in neurophysiology suggests the literalness of this claim. See V. Gallese and A. Goldman, "Mirror Neurons and the Simulation Theory of Mind-Reading", *Trends in Cognitive Science* 2 (1998): 493–501 and P. Ruby and J. Decety, "Effect of Subjective Perspective Taking During Simulation of Action: A PET Investigation of Agency", *Nature Neuroscience* 4 (2001): 546–50.

[24] See P. Ruby and J. Decety, "Effect of Subjective Perspective Taking"; E. Phelps, *et al.*, "Activation of the Left Amygdala to a Cognitive Representation of Fear", *Nature Neuroscience* 4 (2001): 437–41; and J. E. LeDoux, *The Emotional Brain* (New York: Simon & Schuster, 1996).

[25] Literature on simulation of states of others: Martin Hoffman, "Empathy, Social Cognition, and Moral Action", in W. Kurtines and J. Gerwitz (eds.), *Moral Behavior and Development: Advances in Theory, Research, and Applications* (New York: John Wiley, 1984); Alvin I. Goldman, "Empathy, Mind, and Morals", in M. Davies and T. Stone (eds.), *Mental Simulation* (Oxford: Blackwell, 1995); and Robert M. Gordon, "Sympathy, Simulation, and the Impartial Spectator", in L. May, M. Friedman, and A. Clark (eds.), *Mind and Morals: Essays on Ethics and Cognitive Science* (Cambridge, MA: MIT Press, 1996).

278   Peter Railton

internal emulation, rather than via a moral or strategic judgment.[26] It would come as no surprise to Hume or to Smith that Polish police officers were less likely to follow Nazi SS orders to shoot prisoners when they found themselves confronting their terror-stricken victim personally, and that they explained their reluctance in terms of revulsion and fear rather than principled deliberation.[27]

Inhibitions against killing when another is in utter subjugation seem more reliably ensconced in animals than humans, perhaps because humans have a greater capacity to inhibit simulation by cognitive or emotional stereotypes, ideas, and principles. This capacity for idea-saturated thought makes humans more liable to certain kinds of horrifying cruelty, but it also equips them to simulate effectively creatures as intricate as themselves across a wide range of actual or imagined circumstances, for this requires an idea-rich and associatively-articulate imaginative capacity. A wolf might be less likely to kill another wolf in a position of submission than a human, but wolves cannot as yet represent to themselves the prospect of long-term extinction of their own species, or that of other species. Furnishing life-like representations of remote, inferred eventualities belongs in part to the imagination, as classically conceived. Hard-nosed empiricists like Hume felt no embarrassment about giving a large role to the imagination in epistemology, and the skepticism he voiced against Reason as a foundation for morals or science was meant in part to highlight the assistance Reason needed from the imagination, and the feelings and expectations imagination helped to generate.

The imagination serves action and deliberation not only by helping us to weigh alternatives and feel their force; it helps us enlarge and elaborate the range itself. Experience, rich as it is, does not typically wear its alternatives on its sleeve. On the contrary, it tends to encourage a settling of the mind into a view of what is, and always will be, the *normal* course of events—the "natural". Yet to be prudent or moral I must do more than project the familiar and actual—I need to represent to myself an appropriate range of the unfamiliar but possible. Inference is essential here, by helping us explore the full content of what we currently suppose or imagine, but successful inference calls for imagination, too, even in the case of mathematical logic. A logician seeking to prove a new theorem cannot content herself with drawing the implications of a fixed set of premises simply by consistently applying a fixed strategy. She must be able to think flexibly and intelligently about

---

[26] Hume and Smith may not always have distinguished sympathy from empathy. *Empathy*, as the term has come to be used, is a matter of fairly direct modeling of the internal states of others, thanks to a kind of redeployment of one's own psychic substructure. Empathy thus figures as much in competition or combat with others as with cooperation and caring, since it enables one more accurately to attribute internal states to others, even when these states are at odds with what one deems oneself as the right way of looking at things. (Psychology studies this phenomenon in "tasks" like a child's accurate attribution of beliefs to others that they themselves deem false.) An act I feel entirely justified in undertaking might nonetheless stir indignant rage in another, given his particular circumstances or perspective. If I am to conduct myself effectively toward this person, I had better not assume he agrees with me about the justifiability of my act. *Sympathy*, in the modern usage, involves a kind of "shared attitude" or "concern" for another, such that if I empathetically model them, I wish to help.

[27] See Browning, *Ordinary Men*.

appropriate choices and mixtures of premises and proof strategy, keeping alternative courses of action and starting points open even as she works through the path she has chosen. Imagination is thus not opposed to the exercise of serious, theoretically-contrained reason—ideally, it is an active part of it.

Historically, many of the chief contributions of theoretical morality and moralizing to social and political practice have come at precisely this point—proposing and developing imaginatively alternatives *not* taken seriously in the range of "reasonable" possibilities entertained by their more practical and level-headed contemporaries. Political democracy, national identity, the rule of law, the existence of a benevolent supreme being or "moral order", the abolition of slavery, gender equality, ecological responsibility—these ideas took initial form as imaginative speculations at a time when they must have seemed the farthest thing from political or social reality. But thanks to the work of devoted moralizing and philosophizing speculators, these ideas attained forms sufficiently forceful that sufficiently many people felt a compelling desire to struggle to put them into practice. Most philosophical speculation and conceptual elaboration leaves few ripples in the wider world, one supposes, but tracing back some very important ripples typically reveals seminal contributions by individuals who resolutely refused to take existing circumstances and perceived political possibilities as their conceptual horizon, but who disciplined their imaginations enough to elaborate alternative pictures of how things might be that could recruit wider credibility and allegiance, and not always for the good.

Of course, most of the operation of well-developed imagination is very mundane and workaday. A fully-participating faculty of daily thought and action, it enables us to represent "in real time" what otherwise is not currently visible, but would be impossibly complex to reach or appreciate by inference and reasoning. It may for all I know be possible that creatures quite different from us accomplish the tasks of theoretical or practical deliberation without recourse to an imagination—but *we* appear to need it, day in, day out.

If rationality in the narrow sense is reasoning, rationality in the broad sense is an appropriate responsiveness to reasons. A personality psychologist, asked what advice he would give about how to deliberate in a personal decision concerning the future, such as a choice among job offers, replied, "Well, I'd begin by learning as much as I could about the jobs or places, simulate as best I could what it would be like to take either one, and then read my somatic markers." The "somatic markers" in question are positive and negative feelings, arising from emotions aroused by experience or its simulacrum—imagined work conditions, daily life, or futures, which excite (even at an unconsciousness level) responses with positive and negative "valence". Listing the conditions thus imagined would be next to impossible, and would in any case probably depend upon our capacity for the sort of mental rehearsal just described. Asking how they might interact, or weigh, seems equally to depend upon such a personal capacity, assisted by whatever facts or advice one might have access to ("I hate the thought of living in a city, but I haven't ever really done so, and I do seem to have enjoyed what time I spent in Seattle. And the people I know who've lived there seemed to love it.").

Failures of rationality help us diagnose its components. There is intriguing evidence in abnormal psychology that independently-detectable defects in one's capacity to simulate things from a changed perspective, or to link in one's mind cognitive aspects of one's deliberation to "somatic markers" (for example, in cases of brain damage), lead to systematic defects or difficulties in prudential or moral practice, even among factually-informed, intelligent individuals who show good ability to reason abstractly.[28]

If a well-developed imagination, actively engaged with one's capacities to feel as well as think, has a central importance in human rationality in the broad sense, this would enable us once again to see a possible domain of convergence between scientific and phenomenological camps in philosophy, as well as a kind of reconciliation of experiential and literary sources of evidence. Fictive accounts may be thought of as a kind of experiential source in themselves, affording access to "what the lived world is like" from other perspectives in much the same way that sensation affords access to "what the lived world is like" from one's own perspective. Of course, both literature and sensation can be convincing in ways that are not intrinsically tied to representational accuracy. For example, we tend to find certain "narrativizations" of experience compelling, whether this narration is supplied by other authors or by ourselves.[29] Counteracting such effects may have as much to do with broadening the imagined domain of possibilities as lengthening the direct exposure to actualities.

Only if we confuse the question "Is psychological theory itself expressed in terms of systematic, third-personal theories?" with the question "Do psychological theories vindicate only systematic, third-personal sources of evidence in efficacious practical deliberation?" will we be tempted to think that one must chose between an ethics that takes seriously the authority of scientific psychology and an ethics that takes seriously the authority of a well-worked imagination. After all, psychological research itself enables us to see the indispensable role of the imagination in both intuitive and reflective human decision-making, and the specific kinds of positive contribution it makes (as well as the specific kinds of costs its absence tends to create).

Human Nature and Open-Endedness

Nowhere is the need for imagination-aided-by-theory, or theory-aided-by-imagination, greater than in envisaging heretofore unrealized possibilities for our future, since science and medicine are continually enlarging the domain of possible

[28] See esp. Antonio Damasio, *Descartes' Error: Emotion, Reason, and the Human Brain* (New York: Putnam, 1994), and Simon Baron-Cohen, *Mindblindness: An Essay on Autism and Theory of Mind* (Cambridge, MA: MIT Press, 1995) and *Understanding Other Minds: Perspectives from Developmental Cognitive Neuroscience* (New York: Oxford University Press, 2000).

[29] The force, persistence, and even content of memories, for example, tend to be responsive to many factors that can vary independently of representational accuracy, including emotion, narrative structure, visualizability, suggestibility, and so on. Some recent research suggests that when memories are recalled, the neurological encoding of the memory itself is altered, so that what will be retrieved in subsequent recollections has physically changed. For an overview of a range of recent research on memory, see Daniel L. Schacter, *Searching for Memory: The Brain, the Mind, and the Past* (New York: Basic Books, 1996).

human intervention in what we still quaintly call "the course of nature" or "human nature".

I call these ways of talking "quaint", but it might be more straightforward to say that they are systematically misleading. For if we hope to think at all coherently about "the course of nature" or "human nature", we will have to encompass the fact that precisely the sort of causal efficacy often seen as human "meddling" or "tampering" is in reality part of the course of nature, and of human nature in particular. It is part of the course of nature, we would all agree, that beavers build dams—that is just "beaver nature". But in building their dams, beavers dramatically change the environment they inhabit. Moreover, they shape their own evolution—adaptations occur to the specific conditions created or fostered by beaver dams. Many organisms have dramatically reshaped the climate itself, and altered the course of evolutionary history in profound ways. Even the simplest sorts of organisms may have been responsible for the oxygen-rich atmosphere we inhabit today, and which some of them must find toxic and must adapt to evade.

The questions of modern medical technology or scientific investigation cannot seriously be posed in terms of what is "the course of nature" or "human nature", as opposed to "tampering". It is as much a part of human nature to devise and deploy novel, self-reshaping technologies as it is part of beaver nature to build dams. The emergence of settled agriculture appears, for example, to have affected not only human culture, but also human physiology and the world it inhabits. Marx famously took Ludwig Feuerbach to task for treating the cherry tree standing before his study window as a paradigmatic natural object. For the cherry tree he saw is a complex outcome of the domestication and hybridizing of wild cherry trees; the sweet, fleshy fruit that it is its nature to produce so abundantly is a spectacular success of human-directed selection. Agriculture, migration, emergent social formations, medicine . . . all have modified our environment and ourselves. The invention of corrective lenses has meant that near-sighted people like myself face reproductive odds indistinguishable from those with perfect sight. After generations, the result will likely be a gene pool in which tendencies toward myopia are increased. Corrective lenses are thus a rather slow-moving technique for modification of the human gene pool. Is this an impermissible meddling in the course of nature? Surely the plastic device sitting on my nose is not part of the order of nature. Or is it?

If it can result only in a muddle to appeal to the notion of respecting the course of nature in assessing the appropriateness of new technologies or practices, what of "human nature", that venerable touchstone of eighteenth-century Enlightenment thought? Suppose someone argues against gender equality as "contrary to human nature". As things stand with the nature of humans, a marked sexual dimorphism is encoded in the genes, and gender differences have been observed in all known societies. But not always the same gender differences. And even the physical differences between the sexes have evolved in response to past human practices. Changing gender norms, gene therapy, reproductive innovations, changing child-rearing practices or family forms—how can we say that any of these is *fundamentally* different from what has gone before, or takes us outside the realm of moral possibility? And can ethics pretend that some choices are out of our hands when, in fact, they are not? Or pretend that human nature imposes known ultimate limitations—rather than knowable, but potentially revisable, proximate constraints—on what possibilities we may meaningfully consider when? If ethical thought cannot help us in the face of such lack of closure to ultimate questions about human nature, what can? To elect to exclude them, accepting the present *status quo* as the end of the matter, is but a particular way of answering them. Would ethics advise that?

Think first *backwards* rather than forwards in time. Consider any of the horrible diseases, pestilences, or conditions that in the past have been lamented as "inevitable", but with which we no longer live, at least in the developed societies. "Good riddance", we say, contemplating a previous world in which infection and infectious disease took a toll on so many families, and hung as a threat over the heads of all. What sort of question have we in effect answered when we say this? Presumably, we take what we know of the past, and imagine it continuing today. This imagining has a statistical and a phenomenological aspect. We should not, presumably, imagine continued, high infant mortality rates attended by the feelings that *as things now are* typically would accompany the loss in youth of one's brother or sister, or one's child, to a simple infection or infectious disease. For present-day feelings exist in an environment in which such losses are extremely rare. So I must try to imagine life for those to whom such losses were "part of the course of nature", not atypical for a large family. For this I may need recourse to imagination, literature, memoires, or recollections, not to statistics alone.

I would also need a good imagination, for the shape of the question I ask is, "What would life be like for someone whose experience of loss could be expected to be different from mine?" That is, "Would I prefer the life I would have *were I that sort of person, living in that sort of world* over the life I now have, as the sort of person I am, living in the kind of world I inhabit?" If we think any such questions are simply imponderable, then we must also think that questions like, "Is it a good thing, overall, that infant mortality from infection and infectious disease has been dramatically cut?" do not have any serious answer. But I suspect all of us think that they do. Whatever uncertainties attend questions of this shape, it hardly seems right to say that they make no sense.

To be sure, when we contemplate an unprecedented change in the basic facts or possibilities of life, brought on by (say) medical or technological innovation, we face a still more open-ended question. There are no memoirs to read, no recollections to be had. However, there also is no memoir of *my* future, and yet I must make choices that affect not only how I will live, but what *sort of person* I will be in living that life. A young person contemplating choices about education, marriage, children, or career, must be able to deliberate open-endedly. The 20-year-old must try to imagine herself *as she would be* were she to elect one or another different path in life, even given the unprecedented (for her) character of that life. Similar questions confront someone deciding to leave a relatively stable but impoverished existence to emigrate to a new country and culture, or asking whether to enter the military, or a religious order. Such questions are in many respects imponderable—precise weights cannot be assigned, and one can at best triangulate imaginatively from what one knows of oneself, of others, of what seems to be changing or fixed in the world at large, and so on. But we certainly act as if there were such a thing as considering such questions more or less thoughtfully, gathering relevant information or experience, being "too young" to make them, or "about ready to start" making them, learning from others about them, and so on.

Prudence and ethics, then, have long been in the business of asking open-ended questions about what life would be like, not for ourselves as we now are, but for those who would live this life—whether ourselves or others. Baldly intuitive reactions to the possibilities before us are likely to reflect strongly our current selves and attitudes, or prevalent social norms and expectations; a more considered deliberation would call for supplementation by an enlarged domain of information and experience, including general principles, and historical and cross-cultural depth.

An adequate conception of prudence or ethics should help us understand the nature of such reflective thinking, and the conditions under which it is most (or least) credible—and how we should in consequence shape what we do. To insist that values are irredeemably plural and incomparable, that particular past personal or community relations should always take precedence over general, abstract principles, or that we should give greater weight to our "first-order moral intuitions" undermines such reflection. Yet, as Aristotle himself emphasized, choice by its nature submits our thinking to the discipline that some options must be rejected and others embraced, that is, we must act. Whether we like it or not, choice forces us to consider quite different values, relations, and possibilities within a single action-guiding assessment—where trade-offs will have to be made, crystallized in the choices we make vs. the futures we deliberately forgo.

To be sure, intuition must play a role. Even the most complex and rigorous decision-making procedures will guide our deliberative lives only if we attribute some authority to them. And this deference to certain methods of analyzing or evaluating decisions in making actual choices cannot itself, without regress or circularity, be the outcome of these selfsame procedures. But intuition is not a self-contained faculty of privileged moral insight, nor is it unrevisable. Indeed, we can see how it evolves in the face of experience, knowledge, imaginativeness, and care.

Even critics of theory typically make a place for general principles, criteria of rational choice, and schemes of impersonal assessment and commensuration when it comes to matters of "politics and the law", as Williams does in the passage cited above. How could we possibly say what sort of tax scheme is fair and adequate, or what blend of incentive and environmental control is economically sustainable, or what level of immigration is appropriate, without attempting complex calculations of benefits and costs, involving trade-offs of the most diverse sorts of goods? Williams notes as well that questions of "medical ethics" may also require this sort of "theoretical" treatment within ethics.

If we ask what most pressing and controversial moral questions we are likely to face in the coming years, and where common-sense moral thought may need the greatest assistance if it is to be credible, our list is bound to be taken up very largely with questions of social and global distributive justice, intergenerational fairness, the conditions for stable peace and democratic institutions in the face of political and ethnic conflicts, environmental quality, and the development and deployment of medicine, science, and technology. The task of developing adequate means for tackling such "theoretical" issues is nonetheless eminently a case of *practical* reasoning—action will be called for, decision will be inescapable. We as philosophers will do no service to a world that must find its way through these complex issues if we can offer only an appreciation of value in all its quite real diversities, incommensurabilities, and uniquenesses. We must ourselves assist decision by being decisive—working to elaborate sufficiently definite approaches to decision-making to guide actual practice, to take most seriously what deserves to be taken most seriously.

The philosophical "critique of theory" at the turn of the twentieth century has been a salutary counter-weight to the impractically-abstract and psychologically- and historically-underinformed trends in ethical theory that went before. Let us hope that it helps create the climate for a more sober, sophisticated, and realistic flourishing of ethical theory—ethical theories that better inhabit the world, so that we ourselves might better inhabit that world.

12
Projection and Objectification

Rae Langton

1. Autonomy and Projection in Feminist Philosophy

It is hard to say anything uncontroversial about present feminist work in philosophy, let alone about prospects for the future. All the same, I shall begin by picking up two ideas, and saying something about why they have mattered, and will continue to matter. They are the ideas of *autonomy* and of *projection*. These two have mattered to different camps within feminist philosophy, camps that have sometimes disagreed in ways that roughly, though not exactly, mirror an older division between analytic and continental philosophers. I shall be wanting to see how the two ideas unite in a phenomenon of wider interest: that of sexual objectification.

Pioneer feminists viewed women's oppression in terms of women's autonomy and its thwarting, and this concern has remained central to the work of many liberal feminists, and those working in analytic philosophy. On this view, the basic problem has been that women have been cast in the role of human tools, as Aristotle described slaves: women have been treated as beings whose nature is to be directed by another, and whose purpose is instrumental; women have been treated as lacking in autonomy, and have had their autonomy systematically violated or stifled. This links the idea of oppression with that of objectification: when women are treated as tools, they are treated as things, items lacking in agency. Feminists tend in general to have few warm words for Kant, but these might find it in their hearts to concede he was on the right track when he said that 'autonomy is . . . the ground of the dignity of human nature, and of every rational nature'; and that we should therefore 'always treat humanity, whether in our own person or in the person of any other, never simply as a means, but always at the same time as an end.'[1] They may disagree about what, exactly, autonomy is, and how, exactly, it matters; but they agree that it matters. Martha Nussbaum, to take a recent example, offers an illuminating study of objectification that places autonomy-denial at centre-stage. Connected with autonomy-denial, through a variety of different entailments, are a cluster of other features: instrumentality; ownership or possession; fungibility, or replaceability; subjectivity-denial; violability; and denial of agency. I shall be drawing on her study in what follows.[2]

---

[1] Immanuel Kant, *Groundwork of the Metaphysics of Morals*, tr. H. J. Paton, in *The Moral Law* (London: Hutchinson University Library, 1948), 436, 429.

[2] Martha Nussbaum, 'Objectification', *Philosophy and Public Affairs* 24 (1995), 249–91. See also Barbara Herman, 'Could It Be Worth Thinking about Kant on Sex and Marriage?' in *A Mind Of One's Own:*

The second idea I want to pick up is the idea of projection implicit in certain feminist accounts of social construction. Women's oppression stems from the operation of large-scale psychological or linguistic forces, shaped by unconscious and irrational desires, or shaped by the structure of language itself, a 'language of the fathers'. While feminists in this camp are if anything less likely to find warm words for Kant, and would view with suspicion his pronouncements on autonomy and the dignity of human nature, they might find it in their hearts to concede he was on the right track when he said, on a different topic, that 'the order and regularity in the appearances, which we entitle nature, we ourselves introduce'—and when he showed an interest, not in how our cognitions conform to objects, but in how objects conform to our cognitions.[3] Taking this thought to the social world, they might ask how women conform to the cognitions or representations men have of them. They might add that Kant was mistaken in taking projective construction to be a product of reason, rather than irrational desire, mistaken in supposing it yields necessary constraints, and mistaken above all in his blindness to its political significance.

Those who draw on certain theories of language might speak in terms of the constructive power of certain concepts, or the projection of certain grammatical categories; in an extreme example, Luce Irigaray tries to convey the oppressive potency of grammar by proposing that 'I love to you' is an improvement on 'I love you', the latter after all making a direct 'object' of the loved one. Those who draw upon psychoanalysis (sometimes the same theorists) might speak in terms of the projection of unconscious desires.[4] Descartes's dualistic metaphysics, with its denigration of matter, gets interpreted as the projection of unconscious desires to reject one's mother, and insist on separation. Philosophy itself is put on the couch, interpreted as desire-driven belief which unconsciously expresses and perpetuates hostility to women, shaping thought about the world in general and women in particular. (Needless to say, a liberal focus on autonomy receives a similar projective and debunking explanation.) Distinctive features of this approach include the assumptions that belief is driven by desire; that desire-driven belief shapes and constructs the social world; and that the process is largely invisible to the participants. In this camp too one finds a link with a notion of objectification, understood rather

Feminist Essays on Reason and Objectivity, (eds.) Louise M. Antony and Charlotte Witt (Boulder, Colo.: Westview Press, 1993). For some alternative interpretations of autonomy, see, e.g., Relational Autonomy: Feminist Perspectives on Autonomy, Agency and the Social Self, (ed.) Catriona Mackenzie and Natalie Stoljar (Oxford: Oxford University Press, 2000).

[3] Immanuel Kant, Critique of Pure Reason, trans. Norman Kemp Smith (London and Basingstoke: Macmillan, 1980), A126 and Bxvi.

[4] Luce Irigaray proposes implausibly dramatic theses about linguistic and psychoanalytic projection in, e.g., I Love to You (London: Routledge, 1995); and Speculum of the Other Woman, trans. Gillian Gill (Ithaca: Cornell University Press, 1985), which puts Descartes and other philosophers on the couch. It is impossible to refer adequately to the vast literature here, but for another salient example see Jane Flax, 'Political Philosophy and the Patriarchal Unconscious', (eds). Sandra Harding and Merrill Hintikka, Discovering Reality (Dordrecht: Reidel, 1983). Genevieve Lloyd's The Man of Reason (University of Minnesota Press, 1984) is a classic study of the conceptual (though not particularly psychoanalytic) associations between women and matter in philosophy's history.

differently, drawing on grammatical notions of an object, or conceptual associations of women with matter.

Feminist thinkers in one camp sometimes get impatient with feminist thinkers in the other. One side finds the other's preoccupation with autonomy naive, a relic of oppressive, dualistic ways of thinking; finds naive her apparent focus on individual action, and local manifestation of prejudice; and finds naive her apparent neglect of the invisible forces of desire and language. The other in turn finds naive her sister's exaggeration of the power of desire and language; finds frustrating the poetic style which seeks an alternative to the language of the fathers, an authentic woman's voice which in practice thwarts communication; and finds naive her apparent neglect of norms, whether of reason or morality, by which a case for feminism can be argued. Moreover, the background assumptions of psychoanalytic feminism can look philosophically suspicious. The claim that belief is driven by desire, and that belief shapes and constructs the world—these appear to violate rules of direction of fit. Belief aims to fit the world; desire aims for the world to fit it. But the psychoanalytic story violates these rules: instead of belief coming to fit the world, belief comes to fit desire, and the world, somehow, comes to fit the belief.

It is not my aim to referee these disagreements here. Instead I want to look at the twin themes of autonomy and projection, each emphasized by one camp, neglected by another. I shall say something brief about their on-going importance, and consider, in conciliatory spirit, how they unite in an adequate understanding of sexual objectification. I shall be assuming, but not arguing, that each camp is at least partly right. Yes, autonomy does indeed matter. And yes, belief can indeed come to fit desire; the world can indeed come to fit belief; the process can indeed go on in ways invisible to the participants. I shall be interested in the implications of this projective process for autonomy, in sexual objectification.

Section 2 considers how projection might *help* sexual objectification through its generation of certain desire-driven beliefs. I distinguish a number of projective mechanisms, and explore how these projective mechanisms might assist in the treating of women as things.[5] Section 3 considers how projection might *hide* sexual objectification. I focus here on the epistemology of objectification, and how projection might help to mask itself, and the objectification it assists.

Unwise though it is to speculate, it seems unlikely that the importance of autonomy and projection will go away. One needs no crystal ball to guess that the forces of global capitalism will be around for a while, and with them a tendency to treat people not only as consumers but as commodities, items for use and consumption, and that this is likely to have a continuing effect on women's lives, as the ever-burgeoning

---

[5] The distinctions and arguments of Section 2 build on work in 'Humean Projection in Sexual Objectification', which draws upon Hume in more detail; forthcoming in *Sexual Solipsism: Philosophical Essays on Pornography and Objectification* (Oxford: Oxford University Press, 2003). Much other feminist work draws on Hume (see, e.g., Annette Baier, 'Hume: The Reflective Women's Epistemologist?', in *A Mind of One's Own: Feminist Essays on Reason and Objectivity*, (eds.) Louise M. Antony and Charlotte Witt (Boulder, Colo.: Westview Press, 1993)); but I am not aware of material that draws upon his views of projection.

sex industry illustrates. One can anticipate on-going scope for a feminist version of the Kantian idea that there is a dignity in human nature having its ground in autonomy, and that by virtue of this worth 'we are not for sale at any price'.[6] And one needs no crystal ball to guess that the substitution of the virtual for the real will become an increasing fact of life; and that projection will be a topic of increasing importance, as people increasingly substitute virtual action for action, virtual experience for experience, and virtual human relationships for human relationships.

The pornography industry again provides an illustration. But whether projection should matter here is perhaps less obvious. For even if pornography use does involve projection, and even if pornography also objectifies women in ways that deny autonomy, that would not show that the projective aspect of pornography matters. Projection could be a merely incidental feature of pornography, of as little moral interest as other accidental facts about pornography—as, for example, the uninteresting fact that its images supervene on dots of ink, or pixels on a screen.

To see how the ideas of autonomy and projection might connect, I turn now to an account of sexual objectification offered by Catharine MacKinnon which draws explicitly upon both ideas, and in so doing, unites elements from each of the camps I have described.[7] The hope is that this will enable us to see how projection might help, and hide, sexual objectification.

2. How Projection Helps Sexual Objectification

MacKinnon describes sexual objectification as 'the primary process of the subjection of women', and says:

To be sexually objectified means having a social meaning imposed on your being that defines you as to be sexually used . . . . and then using you that way.[8]

This notion of sexual objectification draws in recognizable ways on the first of the two ideas, conveying a Kantian heritage in that notion of 'use', which picks up on the idea of autonomy-denial and instrumentality. Sexual objectification emerges as the idea (drawing here on Nussbaum's elucidation) that certain sexual ways of treating someone may be ways of denying their autonomy, ignoring their subjective inner life, treating them as readily replaceable, treating them as the kinds of things that can be bought and sold, treating them as something merely to be used, something that is a mere tool.

MacKinnon also describes sexual objectification in terms that draw on the second idea: sexual objectification is, she says, 'an elaborate projective system'.[9] She is interested in how objectification 'unites act with word, construction with expression,

[6] Kant, *Doctrine of Virtue*, trans. Mary Gregor (NY, Evanston and London: Harper & Row, 1964), 435.

[7] Notwithstanding the fact that MacKinnon's proposals have been viewed sceptically by members of each camp. See, e.g., Nussbaum, 'Objectification', whose scepticism is directed not so much against the analysis but the legal proposal; Judith Butler, *Excitable Speech: A Politics of the Performative* (NY and London: Routledge, 1997), ch. 2.

[8] MacKinnon, *Toward a Feminist Theory of the State* (Cambridge, Mass.; London: Harvard University Press, 1989), 122, 140.   [9] Ibid. 140–1.

perception with enforcement, myth with reality'[10]. She is interested in how different modes of treatment 'unite': for example when speech 'unites' with act, and when thought 'unites' with coercion. She is also interested in how desire 'unites' with belief and perception: those who exert power over women see the world as a certain way because they *want to see* the world that way; they believe the world is a certain way because they *want to believe* it is that way. What she describes, I suggest, is a kind of *desire-driven* projection.[11]

This theme of projection, desire-driven or otherwise, tends to be absent in the accounts of objectification offered by analytic or liberal feminists; it seems, for example, to be missing in Nussbaum's otherwise admirably comprehensive study.[12] It receives plenty of attention elsewhere in analytic philosophy however, for example in analyses of the epistemology of colour, and of value. Indeed the projective process is given the very label 'objectification' by J. L. Mackie, when he complains of our tendency 'to objectify values', complains of the propensity of the mind to project itself—to 'spread itself on external objects', as Hume put it.[13] Mackie and MacKinnon share an interest in the way desire and belief may unite to create something both wish to call 'objectification', notwithstanding their different concerns; and they share an interest, too, in desire-driven projection. According to Mackie, in objectifying value, we ascribe 'a fictitious external authority' to features that are nothing more than projections of our 'wants' and 'demands', our 'appetites' and 'desires'.[14]

How are we to understand the idea of a desire-driven projection, as it bears on sexual objectification? In what follows I shall describe and distinguish three varieties of desire-driven projection, none of which should seem too unfamiliar. They all have in common a capacity to generate a belief, given a desire. And they all have in common a potential involvement in sexual objectification, or so I shall suggest, drawing on MacKinnon in each case to illustrate their possible workings. My purpose is analytical and exploratory, rather than polemical. I shall assume, without defending, the adequacy of some projective explanatory hypotheses MacKinnon proposes, though I am aware that more defence is needed.

The first mechanism I shall call the *phenomenological gilding* of desired objects, recalling Hume's description of our activity of 'gilding or staining all natural objects with the colours, borrowed from internal sentiment'.[15] This mechanism is distinctive in

[10] Ibid. 122.

[11] Ibid. 140, 122; *Feminism Unmodified: Discourses on Life and Law* (Cambridge, Mass.; London: Harvard University Press, 1987), 58–9 (emphasis added).

[12] An important exception is Sally Haslanger, whose work on this topic has substantially inspired and influenced me; see Haslanger, 'On Being Objective and Being Objectified', in *A Mind of One's Own*. I draw upon this in 'Beyond A Pragmatic Critique of Reason', *Australasian Journal of Philosophy* 71 (1993), 364–84; and 'Feminism in Epistemology: Exclusion and Objectification', *The Cambridge Companion to Feminism in Philosophy*, (eds.) Jennifer Hornsby and Miranda Fricker (Cambridge: Cambridge University Press, 2000); both reprinted (with revisions) in *Sexual Solipsism*.

[13] J. L. Mackie, *Ethics: Inventing Right and Wrong* (Harmondsworth: Penguin, 1990), ch. 1; David Hume, *A Treatise of Human Nature*, (ed.) L. A. Selby-Bigge, revised P. H. Nidditch (Oxford: Clarendon Press, 1978), 167.   [14] Mackie, *Ethics*, 42, 43, 45, 34.

[15] David Hume, *Enquiries Concerning Human Understanding and Concerning the Principles of Morals*, (ed.) L. A. Selby-Bigge, revised P. H. Nidditch, 3rd edn., (Oxford: Clarendon Press, 1975), 294.

generating beliefs about *value* in particular. The second is the familiar mechanism of *wishful thinking*, which can generate a belief that something is so, given a desire that it be so. Its scope goes beyond beliefs about value to beliefs about almost anything. The third mechanism I shall call *pseudo-empathy*, which is an over-hasty disposition to attribute features of one's own mind to other people, animals, or even inanimate objects (I don't address the question of when exactly such a leap counts as 'over-hasty'). Pseudo-empathy can generate a belief, given a desire, when it leaps from one's own desire that something be so to a belief that someone else desires that it be so. While these mechanisms can all generate belief, given desire, they vary in the sorts of belief they can in principle generate, given a desire—phenomenological gilding generating beliefs about value, wishful thinking generating beliefs about almost anything, and pseudo-empathy generating beliefs about the desires of others. To the extent that these mechanisms generate belief, given desire, they violate the aforementioned rule about direction of fit: belief aims to fit the world, not to fit desire. But these beliefs fit desire.[16]

There is a question about what sorts of desires will be relevant to a projective belief implicated in sexual objectification; and I shall be considering broadly sexual desires. More sinister desires might be equally relevant, or more relevant: for example, explicit desires to maintain or exercise power, to dominate or humiliate, to cause pain; but I shall not be attending much to these.[17]

2.1. Phenomenological Gilding   Sometimes projective belief may have its source in a distinctive phenomenology of experience. Our beliefs about colour, for example, are thought by some philosophers to be mere projections based on the phenomenological character of our colour experience. Our beliefs about colour do not, of course, have their source in desire, so this example is different to the projective beliefs we shall be considering. But I want to ask whether there might be something about the phenomenology of desire—by analogy with the phenomenology of colour—which could yield certain beliefs. If there were, this would be a desire-driven mechanism quite different to the familiar mechanism of wishful thinking: my wishful belief in the immortality of the soul does not arise from any phenomenological feature of my desire to avoid death: my life does not *look* to be immortal, in the way that objects *look* to be coloured. If the phenomenology of desire has the capacity to generate beliefs, possible candidates for such beliefs are beliefs about value.

Hume applied his metaphor of 'gilding and staining' to colour and value alike, and may partly have had this phenomenological parallel in mind when he pursued his extended analogy between them. Describing 'the impulse to desire', he said

it has a productive faculty, and gilding and staining all natural objects with the colours, borrowed from internal sentiment, raises in a manner, a new creation.[18]

---

[16] See 'Beyond a Pragmatic Critique' for further discussion.

[17] This is a substantial omission, since such desires may well have a role to play in sexual objectification, given that some of them presumably *aim* to objectify someone, reduce someone to a thing. It is a gap I shall have to leave, and in any case may be a dialectical strength: presumably if sexual objectification can be generated by more ordinary sexual desires, without help of sinister desires to exert power or humiliate, it could all the more readily be generated with their help.

[18] Hume, *Enquiry*, 294. He is here describing taste as the first impulse to desire.

Mackie, following Hume, regards the desire-generated projection of belief about value as partly phenomenological. He also quotes Hobbes—'whatsoever is the object of any man's Appetite or Desire, that is it, which he for his part calleth Good'—and comments on how (in his view) we reverse the direction of dependence, regarding the desire as depending on the goodness, rather than the goodness on the desire. In parallel manner, but for aversion rather than desire, Mackie says we attribute independent disvalue, a foulness, to the fungus that fills us with disgust.[19] To the extent this occurs, Mackie's account of the projection of value (whose sceptical implications don't concern us here) can be seen as describing a projective response to phenomenological features of desire. The thing desired can appear phenomenologically as having independent qualities that justify, demand, or legitimate the desire, making it almost literally *appear* to have independent value, just as a strawberry appears to be independently red. When you desire something, you can project its desirability, aware less of your attitude than of an apparent feature of the object of your attitude. The phenomenology is quasi-perceptual. (To the eye of a hungry Goldilocks, the porridge literally *looks* delicious.) Belief about value may sometimes be belief that is responsive to this distinctive phenomenology of desire. This phenomenological gilding presents us with one sort of desire-generated belief: belief about the value of what is desired.

Let us think about the possible role of phenomenological gilding in sexual objectification. MacKinnon says,

Like the value of a commodity, women's sexual desirability is fetishized: it is made to appear a quality of the object itself, spontaneous and inherent, independent of the social relation that creates it, uncontrolled by the force that requires it.[20]

MacKinnon is here attempting to describe a certain phenomenology of desire, of men's sexual desire, in an oppressive political context. A woman's 'value', a woman's 'desirability' is 'made to appear a quality of the object, spontaneous and inherent'. The sexual value of a woman appears, phenomenologically, as an 'inherent', independent feature, independent of the desire and independent of relevant social forces, seeming authoritative, seeming to justify the belief in the value, and seeming to justify the sexual desire it provokes. This is what I have described as phenomenological gilding. And so far, so innocuous: there is nothing yet to indicate sexual objectification, nothing yet to indicate how this valuing might be involved in treating a woman as a thing. But now: a woman's value, a woman's desirability, is somehow 'like the value of a *commodity*'. What does she mean? Perhaps this. A massive commercial industry, namely the pornography industry, makes certain objects of sexual desire into commodities, items for commercial buying and selling, for easy satisfaction of appetite, for ownership; and it shapes men's desires to attract them to these sexual commodities. When this occurs, men's sexual desires can themselves become, so speak, commodifying desires: the phenomenology of men's sexual desire comes to resemble, in certain aspects, their desires for other commodities, to the extent that their sexual desires for real women can come to resemble, in certain aspects, their desires for other commodities.

[19] Mackie, *Ethics*, 43, 42.   [20] MacKinnon, *Feminist Theory*, 123.

What then would be the implications for belief about a woman's value? If phenomenological gilding is possible, desire can be a source of projective evaluative belief. So a commodifying desire could be a source of a commodifying evaluative belief. The result would be that the value women are seen as having, and believed to have, will be the sort of value that commodities are seen as having, and believed to have.

This in turn would have implications for question about whether and how phenomenological gilding is implicated in sexual objectification. In many contexts, phenomenological gilding is innocent, in moral terms (whether or not dubious epistemologically); indeed it may be better than innocent. Nussbaum wanted to allow that the objectification she describes could, in certain contexts, be a 'wonderful' part of sexual life, as, for example, when lovers (as described by D. H. Lawrence at any rate) might seek a mutual abandonment of autonomy. The same applies here: when one thinks of the power of sexual love to transfigure perception of the loved one, so that through its eyes every bodily feature appears as precious, every gesture illumined—this 'gilding' of the loved one through desire likewise appears as a potentially 'wonderful' part of sexual life.

But with commodified desire, things will be altogether more bleak. Phenomenological gilding allows a transition from desire to belief about value, via the phenomenology of desire; and MacKinnon's thought seems to be that, to the sexually objectifying eye of the pornography consumer, women appear, phenomenologically, a certain way—they, so to speak, 'look' the way pornography looks, not (or not just) because pornography tries to resemble women (which would make the idea trivial), but because pornography's commodified view of women gets transferred, through the eye of the consumer, to women themselves. That is perhaps why MacKinnon says elsewhere that pornography shapes a 'gaze that constructs women as objects for male pleasure . . . that eroticizes the despised, the demeaned, the accessible, the there-to-be-used, the servile'.[21] If phenomenology of desire can prompt belief about value, and commodifying sexual desires lead to women being seen and valued in the way that other commodities are seen and valued, this would result in women being treated as things. Women would be valued as instruments for the easy satisfaction of desire, as ownable, readily exchangeable; and those who value women as sexual commodities would be more likely to treat them that way in their behaviour. One could expect these attitudes to result in autonomy-denying action, as women's autonomy is inadequately attributed, and violated, through harassment and rape.

2.2. *Wishful Thinking*   Wishful thinking is a phenomenon so familiar it needs little in the way of introduction, and while it poses many difficult philosophical questions, they will not be our topic here. It presents a different aspect of Hume's idea of the mind 'spreading itself' on the world. Hume himself thought many of our beliefs have such wishful origins, including, for example, belief in the immortality

[21]   MacKinnon, *Feminism Unmodified*, 53–4.

of the soul: 'All doctrines are to be suspected which are favoured by our passions; and the hopes and fears which gave rise to this doctrine are very obvious'.[22]

Our question is whether wishful thinking might have a role to play in sexual objectification. What salient beliefs might be wishfully prompted by sexual desire? Candidates might be beliefs that help the desire to persist, that seem to fulfil the desire, or that make the desire seem more likely to be fulfilled. A belief in a *matching desire* seems a likely candidate: the belief of the form 'she desires to do what I desire to do' will legitimate the initial desire and make its satisfaction seem more likely. Moreover, it has plausibly been suggested (by Thomas Nagel) that a constitutive component of an ordinary sexual desire is the aim for a matching desire in the other person.[23] (There will be other, more pathological, cases where the desire of the other person is irrelevant, or relevant negatively, as for a sadist who might desire an *absence* of matching desire.) Belief in matching desire would then convey the belief that this component is already satisfied, as well as conveying hope of the desire's complete fulfilment. So we might antecedently expect wishful incentives for belief in matching desire, and in a source that is far from sinister, namely the very desire for mutuality which is so central to sexual life, but that can go awry, if it helps generate merely wishful belief.[24]

We turn now to some candidate examples, most of which are drawn from MacKinnon, though the first is not. They are examples which also make 'wishful thinking' appear a sadly inadequate label (which is perhaps why MacKinnon does not use it).

Example 1: attribution of matching desire, in a scene from *The Innocent*, by Ian McEwan. Leonard, a young and 'kindly' Englishman, and Maria, who is German, meet and fall in love in post-war Berlin. Later on Leonard begins to have a fantasy:

It began . . . with a simple perception. He looked down at Maria, whose eyes were closed, and remembered she was a German . . . Enemy. . . . Defeated enemy. This last brought with it a shocking thrill. He diverted himself momentarily . . . Then: she was the defeated, she was his by right, by conquest, by right of unimaginable violence and heroism and sacrifice . . . He was powerful and magnificent. . . . He was victorious and good and strong and free. In recollection these formulations embarrassed him. But next time round the thoughts returned.

---

[22] David Hume, 'On the Immortality of the Soul', from *Essays Moral and Political* (1741–2), reprinted in *David Hume: Selected Essays*, ed. Stephen Copley and Andrew Edgar (Oxford: Oxford University Press, 1998), 331.

[23] Thomas Nagel, 'Sexual Perversion', in *Mortal Questions* (Cambridge: Cambridge University Press, 1991)—describing not merely a matching desire, but a matching desire which has a complex and iterative Gricean structure.

[24] There is an important ambiguity in the notion of a 'matching' desire, which is roughly the contrast between 'same desire' and 'complementary desire'. I do not attend to this adequately here, though it is a topic of 'Humean Projection in Sexual Objectification', in the volume *Sexual Solipsism* (forthcoming). Depending on how it is described, the projected 'matching' desire may look like the same desire as the man's, or it may look like a desire that complements his. To take Example 1, the desire Leonard attributes to Maria is under one description the same as his ('a desire to entertain this rape fantasy'), under another description very different from his ('a desire to imagine raping' vs. 'a desire to imagine being raped').

They were irresistibly exciting . . . she was his by right of conquest and then, there was nothing she could do about it. She did not want to be making love to him, but she had no choice.

Still later, he begins to imagine himself a soldier forcing himself on a defeated German enemy; and then he found himself

tempted to communicate these imaginings to her . . . He could not believe she would not be aroused by it . . . His private theatre had become insufficient . . . He wanted his power recognized and Maria to suffer from it, just a bit, in the most pleasurable way . . . Then he was ashamed. What was this power he wanted recognized? It was no more than a disgusting story in his head. Then, later, he wondered whether she might not be excited by it too. There was, of course, nothing to discuss . . . He had to surprise her, show her, let pleasure overcome her rational objections.[25]

Leonard uses Maria's body as, so to speak, a screen, his 'private theatre', on which to project the fantasy of Maria (or: anonymous German enemy) as victim of his rape. The process, as it develops, involves wishful thinking: first in the desire-driven attitude which falls short of belief (he does not believe she is a victim of rape, it is merely 'as if'); then in the desire-driven genuine belief that she will find the fantasy exciting too. Does this example involve sexual objectification? Surely yes. There is instrumentality and autonomy-denial merely in this use of Maria as a projective screen, especially given the fantasy's hidden content. And when Leonard still later succumbs to the temptation to share his solipsistic theatre and 'show' her his imaginings, what ensues is something both parties view, or come to view, as attempted rape. This brings us to the more general issue provided by the next example.

Example 2: attribution of matching desire, in certain kinds of rape. MacKinnon says, of the 'system' that is sexual objectification, In this system . . . women men want, want men . . . Raped women are seen as asking for it: if a man wanted her, she must have wanted him.[26] In a case where a woman is genuinely believed to have 'wanted him', either at the time, or later on in *post hoc* rationalization, the rapist desires to have sex with the woman, and projects a matching desire, perhaps wishfully generated.[27] (I shall not speculate about how common such cases of genuine belief are.) Wishful belief of such a kind may also be projected by other people, including, perhaps, jury members and other ordinary women, prompted in the latter case by a rather different sort of desire—a desire, perhaps, that the world should be a safe one. To the extent that wishful thinking is responsible for the attribution of

---

[25] Ian McEwan, *The Innocent* (London: Picador, 1990), taken from 83–5. This scene is also discussed in 'Humean Projection' (where the examples from MacKinnon are also discussed); and in 'Sexual Solipsism', *Philosophical Topics* 23 (1995), 149–87, reprinted in *Sexual Solipsism*.

[26] MacKinnon, *Feminist Theory*, 140–1.

[27] Such cases may be more common in date rape, and raise issues that parallel the Morgan case in British law (where Morgan's friends claimed genuine belief that his wife consented to sex with them); which I discuss briefly in 'Pornography: a Liberal's Unfinished Business', *Canadian Journal of Law and Jurisprudence* 12 (1999), 109–33; partly reprinted in the volume *Sexual Solipsism*, ch. 2, in the section responding to Ronald Dworkin.

matching desire in such contexts, it would be implicated in sexual objectification, in particular the profound autonomy-denial and violation which is rape.

Example 3: attribution of matching desire, in the pornographic film *Deep Throat.*

This elaborate projective system of demand characteristics—taken to pinnacles like fantasizing a clitoris in a woman's throat so that men can enjoy forced fellatio in real life, assured that women do too—is surely a delusional structure deserving of serious psychological study.[28]

This is a peculiar case, in which something like wishful thinking may well be implicated, first in the desire-driven generation of an attitude that falls short of belief, the entertainment of the fiction that Linda Lovelace madly desires throat sex, due to a quirk of anatomy. Genuine beliefs are also generated, according to MacKinnon (who cites evidence about subsequent behaviour), among them a belief that the star, Linda Marchiano, enjoyed what she was doing; and that women, more generally, are likely to enjoy throat sex.[29] Wishful thinking provides a possible explanation (plus the fact that desire is assisted by genuine belief that pornography 'actors' enjoy what they do). Sexual objectification is described here as 'an elaborate projective system', where 'demand characteristics' are projected first on to a fictional protagonist, the projected desire sustaining and legitimating the viewer's own arousal. The wishful shaping of belief is mediated by the shaping of desire: MacKinnon suggests that pornographic fantasy conditions and alters sexual desire; a consumer may subsequently find desirable the prospect of throat sex, which desire in turn provides incentives for attributing matching desire to Marchiano herself, and to other women—notwithstanding the real world absence of science-fiction anatomy. A projective pattern like this is, MacKinnon remarks, a 'delusional structure deserving of serious psychological study'.

How would this projective pattern be implicated in sexual objectification? A small part of the question is whether the envisaged desire attribution objectifies the merely fictional Linda, and here one might be tempted to think it does not: there is (in Nussbaum's terms) no denial of subjectivity or autonomy, but an affirmation, an attribution to the fictional character of an avid and independent desire for throat sex. The process may still be objectifying, though, in its instrumental view of a woman desperate to make herself sexually available to anyone who wants her. A more important part of the question is whether the desire-attribution to the real Linda objectifies her, and here the answer is surely affirmative: her testimony in *Ordeal* tells how she suffered threats to her life, sexual torture, and rape, in the film's making, and that it took that plus hypnosis (to reduce the gag response) to make her do it. The attribution of matching desire to the real Linda obscures all this, and is thus a denial of subjectivity

[28] MacKinnon, *Feminist Theory*, 140–1.
[29] Cf. MacKinnon on the 'realism' of *Deep Throat*: '[B]efore "Linda Lovelace" was seen performing deep throat, no one had ever seen it being done that way, largely because it cannot be done without hypnosis to repress the natural gag response. *Yet it was believed.* Men proceeded to demand it of women, causing the distress of many and the death of some. Yet when Linda Marchiano now tells that it took kidnapping and death threats and hypnosis to put her there, that is found *difficult to believe*'; (see *Feminism Unmodified*, 181, and associated references to relevant empirical data).

which assists the deep instrumentality and autonomy-denial involved in her abuse, and silences her later testimony.[30] Thirdly, there is the question of whether desire-attribution to other real women by consumers later on objectifies those women.[31] Here again the answer again may be affirmative, if one accepts testimony that some consumers later attributed, or tried to attribute, matching desires for throat sex to their partners (resulting sometimes in 'deep throat' assault): such attitudes and consequent behaviour are likely to instantiate particularly serious versions of (in Nussbaum's terms) subjectivity-denial, instrumentality, and autonomy-denial.[32]

Example 4: Attribution of matching desire, through women's supposed capacity for vaginal orgasm—a science fiction about women that was long accepted as orthodox science. MacKinnon's explanation is that because 'men demand that women enjoy vaginal penetration', they acquire the belief, dressed up as science, that 'vaginal orgasms' are the only 'mature' sexuality; and accordingly the belief that women desire penetrative sex because this is their natural route to orgasm.[33] Wishful thinking projects an imagined biological basis for a conveniently matching desire on the part of the woman, and adds whatever legitimation is granted by a scientific establishment—an eery pseudo-science parallel to the science-fiction biology of *Deep Throat*. Does such attribution of matching desire objectify women? One might suppose again that the attitude itself is not objectifying, that on the contrary it attributes an active independent desire to women, a distinct source of pleasure unique to women, that however erroneous, it is at least subjectivity-affirming and autonomy-affirming. This would be too hasty, given that the attitude denies that women have the sexual experiences they have, and asserts they have sexual experiences they lack—something that may count as subjectivity-denial, rather than affirmation.[34]

[30] In 'Autonomy Denial in Objectification' (forthcoming in the volume *Sexual Solipsism*) I add the notion of silencing to Nussbaum's list of features. Cf. 'Objects do not speak. When they do, they are by then regarded as objects, not as humans, which is what it means to have no credibility,' MacKinnon, *Feminism Unmodified*, 182. For an understanding of what the silencing amounts to, and how Marchiano is silenced, see 'Speech Acts and Unspeakable Acts', *Philosophy and Public Affairs* 22 (1993): 305–30, reprinted in *Sexual Solipsism*.

[31] There is also the question of the attribution of desire to women more generally by the film itself: despite being fiction, it may attribute to real women the sorts of desires the fictional Linda is represented as having, in which case the attitude to women in general is at the least an instrumental one. See 'Scorekeeping in a Pornographic Language Game' (co-authored with Caroline West), *Australasian Journal of Philosophy* 77 (1999), 303–19, reprinted in *Sexual Solipsism*, for an argument about how mere fiction makes claims about the real world.

[32] Such testimony was given at the Minneapolis Hearings: *Public Hearings on Ordinances to Add Pornography as Discrimination against Women*, Committee on Government Operations, City Council, Minneapolis, Minn. (12–13 Dec., 1983), vol. 1, p. 60; cited by MacKinnon in *Feminism Unmodified*, 286, n. 65.

[33] *Feminist Theory*, 140–1; also 123. Elisabeth Lloyd cites blindness to 'orgasm-intercourse discrepancy' for women as an example of bias in evolutionary explanations of women's sexuality, 'Pre-Theoretical Assumptions in Evolutionary Explanations of Female Sexuality', *Philosophical Studies* 69 (1993), 139–53: 'Not to have orgasm from [unassisted] intercourse is the experience of the majority of women the majority of the time' (144), citing studies according to which 30% never have orgasm from unassisted intercourse, 20–35% always or almost always do.

[34] 'Treating as an Object' addresses the question of how subjectivity-denial is best understood.

There may also be instrumental thinking involved; how much more useful if the shape of women's sexual desire were the perfect match to that of men! The theorizing in turn perhaps helped to legitimate instrumental sexual use of women by other parties, by silencing, as 'immature' those women whose desires were apparently less convenient.

Example 5: Attribution of matching desire in Freud's 'seduction theory'. The Freudian interpretation of women's testimony about abuse as children bears comparison, according to MacKinnon, with the projective 'system' in pornography use:

Both the psychoanalytic and the pornographic 'fantasy' worlds are what men imagine women imagine and desire because they are what men, raised on pornography, imagine and desire about women . . . Perhaps the Freudian process of theory-building occurred like this: men heard accounts of child abuse, felt aroused by the account, and attributed their arousal to the child who is now a woman . . . Classical psychoanalysis attributes the connection between the experience of abuse (hers) and the experience of arousal (his) to the fantasy of the girl child. When he does it, he likes it, so when she did it, she must have liked it. Thus it cannot be abusive to her. Because he wants to do it, she must want it done.[35]

The psychoanalyst hears a sexual narrative which he experiences as arousing; since sexual desire aims for a matching desire, he desires the woman likewise to experience the narrative as arousing and accordingly to desire to entertain it. Such desire, on the part of the woman, would sustain and legitimate his own desire. Through a process of wishful thinking, there is a transition to belief: he believes the woman herself experiences the telling of the narrative as arousing, and desires to entertain it; and he believes that as a child, she had that sort of experience and that desire. This belief offering in turn a sufficient explanation for the narrative's existence, the narrative is interpreted as desired fantasy, rather than testimony of child abuse. MacKinnon suggests that a similar projective pattern can destroy testimony of rape in the courts today; and that fear of it contributes to the known reluctance of rape victims to testify—the fear that in effect, their testimony becomes pornography.

How would this desire-attribution be sexually objectifying? Despite the fact that it attributes an active independent desire, the attribution nonetheless exemplifies sexual objectification: the attitude is (in Nussbaum's terms) subjectivity-denying in its blindness to the experience of women who had suffered sexual abuse as children. It is also, perhaps, instrumental, in treating the women and their actions—speech acts of testimony about sexual abuse—as if they were themselves pornographic artefacts, as if they were items whose function is to stimulate arousal. As an action of discounting a woman's testimony, the theorizing that followed was a speech act that denied their subjectivity and autonomy, and silenced them. The implications go beyond the particular woman to women more generally: seduction theory perhaps legitimates other sexual abuse and violence by undermining women's credibility, conveying the thought that women's testimony is probably a lie, that women find the thought of abuse arousing, but are too repressed to say so. The most salient

---

[35] MacKinnon, *Feminist Theory*, 152.

initial feature here seems to be that of subjectivity-denial, leading then to significant instrumentality and autonomy-denial, to the extent that it also makes sexual violence more likely, and redress against it more difficult.

2.3. Pseudo-empathy   In arguing for the projective origins of many of our beliefs, Hume cites yet another disposition; he complains of the

universal tendency among mankind to conceive all beings like themselves, and to transfer to every object those qualities, with which they are familiarly acquainted, and of which they are intimately conscious.[36]

Such pseudo-empathic tendencies provide an anthropomorphic explanation for belief in primitive deities; and also for over-hasty belief about the mental states of other people—though how precisely it is to be distinguished from sympathy is a question I shall here leave aside.

Where wishful thinking makes a transition from 'I desire that she desires to do this', to the belief, 'She desires to do this', pseudo-empathy makes a transition from 'I desire to do this' to the belief 'She desires to do this', the agent's own desire directly prompting belief in a matching desire. While pseudo-empathy can be desire-generated, it need not be: any datum about oneself, whether a desire, a belief, an emotion, or a pain, could prompt pseudo-empathic attribution to another of a similar desire, or belief, or emotion, or pain. We are confining our attention to what these projective mechanisms can generate, given a desire.

Most of the examples just considered under the heading of wishful thinking are as open to a pseudo-empathic as to a wishful interpretation, given that what is attributed in each case is a matching desire, a desire that appears to mirror the desire of the person attributing it. Leonard's belief about what Maria desires could be wishful; and it could as easily be the result of an over-hasty leap from his own experience. 'He could not believe she would not be aroused by it . . . He had to surprise her, show her, let pleasure overcome her rational objections.'[37] Is it a wishful move from 'I desire her to desire it; so I believe she desires it'; or a pseudo-empathic move from 'I desire it; so I believe she desires it'? Quite possibly both, working in tandem: the projective belief might be prompted by pseudo-empathy, and sustained by wishful thinking.

Likewise for the examples from MacKinnon. 'Raped women are seen as asking for it: if a man wanted her, she must have wanted him.' Is this the wishful 'I want her to want it; so I believe she wants it'; or the pseudo-empathic, 'I want it, so I believe she wants it'? Again, quite possibly both, working together. The projection of matching desire to the real Linda Marchiano could be a pseudo-empathic leap from what the viewer finds desirable, to belief about what she finds desirable.

---

[36] David Hume, *The Natural History of Religion* (1757), (ed.) H. E. Root (London: Adam & Charles Black, 1956), 141.

[37] The desire he attributes may look like a formal match to his own, but can be readily redescribed as its opposite: Leonard's desire to imagine raping generates a belief about Maria's desire to imagine *being raped*. This complexity, which depends on how the initial desire is described, is one discussed in more detail in 'Humean Projection'.

Pseudo-empathy could similarly be part of the explanation for projection of matching desire in scientific theorizing about vaginal orgasm; and it could be part of the explanation for the projection of matching desire in MacKinnon's hypothesis about the origins of the seduction theory.

How is pseudo-empathy implicated in sexual objectification? This question exactly parallels the question just considered, of whether wishful thinking might be so implicated; and the answer stands or falls with the answer given for wishful thinking. If it seemed plausible that these are indeed examples of sexual objectification, when construed as wishful projection, because of their subjectivity denial, instrumentality, and autonomy-denial; then it should seem equally plausible that they are examples of sexual objectification, when construed as pseudo-empathic projection. So I shall not rehearse the examples case by case, but shall simply assume that the argument about wishful thinking can be extended to pseudo-empathy.

I said I would be sharing some assumptions of psychoanalytic feminists (though leaving aside their substantive proposals): they are right to emphasize the significance of projective desire-driven belief; right also to think that such belief can shape the world; and right to suppose that these processes can be substantially invisible to the participants. In this section I have looked at the first of these, distinguishing three ways in which desire might projectively generate belief, and showing how each can, in certain circumstances, be implicated in sexual objectification. How widespread or systematic their significance might be, how far their importance extends beyond these particular examples, are questions I don't address, but I suspect MacKinnon is right to give projection a central place in the notion of sexual objectification.

There remain the questions of how such projection may help shape the world, and in ways that are in part invisible: and this bears on the issue of how projection may not only help sexual objectification, but also hide it.

3. How Projection Hides Sexual Objectification

Suppose an Evil Genius were to invent a social system that benefits one group of people at the price of subordinating or objectifying another; suppose he were to realize that the system could be helped along by means of a complex pattern of desire-driven projective beliefs on the part of those people; and suppose he were to want the system to evade notice. He ponders, and, after taking advice from the Devil, dreams up a nearly perfect Plan from Hell. It goes like this.

Step 1: Genesis. Make genesis of the projective belief invisible. Nobody will notice where the belief came from, nobody will wonder about its possibly dubious origins. *Step 2: Subjective appearance.* Let the mind create a subjective appearance of confirming evidence for the projective belief. Make it look as though there is confirming evidence for the projective belief to the eye of the observer, by helping the observer see the world a certain way. And make counter-evidence subjectively hard to see, so that evidence proving the belief wrong will not be noticed. *Step 3: Objective appearance*. Let the world create an objective appearance of confirming evidence for the projective belief. Make the world change, so that it produces evidence that really is genuine evidence for the belief, notwithstanding the belief's falsity.[38] *Step 4: Reality*. Let the world make the projective belief true. Make the world change, so that it fulfills the projective belief; in which case it will keep supplying all the evidence one could ever want.

The beauty of this Plan from Hell is that it will work whether or not it is planned (indeed better the less it is planned), and will work just as well in the absence of Evil Genius and his devilish adviser; so one need be no conspiracy theorist to see how effective it might be. Let us take a look at how projection might help to implement it.

Step 1: Genesis. Make genesis of the projective belief invisible. This trick is achieved by the very nature of projective belief. A distinctive feature of projective belief is that it does not convey to the believer its own best explanation.[39] Such beliefs have their origin in non-epistemic features of the believer's psychology, they are not epistemically receptive—but to the believer, they will seem as good as any other belief. This is partly because of belief's direction of fit. Belief, even projective belief, aims to fit the world; and although projective belief fits desire, rather than fitting the world, it must seem to the believer to be aiming to fit the world, or it would not be belief. Desire-driven projection must make its origins invisible if it is to be belief at all: one cannot (usually) be a merely wishful thinker and believe one is a merely wishful thinker. Of course, that does not make wishful thinking, and the like, immune to discovery. But, with some special exceptions, the moment it is detected, it disappears. Its existence depends on its invisibility, to the believer.

This invisibility is not enough to protect a belief in the face of compelling evidence to the contrary. Even a wishful belief *aims* to fit the world, and enough evidence that the world is not as wished will make the belief go away. So the next step, indeed all the next steps, involve doing something about the evidence.

Step 2: Subjective appearance. Let the mind create a subjective appearance of confirming evidence for the projective belief, which seems also to make counter-evidence disappear.

The projective attribution of matching desire, in rape, meets counter-evidence in a woman's refusal, a woman's 'no'. She does not want it, and says so. This counter-evidence will seem to disappear, if from the subjective viewpoint it may not sound as though she is refusing—if, for example, her refusal has been disabled by porno-graphy's lie that women who say 'no' mean 'yes'. Her 'no' will not look like counter-evidence, and may even look like confirming evidence. The projective attribution of

---

[38] Assuming here one can have evidence for something that is false; for an alternative view about evidence, according to which one cannot, see Timothy Williamson, *Knowledge and its Limits* (Oxford: Oxford University Press, 2000).

[39] For further discussion, see, e.g., Peter Kail, 'Projection and Necessity in Hume', *European Journal of Philosophy* 9 (2001), 24–54; and *Projection and Realism in Hume* (Oxford: Oxford University Press, forthcoming); to both of which I am indebted.

matching desire to the real Linda Marchiano meets counter-evidence in her testimony about abuse, in *Ordeal*. This counter-evidence will seem to disappear, when it looks as though she is not describing abuse, but producing more pornography (*Ordeal* was sold as pornography).[40] The projective attribution of matching desire, based on women's supposed capacity for vaginal orgasm, meets counter-evidence in many women's descriptions of their actual sexual experience. This counter-evidence will disappear, if those descriptions sound instead like descriptions of repression, frigidity, or immaturity. The projective attribution of desire to women who narrated to Freud how they were abused as children meets counter-evidence in that very narration. The women were abused, and said so. This counter-evidence too will disappear the minute the projective belief is adopted, and it will appear to be transmuted into confirming evidence; the narrative sounds like an arousing fantasy that anyone would enjoy making up. Belief is supposed to fit the world: but here the world—at least the world *as subjective appearance*—has come to fit projective belief.

Step 3: Objective appearance. Let the world itself change, so that it creates an *objective* appearance of confirming evidence for the projective belief, evidence that goes beyond how things happen to look to the theory-laden eye of a projection-influenced observer; genuine evidence for the belief, even if the belief is false. Pornography will be helpful in supplying it, and so too, sadly, will women themselves.

If one is looking for evidence about what sex is like, pornography may seem to be as authoritative a source as any. True, it is often fiction: but it also makes claims about what real women desire. Pornography's fictional narratives are made against a backdrop of claimed truths about the world, just as a novelist's fictional narrative about Sherlock Holmes are made against a backdrop of claimed truths about London. Pornography will be a source of independent testimony that women's desires are the desires they are projected to be. Coercion and other incentives in the background can help, as when Marchiano and other women are forced or simply paid to be false witnesses about what gives women pleasure. On this way of thinking, pornography has at least two distinct roles to play in projective objectification, in shaping desire (as discussed in Section 2) and in confirming belief. Yes, says pornography, women *do* have the desires you desire, therefore believe, women to have.

Women too will be helpful in supplying the objective appearance of confirming evidence, and what better authoritative source for evidence about women's sexuality than women? Here the projective beliefs will themselves assist the process, in a context of oppression. Women will sometimes be aware of those projective expectations, and—depending on their circumstances—will sometimes respond in a confirming way. In conditions of relative vulnerability and powerlessness, and with penalties for non-cooperation, some women will act in ways that confirm the belief. Had Maria been less assertive, more dependent and vulnerable, she might have had incentives to behave in ways that confirmed Leonard's expectations, notwithstanding

---

[40] It was marketed that way in junk mail I once received: see 'Speech Acts and Unspeakable Acts'.

their falsity. Women of whom vaginal orgasms are expected, and who are penalized as repressed or immature without them, will, as MacKinnon says, have incentives to fake them.[41] Belief is supposed to fit the world, but here again the world—at least the world *as objective appearance*—has come to fit the belief.

Step 4: Reality. Let the world make the projective belief true. If the world changes, so that it fulfills the projective belief, it will keep on supplying all the evidence needed. MacKinnon says,

[The] beliefs of the powerful become [proven], in part because the world actually arranges itself to affirm what the powerful want to see. If you perceive this as a process, you might call it force, or at least pressure or socialization or what money can buy. If it is imperceptible as a process, you may consider it voluntary or consensual or free will or human nature, or just the way things are. Beneath this, though, the world is not entirely the way the powerful say it is or want to believe it is.[42]

We are considering here the thought that the world *as reality* might come to fit the projective objectifying belief: not simply the world as subjective appearance, or the world as objective appearance. This is what MacKinnon has in mind when speaking of how the world 'arranges itself to affirm' the projective belief. MacKinnon describes this as a sort of projective seeing, and a sort of projective belief, that has a self-fulfilling aspect. This fits in with a broader view about how gender works.

If a woman is defined hierarchically so that the male idea of a woman defines womanhood, and if men have power, this idea becomes reality. It is therefore real. It is not just an illusion or a fantasy or a mistake. It becomes embodied because it is enforced.[43]

The idea that the world 'actually arranges itself to affirm what the powerful want to see' is not the transcendental idealism Kant was proposing in saying that objects must conform to our cognitions: the projective attitudes we are considering become true, partly because of the responsiveness of human beings to the attitudes themselves, and to the modes of treating those attitudes generate. The seeing, and the belief, are themselves part of the constraint, given the woman's awareness of them, and given background conditions of oppression. Marilyn Frye makes a similar point:

The arrogant perceiver . . . coerces the objects of his perception into satisfying the conditions his perception imposes . . . He manipulates the environment, perception and judgment of her whom he perceives, so that her recognized options are limited, and the course she chooses will be such as coheres with his purposes . . . How one sees another and how one expects the other to behave are in tight interdependence, and how one expects the other to behave is a large factor in determining how the other does behave.[44]

[41] MacKinnon, *Feminist Theory*, 140–1, 123.

[42] MacKinnon, *Feminism Unmodified*, 58–9. I follow Sally Haslanger in substituting 'proven' for 'proof', see 'On Being Objective'. This passage is also discussed in 'Beyond a Pragmatic Critique' and 'Feminism in Epistemology'.   [43] *Feminism Unmodified*, 119.

[44] Marilyn Frye, *The Politics of Reality* (Trumansburg, NY: The Crossing Press, 1983), 67. I am leaving aside other important ways of understanding construction which draw on language, e.g., speech act theory, or the semantics of natural kind terms.

For example, a wishful attribution to a woman of submissive desire may be self-fulfilling: the woman in question may not merely fake such desire, but actually acquire it. MacKinnon says, 'Subjection itself, with self-determination ecstatically relinquished, is the content of women's sexual desire and desirability'[45],—and she means that this is the content of women's desire, as projected by men, and also as really instantiated by some women. Desire is constrained by what is perceived to be possible; if it seems that any other than submissive desires are futile, desire may conform to this restricted world, and lower its sights. This, by the way, seems like yet another violation of rules about direction of fit: desire is supposed to aim for the world to fit it: desire is not supposed to aim to fit the world. But as the Stoics showed long ago, it can be a wise course to fit one's desires to the world, at least to some degree. The projective expectation of submissive desire can help create submissive desire; and if the desire is really there, of course it will supply evidence that it is there. Belief is supposed to fit the world, but here again the world—this time the world *as reality*—has come to fit the belief.

By way of a less gloomy conclusion, we can note that there will be limits on the extent to which the world can come to fit projective beliefs, limits on the extent to which the world will make those beliefs true. As MacKinnon puts it, 'the world is not entirely the way the powerful say it is or want to believe it is.' For example (and here I draw on Sally Haslanger) projective beliefs that women are *naturally* or *essentially* submissive will be false: there are likely to be mistakes in the modal content of the beliefs in question.[46] Moreover, there are likely to be mistakes in meta-beliefs about projective beliefs. The 'arrogant perceiver' believes the reason his belief is true is that it has come to fit the world; really it is true because the world has come to fit the belief.

If projective beliefs are bound to be at least partly mistaken, that makes sexual objectification epistemologically vulnerable. Its masking can be discovered. The Plan from Hell is, thankfully, not perfect. But, vulnerable or not, the projective system does make sexual objectification harder to notice—and noticing it is surely a first, and necessary, step to doing something about it.

[45] MacKinnon, *Feminism Unmodified*, 148. The projective attribution of submissiveness is a central theme of Haslanger's discussion, which has influenced my views considerably; see 'On Being Objective'.

[46] Haslanger, 'On Being Objective'.

13

Existentialism, Quietism, and the Role of Philosophy

PHILIP PETTIT

the practical need for practical application of philosophy

David Hume remarks in his *Treatise of Human Nature* that while he is consumed by philosophy in his study, being often lost to questions that generate sceptical anxiety within him, he regains his composure as soon as he departs the study and takes up more practical pursuits.[1] The suggestion often read into this remark—fairly or unfairly—is that though philosophy may be a compelling and satisfying pastime, much philosophizing leaves no impact on ordinary experience or behaviour. Philosophy has no place in practice. It is a quiet and inert presence in life, not one that radiates its influence in other spheres.

This quietist vision of philosophy is consistent with many different, more specific views: with the view that it is an amusing, intellectual diversion, for example, or with the view that it is a compulsion from which we need deliverance.[2] But however it is developed at more specific levels, the vision keeps philosophy removed and insulated from practice. It makes philosophy into a self-standing, self-justifying enterprise.

Opposed to the quietist view is the sort of position that we find, for example, in the nineteenth-century, Danish philosopher, Soren Kierkegaard. Often described as the founding figure of existentialist thought, Kierkegaard said of systematic philosophers like Hegel that they are like a man who builds an enormous castle and lives beside it in a shack.[3] Here the image of the place that philosophy has or ought to have—Hegel is deemed, with scant justice, to have been a failure—is very different indeed. Philosophy, so it is suggested, ought to change people who pursue it, shaping the way they perceive and the way they act. It ought to be capable of being lived out in practice—in experiential and behavioural practice—giving a new direction or quality to the experiences and the dispositions of philosophers themselves.

I want in this essay to consider the question that divides quietism from existentialism and to defend a particular line on that question. The essay is in three main sections. In the first I set out a view of philosophy under which it grows out of reflection on the views that shape ordinary practice. In the second section I outline a theory as to how exactly practice commits us to such views. And then in the third

---

[1] D. Hume (1978). *A Treatise of Human Nature* (Oxford: Oxford University Press), 268–9.

[2] L. Wittgenstein (1958). *Philosophical Investigations* (Oxford: Blackwell).

[3] S. Kierkegaard (1951). *The Journals of Soren Kierkegaard* (Oxford: Oxford University Press). 'In relation to their systems most systematizers are like a man who builds an enormous castle and lives in a shack nearby; they do not live in their own enormous systematic buildings.'

section I argue on the basis of that account that, notwithstanding serious difficulties, philosophy can feed back onto the views that inform practice and recast them in various ways. I reject the existentialist vision according to which there is no limit to how far philosophy may lead us to reconstruct ourselves. But I also reject the quietist view that philosophy must leave everything as it was. Under the picture adopted, philosophy can be expected to have a threefold impact—meditative, methodological, and moral—on people's habits of experience and behaviour.

1. From Practice to Philosophy

Philosophy characterized   What is it that distinguishes philosophy from other intellectual pursuits, in particular from pursuits of a scientific character? My own view is that philosophy deals with questions on which we are all already committed, whether we like it or not, and that this existing commitment, controversial as it often is, gives those questions the particular interest they have for philosophers. The domain of philosophical questioning is territory on which ordinary practice commits us to having opinions, however unarticulated and undeveloped those opinions may be; more on the nature of that commitment in the second section. And the opinions to which we find ourselves practically committed in this way are often quite problematic, whether through giving rise to paradox, having implications it is hard to live with, being difficult to reconcile with scientific views, or whatever. The drive to do philosophy, so I propose, arises from the desire to investigate those questions and to determine how far our practice-bound views can be sustained, in what ways they should be amended and revised, and whether such shifts can be implemented in ordinary practice.

Interpreted in this way, the philosophical drive is readily illustrated. It appears in the compulsion to determine whether we human beings can be free or conscious, assuming that we are creatures bound to the natural order; whether the natural order can be bound to necessities of law and causation, assuming that necessities reflect imaginings about what might have been, not observations about what is; whether values and duties have any place in a world we can explore together, assuming that the natural world can be comprehensively characterized in a wholly neutral vocabulary; and so on.

We never philosophize afresh, then, with a completely open disposition on the views we contemplate as alternatives. Whether we accept them or reject them, we always find ourselves already disposed—disposed, willy-nilly—to adopt certain of those views or families of views: for example, to adopt views that give countenance, under a certain interpretation, to the reality of freedom and consciousness, law and causation, value and duty. We always do philosophy in dialogue with positions that already have a hold on us. Philosophy, as we might put it, is an attempt to come to terms with those opinions, endorsing them if they prove worthy of reasoned endorsement and seeking to liberate ourselves from them otherwise. It is an effort to appropriate and own the views that we take on relevant questions—to expose them to the light of reason—and not to allow them to remain with us, unseen and uninvited, in the dark of unreflective opinion.

Philip Pettit

As we ask ourselves about any philosophical question, according to this picture of things, then we have to consider what our existing practices commit us to on the issue, and whether we should maintain that view or try to work our way out of it, developing it in novel ways, or replacing it with an alternative. We have to consider whether such a development or replacement is required by our reflective, argumentative lights. And we have to ask after whether it is one that we can live with in our practice: whether our habits of perception and conduct can be squared with it or amended to make room for the change that philosophical argument may seem to force upon us.

The picture sketched in these remarks suggests that in doing philosophy we will be inevitably torn between two different attractors. On the one hand we will want to embrace the ideas that come to us with our spontaneous, everyday practices, such as the ideas we naturally have about freedom and consciousness, causation and law, value and duty. But on the other hand we will want to reject any ideas that do not hold up in the light of critical reflection and reasoning. Philosophy will be conducted, then, in a field where rival forces pull against one another, holding out competing ideals: fidelity to the manifest image of how things are, on the one side; fidelity to the intellectual image of how things are on the other.[4]

Where will the intellectual as distinct from the manifest image come from? I think that this is a cultural variable and that philosophy, therefore, has represented a different challenge for different generations and societies. In every case the challenge has been formally the same: to examine and if necessary try to revise the manifest image in the light of the intellectual image. But different periods of history have put different intellectual images in play and so the challenge has been substantively different at different times. The Greeks had the problem of connecting the manifest image with the image for which dialectic or reason seemed to argue. The medievals had the problem of connecting it with the image that imposed itself in the light of revelation as well as reason. And the moderns had the problem of connecting it with the image that imposed itself in the light of science as well as reason.

In our culture the primary problem is still raised by science. As contemporary philosophers we have to face challenges presented by abstract reason—say, the difficulties posed in the traditional paradoxes—as every generation has had to do. But what we have to face most pressingly is the challenge that is presented by the scientific image of ourselves and our world. A naturalistic, more or less mechanical image of the universe is imposed on us by cumulative developments in physics, biology, and neuroscience, and this challenges us to look for where in that world there can be room for phenomena that remain as vivid as ever in the manifest image: consciousness, freedom, responsibility, goodness, virtue, and the like. While it still conforms to a pattern that has continued through many ages—so at any rate I am inclined to think—philosophy today is probably more challenging, and more difficult, than it has ever been.

---

[4] The conflict between the manifest and the scientific image of the world is identified as a main source of philosophical questions in W. Sellars (1997), *Empiricism and the Philosophy of Mind* (Cambridge, Mass.: Harvard University Press).

Philosophy and science   This view of philosophy would make for quite a clean contrast between philosophy and the sciences, while still recognizing the continuity between them. Philosophy will be continuous with the efforts of science, so far as it attempts to elaborate theory that has to be squared with scientific results, as just remarked. But it will stand apart from science in having as its remit the elaboration of a position that vindicates or can replace the views that come spontaneously to us in the ordinary course of life.

Consider the issues that physics investigates and think about the answers that it provides in its different bodies of theory. We ordinary thinkers may be possessed of what is sometimes called a folk physics, making unavoidable presumptions about how middle-sized objects will respond to our interventions and how they will interact with one another. But no one thinks that physicists owe a debt of loyalty to their folk selves and are duty-bound to consider how far different views may prove reconcilable with those presumptions, or even with the practice they guide. The questions physicists debate are too far removed from those presumptions and from that practice to be meaningfully subjected to any such requirement. And if some of the questions are ever connected with folk physics, as when people ask whether subatomic physics gives the lie to the ordinary presumption that some bodies are solid—solid, not full of holes—then we immediately think: this is not physics, this is philosophy.

What is true of physics is obviously true also of other natural sciences like chemistry, biology, neuroscience, and the subpersonal psychology of information-processing. But what of human sciences like social psychology, sociology, and economics? Does the view sketched above allow us to say that these are indeed sciences, and not philosophy under other names?

The question is not whether theories developed within the human sciences ever engage with views that turn out to be maintained commonly among the folk; the question is whether they engage with views that are inevitably maintained by the folk, being bound up with certain regular practices. Nor is the question whether those theories ever present a challenge of some sort to views that are tied up with ordinary practice; even the theories of natural science present such a challenge, requiring us to be able to vindicate the views we hold as a matter of practice with the naturalistic vision that they project. The question, rather, is whether the human sciences have a cognitive interest that makes it legitimate for theorists to develop and test their views, as in natural science, without having to worry about how far they can live with those views as ordinary folk, squaring them with ordinary practices.

The answer to this question is surely that yes, the human sciences do lay claim to such an autonomous cognitive goal. From their very beginnings, they were designed to develop an explanatory and predictive stance on individuals and aggregates and, where relevant, to propose policies whereby various forms of social order may be rendered compatible with how it is predicted that people will behave. The platforms of explanation and prediction that are thereby established may include theses that challenge received, practice-bound presumptions, of course—and it may raise a question about their plausibility that they do so—but they are not developed as alternatives that should replace those presumptions in guiding and shaping ordinary practice. They are not developed in the spirit of philosophical investigation.

It is true that many theorists in the human sciences, from Emile Durkheim to Claude Levi-Strauss and Michel Foucault, have often rejoiced in the revision of practical presumptions that they have taken their theories to imply, and that they sometimes seem to have embraced those theories for the very challenge and scandal they present on that front.[5] But to the extent that such theorists have taken this line, they have been generally regarded—quite rightly, from the point of view embraced here—as waxing philosophical, not scientific. Their interest has not been restricted to developing an explanatory or predictive scheme but has encompassed a desire to rethink certain practice-bound presumptions that they no longer find tenable: that is, to explore the possibility of replacing those presumptions with alternative, allegedly more satisfactory principles.

The characterization defended   The view of philosophy and practice that I have been outlining reduces to three propositions: first, that our ordinary practice commits us to holding by certain, potentially controversial presumptions, such as those that bear on freedom, causation, and duty; second, that philosophy addresses those questions, seeking to examine and assess our practical presumptions; and third, that this engagement with received presumptions is what distinguishes philosophy from other disciplines: philosophy is the theory we pursue in areas where, inevitably, we find ourselves already theoretically committed. The aim of the philosopher, under this picture, is to articulate and assess, and perhaps develop and amend, received practical presumptions. The ultimate ideal is to liberate oneself from the hold of ingrained ideas and to endorse only those views that one can square with the intellectual image of the universe—say, the image deriving from science—that one finds compelling.

How to defend this characterization of philosophy? I offer a brief overview of the main areas of philosophical questioning—this, of necessity, is a fairly personal presentation—and try to show that the overview gives support to the three propositions just distinguished.

Most of the matters covered in contemporary philosophy, whether the style of philosophizing is analytical or not, can be represented as falling within one or more of five broad categories. They can be allocated to the philosophy of reason, the philosophy of nature, the philosophy of mind, the philosophy of society, or the philosophy of value. A further category that might be added is the philosophy of religion but I do not consider it here.

The philosophy of reason deals with ideas and principles that govern human inquiry, argument, and theorizing and is the broadest of philosophical enterprises. It encompasses logic, methodology, epistemology, and philosophy of science and its claims are of the most general relevance. It is within the philosophy of reason that

---

[5] For one way in which this frequently happens see the discussion in ch 3, P. Pettit, (1993). *The Common Mind: An Essay on Psychology, Society and Politics*, paperback edition 1996, (New York: Oxford University Press).

we find an examination of concepts like those of truth, consistency, entailment; observation, induction, abduction; evidence, theory, confirmation; and so on.

This area of philosophy bears out my characterization of the discipline. We ordinary folk reason before we ever think about the philosophy of reason, and we also—crucially—give an account of why we reason as we do. We may not get as far as articulating in its most general form a principle like *modus ponens*, according to which the joint truth of a conditional and its antecedent ensures the truth of the consequent, but we will certainly be disposed to recognize and argue for instances of the principle in the course of our reasoning and of our accounting for how we reason. We are already committed to principles of this sort by our practice and the task of the philosophy of reason is to engage with such matters of practical presumption, articulating, and assessing, and no doubt developing and altering, our received views. There may be no cause for rethinking a principle like *modus ponens* but there are other principles—for example, those associated with inductive habits of reasoning—that have occasioned much heart-searching among philosophers.

The philosophy of nature is next to the philosophy of reason in the breadth of its relevance. I think of it as the area of philosophy in which we find a discussion of the notions of space, time, causation; substance, property, relation; possibility, actuality, essence; quantity, number, and other mathematical entities. These are notions that apply across the board and an understanding of what they involve and of how far they can stand up to criticism is crucial to many other philosophical enterprises.

As with the philosophy of reason, the philosophy of nature fits my characterization of philosophy in a fairly straightforward way. We all have ideas about the topics addressed, albeit in only the most inarticulate of modes. These ideas are already implicated in the ways we think about events happening at different times, for example, while assuming that substances persist through time; about some events causing later events while others merely precede them; about certain phenomena being actual, others possible, and yet others necessary or inevitable. The philosophy of nature tries to come to terms with such ideas and to put them in better shape than that which they assume in our untutored responses. In particular it tries to give them a shape—often quite a revisionary shape—that will enable them to stand up in the light of the best scientific theory. Thus the philosophy of time will often try to give an account of our ideas about time—our practically engaged ideas, not our idle speculations—that renders them compatible with the static, four-dimensional image of the universe that contemporary physics supports.

These comments should help to support the claim that the philosophy of reason and nature bears out my characterization of philosophical inquiry. But I should address an objection that is particularly likely to be raised at this point; it has more force here than in other areas. The objection is that while we may make practical presumptions that bear on issues of reason and nature, and while philosophy certainly addresses those issues too, I have done nothing to show that what makes the issues particularly engaging for philosophers is the fact that they are addressed in our practical presumptions. Wouldn't they be equally engaging, even if they had never been addressed in our folk practice and thought?

They would still have a substantive intellectual interest in that event and for many philosophers this is the only interest that legitimates them as questions worth pursuing; it is neither here nor there that they are addressed in our everyday presumptions. Nonetheless I think that there is support available for my view that the connection with everyday presumptions marks them off as questions of distinctively philosophical interest. Two observations in particular are worth making.

The first is that while the philosophy of reason has given rise to quite formal disciplines in which various logics and related systems have been elaborated, these developments are seen in many circles as belonging to mathematics or some other area, not to philosophy proper. The reason that they are seen in this way, I submit, is that they quickly go to a point at which none of our existing practices and ideas is engaged and that at that point philosophers typically cease to be particularly interested. Philosophers are essentially involved in debate with received, practice-bound opinion—opinion that they themselves hold as members of the folk—and when that debate runs out, their involvement flags.

The second observation I cite in support of my view is that something similar— though this is a much more controversial claim—holds in the philosophy of nature. The discussion of substances and properties quickly confronts alternatives that offer different pictures of the ultimate metaphysical building blocks: these may be represented either as property-instances or tropes, for example, or as property-types or universals, so long as compensating adjustments are made on other fronts. Now there will always be an interest in adjudicating between such alternatives, from the point of view of constructing a metaphysics which fits best with natural science. But when the alternatives discussed have been taken to be equally consistent with the practical presumptions we make in respect of substances and properties and the like—and they have sometimes been taken, rightly or wrongly, in that way—then many philosophers have tended to lose interest, describing the enterprise as a form of book-keeping.[6] This tendency is intelligible in the light of my claim that questions have a distinctively philosophical interest only so far as they are taken to be questions engaged, or tied up with questions engaged, in our practice-bound presumptions.

The other main areas of philosophy, under my tendentious taxonomy, are the philosophy of mind, the philosophy of society, and the philosophy of value. The philosophy of mind engages with familiar topics like belief, desire and emotion, language and meaning, consciousness, freedom, and personhood. The philosophy of society deals with the nature of conventions, norms, and laws, the possibility of joint intention, collective rationality and group agency, and the analysis of power, authority, status, and the like. And, finally, the philosophy of value addresses the range of normative issues that arise in aesthetic, ethical, and political discussion: the meaning of beauty, goodness, and obligation, the nature and role of more substantive values in relation to those categories, and the shape that normative argument should ideally take.

---

[6] M. Johnston, (1993). 'Objectivity Refigured: Pragmatism with Verificationism', in *Reality, Representation and Projection*, J. Haldane and C. Wright (Oxford: Oxford University Press).

It hardly needs argument that ordinary practices of reasoning and dealing with one another are organized around ideas on these sorts of topics. The way we talk about ourselves and others, and the overtures we make in relating to others, speak volubly of the presumptions we endorse as to what minds and persons are and how they can be influenced. The way we assume that regularities can have the force of norm or law, and the way we hold fellow members of groups to certain expectations, speak of firmly entrenched presumptions about the nature of collective life. And the sorts of considerations we entertain and produce in arguing about what is desirable in this or that realm, and what is ultimately to be done, display similar presumptions on the nature of value in general and on the particular principles that ought to command our allegiance.

These three areas of philosophy serve as well as the philosophy of reason and nature to bear out the claims outlined earlier. We have received, practice-bound ideas on all of the issues addressed, or at least on questions presupposed to those issues. And it is very plausible that the reason why the issues engage us in philosophy is precisely that that is so. We are conscious as philosophers that whether we like it or not we are going to have views on those matters as an imperative of practice. And we are naturally anxious, given the challenges from the scientific image of the world, to make sure that the views we end up holding are ones we can truly own and defend.

The view of philosophy defended here, I should say, is not fully borne out by the particular demarcations that have grown up within the academy between philosophy and other disciplines. Many questions that I would regard as philosophical are investigated outside philosophy departments and many questions that I would regard as not particularly philosophical are investigated within. But this imperfect alignment is only what we should expect, given the various exogenous presssures on departmental divisions. My view claims to identify a pattern of concern that satisfies two constraints. First, it has a genuine unity in itself, and gives us an attractive way of construing philosophy. And second, it reflects the interests of institutionally identified philosophers to a more or less accurate approximation. Inevitably, then, the view taken has a revisionary aspect and it should not be judged merely by how well it describes the projects undertaken by philosophy professors and only by philosophy professors.

2. Interlude: the Nature of Practical Presumptions

Practical, not intellectual, presumptions   The discussion so far has supposed that there is no difficulty about how ordinary practices can commit us as ordinary folk to endorsing certain presumptions or ideas. But this assumption needs to be addressed, both to fill out the picture of the last section and to prepare for the argument of the next. So how can folk practices commit us to beliefs on the sorts of matters mentioned? How do folk practices come to involve assumptions about what follows deductively or inductively from what, what distinguishes causation from mere temporal succession, what makes someone free or unfree, when a collection of people constitutes a collective agent, and whether the right is always a function of the good?

This question may be variously resolved, consistently with the image of philosophy described in the first section. It is important for me to defend my particular line, however, as it is involved in the argument presented in the next section. The line is that while the ideas to which our practices commit us define something that might be described as a folk theory—a folk theory of causation, freedom, collectivity, morality, or whatever—it is not a theory that is intellectually endorsed so much as a theory that is embraced as a matter of lived know-how. It is a lived theory that gives us necessary points of orientation in the lived world: it is the *Lebenstheorie* that guides us through the *Lebenswelt*.[7]

The practices that commit us to beliefs about the general topics on which philosophy focuses are, in the first place, practices of a discursive and inferential kind.[8] They are the practices in virtue of which certain premises—these may be given in perception or spelled out in judgment—prove capable of moving us to certain conclusions, whether the conclusions be drawn in words or in actions. The transitions that they license will sometimes be capable of formal and deductive representation but equally often they will have a non-formal or non-deductive character.

People display two sorts of beliefs in the inferences that such discursive practices lead them to make. First of all, and most obviously, they can display beliefs about what follows from what. If they instantiate and endorse relevant arguments they can show that they hold the abstract belief that *modus ponens* is a valid pattern of inference; or they can manifest the more concrete belief that certain observations provide support for the conclusion that emeralds are green but do not give any support to the rival conclusion that they are grue: that is, green if observed before a certain time, blue otherwise.[9] Cases of both these kinds, abstract or concrete, all involve procedural beliefs as to what follows from what.

But people, to move to the second case, can also display beliefs about substantive matters in their inferential practices. They do so in what they take to imply, and what they take to be implied by relevant ascriptions: say, imputations of causation, attributions of freedom, descriptions of groups as agents, or conclusions as to the rightness of an action. In being disposed to countenance certain implicators and certain implications for such ascriptions—and only certain implicators and implications—they subscribe to quite definite specifications of causation, freedom, group agency, and rightness. Thus they will subscribe to causation having a temporal direction so far as they argue from something being later in time to the conclusion that it cannot be the cause of a certain event; they will subscribe to its involving a spatio-temporally continuous process so far

---

[7] The word *Lebenswelt* is particularly associated with E. Husserl (1970). *The Crisis of European Sciences and Transcendental Phenomenology* (Evanston, Ill, Northwestern University Press). That work, interestingly, is concerned with what Husserl sees as the unnecessary alienation of scientific concepts from the lived ideas in which they have their roots.

[8] See R. Brandom (1994). *Making it Explicit* (Cambridge, Mass.: Harvard University Press); P. Pettit, (1998). 'Practical Belief and Philosophical Theory,' *Australasian Journal of Philosophy* 76; and Pettit (2000). 'How the Folk Understand Folk Psychology,' *Protosociology* 14: 26–38.

[9] N. Goodman (1973). *Fact, Fiction and Forecast* (Indianapolis, Bobbs-Merrill).

as they argue from something being removed and disconnected to the conclusion that it cannot be the cause of the event; they will subscribe to its being a productive sort of relationship so far as they take causes to be employable as means of bringing about associated effects; and they will subscribe to its being capable of supporting explanation so far as they invoke causes to resolve questions about why the effects occurred.

With any term of this kind, people may differ in some of the implicators or implications that they countenance; some may be disposed to reason from the presence of causation, for example, to the existence of a lawlike connection, while others have no such disposition. How, then, to identify those inferential connections that are involved in the specification of the relationship ascribed by a word like 'causes'? The answer, I suggest, is that in any linguistic community the relevant connections will be identified—more or less strictly—by the connections an interlocutor will generally be expected to find compelling if he or she is taken to be conversable: that is, sufficiently well-equipped in terms of understanding, reasoning capacity, and discursive responsiveness to be worth engaging in discourse. The linguistic community relative to which the privileged connections—if you like, the a priori connections— are identified in this way may be the community at large or it may be a richer sub-community, say a sub-community of experts in which the ascription of conversability involves quite detailed expectations.[10]

I said that the practices that commit us to practical presumptions—that is, shared practical presumptions—are, in the first place, practices of a discursive and inferential kind. The reason for the qualification about this holding only in the first place is that the practices involved also have a decisive role in the way we conduct ourselves towards the world, towards other people and towards ourselves. It would be a great mistake to miss this, for it would lead us to think, quite wrongly, that in the image defended here, philosophy is exclusively focused on matters of language. In all of the cases envisaged what we are disposed to conclude and say is required to fit the way we respond at the level of conduct, and the presumptions we make are often going to be more visible in how we act than in anything we actually spell out in words. And besides, conduct is not always going to be driven by what we are inclined to say; things can also be the other way around. The arguments we spell out in words often articulate inferences that come to us in their original form as spontaneous responses at the level of sentiment and behaviour.

This last observation can be illustrated with reference to the causation case. It is highly plausible that we are equipped by our biology to see certain sequences of movements that are within our power as more or less compelling ways of achieving corresponding ends: this, in the way we drop things in order to make a noise, or we throw things in order to hit a target. Given that we conceive of causes as potential

[10] On conversability in this sense see P. Pettit and M. Smith (1996) 'Freedom in Belief and Desire,' *Journal of Philosophy* 93: 429–49; P. Pettit (2001). *A Theory of Freedom: From the Psychology to the Politics of Agency* (New York, Oxford University Press and Cambridge: Polity). The criterion of the a priori that is invoked here, being social in origin and pliable in application, is quite close to one endorsed by W. V. O. Quine—the great critic of the traditional category—in Quine (1974) *The Roots of Reference* (La Salle: Open Court Publishers).

means for achieving their effects, then, we will often find relations of causation more vividly available to us in this natural disposition than in any more intellectual, language-bound reflection.

The point can also be borne out in the case of freedom. Whenever we think of someone as having freely done something, in particular done something that affects us, then we think ourselves justified in feeling resentful at what they did or gratified by what they did.[11] But our dispositions to feel resentment or gratitude often spring from perceptions that escape our capacity to verbalize and, though they remain subject to discursively generated revision, they are often activated in a more or less spontaneous way. This being so, we are bound to authorize the experience of resentment or gratitude as an experience—strictly, a defeasible experience—in which the fact that someone has acted freely towards us is made more or less primitively compelling.

Practical Presumptions, not Dispositions   So much for the claim that the presumptions that constitute our folk theory in any area are practical, not intellectual presumptions. They are presumptions accepted as a matter of inferential and related practice, not theses spelled out in formulae, contemplated in the abstract and then reflectively endorsed. But why say that they are presumptions at all? Why treat them as varieties of belief?

The practices that we have been describing all exist as dispositions within human speakers and agents, in particular as dispositions that they regulate in the light of one another's responses. Thus the *modus ponens* practice of inference primarily exists as a disposition that people display to recognize in a case-by-case way that, certain sentences they endorse being related as conditional and antecedent, they have reason to assert the consequent of the conditional. Why should we treat this habit of inference as being anything more than that: a habit? Why should we think that it constitutes a belief or set of beliefs that the conclusion follows in this case, in that case, in that other case, and so on? And why, even more spectacularly, should we think that it constitutes a belief in the abstract principle according to which the joint truth of a conditional and its antecedent guarantees the truth of the consequent; why should we treat it as anything more than a disposition to form distinct, case-bound beliefs?

The reason we treat the habit of inference as a belief is that if we are to countenance someone as a conversable interlocutor—as someone there is a possibility of reasoning with—then we expect that if they are challenged about why they move from asserting certain premises to asserting a deductive conclusion, they will be able to do more than shrug. They will be able to spell out the claim that the conclusion follows from the premises, they will be able to recognize what might be evidence for and evidence against that claim, they will be sensitive to how such evidence goes in the course of inquiry and discussion, and so on. There is a striking contrast in this respect with non-inferential habits, such as the habits of putting

---

[11] P. Strawson (1982). 'Freedom and Resentment' in G. Watson, *Free Will* (Oxford: Oxford University Press). See also P. Pettit (2001) *A Theory of Freedom: From the Psychology to the Politics of Agency*.

words together in grammatical form. The grammatical speaker may not be able to lift intuitions as to what is grammatical into the realm of discourse but anyone we treat as conversable will have to be able to do this with intuitions as to what follows from what.

It is no objection to this observation that not every habit of inference can exist in a person's mind in the form of a premise that they explicitly endorse, as Lewis Carroll's story of Achilles and the tortoise shows.[12] Achilles reckons that he can get the tortoise to admit a conclusion, say that q, on the basis of having admitted that if p then q, and that p. The tortoise says that perhaps he will be forced to do so if he is allowed a further premiss to the effect that if it is the case that those premisses hold, then the conclusion follows. When Achilles allows him this premiss, of course, the tortoise asks for a further premiss to the effect that if it is the case that those enriched premisses hold, then the conclusion follows. And when Achilles allows him this too, he makes a similar request. An infinite regress looms and the lesson is that not every rule of inference can exist as a premiss; some rules must exist as habits of moving from premisses to conclusion that are not themselves explicitly endorsed as premisses.

But this lesson is perfectly compatible with the point just argued. The requirement I mentioned is that a conversable speaker must be capable of dealing with a challenge to any inference he or she draws, spelling out a belief as to what follows from what and being able to defend that belief. And this is quite consistent with the Carroll lesson.

So much by way of arguing that the *modus ponens* habit—and by extension any such habit of inference—must be taken to constitute a belief: a presumption maintained in practice-bound mode. But why should we describe the belief as a belief in the abstract principle or formula, not just as a belief that these premisses support that conclusion, those other premisses that other conclusion, and so on case by case? We might choose not to describe it that way, for all that the argument of this paper requires; it is enough for our purposes that the disposition to form case-bound beliefs will rationally require anyone who understands the corresponding formula to embrace the formulaic belief. But there is a long and intelligible tradition of going to the abstract characterization and I see no reason to break with this.

The idea in the tradition is that the disposition to form relevant case-bound beliefs constitutes a single case-by-case way of believing the general formula; in particular, a way of believing it that contrasts with the formulaic mode of giving one's explicit assent to that formula. Take someone who is disposed to believe of every cat that it is a cat and of every cat that, being a cat, it will have incisor teeth. This person need not be immediately disposed to assent to the universal claim that every cat has incisor teeth. But nevertheless they are traditionally said to believe that universal claim: to believe it *in sensu diviso*, as scholastics used to put it, not *in sensu composito*; to believe it in a divided but not in a unified sense.[13]

---

[12] L. Carroll (1895). 'What the Tortoise said to Achilles,' *Mind* 4: 278–80.

[13] The distinction, which derives from Peter of Abelard, is used in D. Lewis (1969). *Convention* (Cambridge, Mass.: Harvard University Press).

In the same way the person who is disposed to reason in the *modus ponens* way may be said to believe the universal principle instantiated in different cases. People who are said to believe the proposition in the divided, case-by-case way will lack one ability that must be present in the unified, formulaic mode of belief: the immediate disposition to assent to the formula. But they will otherwise perform in an inferentially indiscernible manner and the disposition that they display to form relevant case-bound beliefs will give them reason to assent to that formula, should they gain an understanding of it.[14]

What I have argued in relation to *modus ponens* is going to hold, quite obviously, for other habits of inference too. The lesson is that while we ordinary folk hold by things that we may find challenging and contestable as philosophers, we hold by them in a distinctively practical, particularistic way. We embrace matters of belief in the practical ways we reason and conduct ourselves, without necessarily spelling them out—or at least without spelling them out very often—in formulae that we explictly endorse. And though the things we can be said to believe in that way are often abstract and universal in character, we typically embrace them only in a particularistic, case-by-case manner; we may never abstract from cases and formulate them as things that hold quite generally.

That practical presumptions constitute a lived theory—a *Lebenstheorie*—in this way does not mean that they are a second-best to the reflective sort of theory that we achieve when we can spell out explicit claims and show what follows from them. Spelling out a theory in explicit terms has many advantages, in particular the advantage of allowing us to examine it systematically; this is one of the things, as we shall see, that motivates the philosophical enterpise. But not every belief can be held in explicit form, as we know from the Lewis Carroll argument. And in any case there is a respect in which someone who holds a general belief in a practical, particularistic way will have a significant ability that may be lacking in the articulate believer.

Consider the principle that red things look red in presumptively normal conditions, yellow things look yellow, green things look green, and so on. Someone might believe this in the formulaic way, without actually knowing how red or yellow or green looks, and so without being able to make any use of the principle in distinguishing different colours; the person might even be colour-blind. But someone who knows the principle in the practical, particularistic way will know it through being able in suitable conditions to have colour sensations—through being disposed with any sensation of redness or greenness or whatever to register its presence in some manner—and through being disposed in those conditions, so far as the sensation is as of red, to treat it as evidence of redness, so far as it is as of green, to treat it as evidence of greeness, and so on. Holding the belief in the lived way that is tied up with practice requires the possession of a skill that may be lacking in someone who holds it in the explicitly theorized or formulaic fashion. We will return to this point in the final section.

---

[14] See Pettit 'Practical Belief and Philosophical Theory'.

An objection answered   Under this account of the practical, particularistic way in which we hold to folk theories, it may seem that we the folk are a decidedly empiricist, even positivistic lot. We are said to conceive of causation or freedom or whatever as the phenomenon that answers to the assumptions we display in our reasoning habits as to how things connect with one another. Thus we are said to conceive of causation as that sort of relationship that runs from past to future, that does not hold at a spatio-temporal remove, that is capable of subserving a means-end connection, that makes a certain sort of explanation or prediction possible, and so on. But this means that we are said to conceive of causation operationally or functionally, in terms of what it does, and to abstain from any metaphysical speculation as to what it is in itself. And doesn't that sound suspect? Doesn't it sound as if we the folk are being cast in a suspiciously correct, positivistic posture?

The account given of folk theory emphasizes the sorts of views we cannot help but have about causation and freedom and the like, on pain of there being no possibility of reasoned exchange. But the folk may fill out those views in any area with certain more or less metaphysical commitments and those commitments may come to have a certain a priori status in their exchanges. Thus the folk may well think that while causation generally has to satisfy the sorts of connections mentioned, it consists itself in an unanalysable form of contact—a sort of 'biff' or 'oomph'—that explains why those connections generally hold and that might conceivably be realized in their absence. The commitment to the need for such an unanalysable form of contact could show up in their finding themselves unwilling to recognize certain otherwise suitable connections as instances of causation proper; it need not involve the endorsement of any metaphysical formula, though of course it might do so.

On this account the folk, were they to reject the possibility of biff-contact, might be willing to say that the predicate 'causes' should be taken to ascribe that relationship, whatever it is, that satisfies the operational or functional requirements inscribed in our practices of reasoning about causation; this is certainly the line that would fit best with their other reasoning practices. But so far as they think that there is such a thing as biff-contact—so far as they are committed to such a metaphysic— they will display a belief that the predicate should be primarily used to posit the presence of that contact, and that the functional specifications should be taken to serve a purely evidential role. The satisfaction of those specifications would be indicative of causation, under the practice imagined, providing evidence that there is the sort of biff-contact required for one thing to cause another; but it would not establish in itself that causal contact had occurred.[15]

As it is in the case of causation, so it may be elsewhere. Although the folk's views will be established on the basis of how they reason with one another, and on how far that pattern of reasoning is associated with conversability, they may still contain a metaphysical component. Just as their views on causation may postulate an empirically

---

[15] The account sketched here derives from an important paper by David Braddon-Mitchell which shows that this sort of thing may be true of consciousness and that if it is, then that will defuse many contemporary philosophical debates about consciousness. See D. Braddon-Mitchell (2001). 'Qualia and Analytical Condititionals', *Journal of Philosophy* 100(3): 111–35.

unexhausted form of contact between cause and effect, so their views on freedom may postulate an empirically unexhausted form of contra-causal power, their views on consciousness an empirically unexhausted form of self-transparency, and so on. The story told in this section is in no way inconsistent with ascribing such metaphysical leanings to ordinary people.

3. From Philosophy to Practice

Against existentialism   By the account given in the first section, philosophy grows out of the desire to examine and reconstruct the presumptions that we are inevitably inducted into, as we saw in the second section, when we participate in the discursive and related practices that characterize human life. The question to which we now turn—the issue between existentialism and quietism—is whether this reflection on our practical presumptions is capable of making a difference in ordinary life: whether it can shift our habits of inference, so that we read some experiential data differently and are drawn into some different behavioural responses. Is philosophical reflection impotent in relation to the practice from which it springs? Or is it a sort of reflection that can feed back in that way onto ordinary practice?

Under the account given, we should naturally hope that philosophy is not practically impotent in this way. There would be something poignant and depressing about our situation were we able to examine and assess our practical presumptions, discerning various shortfalls and mistakes, but not have the capacity to do anything about putting those failures right. We would have to live in ironic, intellectual detachment from beliefs that we couldn't help but embrace in the hurly burly of the day-to-day. We must seek out any opportunity there may be, then, for allowing philosophical reflection to feed back onto ordinary practice.

The existentialist claim, as I conceive of it, is that there is no problem obstructing the path of such philosophical feedback. The proposal is that we philosophers can throw off received ideas as we find them wanting and replace them with the notions that receive our philosophical *imprimatur*. We can rebuild ourselves plank by plank, ultimately endorsing attitudes and dispositions that are completely at variance with those from which we started. We can even assume the status of a Nietzschean *Uebermensch*, spurning folk wisdom and folk inhibitions in favour of the guidance provided by our personally authorized views. We can seek with someone like Sartre, for example, to reject the self-protective, self-deceptive ideas of the folk and and to espouse the bold and bracing ideal of what is described as authentic consciousness.

It is worth reminding ourselves just how radical a transformation may be required under this image of philosophy. As Sartre interprets his findings, for example, philosophy would require us to give up on the idea that we are anything more than an impersonal sequence of brute impressions and bald decisions; to detach ourselves from all emotion, recognizing it as an attempt in bad faith to hide our free decisions from ourselves; to take the world to be the shapeless, unstructured mess which we can only experience at the cost of feeling a massive nausea; and to accept that relations between people are inevitably a power-struggle about whose representations of the other are to prevail.[16] This is a bleak, tantalizing and wholly alien vision. If we think that philosophy could intrude it into everyday practice, then we probably believe that there are no limits to the transformative power of philosophical thinking.

Such a belief in philosophy's transformative power is not restricted to card-carrying existentialists. Many contemporary philosophers in the analytical tradition think that the philosophical examination of practical presumptions should lead us, so far as we endorse the findings of science, to think that we embrace falsehood when we evaluate actions as right or wrong,[17] when we treat people as having done things freely,[18] when we countenance beliefs and desires as determinants of action,[19] and when we say that time passes.[20] If these philosophers go on to say that we should simply replace our existing false beliefs with what we take to be scientifically warranted truths, reworking our ordinary practices around this new wisdom, then they are just as radical as any self-described existentialists.[21]

I do not think that the existentialist image of philosophy's transformative potential can really stand up. It suggests that there are no limits in the extent to which philosophy may be able to transform ordinary practice and this, in my view, is just facile optimism. The optimism is iconoclastic and enticing but it comes ultimately, so I shall try to argue, from an inadequate understanding of the relationship between belief and practice.

The suggestion that philosophy can transform practice in quite radical ways only makes sense if the practical presumptions that philosophy examines are the determinant of practice, discursive and otherwise, and not the other way around. The beliefs we entertain will have to be the unmoved movers of our practice-bound dispositions to reason this way or that, where the reasoning involved may be purely discursive or may also appear at the level of sentiment and behaviour. In particular, this will have to be so with those more or less general beliefs or ideas that philosophy tries to explicate, examine and—at least in the existentialist image—replace. Such beliefs must be the independent variable and the reasoning practices associated with them the dependent; the direction of determination must run from beliefs to practices.

This picture has a natural appeal. It gives expression to the idea that the beliefs and ideas endorsed by intellect are at the control centre of human response and that what happens at that centre determines everything which takes place on the peripheries of practice. And that idea has been dominant for a very long time in philosophical thinking, constituting what has sometimes been described as a 'logocentric'

[16] J. P. Sartre (1957). *The Transcendence of the Ego: An Existentialist Theory of Consciousness* (New York: Farrar, Straus & Giroux); Sartre (1958). *Being and Nothingness* (London: Methuen); Sartre (1962). *Sketch for a Theory of the Emotions* (London: Methuen).

[17] J. L. Mackie (1977). *Ethics* (Harmondsworth: Penguin).

[18] P. Van Inwagen (1983). *An Essay on Free Will* (Oxford: Oxford University Press).

[19] P. Churchland (1979). *Scientific Realism and The Plasticity of Mind* (Cambridge: Cambridge University Press).   [20] J. J. C. Smart (1963). *Philosophy and Scientific Realism* (London: Routledge).

[21] A good example of someone who takes this view is Paul Churchland, op.cit.

vision: a vision focused on the role of word or *logos* rather than on the role of custom or deed, *ethos* or *praxis*.[22]

But this logocentric picture is at odds with the account given in the last section of how it is that we the folk hold by our practical presumptions. For we saw in the course of explicating such presumptions that if we can be said to believe something like the principle of *modus ponens*, or commonplaces such as those that govern causation, then that is so only because we are disposed to reason appropriately and to justify our reasoning in discourse with others. The mode of existence enjoyed by such general beliefs is not independent of our reasoning habits and practices. The general beliefs exist in us only so far as those habits and practices command our allegiance. They exist in us only so far as we are spontaneously disposed to reason appropriately—at least in presumptively favourable conditions—and are equally disposed to maintain those dispositions under discursive interrogation. Those dispositions are the base on which the possession of the general beliefs supervenes.

If anything of this kind is true—and something of the kind is surely compelling—then we cannot think of the general beliefs in question as attitudes that exist independently from discursive practices, shaping how those practices go. And so we cannot think of them as attitudes that may readily shift under philosophical examination, leading to an automatic adjustment—however long the adjustment may take to stabilize—in the person's discursive practices and in associated responses at the level of sentiment and behaviour. We could only have thought of them in that way if they had been formulaically embraced beliefs, not beliefs maintained in the case-by-case manner of practical presumptions.

Were formulaically embraced beliefs at the origin of our practice-bound responses then they would have constituted a centre of control which philosophy might have infiltrated and transformed. But the centre at which our discursive and related practices are controlled does not lend itself to easy philosophical take-over. That centre exists, paradoxically, at the peripheries where we find this or that particular transition of thought compelling and display it in what we say, in what we feel, or in what we do. It is distributed in the myriad points at which we find ourselves compelled to draw this or that conclusion and find ourselves able to defend the conclusion drawn under the pressure of discursive exchange with ourselves and others. Thus the conviction that causation is from past to future or that there is no causation at a distance manifests itself, not in the mesmerizing spell of an abstract formula, but in the magnetic force with which we find ourselves drawn to conclude that now this event, now that, can or cannot have been the cause of something under investigation.

The lesson is that if we go along with the argument of the last section, then we must reject any easy existentialist optimism about the capacity of philosophy to undo and reform our received, practice-bound ideas. We must recognize that those ideas come

---

[22] My preferred account of the relationship between belief and practice may be described as 'ethocentric', in a word I have used in related contexts; see, e.g., *The Common Mind*. Ironically, this understanding of the relationship has many affinities with the point of view maintained by Martin Heidegger in his allegedly existentialist work. See M. Heidegger (1963). *Being and Time* (New York: Harper and Row).

with the inertia of habits ingrained in us by our biology and our background and that they may leave in place only restricted possibilities for revision and replacement.

Against quietism   But does the lesson argue for quietism, then, leaving us with the unhappy prospect of having to believe in practice what we may find ourselves philosophically unable to endorse? Does it suggest that we may have to live our lives switching between two perspectives, one practical, the other philosophical—one associated with lived experience and behaviour, the other with theoretical reflection—where the perspectives offer visions of different and incompatible worlds? I hope not; and I think not.

Under the account of philosophy presented earlier, it involves the articulation of practical assumptions, whether in the area of reason, nature, mind, society, or value, and the rationalization of those assumptions—this will typically involve giving up some assumptions, and amending others—so that they are internally coherent and coherent with doctrines that are taken to be independently compelling: say, the general lessons of natural science. But any articulation of such assumptions will allow us to draw lessons from them that were not previously capable of being identified, since it is only when we articulate our beliefs that we can begin to examine where they lead. And any revisionary articulation—any articulation that involves rejecting or amending some received ideas—is bound to have lessons that will be particularly surprising. The lessons to be taught by philosophy I describe, for want of better terms, as respectively meditative, methodological, and moral.

The meditative lessons   The meditative lessons I have in mind are those implications that are capable of being absorbed reflectively by people. Such lessons will give people a different take on habits of perception and response that are more or less inevitable and indispensable in human life, leading them to assign a different significance to the experience and behaviour in question.

Think of how we see and read the expressions of others, interpret their actions, and feel resentment or gratification at what they do to us. Think in particular of the concepts that we generate to make sense of these performances, as we introduce talk of the meaning of a glance, the intention or motive behind a piece of behaviour, or the responsibility of the agent for how they treated us. It is extremely unlikely that any philosophical theory which represented these conceptions as groundless could be seriously embraced. But there are many different theories that might be used to support them and, depending on which is embraced, philosophy will give the conceptions—and the performances they inform—a very different significance.

My own preference, for example, supports a construal of the conceptions in question which is reasonably faithful to our intuitions but remains valid within an austere naturalistic picture: a picture under which the entities in the subatomic realm, and the regularities that govern them, fix every other aspect of the world.[23]

---

[23]   P. Pettit (1993). 'A Definition of Physicalism,' *Analysis* 53: 213–23. For my views on intentionality and freedom see *The Common Mind*; and Pettit (2001). *A Theory of Freedom: From the Psychology to the Politics of Agency* (Cambridge: Polity).

That I adopt this picture is not going to change greatly the way in which I carry on in the application of the concepts in question, but it is bound to have an impact on me; or at least it is bound to have an impact if I am a philosopher who internalizes his own views properly. One negative impact it will have is to discipline me in a habit of thought that banishes all suggestion of a non-materialistic machinery at work in the generation of human behaviour: it will inhibit any tendency to draw Cartesian conclusions. And one positive impact it should have is to school me into a sense of continued awe that I, a construct in messy chemical material, should be able to make interpersonal contact with other such constructs and to establish community with them.

I speak of the sort of lesson forthcoming here as meditative in character. The reason for that choice of epithet is that it is a sort of lesson that is easily lost to view in the professional pursuit of philosophy. Letting the lesson resonate and echo in one's everyday awareness requires a discipline of the soul as much as a discipline of the mind and it is not something that is easily taught in the classroom or cultivated in the office. It is not something indeed that fits comfortably with the image of the professional that philosophers are more or less forced to assume. It smacks of religion rather than scholarship or science.

Yet if philosophical reflection is not allowed to have a meditative impact, then it really is vulnerable to Kierkegaard's jibe against systematic thought. The professional philosopher who works from nine to five on his or her views of mind-reading, action-explanation, or freedom and then leaves that work entirely to the confines of the office is pursuing philosophy in a space that is one dimension short of what it might have been. The interest of philosophy is associated in considerable part with the challenge it poses to let the results of philosophical reflection reverberate in one's day-to-day experience and life. If professional philosophy loses touch with that dimension, then it is in danger of degenerating into a routine scholasticism or of being absorbed into other disciplines like the history of ideas or the sociology of thought. Not only that indeed. If professional philosophy loses touch with that dimension, then it will miss out on an important source of confirmation and dis-confirmation for philosophical views: the view that cannot be absorbed in any way within ordinary experience and conduct must for that very reason come under serious question.

I illustrated the meditative challenge with the naturalistic sorts of views that I happen to hold about mind but it applies with all sorts of views, non-naturalistic as well as naturalistic, and it applies of course to views on the whole range of topics covered in philosophy.

Philosophical views on almost any topic can be categorized as non-naturalistic or naturalistic and, in the latter event, as hard naturalistic or soft naturalistic. The non-naturalist will argue that our practical presumptions on the subject in question are inconsistent with science but should still be embraced. The hard naturalist will agree that they are inconsistent but maintain that they therefore have to be rejected. And the soft naturalist will hold that they can be reconciled, though perhaps only after quite imaginative recasting, with scientific claims. The views I used to illustrate the meditative lesson are soft naturalistic in character. But non-naturalists would also have meditatively challenging views—views of a spiritualistic character—to savour and absorb in their everyday practice. And hard naturalists would face the rather different meditative task of finding a way of living with practices that they believe to be grounded in false beliefs. One way of doing this would be to try to think of them as practices pursued or pursuable in the fashion of make-believe games. Another would be to try to see them as habits of reaction that are more or less autonomous in character and only mistakenly treated as modes of believing anything.

The meditative challenge to philosophy not only arises, regardless of whether one is a non-naturalist, a hard naturalist, or a soft naturalist. It also arises in every area of philosophical thought: those involving reason, nature, society, and value, as well as the area of mind. Consider the view of inductive reasoning under which it works with categories of projection that come to us naturally but that have no rationally discernible basis. Or think of the theory of time under which our experience as of time passing is essentially illusory. Or think of the position which represents certain groups as having all the properties for which we naturally look in an agent or person. Or think of the various views that claim to identify the purpose, cognitive or non-cognitive, of evaluation. No matter where one looks across the range of philosophical reflection, one finds views emerging that are going to pose a meditative challenge for any serious mind.

But the influence that philosophy is going to have on practice is not limited to the meditative impact, central though this is. There are at least two other distinguishable domains in which philosophical reflection is likely to change how people might otherwise perceive and behave. I describe these respectively as the methodological and the moral. The meditative lessons of philosophy derive from the particular casting that philosophy gives to views we already hold, albeit in purely practical mode. The methodological and moral lessons come from a different source. They derive from the fact that our practical presumptions, when they are articulated according to the account given in this or that philosophy, often prove to have implications which are new to common sense. The methodological lessons are implications that bear on how the world may be expected empirically to be, the moral on how it should be evaluated.

The methodological lessons   Consider the famous attempt by Galileo to persuade people that objects fall to earth at the same rate, regardless of their weight.[24] It works by inviting people to think a thought experiment through and to agree that what will happen, according to their own beliefs about different aspects of the experiment, shows that bodies of different weights will fall to the earth at the same rate. You are invited to imagine two solid bodies, indiscernible in shape or weight, falling to earth, and to agree that they should fall at the same rate. Then you are invited to imagine them falling with a thread connecting them and to agree that

<hr />

[24] This use of the Galilean model is different from that in F. Jackson (1998). *From Metaphysics to Ethics: A Defence of Conceptual Analysis* (Oxford: Oxford University Press), 78.

they will still fall at the same rate. Finally you are invited to imagine that the connecting thread is rigid like an iron bar and to agree that they will continue to fall at the same rate. And then it is pointed out that the two bodies connected in that rigid way are equivalent to a single body of double the weight, so that you have just agreed that such a body will have the same rate of fall as either of the bodies on its own. Thus your own beliefs about the elements in the scenario envisaged—the claims to which you are invited to agree—are shown to imply, perhaps contrary to your existing view on the matter, that bodies of different weights can fall at the same rate to earth.

This thought experiment turns on the fact that our views on different matters, once articulated, can prove to have surprising implications. And that lesson holds as much of the practical presumptions articulated in philosophy, as it does of the particular, empirical intuitions that Galileo was working with. Unsurprisingly, then, one very common style of argument in philosophy attempts to derive such potentially surprising implications and to paint in the picture of the world that they convey.

It is in this vein that I read many of the most influential—though not necessarily compelling—contributions of philosophy in the last hundred years or so. Here, roughly stated, are some prominent examples.

- Lewis Carroll's demonstration that under our presumptions about reasoning, as revealed in interpersonal exchange, no argument will be supported by its premises alone; there will always have to be a rule of inference that is presupposed in the background.[25]
- Wittgenstein's argument that properly and coherently articulated, our practical presumptions about what following a rule involves, in particular a rule of thought or judgement, entail that a private language is impossible: no one could use an informative, private language to name and keep track of sensations that others could not in principle access.[26]
- Quine's argument that the presumptions we hold in respect of interpreting and translating words, at least when they are spelled out as they ought to be, entail that two equally good manuals of translation could offer inconsistent construals of a sentence in the target language.[27]
- Sellars's argument that everything we are committed to in ascribing mental states to ourselves and others is consistent with our having learned to use mental concepts in the way in which we apparently learn to use terms that are theoretically introduced.[28]
- Strawson's argument that the presumptions involved in sustaining reactive emotions like resentment and gratification entail an ascription of freedom to the subject on whom they are targetted and that disbelieving in someone's freedom is as difficult as the suspension of those reactions.[29]

[25] L. Carroll (1895). 'What the Tortoise said to Achilles,' *Mind* 4: 278–80.
[26] L. Wittgenstein (1958). *Philosophical Investigations* (Oxford: Blackwell).
[27] W. V. O. Quine (1970). *Word & Object* (Cambridge, Mass.: MIT Press).
[28] W. Sellars (1997). *Empiricism and the Philosophy of Mind* (Cambridge, Mass.: Harvard University Press).
[29] P. Strawson (1982). 'Freedom and Resentment', in G. Watson, *Free Will* (Oxford: Oxford University Press).

- John Perry's argument that under our practical presumptions as to what is necessary to make it rational to perform an action, the agent must have beliefs with an indexical content involving concepts like 'I' or 'now' or 'here'.[30]

Just as Galileo's deduction was driven by a thought experiment, so these arguments have often been associated with experiments—better perhaps, intuition-pumps[31]—that are designed to make vivid the possibility or impossibility alleged. We are invited to imagine the frustration of the individual—Achilles in Carroll's famous story—who tries to move by argument an interlocutor who will endorse only what the premises say, and nothing that is merely presupposed; the plight of the person who tries to keep a diary on sensations occurring within them that no one else could in principle access; the problems of the radical translator as he or she finds it possible to translate a sentence in inconsistent ways and can find nothing to make one translation right, the other wrong; the position of human beings at a stage where they can give a behaviouristic account of one another's responses but not a properly mental one; the challenge for the person who wants to suspend reactive emotions in dealing with someone and yet continue to see them as a personal and free subject; and the predicament of someone who is lost in an unfamiliar complex and enjoys access to a map but has no way of telling where on the map is *here*.

Philosophy claims to teach us something potentially surprising by means of contemplating such scenarios, as Galileo claimed to do so by his. And what it teaches us bears in a distinctive way on practice. In particular, it bears on the practice of science and it is for that reason that I speak of methodological lessons. Thus the lessons of the tales rehearsed are, roughly: that we must expect some rules of inference to be hard-wired into any cognitive system; that there is no point in looking for a so-called Cartesian theatre of the mind; that neither is there any point in looking for a museum of meaning in the head; that if we can explain the evolution of a behaviouristic language for describing one another's responses, then it is going to be a short step to having an explanation of how the language of mind might have emerged; that if we can give an account of conditions that would make it appropriate, by our lights, to feel resentment and gratification at a subject, then we will have given conditions under which it is in order to ascribe freedom to that person; and that any story of cognitive architecture must make room for beliefs that are context-involving in the manner of beliefs with indexical content.

The methodological lessons illustrated—they may not be the only lessons supported by the arguments in question—all bear on the challenges and prospects for cognitive science and neuroscience. But not every lesson that philosophy may prove able to teach will be confined to this area. There is room for the same sort of philosophical work in relation to the social sciences. Thus Donald Davidson offers an argument that people who were as alien to us as certain anthropological theories assume would not be recognizable—by our received practices and views—as other

---

[30] J. Perry (1979). 'The Essential Indexical,' *Nous* 13: 3–21.
[31] D. Dennett (1984). *Elbow Room: The Varieties of Free Will Worth Wanting* (Cambridge, Mass.: MIT Press).

minds.[32] And in a similar vein many philosophical accounts of our presumptions about the nature of people and of how they operate argue that it would be impossible to engage interpersonally with any subjects who conformed to the role in which much sociological theory casts them; in that sense they would not count as people.[33] This sort of argument persuaded Max Weber to impose on social science the *Verstehen* constraint of always having to represent human beings in such a way that we could imagine making interpersonal sense of them.[34]

Why should there be room for active exploration of this methodological kind in relation to the human sciences, psychological and social, but not, so it seems, in relation to the natural? There is some room for such work in relation to the natural sciences, as when philosophers put forward schemes under which quantum phenomena are interpreted so as to fit with received ideas about causation, or the theory of natural selection is interpreted so as not to undermine intuitive ideas about altruistic motivation. But it is certainly true that the human sciences offer more fertile ground for such investigations. The reason, I suggest, is that the shared presumptions about mind, persons, and society that are embedded in our ordinary practices are much richer and harder to remove than the presumptions we make about nature, so that the implications they prove to have are bound to carry greater methodological weight.

The moral lessons   The derivation of the moral lessons implied by our practical presumptions is the sort of thing pursued in normative ethics and normative political theory. These disciplines take as given the presumptions of moral reasoning—as already articulated and perhaps amended—and tries to deploy them in the development of views on a range of particular, often quite practical issues. The presumptions that are typically deployed in this sort of argument will bear on how far normative judgement is universalizable, abstracting from particularities of person or context; how far it is driven by reference to paradigm cases, and the judgements they support, how far by reference to principles; and how far issues of what it is right to do or right to institutionalize turn on questions of what is for the best overall: say, what is likely to promote overall welfare.[35] These presumptions are variously recognized and variously assessed by philosophers, of course, and what status they are given is often a function of how satisfactory they prove in the lessons they teach; the same indeed is true of the presumptions from which methodological lessons are derived.[36]

---

[32] D. Davidson (1984). *Inquiries into Truth & Interpretation* (Oxford: Oxford University Press).

[33] Pettit, *The Common Mind* is devoted in good part to showing what social science research programs are feasible by reference to this and to related constraints.

[34] M. Weber (1949). *The Methodology of the Social Sciences* (New York: The Free Press).

[35] On some of those issues see P. Pettit (1997). 'A Consequentialist Perspective on Ethic', in M. Baron, M. Slote, and P. Pettit, *Three Methods of Ethics: A Debate* (Oxford, Blackwell); and Pettit (2001). 'Embracing Objectivity in Ethics', in B. Leiter *Objectivity in Law and Morals*. (Cambridge: Cambridge University Press): 234–86.

[36] See J. Rawls (1971). *A Theory of Justice* (Oxford: Oxford University Press) on the method of reflective equilibrium.

Many of the issues addressed in normative ethics will be questions to which people's answers come fairly quickly, being matters of well-established opinion, if not practical presumption. But many of the issues will be novel and will give the enterprise a surprising and engaging cast. Is abortion on a par with homicide? Is the failure to save the lives of those exposed to starvation equivalent to taking their lives? Is it legitimate to damage embryos in order to further medical research? As society changes and technologies develop, there are a host of ethical issues of this kind that need to be resolved. Thus there will always be occasion for developing received presumptions about matters of morality—as these are articulated in this or that philosophy—and applying them in the resolution of such issues.

But apart from teaching moral lessons that bear on relatively new ethical issues, there is also room for philosophy to play a similar role of this kind in developing views on how society should be best ordered. Unsurprisingly, our practical presumptions do not bear directly on matters as concrete—and in human history as recent—as how best to arrange the affairs of people in relation to one another, in relation to law, and in relation to government. At most those presumptions give us a base for the specification of presumptively relevant values such as those of equality and justice and freedom. Thus philosophy can also assume an engaging moral role in elaborating different ways of understanding such ideals, and different ways of weighting them against one another. And this, of course, is precisely what normative political theory attempts. It tries to derive from a baseline of common, practical presumptions lessons that bear on what sort of state and society we should be seeking.[37]

Conclusion

Although we have to reject the intellectualist picture under which ordinary practice is guided by independently maintained beliefs, and can be adjusted to any revision in those beliefs, still we can see lots of opportunity for the philosophical articulation and examination of received ideas to influence practice. Philosophy has meditative, methodological, and moral lessons to teach and these impact, by any criterion, on ordinary practice. They reshape the perceptions and dispositions that pre-exist the philosophical enterprise and, without amounting to the sort of thing envisaged in existentialism, they certainly give the lie to the quietist picture that seemed to loom as the only alternative. Philosophy is not something, then, for the armchair alone. It teaches lessons that philosophers ought to be able to bring home from the office, and take out of the study.[38]

---

[37] The elaboration of such ideas may often involve looking at past practices of reasoning and seeing possibilities of thought that may have been eclipsed at later points. For an argument that a past tradition of politics and thought points us to a conception of liberty—freedom as non-domination—that is unjustly neglected in contemporary political thinking, see Pettit, (1997). *Republicanism: A Theory of Freedom and Government* (Oxford: Oxford University Press).

[38] My thanks to Brian Leiter and Victoria McGeer for their comments on my argument.

Bibliography

The bibliography contains all the philosophical works referenced by contributors to this volume, organized by area of philosophy (broadly construed). It should provide an illuminating resource for anyone wanting to see what works have been important in philosophy's past, both recent and distant, and which works are likely to be important to its future.

Metaphysics, Epistemology, Philosophy of Language and Mind

Alexander, Samuel, *Space, Time and Deity* (London: Macmillan, 1927).

Annis, David, 'A Contextualist Theory of Epistemic Justification', *American Philosophical Quarterly*, 15 (1978), 213–19.

Armstrong, David M., *A Materialist Theory of Mind* (New York: Humanities Press, 1968).

Ayer, A. J., *Language, Truth and Logic* (London: Victor Gollancz, 1936).

Baier, Annette, 'Hume: The Reflective Women's Epistemologist?', in Louise M. Antony and Charlotte Witt (eds.), *A Mind of One's Own: Feminist Essays on Reason and Objectivity* (Boulder, Colo.: Westview Press, 1993).

Barnes, Barry, and David Bloor, 'Relativism, Rationalism, and the Sociology of Knowledge', in Martin Hollis and Steven Lukes (eds.), *Rationality and Relativism* (Cambridge, Mass.: MIT Press, 1982).

Block, Ned, 'Troubles with Functionalism', in C. W. Savage (ed.), *Perception and Cognition: Issues in the Foundation of Psychology* (Minneapolis: University of Minnesota Press, 1978).

—— 'Inverted Earth', *Philosophical Perspectives*, 4 (1990), 53–79.

—— 'The Real Gap', *Journal of Philosophy* (forthcoming).

—— and Robert Stalnaker, 'Conceptual Analysis, Dualism, and the Explanatory Gap', *Philosophical Review*, 108 (1999), 1–46.

Boghossian, Paul, and David Velleman, 'Color as a Secondary Quality', *Mind*, 98 (1989), 81–103.

Braddon-Mitchell, David, 'There are Zombies in Another Dimension', University of Sydney (2001).

Brandom, Robert, *Making it Explicit* (Cambridge, Mass.: Harvard University Press, 1994).

Burge, Tyler, 'Content Preservation', *Philosophical Review*, 102 (1993), 457–88.

'Individualism and the Mental', in Peter French, Theodore Uehling, Jr., and Howard Wettstein (eds.), *Studies in Metaphysics, Midwest Studies in Philosophy*, vol. 4 (Minneapolis: University of Minnesota Press, 1979), 73–121.

Byrne, Alex, 'Intentionalism Defended', *Philosophical Review*, 110 (2001), 199–240.

Carnap, Rudolf, *Logical Foundations of Probability* (Chicago: University of Chicago Press, 1951).

—— 'The Methodological Character of Theoretical Terms', in Herbert Feigl and Michaal Scriven (eds.), *Minnesota Studies in the Philosophy of Science*, vol. 1 (Minneapolis: University of Minnesota Press, 1956).

—— *The Logical Structure of the World*, trans. R. George (Berkeley: University of California Press, 1967).

Carroll, Lewis, 'What the Tortoise said to Achilles', *Mind*, 4 (1895), 278–80.

Carruthers, Peter, *Phenomenal Consciousness: A Naturalistic Theory* (Cambridge: Cambridge University Press, 2000).

Castañeda, Hector-Neri, *The Phenomeno-Logic of the I*, J. G. Hart and Tomis Kapitan (eds.) (Bloomington, Ind.: Indiana University Press, 1999).

Chalmers, David, *The Conscious Mind: In Search of a Fundamental Theory* (Oxford: Oxford University Press, 1996).

—— 'The components of content', in David Chalmers (ed.), *Philosophy of Mind: Classical and Contemporary Readings* (Oxford: Oxford University Press, 2002).

Chambers, Timothy, 'On vagueness, *sorites*, and Putnam's "intuitionistic strategy" ', *Monist*, 81 (1998), 343–8.

Clark, Austen, *A Theory of Sentience* (Oxford: Oxford University Press, 2003).

Coady, C. A. J., *Testimony* (Oxford: Oxford University Press, 1992).

Collins, John, Ned Hall, and Laurie Paul (eds.), *Causation and Counterfactuals* (Cambridge, Mass.: MIT Press, 2001).

Crane, Tim, 'The intentional structure of consciousness', in Quentin Smith and Aleksandar Jokic (eds.), *Consciousness: New Philosophical Perspectives* (Oxford: Oxford University Press, 2003).

Damasio, Antonio, *Descartes' Error: Emotion, Reason, and the Human Brain* (New York: Putnam, 1994).

Davidson, Donald, 'Causal Relations', *Journal of Philosophy*, 64 (1963), 691–703.

—— 'Actions, Reasons, and Causes' in his *Essays on Actions and Events* (Oxford: Oxford University Press, 1980).

—— 'Mental Events', in Lawrence Foster and J. W. Swanson (eds.), *Experience and Theory* (Amherst, Mass.: University of Massachusetts Press, 1970), reprinted in his *Essays on Actions and Events* (Oxford: Oxford University Press, 1980).

—— *Inquiries into Truth & Interpretation* (Oxford: Oxford University Press, 1984).

—— 'The Structure and Content of Truth', *Journal of Philosophy* (1990), 278–328.

Dennett, Daniel, *Content and Consciousness* (London: Routledge, 1968).

—— *Elbow Room: The Varieties of Free Will Worth Wanting* (Cambridge, Mass.: MIT Press, 1984).

DeRose, Keith, 'Solving the Skeptical Problem', *Philosophical Review*, 104 (1995), 1–52.

Dretske, Fred, *Naturalizing the Mind* (Cambridge, Mass.: MIT Press, 1995).

Droege, Paula, *Caging the Beast: A Theory of Sensory Consciousness* (Amsterdam: John Benjamins, 2003).

Dummett, Michael, *Elements of Intuitionism* (Oxford: Oxford University Press, 1977).

—— *Truth and Other Enigmas* (London: Duckworth, 1978).

—— *Origins of Analytical Philosophy* (London: Duckworth, 1993).

Dupré, John, *The Disorder of Things* (Cambridge, Mass.: Harvard University Press, 1993).

Egan, Andrew, 'Appearance properties?', (forthcoming).

Fain, Haskell, 'Some Problems of Causal Explanation', *Mind*, 72 (1963), 519–32.

Fallis, Don, 'Veritistic Social Epistemology and Information Science', *Social Epistemology*, 14 (2000), 305–16.

Fine, Kit, 'Essence and Modality', in J. Tomberlin (ed.), *Philosophical Perspectives, 8, Logic and Language* (Atascadero, Calif.: Ridgeview, 1994).

—— 'Senses of Essence', in W. Sinnott-Armstrong, D. Raffman, and N. Asher (eds.), *Modality, Morality, and Belief: Essays in Honor of Ruth Barcan Marcus* (Cambridge: Cambridge University Press, 1995).

Fodor, Jerry, *The Language of Thought* (New York: Thomas Y. Crowell, 1975).

—— 'Making Mind Matter More', in his *A Theory of Content and Other Essays* (Cambridge, Mass.: MIT Press, 1990).

—— *Hume Variations* (Oxford: Oxford University Press, 2003).

Foley, Richard, 'Egoism in Epistemology', in F. Schmitt (ed.), *Socializing Epistemology* (Lanham, Md.: Rowman & Littlefield, 1994), 53–73.

—— *Intellectual Trust in Oneself and Others* (Cambridge: Cambridge University Press, 2001).

Foster, John, 'Psychophysical Causal Relations', *American Philosophical Quarterly*, 5 (1968), 64–70.

Foucault, Michel, *Power/Knowledge* (New York: Pantheon, 1980).

French, Peter, Theodore Uehling, and Howard Wettstein (eds.), *Midwest Studies in Philosophy XI: Studies in Essentialism* (Minneapolis: University of Minnesota Press, 1986).

Freud, Sigmund, 'The Dissection of the Psychical Personality', in his *New Introductory Lectures on Psychoanalysis*, trans. J. Strachey (New York: Norton, 1965).

Fricker, Elizabeth, 'Telling and Trusting: Reductionism and Anti-Reductionism in the Epistemology of Testimony', *Mind*, 104 (1995), 393–411.

Gallese, Vittorio, and Alvin Goldman, 'Mirror Neurons and the Simulation Theory of Mind-Reading', *Trends in Cognitive Science*, 2 (1998), 493–501.

Gettier, Edmund, 'Is Justified True Belief Knowledge?', *Analysis*, 23 (1963), 121–3.

Goldman, Alvin, *Epistemology and Cognition* (Cambridge, Mass.: Harvard University Press, 1986).

—— 'Epistemic Folkways and Scientific Epistemology', in Goldman (1992).

—— *Liaisons: Philosophy Meets the Cognitive and Social Sciences* (Cambridge, Mass.: MIT Press, 1992).

—— 'Strong and Weak Justification', in James Tomberlin (ed.), *Philosophical Perspectives*, vol. 2: *Epistemology* (Atascadero, Calif.: Ridgeview, 1988), reprinted in Goldman (1992).

—— 'Empathy, Mind, and Morals', in Martin Davies and Tony Stone (eds.), *Mental Simulation* (Oxford: Blackwell, 1995).

—— *Knowledge in a Social World* (Oxford: Oxford University Press, 1999).

—— 'A Priori Warrant and Naturalistic Epistemology', in James Tomberlin (ed.), *Philosophical Perspectives*, vol. 13: *Epistemology* (Malden, Mass.: Blackwell, 1999), reprinted in Goldman (2002).

—— 'Experts: Which Ones Should You Trust?', *Philosophy and Phenomenological Research*, 63 (2001), 85–110, reprinted in Goldman (2002).

—— *Pathways to Knowledge: Private and Public* (New York: Oxford University Press, 2002).

—— 'Reply to Commentators', *Philosophy and Phenomenological Research*, 64 (2002), 215–27.

—— 'The Unity of the Epistemic Virtues,' in Abrol Fairweather and Linda Zagzebski (eds.), *Virtue Epistemology* (New York: Oxford University Press, 2001), reprinted in Goldman (2002).

—— and Moshe Shaked, 'An Economic Model of Scientific Activity and Truth Acquisition', *Philosophical Studies*, 63 (1991), 31–55, reprinted in Goldman (1992).

Goodman, Nelson, *Fact, Fiction and Forecast* (Indianapolis: Bobbs-Merrill, 1973).

Harman, Gilbert, 'The Intrinsic Quality of Experience', *Philosophical Perspectives* (1990).

Hausman, Daniel, *Causal Asymmetries* (Cambridge: Cambridge University Press, 1998).

Heidegger, Martin, *Being and Time*, trans. J. MacQuarrie and E. Robinson (New York: Harper & Row, 1963).

Holman, Emmett, 'Color Eliminativism and Color Experience', *Pacific Philosophical Quarterly*, 83 (2002), 38–56.

Horgan, Terence, and John Tienson, 'The Intentionality of Phenomenology and the Phenomenology of Intentionality', in David Chalmers (ed.), *Philosophy of Mind: Classical and Contemporary Readings* (Oxford: Oxford University Press, 2002).

Hume, David, *The Natural History of Religion* (London: Adam & Charles Black, 1956).

—— *A Treatise of Human Nature* (Oxford: Oxford University Press, 1978).

Hume, David, *Enquiries Concerning Human Understanding and Concerning the Principles of Morals* (Oxford: Oxford University Press, 1997).

—— 'On the Immortality of the Soul', from *Essays Moral and Political*, reprinted in Stephen Copley and Andrew Edgar (eds.), *David Hume: Selected Essays* (Oxford: Oxford University Press, 1998).

Jackson, Frank, *From Metaphysics to Ethics: A Defence of Conceptual Analysis* (Oxford: Oxford University Press, 1998).

—— 'Mind and Illusion', in Anthony O'Hear (ed.), *Minds and Persons* (Cambridge: Cambridge University Press, 2003).

Johnston, Mark, 'Objectivity Refigured: Pragmatism with Verificationism', in John Haldane and Crispin Wright (eds.), *Reality, Representation and Projection* (Oxford: Oxford University Press, 1993).

Kant, Immanuel, *Critique of Pure Reason*, trans. Norman Kemp Smith (London and Basingstoke: Macmillan, 1980).

Keefe, Rosanna, and Peter Smith (eds.), *Vagueness: A Reader* (Cambridge, Mass.: MIT Press, 1997).

Kim, Jaegwon, 'Causation, Nomic Subsumption, and the Concept of Event', *Journal of Philosophy*, 70 (1973), 217–36.

—— 'Multiple Realization and the Metaphysics of Reduction', in his *Supervenience and Mind* (Cambridge: Cambridge University Press, 1993).

—— 'Lonely Souls: Substance Dualism and Causality', in Kevin Corcoran (ed.), *Soul, Body, and Survival* (Ithaca, NY: Cornell University Press, 2001).

—— *Physicalism, or Something Near Enough* (Princeton: Princeton University Press, 2005).

Kitcher, Philip, 'Veritistic Value and the Project of Social Epistemology', *Philosophy and Phenomenological Research*, 64 (2002), 191–8.

Kriegel, Uriah, 'PANIC theory and the prospects for a representational theory of phenomenal consciousness', *Philosophical Psychology*, 15 (2002), 55–64.

—— 'Phenomenal Content', *Erkenntnis*, 57 (2002), 175–198.

Kripke, Saul, *Naming and Necessity* (Oxford: Blackwell, 1980).

Langton, Rae, 'Beyond A Pragmatic Critique of Reason', *Australasian Journal of Philosophy*, 71 (1993), 364–84.

—— 'Feminism in Epistemology: Exclusion and Objectification', in Jennifer Hornsby and Miranda Fricker (eds.), *The Cambridge Companion to Feminism in Philosophy* (Cambridge: Cambridge University Press, 2000).

Leiter, Brian, 'Prospects and Problems for the Social Epistemology of Evidence Law', *Philosophical Topics*, 29 (2001), 319–32.

Lewis, David, *Convention* (Cambridge, Mass.: Harvard University Press, 1969).

—— 'Causation', *Journal of Philosophy*, 70 (1973), 556–67.

—— 'Postscript to "Causation" ', in his *Philosophical Papers*, vol. II (Oxford: Oxford University Press, 1986), 173–213.

—— 'Causation as Influence', *Journal of Philosophy*, 97 (2000), 182–197.

Levine, Joseph, 'Experience and representation', in Quentin Smith and Aleksandar Jokic, (eds.), *Consciousness: New Philosophical Perspectives* (Oxford: Oxford University Press, 2003).

Lloyd, Dan, 'Leaping to Conclusions: Connectionism, Consciousness, and the Computational Mind', in Terry Horgan and John Tienson (eds.), *Connectionism and the Philosophy of Mind* (Dordrecht: Kluwer, 1991).

Loar, Brian, 'Phenomenal Intentionality as the Basis of Mental Content', in Martin Hahn and Bjorn Ramberg (eds.), *Reflections and Replies* (Cambridge, Mass.: MIT Press, 2003).

Longino, Helen, *The Fate of Knowledge* (Princeton, NJ: Princeton University Press, 2002).

Lycan, William, *Consciousness and Experience* (Cambridge, Mass.: MIT Press, 1996).

—— 'The Case for Phenomenal Externalism', *Philosophical Perspectives*, 15 (2001), 17–35.

Mackie, J. L., *The Cement of the Universe* (Oxford: Clarendon Press, 1972).

Maund, Barry, *Colours: Their Nature and Representation* (Cambridge: Cambridge University Press, 1995).

McDowell, John, 'Virtue and Reason,' *The Monist*, 62 (1979).

—— *Mind and World* (Cambridge, Mass.: Harvard University Press, 1994).

McGinn, Colin, 'Consciousness and Content', *Proceedings of the British Academy*, 74 (1988), 219–39, reprinted in his *The Problem of Consciousness* (Oxford: Oxford University Press, 1990).

McLaughlin, Brian, 'Color, Consciousness, and Color Consciousness', in Quentin Smith and Aleksandar Jokic (eds.), *Consciousness: New Philosophical Essays* (Oxford: Oxford University Press, 2003).

McTaggart, J. M. E., *The Nature of Existence*, vol. 2 (Cambridge: Cambridge University Press, 1927).

Nagel, Thomas, 'What Is It Like to Be a Bat?', *Philosophical Review*, 83 (1974), 435–50, reprinted in David Rosenthal (ed.), *The Nature of Mind* (Oxford and New York: Oxford University Press, 1991).

—— *The View From Nowhere* (New York: Oxford University Press, 1986).

Nozick, Robert, *Philosophical Explanations* (Cambridge, Mass.: Harvard University Press, 1981).

Paul, Laurie A., 'Keeping Track of the Time: Emending the Counterfactual Account of Causation', *Analysis*, 58 (1998), 191–8.

Peacocke, Christopher, *Sense and Content: Experience, Thought, and their Relations* (Oxford: Oxford University Press, 1983).

Perry, John, 'The Essential Indexical', *Noûs*, 13 (1979), 3–21.

Pettit, Philip, 'A Definition of Physicalism', *Analysis*, 53 (1993), 213–23.

—— 'Practical Belief and Philosophical Theory', *Australasian Journal of Philosophy*, 76 (1998), 15–33.

—— 'How the Folk Understand Folk Psychology', *Protosociology*, 14 (2000), 26–38.

Plantinga, Alvin, *Warrant and Proper Function* (New York: Oxford University Press, 1993).

Putnam, Hilary, 'The Meaning of "Meaning" ', in *Mind, Language, and Reality* (Cambridge: Cambridge University Press, 1975).

—— 'Vagueness and Alternative Logic', *Erkenntnis*, 19 (1983), 297–314.

—— *The Many Faces of Realism* (La Salle, Ill: Open Court, 1987).

Quine, W. V. O., *Word & Object* (Cambridge, Mass.: MIT Press, 1970).

—— *Philosophy of Logic* (Englewood Cliffs, NJ: Prentice-Hall, 1970).

—— *The Roots of Reference* (La Salle: Open Court Publishers, 1974).

Rea, Michael, *World Without Design: The Ontological Consequences of Naturalism* (Oxford: Clarendon Press, 2002).

Reid, Thomas, *Inquiry and Essays*, in Ronald Beanblossom and Keith Lehrer (eds.) (Indianapolis: Hackett, 1983).

Rey, Georges, 'A Narrow Representationalist Account of Qualitative Experience', *Philosophical Perspectives*, 12 (1998), 435–58.

Rorty, Richard (ed.), *The Linguistic Turn: Recent Essays in Philosophical Method* (Chicago: University of Chicago Press, 1967).

Rorty, Richard *Philosophy and the Mirror of Nature* (Princeton: Princeton University Press, 1979).
—— *Consequences of Pragmatism* (Minneapolis: University of Minnesota Press, 1982).
—— *Objectivity, Relativism, and Truth* (Cambridge: Cambridge University Press, 1991).
Rosenthal, David, 'A Theory of Consciousness', in Ned Block, Owen Flanagan, and Güven Güzeldere (eds.), *The Nature of Consciousness* (Cambridge, Mass.: MIT Press, 1997).
Sartre, J. P., *The Transcendence of the Ego: An Existentialist Theory of Consciousness* (New York: Farrar, Straus & Giroux, 1957).
—— *Being and Nothingness* (London: Methuen, 1958).
—— *Sketch for a Theory of the Emotions* (London: Methuen, 1962).
Searle, John, 'Minds, Brains and Programs', *Behavioral and Brain Sciences*, 3 (1980), 417–24.
—— *Intentionality* (Cambridge: Cambridge University Press, 1983).
—— 'Consciousness, Explanatory Inversion and Cognitive Science', *Behavioral and Brain Sciences*, 13 (1990), 585–642.
—— *The Rediscovery of the Mind* (Cambridge, Mass. MIT Press, 1992).
Sellars, Wilfrid, *Empiricism and the Philosophy of Mind* (Cambridge, Mass.: Harvard University Press, 1997).
Shoemaker, Sydney, 'The Inverted Spectrum', *Journal of Philosophy*, 74 (1981), 357–81.
—— 'Qualities and Qualia: What's in the Mind?', *Philosophy and Phenomenological Research Supplement*, 50 (1990), 109–31.
—— 'Phenomenal Character', *Noûs*, 28 (1994), 21–38.
—— 'Introspection and phenomenal character', *Philosophical Topics* (2001), reprinted in David Chalmers (ed.), *Philosophy of Mind: Classical and Contemporary Readings* (Oxford: Oxford University Press, 2001).
Siewert, Charles, *The Significance of Consciousness* (Princeton: Princeton University Press, 1998).
Skyrms, Brian, *Causal Necessity* (New Haven, Conn.: Yale University Press, 1980).
Sosa, Ernest, 'Testimony and Coherence', in *Knowledge in Perspective* (Cambridge: Cambridge University Press, 1991).
Stich, Stephen, *The Fragmentation of Reason* (Cambridge, Mass.: MIT Press, 1990).
Stoljar, Daniel, 'Consequences of Intentionalism' (forthcoming).
Strawson, Galen, *Mental Reality* (Cambridge, Mass.: MIT Press, 1994).
Strawson, P. F., *Individuals: An Essay in Descriptive Metaphysics* (London: Methuen, 1959).
Suits, Bernard, *The Grasshopper: Games, Life and Utopia* (Toronto: University of Toronto Press, 1978).
Thagard, Paul, *Conceptual Revolutions* (Princeton, NJ: Princeton University Press, 1992).
—— 'Collaborative Knowledge', *Noûs*, 31 (1997), 242–61.
Thau, Michael, *Consciousness and Cognition* (Oxford: Oxford University Press, 2002).
Thompson, Brad, *The Nature of Phenomenal Content*, Ph.D. dissertation, University of Arizona (2003).
Tye, Michael, *Ten Problems of Consciousness: A Representational Theory of the Phenomenal Mind* (Cambridge, Mass.: MIT Press, 1995).
—— 'Blurry Images, Double Vision, and Other Oddities: New Problems for Representationalism?', in Quentin Smith and Aleksandar Jokic (eds.), *Consciousness: New Philosophical Perspectives* (Oxford: Oxford University Press, 2003).
Van Inwagen, Peter, *An Essay on Free Will* (Oxford: Oxford University Press, 1983).
Vinueza, Adam, 'Sensations and the Language of Thought', *Philosophical Psychology*, 13 (2000), 373–92.
Warfield, Ted, 'Against Representational Theories of Consciousness', *Journal of Consciousness Studies*, 6 (1999), 66–9.

Weinberg, Jonathan, Shaun Nichols, and Stephen Stich, 'Normativity and Epistemic Intuitions', *Philosophical Topics*, 29 (2001), 429–60.

Wiggins, David, *Sameness and Substance Renewed* (Cambridge: Cambridge University Press, 2001).

Williamson, Timothy, *Vagueness* (London: Routledge, 1994).

—— 'Putnam on the Sorites Paradox', *Philosophical Papers*, 25 (1996), 47–56.

—— 'On the Structure of Higher-order Vagueness', *Mind*, 108 (1999), 127–43.

—— 'Truthmakers and the Converse Barcan formula', *Dialectica*, 53 (1999), 253–70.

—— *Knowledge and its Limits* (Oxford: Oxford University Press, 2000).

—— 'Vagueness in Reality', in Michael Loux and Dean Zimmerman (eds.), *The Oxford Handbook of Metaphysics* (Oxford: Oxford University Press, 2004).

Wittgenstein, Ludwig, *On Certainty*, G. E. M. Anscombe and G. H. von Wright (eds.) (New York: Harper, 1969).

—— *Philosophical Investigations*, trans. G. E. M. Anscombe (Oxford: Basil Blackwell, 1972).

Wright, Wayne, 'Projectivist Representationalism and Color', *Philosophical Psychology*, 16 (2003), 515–33.

Moral, Political, and Legal Philosophy

Alexander, Jason, and Brian Skyrms, 'Bargaining with Neighbors: Is Justice Contagious?', *Journal of Philosophy*, 96 (1999), 588–98.

Annas, Julia, 'Moral Knowledge as Practical Knowledge', in E. F. Paul, F. D. Miller, and J. Paul (eds.), *Moral Knowledge* (Cambridge: Cambridge University Press, 2001), 236–56.

Anscombe, G. E. M., 'Modern Moral Philosophy', *Philosophy*, 33 (1958), 1–19.

Aristotle, *Nicomachean Ethics*, trans. W. D. Ross and J. O. Urmson, in Jonathan Barnes (ed.), *The Complete Works of Aristotle* (Princeton, NJ: Princeton University Press, 1984).

Athanassoulis, Nafsika, 'A Response to Harman: Virtue Ethics and Character Traits', *Proceedings of the Aristotelian Society*, 100 (2000), 215–21.

Blackburn, Simon, *Ruling Passions: A Theory of Practical Reasoning* (Oxford: Clarendon Press, 1998).

Brennan, Samantha, 'Thresholds for Rights', *Southern Journal of Philosophy*, 33 (1995), 143–68.

Brink, David O., 'Self-Love and Altruism', *Social Philosophy and Policy*, 14/1 (Winter, 1997), 122–57.

Broad, C. D., 'Self and Others', in his *Broad's Critical Essays in Moral Philosophy* (London: George Allen & Unwin, 1971).

Broome, John, *Weighing Goods* (Oxford: Blackwell, 1991).

Butler, Judith, *Excitable Speech: A Politics of the Performative* (NY and London: Routledge, 1997).

Cicero, *On Moral Ends*, trans. Raphael Woolf (Cambridge: Cambridge University Press, 2001).

Cohen, Joshua, 'An Epistemic Conception of Democracy', *Ethics*, 97 (1986), 26–38.

Cooper, Russell, Douglas DeJong, and Thomas Ross, 'Cooperation without Reputation: Experimental Evidence from Prisoner's Dilemma Games', *Games and Economic Behavior*, 12 (1996), 187–218.

Dancy, Jonathan, *Moral Reasons* (Oxford: Blackwell, 1993).

Darwall, Stephen, Allan Gibbard, and Peter Railton, 'Toward *Fin de siècle* Ethics: Some Trends', *Philosophical Review*, 101 (1992), 115–90.

Deigh, John, 'Freud, Naturalism, and Modern Moral Philosophy', in his *The Sources of Moral Agency: Essays in Moral Psychology and Freudian Theory* (Cambridge: Cambridge University Press, 1996).

Doris, John, 'Persons, Situations, and Virtue Ethics', *Noûs*, 32 (1998), 504–30.

Doris, John, *Lack of Character* (Cambridge: Cambridge University Press, 2002).

Dworkin, Ronald, 'Liberalism', in Stuart Hampshire (ed.), *Public and Private Morality* (Cambridge: Cambridge University Press, 1977).

Estlund, David, 'Democracy without Preference', *Philosophical Review*, 49 (1990), 397–424.

—— 'Making Truth Safe for Democracy', in David Copp, Jean Hampton, and John Roemer (eds.), *The Idea of Democracy* (New York: Cambridge University Press, 1993), 71–100.

Flanagan, Owen, *Varieties of Moral Personality: Ethics and Psychological Realism* (Cambridge, Mass.: Harvard University Press, 1991).

Flax, Jane, 'Political Philosophy and the Patriarchal Unconscious', in Sandra Harding and Merrill Hintikka (eds.), *Discovering Reality* (Dordrecht: Reidel, 1983).

Foot, Philippa, 'Moral Beliefs', *Proceedings of the Aristotelian Society*, 59 (1958–59), 83–104.

—— 'The Problem of Abortion and the Doctrine of Double Effect', in her *Virtues and Vices* (Berkeley, Calif.: University of California Press, 1973), 19–32.

Freud, Sigmund, *Civilization and Its Discontents*, trans. J. Strachey (New York: Norton, 1961).

Frye, Marilyn, *The Politics of Reality* (Trumansburg, NY: The Crossing Press, 1983).

Gauthier, David, *Morals By Agreement* (Oxford: Clarendon Press, 1986).

Gewirth, Alan, *Reason and Morality* (Chicago: University of Chicago Press, 1978).

Gibbard, Allan, *Wise Choices, Apt Feelings: A Theory of Normative Judgment* (Cambridge, Mass.: Harvard University Press, 1990).

Gordon, Robert M., 'Sympathy, Simulation, and the Impartial Spectator', in Larry May, Marilyn Friedman, and Andy Clark (eds.), *Mind and Morals: Essays on Ethics and Cognitive Science* (Cambridge, Mass.: MIT Press, 1996).

Gutmann, Amy, and Dennis Thompson, *Democracy and Disagreement* (Cambridge, Mass.: Harvard University Press, 1996).

Habermas, Jürgen, *The Theory of Communicative Action*, trans. Thomas McCarthy (Boston: Beacon Press, 1984, 1987).

Hare, R. M., *Moral Thinking: Its Levels, Method, and Point* (Oxford: Clarendon Press, 1981).

Harman, Gilbert, 'Moral Philosophy Meets Social Psychology: Virtue Ethics and the Fundamental Attribution Error', *Proceedings of the Aristotelian Society*, 99 (1999), 315–31.

—— 'The Nonexistence of Character Traits', *Proceedings of the Aristotelian Society*, 100 (2000).

Herman, Barbara, 'Could It Be Worth Thinking about Kant on Sex and Marriage?' in Louise M. Antony and Charlotte Witt (eds.), *A Mind Of One's Own: Feminist Essays on Reason and Objectivity* (Boulder, Colo.: Westview Press, 1993).

Hirschman, Albert, *The Passions and the Interests: Political Arguments for Capitalism Before Its Triumph* (Princeton, NJ: Princeton University Press, 1977).

Hoffman, Martin L., 'Empathy, Social Cognition, and Moral Action', in William Kurtines and Jacob Gerwitz (eds.), *Moral Behavior and Development: Advances in Theory, Research, and Applications* (New York: John Wiley, 1984).

Hooker, Brad, *Ideal Code/Real World* (Oxford: Clarendon Press, 2000).

Horkheimer, Max, and Theodor Adorno, *Dialectic of Enlightenment* (New York: Continuum, 1994).

Hurka, Thomas, *Perfectionism* (New York: Oxford University Press, 1993).

Hursthouse, Rosalind, 'Virtue Theory and Abortion', *Philosophy and Public Affairs*, 20 (1991), 223–46.

—— *On Virtue Ethics* (New York: Oxford University Press, 1999).

Irigaray, Luce, *Speculum of the Other Woman*, trans. Gillian Gill (Ithaca, NY: Cornell University Press, 1985).

—— *I love to you* (London: Routledge, 1995).

Kagan, Shelly, 'The Additive Fallacy,' *Ethics*, 99 (1988), 5–31.

—— *The Limits of Morality* (Oxford: Clarendon Press, 1989).

—— 'Replies to My Critics', *Philosophy and Phenomenological Research*, 51 (1991).

—— 'Equality and Desert', in Louis P. Pojman and Owen McLeod, eds., *What Do We Deserve? Readings on Justice and Desert* (New York: Oxford University Press, 1999).

Kamm, F. M., *Morality/Mortality*, vol. I: *Death and Whom to Save from It* (New York: Oxford University Press, 1993).

—— *Morality/Mortality*, vol. II: *Rights, Duties, and Status* (New York: Oxford University Press, 1996).

Kant, Immanuel, *Groundwork of the Metaphysics of Morals*, trans. H. J. Paton, in *The Moral Law* (London: Hutchinson University Library, 1948).

—— *Doctrine of Virtue*, trans. Mary Gregor (New York: Evanston and London: Harper & Row, 1964).

Kierkegaard, S., *The Journals of Soren Kierkegaard* (Oxford: Oxford University Press, 1951).

Korsgaard, Christine M., *The Sources of Normativity* (Cambridge: Cambridge University Press, 1996).

Kupperman, Joel, *Character* (Oxford: Oxford University Press, 1991).

Langton, Rae, 'Speech Acts and Unspeakable Acts', *Philosophy and Public Affairs*, 22 (1993), 305–30, reprinted in *Sexual Solipsism* (forthcoming).

—— 'Sexual Solipsism', *Philosophical Topics*, 23 (1995), 149–87, reprinted in *Sexual Solipsism* (forthcoming).

—— 'Pornography: a Liberal's Unfinished Business', *Canadian Journal of Law and Jurisprudence*, 12 (1999), 109–33.

—— 'Humean Projection in Sexual Objectification', forthcoming in *Sexual Solipsism: Philosophical Essays on Pornography and Objectification* (Oxford: Oxford University Press, 2003).

—— 'Treating as an Object: Doing or Viewing?' in *Sexual Solipsism* (forthcoming).

—— and Caroline West, 'Scorekeeping in a Pornographic Language Game', *Australasian Journal of Philosophy*, 77 (1999), 303–19.

Leiter, Brian, 'Naturalism and Naturalized Jurisprudence', in B. Bix (ed.), *Analyzing Law: New Essays in Legal Theory*, (Oxford: Clarendon Press, 1998).

List, Christian, and Robert Goodin, 'Epistemic Democracy: Generalizing the Condorcet Jury Theorem', *Journal of Political Philosophy* (2001), 277–306.

McEwan, Ian, *The Innocent* (London: Picador, 1990).

Mackenzie, Catriona, and Natalie Stoljar (eds.), *Relational Autonomy: Feminist Perspectives on Autonomy, Agency and the Social Self* (Oxford: Oxford University Press, 2000).

Mackie, J. L., *Inventing Ethics* (London: Penguin, 1971).

—— *Ethics: Inventing Right and Wrong* (Harmondsworth: Penguin, 1990).

MacKinnon, Catherine, *Feminism Unmodified: Discourses on Life and Law* (Cambridge, Mass.: Harvard University Press, 1987).

—— *Toward a Feminist Theory of the State* (Cambridge, Mass.: Harvard University Press, 1989).

McMahan, Jeff, 'Killing, Letting Die, and Withdrawing Aid,' *Ethics*, 103 (1993), 250–79.

Marcuse, Herbert, *One-Dimensional Man* (Boston: Beacon, 1964).

Mill, J. S., *On Liberty* (Indianapolis: Hackett, 1978).

Mills, Charles W., *The Racial Contract* (Ithaca, NY: Cornell University Press, 1997).

Moore, G. E., *Principia Ethica* (Cambridge: Cambridge University Press, 1903).

Morris, Herbert, 'Persons and Punishment', *The Monist*, 52 (1968), 475–501.

Murphy, Liam B., *Moral Demands in Nonideal Theory* (New York: Oxford University Press, 2000).

Nagel, Thomas, *The Possibility of Altruism* (Oxford: Clarendon Press, 1970).

—— 'Libertarianism Without Foundations', *Yale Law Journal*, 85 (1975), 136–49.

—— 'Sexual Perversion', in *Mortal Questions* (Cambridge: Cambridge University Press, 1991).

Nietzsche, Friedrich, *Beyond Good and Evil*, trans. Walter Kaufmann (New York: Vintage, 1966).

Nozick, Robert, *Anarchy, State, and Utopia* (New York: Basic Books, 1974).

Nussbaum, Martha, 'Objectification', *Philosophy and Public Affairs* 24 (1995), 249–91.

Parfit, Derek, *Reasons and Persons* (Oxford: Clarendon Press, 1984).

—— 'Equality or Priority?', The Lindley Lecture (Lawrence, Kan.: University of Kansas Press, 1995).

Pettit, Philip, *The Common Mind: An Essay on Psychology, Society and Politics* (New York: Oxford University Press, 1993).

—— 'A Consequentialist Perspective on Ethics', in Marcia Baron, Michael Slote, and Philip Pettit, *Three Methods of Ethics: A Debate* (Oxford: Blackwell, 1997).

—— *Republicanism: A Theory of Freedom and Government* (Oxford: Oxford University Press, 1997).

—— 'Embracing Objectivity in Ethics', in Brian Leiter (ed.), *Objectivity in Law and Morals* (Cambridge, Cambridge University Press, 2001), 234–86.

—— *A Theory of Freedom: From the Psychology to the Politics of Agency* (Cambridge: Polity, 2001).

—— and Michael Smith, 'Freedom in Belief and Desire', *Journal of Philosophy*, 93 (1996), 429–49.

Pritchard, H. A., 'Does Moral Philosophy Rest Upon a Mistake?', *Mind*, 21 (1912), 21–37.

Quinn, Warren S., 'Actions, Intentions, and Consequences: The Doctrine of Doing and Allowing', *Philosophical Review*, 98 (1989), 287–312.

—— 'Actions, Intentions, and Consequences: The Doctrine of Double Effect', *Philosophy and Public Affairs*, 18 (1989), 334–51.

Rachels, James, 'Active and Passive Euthanasia', *New England Journal of Medicine*, 292 (1975), 78–80.

Railton, Peter, 'Made in the Shade: Moral Compatibilism and the Aims of Moral Theory', *Canadian Journal of Philosophy*, 21 (1997), 79–106.

Rashdall, Hastings, *The Theory of Good and Evil* (London: Oxford University Press, 1907).

Rawls, John, *A Theory of Justice* (Cambridge, Mass.: Harvard University Press, 1971).

—— 'The Independence of Moral Theory', *Proceedings of the American Philosophical Association*, 48 (1974–75), 5–22.

Ross, W. D., *The Right and the Good* (Oxford: Clarendon Press, 1930).

Ross, Lee, and Richard Nisbett, *The Person and the Situation* (Philadelphia: Temple University Press, 1991).

Rousseau, Jean-Jacques, *The Social Contract*, in G. Cole, trans., *The Social Contract and Discourses* (London: Everyman, 1973).

Sayre-McCord, Geoffrey, 'Mill's Proof of the Principle of Utility: A More than Half-Hearted Defense', *Social Philosophy & Policy*, 18.2 (2001), 330–60.

Scanlon, T. M., *What We Owe to Each Other* (Cambridge, Mass.: Harvard University Press, 1998).

Scheffler, Samuel, *The Rejection of Consequentialism: A Philosophical Examination of the Considerations Underlying Rival Moral Conceptions* (Oxford: Clarendon Press, 1982).

—— *Human Morality* (New York: Oxford University Press, 1992).

Sher, George, *Desert* (Princeton, NJ: Princeton University Press, 1987).

—— *Beyond Neutrality: Perfectionism and Politics* (Cambridge: Cambridge University Press, 1997).

Sherman, Nancy, 'The Moral Perspective and the Psychoanalytic Quest', *Journal of the American Academy of Psychoanalysis*, 23 (1995), 223–41.

—— 'Emotional Agents' in M. Levine (ed.), *The Analytic Freud* (London: Routledge, 2000).

Sidgwick, Henry, *The Methods of Ethics* (London: Macmillan, 1907).

Singer, Peter, 'Famine, Affluence, and Morality' *Philosophy and Public Affairs* (Spring, 1972), 229–43.

Skyrms, Brian, *Evolution of the Social Contract* (Cambridge: Cambridge University Press, 1996).

Slote, Michael, *Common-Sense Morality and Consequentialism* (London: Routledge & Kegan Paul, 1985).

—— *Beyond Optimizing: A Study of Rational Choice* (Cambridge, Mass.: Harvard University Press, 1989).

Stevenson, Charles, *Ethics and Language* (New Haven, Conn.: Yale University Press, 1944).

Stocker, Michael, *Plural and Conflicting Values* (Oxford: Clarendon Press, 1990).

—— and Elizabeth Hegman, *Valuing Emotions* (Cambridge: Cambridge University Press, 1996).

Strawson, P. F., 'Freedom and Resentment', in Gary Watson (ed.), *Free Will* (Oxford: Oxford University Press, 1982).

Strum, Shirley, *Almost Human* (New York: Random House, 1987).

Temkin, Larry, *Inequality* (New York: Oxford University Press, 1993).

Thomson, Judith Jarvis, 'Killing, Letting Die, and the Trolley Problem', *The Monist*, 59 (1976), 204–17.

Unger, Peter, *Living High and Letting Die* (New York: Oxford University Press, 1996).

Velleman, David, 'A Rational Superego', *Philosophical Review*, 108 (1999), 529–58.

—— 'Love as a Moral Emotion', *Ethics*, 109 (1999), 338–74.

Warnock, G. J., *Contemporary Moral Philosophy* (London: Macmillan, 1967).

—— *The Object of Morality* (London: Methuen, 1971).

Williams Bernard, *Morality: An Introduction to Ethics* (New York: Harper & Row, 1972).

—— 'A Critique of Utilitarianism', in J. J. C. Smart and Bernard Williams, *Utilitarianism For and Against* (Cambridge: Cambridge University Press, 1973).

—— 'Utilitarianism and Moral Self-Indulgence', in his *Moral Luck: Philosophical Papers 1973–80* (Cambridge: Cambridge University Press, 1981).

—— 'Contemporary Philosophy: A Second Look', in Nicholas Bunnin and E. P. Tsui-James (eds.), *The Blackwell Companion to Philosophy* (Oxford: Blackwell, 1996).

Wolf, Susan, *Freedom Within Reason* (New York: Oxford University Press, 1990).

Philosophy of Science

Achinstein, Peter, 'The Pragmatic Character of Explanation', *PSA* (1984), ii: 275–92, reprinted in David Ruben (ed.), *Explanation* (Oxford: Oxford University Press, 1993), 326–44.

Bacon, Francis, *The Advancement of Learning* (London: Henrie Tomes, 1605).

Brock, William, and Steven Durlauf, 'A Formal Model of Theory Choice in Science', *Economic Theory*, 14 (1999), 113–30.

Bromberger, Sylvain, 'Why Questions', in Robert Colodny (ed.), *Mind and Cosmos* (Pittsburgh: Pittsburgh University Press, 1966), 86–111.

Burtt, E. A., *The Metaphysical Foundations of Modern Physical Science* (London: Routledge & Kegan Paul, 1967).

Bush, Vanevar, *Science: The Endless Frontier* (Washington, DC: NSF, 1990).

Cartwright, Nancy, 'Causal Laws & Effective Strategies', *Noûs*, 13 (1979), 419–37.

Cartwright, Nancy, *The Dappled World* (Cambridge: Cambridge University Press, 1999).
—— 'Measuring Causes: Invariance, Modularity and the Causal Markov Condition', *Measurement in Physics and Economics Discussion Paper Series, DP MEAS 10/00*, Centre for Philosophy of Natural and Social Science, London School of Economics (2001).
—— 'On Herbert Simon: How to Get Causes from Probabilities', Causality Technical Reports, London School of Economics (forthcoming).
Cat, Jordi, 'On Understanding: Maxwell on the Methods of Illustration and Scientific Metaphor', *Studies in the History and Philosophy of Modern Physics*, 32 (2001), 395–441.
Churchland, Paul, *Scientific Realism and The Plasticity of Mind* (Cambridge: Cambridge University Press, 1979).
Crews, Frederick, 'Analysis Terminable', in his *Skeptical Engagements* (New York: Oxford University Press, 1986).
Dowe, Phil, 'An Empiricist Defence of the Causal Account of Explanation', *International Studies in the Philosophy of Science*, 6 (1992), 123–8.
—— 'Wesley Salmon's Process Theory of Causality and the Conserved Quantity Theory', *Philosophy of Science*, 59 (1992), 195–216.
Dray, William, *Laws and Explanation in History* (Oxford: Oxford University Press, 1957).
Earman, John, *Bayes or Bust?* (Cambridge, Mass.: MIT Press, 1992).
Eells, Ellery, *Probabilistic Causality* (Cambridge: Cambridge University Press, 1991).
Feigl, Herbert, and Grover Maxwell (eds.), *Minnesota Studies in the Philosophy of Science*, vol. III: *Scientific Explanation, Space, and Time* (Minneapolis: University of Minnesota Press, 1962).
Feyerabend, Paul, *Science in a Free Society* (London: New Left Books, 1978).
—— *Farewell to Reason* (London: Verso, 1987).
Fine, Arthur, and Mickey Forbes, 'Grünbaum on Freud: Three Grounds for Dissent', *Behavioral and Brain Sciences*, 9 (1986), 237–8.
Fodor, Jerry, 'Special Sciences', *Synthèse*, 28 (1974), 77–115.
Friedman, Michael, *Kant and the Exact Sciences* (Cambridge, Mass.: Harvard University Press, 1947).
—— *Foundations of Space-Time Theories: Relativistic Physics and Philosophy of Science* (Princeton: Princeton University Press, 1983).
Galison, Peter, *Image and Logic* (Chicago: University of Chicago Press, 1998).
Gardenfors, Peter, 'A Pragmatic Approach to Explanations', *Philosophy of Science*, 47 (1980), 404–23.
Garfinkel, Alan, *Forms of Explanation* (New Haven, Conn.: Yale University Press, 1981).
Giere, Ronald, *Explaining Science* (Chicago: University of Chicago Press, 1988).
—— *Science Without Laws* (Chicago: University of Chicago Press, 1999).
Grünbaum, Adolf, *The Foundations of Psychoanalysis: A Philosophical Critique* (Berkeley: University of California Press, 1984).
Harding, Sandra, *Whose Science? Whose Knowledge?* (Ithaca, NY: Cornell University Press, 1991).
—— 'After the Neutral Ideal: Science, Politics, and "Strong Objectivity" ', *Social Research*, 59 (1992), 567–87.
Hempel, Carl, 'Deductive-Nomological Explanation vs. Statistical Explanation', in Feigl *et al.* (1962), 98–169.
—— *Aspects of Scientific Explanation and other Essays in the Philosophy of Science* (New York: Free Press, 1965).
—— 'The Function of General Laws in History', *Journal of Philosophy*, 39 (1942), 35–48, reprinted in Hempel (1965), 231–43.

—— 'Problems and Changes in the Empiricist Criterion of Cognitive Significance', in his *Aspects of Scientific Explanation* (New York: Free Press, 1965).

—— *Philosophy of Natural Science* (Englewood Cliffs, NJ: Prentice Hall, 1966).

—— and Paul Oppenheim, 'Studies in the Logic of Explanation', *Philosophy of Science*, 15 (1948), 135–75, reprinted in Hempel (1965), 245–95.

Hesslow, Germund, 'Discussion: Two Notes on the Probabilistic Approach to Causality', *Philosophy of Science*, 43 (1976), 290–2.

Hitchcock, Christopher, 'Of Humean Bondage', *British Journal for the Philosophy of Science*, 54 (2003), 1–25.

Holland, Paul, 'Statistics and Causal Inference', *Journal of the American Statistical Association*, 81 (1986), 945–60.

Hoover, Kevin D., *Causality in Macroeconomics* (Cambridge: Cambridge University Press, 2001).

Hopkins, Jim, 'Epistemology and Depth Psychology: Critical Notes on *The Foundations of Psychoanalysis*', in Peter Clark and Crispin Wright (eds.), *Mind, Psychoanalysis and Science* (Oxford: Blackwell, 1988).

Hull, David, *Science as a Process* (Chicago: University of Chicago Press, 1988).

Humphreys, Paul, *The Chances of Explanation* (Princeton, NJ: Princeton University Press, 1989).

Hunt, Bruce J., *The Maxwellians* (Ithaca, NY: Cornell University Press, 1991).

Husserl, Edmund, *The Crisis of European Sciences and Transcendental Phenomenology* (Evanston, Ill: Northwestern University Press, 1970).

Jeffrey, Richard, 'Statistical Explanation vs. Statistical Inference', in Salmon *et al.* (1971), 19–28.

Kitcher, Philip, '1953 and All That. A Tale of Two Sciences', *Philosophical Review*, 93 (1984), 335–73.

—— 'The Division of Cognitive Labour', *Journal of Philosophy*, 87 (1990), 5–22.

—— 'The Naturalists Return', *Philosophical Review*, 100 (1992), 53–114.

—— *The Advancement of Science* (New York: Oxford University Press, 1993).

—— 'An Argument about Free Inquiry' *Noûs*, 31 (1997), 279–306.

—— 'The Hegemony of Molecular Biology', *Biology and Philosophy*, 14 (1999), 195–210.

—— 'Real Realism: The Galilean Strategy', *Philosophical Review*, 110 (2001), 151–97.

—— *Science, Truth, and Democracy* (New York: Oxford University Press, 2001).

Kuhn, Thomas, *The Structure of Scientific Revolutions* (Chicago: University of Chicago Press, 1962).

—— *The Essential Tension* (Chicago: University of Chicago Press, 1977).

Lakatos, Imre, 'Falsification and the Methodology of Scientific Research Programmes', in Imre Lakatos and Alan Musgrave (eds.), *Criticism and the Growth of Knowledge* (Cambridge: Cambridge University Press, 1970), 91–196.

Latour, Bruno, *Science in Action* (Cambridge, Mass.: Harvard University Press, 1987).

—— and Steve Woolgar, *Laboratory Life: The Construction of Scientific Facts* (Princeton, NJ: Princeton University Press, 1986).

Laudan, Larry, *Science and Values* (Berkeley: University of California Press, 1984).

—— 'Demystifying Underdetermination', in C. W. Savage (ed.), *Minnesota Studies in Philosophy of Science*, vol. xiv (Minneapolis: University of Minnesota Press, 1990).

—— *Beyond Positivism and Relativism: Theory, Method and Evidence* (Boulder, Colo.: Westview Press, 1996).

Lewontin, Richard, 'Science, Truth, and Democracy', *New York Review of Books* (9 May 2002).

Lipton, Peter, *Inference to the Best Explanation* (New York: Routledge, 1991).

Lloyd, Elisabeth, 'Pre-Theoretical Assumptions in Evolutionary Explanations of Female Sexuality', *Philosophical Studies*, 69 (1993), 139–53.

Longino, Helen, *Science as Social Knowledge* (Princeton, NJ: Princeton, University Press, 1990).

Mackenzie, Donald, *Statistics in Britain: 1865–1930, The Social Construction of Scientific Knowledge* (Edinburgh: Edinburgh University Press, 1981).

Menzies, Peter, and Huw Price, 'Causation as a Secondary Quality', *British Journal for the Philosophy of Science*, 44 (1993), 187–203.

Miller, Richard W., *Fact and Method: Explanation, Confirmation and Reality in the Natural and Social Sciences* (Princeton, NJ: Princeton University Press, 1987).

Morgan, Mary S., 'Learning from Models', in Mary S. Morgan and Margaret Morrison (eds.), *Models as Mediators* (Cambridge: Cambridge University Press, 1999), 347–88.

Nagel, Ernest, *The Structure of Science* (New York: Harcourt Brace, 1961).

Pearl, Judea, *Causality: Models, Reasoning and Inference* (Cambridge: Cambridge University Press, 2000).

Popper, Karl, *Conjectures and Refutations* (New York: Harper Torchbooks, 1965).

Richardson, Alan, 'Explanation: Pragmatics and Asymmetry', *Philosophical Studies*, 80 (1995), 109–29.

Ruben, David (ed.), *Explanation* (Oxford: Oxford University Press, 1993).

Sachs, David, 'In Fairness to Freud', reprinted in J. Neu (ed.), *The Cambridge Companion to Freud* (Cambridge: Cambridge University Press, 1992).

Salmon, Wesley, *Foundations of Scientific Inference* (Pittsburgh: University of Pittsburgh Press, 1965).

—— 'Statistical Explanation', in Salmon *et al.*, (1971), 29–88.

—— *Scientific Explanation and the Causal Structure of the World* (Princeton, NJ: Princeton University Press, 1984).

—— *Four Decades of Scientific Explanation* (Minneapolis: University of Minnesota Press, 1990).

—— Richard Jeffrey, and James Greeno (eds.), *Statistical Explanation and Statistical Relevance* (Pittsburgh: Pittsburgh University Press, 1971).

Scriven, Michael, 'Explanation and Prediction in Evolutionary Theory', *Science*, 130 (1959), 477–82.

—— 'Explanations, Predictions, and Laws' in Herbert Feigl and Grover Maxwell (eds.), *Minnesota Studies in the Philosophy of Science*, vol. III (Minneapolis: University of Minnesota Press, 1962).

—— and Herbert Feigl (eds.), *Minnesota Studies in Philosophy of Science*, vol. I (Minneapolis: University of Minnesota Press, 1956).

Shapin, Steven, *A Social History of Truth* (Chicago: University of Chicago Press, 1994).

—— and Simon Schaffer, *Leviathan and the Air Pump: Hobbes, Boyle, and the Experimental Life* (Princeton, NJ: Princeton University Press, 1985).

Sintonen, Matti, 'The Pragmatics of Scientific Explanation', *Acta Philosophica Fennica*, 37 (1984).

Slezak, Peter, 'Bloor's Bluff: Behaviorism and the Strong Programme', *International Studies in the Philosophy of Science*, 5 (1991), 241–56.

Smart, J. J. C., *Philosophy and Scientific Realism* (London: Routledge, 1963).

Solomon, Miriam, 'Scientific Rationality and Human Reasoning', *Philosophy of Science*, 59 (1992), 439–55.

Spirtes, Peter, Clark Glymour, and Richard Scheines, *Causation, Prediction and Search* (New York: Springer, 1993).

Spohn, Wolfgang, 'Stochastic Independence, Causal Independence, and Shieldability', *Journal of Philosophical Logic*, 9 (1980), 73–99.

Stove, D. C., *Probability and Hume's Inductive Skepticism* (Oxford: Clarendon Press, 1973).

Suppe, Frederick, *The Semantic Conception of Theories and Scientific Realism* (Chicago: Chicago University Press, 1989).

Suppes, Patrick, 'What Is a Scientific Theory?', in Sidney Morgenbesser (ed.), *Philosophy of Science Today* (New York: Basic Books, 1967).

—— *A Probabilistic Theory of Causality* (Amsterdam: North-Holland, 1970).

Van Fraassen, Bas, *The Scientific Image* (Oxford: Oxford University Press, 1980).

—— *The Empirical Stance* (New Haven: Yale University Press, 2002).

von Wright, George H., in *Explanation and Understanding* (Ithaca, NY: Cornell University Press, 1971).

Weinberg, Steven, *Dreams of a Final Theory* (New York: Vintage, 1994).

Wilson, E. O., *Consilience* (Cambridge, Mass.: Harvard University Press, 1998).

Wollheim, Richard, 'Desire, Belief, and Professor Grünbaum's Freud', in his *The Mind and Its Depths* (Cambridge, Mass.: Harvard University Press, 1993).

Woodward, James, 'Explanation, Invariance, and Intervention', *PSA* (1996), ii: S26–41.

History of Philosophy

Alcinous, *Handbook of Platonism*, trans. John Dillon (Oxford: Clarendon Press, 1995).

Annas, Julia, 'Royaume-Uni: III: La philosophie antique', in Raymond Klibansky and David Pears (eds.), *La philosophie en Europe* (Paris: Gallimard, 1993), 398–404.

—— *The Morality of Happiness* (Oxford: Oxford University Press, 1993).

—— and Jonathan Barnes (eds.), *The Modes of Scepticism: Ancient Texts and Modern Interpretations* (Cambridge: Cambridge University Press, 1985).

—— and Christopher Rowe (eds.), *New Perspectives on Plato, Modern and Ancient* (Cambridge, Mass.: Harvard University Press 2002).

Aristotle, *Categories*, trans. J. L. Ackrill (Oxford: Oxford University Press, 1963).

Armstrong, A. MacC., 'Philosophy and its History', *Philosophy and Phenomenological Research*, 19 (1959), 447–65.

Atherton, Margaret (ed.), *Women Philosophers of the Early Modern Period* (Indianapolis: Hackett Publishing Co., 1994).

Ayers, Michael, 'Analytical Philosophy and the History of Philosophy', in Jonathan Rée, Michael Ayers, and Adam Westoby (eds.), *Philosophy and its Past* (Highlands, NJ: Humanities Press, 1978).

Barnes, Jonathan, *The Toils of Scepticism* (Cambridge: Cambridge University Press, 1990).

Bayle, Pierre, *Dictionnaire Historique et Critique* (Rotterdam: Reinier Leers, 1697).

Becker, Lawrence, *A New Stoicism* (Princeton, NJ: Princeton University Press, 1998).

Beiser, Frederick C., *The Fate of Reason: German Philosophy from Kant to Fichte* (Cambridge, Mass.: Harvard University Press, 1987).

Bennett, Jonathan, *A Study of Spinoza's Ethics* (Indianapolis: Hackett, 1984).

Bett, Richard, *Pyrrho, His Antecedents and His Legacy* (Oxford: Oxford University Press, 2000).

Brandes, Georg, *Friedrich Nietzsche*, trans. A. Chater (London: Heinemann, 1915).

Brittain, Charles, *Philo of Larissa: the Last of the Academic Sceptics* (Oxford: Oxford University Press, 2001).

Broad, Jacqueline, *Women Philosophers of the Seventeenth Century* (Cambridge: Cambridge University Press, 2002).

Brucker, Jakob, *Historia Critica Philosophiæ* (Leipzig, 1744).

Burnyeat, Myles, 'Aristotle on Understanding Knowledge', in E. Berti (ed.), *Aristotle on Science: the Posterior Analytics* (Padua: Editrice Antenore, 1981), 97–139.

Burnyeat, Myles, and Michael Frede (eds.), *The Original Sceptics: A Controversy* (Indianapolis: Hackett, 1997).

Canto-Sperber, Monique (ed.), *Philosophie grecque* (Paris: Presses Universitaires de France, 1997).

Charles, David, *Aristotle's Philosophy of Action* (London: Duckworth, 1984).

Clark, Maudemarie, *Nietzsche on Truth and Philosophy* (Cambridge: Cambridge University Press, 1990).

—— 'On Knowledge, Truth, and Value: Nietzsche's Debt to Schopenhauer and the Development of His Empiricism', in Christopher Janaway (ed.), *Willing and Nothingness: Schopenhauer as Nietzsche's Educator* (Oxford: Oxford University Press, 1998).

Cohen, G. A., *Karl Marx's Theory of History: A Defense* (Princeton, NJ: Princeton University Press, 1978).

Cohen, Leslie, 'Doing Philosophy is Doing its History', *Synthèse*, 67 (1986), 33–50.

Cooper, J. M., *Reason and Emotion: Essays on Ancient Moral Psychology and Ethical Theory* (Princeton, NJ: Princeton University Press, 1999).

Curley, Edwin, 'Dialogues with the Dead', *Synthèse*, 67 (1986), 51–6.

Danto, Arthur, *Nietzsche as Philosopher* (New York: Macmillan, 1965).

Easterling, P. E. (ed.), *Cambridge Companion to Greek Tragedy* (Cambridge: Cambridge University Press, 1997).

Everson, Stephen, 'Psychology', in Jonathan Barnes (ed.), *The Cambridge Companion to Aristotle* (Cambridge: Cambridge University Press, 1995).

—— *Aristotle on Perception* (Oxford: Oxford University Press, 1997).

Fine, Gail, *On Ideas* (Oxford: Oxford University Press, 1993).

Garber, Daniel, *Descartes's Metaphysical Physics* (Chicago: University of Chicago Press, 1992).

Garrett, Don, 'Does History Have a Future? Some Reflections on Bennett and Doing Philosophy Historically', in *Doing Philosophy Historically* (Buffalo: Pergamon Press 1989).

—— *Cognition and Commitment in Hume's Philosophy* (New York: Oxford University Press, 1997).

—— 'Owen on Humean Reasoning', *Hume Studies*, 26.2 (2000), 291–303.

—— 'Spinoza's Theory of Mind and Imagination', presented at the American Philosophical Association Eastern Division Meetings (2001).

—— 'Spinoza's *Conatus* Argument', in John I. Biro and Olli Koistinen (eds.), *Spinoza: Metaphysical Themes* (New York: Oxford University Press, 2002), 127–58.

Gaukroger, Stephen, *Francis Bacon and the Transformation of Early Modern Philosophy* (Cambridge: Cambridge University Press, 2001).

Gemes, Ken, 'Nietzsche's Critique of Truth', in John Richardson and Brian Leiter (eds.), *Nietzsche* (Oxford: Oxford University Press, 2001).

Gosling, J. C. B., and C. C. W. Taylor, *The Greeks on Pleasure* (Oxford: Clarendon, 1982).

Gotthelf, Allan (ed.), *Aristotle on Nature and Living Things* (London: Mathesis Publications/ Bristol Classical Press, 1985).

—— and James Lennox (eds.), *Philosophical Issues in Aristotle's Biology* (Cambridge: Cambridge University Press, 1987).

Gracia, Jorge J. E., *Philosophy and Its History: Issues in Philosophical Historiography* (Albany: State University of New York Press, 1992).

Griswold, Charles (ed.), *Platonic Readings, Platonic Writings* (New York: Routledge, 1988).

Guthrie, W. K. C., *The Sophists* (Cambridge: Cambridge University Press, 1971).

Hare, R. M., *Plato* (Oxford: Oxford University Press, 1982).

Horn, George (Georgius Hornius), *Historiae philosophicae libre VII successione sectis et vita philosophorum ab orbe condito ad nostram aetatem agitu* (Lugdini Batavorum, 1655).

Hurka, Thomas, 'Nietzsche: Perfectionist', in Brian Leiter and Neil Sinhababu (eds.), *Nietzsche and Morality* (Oxford: Oxford University Press, forthcoming).

Inwood, Brad, *Ethics and Human Action in Early Stoicism* (Oxford: Oxford University Press, 1985).

Jesseph, Douglas, *Berkeley's Philosophy of Mathematics* (Chicago: University of Chicago Press, 1993).

Kail, Peter, 'Projection and Necessity in Hume', *European Journal of Philosophy*, 9 (2001), 24–54.

—— *Projection and Realism in Hume* (Oxford: Oxford University Press, forthcoming).

Kemp Smith, Norman, 'The Naturalism of Hume', *Mind*, 14 (1905), 149–73.

—— *The Philosophy of David Hume* (London: Macmillan, 1941).

Kitcher, Patricia, *Kant's Transcendental Psychology* (New York: Oxford University Press, 1993).

Klagge, J. C., and N. Smith (eds.), *Methods of Interpreting Plato and His Dialogues* (Oxford: Oxford University Press, 1992).

Kuklick, Bruce, 'Seven Thinkers and How They Grew: Descartes, Spinoza, Leibniz; Locke, Berkeley, Hume; Kant', in Rorty, Schneewind, and Skinner (eds.) (1984).

Laks, André, 'Herméneutique et argumentation', in *Débat*, 72 (1992), 146–54.

Lear, Jonathan, *Open Minded: Working Out the Logic of the Soul* (Cambridge, Mass.: Harvard University Press, 1998).

Lehrer, Keith, *Thomas Reid* (London: Routledge, 1989).

Leiter, Brian, 'Nietzsche and Aestheticism', *Journal of the History of Philosophy*, 30 (1992), 275–90.

—— 'Classical Realism', *Philosophical Issues*, 11 (2001), 244–67.

—— *Nietzsche on Morality* (London: Routledge, 2002).

Lennon, Thomas M., *The Battle of the Gods and Giants: the Legacies of Descartes and Gassendi, 1655–1715* (Princeton, New Jersey: Princeton University Press, 1993).

—— *Reading Bayle* (Toronto: University of Toronto Press, 1999).

Lennox, James, *Aristotle's Philosophy of Biology* (Cambridge: Cambridge University Press, 2001).

Lloyd, Genevieve, *The Man of Reason* (Minneapolis: University of Minnesota Press, 1984).

Loeb, Louis E., *From Descartes to Hume: Continental Metaphysics and the Development of Modern Philosophy* (Ithaca, NY: Cornell University Press, 1981).

Marks, Joel, and Roger Ames (eds.), *Emotions in Asian Thought: A Dialogue in Comparative Philosophy* (Albany: State University of New York Press, 1995).

Mercer, Christia, *Leibniz's Metaphysics: Its Origins and Development* (Cambridge: Cambridge University Press, 2001).

Mitsis, Phillip, *Epicurus' Ethical Theory* (Ithaca, NY: Cornell University Press, 1988).

Morgan, Kathryn, 'Socrates and Gorgias at Delphi and Olympia: *Phaedrus* 235d6–236b4', *Classical Quarterly*, 44ii (1994), 375–86.

Nadler, Steven M., *Arnauld and the Cartesian Philosophy of Ideas* (Princeton, NJ: Princeton University Press, 1989).

—— *Malebranche and Ideas* (New York: Oxford University Press, 1992).

Nehamas, Alexander, *Nietzsche: Life as Literature* (Cambridge, Mass.: Harvard University Press, 1985).

Nussbaum, Martha, *The Fragility of Goodness: Luck and Ethics in Greek Tragedy and Philosophy* (Cambridge: Cambridge University Press, 1986).

—— and Amelie Rorty (eds.), *Essays on Aristotle's De Anima* (Oxford: Oxford University Press, 1992).

Owen, David, *Hume's Reason* (Oxford: Oxford University Press, 1999).

Pellegrin, Pierre, *Aristotle's Classification of Animals*, trans. A. Preus (Berkeley: University of California Press, 1986).

Penelhum, Terence, *Butler* (London: Routledge & Kegan Paul, 1985).

Pippin, Robert B., *Hegel's Idealism: the Satisfactions of Self-Consciousness* (Cambridge: Cambridge University Press, 1989).

Rée, Jonathan, Michael Ayers, and Adam Westoby (eds.), *Philosophy and its Past* (Hassocks, Sussex: Harvester Press, 1978).

Richardson, John, *Nietzsche's System* (New York: Oxford University Press, 1996).

Ricoeur, Paul, *Freud and Philosophy*, trans. D. Savage (New Haven, Conn.: Yale University Press, 1970).

Rorty, Richard, 'The Historiography of Philosophy: Four Genres', in Richard Rorty, J. B. Schneewind, and Quentin Skinner (eds.) (1984).

——J. B. Schneewind, and Quentin Skinner (eds.), *Philosophy in History: Essays in the Historiography of Philosophy* (Cambridge: Cambridge University Press, 1984).

Rosen, Michael, *On Voluntary Servitude: False Consciousness and the Theory of Ideology* (Cambridge, Mass.: Harvard University Press, 1996).

Rosenthal, David M., 'Philosophy and its History', in Avner Cohen and Marcelo Dascal (eds.), *The Institution of Philosophy: A Discipline in Crisis?* (La Salle: Open Court, 1989).

Russell, Bertrand, *A History of Western Philosophy* (New York: Simon & Schuster, 1945).

—— *A Critical Exposition of the Philosophy of Leibniz* (Cambridge: Cambridge University Press, 1900).

Schacht, Richard, 'Nietzsche's *Gay Science*, or, How to Naturalize Cheerfully', in Robert Solomon and Kathy Higgins (eds.), *Reading Nietzsche* (New York: Oxford University Press, 1988).

Schmaltz, Tad M., *Malebranche's Theory of the Soul: A Cartesian Interpretation* (New York: Oxford University Press, 1996).

—— *Radical Cartesianism: The French Reception of Descartes* (Cambridge: Cambridge University Press, 2002).

Schneewind, J. B., *The Invention of Autonomy: A History of Modern Moral Philosophy* (Cambridge: Cambridge University Press, 1998).

Schofield, Malcolm, 'Likeness and Likenesses in the *Parmenides*' in C. Gill and M. N. McCabe (eds.), *Form and Argument in Late Plato* (Oxford: Oxford University Press, 1996).

Schopenhauer, Arthur, *On the Will in Nature*, trans. E. F. J. Payne (New York: Oxford University Press, 1992).

Sedgwick, Sally (ed.), *The Reception of Kant's Critical Philosophy: Fichte, Schelling, and Hegel* (Cambridge: Cambridge University Press, 2000).

Sextus Empiricus, *Outlines of Scepticism*, trans. Julia Annas and Jonathan Barnes (Cambridge: Cambridge University Press, 2000).

Skorupski, John, *John Stuart Mill* (London: Routledge, 1989).

Sorabji, Richard, *Emotion and Peace of Mind: from Stoic Agitation to Christian Temptation* (Oxford: Oxford University Press, 2000).

Stanley, Thomas, *The History of Philosophy* (London, 1655).

Stroud, Barry, *Hume* (London: Routledge, 1977).

Taylor, Christopher, 'Aristotle's Epistemology', in Stephen Everson (ed.), *Epistemology* (Cambridge: Cambridge University Press, 1990), 116–42.

Walton, Craig, 'Bibliography of the Historiography and Philosophy of the History of Philosophy', *International Studies in Philosophy*, 5 (1977), 135–66.

Williams, Bernard, *Descartes: The Project of Pure Enquiry* (Harmondsworth: Penguin Books, 1978).

Wilson, Catherine, 'The History of Modern Philosophy' in Oliver Leaman (ed.), *The Future of Philosophy: Towards the Twenty-First Century* (London: Routledge, 1998).

Wilson, Margaret, 'History of Philosophy Today; and the Case of the Sensible Qualities', *Philosophical Review*, 101.1 (January 1992), 191–243.

Wolff, Jonathan, *Why Read Marx Today?* (Oxford: Oxford University Press, 2002).

Wolff, Robert Paul, 'Methodological Individualism and Marx: Some Remarks on Elster, Game Theory, and Other Things', *Canadian Journal of Philosophy*, 20 (1990), 469–86.

Wolfson, H. A., *The Philosophy of Spinoza: Unfolding the Latent Processes of his Reasoning* (Cambridge, Mass.: Harvard University Press, 1934).

Wolterstorff, Nicholas, *Thomas Reid and the Story of Epistemology* (Cambridge: Cambridge University Press, 2001).

Wood, Allen W., *Hegel's Ethical Thought* (Cambridge: Cambridge University Press, 1990).

Woodruff, Paul, 'Plato's Early Theory of Knowledge', in Stephen Everson (ed.), *Epistemology* (Cambridge: Cambridge University Press, 1990).

Zöller, Günter, Fichte's *Transcendental Philosophy: the Original Duplicity of Intelligence and Will* (Cambridge: Cambridge University Press, 1998).

Index

This index was prepared by Ian Farrell.